Crafting Lives

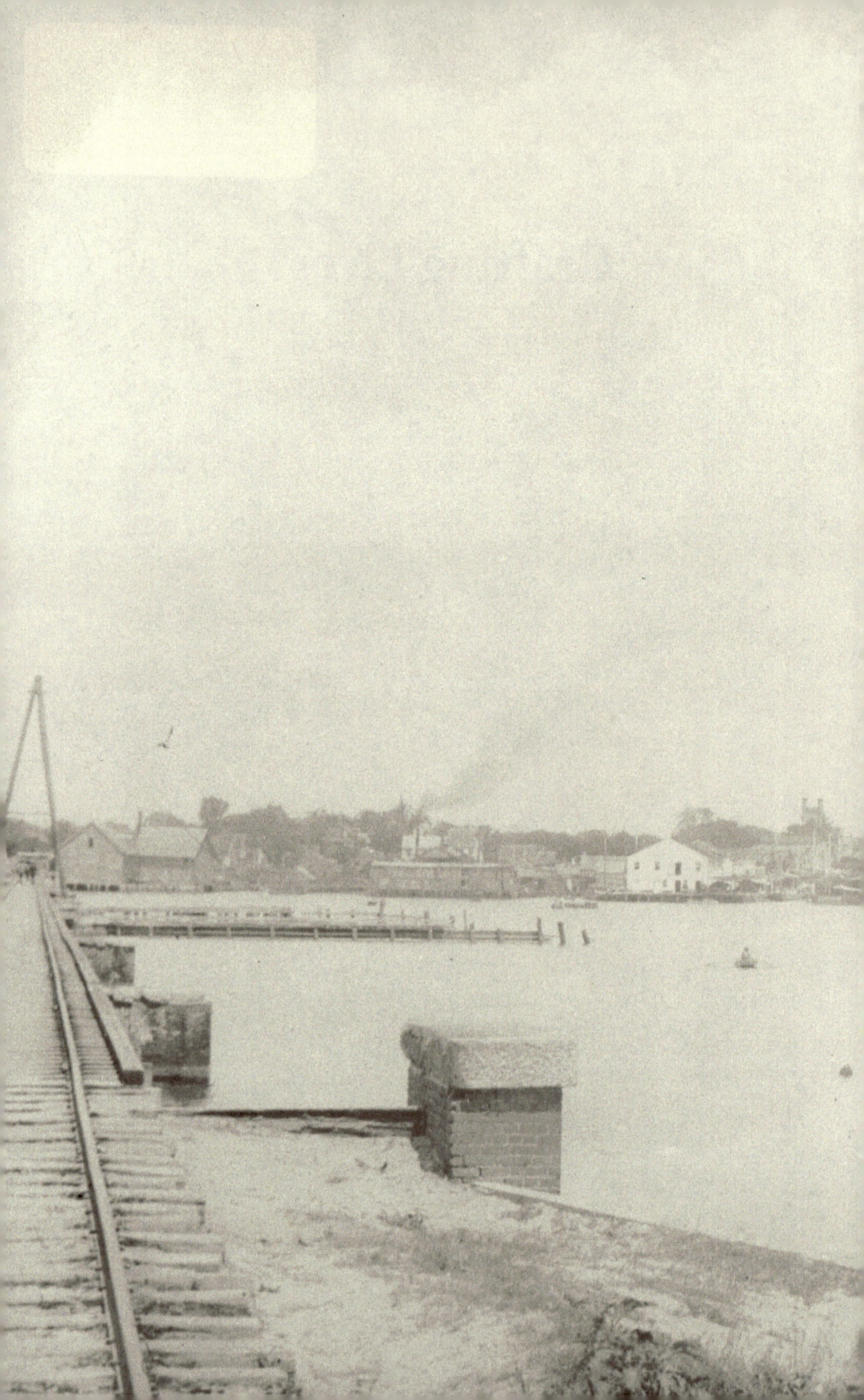

Crafting Lives

African American Artisans in New Bern, North Carolina, 1770–1900

CATHERINE W. BISHIR

The University of North Carolina Press
Chapel Hill

Set in Calluna

The paper in this book meets the guidelines for permanence and durability of the Committee on Production Guidelines for Book Longevity of the Council on Library Resources.

Library of Congress Cataloging-in-Publication Data
Bishir, Catherine W.
Crafting lives : African American artisans in
New Bern, North Carolina, 1770–1900 / Catherine W. Bishir.
pages cm
Includes bibliographical references and index.
ISBN 978-1-4696-0875-4 (hardback)
ISBN 978-1-4696-2657-4 (pbk.)
ISBN 978-1-4696-0876-1 (ebook)
1. African American artisans—New Bern—History—19th century.
2. Artisans—North Carolina—New Bern—History—19th century.
3. African Americans—North Carolina—New Bern—History—19th century.
4. New Bern (N.C.)—History—19th century. I. Title.

F264.N5B56 2013
305.896'0730756192—dc23
2013018943

THIS BOOK WAS PUBLISHED WITH THE ASSISTANCE OF

Jim and Gail Bisbee

Carolyn Moore Bland

Ken and Ellen Chance

Jim Congleton

Empire Properties

First Citizens Bank, New Bern, North Carolina

Bernard George

John and Katherine Haroldson

George and Emily Henson

Bill and Nancy Hollows

Myrick Howard

Joe and Nancy Mansfield

Bob and Carol Mattocks

John Robert and Alison Mattocks

Nelson McDaniel

Champ and E. T. Mitchell

William Price

Swiss Bear

John and Susie Ward

William Smith and Margaret Norris Ward Bequest

Ben Watford

Z. Smith Reynolds Fund of
the University of North Carolina Press

In memory of Kay Phillips Williams

NOVEMBER 6, 1942–OCTOBER 14, 2012

Contents

Introduction *5*

ONE

The Setting:
New Bern from the Colonial Period to 1900 *19*

TWO

The Fruits of Honest Industry: Black Artisans in New Bern's "Golden Age," 1770–1830 *37*

THREE

Hundreds of Fine Artisans:
Leaving and Staying, 1830–1861 *97*

FOUR

Worthy to Be Free, Worthy to Be Respected:
Civil War, Union Occupation, and Presidential Reconstruction, 1862–1866 *151*

FIVE

We Can and Will Do More:
Artisans and Citizens, 1867–1900 *193*

Conclusion *255*

Appendix: Biographical Summaries *259*

Notes *293*

Bibliography *343*

Acknowledgments *357*

Index *361*

Illustrations and Maps

Illustrations

New Bern Fish, Oyster, and Game Fair *21*
Engraving of New Bern *29*
Fish Market *34*
"Co. G's Cook House at Newbern, Nov. 1862" *41*
John R. Donnell House *43*
Craven County Jail *44*
John Rice Green House, stair hall *92*
Sarah Rice gravestone *94*
"Profile of a Young Man Wearing a Hat" *102*
"Negro Church at Beaufort, Dec. 7, 1862" *110*
William Hollister House *113*
Craven Street *128*
John H. Scott and family *143*
John Patterson Green *144*
Sketch map of New Bern, 1864 *154*
"The Freedmen's Blacksmith and Wheelwright Shop" *157*
James Walker Hood *161*
"Negro volunteers passing Episcopal Church, New Bern NC" *165*
Abraham H. Galloway *177*
King Solomon Lodge *186*
Sylvia Conner *202*
Craven County Courthouse and Jail *203*
Gaston House Hotel *206*
Joseph C. Price *222*
George H. White *225*
Ebenezer Presbyterian Church *227*
St. Peter's AME Zion Church *229*

North George Street *243*
Allen G. Oden *246*

Maps

New Bern and environs *2*
New Bern, ca. 2010 *3*
New Bern, ca. 1770 *4*
New Bern, ca. 1825 *39*
New Bern, ca. 1860 *99*
New Bern, ca. 1885 *195*

Crafting Lives

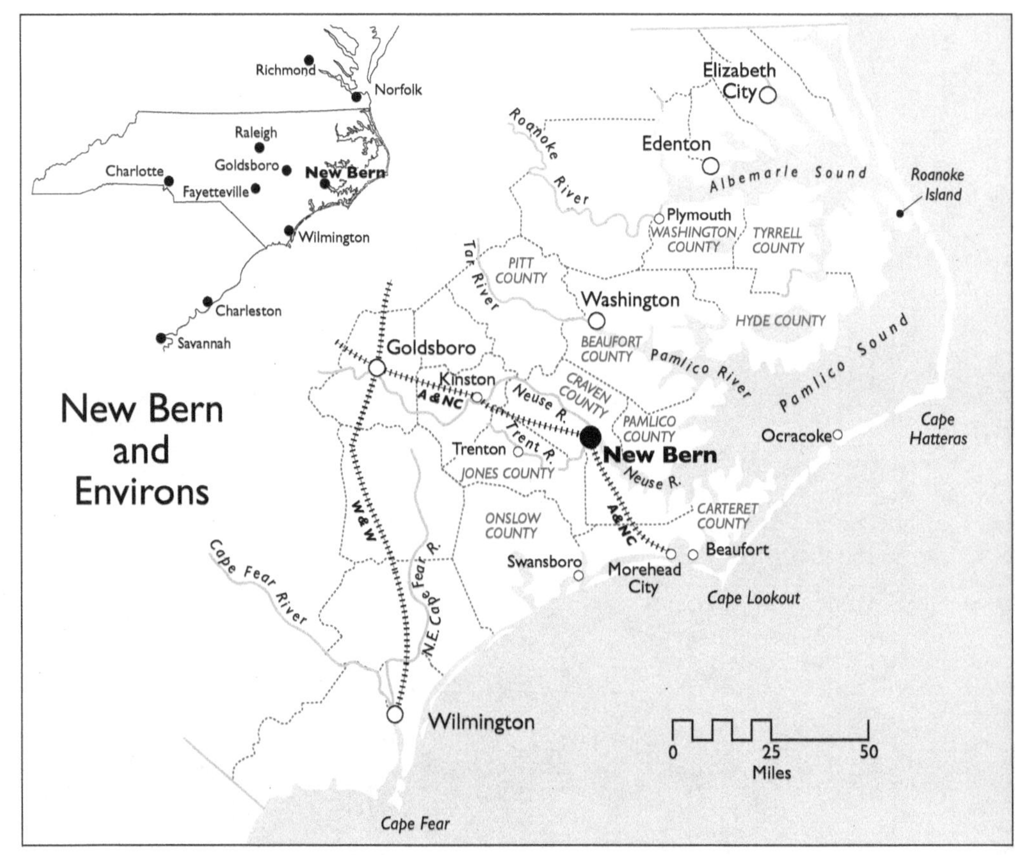

New Bern and environs. Map by Michael T. Southern.

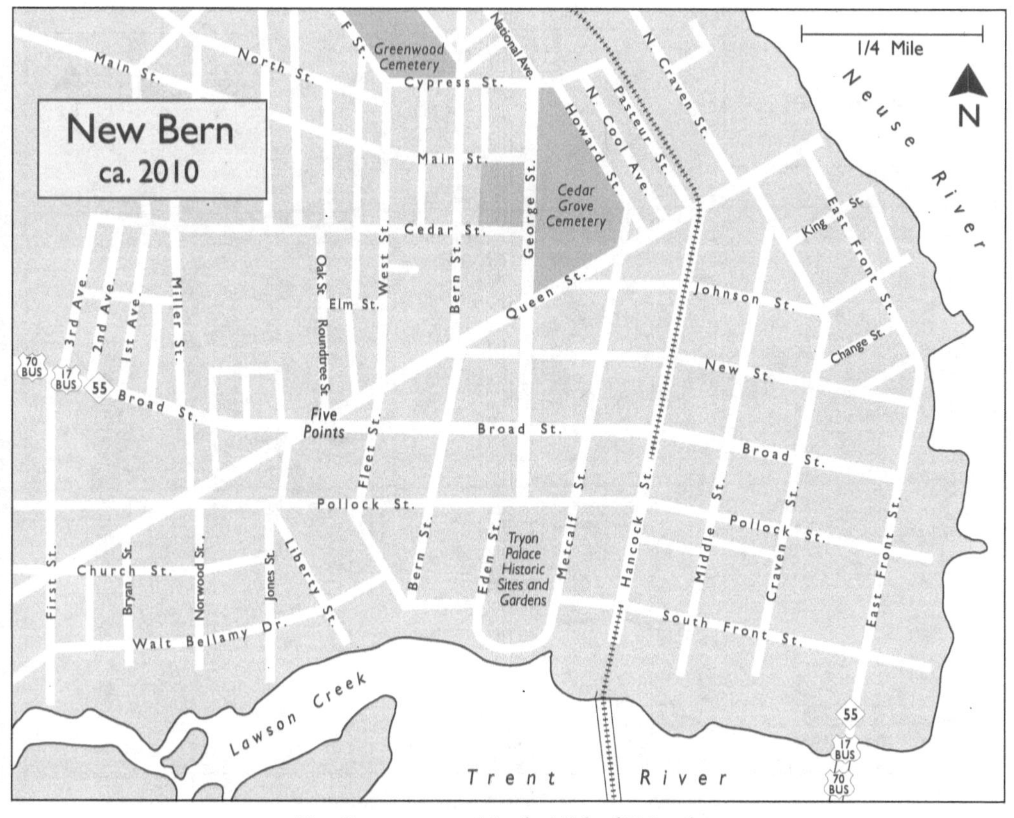

New Bern, ca. 2010. Map by Michael T. Southern.

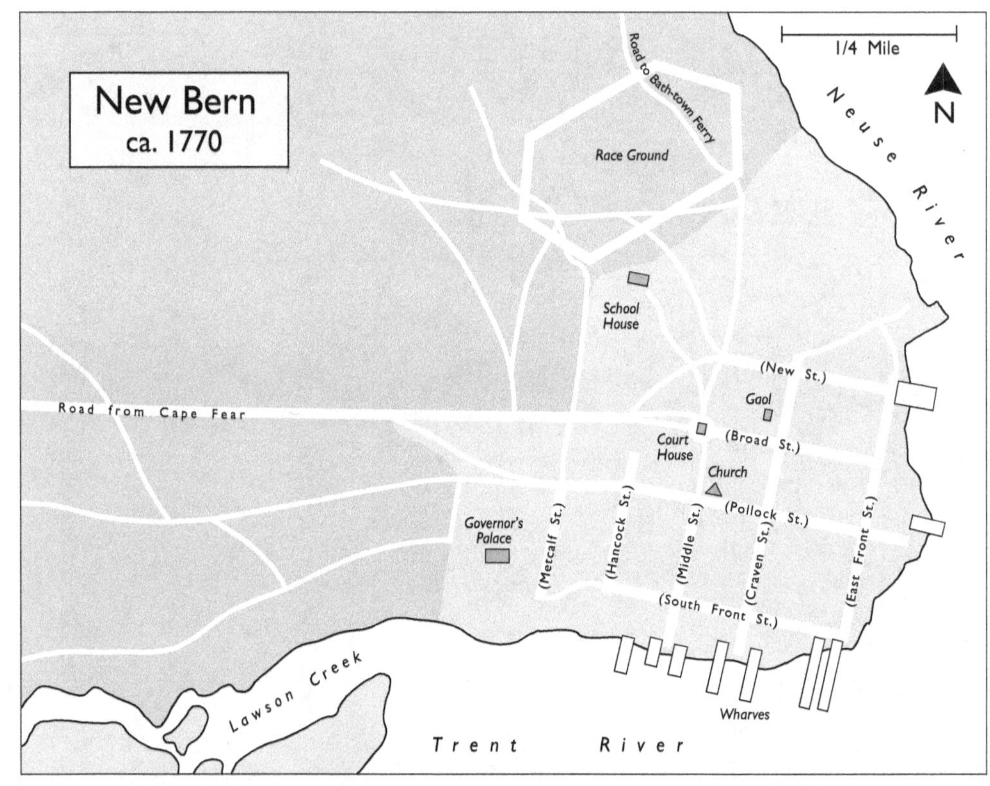

New Bern, ca. 1770. Map by Michael T. Southern.

Introduction

As a workman, my father was without a superior, in that section of the state. He designed and executed all styles of clothing and uniforms which the trade demanded, even going back to old continental styles and theatrical costumes.

—John Patterson Green, *Fact Stranger than Fiction* (1920)

John R. Green was a tailor, employing several journeymen and apprentices, who turned out a good style of work. . . . He was a bright mulatto, and always dressed in the latest fashion, making his own figure an advertisement of his proficiency in the art of improving the looks of men. [He] was much respected for his modest, unassuming behavior, though he possessed wealth enough to put on airs.

—Stephen Miller, "Recollections of New Bern Fifty Years Ago" (1873)

As an artisan of color, New Bern tailor John Rice Green (1793–1850) lived a life of paradox. Born a slave and apprenticed to a white master tailor, he learned and practiced his trade in bondage as did most black artisans in the South. By working extra hours he saved the money to obtain his freedom in young adulthood while also teaching himself to read and write. After his emancipation in 1818, he became a prosperous master craftsman with his own apprentices and slaves. Green spent his life in a setting dominated by the institution of slavery where he developed and maintained lasting connections with friends and family members still enslaved, fellow free people of color, and leading white citizens. Through his relationships, coupled with his skills, industry, and thrift, Green, like hundreds of other American artisans, found opportunities to attain a degree of economic autonomy and community stature. Whatever his accomplishments, as a man of color he also employed carefully honed techniques of "modest, unassuming" racial deference essential to his success in a racially defined southern city, while mustering resources of hope and inner strength, family ties, and craft pride to maintain his and his family's self-respect within that setting.

Green shared with other artisans certain intangible as well as tangible benefits of craft skills and identity. As a successful tailor he attuned himself both to the larger world and to his immediate community as he kept abreast of current styles and local and individual preferences. Day after day, he measured his clients' forms and listened to their needs and desires. He laid out patterns and fabric on a broad table, wielded scissors and shears to cut each section of a coat, trousers, waistcoat, or shirt. He sewed these together, hemmed and pressed the garment, and attached buttons or trim. After making any final adjustments, he presented the finished garment and the bill for the job. His role as an artisan also enabled him to lift his sights above the workbench and to look toward a broader horizon.

Through the exercise of craft skills—whether as a tailor, dressmaker, house carpenter, or wheelwright, and whether enslaved or free—artisans experienced some degree of mastery over both the process and the products of their trades. By extension, many of them, like Green, could imagine and then pursue strategies to shape their own situations, however narrowly or broadly, and thereby to craft their lives in slavery or in freedom. "If we cannot first imagine freedom," as one writer puts it, "we cannot actually achieve it."[1] For John Rice Green, this larger view included developing his identity as an artisan, earning and saving money to achieve his freedom and acquire property, participating in church and civic life, and assembling the means to establish and protect a free family and help liberate others.

THIS BOOK IS ABOUT African American artisans who plied their trades in the small, majority-black port city of New Bern, North Carolina, from the late eighteenth century to the twentieth century. It has as its immediate purpose to portray a specific group of men and women, their families and friends, their slaves and owners, employees and employers, fellow citizens and church members—in a particular place through time. Through the admittedly sparse record of their experiences, we can consider the complexity and contradictions of their lives, their limitations and accomplishments, and their changing trade, family, and political roles.

More broadly, through the lens of New Bern's example, this group biography depicts an important class of Americans—artisans of color in the urban South—whose story is seldom told, and thereby highlights the experiences of a group vital to the history of American crafts, labor, social, and political life. The popular stereotype of African American southerners focuses on their labor in fields and forests, as servants and laborers, or minimally skilled craft workers. But in fact from the earliest years of Euro-African settlement in America men and women of African descent practiced craft trades in urban as well as rural settings, where they often constituted a major part of the skilled workforce.[2] Their numbers varied from one locale to another and from one period to another, but by any yardstick black southerners composed a significant proportion of America's artisan population throughout the eighteenth and nineteenth centuries.

This study explores the experiences of New Bern artisans of color from two interwoven perspectives. On the one hand, it uses their example to depict in detail, and when possible in personal terms, aspects of the lives of urban black artisans that New Bernians shared with their counterparts throughout the region. From New Orleans and Charleston to Richmond and Baltimore, enslaved and free black artisans found that, in contrast to conditions in the countryside, in town they were likelier to observe and do business with a wide range of black and white people, to hone their skills and learn strategies from other enslaved and free blacks, and to gather with people of diverse backgrounds and political views in churches, taverns, and workshops. Towns and cities also offered prime opportunities for blacks to gain their freedom and, especially after emancipation, to participate in political and civic life. In the early national and antebellum eras, urban life in New Bern had more in common with that of the mid-sized river ports of Wilmington and Fayetteville, North Carolina, and Richmond and Petersburg, Virginia, than with that of the big, rich cities of New Orleans or Charleston, or, at the other extreme, the little courthouse and market towns of a few hundred people each that dotted the region. After the Civil War and emancipation, the various economic and political differences that distinguished North Carolina from other states related New Bern more directly to its sister North Carolina cities, including both the old river ports and the growing industrial towns of the Piedmont.

Whatever it shared with other communities, New Bern's particular character framed the lives of its black and white inhabitants and was shaped by them. It, along with every town in every period, had distinct racial, political, legal, economic, and cultural characteristics that created the social environment for all.[3] For more than a century, artisans of color found New Bern an exceptionally promising place to develop their skills, shape their lives, and to establish, advance, and protect their identities as artisans. Among the intersecting threads that created its distinct character were its majority-black population, the wealth and sophistication of early town leaders, the rise of a substantial free black population, the state's comparatively lax racial laws, and the relatively tolerant and even supportive attitudes of some leading whites toward black freedom and advancement.

As in any story, unpredictably important events highlight the role of contingency and luck in the town's character and history: the presence of the son of a leading merchant and an Ibo woman who nurtured New Bern's remarkable group of free black people; the quick Union capture of the town early in the Civil War, which enabled it to become a hotbed of black political leadership; postwar Democrats' ploy to limit black and Republican political influence by gerrymandering New Bern and Craven County into a predominantly black congressional district, which bolstered the black political leadership—made up primarily of artisans—long after the end of Reconstruction. There is also the story of what did not happen—the burst of the financial bubble that terminated the town's early national–period "golden age"; the failure of antebellum leaders to build competitive rail and shipping connections; and, from the mid-nineteenth century onward, a pattern of modest growth in population and industrial development that maintained much of the scale and feel of the earlier town, in which artisans continued to play important economic and social roles.

As depicted in Chapter 1, "The Setting," while its size might label it a town rather than a city—indeed, it called itself a town until after the Civil War—New Bern's early stature as a principal port, colonial capital, and the largest urban place in the state, together with its complex social and economic life and some of the colony and state's most sophisticated urban architecture, gave it the presence of a small city within its temporal and geographical context. In this port town, characterized by a white mercantile and planter elite and a majority-black population, there were opportunities for skilled artisans, together with prospects for fellowship and community for people of color. Like their counterparts in other southern cities, New Bern artisans of color found their own ways of navigating their community's web of race and power, custom and law.

ALL ARTISANS—no matter what their race, status, or trade—grounded their social and economic identity in the mastery of the expertise required to produce material objects their communities needed and valued. Based in access to training through apprenticeship or other means, their craft proficiency—combined with industry and thrift, good luck and connections—could open the way to positions well above that of the unskilled laborer without depending on the accumulation of capital that defined the upper classes.[4]

The status of artisan was especially significant for southern blacks. In New Bern's and many other southern cities' steep class and racial hierarchies, even the most successful white artisans remained far below the elite establishment, ranking above the laboring classes and enslaved people but well beneath the propertied gentry at the top of the social and economic ladder. This stratified situation prevailed in most southern cities even when more egalitarian ideals improved artisans' status in some northern cities. In many cases, southern white craftsmen believed that even their relatively low perch on the economic scale was threatened by competition from enslaved and free black artisans.[5] For people of color in New Bern, as elsewhere, the ladder was severely truncated at the top. From the colonial period through most of the nineteenth century, the social and economic rung occupied by artisans (along with a few barbers, teachers, and ministers) marked the top of the ladder for blacks, however talented they might be. With rare exceptions, New Bern's leading black artisans dominated among the town's most prosperous, best educated, and most respected people of color.

New Bern's black artisans participated in a venerable and widespread tradition in North Carolina. In 1711 Anglican missionary John Urmston observed that whites in the young colony of North Carolina had "a bad time" unless they had "great numbers of slaves who understand most handicrafts," and in the 1730s traveler John Brickell found in eastern North Carolina "several Blacks born here that can Read and Write, others that are bred to the Trades, and prove good Artists in most of them." Although many black craftspeople served the farms and villages of the predominantly rural colony and state, others clustered in the small but growing towns. As was true elsewhere in the South, in every North Carolina community with a significant black population, slaves and sometimes free people of color practiced artisan trades along with and often alongside white craftsmen. So widespread was white reliance on black workmen that a white visitor who admired the substantial buildings and craft productivity of the Moravian settlement of Wachovia in 1773, upon learning that there were only two blacks there, was "the more surprised to find that white people had done so much work." Using the term "mechanic" in a traditional sense that encompassed artisans in a range of handicrafts, a North Carolina politician commented in 1828, "What branch of mechanic have we in our country in which we do not find negroes often distinguished for their skill and ingenuity? In every place we see them equaling the best white mechanics."[6]

Until the Civil War and emancipation, the southern white establishment had an interest in providing craft training for enslaved and free blacks. Slaveholders profited from their skilled slaves' enhanced earnings and sale value, and they and other members of the community hired skilled slaves as needed. As we shall see, apprenticeships for free black children and white orphans provided social controls over both groups and gave them support and skills to prevent them from becoming a public burden. After emancipation, white attitudes and public policies changed, with the result that black rather than white artisans took on most of the training of black youths in skilled trades.

However it was structured, craft training opened doors for thousands of young people of color. Artisans could earn far more money than unskilled workers—at least two or three times as much per diem. Even for enslaved artisans whose work chiefly profited their owners, their wages could add up if they worked extra hours or were hired out and allowed to keep a portion of their pay. Artisan trades also provided opportunities to form relationships with a wide range of community members, including both fellow people of color and influential whites, and to establish reputations for high-quality work and solid character.

Few black artisans grew wealthy, but many attained a modest "competency," and their experiences and achievements enabled them to establish a ground upon which they could stand and face the world. Male artisans such as John Rice Green, in slavery but especially in freedom, employed their occupational status and earnings to claim their manhood despite whites' insistence on sole dominance, by forming and protecting stable families and by developing individual and group self-esteem through church and community leadership. Women's artisan skills, besides enabling them to earn a living, allowed them to share in white gender roles. Unskilled female slaves often labored in the fields or in town at the same tasks as men, but white gender distinctions generally assigned female artisans of both races to garment-making trades. Both black and white married women, such as the freeborn tailoress and dressmaker Temperance Green, John Rice Green's second wife and the mother of his children, often employed their sewing or weaving skills to supplement their husbands' income in supporting their families. Especially important, as Temperance demonstrated after her husband's death, single and widowed needlewomen could earn a slender living while also claiming a feminine niche considered respectable for women of both races. Grounded in their skilled trades, black men and women artisans could and did employ their determination and their skills to work for freedom for themselves and others, to develop their relationships, and to assume leadership in many arenas.

Scholars have long recognized that throughout the nation's history African Americans played vital roles in skilled craftsmanship and in economic and civic life.[7] Several regional and local studies have documented the presence of black artisans in specific times and places, including antebellum New Orleans, Charleston, and Baltimore, Petersburg, and Richmond.[8] A few outstanding black artisans, such as the antebellum free cabinetmaker Thomas Day of Milton, North Carolina, and the twentieth-century blacksmith Philip Simmons of Charleston, South Carolina, have gained scholarly attention because of their distinctive handiwork.[9] The enslaved seamstress Elizabeth Keckly worked in Hillsborough, North Carolina, and elsewhere before gaining fame as confidante and dressmaker to Mary Todd Lincoln.[10] Craftsmen, including blacksmith Gabriel in Virginia, carpenter Denmark Vesey in Charleston, and caulker Frederick Douglass in Baltimore, figured prominently among antebellum leaders of rebellions and abolitionism. Accounts of black political leadership during and after Reconstruction show that many of the freedmen who held political office were artisans.[11]

What is missing, however, is consideration of urban southern black artisans as individuals and as a group through time in the context of a local framework. New Bern artisans of color appear occasionally in cameo parts in larger studies—including Donum Montford as an emancipated black slaveholder; the emancipated spinner Amelia Green as a determined emancipator of her children; freedman and cooper Virgil A. Crawford as a voice for freedmen's hopes on Emancipation Day; and carpenter Israel B. Abbott and cooper Edward R. Dudley as combatants in post–Civil War politics. But rarely do these craftspeople have more than walk-on roles. With the exceptions of recent works on Edward Dudley's family or the radical political leader and brickmason Abraham Galloway, they seldom appear as people with lives and careers extending through time or as members of families and communities.[12]

As a locally focused, longitudinal study, *Crafting Lives* allows these and other men and women to appear not merely as snippets or in brief quotes but as people interacting with others through changing times. It enables us to consider their intertwined roles as family members bolstering kinship ties; as workers engaged in varied occupational and economic roles; as men and women striving for freedom, education, and opportunity through self-propelled mobility and other strategies; and as leaders in churches, uplift organizations, and political life during the Civil War and for many years afterward. It presents a narrative that complements existing literature by depicting in detail and giving human personality to the experiences and identities of black artisans through time in a single community.[13]

New Bern's relatively small size offers advantages for a fine-grained local study. By focusing on a specific class of people—artisans of color, who never numbered more than a few hundred at any given time—in a compact community of a few thousand souls, it is possible to assemble information in ways seldom feasible for a larger population segment, and thereby to discern individual stories and larger trends that enrich or complement previous generalizations about black artisan life. Moreover, events specific to New Bern generated situations in which black artisans dealt with unusually promising opportunities and stunningly oppressive restrictions in rapid succession. The city's dynamic history highlights ways in which these artisans confronted new challenges, using their imaginations, skills, and relationships to negotiate their place within their circumstances and sometimes to reshape those circumstances.

The arcs of this narrative—a rollercoaster ride rather than a single arc—place black artisans' lives and actions within the context of larger events nationally, in the state, and in New Bern. Following a brief depiction of the town itself (Chapter 1), chronologically arranged chapters address its artisans' experiences and identity in four principal periods: the relatively flexible early national period (Chapter 2); the increasingly restrictive antebellum years (Chapter 3); the burst of liberty and opportunity during Union occupation of the city (Chapter 4); the long-sought freedom, economic autonomy, family unification, and political participation of the immediate postwar era, followed by the political and racial strife of the last decade of nineteenth century and the drastic restrictions imposed at the turn of the twentieth century (Chapter 5).

THROUGHOUT THE NARRATIVE, certain themes recur, including changing definitions of the meaning of race; black artisans' exercise of agency individually and as members of a group; and their roles within the larger picture of American artisan identity. In such ways, their story contributes concrete and specific human detail to ongoing conversations about African American and American artisan history.[14]

Over the years from the American Revolution to the turn of the twentieth century, as they sought to fulfill their hopes, New Bern's black artisans dealt with shifting definitions of the meaning of race in America.[15] It is well established that Americans have employed ideologies of race in changing ways, and in particular that whites have used racial categories to advance their own interests. From the colonial period and early Republic to the onset of the Jim Crow era and beyond, black New Bernians encountered changing concepts and consequences of what it meant to be "white" or "colored," and they varied their strategies accordingly.

Central to the story is the sense of agency that artisans like John Rice Green and Temperance Green developed through their skills and personal connections—the belief, or at least the hope, that along with producing useful and well-crafted objects, they could find ways to shape their lives and advance their situations and those of their families. Time and time again, they found or created paths of opportunity through the interstices of racially oppressive laws and customs. In every period these skilled men and women used whatever power and leverage they possessed toward certain basic goals: to form and protect stable families; to exert some degree of control over their time and their work; to make enough money to establish a home and support a family; to associate freely with friends and family; to speak and to worship without interference; to gain positions of respect and influence within their community; and, for men, to vote and organize for their own and future generations' rights and advancement.

Most strikingly, in their actions and attitudes New Bern's black craftsmen embodied many traits of American artisan identity, and when they had a public voice, they invoked the principles of the American Revolution and the U.S. Constitution and claimed their place as citizens in terms that some scholars have identified with American artisanal republicanism and identity—that is, the philosophy by which early American mechanics defined their vision of the ideal republic and their proper place in it.

Looking mainly at white men in northern cities, historians have pointed to a "core set of values" that gave American artisans a "special identity as productive members of the new Republic." Claiming an honorable social position grounded in "honest industry," they invoked the ideals of the American Revolution and the rhetoric of the French Revolution and Jeffersonian republicanism as they engaged in political life in order to advance and protect their social and economic status against political and economic pressures.[16] When they marched in protests or in patriotic parades, these northern white craftsmen, like their counterparts in Europe, proceeded in trade groups and displayed the tools or the products of their crafts—Boston ship builders had a model shipyard on a float pulled by thirteen horses in a parade in 1788—as symbols of their status. Successful northern artisans such as silversmith Paul Revere had their portraits painted while holding products of their craft or working at their trades. As artisans they defined their identity and status through the possession of skills and tools essential to the creation of valuable handicrafts, an emphasis on thrift and "industry" (hard work) resulting in economic independence and the ability to earn a "competency" sufficient to support a family and own a modicum of property, a sense of mutuality and belonging within a larger class group that provided assistance and support, participation in civic and political duties, and "respectability"—as denoted by sobriety, morality, and propriety in their style of living—a quality that correlated with the nineteenth century's emerging middle-class ideals.[17]

Complementing works on white artisans in northern cities, studies such as those in *American Artisans: Crafting Social Identity, 1750–1850* have expanded the focus to other locales, suggesting that while craftspeople everywhere "used their artisanal status to assert their social identity," artisans in different settings differed in their strategies as well as in their ultimate goals. This broader focus reveals that "the issues of mechanics' identity and independence encompass more than the rise of artisanal republicanism and the creation of the working and middle classes."[18]

Particularly relevant to the present study are projects that consider how artisan identity developed for whites and blacks amid the distinctive racial conditions of the antebellum South. Only in a few southern cities, and seldom in North Carolina, did white artisans in the South self-identify as a class group based on occupational status.[19] Southern white artisans most often called up the rhetoric of artisan identity in times of economic stress to protest against competition from black craftsmen or laws and practices that favored the propertied elite over working people.[20] Many ambitious antebellum white artisans sought to become slaveholders and even planters themselves. Others, before and especially after the war, strove to join the managerial, professional, and industrialist classes.[21]

Especially challenging is the largely unaddressed question of artisan identity among southern black craftsmen. Thousands upon thousands of American craftspeople belonged to this social, racial, and geographical category, making their experience a vital part of the picture of American artisan life. Yet as James Sidbury states in an essay about enslaved craftsmen in early Richmond, the subject of black and especially enslaved American artisans' identity has gained scant attention from scholars, in part because their story "fits awkwardly into the existing literature on the history of artisans in America" and indeed "calls into question the relevance of traditional definitions of artisanship for slave societies."[22]

Since slaves could not own even themselves, much less their tools, how could they embody the artisan's defining quality of possession of skills and tools? With their skills employed to profit their owners and their families subject to dispersal by an owner's whim or need, how could enslaved artisans attain the goal of an independent "competency" or support a family as white artisans sought to do? How could enslaved artisans or even free blacks expect to follow white artisans' customary path from apprentice to independent master or mistress or hope to participate in society as an artisan-citizen? Given the South's racialized definitions of class, how could enslaved or free black artisans establish themselves as a respectable class group? With the South's antebellum restrictions on free black suffrage, how fully could they share in the ideals of artisanal republicanism and citizenship? After emancipation and enfranchisement, how did newly freed artisans affirm their citizen identity and their place in the American republic in the face of white backlash? Faced with white efforts to limit blacks' economic advancement coupled with the growth of mass production, how could black artisans gain the economic independence that lay at the heart of artisan identity? Given the deferential racial customs of the South, what did respectability mean to artisans of color? What degree of mutuality was possible among unfree workers and free ones, or for freedpeople circumscribed by racially based restrictions?

New Bern provides an opportunity to explore such questions through studying the actions and—when the record permits it—the rhetoric of the community's black artisans. In New Bern, as in most southern cities, it is easy to see how white concepts of race often stifled blacks' development of identities as artisans and citizens. But in New Bern, especially during periods when the city's people of color had opportunities to define their lives as free people and as citizens, we are invited to ask, "What did these artisans do when they could?" The evidence suggests that what they said when they had a public voice and, especially, *what they did when they could* embodied essential values of American artisan and citizen identity.

From the colonial period to the Civil War, enslaved and free artisans of color in New Bern and other locales, like artisans everywhere, worked to convey trade skills to the younger generations. Despite the obstacles, they strove to attain their freedom through escape and manumission, to support the liberation of others, and to assert their roles as husbands and wives and parents. Through the early national period, especially in New Bern, some artisans born in slavery had a real hope of obtaining their freedom and even advancing to the position of masters in their trades. As long as state law allowed them to do so—until 1835—free black men in New Bern, including the artisans who constituted a significant portion of the local electorate, asserted their citizenship by voting regularly and for politicians who protected their rights. While accommodating the rituals of racial deference with "modest, unassuming" behavior, black artisans also constructed personae that projected social respectability and mastery of skills. In 1811, as we shall see, the recently manumitted carpenter Thomas Newton identified himself as a "Master" of his trade and used traditional artisanal language when he stated that he had earned the money to buy and free his wife "by the fruits of his honest industry."[23] Leading artisans also used the fruits of their industry to become slaveholders and masters of apprentices and to enable their children to better themselves through education as well as the acquisition of trade skills. Confronted in the 1850s with growing threats to their status and liberty, many free black artisans, including John Rice Green's widow Temperance Green, left New Bern for the North to establish new lives rather than lose the economic and social ground they had struggled to attain. Other free black artisans and most enslaved ones stayed in New Bern, employing—like other people of color across the South—their skills and industry, networks of kin, participation in churches and civic organizations, and webs of communication to extend their political knowledge and their sense of themselves as potential citizens.[24]

Once the Civil War brought freedom—which came early in New Bern, with Union military occupation from 1862 onward—formerly enslaved as well as already free artisans promptly put into practice the political ideals and goals they had had to repress for years. Black artisans and their allies led in the Equal Rights Leagues, staging parades and other public events that promoted their cause, thus taking the reins in early campaigns for full citizenship. Fittingly indeed, at the North Carolina Freedmen's Convention of 1865—which New Bern's black artisan-leaders organized and dominated—the convention leaders employed the language of artisan identity in predicting the future of black advancement: "[We] will prove by our habits of industry and respectability, that we are worthy of citizenship among the people of North Carolina."[25]

From 1865 onward a group of formerly enslaved as well as previously free black artisans emerged as leading master craftsmen and property owners. They also continued in public leadership roles established during their wartime experiences, and they and their successors persisted in such roles through most of the century. They used their artisan status to advance larger goals, especially the attainment of equal political rights and educational opportunities that opened the door for advancement for their children and the coming generations. Time and time again, as they navigated the unfamiliar and ever shifting terrain of life and work after emancipation, New Bern artisans of color embodied and expressed core traditions of American artisan identity and citizenship in ways adapted to the circumstances in which they plied their trades and lived their lives.

Finally, this book is, as historian Glenda Gilmore wrote of *Gender and Jim Crow*, her New Bern–based study of Progressive Era black women, "a book about hope."[26] As we will see throughout the narrative, artisans of color in

New Bern, like individuals in many times and places, employed multiple strategies to form and to pursue their hopes. Through their sense of purpose and their navigation of racial mores, and especially through their capacities as informed and tenacious artisans and citizens, they worked to fulfill the hopes they shared with many others—for freedom, a safe family, a decent education, the right to vote, a comfortable home, a place in the community. During the Civil War one observer called the occupied town a "Mecca of a thousand noble aspirations." While many had to defer or give up their dreams or see their achievements vanish, a remarkable number of New Bern's black artisans saw at least some of their hopes become reality.

Crafting Lives thus offers a new perspective on the lives and strategies of an understudied group of American artisans. Instead of singling out a few outstanding craftspeople as anomalies, we can perceive them as individuals within a personal and temporal context, as part of a community and of a long continuum. Rather than viewing black artisans as an undifferentiated group or attempting to characterize a universal slave or freedperson's experience, we can glimpse the outlines of individual lives as well as of various classes and levels of accomplishment. We can observe how these artisans employed their skills and connections to navigate the pitfalls and opportunities of an ever-changing, racially configured landscape. Throughout the years, black artisans, like John Rice Green, dealt constantly with the powerful and shifting tensions between the demands of "knowing their place" in the American South and their dream of claiming their proper place in the ideal American republic.

Just as every town and city across the South and across the nation had its own distinctive character, so too did black artisans' lives play out differently in different communities. No other place replicated New Bern's particular opportunities and limitations. Still, the story of this one small city and the stories of its black craftspeople can expand our understanding of the broader saga of American slavery and freedom. Through these black New Bernians' experiences, both typical and atypical of their counterparts elsewhere, we can perceive more fully the roles of southern black urbanites in the larger picture of American artisan identity. It is my hope in writing this book that their stories will open doors to further studies and broader questions about black artisans' lives and identities throughout the nation.

ONE

The Setting

New Bern from the Colonial Period to 1900

Complaint having been made that certain persons have lately introduced into this Town a Machine called a flying horse machine [carousel] to which many idle and disorderly persons resort to in the night time as well as in the day whereby the peace of the Town is disturbed, and the Subordination of the Slaves and free Negroes is lessened. It is therefore ordered that hereafter it shall not be lawful for any person whatsoever to use any such machine for the entertainment of any person within this town after Sun down under the penalty of Five pounds for every offence—and further that if any said person shall presume to admit any Slave, free Negro or Mulatto to ride on the sd horses or any of them, or to be within the inclosure when the same is exhibited he, she or they shall forfeit five Pounds for every Offence.

—New Bern Town Council Minutes,
July 25, 1803

For most of its history, New Bern, North Carolina, was a majority-black community in which people of every color and condition interacted daily. Some aspects of its story differed from those of other southern cities, just as those cities differed among themselves. Among the town's particular characteristics were its early status as a colonial capital and principal port; its unusually large proportion of free people of color; its status as a liberated city occupied by Union forces from 1862 through the duration of the war; and its role as a center of black political leadership from the mid-1860s until black disfranchisement in 1900. New Bern also shared much with its sister southern cities, including a defining feature of southern towns—the proximity and interaction of black and white residents. Visitors from the North or other countries sometimes found this situation startling, even objectionable. But for southern urbanites, it was simply a fact of life.

Amid the hierarchies of race and class, individual paths and personal relationships often crossed racial boundaries. Whatever the efforts of white authorities to exert control, white and black, free and enslaved people met in the marketplace and elsewhere to exchange goods and services and to share pleasures. Free black and white people bought and sold property to one another, including slaves until the Civil War. Blacks and whites attended auctions of debtors' and decedents' household goods, flocked to the race track, gathered to witness political orations and public whippings and hangings, and grasped the chance to whirl on a "flying horse." Colonial and antebellum New Bernians of every rank and hue encountered one another in religious revivals and in established churches. And while some parts of town had a preponderance of one race or the other, the homes and workshops of blacks and whites were dispersed throughout the community.

In private, men and women of every race and status engaged in sexual relationships, with white men often taking black mistresses, free or enslaved; in some cases their children were recognized locally, and a few became leaders in their trades or in the community. Free women and men of color married enslaved partners despite laws against such unions and the lack of legal standing for their marriages, and many black parents raised their children to remember family members who had been sold away. In common with most southern cities, but in contrast to many northern locales, free and enslaved black apprentices in New Bern lived in the households of both black and white master artisans throughout the antebellum period. Likewise in common with sister southern towns but unlike most northern

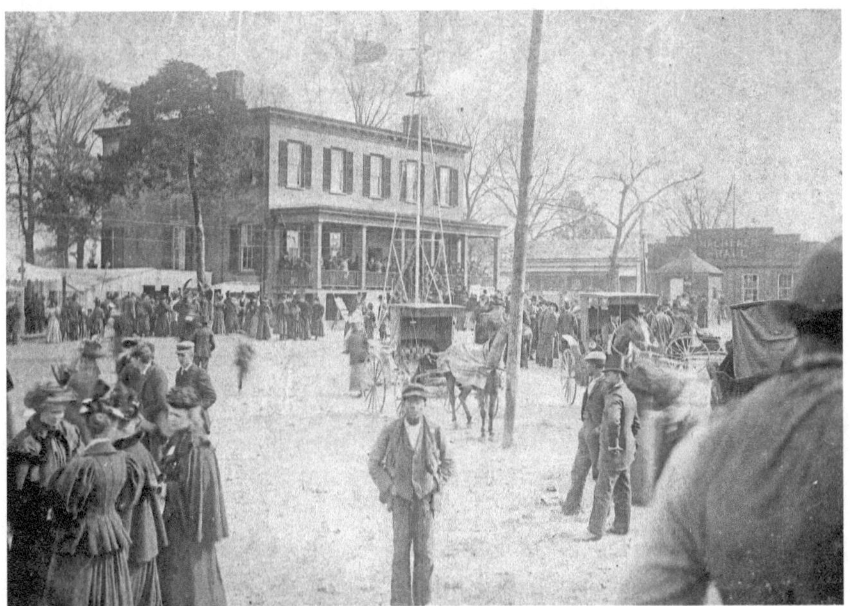

New Bern Fish, Oyster, and Game Fair, New Bern, February 26, 1897. Typical of the nineteenth century, the fair attracted both black and white attendees. The rear of the Moses Griffin School (discussed in Chapter 3) is shown in the background. Courtesy of the New Bern Historical Society, New Bern, North Carolina.

ones, New Bern's enslaved, free black, and white artisans worked alongside one another in shops, on construction sites, and along the wharves and waterways. As elsewhere, the mid- and late nineteenth-century city saw growing separation of races and classes both in residential patterns and in membership in churches and other community institutions. Such divisions increased after the Civil War as whites erected new barriers and newly emancipated blacks sought greater autonomy. Even so, at the end of the nineteenth century the lines of Jim Crow segregation had not been fully drawn.

Throughout the years covered in this book, residents of New Bern maintained familiar patterns of connections along with hierarchy, mutual knowledge along with social distance. Black and white people moved constantly throughout the city, going in and out of shops and houses, to the wharves and back, watching and being watched. Little boys, especially, followed their curiosity through town. One who grew up as a free boy of color in antebellum New Bern recalled, "There was not much 'going on,' in that old town, on land or on water, in those days, which I did not see. If there was to be a sale or hiring of slaves on the auction block, I was near at hand, to note every word, cry or movement; if any one was to be lashed, at the whipping-post, there [I] was . . . to behold it." Returning home from his explorations, he met with a warm reception even if he had "neglected some domestic duty, in order to keep tab on the varied county and municipal affairs." Central to the experience of the town's black artisans—and to that of most New Bernians and residents of other small and medium-sized towns—was the community's compactness and intimacy. People of every race and status knew one another—knew their names, their faces, their families, their relationships, and, in the largest sense, knew their "business."[1]

New Bern was no ordinary small town, for despite its modest size—fewer than 1,000 people in the late colonial period and just over 9,000 by the end of the nineteenth century—it has a long and complex history. Founded in 1710 at the confluence of the Neuse and Trent Rivers, by the late eighteenth century New Bern had developed into a "city-like" place with a full range of classes, dominated by a white mercantile and planter elite who profited from the coastwise triangular trade among the Carolinas, the West Indies, and New England.[2] Like many ports, it had a cosmopolitan flavor owing to the comings and goings of sailors, artisans, merchants, and lawyers from the Caribbean, northern cities, Great Britain, and continental Europe. Grounded in its stature as a colonial capital and a port of regional significance, from 1790 through 1830 it was the largest town in a state sometimes called "civitas sine urbe."[3]

New Bern, like other principal towns in the colony, was laid out in a formal grid adapted to the topography and the main roads to other communities. Oriented to the site rather than to cardinal directions, the town extended back from the apex of the riverine triangle, with businesses and wharves clustered near the sheltered Trent River waterfront. Principal public buildings stood a few blocks back from the water, and, along with residences and other large and small structures, slave houses, garden lots, and industrial sites appeared in decreasing density toward the edges of the grid. The town plan and scale as depicted in C. J. Sauthier's 1769 town map persisted essentially unchanged at the town core, while growth expanded the grid west and north.

Because of North Carolina's "inconvenient geography," New Bern, like other Tar Heel towns, remained small in size and wealth compared to such well-situated southern ports as New Orleans, Charleston, Richmond, Petersburg, and Baltimore. The rivers that converge in New Bern drain a large agricultural and forested hinterland, but, as was true of all of North Carolina's ports, difficulties of navigation hindered the town's growth in trade, wealth, and size. Above New Bern, the Trent River reaches only a short distance into the agricultural zone. Although the Neuse extends some 275 miles inland, shipping was difficult beyond forty or fifty miles upriver. To compound the problem, below New Bern the Neuse opens not into an ocean harbor but into the Pamlico Sound, a broad expanse separated from the Atlantic by barrier islands with shallow and oft-changing inlets. Captains of seafaring vessels bound to or from New Bern had to offload goods or change vessels at Ocracoke Inlet, and some hired pilots to navigate the sound, thus increasing the cost and time of transport and reducing profits on goods traded through the port.

Whatever its limitations as a port, New Bern had the advantage of being located roughly midway along the North Carolina coast, and its status rose when royal governor William Tryon selected it in 1765 as the de facto capital of the colony. He employed English architect John Hawks to build the governor's residence and seat of government now known as Tryon Palace and enhanced the town's prominence as well as its architectural panache. The community and its patriot leaders—who included early state governors—played important roles during the American Revolution and the postwar years. Even after Raleigh was established inland as the new capital in 1794, New Bern struck a visitor in 1802 as a "trading and growing town," with from 700 to 1,000 houses and some "respectable brick edifices," including a new courthouse.[4]

New Bern maintained its position as the state's largest city through the early national period, with about 2,500 people in 1800, more than 3,600 by 1820, and just over 3,700 in 1830. Its population, though small, placed the town in good company among southern cities: in 1820 it stood eighth among them. Density increased within the original town grid and northward on streets from Broad to Queen, and wharves and industries appeared along the Neuse as well as the Trent waterfront. New areas were platted north and west of the old town, again adapting the grid to accommodate property lines and natural features, with Lawson Creek, a tributary of the Trent, marking the southern boundary of a tract developed west of the original grid.

During what observers later regarded as its "golden age," the town—known as the "Athens of North Carolina"—was home to some of the state's most illustrious political figures and elite families and was noted for its good schools, fashionable social life, and elegant architecture. Visitors in the 1820s found it a "vortex of fashion," where "the gayest of the gay" lived a life "full of extravagance and fine dressing." A former New Bernian on a visit home described one woman's house as "like a palace she has the most splendid drawing room I ever beheld, quite new and the latest fashion, she told us the furniture of that room cost 1500 doll[ar]s."[5]

Many a traveler who struggled through eastern North Carolina's small villages, swamps, and forests greeted the town's urban comforts with relief and admiration. Although the governor's palace burned in 1798, stylish and substantial new buildings, in brick as well as frame, defined the cityscape, including handsome, towered churches, a brick academy and a Masonic hall built in the classical spirit of the palace, well-finished commercial buildings, and costly residences. Except for commercial rows, most buildings, including houses, were freestanding, in keeping with residents' preferences. Free workers' dwellings, slave quarters, workshops, and outbuildings stood among the larger buildings and formed clusters at the expanding perimeters of town.

From the late colonial period onward, New Bern and surrounding Craven County had a substantial black population that included both slaves and an unusually large number of free people of color. Free black families had lived in Craven County since the early eighteenth century, and many descended from immigrants from Virginia and Maryland, including the Dove, Carter, Copes, George, Godett, and Spelman families.[6] During the colonial period, most free blacks in the county—like those throughout North Carolina—owed their status to free maternal forbears. New Bern jurist William Gaston affirmed in 1835 that, according to aged residents, there were "scarcely any emancipated Slaves in this State" before the American Revolution, and the free people of color were "chiefly Mulattoes, the children of white women."[7] In 1790, the first United States census counted in Craven County (including New Bern) 337 free people of color, 3,440 whites, and 3,858 slaves. Some other eastern North Carolina towns and plantation counties also had large black populations, but in the state as a whole, large slaveholders were few, and black people (including a tiny number of free blacks) constituted only about one quarter of the total population.[8] During the early national period, as New Bern's free black population increased faster than did the overall population, the community became one of North Carolina's chief centers of free black life. In 1800 the first census to count the town separately from the county showed that the town's population of 2,467 included a slight majority of slaves over white residents plus 144 free people of color, and by 1820 there were 268 free blacks in town along with 1,475 whites and 1,920 slaves.[9]

As in many antebellum southern cities, black New Bernians worshipped in racially mixed, if physically separated, congregations in which blacks were often assigned to the balconies or to separate services. The small Catholic congregation begun by 1821 was evidently unusual in holding joint services for all: in 1839, after meeting in rented or borrowed spaces for several years, their bishop encouraged the group to build its own church "to keep our people together, negros as well as whites, which will neither leave us at the caprice or bigotry of others."[10] Methodists and some other denominations held revivals where men and women of all classes and races joined in emotional services that alarmed staid white citizens.

Most churchgoing black New Bernians attended the Methodist Meeting House, a majority-black congregation with an expressive style of worship. The strength of Methodism in North Carolina reflected the influence of itinerant missionaries such as Francis Asbury, who ministered to blacks as well as whites and opposed slavery. As early as 1796 New Bernians, including hundreds of slaves, gathered to hear Asbury preach. In about 1800 the congregation erected a meetinghouse on Hancock Street, and by 1808 the congregation of 781 souls comprised 201 whites and 580 blacks. When white Baptist minister Samuel Wait came to New Bern in 1827, he attended a Methodist service and commented, "Nearly all the blacks in town who have made a profession of religion, belong to that church."[11]

By 1820 other denominations had established or revitalized congregations, including Baptists, Presbyterians, and Episcopalians, which all had black as well as white worshippers. Christ Episcopal Church, long associated with the landed gentry, lagged after the American Revolution but took on new life in 1817 with the organization of the North Carolina diocese; its rector Richard Sharp Mason, who arrived in 1818, initiated a ministry among blacks, and the parish register recorded the baptisms, marriages, and burials of slaves and free blacks along with whites. By the mid-1820s, both the Episcopalians and the Presbyterians had erected costly and handsome new churches. Along with expressing their congregations' devotion and status, these edifices also displayed the local prosperity that attained its apex by that time and would begin to decline by the end of the decade.

THE ANTEBELLUM PERIOD brought a severe downturn in New Bern's fortunes and its ranking among the state's cities. During the 1820s and 1830s, the state as a whole experienced economic problems and outmigration that earned it the nickname of the "Rip van Winkle State." New Bern, like most of North Carolina, suffered from the dearth of good transportation and profitable enterprises. Beginning in the mid-1830s, however, and increasingly in the 1840s and 1850s, progressive state leaders and entrepreneurs in Charlotte, Fayetteville, Raleigh, Salisbury, and Wilmington campaigned for and attained educational advances and internal improvements, including railroads and plank roads. Although the scale of these projects and the economic and urban growth in North Carolina never rivaled the topographically advantaged and more entrepreneurial cities of other southern states, nonetheless these investments brought what progressives called a "Spirit of Improvement" that benefited the economy and slowed outmigration.

Besides sharing in the general depression in the "Rip van Winkle State" during the second quarter of the nineteenth century, New Bern experienced an especially sharp plunge in the late 1820s as Caribbean trade dropped off; the old problems of navigation intensified as ships grew larger; and a local banking crisis burst credit-based bubbles for many. A scheme to build a shipping canal from the Neuse below New Bern to the good ocean harbor at Beaufort fell far short of its sponsors' hopes. Almost overnight, it seemed, the city that had been the "gayest of the gay" collapsed into depression. Many people left town, including numerous free people of color, during the 1820s. One observer commented in 1830, "The continued show and dash of those who are insolvants, may be compaired to a candle in the socket. Just before it sinks it brims up with more brilincy, sinks and is no more seen. There will be a dash with sums perloined from creditors until it is extinguished, and then they will sink to be seen no more." In 1834 a prominent white New Bernian wrote, "Our town is full of idle, discontented people, whose vicious appetites seem to crave scandal for their daily food, the place is hardly fit for an honest man to live in; & the country seems to be so impoverished as to afford no business worth pursuing—The times seem to be evil indeed."[12]

The mood and self-image of the citizenry drooped, and more people moved away. According to a later account, in contrast to other cities' "energetic, enterprising" mercantile leadership, antebellum New Bernians "failed to partake of the public spirit which animated the merchants of her sister town, Wilmington, and quietly folding their arms in fancied security, suffered the Wilmington and Weldon railroad to be constructed a few miles in their rear, without securing a connecting link, thus effectually cutting themselves off from the largest portion of their rightful heritage."[13]

In 1840 Wilmington, with its deep river port on the Cape Fear and its newly completed railroad, was almost twice the size of New Bern. By 1860, profiting from its multiple railroad lines and its river trade with Fayetteville and the plank road that linked that town to the North Carolina Piedmont, Wilmington had grown to nearly 10,000 people. New Bern's population as well as its fortunes actually shrank between 1830 and 1840, producing a hiatus in building and a decline in many trades. During the 1840s, local business rallied somewhat with growth in the international turpentine market, and a local newspaper took comfort in 1844 in the fact that "our mechanics for a few months have been busily employed, which we always consider a good indication." The town grew to 4,681 in 1850 and to 5,432 in 1860 and saw new investment in construction and other enterprises. In 1858, after years of effort from its more progressive citizens, the city celebrated the completion of the Atlantic and North Carolina Railroad, which linked New Bern east to Morehead City and west to Goldsboro and thence to points west, north, and south. The railroad facilities at the northeast corner of town spurred enterprises along the Neuse waterfront and encouraged workers to settle in adjoining neighborhoods. Although New Bern never regained its earlier primacy—the "golden age" remembered by many—in 1860 its fortunes were on the upswing and its workshops, construction sites, wharves, and railroad yards bustled with black and white workers.[14]

By the 1850s certain sectors of life showed growing separation of races and classes akin to trends in other southern cities. Whereas for years both blacks and whites had been laid to rest in Cedar Grove Cemetery, shortly before the Civil War, Greenwood Cemetery was established for black burials.[15] During the 1840s, when the nation's northern and southern Baptists and Methodists separated over the issue of slavery, their local congregations divided along racial lines, with the whites constructing new churches and leaving the older sanctuaries to the black members.[16] In 1843 the 284 white members of the Methodist congregation moved into a new sanctuary, while the 803 black members continued in the old meetinghouse and received their own (white) minister from the North Carolina Methodist Conference. Known by 1847 as Andrews (Andrew, or Andrew's) Chapel, it was by far the largest congregation in town. Its role in community life paralleled that of black Methodist groups in Raleigh, Fayetteville, and Elizabeth City and Baptist ones in Richmond and Petersburg and other cities.[17]

The city maintained its familiar balance of whites and slaves—with 1,954 whites and 1,927 slaves in 1850—but saw dramatic growth in the free black population. Much of this increase came in the 1840s, when the number of free blacks in town rose from about 418 to 800—more than 17 percent of the total population. In 1850 both the number and the proportion of New Bern's free people of color surpassed those in any other North Carolina town, including the much larger city of Wilmington.[18]

New Bern's racial makeup was also remarkable within a national context. In 1850 the town's ratio of free people of color to the overall population exceeded that of nearly all southern cities, including Baltimore, Richmond, Charleston, and New Orleans, in each of which free blacks constituted 10 percent or less of the total population. Only Petersburg, Virginia, where industrial development drew free black as well as enslaved workers, had a ratio comparable to New Bern's, with free blacks making up about 18 percent of its total population.[19] In 1850 almost 30 percent of free New Bernians were black, and a similar proportion of black New Bernians were free. Although outmigration in the 1850s reduced the number of free blacks while the slave and white populations grew, nevertheless New Bern's free black population in 1860 still exceeded that of any other North Carolina city.[20]

NEW BERNIANS' EXPERIENCES during the Civil War were unique in the state and nation. Occupied—or liberated—by Union forces from early 1862 onward, the city was transformed overnight as the local white population all but vanished, while the black population soared as fugitive slaves arrived from near and far. Many white New Bernians, like their fellow North Carolinians, had opposed secession and hoped to avoid war, but once the state seceded, on May 20, 1861, most supported the Confederacy. Early Union strategy focused on capturing North Carolina's northern and mid-coastal zone as a base of operations. After taking Hatteras in 1861 and then Roanoke Island, Elizabeth City, and Edenton, Union forces led by General Ambrose Burnside entered New Bern on March 14, 1862, and soon captured nearby Beaufort, Plymouth, and Washington, North Carolina.[21]

The Union troops arrived in New Bern to find that the whites, especially the leading "secesh" citizens, had departed inland by trainloads, as well as by carriage and wagon and on foot, to take refuge in Confederate territory

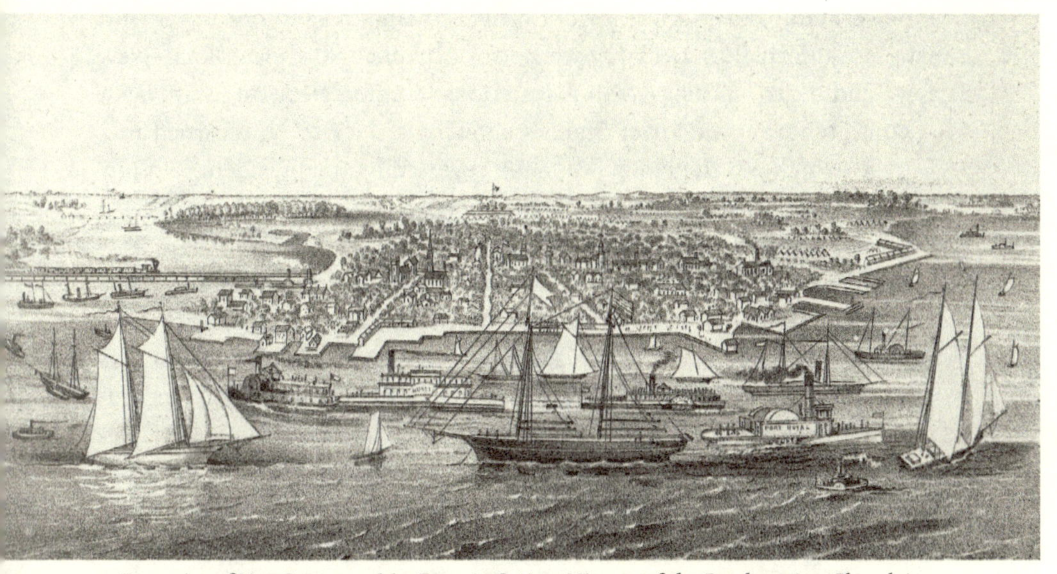

Engraving of New Bern, ca. 1864. From L. C. Vass, History of the Presbyterian Church in New Bern, N.C.: With a Resume of Early Ecclesiastical Affairs in Eastern North Carolina, and a Sketch of the Early Days of New Bern, N.C. *(Richmond: Whittett and Shepperson, 1886). This view looks west from the Neuse River, with the Trent River on the left, crossed by the railroad bridge. Courtesy of the State Archives of North Carolina, Raleigh.*

("Dixie") beyond Union lines. Most stayed away for the duration of the war. Some local slaves were taken or sent inland, but many stayed behind, along with most of the free people of color.[22] Military administrators replaced the local civilian government. Protected by Union troops and free of the long-dominant local white minority, New Bernians of color experienced a new world of possibilities.

Within a week of occupying the city, General Burnside reported that it was "overrun with fugitives," as thousands of slaves from miles away made their way to freedom "through woods and swamps from every side."[23] Questions over the fugitives' status sparked a local controversy entwined with evolving Federal policy. In 1861, at Fortress Monroe in Virginia, Union officials had designated the unexpected number of fugitive slaves coming behind their lines as "contrabands" of war and protected them against claims of their former owners. In coastal South Carolina the 1861 Union capture of the Sea Islands and the town of Beaufort likewise attracted many slaves to seek sanctuary. In a short-lived attempt to encourage North Carolina to rejoin the Union, in May 1862 President Abraham Lincoln appointed

Edward Stanly (a Unionist, former New Bernian, and son of John Stanly, late of California) as civilian governor of occupied North Carolina—New Bern and nearby locales—with instructions to enforce existing state laws. A contretemps ensued over Stanly's allowing a slave to be returned to a former owner, but the policy was soon reversed by the president. On July 17, Congress passed the Second Confiscation Act, stating that slaves of rebel owners who had come into Union lines were "forever free."[24]

As a haven of liberty, the town—which had about 5,000 black and white residents in 1860—nearly doubled in size within a few months. By the end of 1864 there were over 6,500 black residents in New Bern proper and as many more in hastily built emergency settlements outside the city, including the village across the Trent River that became known as James City. Despite repeated attacks by Confederate forces and the Confederate recapture of nearby Plymouth and Washington, New Bern remained in Union hands. Talented and ambitious artisans and others arrived from near and far to join the town's established residents of color and make New Bern a place of unprecedented black political and economic life.

AFTER THE WAR, as white and black New Bernians returned home and more newcomers arrived, residents of the city possessed a strong base of skills, enterprises, and community institutions. At first, the local economic situation looked promising, as established businesses recovered and new ones began. But New Bern shared with much of the South a lack of capital, and its leaders were slow to adopt the booster strategies or attract the entrepreneurs that generated New South advances in competing cities. In contrast to New Bern, within a few years after the war Wilmington's trade and growth bounced back with new energy, as its multiple rail and steamship connections boosted profits from trade in agricultural and forest products and new factories and businesses blossomed. Similar growth and energy boosted the fortunes of the piedmont towns of Charlotte, Winston-Salem, and Greensboro, where newcomers and established citizens invested in new factories and railroad connections.

In New Bern, although shipping rebounded, the financial problems and bad physical condition of the Atlantic and North Carolina Railroad, compounded by the lack of competing rail lines, retarded economic growth. A full fifteen years after the war, the city directory reported that townspeople were still "busily employed in . . . *getting ready* for a higher and more reliable commercial progress" (emphasis added), and pointed to a few new factories—all employing semiskilled or unskilled labor to process local materials—as evidence of progress. Acknowledging that "the old elements of commercial prosperity and power have vanished into the past, never to be restored," the writer envisioned "at least an encouraging probability of such a measure of local opulence and success as we have not known for many years."

In the 1880s and 1890s, outside investors expanded the exploitation of the region's forests, and some additional rail lines were built. With at least a dozen sawmills and planing mills employing scores of workmen by the mid-1890s, the timber industry fueled the economy through the decade and into the next century. New businesses included a bottling plant for a local pharmacist's beverage, invented in 1893 and named Pepsi-Cola in 1898. Forestry and agriculture, including a burgeoning truck-farming industry, along with the business of catching and packing fish and oysters for export, kept merchants and workers busy and the wharves lively.[25]

Postwar New Bern shared certain characteristics with its sister cities in the state. While the piedmont industrial towns of Charlotte, Winston-Salem, and Greensboro barreled ahead in their race to excel in wealth and size, they all remained small compared to New South cities elsewhere. Wilmington, at about 20,000 people, was the state's largest city in 1900. At about half that size, New Bern ranked seventh among the state's urban places. Although New Bern's proportion of black people—more than 60 percent—exceeded that of the state's other cities in 1890 and 1900, nonetheless Wilmington, Raleigh, Charlotte, Winston-Salem, and Fayetteville had populations that ranged from 30 percent to more than 50 percent black.

As New Bern grew at a stately pace from about 5,000 in 1860 to about 9,000 in 1900, its black and white citizens developed a typical range of community institutions. Its first city directory, published in 1880, listed three black Masonic lodges and three white ones, and one black and one white Good Templars chapter. There were five white churches and eight black ones—the latter comprising two African Methodist Episcopal Zion (AME Zion) churches, two Baptist churches, and one each for African Methodist Episcopal (AME), Christian, Episcopal, and Presbyterian worshippers.[26] A Catholic church for blacks soon followed. Most black New Bernians associated with the Baptist, AME, and AME Zion congregations, which were independent of white oversight and supported development of social, educational, and political as well as religious leadership.

Despite changes wrought by emancipation and the beginnings of industrialization, life in New Bern seemed "old-fashioned" to many. The customary habits of familiarity and mutual knowledge interacted with the era's evolving social and economic tensions and distances between classes and races. Most New Bernians, especially those of color, were native North Carolinians—some local, some from other parts of the state—but there were several groups of newcomers, including former Union soldiers stationed there during the war and other northern and European immigrants who established factories, plied specialty trades, or opened retail businesses.[27]

The expansion of the postwar town plan perpetuated the layout established in the colonial period. Wharves and industrial plants grew more numerous along the riverfronts and near the railroad. The central area, from South Front Street to Queen Street, contained the principal business houses and churches as well as new and old residences, ranging in size and quality from industrialists' mansions to working people's homes. The period also brought continuous westward and northward expansion of gridded developments aimed primarily at black and some white working people. After a postwar hiatus in major construction, a massive new courthouse rose in the 1880s to replace one burned years earlier, and it was followed by the federally sponsored building of an imposing United States Post Office in the 1890s. New stores, churches, and residences displayed generally conservative versions of current styles of architecture akin to those in towns throughout the state and region. As freedmen formed their own churches, they worshipped initially in modest structures but within a few decades erected substantial sanctuaries that served as focal points for the growing and increasingly black suburban areas.

Essential to the town's political life was its strong black majority. After the congressionally mandated amendment to the state constitution in 1868 to grant universal male suffrage, New Bern and Craven County became a bastion of black and Republican political voters. Although North Carolina Conservatives (renamed Democrats during the 1870s) regained control of state government in 1870 and ended Reconstruction in 1876, throughout the century at least a few black men, all Republicans, continued to represent Craven County in the legislature and to serve as city aldermen and in other local offices. In 1872 the legislature redrew congressional districts and placed Craven County in the gerrymandered "Black Second" district to minimize the impact of Republican voters on the state in general—and in the process encouraged black officeholding within the district.[28]

The 1890s brought political upheaval for New Bern as for the state at large. Throughout the South, Populists and Republicans mounted challenges to Democratic dominance, but only in North Carolina did Democrats lose control of both the legislature and the governorship. In 1894 the state's Populists and Republicans, who had little in common except their desire to oust the Democrats, formed a Fusionist alliance and won a legislative majority, and they repeated their victory in 1896 and put a white Republican in the governor's office. Fusionism brought new openings in black political life, including greater representation in the legislature and in local offices in New Bern and elsewhere. In 1898 the frustrated Democrats launched a "white supremacy crusade" that produced a statewide Democratic sweep on November 8, followed two days later by a violent Democratic coup in Wilmington. The Democrats followed up with a second white supremacy campaign in 1900. This election also included ratification of a state constitutional amendment to disfranchise nearly all blacks and give whites control of the political process. With the turn of the new century, the page turned on a new era of black disfranchisement and Jim Crow segregation in North Carolina and the American South.

In New Bern, as elsewhere in the South, the new century brought new expressions of social and racial identity and of economic and political life that continued some threads from the eighteenth and nineteenth centuries while breaking off others. The contrast between persistent and broken threads is especially sharp in the material vestiges of New Bern's history. Although local black and white artisans produced thousands of objects of wood, metal, and textiles over the years, scarcely any of those made in New Bern survive. The few known locally made craft items are silver and fine furniture. Although some of the silver is documented to New Bern craftsmen (all of them white), none of the few extant pieces of Pamlico Sound–area furniture has been ascribed to a specific maker.

Among the reasons for the dearth of surviving local craft artifacts are wealthy New Bernians' taste for imported goods and the late development of the practice of identifying and collecting southern crafts. Many New Bern pieces vanished during the Civil War, when the elite left town in advance of Union troops and the contents of the houses they abandoned disappeared in various directions. As elsewhere, most of the tools, horseshoes, barrels, wagons, shoes, and clothing made by local artisans were worn out or tossed aside, while some treasured possessions were sent to faraway heirs or accompanied their owners who moved away. City fires,

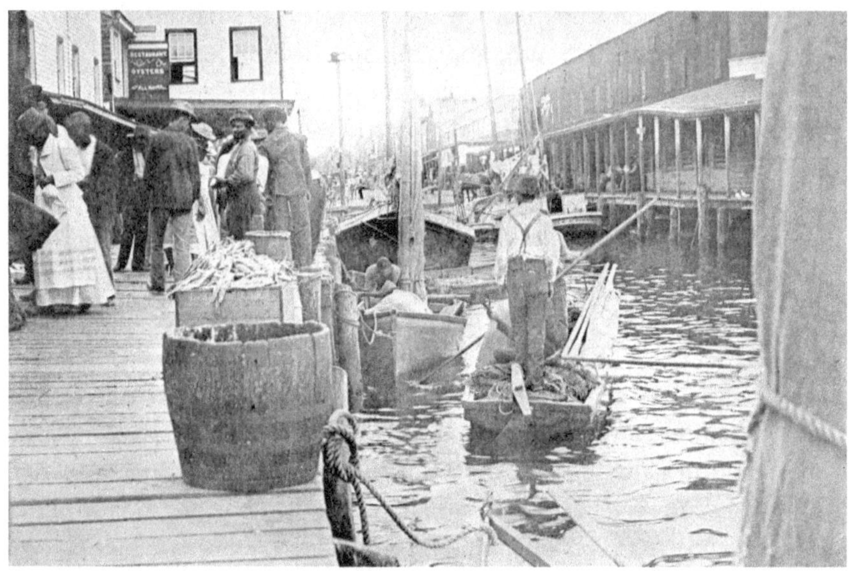

Fish Market, New Bern, 1906. The docks and surrounding buildings that extended into the Trent and the Neuse have been destroyed. Courtesy of the State Archives of North Carolina, Raleigh.

especially the Great Fire of 1922, destroyed untold quantities of furniture as well as family Bibles, photographs, diaries, and letters. So, too, although black craftsmen worked along with whites on most building projects, the best-documented New Bern buildings have been lost, so that we have yet to learn whose hand carved a certain molding, smoothed a plaster wall, or laid up a fine brick chimney.

Because of these losses and the absence of documents or traditions linking a given artisan to a given artifact, in New Bern, in contrast to some locales, it is not yet possible to trace the workmanship, style, or design influences of any of the city's artisans of color. In time, new objects or information may surface to tie more works to their New Bern makers. What survives, however, is the saga of the remarkable lives New Bern's black artisans crafted for themselves, their families, and their fellow New Bernians over a period of more than a century.[29]

The theme of persistent and broken threads also defines the physical setting in which the town's history took place. A remarkable number of high-quality buildings have survived from the eighteenth and nineteenth centuries to define the town's human scale and distinguished architectural character, especially in the central blocks, which include modest and grand buildings of every era. What is missing in New Bern, as in many towns, are most of the neighborhoods and the workaday settings in which the people who appear in this study spent much of their lives. The 1922 fire devastated most of the predominantly black neighborhoods north of and adjoining Queen Street; in subsequent years churches there were rebuilt, as well as some of the homes and businesses. Public housing and urban renewal projects leveled additional blocks in this area and in the old neighborhood north of Lawson Creek. Redevelopment likewise swept away the mixed-use riverfront areas including the old wharves and black and white businesses adjoining South Front Street.

Today's visitor or the traveler returning home often glimpses New Bern first from the soaring Trent River and Neuse River bridges. These panoramic views capture not only the city's changes but essential continuities—the confluence of the broad rivers, the renewed boating activity at the waterfront, the commercial sector stretching back from the waterfronts, and a cityscape where church spires of many eras still rise above the greenery to spike the skyline. From this vantage, atop the product of twenty-first-century technology, it is possible to use the mind's eye to imagine the town of earlier times. Within the context of this riverine triangle and its long history of opportunity and oppression, hard times and prosperity, New Bern's craftspeople of color from the late eighteenth century to the turn of the twentieth century used their skills, their relationships, and their hopes to construct their identities as artisans and as citizens.

TWO

The Fruits of Honest Industry

Black Artisans in New Bern's "Golden Age," 1770–1830

LOST: A few weeks ago, between the Subscriber's House and Mr. Hall's Book store, a DIAMOND for cutting glass with a white bone handle, on which are inscribed the letters D M—A reward of one Dollar and fifty Cents will be given to any person who shall restore it to the owner.

—Donum Mumford [Montford],
New Bern True Republican,
April 2, 1810

The notice in the New Bern newspaper described a small object in simple terms intended to restore it to its owner. The wording also implied much about the owner's identity and the community in which he lived and worked. The specialized tool indicated that he cut and installed window panes as part of his trade. Its diamond head, for scoring precise lines, identified it as an implement of high quality, and its monogrammed handle suggested his attachment to it. The reward of $1.50—a day's pay or more for a skilled worker—revealed his strong desire to regain the lost object and his financial capacity to offer such a sum. The laconic reference to the location where he had lost the glass cutter revealed that the community was small enough and Donum Montford and his place of residence so well known that newspaper readers would know where to look for it.[1]

At the time he placed the notice in 1810, plasterer and brickmason Donum Montford was about forty years old, a newly married head of household, and a master craftsman who had five local children as his apprentices. He and his wife, Hannah, made their home among white and black neighbors, and they became members of Christ Episcopal Church. He owned slaves and real estate, and as a male taxpayer he qualified to vote.

In 1810 Montford had been a free man for just over five years. It is easy to imagine that he had received his diamond glass cutter as a gift on the occasion of his manumission in 1804 or bought it himself as a token of his status. However he came to own it, he likely valued it for more than practical reasons. The possession of craft tools was an established symbol of artisan identity. During and after the American Revolution, urban white craftsmen in the North brandished the tools of their crafts as they marched in parades, trade by trade, to assert their patriotism or defend their economic position. Although such a scene was seldom replicated in North Carolina, artisans here, as elsewhere, understood the meaning as well as the utility of owning tools.[2] When a master artisan presented his graduating apprentice with tools to begin his trade, or a parent bequeathed tools to a child who followed in his or her craft, the transfer marked a life stage as well as meeting a practical need. Seldom did apprentice bonds specify the items to be given, though in one case in piedmont Rowan County in 1805 the county court bound Sam, a free boy of color, to Joseph Clarke to learn the blacksmith's trade and ordered Clarke to give Sam "when of age an Anville, Sledge & Hammere Shoeing tools, & two pr. of Tongs."[3] In contrast to a slave, who legally owned nothing, not even himself, a free artisan took pride in owning his tools. Whether Montford retrieved his glass cutter or

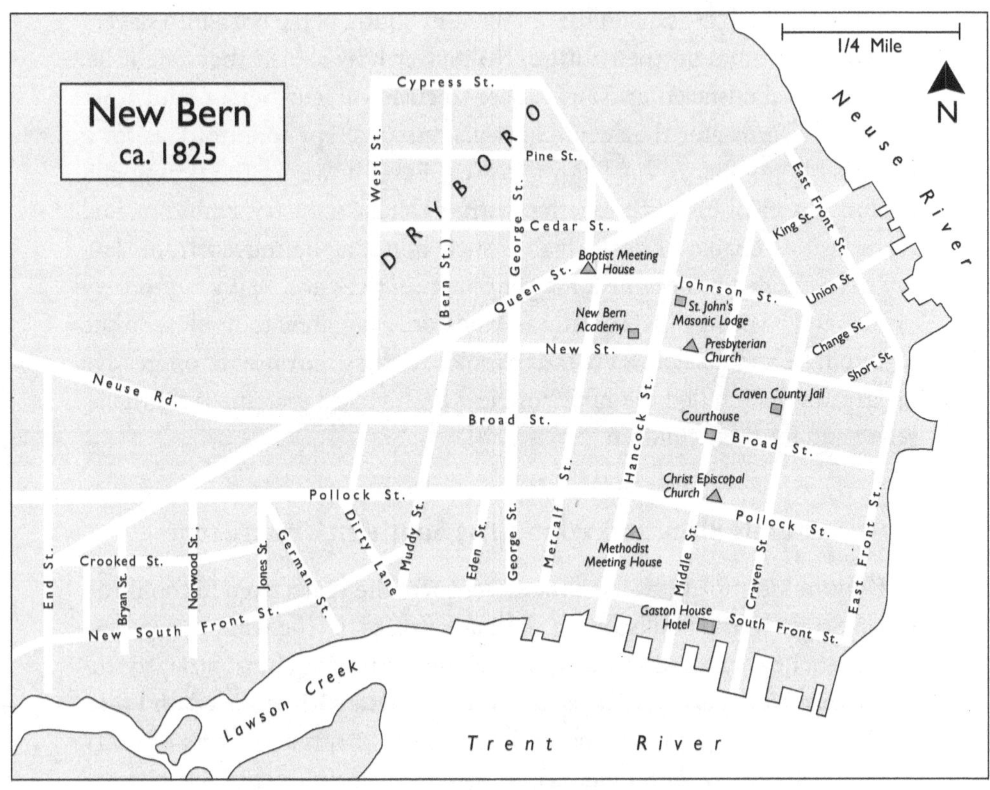

New Bern, ca. 1825. Map by Michael T. Southern.

not—which, as we shall see, he may have done—his initials on it, like his advertisement for its return, denoted his attachment to this emblematic possession of an artisan.[4]

Montford's advertisement for his glass cutter also leads us into the complex world of black artisan life in early national–period New Bern. As a man who spent roughly half of his life in slavery and half in freedom, Montford shared many experiences with the thousands of enslaved and free black craftspeople who constituted much of the skilled workforce of the urban South. In slavery and in freedom, he participated in dimensions of black artisan life that New Bern had in common with other southern cities. But his experiences also reflected the city's particular character and circumstances: during the decades following the American Revolution—later recalled as the town's "golden age"—New Bern's prosperity and especially the values and actions of its illustrious white and black leaders combined to create an era of unusual opportunity for artisans of color.[5]

For most black artisans in the antebellum South, being born into slavery placed clear limits on their future. No matter how skilled they might be, seldom could enslaved artisans expect to trace the customary path from apprentice to master that white artisans pursued. For Montford, as for a remarkable number of his fellows in New Bern, however, the timing and circumstances of his birth together with his skills, industry, ambition, and relationships enabled him to realize such hopes as he moved from slavery to freedom and became a master of apprentices and slaves, a property owner, and a voting citizen. Only as Montford's life drew to its close in the 1830s did he and his fellow artisans of color witness the onset of oppressive racial laws that chilled the hopes of New Bern's black craftsmen for themselves and for their children.

Artisans Black and White: The Southern Urban Scene

As Donum Montford traversed the streets over the years, from his home on Broad Street to the bookstore or the marketplace, to the wharf, work site, or church, he witnessed scenes akin to those common in most other southern towns. New Bern, like its sister cities, bustled with enslaved and free, black and white artisans along with hundreds of other workers of every color and status. Whether blacks composed a majority of the local population, as they did in New Bern and a few other towns, or a substantial minority, as in many southern cities, black artisans formed a constant presence in the human and economic landscape.

Montford and his contemporaries lived in a prime era for handicrafts all across America. Especially in the South, where industrial mass production had only begun, the work of local craftsmen still defined the economy and character of most communities. Although port towns like New Bern imported many items from northern or foreign cities, daily life for most townspeople took place amidst the products of their neighbors' handicrafts, as they drove carriages through the streets, welcomed or served guests in rooms adorned with stylish moldings and warmed by efficient fireplaces, noticed a smartly tailored coat on a passerby, packed fish into barrels, weeded a garden with an iron-headed hoe, or went to sea in a well-caulked ship.

In his daily rounds Montford, like most urban southerners, encountered scores of black and white craftspeople, from youths to aged men and women, busy in a wide range of trades. If he wanted a new coat, he could

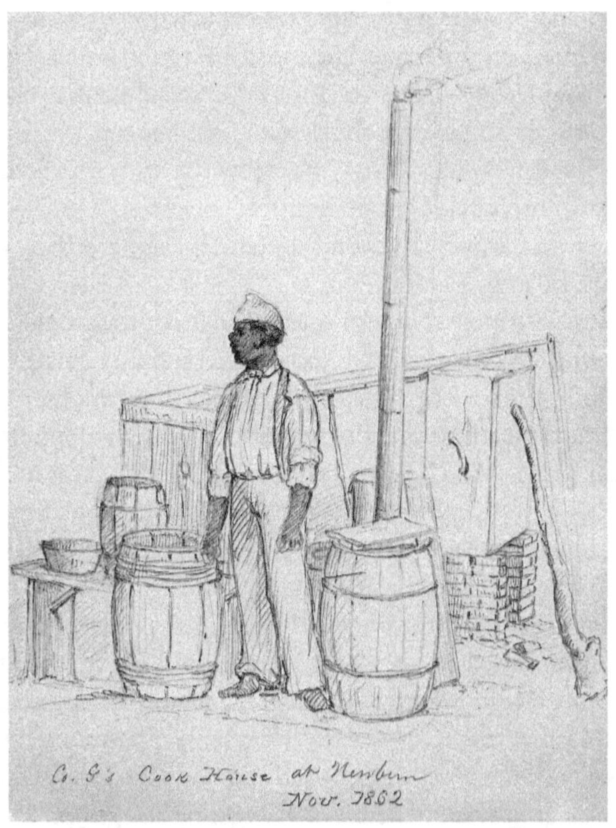

"Co. G's Cook House at Newbern, Nov. 1862." James Wells Champney Sketchbook. The drawing illustrates the ubiquitous use of wooden casks typically made by local coopers. Courtesy of the Outer Banks History Center (Manteo), State Archives of North Carolina, Raleigh.

visit the shop of white tailor Reuben Bell, where black and white apprentices and journeymen plied their shears and needles, or he might search out free black tailor John Bragg and his family of needleworkers. If he decided to purchase a silver tablespoon for his wife, he might consult one of the local white silversmiths, such as Freeman Woods or William Tisdale, but when he needed to have his tools or his wagon repaired or a horse shod, he could turn to the slave Willoby or another enslaved blacksmith at white blacksmith William Conway's forge. To replenish his supply of barrels and buckets to transport oyster shells or mix lime mortar, he went to a workshop where enslaved coopers, such as Abram, America, and Bill, shaped, heated, and bent wooden staves and bound them together with iron bands to form containers large and small. At the waterfront, jostling with black boatmen, pilots, and vegetable hucksters, he could watch enslaved ship carpenters Tom and Henry ascending and descending the mast of white merchant Thomas McLin's schooner, *Rapid*, as they repaired the vessel on behalf of white shipbuilder Thomas Sparrow.[6] At his brick kiln and at construction sites throughout town, Montford expected to practice his trade in company with his own slaves and apprentices along with a familiar cast of artisans black and white.

In common with most southern cities—and in contrast to the situation in the North—the city's black and white, enslaved and free artisans frequently worked together. Southern artisans who traveled north observed that life and labor in the North were more segregated than anything they had experienced at home. What a northern visitor to New Bern found unusual or even objectionable Montford and his fellow residents took for granted: in every local building project for which records identify the workmen, artisans of both races were on the job.

In 1816 and 1817 Montford regularly passed the site on Craven Street, near Queen Street, where craftsmen familiar to him were building a residence for white attorney John R. Donnell. Typifying the city's best Federal-period architecture, the freestanding two-and-one-half story dwelling had brick walls expertly laid in Flemish bond and every intricate detail of woodwork and plaster beautifully rendered. Directing the project as well as executing the elaborate carpentry was white house carpenter Asa King, who had several other notable buildings in town to his credit and likely had enslaved carpenters working with him. The principal brick contractors were white brickmasons Wallace Moore and Joshua Mitchell. Most of the other artisans were black, including free painter Benjamin Wade and slaves such as brickmason Daniel and carpenters Elijah and York. Montford supplied bricks from his brickyard, and Donnell also paid "Mr. Forbes's Boys"—slaves of merchant Stephen Forbes—to select bricks from Forbes's kiln. Donnell employed "negro Boston" for framing two houses at "Mr. Kings Saw Pit," where Boston laid out and with the help of other hands assembled and raised heavy timber frames from the joists and beams cut by sawyers who were probably slaves as well.[7]

A few years later, Montford participated in the diverse workforce at a major public construction project—the Craven County Jail, a few blocks south on Craven Street. In 1821 he and his workmen fired 100,000 bricks at his kiln and hauled them to the building site as a portion of the more

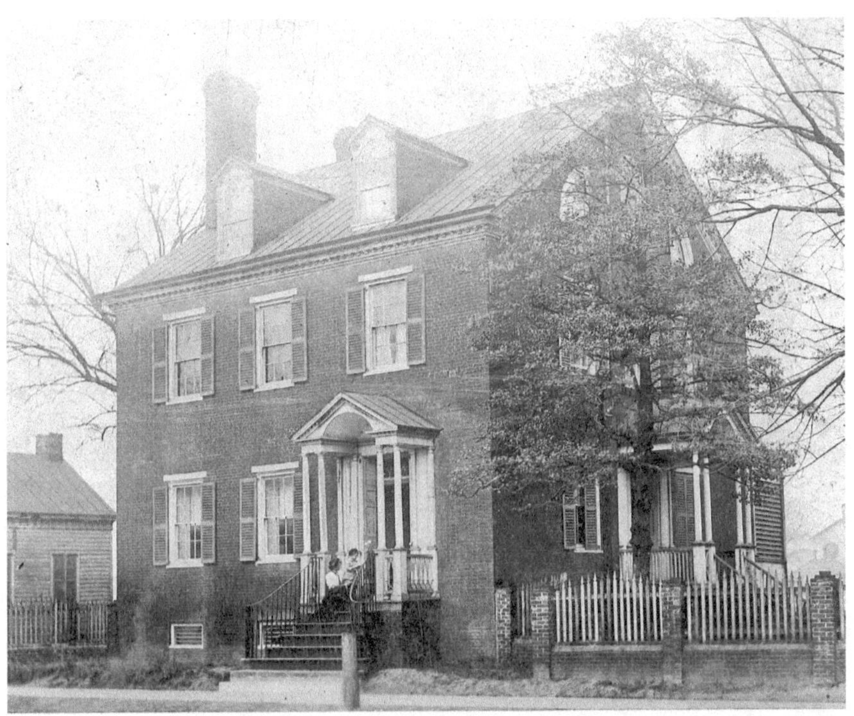

John R. Donnell House, New Bern. Courtesy of New Bern Firemen's Museum, New Bern, North Carolina.

than 400,000 bricks needed for the job. White brickmason Joshua Mitchell spent day after day laying up the Flemish-bond brick walls at the rate of fifteen shillings per day, sometimes with his slave Jacob, who "worked with me at Jail." In 1822 and 1823 white house carpenter John Oliver and his slaves raised the roof, installed skylights, and finished and fitted the windows, doors, and partitions. Montford returned in 1824 with his artisans Tony and Lawson to lathe and plaster the interior walls, caulk around the door and window openings, and apply whitewash with the help of his laborers Charles, Edmond, and Romey. Throughout the city's years of prosperity, similar scenes played out on nearly every block in town.[8]

New Bern's mercantile wealth, coupled with the centrality of artisan crafts in this period, provided good prospects for all artisans, black and white. Elegant houses, churches, and civic buildings showcased thousands of hours of skilled handiwork by master craftspeople, apprentices, journeymen, and slaves. Despite the local practice of importing columns, stonework, and superior types of bricks, the master carpenter or brickmason

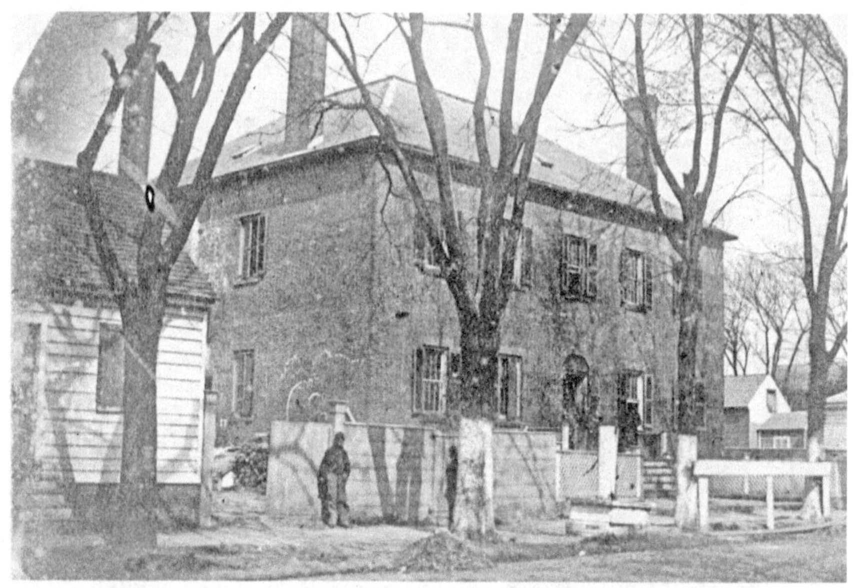

Craven County Jail, New Bern. Photograph ca. 1862. Courtesy of the North Carolina Collection, University of North Carolina at Chapel Hill Library.

not only wielded his plane or his trowel but took a lead role in planning and managing construction of buildings from start to finish. The principal economic engines—shipping, the production of naval stores, fishing, and agriculture—generated work for shipbuilders, coopers, blacksmiths, and carpenters. The fashion-conscious elite complemented their purchases of New York or Philadelphia goods with coats and gowns, boots and slippers, cabinet pieces and chairs and tables, and fine silverware made by New Bern artisans. The city's craftsmen also profited from farmers and villagers who came to town to purchase their products, while New Bern carpenters and brickmasons hired by out-of-town employers spread the town's architectural influence into Carteret, Beaufort, Jones, Hyde, and Tyrrell Counties.

Along with barbering, a traditionally black occupation in the South, artisan crafts generally represented the most lucrative occupations open to men of color and, like barbering, could provide opportunities for contact with elite whites.[9] Professions such as the law or the academy lay out of reach for essentially all antebellum black North Carolinians—the free black schoolteachers John Chavis in Raleigh and John Stewart Stanly in New Bern were rare exceptions—while custom as well as apprentice laws encouraged artisan training for free blacks. Artisans' and barbers' pay exceeded by double and triple and more per day the wages paid to laborers. In 1813 the emancipated barber John C. Stanly charged attorney Edward Graham ten shillings per month for his daily shaves, and in the 1820s Donum Montford made twelve shillings sixpence ($1.00) per day for his and his artisans' plastering and five shillings a day for his laborers.[10] Artisans, along with a small number of barbers, predominated among the wealthiest free New Bernians of color, and they also numbered among the enslaved people who earned and saved money to obtain their own and others' liberty. Not surprisingly, parents of free and enslaved black children often arranged craft apprenticeships to equip them for profitable work. Barber John C. Stanly made sure that his children learned trade skills along with gaining an education: although his son John Stewart Stanly, as noted, became a merchant and schoolteacher, Benjamin Stanly followed his father in barbering, Catharine and Frances learned the dressmaker's craft, Charles became a tailor, and grandsons John and Osborne mastered the joiner's trade.[11]

Crafts in early national–period New Bern were sufficiently important, and thus rewarding and prestigious, that a few of the town's premier white artisans, while always distinct from the merchant-planter-lawyer upper crust, occupied positions in the upper-middling as well as working classes. Nor were any artisan trades in early nineteenth-century New Bern identified as "Negro work," for white master artisans and journeymen worked at every craft that blacks did.[12] So too, with the exceptions of silversmithing and gunsmithing, free black and enslaved artisans practiced all the major crafts from shoemaking and dressmaking to blacksmithing and coopering, as well as bricklaying, carpentry, and shipbuilding.[13] Although there is scant evidence of enslaved or free black furniture makers in New Bern, there were at least a few, such as the slave Sam, who was "brought up to the cabinet maker's business but ha[d] for five or six years past worked at the carpenter's trade" before he ran away in 1789. He was believed to have headed for Charleston, perhaps in hopes of finding work in his specialty.[14]

The roster of New Bern's leading white craftsmen in the early national period included such respected citizens as brickmasons Joshua Mitchell, Bennett Flanner, and Wallace Moore; house carpenters John Dewey, John Oliver, Martin Stevenson, Uriah Sandy, Asa King, and Hardy B. Lane Sr.; shipbuilder Thomas Sparrow; furniture makers Robert Hay, Gabriel Rains, Thomas Youle, and Richard and Joseph Hall; painter William Charlotte; tailors Reuben Bell and John Louis Durand; and silversmiths William and Nathan Tisdale and Freeman Woods. John Hawks, the English architect who designed Tryon Palace in the 1760s, stayed in town until his death in 1790, and for a brief period after 1800 English-born carpenter and architect William Nichols lived and worked in New Bern. Most of these men owned or at least employed slaves.[15]

In contrast to free artisans, most of the city's large but unknown number of enslaved craftsmen—house carpenter Abraham, blacksmith Thomas Bowman, tanner Joe, carpenter and seaman Sam, and many others—had their names enter the record chiefly when they were bequeathed, sold, or hired out and when they escaped captivity.[16] Some, as we shall see, belonged to free artisans whom they assisted in their trades, but many were owned by nonartisans who hired them out to free artisans and other employers and thereby profited from their earnings.

After the turn of the nineteenth century, newly manumitted craftspeople such as Donum Montford moved into the ranks of the leading free artisans in New Bern. Tailors John Rice Green and John Bragg, painter Ben Wade, and carpenters Thomas Newton, James York Green, and James's brother Rigdon Green joined Montford as free men by the late 1810s. Others, including house carpenter William H. Hancock (possibly born free) and the manumitted plasterer and brickmason Abram Allen, soon embarked on their careers. Some gained a place in local memory for their excellence. John Bragg's tailoring expertise led "prominent people . . . to move their custom to the shops at which he was employed in order that he might work on it," and Hancock was remembered as a "skilled carpenter and builder, who had planned and constructed some of the most ornate buildings in our home town."[17]

BESIDES THE CITY'S OPPORTUNITIES for skilled craft employment, the racial and social climate in early national–period New Bern also encouraged the development of black artisan and citizen identity. The reasons for the community's particular character in this period are not altogether clear, but in addition to the relative leniency of North Carolina's racial laws before the 1830s, key factors included the long-established population of free people of color in Craven County, the attitudes of certain local elite white leaders, and the actions of people of both races in supporting black New Bernians' pursuit of freedom and prosperity.

Craven County's large and independent rural population of free people of color, including families who had lived there since the 1740s and 1750s, took a role in shaping local white and black views. Often combining crafts with farming and fishing, county artisans typically accepted children from neighboring families as apprentices in carpentry, shoemaking, and coopering, and children from these families also entered apprenticeships with New Bern artisans. Artisans and other county men of color strengthened their identity as citizens through military service in the American Revolution and in the local militia. Free blacks from the county also made visits to town and were well known there, and by their accepted presence and methods of navigating racial boundaries they set an example for slaves and whites as well as fellow free blacks.

Soldier, Citizen, Artisan

Epitomizing the complexity of artisan-citizen identity for free blacks was Craven County cooper and Revolutionary War veteran Asa Spelman, who managed an effective blend of achievement and deference. Stories told by white memoirist John D. Whitford a century later evoke the attitudes of Spelman's day and of Whitford's. During his trips to town to collect his soldier's pension, Spelman regaled New Bernians with tales of "his acquaintance with Mars[e] General Washington and of his own exploits in the Revolutionary War. Just how much fiction was mixed with the truth no one knew." In 1791, when George Washington visited New Bern, Spelman at last found public vindication. In an event witnessed by many black and white New Bernians, the former president "happened to meet" Spelman. As Whitford recounted,

> [The] test is about to be made of Asa's truthfulness. There stands Washington in his presence, with all that dignity which threw such majesty around him wherever he might be. "Why Asy," as the negro approached, exclaimed the great man, "how came you here. I am glad to see you," at the moment extending his hand, which of course was grasped with becoming pride and respect. Next to Washington that day, "Asy" was the hero of the occasion. But he knew his place and did not attempt to exceed the proper limits. Therefore he was respected until bowed with the weight of near ninety years he sank down in a patriot's grave. His name is on the Craven County list of Revolutionary patriots.[18]

Thirty years later, "All the remaining heroes of the Revolution who were to be found in New Bern and vicinity were invited and present at [a] dinner.

... Asa Spelman, the old negro, was not left out. He was there but knew well his color and place thus was treated well and deserved to be."[19] For Spelman, such events affirmed his standing as a citizen and his connection to the American Revolution, while Whitford's account reminded readers that, however distinguished the old soldier's legacy, respectability went hand in hand with performances of deference attached to "color and place."

Law as well as custom shaped the setting for black artisan life. Even in the context of North Carolina's relatively lax racial laws, New Bern authorities seem to have been notably flexible in their regulation of local slaves and free blacks, and whites conducted business with enslaved and free blacks.[20] When the state passed laws in 1785 to regulate black activities in Wilmington, Washington, Fayetteville, and Edenton, New Bern was not included, perhaps because its leaders preferred to manage their community as they saw fit. In 1787, likely in response to their experiences in New Bern during North Carolina General Assembly sessions there, state lawmakers bore down on the town in terms that portrayed its character. Objecting to "the conduct of idle and disorderly slaves, free negroes, and persons of mixed blood in the said town" as well as to the practice of whites trading openly with slaves, legislators insisted that such activities be "properly restrained." They enacted a law requiring New Bern to pass "such regulations ... as will prevent the mischiefs and evils at present existing."[21]

New Bern authorities complied, but, as in cities from Baltimore to New Orleans, the nature of urban life made "proper restraint" of blacks and their interaction with whites well-nigh impossible.[22] As elsewhere, the city's frequent reiteration of such ordinances revealed a lively and racially porous community life. Slaves and free blacks arrived in town without proper identification, preached to other blacks without supervision of a white minister, and assembled in public and in secret. Despite penalties that included jailing and whippings, male and female slaves sold beer and cakes on the wharves and in the streets without licenses; operated tippling shops; hired themselves and found work without permits; and lived away from their owners. Whites, free blacks, and slaves traded, gambled, drank, and danced with one another, and as white authorities feared, shared conversations about politics and freedom as well as how to find a good meal or a partner. "Country Negroes" came to town on Sundays without passes, and black and white shopkeepers "trad[ed] with Slaves without a written permission from the owner."[23] At the other end of the spectrum, leading black artisans such as Donum Montford lived circumspect lives, demonstrating like Asa Spelman their mastery of "color and place" and cultivating valuable relationships with powerful local whites.

Of critical importance to New Bern's favorable setting for artisans of color were its distinguished white citizens who engaged in manumissions and supported the rights of free people of color. Throughout the nation, the period after the American Revolution brought a "wave of manumissions" in the spirit of the universal rights of man. In some locales, manumissions dropped off within a few years and conditions for free blacks deteriorated.[24] In New Bern and some other communities, however, manumissions continued and even increased in the 1810s and 1820s. Numerous members of leading white planter and lawyer families, including widows and children of large slaveholders, took steps to assure the "blessings of liberty" for selected slaves, including artisans such as Donum Montford, and, as we shall see, when emancipated artisans like Montford sought to free or help free others, prominent white attorneys assisted their efforts.

These actions took place in a time and place where leading political figures saw the institution of slavery as flawed and even immoral despite their deep engagement in it. A visiting minister preaching against slavery in the 1820s found that New Bern's slaveholders could "bear to be reasoned with on the great evils of slavery" and commented that a large audience heard his sermon on the topic "without marks of displeasure."[25] To some extent these attitudes reflected the mindset of many elite southerners in the first decades after the Revolution, before economic and generational changes and resistance to northern abolitionists took their toll.[26]

But the atmosphere and opportunities in New Bern also represented the influence of key leaders whose backgrounds, political affiliations, and personal philosophies led them to speak and act with unusual tolerance and sympathy for their black neighbors. Although all were slaveholders, in contrast to many whites who saw all blacks in monolithic terms, they could perceive subtle differences among their fellow human beings and act accordingly. William Gaston, New Bern attorney and legislator and North Carolina Supreme Court chief justice, gained recognition for speaking against slavery and for his legal opinions supporting the human rights of both slaves and free blacks.[27]

Gaston's friend and fellow Federalist John Stanly likewise defended free blacks' rights, and he and Gaston and their friend Edward Graham often aided in manumissions by serving as attorneys for both free blacks and whites seeking to free slaves. Although Graham shared with Gaston and Stanly a Princeton education and a Federalist political philosophy, unlike them he was not a native New Bernian. He was a New Yorker who had read law with manumission proponent John Jay, the first chief justice of the United States Supreme Court, before coming to New Bern and entering civic leadership, and he likely carried forward his mentor's ideals in helping many New Bernians obtain their liberty. Recognizing these men's attitudes and authority, black New Bernians regularly turned to them for legal assistance and representation of their interests and, as we shall see, supported them with their votes. Although some prominent white New Bernians held differing beliefs, these and other elite men and women who held similar values took key roles in shaping their town's "golden age."

Thus while racial and social hierarchies remained firmly in place and while slavery's grounding in violence could never be forgotten, during New Bern's early national period there existed a degree of acquaintance, cooperation, and even civility between some whites and some persons of color, as well as the realistic hope for at least a few slaves to gain their own and their families' freedom with the support of white citizens. Although only a modest number of the town's enslaved artisans actually obtained their liberty or became master artisans, property owners, or voters, enough did so to give the city a character remarkable in the state and nation. By their example and their support of others, these craftspeople demonstrated to enslaved people and to whites alike the real possibility of black artisan-citizenship in their time and place.

Most Valuable Negroes: Artisans in Bondage

Like most people of color in the slave South, the majority of New Bern's antebellum black artisans spent much or all of their lives in bondage, plying their skills for the benefit of their owners and employers. Most of the town's leading free artisans of color, like John R. Green and Donum Montford, had begun their lives in slavery, and many more remained in bondage. The general picture of artisan slavery in New Bern, including artisans' craft training, modes of employment, and efforts to win freedom, resembled that in such cities as Wilmington, North Carolina, and Petersburg and Richmond, Virginia, and to some extent Charleston, South Carolina, and Baltimore, Maryland.

Enslaved craftsmen, like whites and free blacks, possessed skills that ranged from the most basic to highly refined.[28] More than their condition of freedom or servitude, the quality of artisans' work reflected their natural abilities and opportunities for training, along with the market for fine workmanship. Like those of free craftsmen, enslaved artisans' public and private identities and their earning power were bound up in the skills they had mastered, and for those enslaved, their skills also defined their value as property. Some enslaved craftsmen, like free ones, turned out practical items adequate for their purposes, including Abraham, a "tolerable good carpenter and shoemaker," and James York Green, who had earned a good reputation in bondage and was "tolerable" at carpentry.[29] Others gained recognition for fine work, such as Sam, an "excellent Ship & House Carpenter," and an anonymous "First rate house carpenter" offered for sale by white cabinetmaker John Nelson. Although sellers may have exaggerated some claims, they could not go too far without straining local credibility. Three house carpenters—presumably so well-known as to require no introduction—were advertised for sale by John Oliver in 1821 as being "perhaps equal to any in Newbern," and when Oliver's administrators proffered the three carpenters again in 1823, they described them as "equal to any in the state."[30]

As in many southern cities, no records indicate the number of enslaved artisans in New Bern. Although it is tempting to make estimates based on the number of slaves owned by artisans, the prevalence of slave hiring precludes that approach. Some enslaved craftsmen did belong to other artisans: several leading free artisans owned slaves, including some who shared their trade skills. But most free black and white artisans owned only a few slaves, if any, and these typically included laborers, domestic servants, children, and elderly people as well as able-bodied craftsmen. If runaway notices and sales advertisements, wills, and estates inventories are any indication—and clues of occupational identity are spotty for both owners and slaves—few enslaved artisans belonged to other artisans. All evidence suggests that, as exemplified by the young Donum Montford and John Rice Green, most of the city's enslaved artisans belonged to non-artisans—to lawyers and planters, merchants and doctors, and their widows and orphans—who relied on their wages for income.[31]

Slave artisans often learned their trades because their owners wanted to enhance their value for hire or sale. When slave dealer John Gildersleeve advertised to purchase 100 young blacks he noted, "An extra price will be given for mechanics." Although some slaves acquired craft skills informally, slaveholders often arranged apprenticeships for promising youths, sharing the strategy of a western North Carolina slaveholder who asked his father to send him one of his slaves "that you might think ingenious," whom he planned to bind out to a carpenter or bricklayer.[32]

Slaveholders sometimes set up apprenticeships for their slaves as investments to benefit their heirs. A youth named Abraham was in training with house carpenter William Paxton in 1791 when his owner willed him to a nephew, with the condition that he should continue with Paxton for a term of five years. A boy named Jack, who belonged to Governor Richard Dobbs Spaight Sr.'s widow Mary Jones Spaight, was bound to Alexander Mitchel to learn the carpentry trade and continued his apprenticeship after her death to benefit her heirs.[33] Abram, a child owned by the widow Ann Blackledge, showed sufficient potential that she specified in her will that he was to be taught the trade of cooper and remain with her son William until Abram was twenty-one. Then the young cooper was to be given to her granddaughter Ann B. Hatch "or if she be dead to my grandson Richard B. Hatch unless my son William prefers to keep him and pay the said Ann B. or Richard B. Hatch $500," indicating the substantial value anticipated for a skilled slave.[34]

For some young slaves, owners took into consideration their aptitudes and physical attributes in selecting their trades. As a boy, John Rice Green, also owned by Mary Jones Spaight, was "of such small and delicate frame, even up to the time when he entered his 'teens,' that, it was somewhat of a problem, what disposition should be made of him,—a laborious occupation for him was 'out of the question.' . . . Finally, it was determined to apprentice him to a tailor." The concern over the lad's welfare likely reflected the influence of his mother, Sarah Rice, the beloved nurse of the Spaight children, who was singled out in Mary Jones Spaight's will for subsequent manumission and a gift of £100. In 1806, at age thirteen, Sarah's son, known as "Jack the weazel" for his small size, "first crossed his legs, on the 'board' and commenced a career, which continued for forty-three years." Four years later, the administrators of Mrs. Spaight's estate listed among her nineteen slaves "John a Boy bound to Reuben Bell to learn the Taylors trade."[35] Richard Dobbs Spaight Jr. inherited and later manumitted John, the tailor.

Enslaved craftsmen's apprenticeships often became part of their community identity. Whereas white artisans cited in their advertisements their "regular" apprenticeships or northern training, slaveholders used the identifying history of an artisan's training to find runaways. When plasterer Ulysses, aged about twenty-eight, ran away in 1818, his Hyde County owner accompanied the fugitive's physical description with the statement that Ulysses had "served his time" with New Bern master artisan Donum Montford.[36] Apprenticeships for slaves were regarded as sufficiently important to warrant legal action if the terms of the apprenticeship were not met. In 1810, a "mulatto" boy named George was bound by his owner, merchant Stephen Forbes, for a term of four years to learn the house carpenter's trade from white carpenter John Oliver. But in 1815 Forbes took Oliver to court, claiming that he failed to meet the bargain and demanding damages of £250.[37]

Along with arranging for their training, owners of enslaved artisans often provided them with the tools to practice their trades. When the executrix of planter Benners Vail's estate offered several craftsmen for hire in 1816, she followed common precedent in assuring potential employers that "the tools of the tradesmen will be furnished them."[38] In the world of free artisans, ownership of tools was an essential complement to their skills in defining their identity, but for enslaved artisans, the question of possession was subject to different perspectives held by the slaveholder and the craftsman. New Bern attorney John Donnell recorded his purchase of carpenter's tools "for Simon" in terms that could have had different meanings for the two men.[39] In 1786, white carpenter Shadrach Fulsher left most of his personal goods to his wife Mary and his son William, but he exempted his working tools, which were to be "kept at the discretion of my heirs for my Negro Windsor to work with, and to be left with him as he is hereafter left." Shadrach bequeathed his slaves to Mary for her lifetime and then to his son, but he stated that Windsor and his tools were to go to his nephew, New Bern ship carpenter Thomas Fulsher.[40] In legal terms, the slaveholder retained ownership of the tools the enslaved artisan used along with the person of the workman. Yet in terms of use and association, artisans like Simon or Windsor might well have considered them as much theirs as their owners' possessions. When shoemaker Cupid escaped from his Nash County owner in 1817, aiming for New Bern or another port, he carried away shoes, leather, and tools "suitable for his trade." He likely combined his sense of virtual ownership by use with his need to practice his trade on the run.[41]

If enslaved artisans learned their trades and mastered the use of tools because of decisions made by others, they often acted on their own behalf in learning to read and write. In doing so, they enhanced their personal power and agency both through the act and status of becoming literate and by employing the practical benefits literacy brought. Some mastered writing as well as reading, while some could read but not write. Literate slaves could read the Bible, keep up with and share news from other cities, and read abolitionist literature and other forbidden documents. Those who could both read and write could maintain contact with friends and relatives near and far, and could help themselves and others escape bondage by forging free papers or slave passes. When cabinetmaker and carpenter Sam ran away toward Charleston in 1789, his owner stated that he could "read and I believe write" and predicted that he would "endeavor to pass for a free man."[42] Ulysses, the slave who learned the plastering trade from Donum Montford, could read and write "tolerable well" when he escaped in 1818. When Ulysses ran away again almost twenty years later, his owner surmised that he had forged a pass and might try to reach a northern state.[43]

Through the early national period, educating slaves in North Carolina was not a dangerous proposition. In contrast to states that outlawed such instruction, although some individual slaveholders forbade the practice, North Carolina's legislature resisted such a step throughout the 1820s. When the topic arose, the debate revealed that many whites believed that the duty to teach slaves to read the Bible outweighed the dangers associated with reading abolitionist literature. When Donum Montford accepted Abram Allen as an apprentice and his slave, he promised that the youth would learn to read and write, and so he did. While still enslaved, the young tailor John Rice Green, like other ambitious slaves, devised a strategy to educate himself. He acquired his own copy of "Webster's Spelling Book," which became "his inseparable companion, by night and by day; and, with the assistance of a blind man, whom, at times, he led through the street, he was gradually inducted into the mystery of reading." Green "would call the letters of a word, and the blind man would tell him how to pronounce it," so that before long the boy was reading.[44]

Enslaved artisans such as John Rice Green who worked with whites and free blacks as well as fellow slaves also gained opportunities to form relationships across racial lines and to learn techniques of doing business in the community. White house carpenter Hardy B. Lane Sr. employed slaves, white and free black apprentices, and his own sons in his workshop. As an enslaved apprentice in the shop of white tailor Reuben Bell, where most of the other workers were white, John Rice Green remembered being "picked on" by other apprentice boys, but he also expressed gratitude for the "protection often extended to him by a Frenchman, Durand by name."[45] Green's memory of the kind Frenchman also highlights the cosmopolitan nature of the community, where Europeans appeared as craftsmen, music and dancing teachers, bakers and confectioners, bringing their own perspectives to their interactions with local workmen of every station and race.[46]

Although it is well known that black and white men worked together on construction sites, seldom do records reveal details of their interactions on the job. One unusually well-documented New Bern project likely typifies many others—the 1772 repairs to the Governor's Palace (Tryon Palace) and construction of outbuildings, which involved constant and close association between blacks and whites. White carpenter-cabinetmakers Jarvis Buxton and John West kept daily records of their tasks and those performed by slaves Jim, Will, Pompey, Mallett, and Spooner. Buxton and West charged eight shillings a day for their own work; the other artisans earned between six shillings and seven shillings sixpence per day; unnamed "Negroe Labourers" made about three shillings; and several "boys" made one shilling fourpence per day.[47]

From June through October, ever-changing teams of carpenters proceeded from one task to the next, not only working at the same construction site but sharing tasks. Sometimes black and white men completed a job together, and sometimes Buxton or West began a project along with the slaves, who then finished it on their own. On June 29, 1772, Jarvis Buxton reported on the work done inside the palace: "Myself and Will 1 day Each & Mallett ½ day taking down the Pictures and preparing . . . the Wainscot." Jarvis Buxton, Will, and Mallett continued together on the wainscot the following day, but thereafter Buxton moved to another job and Will and Mallett completed the wainscot without him. For the Pigeon House (where the brick walls were erected by white bricklayer Thomas Lippiner and some unnamed black men), Jim sawed the joists and plates for the roof and worked with Buxton to frame it up while Pompey sawed lumber and made shingles. In September, Buxton and Jim were joined by Spooner and other men, and together they finished the Pigeon House in October.[48] Neither these nor any other records reveal whether such proximity and cooperation bred mutual respect or an exchange of views or expertise among the participants. There is no way to know if their experience encouraged Jim or Pompey to aim for greater liberty, or if Buxton or West treated these men any differently because of their shared work and workmanship.

SLAVE HIRING

Although white carpenter Jarvis Buxton might have owned Jim, Will, Pompey, and other slaves who worked with him at the Governor's Residence, it is also likely that he hired at least some of these men from other owners. As it developed in New Bern and throughout the South, the practice of slave hiring produced a "hybrid" form of slavery that was especially prevalent in urban settings. Although slave hiring had its risks for all parties—the owner, the hirer, and the slave (who might be especially subject to abuse by a hirer)—it offered such advantages to the owners and employers that it was practiced in nearly every southern town and in many rural areas. Some authorities believe it was not only central but essential to the functioning and even the survival of urban slavery.[49]

Hiring shaped the lives of many enslaved artisans just as it did the economy as a whole, and it often offered skilled slaves greater latitude and autonomy in plying their trades than they would have had otherwise. The financial arrangements generally took one of two forms. In one prevalent approach, the slave's owner and the employer struck a bargain in which the employer paid the owner a certain sum for the slave's work and sometimes specified an amount that the worker could keep from his or her earnings. By contrast, "self-hiring" or "hiring themselves" gave enslaved workers a much greater role in making the arrangements. In this widespread but often controversial practice, the owner permitted his or her slaves to find their own employers and receive their pay directly, from which the slaves paid "wages" to their owner, thus hiring themselves from the owner. Considered by some observers to be quasi-free, slaves who hired themselves had the greatest opportunity for autonomy and individual identity within the limits of slavery. They could develop a sense of the value of their skills, select their employers, and negotiate bargains with their owners as well as their employers. Self-hiring was especially prevalent in towns and cities, where a large if unquantifiable proportion of slaves were self-hired at any given time, including "town Negroes" and others whose owners sent them or allowed them to go into town to find work and sometimes to live on their own and to stay away as long as they pleased.

State and local lawmakers struggled to balance the economic benefits of slave hiring, especially self-hiring, against the perceived problems. In the immediate post-Revolutionary era, state and local laws addressed chiefly the economic aspects of the practice. When the North Carolina legislature enacted a law in 1785 to regulate slave self-hiring in Wilmington, Fayetteville, Washington, and Edenton, the preface to the bill acknowledged that it was "customary for many persons, as well in the country as in the several towns in this State, to permit their slaves to hire themselves out from day to day, by which great profits are acquired." Probably in response to complaints from officials in those towns, the lawmakers required slaveholders who profited from their slaves' work in the towns to "contribute more than the ordinary taxes towards [the towns'] support," while still "permitting slaves to hire themselves under proper restrictions and regulations" that would be "convenient" for potential hirers. Recognizing self-hiring as a fact of urban life, the laws of 1785 made no attempt to halt the practice but only to regulate it by requiring fees and badges. Two years later, under pressure from the legislature, New Bern followed suit. Within a decade, however, growing concerns over slaves' potential autonomy and fears of rebellions fomented by unsupervised slaves spurred the legislature in 1794 to forbid slaves to hire their own time "under any pretense whatever." Leaders from Wilmington and New Bern promptly objected, citing "the difficulty of obtaining white laborers," and obtained exemptions for the mutual benefit of slaveholders and employers.[50]

New Bern's initial slave-hiring regulations addressed mainly economic issues. They sought to protect town slaveholders' profits against competition from slaves "from the country" and to exclude strangers and runaways by requiring that only slaves who belonged to or were hired by townspeople could obtain badges for hiring out. In 1802, in the wake of the slave blacksmith Gabriel's failed insurrection plot in Richmond, New Bern authorities sought to exert greater control over their town's slave population. They authorized the town sergeant to seize and jail as runaways all slaves "found in the Town with or without a pass except . . . such as belong to or is hired to some inhabitant of the town or such Negroes from the Country as are attended by some white man." A few years later, local ordinances limited to 100 the total number of slaves to be hired out and, in order to distinguish "town Negroes" from others, required that all male slaves fifteen years of age and older who "belonged to the town" had to carry identification or risk punishment by thirty-nine lashes.[51] Yet because white slave owners and employers found that the advantages outweighed the potential risks, slave hiring and self-hiring persisted despite whites' frequent complaints about abuses of the system.[52] For dozens of enslaved artisans in New Bern, hiring offered a life that interwove legal servitude and personal autonomy, and which sometimes enabled them to negotiate with both their owners and their employers to define their roles as artisans and individuals.

A House Carpenter Hired Out

The experiences of the enslaved house carpenter Ben illustrate the business details of slave hiring in New Bern. Employed by at least three of the city's leading white house carpenters, Ben left his handiwork on some of the city's premier buildings of those years, including those credited to his white employers. His activities thus highlight the role of hired slaves in contributing to the unified character of the local architecture of the era. Although no narrative of Ben's life survives, records made by his owners provide clues to his activities from 1817 to 1825. For several years Ben belonged to white carpenter John Oliver, who likely assigned him to his various projects. In 1817 Oliver hired Ben out to white carpenter Uriah Sandy, who was in 1819–22 the contractor for New Bern's imposing First Presbyterian Church. In a typical hiring agreement, Sandy promised to pay Oliver the sum of $120 ($10 per month) for a year's "hire of Negro Man Ben also to find him, one Winter Suit of Cloths and Two Summer Suits, One Blanket and one pair of Shoes and pay his Taxes" (the head tax paid on slaves and possibly the fee for a hiring license). Such agreements might be made at any time of year, but they most often occurred when slaveholders, slaves, and potential hirers gathered at the market house or courthouse on the traditional "hiring day" of January 1 to make bargains for the upcoming year. Hiring agreements often terminated at Christmas, marking the end of the work year and the beginning of a traditional holiday week for slaves.[53]

After a few years, Ben experienced another change. He was likely one of the three outstanding house carpenters offered for sale by John Oliver in 1821 and whom Oliver's agents advertised in 1823 as equal to any in the state. Attorney John R. Donnell, who made a practice of acquiring slaves for hiring out, found the advertisement credible and recorded in his letter book his purchase of Ben for $615 at John Oliver's sale on July 1, 1823. Samuel and Joseph Oliver, who managed the sale, deeded "a negro man carpenter, Ben," to Donnell that very day. After buying Ben, Donnell also bought tools for his use, including an adze and two pairs of compasses from Mr. Clark ($1.30), a fore plane and jack plane from Mr. Forbes ($2.75), a broad axe from Mr. Franklin ($2.25), and a hand saw, square, and chisels from Mr. Dunn.[54] This was standard practice for Donnell. Just the year before, as we have seen, Donnell spent $25.35 for a more elaborate set of tools for his slave Simon to use while hired out: sash planes, ovolo planes, fore planes, molding planes, a tenant saw, rabbit planes, a brace and bits, a handsaw, one lot of chisels, a rasp, nippers, gimlets, a hammer, a screw augur, a plow (plane), and more, which indicated the high level of Simon's craftsmanship.[55] Although Donnell legally owned these tools, in practical terms they formed part of Ben's and Simon's kits and contributed to their identity as artisans as well as improving their prospects for profitable employment.

Within several months Donnell hired Ben out to white house carpenter Martin Stevenson, with "his time commencing" on December 14, 1824. Stevenson was involved in building some of the city's premier edifices, and Ben probably worked with him on those projects. Donnell and Stevenson agreed that Stevenson would pay Donnell for Ben's services but also allowed some recompense to Ben. Donnell recorded that Stevenson was to pay him "$18 per month of 26 working days he to be accountable for the whole time, unless he is sick when I am to have immediate notice—of this I allow him to pay Ben $1.50 per week provided Ben has lost no time & not misbehaved during the week (out of this $1.50 Ben is to board and clothe himself—my object being to reserve $12 per month to myself)." If all went well Donnell could hope to recoup Ben's purchase price within five years. For Ben, saving a like amount toward possible manumission, even if he worked additional hours on his own time, would have taken far longer. Nevertheless this arrangement, whether made at Ben's request or standard for Donnell or Stevenson, marked an improvement over John Oliver's bargain with Uriah Sandy, for it gave Ben control over a portion of his earnings.[56]

The following year, Ben evidently played a role in selecting his employer, thus taking another step to shape his situation within the bounds of slavery. After working for Stevenson through February 1825, Ben was hired out to another man, but soon Donnell noted his apparent dissatisfaction: "Ben commenced work with Mr. Jarvis on Friday 27 May 1825 at $18 per month $6 to be paid to Ben and quit as he [Ben] stated to me on Tuesday 12th day of Sale at Beaufort when Mr. Jarvis [was] absent at 10 o clock." On Wednesday, July 13, Donnell noted Ben had "commenced 2 month with Antony (Portg), he to find him and pay me $12-month of 26 working days." The pronoun "he" is ambiguous and might refer to Ben hiring himself and paying his owner wages, or possibly Ben had found a new employer to pay Donnell for his time.[57]

Whether Ben "hired himself" or not, many slave craftsmen did so. Self-hiring, as we have seen, was the nearest to freedom that most enslaved artisans came. John R. Donnell and his enslaved plasterer Shade Green had an arrangement for years in which Green worked on his own and paid Donnell regular wages. Their financial dealings sometimes also involved negotiations between the slaveholder and the slave. When Donnell settled up "with Shade this 16th March 1823 for his wages . . . leaving him in debt $36," he noted, "He pays [me] wages at the rate of eight Dollars per month." Donnell listed "credits" to Shade Green, such as fifteen dollars for white-washing at Donnell's house and plastering the home of Donnell's brother-in-law Charles G. Spaight. He also credited Green with "one months wages while traveling with me—$22.00," suggesting the amount of Green's usual earnings. Their dealings occasioned compromises on Donnell's part. He noted on February 23, 1829, "Within the last year Shade has paid me $85.05 (including work done for me and 1½ month allowed for absence with me) having $10.95 due of wages of that year—I have told him that I would strike out of my account the forward balance against him about $209 if he would make up the balance of $10.95 for last year and keep up his wages from the first of this year. I therefore open on next side a new account with him."[58]

The enterprising Shade Green, like other self-hiring artisans, may have used his earnings to acquire his freedom. Although no record of his manumission has been found, in 1840 the census listed Shadrach Green as a free man of color and head of a large free black household living on the edge of town near tailor John Bragg and his family. Shade Green was a friend, though not a kinsman, of tailor John Rice Green and was described by John's son as "a man of means, and well reputed in the community where he lived." He also "possessed on his premises a well of crystal water with a pump extending into it. This water was used, gratis, by every one, within half a mile, who thirsted for it."[59]

Although John R. Donnell acquired and hired out slaves as a business venture, many of New Bern's enslaved artisans labored to support widows and children who had inherited them. As we have seen, some slaveholders arranged artisan training for slaves to assure income for their heirs, and when they made their wills, they reiterated such purposes. Planter David Witherspoon, owner of fourteen slaves, directed in his will of 1801 that his executors hire out his carpenter Jack and two other slaves by the month, with "their wages appropriated to the use of my son [John]."[60] White blacksmith James Sanders, who bequeathed his blacksmiths Willoby, Ben, and

Harry, along with two sets of blacksmith tools and six other slaves, to his wife Mary in 1785, expressed special concern for educating his children and recommended that his executors hire out "my best Negroes, particularly my tradesmen, yearly, which will be much more to the advantage of my wife and children than otherwise, or that only such [slaves] might be reserved from hiring as might be of immediate use in my family." The three blacksmiths earned a regular income for Mary and the Sanders children for several years.[61]

When craftsmen were hired out, as when they were sold, they often faced separation from their families and from home. Such events often followed the death of an owner. While some slaves genuinely grieved the loss of a particular owner, for many, their grief reflected fears of what might happen to them and their families. The enslaved artisans of planter Benners Vail faced dispersal in 1816 when Elizabeth Vail, his widow and executrix, took on the administration of his estate. Some of them could hope for some stability, albeit with a new master, for Mrs. Vail advertised for lease a mill site together with "negroes skilled in the management of the Mills, Coopers & Carpenters who can be hired."[62] She also offered for hire separately "a number of valuable Negroes, among them are Ship & House Carpenters, Caulkers, and Blacksmiths," whose new employers might take them to distant sites for long or short periods. Following the 1802 death of former governor Richard Dobbs Spaight Sr., his estate in 1804 included eighty-nine slaves, including Jim, a fifty-nine-year-old shoemaker valued at $175, and Tom, a fifty-one-year-old blacksmith valued at $450. Spaight's executors hired out his slaves over the years—as many as thirty-four in a single year—to benefit his widow, Mary Jones Spaight, and their minor children. Eventually the executors distributed the Spaight slaves among the surviving heirs in and around New Bern.[63]

Meanwhile, the blacksmiths Willoby and Ben, who had worked for years to support the widow Mary Sanders, likewise found that their owner's death brought abrupt changes. In her will of 1791 Mrs. Sanders directed her executor to sell Willoby and Ben, together with "all my Smiths tools and my household furniture." Ben died, but Mary's son-in-law, Charles Hatch, bought Willoby and the blacksmith's tools and shop, paying $260 for Willoby, $7 for the blacksmith shop, and $15 for the tools Willoby would use: "2 Anvills, 1 pair of Bellowes, three Sledge hammers, 2 hand hammers, 4 pairs of Tongs, 2 Vices, 1 Bick Iron, 1 Sett hammer, 1 Tool to make Nails, 1 cow Hammer." By 1807 Willoby had been sold again and was owned by Thomas

Hyman and William Conway, partners in a blacksmith shop.[64] Similar sagas occurred over the years as enslaved artisans along with other slaves were sent hither and yon to benefit and settle the estates of their former owners.

RUNNING FOR FREEDOM

Confronted with the jolting changes wrought by the deaths and needs of their owners, artisans, like other slaves hired out to distant sites, often escaped and headed home. A substantial proportion of runaways were slaves hired from estates or sold in the wake of their owners' deaths. When carpenter Mark Ralph was hired from the estate of William Shepard of New Bern, his new employer took him more than thirty miles inland to a Pitt County plantation. Although he was fifty years old and past the age of hasty departures, Ralph soon escaped. His owner believed he was on his way to New Bern "in which place and its neighborhood he is well known and where he is probably lurking." The uncertainties of estate management also offered slaves the chance to slip away and remain at large. Carpenter Jacob, a "valuable Negro, having sold some years since for 800 dollars," had been hired from the estate of his late owner on January 1, 1814. He ran away on about May 1, but the hirer failed in his duty to advertise for Jacob's return, and not until July 1 did the frustrated estate administrator take on the task. By that time, he surmised, the "artful and cunning" Jacob, who was believed to be passing as a free man, had made his way to Elizabeth City to board a ship to the North.[65]

Runaway slaves moved constantly to and from towns and across the countryside throughout the region, often heading for cities where they hoped to find work without too many questions being asked. The hundreds of runaway notices that filled antebellum newspapers depict a vast number of people walking surreptitiously across the state and the region. Most of the runaways whose owners guessed at their motives were said to have slipped away in order to return home, reunite with family members, or find a point of departure by sea.

In the New Bern area, as elsewhere, artisans constituted a significant proportion of runaways who stayed away long enough to propel their owners or hirers to pay for advertisements for their return. Enslaved artisans had certain advantages that enabled them to succeed in their escapes, including the "cunning" that arose from dealing with whites and the knowledge that their skills could help them to find employment in a new setting. Of 134 documented runaways in North Carolina in the period 1748–75, 10

James, a Blacksmith

Although most advertisements for runaway slaves supplied little more than a name, a trade, and an approximate age, some provided vivid descriptions. James, a blacksmith "most used to making axes," who ran away in 1791 at age twenty-one, was five feet seven or eight inches tall, with a "yellowish complexion" and "small legs and very large feet—has a bold look, speaks good English and can tell a smooth tale—born on Trent river." He already bore signs of a hard life, "stoop[ing] forward in his knees and body as if he had a burthen on his back—his back is marked with the whip, he has a scar on one of his elbows occasioned by a burn," perhaps sustained at the forge where he worked. In contrast to the plain garb of many slaves, James carried with him an extensive wardrobe: "one blue coat dyed in the cloth and turned whitish where it is worn, middling fine cloth, also a tight bodied coat, with holes at the elbows and under the arms, and a rent in one shoulder; also a sky blue homespun [coat] and a jacket of nearly the same—also a homespun white linen jacket, a pair of corduroy, and a pair of buckskin breeches, new last fall but worn in the crotch, two pair of tow trousers, two shirts and a fine new white shirt . . . and a pair of sky coloured stockings—a new wool hat with a purple ribbon round it and an old rackoon one. . . . All masters of vessels and others are forwarned of harboring or carrying him off at their peril."

Aaron Lambert, Jones County. *North Carolina Gazette* (New Bern), September 24, 1791, *SLF*, 3.

percent were described as artisans. The proportion rose to about 13 percent during the period between 1775 and 1840: out of 2,661 slaves described in runaway notices in North Carolina newspapers, 339 possessed at least one skill; about a third of these skilled runaways were carpenters and blacksmiths, followed by shoemakers and coopers. Few if any women artisans appeared among the runaway notices in New Bern–area newspapers. Like other runaways, most of the escaping craftspeople were men from their late teens into their thirties—of an age to undertake such a risky and demanding venture.[66]

New Bern's position as a port, together with its large population of slaves and free people of color, made the city a compelling destination for fugitives. Some of the runaway notices in local newspapers sought the return of local slaves, but many described slaves from other places who were thought to be heading for New Bern or other ports to escape by sea. Some had made journeys that required great tenacity and a working knowledge of geography. Dick, a blacksmith who had made two previous attempts to escape to a free state, ran away from Leaksville in the northwestern Piedmont; his owner, textile industrialist John Motley Morehead, believed that he was heading east to board ship in New Bern or Wilmington. An unnamed blacksmith, raised in New Bern and formerly owned by Governor Abner Nash, ran homeward from piedmont Caswell County. His owner surmised that he had gone to New Bern to "get on board some vessel" and expected that his brothers Abram and Tom would "keep him secreted until he can get off."[67] At any given time, the city's majority-black population included an uncounted number of fugitives hiding out or living with friends or family and planning to make a lasting escape.

Advertisements for runaways illuminated the depth and breadth of slave networks of family and friends to whom fugitives turned for refuge. Bricklayer "Frank or Frank Burr" was a well-dressed, talkative, and literate artisan "raised by John Devereux," the wealthy merchant from whom his New Bern owner James G. Stanly had purchased him. When Burr ran away in 1820, Stanly listed his likely destinations: he might go to his wife at Durant Hatch's plantation in Jones County or to his father at Mr. Pollock's farm near Trent Bridge, but it seemed probable that he was "lurking about" another Pollock plantation on the Roanoke River a hundred miles north of New Bern, "where he has connections." Burr's former owner Devereux had married Frances Pollock, a member of a distinguished and wealthy planter family—thus Burr's link to the Pollock plantations and their extensive slave networks.[68]

Runaway notices also reveal much about slaves' naming patterns. Although many slaves actually had only one name (a first name), runaway advertisements reveal that some, like Frank Burr, had last names as well, which they and their friends employed even if whites did not. In these notices, if not at other times, slaveholders acknowledged both the first and last names of runaways to maximize the chances of recapturing them, as did the slaveholder who advertised for "Allen, calls himself Allen Woodard . . . a pretty good house carpenter and a very ingenious negro."[69] Slaves known by one name during bondage often took a last name when they gained their freedom, but some slaves, such as Rigdon Green, John Rice Green, and James York Green, had two or even three names before they were emancipated. The master carpenter known as Tom Newton before his manumission signed his name as Thomas Newton as a free man.

A Painter Bent on Freedom

The experiences of one determined runaway artisan, New Bern painter "Tom, or Tom Whitfield," evoke those of many other runaway craftsmen. In 1821, when he was about thirty-five years old, Whitfield ran away from Rachel McCabe, who surmised that he was "probably lurking" at the home of his wife, who lived at Mr. William Gaston's mills. Captured and sold far from home, by 1825 Whitfield escaped again, and R. Powell of Smithfield advertised for his return, noting that he had formerly belonged to the late Mrs. McCabe of New Bern, where he was "well known as a House Painter, having followed that business several years."[70] This was a typical advertisement, for slaveholders often identified runaways as being well known locally: far from being invisible or anonymous to white citizens, many enslaved craftsmen had strong local identities.[71] Some advertisers even stated that there was no need to describe a certain runaway because he or she was so well known in the locality.[72] It was chiefly when slaveholders believed their slaves had made for a distant destination where they were not known that they paid to publish lengthy descriptions of the fugitives' bodies, expressions, clothing, and habits. Isaac, a shoemaker who ran away in 1800 from Durant Hatch of Jones County, had formerly belonged to "Abner Nash, Esq., deceased" and was thus "well known in the town & vicinity of Newbern." But because Hatch believed that Isaac had headed for Virginia by way of Halifax or Edenton, North Carolina, he paid the Edenton newspaper to print a lengthy advertisement that described the tall, thin, yellow-complexioned shoemaker in detail, including his chipped front tooth and "remarkable small foot."[73]

Believing that Whitfield had returned to New Bern, Powell surmised that the rebellious painter planned to board a ship to the north and therefore announced, "Masters of vessels and others are forbid carrying away or harboring said Negro." It was standard practice to post an official warning invoking legal penalties to prevent ship captains from permitting fugitives to board their ships. So many runaways sought to reach freedom by sea that in 1791 the legislature forbade ship captains from allowing any slaves on board their vessels without a pass from a justice of the peace or the slave's owner, and in 1792 the state enacted a death penalty for taking fugitive slaves out of the state. Some slaveholders added to their warnings to masters of vessels against taking a certain slave on board that "the penalties of the law will be enforced against all such offenders."[74]

Although Whitfield evidently failed in this attempt, he did not give up. Recaptured, sold, and resold, despite his reputation as a chronic runaway he continued to find work and to be "well known in and about Newbern as a House Painter." After biding his time for four years, in 1829 he ran away from Henry Mitchell of New Bern, who had bought him from an interim owner. Mitchell took the extreme step of designating Whitfield as an outlaw, stating "if in the act of taking him, he should resist and be killed, I will not hold the person so killing, responsible for his value." By outlawing a runaway, an owner legally authorized members of the public to attempt to capture the fugitive, and if the runaway resisted capture, to kill him "as they may see fit, without accusation or impeachment of any crime." Whitfield was either captured or returned voluntarily because of the threat of death. But he did not stay in bondage long. Mitchell decided to send him out of the state, probably to the slave-hungry western or southwestern plantation territories. In 1831 Mitchell advertised, "Ran away from subscriber's agent while passing through Rockingham County, NC . . . 3 negro men," including Tom Whitfield, about 40 years old, "well made, quite dark complexion, his eyes are generally a little red." Mitchell offered a token reward of ten dollars for each slave.[75] Whether Whitfield made good his escape and began a new life as a free painter remains unknown.

An Era of Manumissions

. . . your petitioner Thomas Newton . . . was the property of Benjamin Woods Esqr in his life time and that in conformity to the intention and desires of his said master often times expressed the Executrix of Mr Woods was pleased to obtain leave from this Worshipfull Court to give your petitioner his freedom which has been confirmed to him accordingly. And your petitioner further sheweth that he has a wife named Sarah late the property of Mr. John Devereaux, and that your petitioner has been enabled to purchase his wife from Mr. Devereaux by the fruits of his

honest industry. . . . And your petitioner being Master of the Carpenters business is able to maintain himself wife & children . . . and is therefore anxious to procure his wifes freedom And humbly prays your worships to grant him a license for this purpose upon your petitioner entering into Bond with securities agreeably to the acts of Assembly in such case. . . .

Thomas Newton by E. Graham, his Atto.
—Craven County Petitions, 1811

For a remarkable number of New Bern artisans during the post-Revolutionary period, freedom came through manumissions. Blacks as well as whites had heard the Revolutionary messages of liberty and equality, including the inspiring phrases of the Declaration of Independence, and they used whatever resources they possessed to work for freedom. New Bern carpenter Thomas Newton, like Donum Montford and John Rice Green, typified the artisans who learned and practiced their crafts in bondage for many years before opening new chapters as free men and masters of their trades. Although numerous artisans in cities throughout the South found paths to emancipation, in New Bern an unusually large number of private manumissions produced an ensemble of free artisan-citizens of color who shaped the city's exceptional character as a home and haven. Using abilities developed in their craft trades, many of the city's leading black artisans employed their vision and imagination, profitable skills, relationships, and determination to obtain their own liberty and that of their families and friends.

Couched in the language of artisan and manhood identity, Thomas Newton's petition touched on the myriad factors that, as we shall see, made his and others' freedom and craft status possible. Especially important was his reference to the "acts of the Assembly," for at that time North Carolina laws concerning manumission were fairly lenient. Moreover, manumissions often involved the support of prominent white citizens such as those cited in Newton's petition, including his and Sarah's prestigious former owners, Benjamin Woods Esq. and merchant and planter John Devereux, and Newton's attorney, Edward Graham. Newton also asserted his artisan identity by reiterating the customary phrase of employing the "fruits of honest industry" to purchase his wife. Having imagined and pursued freedom and developed his craft abilities for years, he claimed his status as a "Master of the carpenter's business" and as a free man able to maintain his own free family.[76]

Under North Carolina law, as under the law of some other colonies, slaveholders in the early colonial period could free a slave at will for honest and faithful service. (The law required the freedperson to leave the colony, but this measure was frequently ignored.) Manumission laws varied over the years from one colony and state to another. In 1741, to counter Quakers' multiple manumissions, North Carolina added meritorious service as a requirement together with licensing by the county court. But this provision, which distinguished North Carolina from other colonies, did not prevent individual manumissions; especially in the cases of children the courts often ignored the meritorious service requirement. After the Revolution, manumission laws followed colonial precedents except for the addition of a few new requirements that complicated the process but did not halt it. As Newton's petition acknowledged, a law of 1801 required the emancipator to post bond to assure that the freedperson would not become a public burden. In 1818 the legislature shifted authority for manumission from the county court to the superior court.[77]

In New Bern, as throughout much of the country, the first decades after the American Revolution brought a "wave of manumissions," as the ideals of liberty and the rights of man inspired some slaveholders to free their slaves. In contrast to some parts of the South where the wave ebbed in the new century, in New Bern manumissions gained momentum and continued through the 1820s.[78] When members of prestigious families, including heirs of Revolutionary patriots, freed selected slaves or assisted in other manumissions, they not only added to the city's free black population but also lent authority and prestige to the idea of private manumissions and the acceptance of certain free blacks as community members and citizens. With the chain of manumissions thus begun, emancipated New Bernians such as Donum Montford and Thomas Newton set about freeing others, so that a growing number of local black artisans modeled roles both as freedmen and as emancipators.

Petitions for manumissions often echoed the spirit of the American Revolution by citing the "blessings of liberty" and praising the person to be freed in terms of artisan-citizenship virtues. In 1812, supporters of manumission for carpenter James York Green explained that he had not only performed meritorious service, but was also a "a sober, honest and industrious fellow and in their opinions would not disgrace the character of a free man."[79] Of carpenter Bacchus and his wife Sukey, their emancipator stated in 1811 that "in industry fidelity and honesty & in all the qualifications of *good citizens*" (emphasis added), the two would "not suffer by a comparison with any free persons of their colour."[80] In contrast to later years, when the very idea of blacks as citizens came into question, the standard phrase in many manumission bonds and petitions—such as that for tailor John Rice Green in 1818—stressed that the freedpersons would behave as "honest and peaceable citizens."[81]

To begin the process of manumission, the slaveholder petitioned the court or legislature for permission to free a specific slave or slaves and posted the necessary bond. After obtaining permission, the emancipator had to execute a deed of manumission to the person to be freed in order to make the action legal. It was usual, though not required, to register the deed of manumission with the county to create a permanent and public record. In the case of John Rice Green, his owner Richard Dobbs Spaight Jr. posted bond and gained permission to free him in March 1818 and followed up with a deed to Green in May, which Green registered at the following September court session. When the emancipated carpenter James York Green freed his mother, Violet, and his brother Rigdon in that same year, he petitioned the court in September and signed the deed of manumission in November, and it was registered in December. Sometimes, however, emancipators waited for years to execute the necessary deeds, or the documents were lost or forgotten, lapses that could slow or even prevent the slave's liberation.[82]

Less reliable than deeds of manumission, as many slaves learned to their loss, was emancipation by will. For the slave owner, this method had the advantage of retaining the slave's person and services as long as needed while rewarding faithful service or salving a slaveholder's conscience. For the slave, it guaranteed nothing, since the emancipation was not effective until the decedent's debts were paid and the estate was settled, so that the promised liberation might take years—or never come. In 1812 white blacksmith William Conway bequeathed to "my Negro man Willoby, a blacksmith, his freedom" and, in terms that expressed shared ownership of an individual, to "my Negro man Larry, a blacksmith, my proportionate share of his time" plus $250 "to enable him to purchase the other half of himself." Willoby, as we have seen, had been transferred from one owner to another and was, like Larry, probably anticipating his freedom under Conway's will. After Conway's death, his executors listed one Negro man, Willoby, and "one half of Negro man Larry" to be emancipated. But when the executors balanced the accounts, they found that Conway's debits exceeded his assets, and the sheriff sold Willoby and Larry to pay their former owner's debts.[83]

For many New Bern artisans, despite the perils and uncertainties, the racial conditions and laws of the early national period enabled them to hope for and often to achieve freedom through legal means. Although there is no record of the total number of manumissions or of the proportion of local free blacks who were manumitted rather than born free, manumission documents from the 1780s through the 1820s identify more than 250 Craven County slaves whose owners sought to emancipate them. Since some manumissions went unrecorded, these represent but a fraction of the total.[84]

Central to the story of manumissions and the advancement of artisans and other blacks in New Bern was an exceptional man who spanned the categories of race and class—John Carruthers Stanly, the emancipated and wealthy mixed-race barber. He freed numerous people himself and took instrumental roles in the manumission of many others. Born in 1774, Stanly was generally recognized as the son of wealthy white merchant and Revolutionary War privateer John Wright Stanly and an enslaved Ibo woman. As a young slave, he established a profitable tonsorial business and saved much of his earnings. At age twenty-one he was freed by his owners, ship captain Alexander Stewart and his wife, Lydia Rellier Stewart. Stanly soon acquired two young slaves whom he trained to work in his shop, where his customers included some of the city's leading white men.

Rapidly accumulating property in slaves and real estate in the town and county, Stanly became one of the richest men in New Bern and, with more than 100 slaves at one time, evidently the largest slaveholder of color in the South. Although his father had died when John C. Stanly was sixteen and still enslaved, the barber maintained a relationship with his white half-brother and exact contemporary, attorney and political leader John Stanly. As soon as he could, John C. Stanly acquired and emancipated his wife, Kitty Green, and their three children, John Stewart Stanly, Catharine Green Stanly, and Eunice Stanly. His and Kitty's younger children were born in freedom. Stanly took pains to educate his children, and the family lived in genteel style, first in their house on Johnson Street and then in a larger residence on New (Neuse) Street. Because of Stanly's local stature and his experience in liberating his family, both slaves and slaveholders turned to him for aid. He freed or helped to free an unequalled number—at least forty—of New Bern and Craven County people.[85]

"John C. Stanly (known as Barber John) . . . [owned] a considerable number of slaves, two of whom, Brister and Boston, were skilful barbers, and kept the shop in good reputation. Brister related the circumstance of Dr. Hugh Jones once taking his seat for a shave, and, drawing the sword from his cane, threatened that if he was cut or scratched by the razor, he would run his sword through the body of the operator. The shaving was completed without any accident. On being asked if his hand did not tremble with such danger before him, Brister replied, that he had made up his mind to save his own life by cutting the throat of Dr. Jones, if it became necessary. He also made a remark as to the peculiarity of Bishop England's beard, which I have forgotten."

Stephen Miller, "Recollections of Newbern Fifty Years Ago."

Strategies for Liberation

Donum Montford was among the first New Bern artisans liberated with Stanly's assistance. The strategy the two men employed, with the cooperation of Montford's owners, illustrates the complexities of manumission and the roles of black as well as white participants. In 1804, aged about thirty-three, Montford had belonged for all or most of his life to the elite white Cogdell family. Richard Cogdell, a Revolutionary-era political leader, died in 1787, leaving young Donum and other slaves to his wife, Lydia Duncan Cogdell, for her lifetime and then to their youngest daughter, Lydia Cogdell Badger. Over the years Montford doubtless plied his plastering and bricklaying skills for the benefit of the widow Cogdell and her household, while salting away savings toward eventual liberation. On September 10, 1804, the two Cogdell women, both widowed, sold "a mulatto boy slave named Donum" to John C. Stanly for $500. On the next day, Stanly signed a deed to Montford that "liberated, emancipated, and forever set free . . . the said mulatto boy by the name of Donum Montford."[86]

Although the documents gave no reasons for Stanly's intermediate role, it is likely that Montford had accumulated money for his purchase and emancipation and that, with the Cogdell women willing to support his hopes, he and Stanly had formed this plan. In a similar situation some years later, Raleigh slave Lunsford Lane approached his owner and "asked her if she would sell me to be made free." When she agreed, Lane arranged with her and a local white man "for the latter to take my money and buy of her my freedom, as I could not legally purchase it." It is also possible that white attorney John Stanly took a role in planning Montford's manumission; a defender of free blacks' rights who freed some of his own slaves, he was not only John C. Stanly's half brother but also the nephew of Lydia Cogdell through his mother Ann Cogdell Stanly, and likely well acquainted with Montford. In any case, through this double transaction Montford gained his liberty, John C. Stanly's intermediate role disconnected the manumission from possible entanglement in the Cogdell estate, and Lydia Cogdell and Lydia Badger received a welcome return without taking money directly from Montford.[87]

Once free, Montford worked with Lydia Cogdell in a strategy to free another Cogdell slave. On March 3, 1806, the two signed an agreement wherein Mrs. Cogdell *gave* to Donum Montford her eleven-year-old slave Abram Moody Russell—"free and clear from all charges Debts or demands due or to become due from the said Lydia Cogdell to any person whatsoever." Though prestigious, the family was no longer as wealthy as in the past. Mrs. Cogdell and Montford likely made this arrangement in anticipation of her pending death and to protect Abram from the uncertainties of being freed by will; she died just a month after signing the document. In their agreement, Montford promised to raise Abram, whom he later identified as his nephew, in his home as his apprentice, to teach him the skills of brickmason and plasterer, to assure that he learned to read and write, and to free him when he reached the age of twenty-six. For the last five years of Abram's term, Montford was to pay his wages to Mrs. Cogdell's estate for the benefit of Lydia Badger's children, who included George E. Badger, later a prominent attorney and political figure. Montford followed through on his promises, and—surely with the concurrence of the Badger family—freed Abram ahead of schedule, at age twenty-one, in 1816. In Montford's petition for Abram's manumission, he enlisted the aid of the recently freed carpenter James York Green. Upon his emancipation Abram became known as Abram Moody Russell Allen.[88] After working in New Bern for a time, he moved to Washington, North Carolina, where he lived a long life as a free black artisan and devoted Episcopal churchman.

Although little is known of the specific relationships among Montford, Allen, and the Cogdells, certain phrases hint at the connections between blacks and whites in these families as in the larger community. The 1806 agreement cited "the good will and regard which the said Lydia Cogdell bears toward the said Donum Montford" as the reason for giving Abram to him. A few years later, Lydia Cogdell Badger inscribed the names of both Donum Montford and Abram Moody Russell Allen among the names of white family members in her family Bible. A half century onward, Abram Allen took pride that he had been "reared with Badger and the Stanly's," referring to Lydia's son George E. Badger, a political leader who, like Abram Allen, was born in 1795 and whose grandmother Lydia Cogdell had enabled Allen to become free.[89] Whether Montford or Allen was the son of a white member of the Cogdell-Stanly family or of one of their friends remains unknown.

A number of prominent artisans of color were recognized in the community as children of known white fathers and enslaved mothers. In the late nineteenth century North Carolina historian John Bassett learned from old-timers about the leading free black craftsmen that "most of them were mulattoes, not a few of them were set free by their fathers and thus they fell easily into the life around them. This mulatto class was partly due to the easy sexual relations between the races. A white man who kept a negro mistress ordinarily lost no standing in society on account of it. The habit, though not common, was not unusual. Often the mistress was a slave, and thus there were frequent emancipations either by gift or by purchase of liberty, till the stricter spirit of the laws after 1831 checked it."[90]

Tailor John Rice Green, according to his son John P. Green, was known as the son of Congressman John Stanly (a son of John Wright Stanly) and Sarah Rice, a favored slave in the distinguished Spaight family. Proud of his ancestry, John P. Green presented evidence of his father's parentage: "Sarah Rice, John R. Green's mother, declared that Stanley [*sic*] was his father; John Stanley, on his 'dying' bed, sent for my father and to him in person, acknowledged his paternity, giving him at the same time, a steel engraved likeness of himself,—which we still have, in our family; My father, it was generally conceded, bore a more striking resemblance to Stanley, than any other of his sons,—except that, he was a shade darker; It was common rumor, in that community, that Stanley was his father."[91]

In several cases the slave's owner was also his father, who took steps to free his child. Such was evidently the situation for the mixed-race carpenter Nathan Chapman, whose owner, Samuel Chapman, a married white planter with white children, specified in his will that "Nathan the eldest son of my negro woman Juliet" was to be emancipated and bound to out to learn a trade. Samuel also designated a share in a local bank to go to Nathan when he reached age twenty-one. Of the thirty slaves named in Samuel's estate, only Nathan was noted as "mulatto," and only he was freed, while Juliet and the other slaves were willed to family members.[92] After Samuel's death in 1807, his white family duly carried out his wishes: his son Henry as executor promptly initiated steps to free Nathan, and after Henry's premature death, Samuel's widow Catharine and two new executors completed the manumission of "mulatto boy Nathan, son of Juliet" in 1810. Although Nathan was too young to have rendered meritorious service, the court authorized his emancipation nonetheless. In 1811 one of Chapman's executors bound out the thirteen-year-old Nathan to learn the carpentry trade from William B. Green. In Green's shop Nathan would have worked with Green's still-enslaved house carpenter James York Green. Aided by his father's gift of money, at adulthood Nathan promptly established his own shop and began taking his own apprentices.[93]

EMANCIPATED EMANCIPATORS

Especially important, as the city's free craftspeople of color grew more numerous and prosperous, they like Donum Montford took an effective role in strengthening the free black class by emancipating and helping to emancipate others. Shortly after his own liberation, Montford supported one John F. Smith in freeing a slave named Douglas in 1811 by helping to post bond. In 1814, with the help of John C. Stanly, the emancipated carpenter Robert Lisbon liberated his enslaved artisan, Robert W. Conway. In 1816, as we have seen, the recently emancipated James York Green joined Donum Montford in posting the £300 bond to free Abram Moody Russell Allen, and he provided similar support in other manumissions. The emancipated tailor John Rice Green likewise helped free others, as when he cosigned for a £300 bond to emancipate fellow tailor Boston Ferguson in 1829.[94] Some artisans of color enlisted prominent whites as securities in liberating other blacks, while in other cases free blacks alone were involved.[95]

These emancipated emancipators frequently engaged leading white attorneys to facilitate the process, a fact that highlights the willingness of prominent and well-educated whites to support manumissions on a regular basis. Thomas Newton, as we have seen, employed attorney Edward

Graham to help him emancipate his wife. The emancipated carpenter Robert Lisbon freed his wife, Venus, with the aid of attorney and state supreme court justice William Gaston, and when Lisbon arranged to "secure the blessing of liberty" for his daughter Myrtilla, his attorney was Congressman John Stanly.[96] When carpenter James York Green manumitted his mother, Violet, and his brother and fellow carpenter Rigdon Green in 1818, his attorney was Edward Graham, who was instrumental in numerous manumissions in his adopted community and who likely helped compose Green's statement that he had purchased Violet and Rigdon "under a deep conviction that it was an act of duty and piety . . . in order to redeem his Mother and brother aforesaid from the state of Slavery."[97]

For emancipated people with families in bondage, the acquisition and liberation of family members was a top priority. Leading free black artisans often possessed the resources, connections, and sense of agency to accomplish these acts of "duty and piety." Acquainted with the vagaries of fortune, they recognized that while they owned their family members they could protect them and that emancipation by will often succeeded, but these measures did not guarantee their families' freedom. Only by freeing them directly could free people guard their enslaved children, spouses, or parents from being torn from them or sold after their own deaths. Thus in her 1796 petition to manumit her daughter Princess, the emancipated spinner Amelia Green explained that it was "with much toil and industry" that she had raised the money to purchase Princess with the purpose of granting her freedom. Perhaps advised by her attorney—Edward Graham again—she informed the justices that she was "far advanced in life" and feeling the "infirmities of age growing upon her," as she "contemplat[ed] the awful event of her Death at no very Distant period, an event (which, unless the goodness of Your worship prevents) might frustrate [her] pious intention."[98] It was to prevent this outcome that she sought and gained permission to free her daughter.

Amelia Green had worked for years as a spinner to purchase her own freedom in 1785 from Robert Schaw for £100. Moving from the Wilmington area to New Bern between 1789 and 1795, she joined an important family network through the marriage of her granddaughter, Kitty Green, to barber John C. Stanly, who had purchased and freed Kitty and probably advised and supported Amelia in her efforts to purchase and free her children. Amelia bought her daughter Nancy from William Tryon Howe in 1794 for £120 and Princess from Isabel Chapman in 1795 for £100. After freeing Princess in 1796, in 1801 she petitioned to free Nancy; and in 1806 Amelia and Nancy purchased and freed Amelia's daughter and Nancy's sister, Harriet. Amelia Green lived to a ripe old age in her tidy home on Broad Street after seeing all her children and most of her grandchildren freed.[99]

An evocative expression of a parent's concerns appears in Donum Montford's petition of 1827 to free his eighteen-year-old son, Nelson, whom he had trained in his craft. Knowing the uncertainties of emancipation by will and likely aware of mounting white resistance statewide toward manumission, Montford employed Congressman John H. Bryan as his attorney. Although Bryan probably helped phrase the petition, its content surely embodied Montford's own experiences and feelings. Implying that while he lived he could protect his child from the harsh reality of his condition, Montford stated that, being "advanced in years," he was "apprehensive that in case of his death his said son who is his only child *may be reduced* to slavery" (emphasis added). To prevent this fate, he "humbly prays your Honor that [Nelson] may be emancipated agreeably to the acts of assembly in such case." In 1828 Montford posted £300 bond for Nelson's manumission; his witness was John Stewart Stanly, the son of John C. Stanly, who had emancipated Montford a quarter century earlier.[100] Within only three years, as we shall see, North Carolina enacted laws that raised nearly insurmountable barriers to such actions.

A Family Network of Emancipation

In manumissions, as in all aspects of life, webs of kinship knit together many enslaved people who supported one another in their efforts to protect their families and advance their conditions. One especially striking network linked several men and women owned by heirs of planter, governor, and Revolutionary patriot Abner Nash. At Nash's death in 1786 he left an estate of 110 slaves to his widow and young children. Although some of the Nash slaves were sold—and some, as we have seen, escaped bondage with the help of their kin—others descended to Abner Nash's children. Born and raised in the thick of the Revolution, Nash's children, as well as his slaves, likely imbibed something of the era's spirit of liberty. After coming of age the Nash heirs freed or arranged to free selected slaves. A man named Virgil was one of the first Nash slaves emancipated when he was freed in 1807 by Abner Nash's son Frederick with the support of his brother-in-law George H. Burgwin. Other family manumissions soon followed.[101]

Far from being passive recipients of freedom, Nash slaves actively pursued it. A key figure was carpenter Bacchus (Backus) Simmons. In 1809 attorney Edward Graham reported from New Bern to Frederick Nash in Hillsborough that the latter's slaves Bacchus and Sukey had been sold for $600 to William Conway and John C. Stanly. The sale was evidently part of a plan, probably facilitated by Stanly and Graham, to achieve Bacchus and Sukey's goal of freedom. Two years later, when attorney Graham presented William Conway's petition to free the couple, he explained that Conway had "become the purchaser of said slaves under a trust that upon the performance of certain Conditions on their part your petitioner would release his claim upon the said slaves and *assist them* [emphasis added] in an application . . . for their freedom."[102] Although the conditions were not specified, clearly the "honest and industrious" Bacchus and Sukey—who possessed "all the qualifications of good citizens"—had met them and were taking action to obtain their promised freedom. As a free man, Bacchus Simmons immediately began to acquire property—including land purchased from John C. Stanly less than six months after his emancipation—and to help fellow Nash slaves toward freedom.

At about the same time that Bacchus Simmons became a free man, Abner Nash's eldest daughter, Margaret Nash Haslin, arranged for manumission of some of her own slaves. She had already freed Phoebe, her mother's favorite slave, but shortly before her death she took further steps. Aware of the problems of emancipation by will, in 1811 Margaret bequeathed her young shoemaker Macklin to his father, the emancipated carpenter Thomas Newton, with the provision that he should free Macklin upon his maturity, an act that Newton accomplished in 1818. She also left her slave Rachel and Rachel's children to John C. Stanly, with instructions for him to liberate them. On June 13, 1816, Stanly followed through by petitioning to emancipate Rachel and her family—Kelsey, Hannah, Amy, Ketty, John, and Alfred—who were "of good moral character, sober & industrious." Implying that these slaves had taken a proactive role in obtaining their freedom and probably that they had saved money for the purpose, Stanly stated that *they* were "ready if emancipated to give the bond required by law that they shall not become chargeable to the parish." On June 16, carpenter Bacchus Simmons joined with one John Templeton in posting bond for the family's liberation in the sum of £2,800 to guarantee that they would "behave as honest and peaceable citizens."[103]

Meanwhile, by 1815 Virgil Crawford, a farmer and something of a carpenter

—and almost certainly the Virgil freed in 1807 by Frederick Nash—had married a woman named Lydia, whom he held as a slave along with most of their children. Facing his death, Crawford specified in his will that his wife and children should be emancipated and appointed "my friend John C. Stanly" as trustee of his estate. He also took the extra precaution of bequeathing Lydia and the children to Stanly, "it being understood that he receives them as a sacred trust, to pursue the necessary measures for their emancipation." As promised, Stanly sold all of Crawford's property "except his wife and Children which I have made free as directed by his will." With the proceeds of the estate, Stanly purchased another Crawford daughter, Virchey, for $206 from Ann Nash, a daughter of Abner Nash, in order to free Virchey along with the rest of her family. Stanly petitioned the court in 1815 for permission to free Lydia and her children, Virchey, Mary, Susan, Virgil, and Fred. Carpenter Bacchus Simmons came to the aid of this family as well by posting the bonds of £200 to the governor and £100 to the county court, a duty he again shared with the freed carpenter, James York Green, to guarantee that the "said negroes so liberated . . . [would] behave as honest and peaceful citizens."[104]

Simmons continued his assistance to the Crawford family by taking two of the "orphan" children into his home as apprentices in 1821—Mary, aged seven, as a spinster, and Virgil, twelve, as a carpenter—and thus gave them fatherly guidance and support and the skills to make a living. For the young Virgil Crawford, Simmons opened the door to the ranks of free artisan-citizenry. Strengthening the widow Lydia's economic independence, Simmons sold to her for fifty dollars part of his lot #357 in New Bern in 1836, and another part of it for eighty dollars in 1846, making them neighboring property owners on German Street. By 1830 Lydia's son Virgil Crawford, born about 1809, had completed his apprenticeship and was living in Washington, North Carolina, and in 1850 he was identified in the census as a mechanic. His son, Virgil A. Crawford, born in the early 1830s, probably to an enslaved mother, would become a cooper and leading citizen and political figure in post–Civil War New Bern.[105]

The Blessings of Liberty: Free Artisans and Citizens

Newly emancipated artisans such as Bacchus Simmons, John Rice Green, Donum Montford, and Thomas Newton entered into their roles as free people with a strong sense of purpose. For years, they had imagined and worked toward freedom, and once free they wasted no time in moving forward. Now able to keep the wages their skills commanded, they began immediately to acquire property, take their own apprentices, establish and protect their families, participate fully in church and civic life, and, as we have seen, help friends and family become free and advance. Whatever the restrictions state laws and social mores placed on free people of color, they partook avidly of the blessings of liberty they had achieved.

One treasured aspect of freedom was the ability to travel and to move from one locale to another. To be sure, existing state law forbade free people of color from returning to the state after spending time away, and a law enacted in 1826 prohibited the immigration of free blacks into the state. These measures, however, did not address free blacks' movement within the state. When traveling away from home, free people of color needed to carry proof of their status to avoid being identified as illegal immigrants or runaway slaves, but they could nonetheless move about the state to visit family and friends or conduct their business. As a free woman, Amelia Green could and did move from New Hanover County to New Bern, purchase her daughters from their owners in the former county, and enable them to become free in New Bern. Free blacks involved in construction, like whites, were most apt to travel for work because of the site-specific nature of building. In 1819 Donum Montford went nearly 100 miles north to the plantation of Ebenezer Pettigrew in Tyrrell County, where he delivered bricks and lime, built the foundation for a smokehouse, and mended plaster. Within two years after his emancipation in 1818, house carpenter Rigdon Green embarked on the first of a sequence of moves on a path of upward mobility. By December 1820 he was in Fayetteville and sufficiently established to take an apprentice, Robert Hazle, aged thirteen, to the carpenter's and joiner's trade. In 1826 Green moved to Edenton, where in March 1827 he took a free "mulatto" apprentice, Goldsmith Lloyd, aged seventeen, to the house carpenter's trade. He remained in Edenton for some twenty years and acquired substantial property in land and slaves before moving back to New Bern.[106]

For free black artisans such a seemingly simple matter as the possession of their working tools represented not only an economic investment but also an important symbol of their status as artisans and as free men. As we have noted in reference to Donum Montford, for artisans in America, as elsewhere, possession of tools ranked along with mastery of skills in establishing artisan identity. For emancipated artisans, especially those newly free, ownership of tools had special significance as marking their transition from slaves to free people capable of legal ownership. Some tailors and shoemakers needed only a small kit of cutting and sewing implements, but masters of these trades, such as tailors John Bragg and John Rice Green, required more extensive equipment, patterns, and workbenches. The free spinner Amelia Green owned two spinning wheels, one for wool and one for linen.[107] A journeyman carpenter could manage with a few basic tools, but a master artisan such as Thomas Newton possessed a large chest full of hammers, saws, chisels, gouges, and planes of different types. Typically manufactured in the North or abroad and shipped to local merchants, tools often constituted a craftsman's most valued and valuable personal possessions. For artisans of both races who did not own land or slaves, their tools typically constituted a substantial part of their estates.

As a free man, Thomas Newton could also designate the distribution of his working tools after his death. In his will of 1826 Newton bequeathed most of his tools to his free carpenter son, Mars Newton, and left a few others—a jack plane, a fore plane, and a hand saw—to his apprentice, Kelso (Kelcy) Davis. At this point Davis was still being held as a slave by John C. Stanly, but Newton bequeathed him the tools nonetheless.[108] Donum Montford made no special disposition of his tools in his will, and most of his tools and equipment were sold from his estate. A few remained in the hands of his heir, executor, and former apprentice, Abram Allen. Among these was an object Montford once had lost but later found or replaced: "1 Dimond to cut Glass."[109]

FREE BLACK MASTERS AND APPRENTICES

For free artisans of color, as for their white counterparts, acquisition of skills through the established apprentice system played a central role in defining their careers and their position in the community. Access to craft training was essential to becoming an artisan rather than a laborer. Most artisans who were born free or emancipated in childhood learned their trades through apprenticeships, some informally from a parent or sibling, others through formal agreements registered or arranged by the county court. Especially important, as we shall see, emancipated artisans such as Abram Allen, Donum Montford, Thomas Newton, and Bacchus Simmons, who had learned their skills in slavery, asserted their roles as artisan-citizens by taking apprentices to their trades and thus advancing both their own stature and the prospects of the next generation of their fellow people of color.

Under state law many free children of color, like white children, entered apprenticeships through county court action or a voluntary binding out recorded by the court. Some children were bound out from toddlerhood to adulthood, while older youths entered apprenticeships for just a few years. The apprentice bond, or indenture, was a contract between the master and the court—not between the master and the apprentice. As required by law, the document stated that the masters or mistresses must provide their apprentices with "fit and necessary" clothing, diet, and lodging—typically in their own households—and instruct them or have them instructed in the "art and mystery" of the specified trade, as the old phrase went.[110] From 1762 onward, North Carolina also required the master or mistress to teach the apprentice, or cause him or her to be taught, to read and write. This requirement, despite occasional proposals to end it for black apprentices, persisted unchanged until 1838.[111]

Although North Carolina's eighteenth-century apprentice laws did not explicitly address race, their provisions brought many children of color into the system. Early apprentice laws focused on placing "baseborn" children and "orphans" with responsible (typically male) adults to prevent them from becoming a public burden. Because the term "orphan" referred to any child without a legal father, and state law forbade interracial marriages and gave no legal standing to enslaved parents, many free black children with two living parents, including some who considered themselves married, were identified as baseborn or orphans and were thus subject to binding out.[112] In 1801, the legislature passed the first law explicitly aimed at free apprentices of color—in this case, to protect these vulnerable children from abuses such as kidnapping or enslavement. Every master or mistress of a free black apprentice had to post bond with the court, guaranteeing to keep the child in the county and to present the youth in court on completion of the apprenticeship.[113]

These laws assured that great numbers of free children of color obtained craft training that enabled them to pursue lines of work that would have been impossible or unlikely otherwise. During the first quarter of the nineteenth century, more than sixty free black children in New Bern and Craven County were bound to at least a dozen skilled crafts, including those of the blacksmith, boatbuilder, bricklayer, brickmaker, carpenter, caulker, chairmaker, cooper, house carpenter, plasterer, ropemaker, seamstress, ship carpenter, shoemaker, tailor, tanner, trunkmaker, and turner.[114] A large number of free black as well as white children were assigned to other occupations, with boys often learning the trades of farming and boating and girls typically bound out as "spinsters," a term that seems to have applied to general housework as well as to spinning.

Many of Craven County's free black apprentices during the post-Revolutionary decades came from rural families, such as the Carters, Godetts, and Doves, who comprised the majority of the free black population. Most of these children were assigned to neighbors of their own race, but after 1800 more were assigned to white and black masters in town. After completing their apprenticeships, most of these county youths returned to their home communities to carry on their trades, which they often combined with farming or fishing.

As New Bern grew and flourished, more town artisans needed and could support apprentices, including black youths from town and county. In contrast to racially restrictive practices farther north, white artisans in New Bern, as in many other southern communities, displayed no squeamishness about race when they took free and enslaved apprentices of color into their workshops and households. In Baltimore, white artisans were unwilling to train free blacks in their trades, and in Cincinnati a white master artisan was arrested for taking an apprentice of color.[115] Most of New Bern's leading white artisans, however, accepted black apprentices as well as white ones for most of the antebellum period.

A flurry of carpentry apprenticeships for youths of both races came in the late 1810s, when leading white house carpenters John Dewey and Uriah Sandy prepared to contract for the imposing First Presbyterian Church. Selecting youths of sufficient age to take productive roles right away, in 1817 Dewey took sixteen-year-old free black Tom Long to his trade, while Sandy signed on three youths of color—James Thornton, Elijah Moore, and William Hancock—the last of whom would become a successful master artisan. In Sandy's workshop, these and other black youths encountered his white apprentices and probably learned skills not only from Sandy but from the accomplished slave carpenter Ben, whom Sandy hired in 1817 from John Oliver. These apprentices and the white builders' slaves and employees worked together to execute the construction and finish the intricate classical details of their masters' projects, which, like the First Presbyterian Church, displayed hundreds of hours of artisans' skilled work.[116]

In addition to those assigned to master artisans, some apprentices bound out to craft trades were assigned to merchants and lawyers who delegated their training to free or enslaved craftsmen. White merchant William Lawrence took Thomas Harris, a free black boy of eleven, as an apprentice cooper in 1799 and likely placed him with a master artisan. Barber John C. Stanly, who took many apprentices to trades besides his own, followed a similar course. In 1804, with his own house on Johnson Street under construction, Stanly took four free black apprentices to the carpenter's trade and probably put them to work under the carpenters employed on his project.[117]

Many of the free black girls who were bound out as spinsters entered the households of black or white artisans, merchants, and attorneys, often in company with their brothers who were bound to other trades. When Donum Montford took orphan Richard Johnson, aged eleven, as an apprentice to the plastering trade, he also accepted responsibility for Richard's sisters, Abbey and Polly, as apprentice spinsters, who likely worked with Hannah Montford or another woman in the Montford home. Only occasionally did the court bind out girls of color to more specific crafts. Mary, a free girl of color, aged six, was bound to the elite white widow Lydia Badger in 1816 to learn the skills of a "sempstress" from Lydia or another household member. In an unusual case, Peggy, a free girl of color, aged twelve, was bound to Michael Guillet in 1811 to learn the trunkmaker's craft.[118]

By the first years of the nineteenth century, free black master craftsmen in New Bern claimed important new roles as artisan-citizens. In a step that demonstrated community support for their skills and character, the county court began to assign apprentices of color to the town's leading black craftsmen within just a few years of their emancipation. Because apprentice bonds do not identify the race of the master or mistress, only that of the apprentice, it is difficult to know how often such assignments took place in other communities; as noted earlier, such arrangements had been made among free blacks in rural Craven County for years. For New Bern's growing class of free black artisans, taking apprentices played a vital role in their own advancement. To expand their businesses they needed—and could support—apprentices to accomplish their work, and for a free black artisan especially, court assignment of apprentices was an official and visible affirmation of his mastery of his trade and his place in the community.

In 1807, three years after his manumission, Donum Montford took his first court-assigned apprentices: Jacob Harris, aged eight, as a plasterer and bricklayer; Garrison Hasle (Hazel), aged eight, as a bricklayer; and Patience Hasle, aged eleven, as a spinster. Three years after being freed in 1812, house carpenter James York Green took as apprentice carpenters Henry and Robert Hasele (Hazel), aged eight and ten, and Bill Dove, aged thirteen, as the first of many such free black children he took into his home and his shop. And in 1821, Abram Allen, emancipated in 1816, took Lewis Dove, aged eleven, to learn the plasterer's and mason's trade.[119] Most if not all of these children, judging from their surnames, came from free black families long established in the county.[120]

As far as can be determined, all of the apprentices the Craven County court assigned to black masters were children of color; no white apprentice is known to have been assigned to a black master or mistress.[121] In addition to expanding the opportunities for black children to become skilled workers, these master artisans enabled them to grow up with an accomplished adult of their own race as a model and authority figure, live in a free black household, and become part of a growing network of free artisans of color in New Bern and beyond. During this period, too, these children of color not only learned their trades from artisans of their own race but could readily imagine becoming master artisans themselves and establishing themselves as heads of households and respected citizens. As we shall see, such was the case with Jacob Harris, Donum Montford's first apprentice after his own emancipation, who mastered the skills of bricklaying and plastering and within a few years began his career as an artisan who passed along his skills to the next generation and raised a large family of educated free people of color.

FREEDOM AND FAMILY, HEARTH AND HOME

The overriding goal toward which most free black artisans directed their energy and their earnings was the formation and protection of stable families. As slaves, many of them had experienced destructive interventions in their family lives and suffered painful separations from spouses or children. Some had been able to maintain their families in slavery, and as free people they pursued the same course. Carpenter Bacchus Simmons and his wife Sukey obtained their freedom together. Barber John C. Stanly and carpenters Thomas Newton and Robert Lisbon married and had children in slavery, and as soon as they were free devoted themselves to acquiring and liberating their spouses and children. Other artisans married soon after their manumissions, such as carpenter James York Green, who wed Mary Neal, a free woman of color, on September 26, 1812, just two weeks after the court authorized Green's liberation. Five years after his manumission in 1804, Donum Montford married the emancipated and well-connected Hannah Bowers, who was remembered locally as the childhood nurse of political leader William Gaston, who had been caring for young William on the day in 1781 when his father, Alexander Gaston, was shot in cold blood by a British soldier. The widow Margaret Gaston, in keeping with her late husband's wishes, obtained an act of the legislature that made Hannah "emancipated and made free to all intents and purposes" and "entitled to all the privileges and benefits of a free person in as full and absolute manner, as if . . . born of a free woman."[122]

By marrying a free woman or by obtaining his enslaved wife's freedom, a man asserted his manhood by assuring that his wife would not be subject to sale or abuse according to her owner's need or whim, and that any children born to the couple thereafter would likewise be free. In 1827 tailor John Bragg, who may have been freeborn or emancipated, married Caroline Ferrand, who had been manumitted with the aid of tailor John Rice Green just months before their wedding.[123] Some enslaved men, such as John Rice Green, wed free black women despite the law against it. Green soon found that after marrying a free woman—his first wife, Sally McClure—"he could no longer endure the yoke of slavery" and redoubled his efforts to attain his own freedom. A year after he was manumitted in 1818, the Christ Church parish register recorded the couple's legal marriage: "September 4th, 1819, At their own house, John Green, a free coloured man to S McClure, a free coloured woman."[124]

Having "their own house" provided free people of color with another important indicator of stability and stature and underscored their identity as independent artisans and citizens. As in many southern cities of the period, black artisan families resided among black and white neighbors throughout New Bern.[125] Most artisans, like other working people, rented living quarters or lodged with family or friends, but the most successful acquired their own homes, including some in prestigious central locations. In 1820, emancipated artisans including Donum Montford, John Rice Green, and Amelia Green, as well as barber John C. Stanly, were living side by side with elite whites and their slaves. In making records of some such areas, census takers not only marked the census categories for whites, slaves, and other free people, but sometimes distinguished races by citing whites as "Mr." or "Mrs." while listing free people of color by name only. Tailor Green was the only man on his block not identified as "Mr."; his white cabinetmaker neighbor was listed as "Mr. Gabriel Rains."[126]

The city's artisans of color also participated in patterns of racial residential separation, which began earlier in New Bern than in most North Carolina towns. By the 1820s, in addition to the free people of color living in central New Bern, memoirist Stephen Miller recalled "quite a large population of the free negro class, who lived chiefly to themselves in the outskirts of the town." Although similar trends had begun in such cities as Petersburg and Richmond, they developed much later in Wilmington, Raleigh, and Fayetteville.[127] The pattern in New Bern and the Virginia cities resulted in large part from the size and proportion of their free black populations: in 1820 New Bern's 3,700 residents included 144 free blacks, compared to only 19 in Wilmington and 67 in Fayetteville. Some free black New Bernians settled in outlying areas because of poverty or a shortage of housing downtown. But the growing free black presence in the suburban sectors also reflected the financial resources of free black artisans, their determination to assert their autonomy by owning property, and perhaps their desire to live beyond immediate white oversight. Frequently working through John C. Stanly, who constantly bought and sold property, free black New Bernians took opportunities in the western and northern sectors to buy real estate at prices they could afford. Whatever their motives, the trends they initiated shaped the city's racial residential patterns for years to come.

West of downtown and adjacent to New South Front Street and Lawson Creek, the grid of streets laid out in the late eighteenth century had long been home to residents and property owners of both races. By 1815 carpenter Thomas Newton owned the house on Jones Street where he and his family lived. Nearby was the carpenter Bacchus Simmons, who had bought his property from John C. Stanly in 1811, right after his own emancipation. By 1820 their immediate neighbors included other free blacks as well as whites and slaves.[128]

During the same period, a large contingent of free black craftsmen and their families settled north of town in an area that included the suburban development north of Queen Street called Dryboro. Authorized in 1806 and platted as a grid by a white landowner, Dryboro initially drew white investors. Some lived there, while others had rental property or let their slaves live there, such as the "negro woman Isa," who in 1827 lived in a house owned by her mistress, Elizabeth Hatch. As the city's free black population increased, a growing number of emancipated artisans bought or rented homes in and near Dryboro. Two years after James York Green was emancipated in 1812, he bought a Dryboro lot from John C. Stanly, and over the years he bought and sold several properties there. Tailor John Bragg owned his family home not far from Green's, and they were soon joined by more artisans and families of color.[129]

In a time and place where the vast majority of free blacks as well as whites were landless, possession of even a small property represented a substantial advance, and it was especially meaningful for formerly enslaved people who had not been able to own even themselves. Property ownership was a qualification for voting until 1835 as well as a symbol of status, and it provided both stability and potential collateral for artisans to expand their businesses or to address their debts. Leading artisans who acquired town lots in the period included Donum Montford, John Rice Green, James Y. Green, Bacchus Simmons, Robert Lisbon, Thomas Newton, and the younger carpenter William H. Hancock. Most owned only their homes, but some, including Montford, both Greens, and Hancock, acquired additional property. Newton and Montford, like John C. and John S. Stanly, both bought rural property where they or their slaves operated farms.[130]

FREE ARTISANS IN "COLORED SOCIETY"

During the 1810s and 1820s, some of New Bern's leading artisans of color grew sufficiently prosperous and prominent to constitute what one participant termed "colored society." Although most craftsmen of both races practiced their trades and raised their families without gaining an education or accumulating wealth, a substantial number of New Bern artisans of color—both freeborn and emancipated—used their relatively high wages to pursue those goals and model a genteel way of life. They anchored their success and their identity on the same bases as did leading white artisans: formation of stable families and support from extended families, possession of high-quality skills often learned from a master artisan, natural ability and intelligence combined with a degree of self-esteem, a reputation for excellent work, property in land and slaves, and a "respectable" deportment of sobriety, uprightness, industry, and, in the case of black artisans, public restraint and modest behavior. With the exception of barber John C. Stanly and his family, New Bern's elite of color in this period consisted entirely of successful artisans and their families. During a quarter of a century and more, their hard-won freedom, coupled with their respectable behavior, craft expertise, and network of black and white connections provided what seemed to be an unusually solid grounding for the lives of people whose status fell between that of free white citizens and that of enslaved people.

Through their use of myriad strategies they strove to protect this status against whatever threats the larger world might offer.

For a few black craftsmen in New Bern, ownership of slaves as well as real estate not only increased their wealth and earning power but also solidified their position among the white slaveholders who dominated the community. However great the emphasis on liberty as part of artisan identity in the North might be, for black as well as white southern artisans, possession of slaves strengthened and sometimes helped protect their independence and stature as citizens. More than once, when whites expressed concerns that free blacks might encourage slave rebellions, others pointed to free blacks' ownership of slaves to dispel their fears. Within two years after his own emancipation in 1818, tailor John R. Green bought the slave Peter Henrion, aged fifteen, for $550; and in 1827 he paid his former owner, Richard Dobbs Spaight Jr., $700 for "mulatto Peter a carpenter . . . commonly called by the name of Peter Dewey." Green also owned Henry, Nicey, and Tempe, whom he mortgaged at one time to Spaight; and Maria, whom he mortgaged to attorney Edward Graham.[131] In 1830 the ten black slaveholders in town included Montford, who had ten slaves; John Rice Green, with six; and James York Green, with four.

Apart from circumstances in which they owned immediate family members, it is hard to determine when free blacks acquired slaves for strictly economic reasons, and when they did so for mainly benevolent reasons. Such motives were often mixed and varied from one slaveholder and situation to another. John Rice Green's son later insisted that his father bought some of his slaves at their own request in order to emancipate them; and when free black carpenter James York Green purchased the recent runaway brickmason Frank Burr in 1822 and immediately mortgaged him to the owner of Burr's wife, he may have been acting at least in part for Burr's benefit.[132]

In accepting the gift of Abram Moody Russell Allen as his slave and apprentice and fulfilling his promise to set him free, Donum Montford acted chiefly out of concern for the boy's welfare. But Montford also had a large workforce of enslaved craftsmen and laborers whom he probably owned chiefly for economic purposes. In 1820, his household included twelve free people of color (including ten workmen) and twenty-two slaves. "Whenever a job was to be done expeditiously, he was apt to be employed," recalled memoirist Stephen Miller, "as he could always throw upon it a force sufficient for its rapid execution." Montford, like other slaveholders, used his slaves as well as his real estate as collateral for loans and mortgages. Montford seldom freed his slaves, and those only the ones closest to him: his apprentice Abram Allen in 1816; his son Nelson in 1828; and by his 1838 will, effective after his widow's death, "my man Isaac," the bricklayer and plasterer Isaac Rue.[133]

Unlike in some locales, in New Bern status in the free black community did not require a long legacy of freedom.[134] As we have seen, many of the leading artisans were born to enslaved mothers and elite white fathers. Some knew of their parentage, such as tailor John Rice Green, son of Congressman John Stanly. In such cases where "common rumor" identified a prestigious father, that local knowledge might enhance the child's stature and connections among people of both races.[135] Of carpenter Rigdon Green it was said that, although he was born in slavery, "yet the circumstances of his birth were such as to identify him with his master . . . and hence the fact that he was educated, and taught the trade of a carpenter and became a master builder."[136]

Whether related by kinship or not, leading black artisans cultivated relationships with prominent whites as clients and sometimes as financial backers or protectors. As well as serving as contractor on major buildings, Donum Montford was asked to participate in 1832 with leading white builders Bennett Flanner, Joshua Mitchell, and Hardy B. Lane in assessing the structural condition of Christ Episcopal Church. On at least one occasion Montford obtained financial assistance from Raleigh attorney George E. Badger, the son and grandson of his former owners Lydia Badger and Lydia Cogdell. Tailor John R. Green fashioned clothing for the white elite—including a "great coat" that cost $6.25 for John R. Donnell, the brother-in-law of his former owner—and on occasion he turned for assistance to his former owner, Richard Dobbs Spaight Jr.[137]

Members of the free black elite also enhanced their status and their ties with the white leadership by affiliating with the prestigious congregations of First Presbyterian and Christ Episcopal Churches. The services were restrained in comparison to the robust worship style of the Methodists, and members tended to be educated and prosperous. Lydia Stewart, the white woman who had owned and emancipated John C. Stanly and continued as a family friend, was a founder of First Presbyterian Church in 1817, and Stanly and his family followed her example in affiliating themselves with the church. Kitty Stanly was among the church founders, and John C. Stanly was the only person of color among the original pew holders—and

Bryan v. Wadsworth

Whatever their racial identification with fellow blacks and their sympathies with those still enslaved might have been, Donum Montford and other emancipated slaveholders sometimes defended slave ownership against legal challenges. An example appears in the case of *Abram Bryan v. William Wadsworth.* In 1806–8, with help from John C. Stanly, the white slaveholder Elizabeth Henry obtained court permission to free several of her slaves as she saw fit. For some, such as the cooper Harry, she executed deeds of emancipation, but for others she did not take further action and freed them only in her will. Before her death in 1825, Mrs. Henry sold her slave Abram Bryan in 1820 to Thomas Wadsworth, who in turn sold him to William Wadsworth. Several years later, Abram Bryan sued Wadsworth for his freedom, insisting that he was free because of the license obtained by Mrs. Henry many years before. In 1835 the case proceeded to the state supreme court, where Justice William Gaston stated the court's ruling that the license to emancipate did not confer freedom—only the deed of manumission or the will of the owner could accomplish that. Among the New Bern men who signed a bond in support of defendant Wadsworth were artisans Robert Conway, Jacob McClure, and Donum Montford—all of whom were born in slavery and emancipated as adults; the latter two are known to have owned slaves themselves. Abram Bryan remained enslaved.

Craven County Civil Actions Records, 1831, NCA&H; CCDB 43: 257; *FFV*, 52, 56; Elizabeth Henry, Estates Papers, CCEP. Bassett, *Slavery in the State of North Carolina*, 31–32, notes that *Bryan v. Wadsworth* established that permission to liberate did not constitute liberation. The race of the signers of Wadsworth's bond was not indicated. It is noteworthy that Abram Bryan as a slave had standing to pursue a lawsuit.

the only one who owned not just one but two pews, discreetly located at the rear of the sanctuary.[138]

Especially striking was the preference of leading artisan families of color for Christ Episcopal Church, the church home of most of the local white aristocracy. Tailor John Rice Green, an ardent Episcopalian, was, according to his son, one of only three men of color who owned and occupied pews on the main floor (he did not name the other two), while the other black worshippers sat in the balcony.[139] Normally the church clerk noted the race and sometimes the enslaved or free status of black parishioners in recording their baptisms, weddings, and burials. But for some established free members of color, as for whites, he noted only their names, not their race. The scribe identified newly freed John Rice Green and his bride, Sally McClure, as "colored" when they married in 1819, but within a few years cited them only by name. No race was noted when free black tailor John Bragg wed Caroline Ferrand at the home of John Rice Green in 1827, or when carpenter Rigdon Green married Caroline Allen "at the house of the mother of the bride" the same year.[140]

For people of all races in New Bern, their self-presentation in their homes and clothing served as markers of status that were especially important in the style-conscious little city. Many free artisans of color applied their earnings to providing decent and comfortable homes for their families, and some used the quality and furnishings of their residences to demonstrate their genteel taste and way of life in terms understood by both blacks and whites. Judging from the few surviving homes of free people of color, the most prosperous people of color had houses built and furnished in a manner comparable with those of leading white craftsmen. Employing his usual discretion, the rich barber John C. Stanly lived in a frame house equivalent to the houses of New Bernians of the artisan class rather than emulating the white elite, as his wealth might have permitted. Emancipated spinner Amelia Green lived in a neatly finished one-story house on Broad Street. The prosperous tailor John R. Green's two-story frame house on Johnson Street was of fairly modest scale, but the interior was adorned with intricate and stylish woodwork similar to much grander New Bern houses of the period.[141]

Besides providing comfortable homes for their families, some black artisans commissioned handsome gravestones to honor family ties. For many years, slaves and free blacks as well as whites were interred at Cedar Grove Cemetery, founded in 1799 by Christ Church on land north of Queen Street and expanded over the years as a municipal cemetery. Here were buried from Christ Church John Rice Green's first wife, Sally (Sarah), and Donum Montford and his wife, Hannah, to name but a few. Handsomely carved and lettered stones marked the graves of some, while others had simpler stones or wooden markers. (Because of the dearth of good local stone, stone markers had to be imported from the North at great expense.)

Among the few surviving grave markers for antebellum black New Berni-

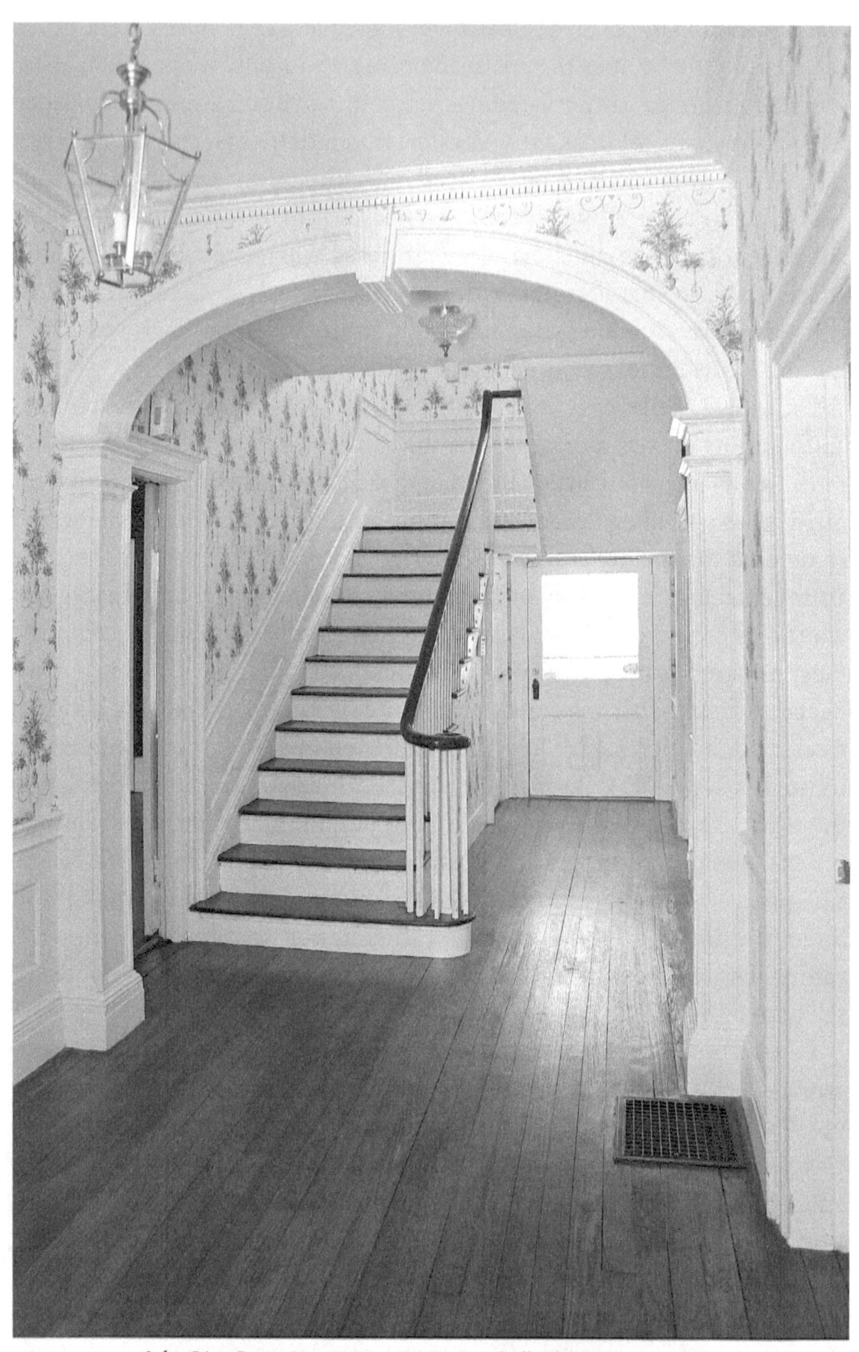

John Rice Green House, New Bern, stair hall. Photograph 2012 by Penne S. Sandbeck, New Bern, North Carolina.

ans is the beautifully executed stone for John Rice Green's mother, Sarah Rice, who died in 1821, just five years after she was freed by the Spaight family. The inscription reads, "Here are deposited / the remains of / SARAH RICE / who departed this life / July 19th 1821/ aged 45 years 8 months and 6 days / Blessed are the Dead which die in the Lord." It is not known whether the marker was commissioned by the Spaights or by Sarah's son John, freed in 1818, perhaps using for the marker some of Sarah's £100 bequest from her former owner, Mary Spaight. If her stone was representative of others long lost, the city's leading black residents took great care to recognize their family members with respect in death as in life.[142]

These accomplished free people of color also safeguarded themselves and their families by balancing their genteel taste with judicious modesty, a strategy not lost on white observers. Memoirist Stephen Miller, as we have seen, remembered that tailor John R. Green, who dressed in the "latest fashion," was "much respected for his modest, unassuming behavior, though he possessed wealth enough to put on airs." John C. Stanly, a master of balancing acts, Miller recalled, was "a man of dignified presence [who] lived in fashionable style, his sons and daughters being well educated, and always making a good appearance as bright mulattoes"—but "uniformly courteous and unobtrusive." Another white memoirist noted that, although Stanly "lived extravagantly in the time of his prosperity," he was "always properly dignified and temperate."[143] In petitioning for his son's freedom, Donum Montford reminded court officials that he had "always endeavoured to conduct himself with humility and honesty" and promised that his son was likewise "honest, sober & industrious and of humble & peaceable deportment."

HONEST AND INDUSTRIOUS MECHANICS: ORDERLY GOOD CITIZENS

For a more than half a century after the American Revolution, however circumspect their deportment, New Bern's leading free black craftsmen demonstrated publicly their status as citizens by regularly exercising their treasured right to vote. The state constitution of 1776 made no racial distinctions in authorizing all free men twenty-one and older who paid taxes to vote for members of the state House of Commons, and those who owned at least fifty acres of land to vote for the state Senate. (These bodies in turn chose the governor and congressmen.) By the early nineteenth century,

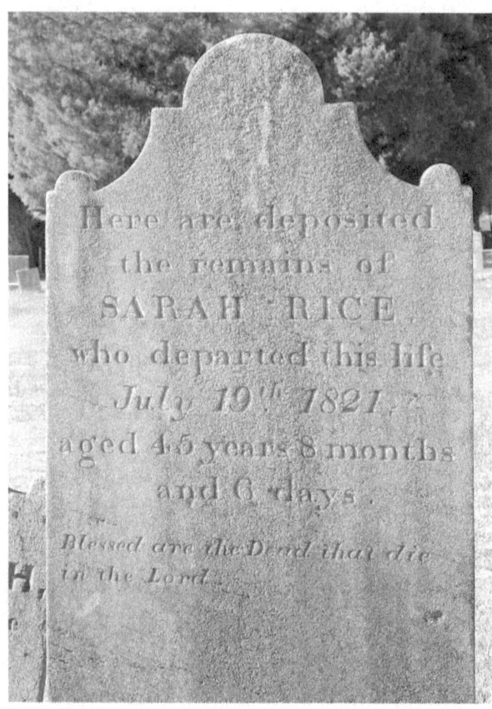

Sarah Rice gravestone. Photograph 2012 by Penne S. Sandbeck, New Bern, North Carolina.

North Carolina was one of the few states in the nation in which blacks could vote. In some locales in the state, few black men actually voted, whether as a result of white intimidation or a sense of futility given their small numbers. In New Bern and Craven County, however, as in a few other places with many free people of color, blacks voted in substantial numbers, a phenomenon that reflected white tolerance and even support for the black franchise as well as these voters' sense that they were sufficiently numerous that their ballots could have an impact.

Because of the city's unusually large number and proportion of free men of color, including those who paid taxes, as many as thirty to fifty black men voted in a total electorate of 200 to 300, and thus constituted a political force to reckon with. Memoirist Stephen Miller recalled seeing candidates John Stanly, William Gaston, Edward E. Graham, and Richard Dobbs Spaight Jr. "paying special civilities to the colored voters; nothing, however, to the extent of undue familiarity." Generally the free black voters supported Federalists, such as Stanly, Gaston, and Graham. Some artisans of color had personal ties with candidates, such as John Rice Green, the son of John Stanly, who was manumitted by Richard Dobbs Spaight Jr., as a young adult, and Donum Montford, linked through his wife, Hannah, to William Gaston. One observer noted that many of the black voters were "mechanics," and indeed, except for John C. and John S. Stanly, nearly all the black men who paid taxes in New Bern between 1815 and 1819—the last year for which local tax records are available before the 1840s—were craftsmen such as Montford and Green, Thomas Newton, James York Green, Bacchus Simmons, and Robert Lisbon. For such voters, the franchise represented the very essence of the artisan-citizenship for which they had worked for much of their lives.[144]

Through the first decades of the century, despite occasional controversies, New Bern's black voters exercised their rights regularly with the support of the local white establishment. In 1814, when Federalist John Stanly won a seat in the state House of Commons in a vote of 132 to 104, his opponents complained that thirty-two black votes had won him the election. A group of armed white thugs hired from a ship in port menaced the polls and then proceeded to Stanly's residence, where they attacked "some free coloured people, whose support he had received in the Election" and who had gathered with Stanly's "servants" in a building on his property, either to celebrate the victory or escape the thugs. A local newspaper editor condemned the "outrage" and claimed that of the thirty-two voters "whose complexions had more or less of an African tinge" only twenty-five had voted for Stanly, not enough to determine the outcome. He observed that the black voters included "two who collectively possess no small stake in the Country, and have paid a direct tax for its support, of upwards of sixty dollars." In the spirit of the American Revolution and republicanism, the editor affirmed the constitutional guarantee of "equal rights of all Freemen," and he employed the definition of artisan-citizenship in identifying most of the black voters as "honest and industrious mechanics . . . and orderly good citizens."[145]

JOHN STANLY'S WHITE SON EDWARD, who was four years old at the time of the incident and who recalled voting as a young man along with free men of color, painted too rosy a picture when he referred to early national–period New Bern as a "paradise for negroes," but he was accurate in recalling its character as remarkable.[146] Toward the end of the town's "golden age," New Bern artisans of color could glimpse hints of the changes ahead that would shrink their options, endanger their economic and social positions, and spur them to make difficult new choices during three decades of growing racial animosity and restrictions. When the Civil War opened up a new world of liberty and New Bern's black artisan-leaders pressed for equal rights, they drew upon the models of black citizenship from their city's remembered past.

THREE

Hundreds of Fine Artisans

Leaving and Staying, 1830–1861

The bearer of this, Cicero or Cicero Richardson, a mulatto boy about 13 or 14 years of age was born of a free mother in this town. He is about leaving here as we understand for Fayetteville, and this certificate is given as testimony of his freedom. His grandmother is a well know[n] huckster or cake woman by the name of Caty Webber. New Bern, Feby 17, 1832. Jn H. Bryan, Thos. S. Gooding, Readin Bourden, John Diuguid, James W. Bryan, M. C. Manly. If any difficulty should occur Cicero can hand this paper to Louis D. Henry who is acquainted with the signers

—Cumberland County Apprentice Bonds

Cicero M. Richardson set out from New Bern to enter an apprenticeship with Fayetteville free black brickmason Jacob Harris, inaugurating what would prove to be a long and successful career as a brickmason and plasterer. His journey came early in a period of mounting challenges for New Bern's artisans of color. Local economic problems and the state's tightening racial restrictions undercut many opportunities and rights upon which these artisans had grounded their hopes for freedom, citizenship, and advancement. In common with urban blacks throughout the increasingly polarized South, slaves strove to expand their freedoms while whites sought to reduce them, and free blacks worked to protect their precarious positions and remaining rights while whites imposed new limitations.[1]

Because of the attitudes and accomplishments of previous years, New Bern's situation for people of color still compared favorably with that of many antebellum communities. Nevertheless, events at the state, regional, and national levels inexorably altered the city's racial, social, and economic dynamics and reduced the prospects for its black residents. As they confronted these changes, New Bern's artisans of color persisted at their trades and relied on their networks of connections to protect their families, maintain their stature as artisans, and convey their skills to the next generation. Only late in the antebellum period did the city's leading artisans give up on their home community and head north to reestablish themselves as artisans and citizens in a new setting.

When Cicero Richardson left New Bern in 1832, the town was mired in an economic depression that limited opportunities for all artisans, especially brickmasons, while Fayetteville needed construction workers to rebuild after a devastating citywide fire in 1831. As Richardson and his family knew, a boy of color leaving home in February 1832 set out at a perilous time, for eastern North Carolina was still aflame after the Nat Turner Rebellion in Virginia the previous August and his capture in October and execution in November. White North Carolinians, like Virginians, vented their fears of further slave insurrections on both free blacks and slaves. For black North Carolinians, whether free or enslaved, travel away from home had always necessitated carrying a pass from an owner or proof of free status and a letter of protection. In 1832 a potent certificate of protection was especially vital.[2]

Cicero Richardson's letter of passage and his move to Fayetteville also highlighted the interracial and supra-local connections that artisans of color employed to support one another in such trying times. His friends in New

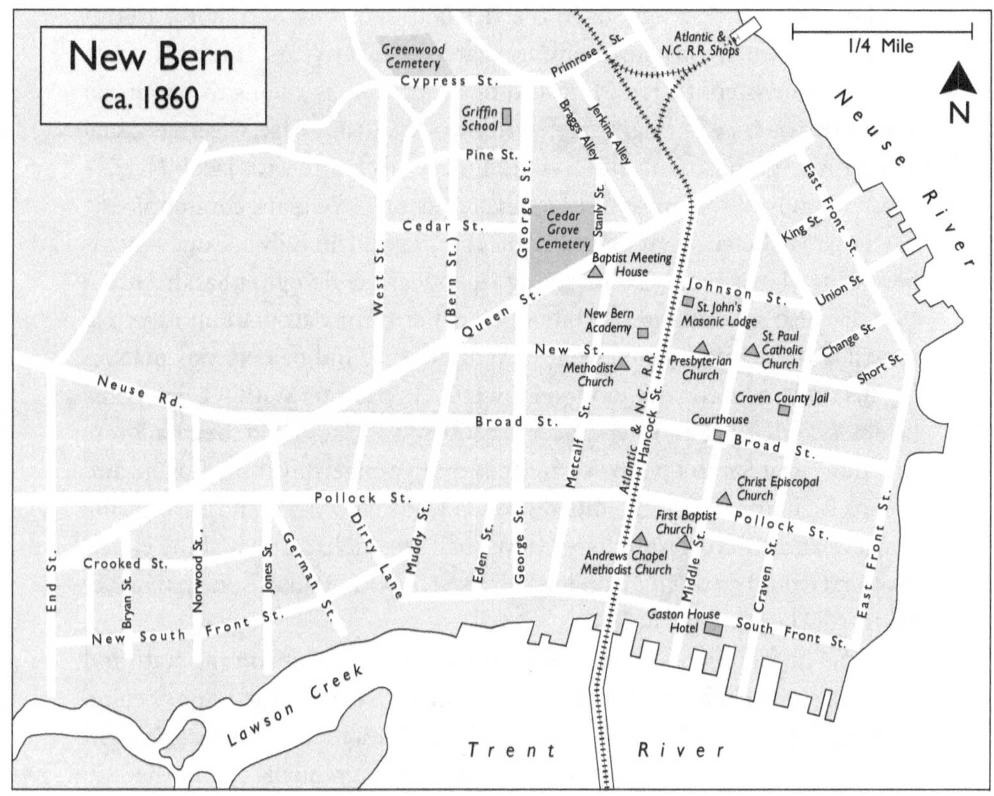

New Bern, ca. 1860. Map by Michael T. Southern.

Bern had armed him with a document that carried unassailable authority: John H. Bryan was a former legislator and congressman; his brother James was a rising lawyer; and Louis D. Henry, in Fayetteville, who had read law with his uncle, Edward Graham, in New Bern, was the speaker of the state House of Commons.[3]

Cicero had an intimate link with the Bryans through his maternal grandmother, Caty or Catherine Webber, longtime nurse and favored slave of the Bryan family, whom James Bryan had freed in 1827 when she was fifty years old.[4] She might well have arranged for her grandson's pass from the Bryans, but her prominent free black friends John C. Stanly and Donum Montford might also have taken a role. Stanly had joined the Bryans in supporting Webber's manumission, and Montford cooperated with Stanly and the Bryans in conveying town property to her.[5] In another connection, Fayetteville brickmason Jacob Harris was the first child apprenticed to Montford after the latter's emancipation; given the ties between New Bern and Fayetteville, the two men may have communicated over the years. It is not known whether Harris contacted Montford or other New Bernians to recruit an apprentice or New Bernians suggested the idea. In any case, Cicero became Montford's "grandson" in the craft and made his home with Jacob Harris's artisan family in the midst of Fayetteville's strong free black community.[6]

Cicero M. Richardson completed his training and literally became a member of the Harris family by marrying Jacob Harris's daughter Sarah Ann in 1841. He also inherited real estate in New Bern from his grandmother. He returned there briefly, then went to Wilmington, and by 1850 was practicing his trade near the new railroad town of Goldsboro.[7] Within a few years, he embarked on yet another move: by 1860 he and Sarah and their children, together with Sarah's widowed mother and younger brothers Robert and Cicero Richardson Harris, joined friends from New Bern and Fayetteville in Cleveland, Ohio.[8] From there, as we shall see, Richardson and the Harris brothers would go on to distinguished careers, with Richardson's namesake eventually becoming a bishop.

As the unfolding of Richardson's career reflects, events on the state and national scene shifted the economic terrain for New Bern artisans of color. Although in much of North Carolina the late antebellum period brought new investments in transportation and trade that gradually awoke the "Rip van Winkle" state, for New Bern and its artisans of color the era brought a different trajectory. The financial downturn of the late 1820s and 1830s proved especially severe and long lasting, and not until the completion of the railroad in the late 1850s did New Bern's economy engage fully in the state's "Spirit of Improvement." The extended depression brought hard times for all artisans and especially for those who constructed fine buildings and produced luxury items.

Along with their colleagues elsewhere in the state during the "Rip van Winkle" era, some of New Bern's leading white artisans bowed out: Martin Stevenson gave up house carpentry for the funeral business, and his colleague Asa King traversed the state in search of work in the 1830s and eventually joined the flood of emigrants to Alabama. Bennett Flanner, a leading white brickmason in the 1820s, put down his trowel by 1835 to become a merchant and in the 1840s moved to Wilmington to enter the turpentine trade.[9] Talented youths like Cicero Richardson, who might have stayed in town in better times, tried their luck elsewhere. Donum Montford's protégé Abram Allen left New Bern by 1830 for nearby Washington. Such was the decline from New Bern's previous level of crafts that when David Paton, architect of the State Capitol, wrote to white carpenter Hardy B. Lane in 1839 in search of eight "first rate Joiner's" to help complete the capitol, Lane responded, "I do not believe their could be one procured from this place that would answer the purpose desired."[10]

Despite the discouraging economic situation, some New Bern artisans of both races persevered.[11] Like their counterparts elsewhere, house carpenter Lane and other white artisans organized a local Mechanics Association in 1841 for mutual aid.[12] At the same time, the social and economic gulf widened between even the most respected mechanics and the slaveholding elite. A local story related that one day a "gentleman" approached leading white builder Hardy B. Lane to inform him that his son was studying medicine in hopes of becoming a physician, but if the boy failed, he would send him to Lane to learn the carpentry trade. Lane retorted, "I want you to understand right here in your tracks it does not take the biggest fool you ever saw in your life to make a carpenter."[13] Joined in his trade by younger white carpenters, including his sons, Frederick, John, and Hardy B. Lane Jr. and apprentices Robert Hancock and Alonzo Willis—all of whom succeeded as mature artisans—Lane continued in the trade until his death in 1856.

Free black artisans likewise soldiered on at their trades. Among the older generation, Donum Montford and John Rice Green stayed in town despite financial reverses, as did tailor John Bragg and Montford's former slave, Isaac C. Rue. They were joined by younger free black artisans, such as carpenter William H. Hancock, blacksmith Richard Hazel, and brickmason Daniel Harris, who may have been born free, and who prospered at their crafts. Other craftsmen made modest livings working for other artisans and eventually for the railroad. If there were few opportunities for high pay, there was still work to be had. Indeed, it is possible that as hard times drove white artisans away more work was available to those who, willingly or not, stayed in town and accepted lower rates of pay.

During this period, the city's white building artisans were among the first in the state to move beyond their traditional handicrafts into mass production. The pioneer in the trend was Hardy B. Lane's former apprentice carpenter Alonzo Willis, who went north in 1848 to obtain machinery for his steam-powered factory on East Front Street, where he produced building materials "in the best style, at short notice, and at New York prices" under the mantra, "Sell cheap and a heap of it." Cabinetmaker and carpenter George Bishop began the second such enterprise in 1850, and by 1860 his

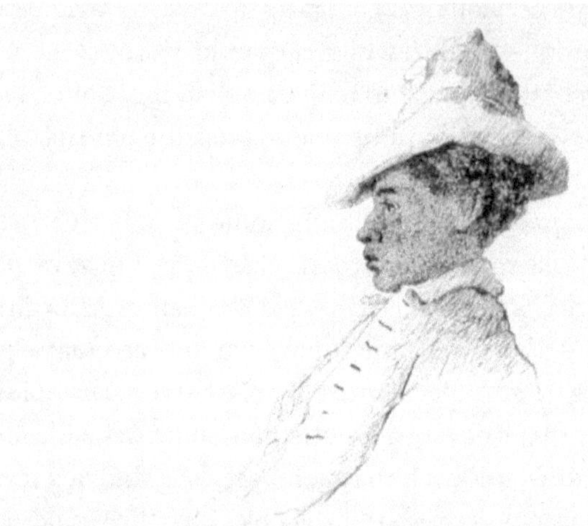

"Profile of a Young Man Wearing a Hat." Edward Graves Champney Collection. This Civil War–era drawing of an unidentified young man was made by Edward Graves Champney during his visit to Hatteras Island and the New Bern area. The image is suggestive of the many apprentices, artisans, and others in antebellum New Bern for whom no images have been located. Courtesy of the Outer Banks History Center (Manteo), State Archives of North Carolina, Raleigh.

sash and blind factory was the largest in the state, employing eleven men and producing $8,000 worth of building materials—and thus reducing the demand for carpenters' handiwork, whether they were black or white.[14]

Perilous Times

For black artisans, there were far worse problems than local economic troubles. In New Bern, as throughout the state and much of the South, the antebellum period brought a sea change in racial attitudes and legal restrictions. The years around 1830 marked a "dividing point" for blacks in North Carolina. Whereas in the early national period public sentiment in North Carolina was relatively lenient toward free blacks, and "slaves were encouraged to obtain their freedom . . . and public leaders favored gradual emancipation and colonization," from the 1830s onward lawmakers responded to white fears of slave insurrections and resentment of abolitionism by enacting restrictions that amounted to a "Black Code."[15] The hostile mood invaded even New Bern and combined with new state laws to undercut the rights, security, and prospects of its most respected black artisans.

As early as 1826 the state legislature took steps to reduce free blacks' autonomy by authorizing the arrest and binding out of any free person of color who lacked "regular and honest employment." Particularly invasive, the law permitted county courts to bind out as apprentices not only orphans but any free black child who lived with parents not "habitually" employed in "some honest industrious occupation."[16] Especially controversial was a law forbidding free blacks from entering the state, a measure that engaged two days of discussion in the legislature. New Bern legislator John Stanly led a minority who insisted that mobility was a natural right of citizens and that such restriction of free people was contrary to the Bill of Rights. Although his opposition was in vain, Stanly and a few others expressed not only their own perspectives but the interests of the communities they represented.[17]

Conditions for blacks in North Carolina worsened when the legislature convened in November 1830 at the height of white alarm over black abolitionist David Walker's *Appeal* of 1829. To curtail slaves' ability to read such tracts and to communicate with abolitionists and one another, the legislature of 1830–31 forbade teaching slaves to read or write, with fines for whites and whippings for blacks who did so. Seeing free blacks as potential agents of slave rebellion, the legislature further restricted their mobility by requiring them to obtain licenses to peddle goods outside their home counties and by prohibiting any free black who left the state for more than ninety days from returning. Especially important, to stem the growth of the free black population, the legislature raised the financial barriers to manumission to prohibitive levels.[18] This last measure struck a debilitating blow at black craftsmen's long-standing ability to earn their way to their own freedom and the status of master artisan and their capacity to help others obtain their liberty.

Just months after the 1830–31 legislative session, the Nat Turner Rebellion of August 1831 in southern Virginia further stoked white fears. As rumors of additional slave plots swept eastern North Carolina, whites captured and killed blacks whom they suspected of planning insurrections and intensified enforcement of the recently passed black laws.[19] New Bern remained relatively calm. After hearing of "black banditti" in nearby Duplin County, town officials called up the local militia but also sent a messenger to verify the rumors. The stories proved false, and the town returned to normal sooner than did what William Gaston called the "panic stricken sections of the state."[20] Local white leaders like Gaston were well acquainted with the city's "honest and peaceable" free black citizens, some of whom were slaveholders themselves, and these citizens in turn maintained protective connections with Gaston, John Stanly, and other political figures.

WITHIN A SHORT TIME, however, such relationships succumbed to the fallout from the Turner insurrection. Although the legislature of 1830–31 curtailed many freedoms previously held by people of color, free blacks in North Carolina still possessed the right to vote by the same rules as whites. Simple legislative action could not undo the 1776 state constitution's colorblind suffrage provisions. Ironically, it was the very success of the city's "honest and industrious mechanics" of color in constructing a stable and productive community and in fulfilling their duties as citizens and voters that spurred white attacks on their constitutional civil rights.

During the late 1820s and early 1830s, as the number of free people of color increased in New Bern, so did their proportion of the local electorate: they constituted as many as 50 or 60 of some 300 voters and included a substantial number of artisans. Tension over black political rights came to a head in New Bern in November 1831, just days after the execution of Nat Turner, which dominated headlines in New Bern newspapers for weeks. As would be the case more than once in North Carolina, it was political competition, not their own racial fears, that led white political strategists to assert a fictional link between black suffrage and the threat of black violence.

The issue arose with a close election for a seat in the state House of Commons that pitted Federalist William Gaston against Democrat Charles B. Shepard. Gaston, as we have seen, was supported by many free black voters, whereas Shepard, according to his brother-in-law John H. Bryan, was "violently opposed by the free negroes." When Gaston won on November 28 by 146 votes to 145, Shepard's allies instantly objected to "the influence of negro votes in the decision of our elections." Shepard's kinsmen John H. and James Bryan (notwithstanding their assistance to individual persons of color) and three other white men prepared a memorial to the legislature, which was signed by 163 citizens and sent to Raleigh.[21]

Their petition began simply enough by complaining that "many of the free negroes residing in . . . Newbern, claim the right of voting for a Representative of said town in the House of Commons and that fifty or more actually exercise that right." Besides objecting to the black voters' effect on this particular election, the petitioners raised the ante by appealing to racial fears to call into question North Carolina's long-standing constitutional provision of male suffrage without reference to race. Invoking the

Nat Turner panic, they claimed that the very sight of black men voting and being courted by white politicians would excite "a spirit of discontent and disorder among the slaves" at a time when "recent occurrences" necessitated keeping slaves "in a state of discipline and subjection" to prevent "the most calamitous of all contests, a *bellum servile*." The writers thus asked the legislature to "determine the true construction of the Constitution" on the matter.

"A Citizen" of New Bern—possibly Gaston—sprang to the defense of free black suffrage, which he said had been exercised for "more than half a century without its being formally questioned." "During the golden age of our ancient city," the writer stated in the local newspaper, "free persons of colour voted without molestation." He wondered, "What may have given rise to the present investigation into the rights of this portion of our population, we know not—we are not aware that at any of our late elections, they have abused their privilege, which they now exercise either by corrupt or injudicious votes." Another writer responded plainly that the investigation had arisen "because, in the recent contest, the very respectable majority of from twenty to thirty white voters, were defeated in their election by the free negroes. This is the immediate cause of the present endeavor to prevent them from voting in future."[22] The New Bern petition, among other factors, pushed the legislature to authorize the state Constitutional Convention of 1835 to address the issue of free black suffrage.

At the convention in Raleigh, advocates on both sides used language that echoed the 1831 exchange in New Bern. As they called on the legacy of the American Revolution and the state constitution to support their positions, their rhetoric revealed radically divergent views of race and citizenship. Gaston and others stated that, by law, free people of color were citizens and therefore entitled to vote under the same rules as whites. If allowed to maintain their rights as citizens, these speakers argued, free blacks would bolster public safety by allying with whites rather than slaves. James W. Bryan and his allies, on the other hand, cited a long roster of documents and insisted that, simply by virtue of race, no Negro could be considered a freeman or a citizen, and that nothing in the state constitution or the intent of the founders supported Negro suffrage.

The delegates voted initially for disfranchisement by a margin of sixty-six to sixty-one. Gaston and his allies proposed compromises before the final vote. A Fayetteville newspaper reported, "Strenuous efforts were made to except from the sweeping disfranchisement" blacks who owned property worth $250 or more, "but in vain." The original amendment carried. Tying citizenship not to free status, property, or education, but solely to race, it asserted, "No free negro, free mulatto, or free person of mixed blood, descended from negro ancestors to the fourth generation inclusive (though one ancestor of each generation may have been a white person) shall vote for members of the Senate or House of Commons." The *Raleigh Register* and the *New Bern Spectator* regretted the effect on property-holding men of color but supported ratification nonetheless. The amendment was ratified by popular vote in the fall of 1835.[23]

Disfranchisement hit New Bern's free black artisans hard. Many of them had voted for years, and some could have continued to do so if Gaston's compromise had passed—as it nearly did. After 1835 even the wealthiest and most respected free blacks lost their political rights and voice. If John Stanly had been alive and able to run for office (he died in 1833), neither his half brother John C. Stanly nor his son John Rice Green could have voted for him again. With the loss of suffrage, free blacks experienced a concomitant decline in their civic influence. No longer did white political leaders need to maintain relationships with black voters or vie for their votes, and no longer were North Carolina officeholders accountable to all free men, only to those who were white. Without free black voters to oppose him, Charles B. Shepard won a legislative seat and soon captured a seat in Congress. From there he railed against abolitionist attacks that put "the South & its institutions . . . in the greatest danger."[24]

In the ensuing years, shifts in sectional politics, including southern white resistance to abolitionism, hardened proslavery attitudes and increased white hostility toward free people of color. In New Bern the deaths of key white leaders, including Stanly in 1833 and especially Gaston in 1844, reduced the influence of those who sought to ameliorate conditions for enslaved and free blacks.

New Bernians of color recognized all too well the significance of the loss of their longtime friend William Gaston, who died unexpectedly in Raleigh on January 23, 1844. The newspapers brimmed with encomiums from far and wide. On February 10, 1844, the city's free people of color assembled at the white St. John's Masonic Lodge to plan their own tribute to Gaston, who was to be reinterred in New Bern following a funeral at the Catholic church he had helped found. The leaders at the meeting were established free black artisans: carpenter James York Green as chair, blacksmith Richard G. Hazel as secretary, and tailor John Rice Green as a principal speaker. At a time when many towns forbade or discouraged blacks from assembling, such a meeting was remarkable indeed; the gathering is the only known meeting of its kind in antebellum New Bern. The purpose, public nature, and prestigious location of the gathering all demonstrated free black citizens' stature in the community.

The assembly resolved to honor Gaston in several ways. In a private gesture, the group planned to send to the Gaston family a copy of the proceedings of their meeting honoring their beloved friend. The document, signed by James Y. Green and Richard G. Hazel on February 29 and delivered to Gaston's son Alexander, provides a rare record of free black New Bernians' own voice. In their statement of admiration and grief for Gaston, they also revealed their own perspectives and concerns and their sense of their identity and place in their home community.

Those gathered at the assembly of February 10 also resolved to give public expression of their respect for their friend and of their identity as citizens despite their loss of the franchise. They planned to participate in the civic ritual of wearing black mourning crepe on their sleeves and to "attend the funeral and walk in the procession." The *New Bernian* of March 5, 1844, reported that on the day of the funeral "it appeared to us that nearly the whole town, white and coloured, were assembled in the church and in the immediate vicinity" and that some 1,500 to 2,000 people walked in the funeral procession, which was the largest known in town history. For New Bern's free people of color, their statements and actions at Gaston's death carried special weight amid the growing racial restrictions in the state and region when they had already lost key rights and now had lost their most powerful friend and protector.[25]

Amid the increasingly troubled years from 1830s through the 1850s, New Bernians of color, like other southern blacks, strengthened their own community institutions. As they saw new legal restrictions close in around them, they concentrated their efforts on the arenas where they could build mutual support and find avenues for advancement. Some leading black artisans and their families continued to participate in the predominantly white Presbyterian and Episcopal congregations, while the majority of blacks, whether free or enslaved, associated with the Methodist Meeting House. Shortly after the north-south division of Methodists nationally, in 1843 the congregation divided by race, with the whites constructing a new sanctuary and the blacks retaining the old one. By 1847 the black Methodist congregation—still the largest in town—was known as Andrews Chapel.

"A Well Tryed Friend": Free Black Newbernians' Tribute to William Gaston, February 29, 1844

Pursuant to notice the free people of colour assembled in St. John's Lodge in this town on the evening of the 10th to make arrangements for paying a suitable tribute of respect to the memory of their deceased friend & fellow townsman Judge Gaston.

The meeting was organized by calling James Y. Green to the chair and appointing Richard Hazle Secretary. The chairman in a few appropriate remarks explained the object of the meeting. And thereupon Jn[o]. R. Green arose & after paying a becoming tribute of respect to the memory & virtues of the deceased submitted the following preamble & resolutions which were adopted. Our beloved townsman our generous friend & kind protector Judge Gaston is no more he died at Raleigh on the 23[d] Jany of apoplexy. We have come together on this mournful occasion to express our feeling of sorrow, deeply sensible of the loss we have sustained in the death of Judge Gaston.

Others have spoken of him as a great statesman a learned Judge a ripe scholar, they are better judges of these things than we are, in our humble situation we shall confine ourselves to his walks among us. As our neighbor our friend & kind protector it is my priviledge to speak on this subject from personal observations having been acquainted with him for the last thirty years.

Where so many virtues & graces are blended in the same individual it is not easy to particularize. Judge Gaston was an example in word and conversation in spirit in purity. He was a friend to the Widow & the orphan, he was the poor mans friend, he was a kind & indulgent master & though a large slave holder the most of his servants can read & write, the consequence is they are a most intelligent set of people. Judge Gaston was a friend to Emancipation he not only emancipated several of his own people but he bought others & set them free, and so soon as the relation of master & servant ceased to exist he became a generous friend & kind protector. Judge Gaston was a well tryed friend of the free man of colour in every situation in which he has been placed he has shown himself to be their faithful constant friend, we have many warm & ardent friends but none more sincere than he was. . . .

Judge Gaston . . . was a Christian in deed & in truth his religion was not a thing of forms & decencies. . . . Judge Gaston loved his home he loved his country & though the stranger should assail it with reproachful epithets yet still his course was onward the old North State forever was his song he went on his way rejoicing.

[We] Resolve

Therefore that we sincerely sympathize with the family of the deceased & our fellow townsmen in the loss we have sustained in the death of Judge Gaston—

That we will through the day of the arrival of the corpse cease from all business & then put crape upon our left arms & ware it thirty days, that we will attend the funeral & walk in procession—

That we hold ourselves ready at all times to join with our fellow townsmen in subscribing to raise a suitable monument to his memory—

That so soon as a correct likeness of our deceased friend can be obtained we will subscribe for a sufficient number to place one in the dwelling of every free man of colour in our town—

That a copy of these proceedings be signed by the chairman and secretary & sent to the family—

Newbern February 29th 1844—James Y. Green President

Richard G. Hazel

James Y. Green and Richard G. Hazel to Alexander F. Gaston, February 29, 1844, William Gaston Papers, SHC.

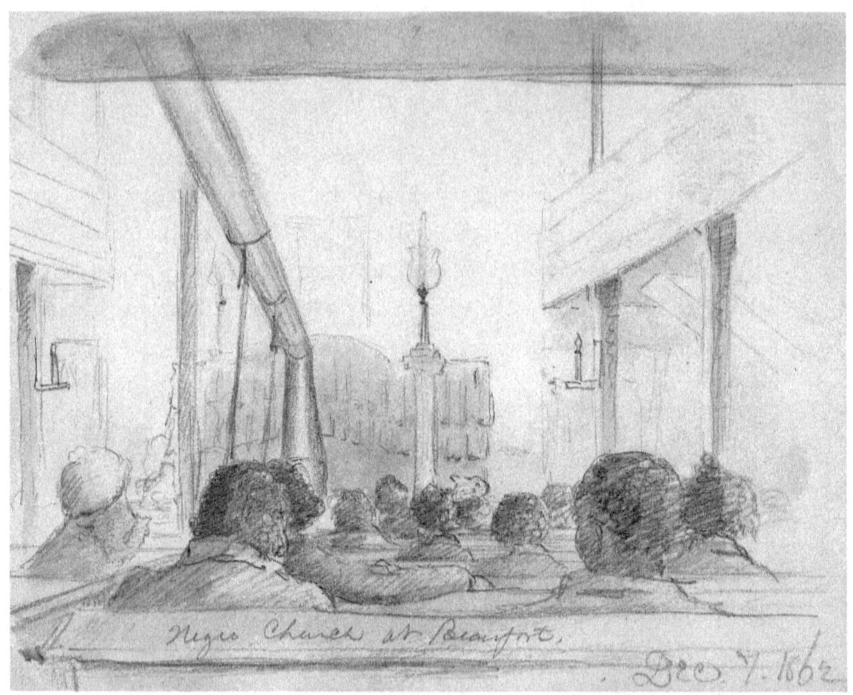

"Negro Church at Beaufort, Dec. 7, 1862." James Wells Champney Sketchbook. This drawing of the Methodist church in Beaufort (now known as Purvis Chapel) evokes something of the character of the larger Andrews Chapel Methodist Church in New Bern, for which no comparable images have been found. Courtesy of the Outer Banks History Center (Manteo), State Archives of North Carolina, Raleigh.

Class leaders and elders included slaves such as carpenter Richard Tucker, cooper Amos York, and bricklayer Thomas Battle, and free men like brickmason Isaac Rue and carpenter Joseph Green. Within the meetinghouse walls, as a white New Bernian recalled, enslaved and free blacks learned to "exhort, with great earnestness and power and to present the Gospel with simplicity and truth."[26] Even with the white minister assigned to them, they could put aside performances of racial deference to interact freely with one another; worship according to their own preferences and traditions; and develop their confidence and skills as community leaders.

Often in association with their churches, black artisans and their friends focused on schooling for their own and other black children. Although state law forbade teaching slaves to read and write, it placed no restrictions on teaching free blacks, nor did the city fathers prevent such instruction.

The state's public schools were for whites only, but black and white teachers in New Bern operated private schools for free children of color. Black artisans, whose earnings could pay the modest tuition and who strove to boost their children's prospects, numbered among the principal supporters. The best known such school was the academy that John Stewart Stanly, the emancipated son of John C. Stanly, operated with his wife, Fanny, until the late 1850s. In 1850, the census counted some thirty-eight free black children attending school; twenty of them lived in free black artisan households, including those of blacksmith Richard Hazel, tailors John R. Green and John Bragg, carpenter William H. Hancock, plasterer Isaac Rue, and mechanic George A. Rue.

Most remarkably, long after state law forbade the practice, New Bern authorities tolerated schooling for slaves. Edward Stanly (the white son of John Stanly), who grew up in New Bern, asserted, "It is a fact well known to residents in Newbern, that, for many years before the rebellion, there were schools for negroes in that town. One school was taught by a free-woman, the wife of a slave, a carpenter—an honest, worthy man, who was living in that town in 1862. I know one gentleman who had a slave who was a pupil in that school." Stanly also cited a school taught on Sundays "by a white woman, where the negroes learned to read. In the year 1856 and afterwards, both the Methodist and Episcopal churches sustained Sunday Schools for colored children, where they were taught to read."[27]

Continuity and Change: Black and White Artisans at Work

Along with the connections and opportunities they pursued through their churches and schools, black artisans in New Bern, like their counterparts throughout much of the South, maintained important continuities in their work settings. Whatever the effect of sectional tensions, in many ways the workaday lives of enslaved and free, black and white artisans changed little during this period from patterns of earlier years. In 1840, when Cicero Richardson was in New Bern and sold the property his grandmother had bequeathed to him, the local scene showed few signs of change since his departure in 1832.[28] Key individuals had died, to be sure, including Cicero's grandmother and her friend Donum Montford. John C. Stanly had lost most of his fortune, which some attributed to his assistance to his heavily indebted half brother John Stanly. But tailor John Rice Green and his family still operated his workshop through the 1830s and 1840s; carpenter William

H. Hancock and blacksmith Richard Hazel prospered at their work; and these and other men trained local youths in their trades.

Cicero Richardson, like any other visitor to town in 1840, would have encountered the familiar sight of black and white, enslaved and free artisans working together. Such was the case at the prominent corner of Broad and George Streets, where white merchant William Hollister embarked in 1839 on construction of a large frame house as one of the town's first major building projects since the mid-1820s. The house followed the locally familiar side-passage form with Federal-style proportions and finish that might have appeared old-fashioned in some cities. In addition to workmen identified only as "carpenters" or "negroes," the free artisans Hollister named in his accounts included Hardy B. Lane Sr. as lead contractor, white carpenter Robert Hancock, black carpenter William H. Hancock, and black painter Ben Wade. The only plasterer or bricklayer Hollister identified was Isaac C. Rue, who was probably still enslaved and hiring his time from Donum Montford's widow, Hannah, who lived across the street from the Hollister house.[29]

What a stranger to town would not have realized but was clear to a native such as Cicero Richardson was that all of these artisans were longtime New Bernians who had weathered many lean years. Lane was about fifty-seven years old, Wade about sixty, and Rue about fifty-two. In contrast to the more dynamic building practices in Wilmington, Fayetteville, and Raleigh, where fires and rising ambitions prompted major construction projects and attracted artisans of diverse backgrounds, none of the craftsmen who built Hollister's house had come to New Bern from elsewhere, and only Robert Hancock and William H. Hancock were in the mid-prime of their lives. Little wonder that after his stay in New Bern Cicero Richardson moved on to Wilmington and then to Goldsboro by 1850.[30]

As well as showing continuity in its population of individual artisans, antebellum New Bern generally continued familiar patterns of racial balance among craftspeople. Whites still held the specialty trades of silversmith and gunsmith. Both blacks and whites worked in carpentry, tailoring and dressmaking and shoemaking, painting, coopering, and wagon- and carriage-making. An exception came in the local transformation of two important trades that New Bern whites abandoned. In 1850, in contrast to previous decades, when men of both races labored at their forges, the census showed not a single white blacksmith in town, compared to six free black and an

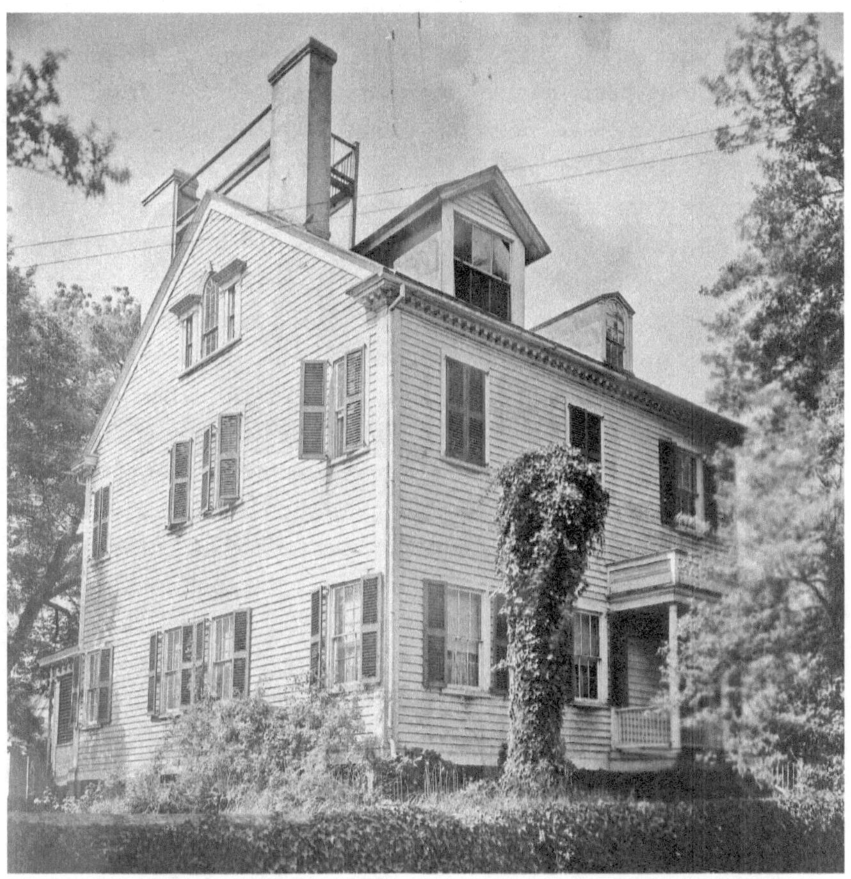

William Hollister House, Broad Street, New Bern. Photograph by Bayard Wootten. Both dormers were originally like the smaller one on the right. Courtesy of the New Bern Historical Society, New Bern, North Carolina.

unknown number of enslaved blacksmiths. The reasons for the change are unclear: demand for blacksmiths' work continued even in hard times and despite competition from factory-made hardware, tools, and equipment. Nor was the physically demanding craft of blacksmithing always considered "Negro work": in antebellum Wilmington, Fayetteville, and Raleigh, white as well as black men operated their forges, including some who accrued substantial property.[31]

Equally striking was the near disappearance of whites among the city's brickmasons. For years, New Bern whites as well as blacks had held prominent positions in the trade, and in antebellum Wilmington, Raleigh, Hillsborough, and Salisbury the numerous white brickmasons included several prosperous citizens. The change in New Bern likely reflected its economic troubles and long hiatus in masonry construction. A few white brickmasons appeared briefly, such as one Joshua Denby who took white orphan William Jones to learn the "art and mystery" of the brickmason's and plasterer's trade in 1843. When local brick construction picked up in the late 1840s, however, essentially all the bricklayers as well as the plasterers were black men, and no white masons appeared in the 1850 census of New Bern.[32]

During the late 1840s and especially the 1850s a gradual upswing in the local economy warmed prospects for artisans in all crafts. Construction of the Moses Griffin School complex, begun in 1848 with a bequest from a local citizen, illustrated the town's continued reliance upon enslaved artisans. The school included a large, brick main building handsomely finished in Greek Revival style (see the photograph of the New Bern Fish, Oyster, and Game Fair in Chapter 1) and various secondary structures. Veteran house carpenter Hardy B. Lane was "architect" and chief builder for the project along with newly minted white brickmason William H. Jones. Most of the other artisans were enslaved. Some belonged to Lane, but several were hired from other owners. They included house carpenter "Dick," or Richard Tucker, who earned for his owner, John D. Flanner, seventeen shillings sixpence per day; and several brickmasons, including Joe, who made twenty shillings a day, almost as much as Jones's twenty-five shillings. The only identifiable free black artisan on the project was Isaac C. Rue, liberated at last, who charged fifteen to twenty shillings a day for building fireplaces and chimneys and mending plaster. Sometimes signing his bills with an "X", by the end of the project he was signing his name for receipts for his own work and that of his employees.[33] Of New Bern's eight free men in the trowel trades—all black—only Rue owned significant property: in 1850 he was a married head of household who owned $500 worth of real estate and one slave, a nineteen-year-old black man.[34]

Slavery and the Vanishing Hope of Freedom

Only because he had been freed by Donum Montford's will had Isaac C. Rue gained his liberty during the 1840s. Of all the racially restrictive laws enacted by the legislature of 1830–31, the new barriers to manumissions had the most dramatic impact on New Bern artisans of color, and few other New Bern artisans moved from slavery to freedom after 1830. Whatever the desire of black and white slaveholders to free selected slaves might have been, the new requirements all but ended the practice.[35]

The intentionally burdensome manumission law required a potential emancipator to publish a notice in the *State Gazette* and to display another at the local courthouse for six weeks in advance of presenting a petition to the court. Worse, the amount of bond to be posted rose to a prohibitive level of two securities of $1,000 each for every slave to be liberated (half that for persons aged fifty years and older), which exceeded the value of nearly all slaves. These measures put manumission beyond the capacity of all but the wealthiest slaveholders. Slave owners could still emancipate by will—until a law passed in 1861 forbade that practice too—but the slave had to wait for two years after the owner's death (and until the will was probated and all debts were settled) to become free. Although a few individuals were freed after 1831 by wills or legislative acts or rare instances of private manumissions, the days when enslaved artisans could work and save for their freedom, hope to purchase and free their family members, and help their friends obtain their liberty had come to an end.[36] Whatever their skills, hopes, and capacity to earn and save money, most artisans who came of age after 1830—such as Hardy B. Lane's carpenters Bill (aged thirty in 1856), Mingo (twenty-eight), and Donum (twenty-six)—could expect to stay in bondage for the rest of their lives. Within a decade what seemed a permanent condition would alter forever, but until the Civil War the prospect of freedom seemed beyond the reach of most enslaved artisans.[37]

Although there are no figures on the number of slaves in New Bern who were hired out or hired themselves, evidence indicates that the practice not only continued but expanded in the late antebellum era. As slaves' selling prices rose in response to demand from the southwestern cotton fields, free artisans and other employers hired slaves rather than purchasing them, especially when they needed expensive skilled workers. Hiring wages also increased, providing slaveholders with a good return on slaves they rented out for long or short periods or permitted to hire themselves.[38] When free black carpenter Rigdon Green hired several slaves from heiress Mary McKinley on January 1, 1840, the rate of $198 per slave, to be paid on January 1, 1841, suggests that they were skilled artisans. In a customary pattern, the hiring agreement specified that each worker was to have a certain sum—$48 in this case—for himself. Both hirer and owner may have had special sympathies for the workmen: Green had been enslaved until his brother James York Green emancipated him, and Mrs. McKinley had provided in her will for her slaves to be freed at her death. McKinley died by year's end, and when Green settled up with her estate, her executors gave the workers their payments—potential nest eggs for their lives in freedom.[39]

A House Carpenter Hired Far from Home

Some enslaved artisans, including those who possessed exceptional skills and whom their owners trusted, were sent long distances to make money for their owners. Although some suffered from mistreatment in their new settings, others found opportunities for autonomy and valuable experiences. During the 1830s, with construction at a standstill in New Bern, banker Charles Dewey sent his house carpenter Jack Dewey more than 100 miles west to Raleigh and Hillsborough to work for banker and planter Duncan Cameron and his son Paul, who were among the richest men in the state. During his tenure with the Camerons from 1833 through 1835, Jack Dewey earned for his owner the welcome sum of $100 for a six-month term.[40] Dewey had previously worked in New Bern with the accomplished white house carpenter Asa King, who also left New Bern to work for Duncan Cameron in 1833.[41]

Given a copy of the plans, Dewey helped build Paul Cameron's frame house, Burnside, at the edge of Hillsborough. Reflecting Dewey's autonomy, Paul reported to Duncan, "I went . . . to H'borough to see how Jack and his company had employed themselves. They had not gone on as well as I had expected in laying down the floors—but said that they had waited until all the flooring plank had been carried up so that a selection might be made of the best for the floors of the lower rooms." Moving regularly from town to town, Dewey also worked on Duncan's projects in Raleigh, including his suburban residence on the Hillsborough Road and possibly buildings at the present St. Mary's School across the road. In 1834, Paul queried his father, "What has become of Jack—I hope that you will get him off at the very earliest day—as I am resolved to make a finish of my house in short order." In Raleigh Dewey probably visited the most important construction site in the state: the monumental State Capitol, then rising a few blocks east of Cameron's house. Cameron was one of the commissioners for the project, and New Bern carpenter Asa King worked there late in 1833. Dewey's sojourn in the Piedmont expanded his horizons and affirmed his ability to operate on his own. His interaction with men such as Hillsborough's white master brickmason John Berry at Burnside or northern builder William Drummond at Duncan Cameron's Raleigh projects likely enhanced his expertise. In the process he left his mark and possibly his influence on buildings far from New Bern.[42]

The custom of self-hiring likewise persisted on a large scale. Some whites continued to complain about the independence it allowed and the example it set for other slaves. Nevertheless the advantages to slaveholders and employers assured its continuation. Some slaveholders allowed slaves great latitude in conducting their affairs, including owners who might have wished to emancipate certain slaves but could no longer do so. Enslaved artisans, especially those who earned good rates of pay and were able to keep a portion of their earnings and to work extra hours on their own, used the system to carve out a degree of autonomy, to save money, and to benefit their families. Blacksmith Scipio, who belonged to white physician Isaac Hughes, was recalled as having "*owned* and operated" (emphasis added) a livery stable, where he employed his skills to shoe horses and repair vehicles. Also known as Scipio Hughes, in 1838 he attended the estate sale of John Oliver and bought such domestic items as china plates, two basins, and a ewer, indicating that he maintained at least a modest household of his own.[43]

New Bern blacksmith George S. Fisher, born a slave about 1822, came of age too late to earn his way to freedom, but he gained recognition nonetheless. His owner, Elizabeth Smith, placed him as an apprentice blacksmith with white mechanic and merchant Zaccheus Slade, and thereafter Smith hired him out to Slade, who considered him "an ingenius workman" and "the most skillful of his race that he ever saw." He "wrought steel plows, cultivators, etc., and would make alterations in Northern made agricultural implements by which they would be better adapted to use on Southern farms." Working extra hours "at night and during the half holidays given to him by Mr. Slade who hired him from his owner," Fisher saved more than $1,000, and although he lost his money during the Civil War, he emerged after emancipation as a prosperous artisan and citizen.[44]

Likewise born too late to buy his own or his family's freedom, house carpenter Richard Tucker employed his good wages—seventeen shillings sixpence at the Griffin School—to benefit his family within the strictures of bondage.[45] In about 1835 he married Emeline, the slave of New Bern white shoemaker Raymond Castix, and over the years the couple had fifteen children. Their firstborn children belonged to Emeline's owner, who sold away at least seven of them. Although much of Tucker's earnings went to his owner, white merchant John D. Flanner, like other enslaved artisans he worked extra hours and saved money. According to one account, Tucker persuaded Flanner to buy Emeline and their youngest child, "which with Richard's help he did, for $800." The Tuckers' children born thereafter belonged to Flanner and lived with their parents. The still enslaved carpenter "paid his owner $15 a month for his time, and in addition to this, fully supported himself and his family." Like George Fisher, Richard Tucker moved quickly into community leadership when freedom came, as well as bringing many of his children back together.[46]

ALTHOUGH SOME ENSLAVED ARTISANS carved out niches of relative autonomy, for those determined to gain their liberty, the principal route to freedom after 1831 was by running away. Although this path became increasingly dangerous as lawmakers expanded the powers of slave patrollers and increased penalties for harboring or assisting runaways, nevertheless many slaves continued to escape for short and long periods and sometimes for good.[47]

Slaveholders took every possible step to close off the escape routes by sea, which made New Bern such a compelling destination, while slaves continued to find their way onto northbound ships. In 1836 white carpenter Thomas Bragg of Warrenton, formerly of New Bern, advertised in New Bern and Norfolk newspapers for Dick, "a first rate carpenter by trade" and an "artful cunning fellow" who had "a mother in New Bern, where he will go." He and another slave had escaped in Washington, North Carolina, a good distance from Warren County but not far from New Bern. Anticipating that the two would attempt to board a ship bound toward freedom, Bragg cautioned "masters of vessels . . . not to take them out of the State, at their peril."[48] When two or three slaves escaped to the North within a single year, in 1854, a New Bern newspaper editor speculated that they had help from free sailors of color and called for new restrictions on such seamen.[49] These methods served many runaways, including brickmason Abraham Galloway, who, with help from the captain, hid on a Philadelphia-bound ship docked at Wilmington and, as we shall see, made his way to Canada before returning south during the war and leading the cause for freedom in New Bern and beyond.[50]

Resistance by Refusal

In one case, slave artisans' condition of servitude enabled them to take a stand against abuse, which was meaningful, though ultimately futile. When young John P. Green, the tailor's son, was helping in the workshop of a family friend, "Uncle Balaam" Jones, in the 1850s, "Mr. [John] Hancock, the town sergeant, came into the cooper-shop and exclaimed, 'I want one of your men to make me a paddle!' The men, one and all, knowing the purpose of torture that the paddle would be put to, stoutly refused to make it. This they could do with safety, at that time, for they were slaves, and knew that their masters would uphold and protect them in the refusal. It is not so in the south now. 'Well,' said the official, 'give me a drawing knife and a brace and bit, and I will make it myself.' He was 'as good as his word,' for in a jiffy, he had the instrument made and bored full of holes. He then took his departure, carrying the paddle with him." Green surreptitiously followed the sergeant to a remote site where, as the slave artisans had anticipated, the official wielded the paddle to torture a slave accused of conspiring to blow up the house of a prominent citizen, trying in vain to force him to reveal the names of his co-conspirators.

John Patterson Green, *Fact Stranger than Fiction*.

Free Artisans of Color: A Growing Community

Despite the tightening restrictions on manumission, New Bern's population of free people of color continued to grow, and free black artisans took major roles in the local economy and society. In 1850 the United States census—the first to identify occupations (for free males only)—revealed for the first time the number of free black artisans in the city. In that year, about 60—almost 20 percent—of New Bern's 330 free boys and men of color were working at artisan trades. Free black men were almost twice as likely as whites to become artisans, for only about 110—12 percent—of the town's 929 white males plied skilled crafts.[51] This meant that more than a third of New Bern's free male artisans were black. As a result, unlike free black craftsmen who lived in communities with only a few successful free people of color—the lonely situation of the famed cabinetmaker Thomas Day, who was the sole free black man of his educational and class level in Milton or for miles around—free black artisans in New Bern could participate in community life amid many of their fellows, a situation that provided mutual aid and companionship and likely attracted other talented free blacks to town.

Even with the new restrictions, a few slaveholders found ways to liberate selected slaves, including their own children. Such was the case of tailor Freeman Morris, one of three mixed-race children born to the enslaved woman Patty and her unmarried white owner William S. Morris. In 1828 William took Freeman, Albert, and Harriet, aged eight to twelve, to Pennsylvania, where he freed them but was unable to "place them where their moral interests and future usefulness could be protected." When William brought the children back to North Carolina, he petitioned the legislature in 1829 "to recognize the validity of their emancipation" in another state, but his plea was rejected. Within two years, the state enacted newly prohibitive barriers to manumission while still allowing emancipation by will. In his will of 1831, William Morris directed his executor, white house carpenter Hardy B. Lane, to sell all his property at his death except "my negro woman Patty and her 3 mulatto children Harriett, Albert, and Freeman," and instructed Lane to take the children "beyond the limits of this state to some state or country where emancipation is unrestricted by law, and cause them to be emancipated." He designated half the proceeds of his estate to the purpose and their support. By the time he republished his will in 1838, Morris had found a way to free the children, and he bequeathed his property in trust to Patty for her lifetime and then to the three children. After his death in 1848 his executors disposed of his property accordingly. By 1850 Freeman and Albert Morris were not only free but working as respected local tailors.[52]

Two well-known artisans, Park Lawrence and Isaac C. Rue, obtained their liberty after 1831 by their owners' wills. Lawrence, born in Africa about 1770, was according to his obituary "brought to this country" at age twenty-six and sold to the family from whom he took his surname. He soon learned the carpenter trade and also how to read. In 1845 the widow Catharine Lawrence's estate included "Negro Man Park Freed by the Will." In 1860 the census identified Park Lawrence as a ninety-year-old free carpenter from Guinea, and at his death in 1871 at age 101 the local newspaper singled him out for his great age, distinctive accent, and vivid tales of his homeland.[53]

As we have seen, Isaac Rue, born in 1788, was emancipated by the 1838 will of Donum Montford, subject to the life estate of his widow Hannah. Montford, who had seen the recent tightening of the law and anticipated the possibility of further restrictions, directed his executor, Abram Allen, whom he had freed almost twenty years earlier, that if it became impossible to free Isaac, he was to give him a pass "to some of the northern states and $100 cash."[54] Hannah died in 1846, and by 1850 Isaac Rue was a free man. He continued and prospered at his trade until his death in 1880 at age ninety-two.[55]

APPRENTICESHIPS AND FREE PEOPLE OF COLOR

By the 1840s and 1850s, most of the free black artisans in town had been emancipated before 1831 or were born free and learned their trades through apprenticeships. Court-authorized apprenticeships for black as well as white children continued through the period, including those spurred by the law authorizing county courts to bind out free black children whose parents were not regularly employed. Although some parents objected to involuntary apprenticeships, others sought out apprenticeships. In 1839, Sally Lewis, a free woman of color, asked the court to "bind my daughter Elizabeth a free girl of color to Capt. Jacob Johnson and his wife Rebecca Johnson until she is eighteen years old to Learn the Seamstress Trade." Rachel Wilson, a freeborn black woman from Carteret County who had come to New Bern about 1813 upon completion of her own apprenticeship and married an enslaved man, Peter Wilson, affirmed in 1833, "I wish the court to bind my son John Wilson [aged about thirteen] to Mr. Hardy Whitford to be lernt the shoemaking bizeness." In 1850 Rachel and Peter's fourteen-year-old son David Wilson was an apprentice carpenter in the household of white house joiner Robert Hancock, laying the foundation for what proved to be a long career. For such children, especially those with enslaved or absent fathers, apprenticeships offered both the opportunity to learn valuable skills and homes with citizens who could protect them along with providing their keep.[56]

In some respects New Bern and Craven County provided unusually good situations for free black apprentices. In 1838 state law excused masters and mistresses of free black apprentices from the requirement to teach them to read and write. Some counties then printed different forms for free black and white apprentices or marked through the wording about reading and writing. Craven County court officials, however, continued using the older forms well into the 1850s, and the majority of apprentice bonds for free blacks included the clause to teach them to read and write.[57] Craven County officials also complied with the established state law that protected free black apprentices by requiring their masters or mistresses to post bond to keep the child in the county and present him or her to the court at the end of the apprenticeship; in many cases only these bonds reveal free black apprentices' racial identity.

Other changes in the apprenticeship system, however, worked to the detriment of New Bern's black artisan class. From 1830 onward, the number of black master artisans assigned apprentices by the county court fell precipitously, a shift that undercut their stature and their prospects. Economics surely played a role in the decline, for depressed conditions from the late 1820s into the 1840s reduced all artisans' capacity to support and employ apprentices.[58] But the drop in apprentices bound to black masters was more abrupt than for white masters, whether for economic reasons or because of white concerns over giving authority to black artisans. That Donum Montford had court-assigned apprentices as late as 1834 was unusual; his fellow artisans of color, such as James York Green, who had taken numerous apprentices in earlier years, received no more apprentices from the court after about 1830.[59]

Even more telling was the decline in the number and proportion of free black children assigned to learn skilled trades from masters of either race. Because Craven County apprentice bonds sometimes omitted racial identity for free black children, any estimate of their number falls short of the actual total. Still, it appears that while the court continued to bind some free blacks as artisans, such assignments dwindled from the 1830s onward, and more black children entered apprenticeships as servants, spinsters (usually meaning general domestic workers), and farmers (farm laborers).[60]

Some free black children of color, however, were still bound out to learn skilled trades from white masters. In contrast to many northern cities, New Bern, like many southern communities, had no rule or custom against having free black or enslaved apprentices in the same shops as whites.[61] In 1838, three boys from the free black Little family entered apprenticeships with white house carpenter Hardy B. Lane. In his home and workshop they encountered both his slaves and his carpenter sons, Frederick, Hardy Jr., and John, as well as white apprentice carpenter Alonzo Willis, an orphan bound to Lane in 1834.[62] Free black shoemaker Moses Hill began his long career with rich white shoemaker Raymond Castix, who took numerous black apprentices in the 1840s and operated something of a shoemaking factory.[63] White house carpenter Robert Hancock continued his practice of training free black apprentices, including John and Marshall Wilson and William Mitchell in 1854. The next year, Cicero Mason, a free black, aged fifteen, was bound to white merchant John D. Flanner to learn the house carpenter's trade—perhaps from Flanner's enslaved house carpenter, Richard Tucker—and helped build Flanner's stylish Italianate house.[64]

Despite the change in court practices, free black artisans found other ways to employ black apprentices and pass along their skills. Following age-old custom, many trained their own children and grandchildren, such as house carpenter William H. Hancock, who took his son Richard as his apprentice when the boy was thirteen and kept him "at the bench" until he reached his majority. Isaac C. Rue likely trained his grandsons Edward and Isaac Richardson in the brickmason's and plasterer's trades, and tailor John Bragg conveyed skills to four of his children—Elizabeth, Sarah, Henry, and Cicero—all of whom worked in his shop and later plied the tailoring trade on their own.[65] Leading black artisans also took apprentices from outside their families. William Alston, a member of a notable free black Raleigh family, came to New Bern for an eight-year apprenticeship with tailor John R. Green and went on to study at Oberlin College and become an Episcopal priest in Philadelphia and New York.[66] In 1850, house carpenter Rigdon Green had two black apprentices in his home, Charles Skinner and James Dixon, whom he might have brought from Edenton. House carpenter William H. Hancock trained other free black youths besides his son Richard, including Charles McLin, aged eighteen, and Stephen Bragg, seventeen, carpenters in his household in 1850. Although some apprenticeships had always been arranged without leaving a court record, it is likely that as the court assigned fewer children to black master artisans, these craftsmen arranged apprenticeships outside of court channels for their own benefit and that of the youths they instructed.

An Apprentice's Tale

Alexander Herritage Newton was the only Craven County black youth bound by the court to an artisan trade in 1852. Born on Craven Street in New Bern, he was the freeborn son of Mary Newton, a free woman of color, and her husband Thaddeus Newton, who was owned by the Custis family. Mary, aged thirty-six in 1850, headed a household in the Dryboro suburb that included her five children; as a slave, her husband was not named in the census. She was one of several free women who took the surnames of their enslaved husbands and gave them to their freeborn children. Because of his father's status, the court identified Alexander as "a free boy of color, an orphan" when he was bound out at age seventeen to merchant Jacob Gooding to learn the bricklayer's and plasterer's trade. It is not known whether the court singled out Alexander or his mother sought out the apprenticeship, but given her position and Alexander's age, it is likely that she took the initiative.[67]

Like other nonartisans who took apprentices to skilled trades, Jacob Gooding placed Alexander under his foreman, Henry E. Bryan, an enslaved artisan hired from another owner. The youth chafed under his apprenticeship, and on one occasion, his disobedience sparked conflict that revealed the workshop dynamics among free and enslaved persons. After defying an order from Bryan, and engaging in a scuffle with him, he was "in for punishment, and being a free boy [neither] the slave overseer nor his master could punish me. I was reported to my employer." The employer (probably Gooding), gave Newton thirty-nine lashes, the most allowed under the apprentice code, which put him out of work for three weeks. Acknowledging his strategy of passive resistance, Newton recalled, "I suppose that I could have gone to work sooner, but I was determined that my punishment should cost my employer something as well as myself."[68]

Soon after this, the enslaved foreman, Bryan, also disobeyed the master and faced a whipping. Young Newton defied the law by coming to his aid: "I dressed this slave up in a woman's garb and conducted him through the streets to the house of one, Mr. Primrose, a man who stood high in the community, and held the confidence of all slaveholders as one of them and one of their defenders and supporters." Newton got Bryan safely into Primrose's kitchen, and "with the assistance of the slaves in charge of the kitchen, we placed him in the attic at the rear of the house, above the kitchen." Despite a reward posted for his capture, Bryan remained undiscovered. After "things quieted down," Newton and his friends put Bryan on the "mystic train"—as Newton termed the "underground railroad," which in New Bern usually meant a northbound ship—to "send him to a clime where he enjoyed his freedom."[69]

After orchestrating Bryan's escape, Newton completed his apprenticeship early and received from his master "$6, a suit of clothes, set of tools, and a Bible, and the advice to be a good boy." He found another employer, but after being ordered to work on the July Fourth holiday, his spirit of independence broke out, and he "made up my mind not to work that day. Of course, this was disobedience and would have called for punishment. So I had to do something." Rather than face another whipping, he "cleaned up [his] tools, packed them away, and on the fourth of July, 1857 left for Beaufort, N.C." He found a job as a cook on a ship bound for New York.

In New York, Newton became part of an important network of people of color and their allies working for freedom. His mother was already there, collecting money to buy her husband's liberty with help from leading abolitionists. Some of these, such as Robert Hamilton, the black publisher of the AME *Anglo-African* newspaper, helped Newton find work in his trade, and he also attended school. In 1859 Newton first heard sermons from black preachers of the AME church, including New Bernian émigré George A. Rue, who inspired him to "serv[e] God in the uplifting of my people." In the same year, he married Robert Hamilton's daughter Olivia, thus linking himself with New York's progressive black leadership. During the Civil War, he joined the 29th Connecticut Colored Volunteer Infantry, which was one of the first black regiments in the country. After serving through the war, Newton was ordained an AME minister and spent most of his life in the North, with a brief period as pastor at the New Bern church founded in 1865 by George A. Rue. Like many ministers who had begun their working lives as artisans, Newton supplemented his income or helped his congregations with his bricklaying skills, "not fear[ing] to take off my coat, roll up my sleeves, and go to work."[70]

For Alexander Newton, as for other youths of color, the apprentice system, designed mainly for discipline and social control, proved to be an important avenue toward advancement. As Newton later recalled, during the years of slavery "there were many young men of the race who learned well some trade. They were apprenticed, as in my case, to some good workman, for at least four years or more. At the end of that time they were efficient, practical workmen who, if free, could command good wages. So that hundreds of fine artisans came out of slavery who were able to begin at once the laying of the foundation of the history of a free people."

FAMILIES AND HOMES

Free artisans of color had greater control over their family situations than did slaves and likewise sought to establish stable families, though many, like Newton, suffered the effects of slavery when their parents, mates, or children were slaves. A good number of free people of color who were listed as single people in the census, such as Alexander Newton's mother, Mary, were married in their own eyes, if not in the eyes of the law, to enslaved spouses who were not named in the census. Some free women of color listed as single may have been involved in interracial relationships: as white attorney James W. Bryan complained in 1854, "a large number of our young men and several of our merchants . . . have negro wives or 'misses' and keep them openly, raising up families of Mulattoes!" Even if both partners wished to marry, interracial marriages were forbidden by law. "Negro wives" who were free likely appeared as single women, sometimes living with their freeborn children.[71] Other single artisans, especially young people like twenty-year-old free black brickmason William Johnson, boarded or lodged in the households of others. This was a common practice among both blacks and whites, providing housing for many and supplying extra income to those with room to spare. Johnson lived with several boarders in the household of widow Lydia Crawford—probably the woman freed by John C. Stanly after her husband Virgil's death—who, like many women, employed her housekeeping skills to earn a living.[72]

Most leading black male artisans, however, were married and headed households that included their free wives and children. Artisans' earnings offered an advantage in establishing and providing for families, while their positions as family men bolstered their stature in the community. As we have seen, by marrying a free woman, a man could assure that their children were born free. Some young couples made their homes with older family members, like emancipated tailor Freeman Morris, aged thirty in 1850; his wife, Maria, aged twenty-six; and their baby Hannah, all of whom lived with Maria's mother, Mary Allen, in the household headed by Maria's property-owning grandmother Eliza Allen. More often, married male artisans headed their own households. House carpenter William H. Hancock at age forty-five maintained a home that included his wife, Mary, thirty-six, and their seven children, ranging in age from eighteen-year-old carpenter Richard Mason Hancock to baby Coleston. Blacksmith Richard Hazel married Ann Nash Newton, a daughter of emancipated master carpenter Thomas

Newton, at Christ Church in 1833; by 1850 their household included four children plus Ann's widowed mother Sarah Newton, aged eighty, who had been freed by her husband Thomas almost forty years before.[73]

These artisan families made their homes in neighborhoods that grew more racially distinct in the late antebellum years. Throughout the period New Bern, like most southern towns, displayed a mix of races, classes, and uses—residential, commercial, and light industrial—in many parts of town. When an old-time white New Bernian recalled antebellum residents block by block, she named many whites and a few free blacks living as neighbors, as well as many "negro houses" and "servants' rooms."[74] As the city's free black population grew, however, many people of color continued earlier trends by making their homes in the increasingly black, racially mixed suburban areas.[75] In contrast to other North Carolina towns, which still had only a few free people of color who typically lived in dispersed patterns, New Bern had more in common with Virginia cities with large free black populations who tended to concentrate in certain racially mixed areas.[76] Yet New Bern also differed from the Virginia pattern, for while Richmond's white elite withdrew from the mixed waterfront and industrial sectors to establish homes on higher ground, leading white New Bernians, along with many of their slaves, kept their residences and businesses in the central city and nearby blocks.[77]

With central New Bern maintaining its prestige and high property values, by 1850 only a few free blacks still lived there, chiefly leading artisans and property owners who had been there for years. Blacksmith Richard Hazel and his family lived in the heart of town and operated a bakery at the prime corner of Broad and Middle Streets near the county courthouse.[78] Joiner John Stanly, grandson of John C. Stanly, lived with his schoolteacher parents, John S. and Fanny Stanly, not far from his dressmaker aunts Catharine and Frances. Although tailor John Rice Green lost most of his fortune before 1850 and moved to a more modest residence, he and his family still lived among white neighbors such as house carpenter John Lane and silversmith William Tisdale. Property-owning black artisans also created a lasting pattern along George Street in a central axis from South Front Street north to Queen Street and beyond. They included tailoress Elizabeth Bragg near the corner of George and Front; Donum Montford and later his widow at Broad and George; and Isaac Rue and his family near George just south of Queen. Rue's daughter Sarah and her husband, caulker Simon Richardson, and their children lived nearby, with black neighbors on one

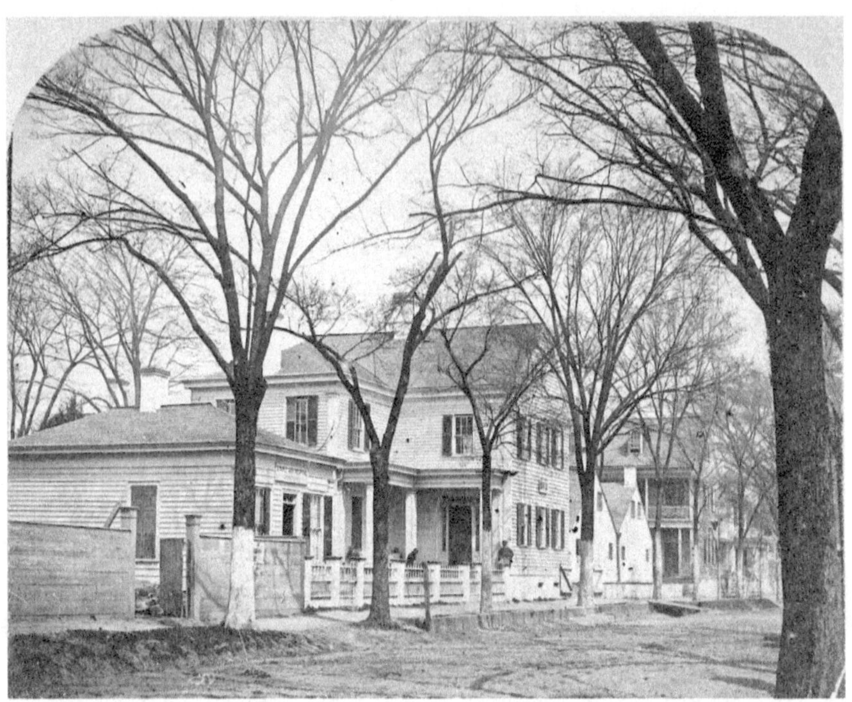

Craven Street, New Bern, ca. 1863. The photograph shows a representative antebellum residential streetscape in New Bern: the west side of Craven Street, looking north from Broad Street. It was made during the buildings' use as a Civil War hospital. The Coor-Cook House (later moved) and its accompanying office appear in the foreground and the Coor-Gaston House, the longtime home of William Gaston, in the background; the small gabled buildings in between were built as hospital wards. Courtesy of the North Carolina Collection, University of North Carolina at Chapel Hill Library.

side and whites on the other. Free black residents also branched out from George along Queen and nearby streets. How this pattern originated is unknown, but it began early in the nineteenth century and continued until well after 1900.

North of Queen Street, the racially mixed suburb encompassing the original Dryboro developed a distinct identity as black homeowners as well as renters moved there in increasing numbers. Laborers, sailors, domestic servants, and artisans of both races who rented houses or rooms were interspersed among those who had taken advantage of the moderate prices to acquire their own homes, valued from twenty-five to a few hundred dollars. A skilled artisan in New Bern earned from $1.00 to $2.50 per day and a laborer or servant perhaps a quarter to half of that; to save enough money to buy or build a home in this neighborhood was a challenge but not impossible. As a result, not only did New Bern have an unusually large proportion of free people of color but a remarkable number of free black property owners. Representative of many was Alexander Newton's mother, Mary, who owned property valued at $100; her enslaved husband, Thaddeus, had likely contributed his earnings toward the purchase of his family's home. Some of the Newtons' neighbors held property worth $300 to $500, including tailor John Bragg and carpenter James York Green, who had bought and sold property in Dryboro for years. Other notable artisan families in the neighborhood included those of James's carpenter brother Rigdon Green and master carpenter William H. Hancock.[79]

"COLORED SOCIETY"

These and other leading black artisans and their families formed an important presence in the social and economic fabric. The "colored social circle" that included John P. Green's parents, John and Temperance, was not only "satisfying and uplifting" to its members but large enough to provide mutual support and a sense of community.[80] Its members had defined themselves as artisans and citizens in the years before 1830, and most had business or family relationships with white leaders. Although some were freeborn, most owed their status to the previous era of manumissions. As they confronted one new restriction after another, their group provided an important survival mechanism and strengthened the base from which they dealt with the growing threats to all free people of color.

In contrast to some elites of color in other places, in New Bern freeborn status was not a criterion for acceptance in the "colored social circle," nor was fair complexion. Although some of the New Bern leaders were light skinned and occasionally taken for white, others were dark complexioned. John P. Green singled out the dark-skinned William H. Hancock and Richard Hazel and commented that Hazel—"One of the well to do and most highly respected" in the group—was "a man of pure Negro blood." "There was not amongst us any of that, squeamishness with respect to the varying shades of color," asserted Green, for "all that was required of a person knocking at the door of our social circle for admittance, was fitness; my dear father, who was one of the leaders of the colored society, in the old town, always stoutly maintained that, persons seeking association with others should be congenial and meritorious; and this theory was acted on, until the emigration of the families composing the circle annihilated it."[81]

Despite their local stature, none of these black New Bernians attained wealth comparable to that of those in richer cities. In 1850, only four—all artisans or their spouses—owned realty worth as much as $500. Blacksmith Richard Hazel's real property was valued at $2,000, and those with $500 in real estate were carpenter James York Green, plasterer and brickmason Isaac C. Rue, and Ann Green, the wife or widow of plasterer Shade Green. Mechanic George A. Rue, tailor John Bragg, and dressmaker Catharine Stanly were among a dozen with property valued between $200 and $500 (Stanly's holdings would more than double by 1860).[82] By comparison, several Wilmingtonians of color possessed real property worth upwards of $800, and a few had real property worth more than $1,000. New Bern's Donum Montford, like John C. Stanly, once held greater wealth in land and slaves, but both lost most of their property before their deaths. When Montford died in 1838, he owned six slaves, compared with twenty-two in 1820 and ten in 1830. In 1850 New Bern's eight black slaveholders, who owned from one to four slaves each, included six artisans—Rigdon Green, John Rice Green, William H. Hancock, Richard Hazel, Isaac C. Rue, and Catharine Stanly—plus Catharine's brother John S. Stanly and one Caroline Lane. The Greens, the Stanlys, and Rue were all former slaves.[83]

The most successful artisans also acquired household possessions to provide their families with comfortable homes as well as to convey their status and genteel taste. The children of John C. Stanly, including his dressmaker daughters Catharine and Frances, enjoyed the middle-class domestic settings established by their parents. Some people treasured favorite items even (or especially) after suffering financial reverses. John P. Green recalled that he was born in 1845 "'with a silver spoon in my mouth,' and rocked in the cradle of luxury (a mahogany cradle, to be explicit)." After his father, tailor John Rice Green, lost his health and wealth, and a fire destroyed the family home, his mother "still retain[ed] a few pieces of the furniture, and broken sets of silver-ware, rescued from the flames," which reminded her and her children of the way of life they had once enjoyed.[84] Such memories of mahogany and silver were not just figments of rose-colored childhood imagination. At the estate sale of white silversmith Freeman Woods in 1835, men of color joined whites in purchasing luxury items: John C. Stanly bought a looking glass and a breakfast table; William H. Hancock bought a bed and a decanter; and Richard Hazel took home several pieces of china and a waffle iron. Despite financial reverses, Donum and Hannah Montford had in 1838 a full complement of household goods in their home on Broad

Street, and they could welcome their friends to rooms graced with a secretary desk, a sofa, a mahogany candle stand, a dining table, and a breakfast table. They could dine in good style with plates of Liverpool ware, silver teaspoons and tablespoons, decanters and wine glasses, terrines and oyster dishes. Probably in their parlor they displayed their family Bible and their two pictures, one of Napoleon and one of Christ on the Cross.[85]

Leading artisans also devoted attention to their children's education and sent them to several years of school before they entered apprenticeships in skilled trades. Richard M. Hancock stayed in school until age thirteen before starting his apprenticeship with his father, William. When Alexander Newton entered his apprenticeship at age seventeen, he had already learned to read and write at the private school run by John Stewart Stanly and his wife, Fanny.[86] In addition to providing opportunities for local black children, the Stanlys' school built up the supra-local network of free families of color. As former student John P. Green recalled, "Colored students came to Mr. Stanley's school from all parts of the state" and made lasting friendships with their schoolmates from other communities.[87]

A few parents in this group sought to enlarge their children's opportunities beyond the local possibilities. This meant sending their children north, with the likelihood that, once introduced to a different life—and because of the state law forbidding free blacks gone more than ninety days from reentering the state—they would not come back.[88] Like John Rice Green's apprentice, William Alston, these New Bernians usually chose Oberlin School and College in Ohio, one of the few antebellum institutions of higher learning in the country that accepted students of color. In 1852 John S. and Fanny Stanly enrolled their daughter Sarah there, which launched her career as an educator in the North. Richard and Ann Nash Hazel sent their daughters Ann and Elizabeth to Oberlin, where Ann graduated in 1855. Rigdon and Caroline Green likewise sent their children to Ohio schools, including Benjamin, who became a book agent in Cleveland.[89]

Most of these leading artisan families continued their attachment to prestigious and predominantly white churches where, despite deteriorating racial attitudes in the broader world, they seem to have been treated with tolerance and some degree of respect by their white coreligionists. The Stanly family maintained their devotion to the Presbyterian church, where carpenter James York Green was also active.[90] Among the elite of color at Christ Church, Donum and Hannah Montford were singled out as "colored communicants," and Hannah was cited at her death as "Mrs.

Hannah Montford"—an unusual title of respect for a white to apply to a person of color. John Rice Green, according to his son, was one of only three free black members of the church who had a pew on the ground floor. The others may have included the prosperous house carpenter William H. Hancock and his wife, Mary Ann Hancock, who had at least four children baptized there, including their eldest son, named for rector Richard Sharp Mason. Some whites resented their presence: elderly attorney James W. Bryan complained in 1854, "Our society is in a deplorable condition and I think in a few more years the Negroes will take and rule the place. The displays made by them here on Sunday is perfectly astounding—they dress *elegantly* and have taken the Episcopal church—The pastor has a tremendous Sunday school of *the Negro Elite*—they have flocked in the school."[91] Despite such attitudes among some whites, the leading black artisans continued their affiliation with the church and thereby strengthened their relationships with one another and with some leading whites.

More remarkable than participation in an elite congregation was the role of free black house carpenter William H. Hancock in New Bern's white Masonic lodge, St. John's, where he was not only a member but an officer. The prosperous and literate Hancock evidently became a member in 1846 and remained one into the 1850s, serving in the office of the tyler who guarded the door and took other ceremonial roles. He won a place in local lore: a Union soldier and Mason stationed in New Bern during the war heard about the "black man who had been made a Mason of the Lodge that he might be Tyler." New Bern memoirist John D. Whitford remarked in the 1880s on Hancock's membership in the lodge of which he himself was a member, and John P. Green commented, "Mr. Hancock was the only tyler, of a white Masonic lodge, in a slave state, that I have ever heard of or seen, marching, with drawn sword, at the head of a white Masonic procession. Where he was made [Mason] or how he won recognition in that town, twenty years before the Civil War, is more than I can explain; and what makes his treatment the more remarkable, lies in the fact that, though not a pure blooded Negro, yet his color was pronounced—unmistakable."[92]

Hancock's role, however it came about, offers hints of relationships that existed between at least some whites and the most "respectable" free men of color in the community, who occasionally transcended racial barriers and, within limits, valued one another for their merits. For Hancock and his friends, as for their counterparts in other southern cities, although class could never trump race, it was often an ameliorating factor. Such relationships likely supported their hopes that hard work, respectable behavior, and adherence to community mores could still bring rewards for a class of people increasingly under attack.

Parting Ways

Whatever rays of hope might flicker for a few individuals, during the 1850s conditions worsened relentlessly for black artisans. A generation of white leaders like William Gaston and John Stanly, who acknowledged the evils of slavery and supported the citizenship of free blacks, gave way to proslavery advocates who took the opposite stance. White southerners fearful of abolitionism and slave insurgencies often targeted free blacks as potential incendiaries, and white workers' complaints about black competition mounted. Civic officials grew more aggressive in enforcing racial laws, and whites invaded the homes of even the most respectable black citizens in search of weapons or to harass them and their families.[93]

Beginning in the 1840s, as part of a larger movement in the South, whites held rallies across North Carolina to object to competition from "free negro mechanics" and sent a flurry of petitions to the state legislature demanding restrictions and special taxes on free black mechanics and measures to encourage or force them to emigrate to Liberia. How the movement originated and why it spread so fast remains an open question. Free black mechanics were so few in North Carolina as to present little threat to whites, especially in western piedmont counties like Rowan, which produced one of the bitterest petitions.[94]

In 1850 a memorial of this type was printed with the heading, "Sundry Citizens of Craven County." The county, of course, had long been the home of free black artisans, some of whom had worked alongside and for white artisans. Speaking for "citizens" rather than just mechanics, the memorial claimed that the "White Mechanics of Our State"—not just local ones—were suffering "serious injury" from "free negro mechanics." Not only by keeping wages low, but by degrading white artisans by making them work "side by side with negro labor," the writers claimed, the employment of free black craftsmen prevented the "advancement of Architecture" and kept away (presumably white) "genius and talent." In addition to calling for a special tax on all free black mechanics, the petition sought to tax all free blacks to pay for removing them to Liberia. The circumstances and the authorship of this petition are puzzling. The only copy found in legislative papers has "Craven" marked through and "Beaufort" written in, and the signers have typically Beaufort County names.[95] It is not known whether any such memorial was actually forwarded from Craven County, but it is tempting to speculate that its promoters failed to attract enough signers or even met with sufficient local opposition that they gave up the project.

As antiblack attitudes increased regionally, other voices raised objections to practices central to New Bern's slave economy. A negrophobic local newspaper editor took especially extreme positions. He began one tirade with the usual complaints about self-hiring. While acknowledging that "many worthy slaves . . . without abuse" enjoyed "greater privileges than the law permits," he demanded a halt to the practice. Employing the common bugaboo of slave rebellion, he claimed that self-hiring was inherently "prejudicial to the general content of our slaves, as it exalts one slave into nothing less than a freeman, excepting the privilege of voting, while his associates are under the immediate direction of their masters."[96] Going still further, the editor objected to the sheer existence of skilled slaves in terms akin to the 1850 petition concerning free blacks. "We do not believe it proper for those slaves to be initiated in trades of all kinds and brought into direct competition with the white laborers. At the North . . . they are not allowed to work at the same bench with the white mechanics, and why should it be so here." He sought to "place the slaves at their legitimate work—ditching, ploughing, making turpentine, getting shingles, clearing forests, draining low lands &c." By so doing, "we will . . . fill up our town with high-minded, industrious [white] mechanics, and place the slaves out of the way of all communication or contact with abolitionists, either at home or abroad."[97] Such views, it seems, did not represent the dominant white perspective in New Bern, where the elite profited from enslaved artisans and the civic authorities recognized their centrality to the economy and maintained a fairly loose hand concerning slave hiring. As in the state as a whole, despite white workers' complaints in the 1850s, the slaveholding power defeated any efforts to restrict their use of their enslaved workers, and slave artisans continued to hire themselves and to profit from their own skills.[98]

In political life, as well as in labor matters, New Bern people of color continued to find areas where white authorities turned a blind eye toward racial laws, to the dismay of some less tolerant white observers. A revelation of local practices appeared in a letter in the *New Bernian* of July 9, 1852. "A Citizen" objected that local men with a "prohibited" fraction of "mixed blood" were voting in state elections, with the permission of poll inspectors. Worse, if a poll inspector was reproached for failing to scrutinize voters sufficiently, "it is at once replied that it is not the officer who carries out the law who can be blamed, but the law itself if there is a fault." Whether the poll officers' responses referred to the intent of the law or to the difficulty of applying the racial formula, they may also reflect their reaction to others meddling in their business. How often and by whom such voting took place is unknown, but the evidence of the practice in the 1850s, like William H. Hancock's membership in St. John's Lodge, suggests the ongoing complexity of New Bern's racial constructions and relationships.[99]

New Bern's schools for enslaved children likewise drew the ire of certain whites. The irascible editor of the *New Bern Weekly Journal* complained in 1854 of the "notorious fact, that day schools are kept in the town of Newbern to enlighten the heathen minds of our slaves—teaching them reading and writing. It is not necessary to say one word on the effects of this, as all can see it is a school rendering its pupils fit agents for the Northern abolition[ists], and it should be stopped at once." As a result, he railed, "we are informed that our slaves here are in the habit of corresponding with individuals of all parts of our country without any examination of such correspondence; and many receive public journals from the North that are freighted with the most heretical abolition doctrine; all of which is contrary to our statutes."[100]

Events proved the editor right. When the black New York publisher Robert Hamilton visited New Bern in 1863, he called attention to his host, barber Clinton D. Pierson (Pearson), a slave whose owner permitted him to travel widely and learn to read, enabling him to serve as a conduit of news, apparently without interference. "Our readers will understand perfectly what he is when we state to them that he has taken the *Congressional Globe* and the *New York Tribune* for years, even when the only other copy was that sent in exchange to the newspaper of the town."[101] When Union troops liberated New Bern in 1862, they were amazed to find that many slaves could already read and write. Early in the occupation, a Union soldier marveled at two young girls of color who came into camp asking if the soldiers had papers and magazines to give away. One soldier responded, "If you can read this verse you can have this book." To the "astonishment of the soldiers, the black girl took the book and read the poetry, after the style of Hiawatha, beautifully. She got the book, but where did she learn how to read? It had long been a serious offense to teach the negroes letters."[102]

In the tense legislative session of 1860–61, state lawmakers enacted laws that terminated many of the rights blacks still possessed. Amid the secession crisis, the legislature abolished emancipation of slaves by will, thus blasting most slaves' remaining hopes for manumission and parents' plans to liberate their enslaved children. A law to "prevent free Negroes from having the control of slaves" forbade free blacks from buying, apprenticing, or hiring slaves "for any length of time." Along with reducing free blacks' capacity to operate their trades and train enslaved youths, this law also prevented them from acquiring and protecting their enslaved spouses or children.[103] By the eve of the war, most of the rights that had undergirded the development and success of New Bern's robust free black artisan-citizen class had vanished.

THE BLACK "HEGIRA"

By the time these laws passed, most of New Bern's leading free artisans of color had left. Having done everything in their power to define decent lives for themselves and their families at home, they took command of their situation in the only way still open to them—by "voting with their feet." Some who departed in the 1850s went to Liberia, such as tanner Daniel Williams, born in slavery, and his free brickmason son. Isaac C. Rue and a few other New Bernians kept up with colonization and related issues by subscribing to the American Colonization Society's *African Repository* but chose not to emigrate. Most of the New Bern black artisans who left town in this period joined friends and relatives in northern cities.[104]

For years, wariness of change and fear of hostility elsewhere discouraged moves for some free black artisans. Those deeply invested in families, friends, and clients likely judged it best to stay in the community where they were known. Tailor John Rice Green, his son recalled, explained himself in metaphorical terms: "So fond was [he] of sea-food," that when people of color began leaving New Bern for the North and "he was asked, whether or not he intended to join in the procession, he answered, that he would never leave North Carolina, until he could carry the Neuse and Trent rivers with him."[105]

During the 1850s, as the younger Green recalled, "the slaveholders became greatly excited" that growing abolitionism would jeopardize "their favorite, degrading, institution of slavery," and "the enlisting of men, drilling of soldiers, searching of colored residences for firearms, and cruelly whipping the owner, when an old fowling-piece was found" convinced many blacks that "a reign of terror seemed imminent." Hence "a majority of self-respecting colored families, in all parts of the South began to 'sell out, pack up and get out,' while, as one expressed it, 'the getting was good.' This was especially true as regarded the colored families, long resident in old Newbern; they 'stayed not on their going,' but, sold their possessions and went—some to New York, some to Philadelphia, a few to Boston and New Haven; but the majority to Cleveland and Oberlin, Ohio." Although far from rivaling later black exoduses, this movement encompassed hundreds of southern blacks: Green termed it a "hegira," the mass departure of a people to escape perilous conditions evoking Mohammed's escape from Mecca. A pattern of chain migration developed as a few individuals ventured north and then "began, without delay, to write persuasive letters, to the dear ones left behind, exhorting them to follow their example."[106]

The exodus drew away many of the most accomplished and promising people of color in their communities. Those from New Bern included the Stanlys, Greens, Morrises, Hazels, and Hancocks, who had enjoyed the best social and economic situations among local free people of color. Despite (or because of) their fortunate position and strong sense of identity, when white oppression exceeded their tolerance levels, they led the exodus, taking with them their skills, their educations, and their hopes for the future. They could see the direction that events were taking, and they had become accustomed to having at least some opportunities for success and autonomy. They had devoted themselves to training and educating their children, for whom their home community offered ever shrinking prospects. They also possessed the freedom to leave, funds to undertake a journey, connections with other families, and the confidence and abilities to make a new life in a new place. Years later, an aged white citizen of Fayetteville, another principal point of exodus, commented to writer Charles Chesnutt in terms that applied equally to New Bern, "Those were our best colored people. It was a loss to the town when they left." Chesnutt, whose parents participated in the movement, replied, "Yes, but they couldn't live here. Things were getting too warm for them. You had taken away their suffrage; the laws were becoming more and more severe toward free colored people; and they felt their only safety lay in emigration toward a freer clime. They didn't even know how soon they themselves would be made slaves."[107]

Some of the émigrés, familiar with New England's abolitionist history, headed for that region. The educated and property-owning mechanic George A. Rue and his family moved to New Haven, Connecticut, as some of the first New Bernians in that city. Evidently licensed as a preacher at

Andrews Chapel, Rue appeared in the New Haven city directory in 1852 as the Reverend George Rue, colored, a joiner by trade. He affiliated with the AME church and was ordained as a deacon in 1855, and by 1860 he was serving a congregation in Newport, Rhode Island. Rue traveled extensively, made the acquaintance of abolitionist leaders including Frederick Douglass, and became an eloquent opponent of slavery.[108]

Other New Bernians soon joined the colony of North Carolinians of color in New Haven, which grew from six in 1850 to fifty-eight in 1860. An early twentieth-century historian highlighted a group of "remarkable colored mechanics" from New Bern and Washington, North Carolina, who established their identity in New Haven as "worthy artisans and citizens." Prominent in the group was William H. Hancock, the New Bern house carpenter, churchman, and Masonic tyler, who arrived with his family between 1853 and 1855. By 1860 three of his and Mary's grown children—a dressmaker, a seamstress, and a wheelwright—were contributing to the household, which also included younger children born in Connecticut. The eldest son, Richard Mason Hancock, lived with his parents initially but by 1860 had married and moved on.[109]

Richard Mason Hancock exemplified the talented individuals who left New Bern in early manhood. After completing his apprenticeship with his father and seeing the limitations he faced in his native state, he probably paved the way for his family's move. In 1852 he was in New York, assisting fellow New Bern émigré, blacksmith Cornelius Sawyer, in selling property in New Bern. After working as a joiner in New Haven for a few years and marrying Mary Beman, the daughter of a prominent local minister, by 1860 he moved with his wife and their daughter to the Erie Canal city of Lockport, New York, where he worked as a ship carpenter and soon mastered the exacting trade of patternmaking for casting industrial components. In 1862 Richard, recently widowed, moved on to Chicago, which was whirring with wartime manufacturing. He advanced to become foreman of the large Eagle and Liberty Pattern Works shop, and thanks to an enlightened white employer gained national recognition as the black manager of a white workforce. In his adopted city Hancock became a "public-spirited and progressive citizen; a member of several societies, in some of which he holds a high rank, notably the Masonic fraternity; a vestryman of St. Thomas' Episcopal Church, and an interesting talker at the literary sessions of the Prudence Crandall circle."[110]

An especially large number of New Bern black artisans and their families chose Cleveland or Oberlin, Ohio, as their destination. Both towns were renowned centers of abolitionism that attracted a major part of the southern black hegira. A local historian observed that these "early Negro residents" were of "an unusually high type" who had "some means, some education, some ambition, and a trade or occupation which made them seem desirable acquisitions." The city thus "received a class . . . who were in many respects better fitted to begin life anew than most migrants" and who "established standards of life and conduct for the Cleveland Negro-Americans." Despite some racial tensions and restrictive black laws, the newcomers had opportunities greater than those back home. They sent their children to public schools, formed Masonic and other fraternal groups, entered into church life and leadership, and worked to expand their political rights.[111]

The first North Carolina émigrés to Cleveland and Oberlin soon persuaded their friends and families to follow. In 1850 the census showed only 8 colored North Carolinians in Cleveland, but by 1860 there were 120 in that city and 135 more in nearby Oberlin. (The actual number was larger, because the census listed several of the fair-skinned Carolinians as white.) A noted "pioneer" among the North Carolinians was plasterer and bricklayer Cicero M. Richardson, who had left New Bern for his apprenticeship in Fayetteville almost twenty years before. Having arrived in Cleveland from Goldsboro in 1850 or 1851, by 1860 he had $5,000 worth of real estate; his wife, Sarah, was a printer; and all but the youngest of their seven children were in school. Nearby lived Sarah's widowed mother and siblings from Fayetteville, including Robert, a mechanic aged twenty-two, and Cicero Richardson Harris, aged fifteen.[112]

Arriving soon after Richardson was New Bern tailor Freeman Morris, who had been acquainted with idea of living in a free state since his boyhood, when his white father took him north in hopes of setting him free. He and his wife Maria, their children, and Maria's mother were in Cleveland by 1851 or 1852, and by 1853 Morris had a merchant tailor shop in a prestigious downtown location. When race leader William Wells Brown visited Cleveland in 1857 and lauded its black citizenry in his newspaper, *The Liberator*, he singled out "Mr. Morris" from North Carolina as an educated man and a merchant tailor with "a fine run of customers," while his wife "would do honor to any society in which she might appear."[113]

Morris, who had seen free black men voting during his childhood in New Bern, took a precedent-setting role in Cleveland's political life. In 1859, after local election judges refused to recognize his vote, the Cuyahoga County Court "sustained the right of Freeman H. Morris, a mulatto, to vote in the city election." The ruling "declared the law prohibiting persons of any Negro blood from voting was unconstitutional. The court held that under the state constitution all persons with more than one-half white blood were legally white." In addition to having a white father, Morris must have argued, his mother Patty was partly white. This and other rulings "opened the way" to the ballot for Cleveland men of color.[114]

Other leading New Bern families decided to move to Ohio after sending children to school there. They realized that their children would not return home, and they had witnessed or heard about the differences between their home town and life in Cleveland and Oberlin. After New Bern schoolteachers Fanny and John S. Stanly sent their daughter Sarah to Oberlin College in 1852, they and most of their extended family moved to Cleveland. Blacksmith Richard Hazel and his wife, Ann Nash Newton Hazel, who enrolled two daughters at Oberlin in the early 1850s, soon followed suit.[115] Carpenter Rigdon Green and his wife, Caroline, who sent their children to school in Ohio in the mid-1850s, moved to Cleveland in 1859 to reunify the family. Green clove to the Episcopal church, and at his death at age ninety-one, in 1887, the preacher recalled that his "churchmanship was that of the school of the great Bishop Ravenscroft, of North Carolina, for whose memory he always expressed the most profound veneration."[116]

Although some families went north together, others separated as a result of the exodus. While Rigdon Green moved to Cleveland, his older brother James York Green, then in his sixties, chose to stay in New Bern. When John S. Stanly and most of the Stanly family moved north, John's two sisters, dressmakers Catharine and Frances Stanly, stayed behind as the only family members remaining by 1860. Tailoress Sarah Bragg Stanly, a daughter of tailor John Bragg and the widow of tailor Charles S. Stanly, the youngest son of John C. Stanly, joined the Stanly family in Cleveland, and her brother Cicero Bragg, a tailor of eighteen, moved there and lived with her and her four children. Her parents, tailor John Bragg and his wife Caroline, remained in New Bern for a time, but by 1864 they too had moved to Cleveland and were living with Sarah and her children, leaving their other grown children, tailoress Elizabeth, tailor Henry, and butcher George, in New Bern.[117]

A Dressmaker's Journey

The story of the widowed tailoress and dressmaker Temperance Green, as told by her son, depicts the strategies involved in one artisan family's move north. Upon the death of her husband, tailor John Rice Green, in 1850, Temperance and her children moved into a small house on Cedar Street in Dryboro, which her husband had protected for them against debts incurred during his years of ill health and financial problems.[118] For the well-born and class-conscious Temperance, the move marked a drastic comedown from their former neighborhood. Not only was the house "a rude cottage, in an obscure section of the old town" beside the graveyard, but the neighboring dwellings were "tenanted by persons, the like of whom she had never known as associates; and who, on occasions, would publicly proclaim, in clarion tones, 'It makes no difference how high the Eagle flies in the air, he's got ter come down ter git 'is support!!'"[119]

For several years, Temperance and the children made do with help from black and white friends and by planting a garden and raising chickens. Especially vital were her skills as a needlewoman who could "make any article of wearing apparel, for either man or woman,—from a shirt to a 'Prince Albert' coat, and she knew how to 'card' wool or cotton, spin with the wheel and weave at the loom." She could gather cotton from the plant and, "without assistance, card, spin, weave and manufacture it into a suit of clothes." Strict in her devotion to thrift and industry, Temperance let her family "eat no idle bread" and put her children, Sarah Rice Green, Catharine Stanly Green, and John Patterson Green, to work. Although she could provide but a slender living for her "fatherless children," she rejected several offers of marriage. When asked why, "Her curt answer was that she would not place her children under any step-father, to be treated in accordance with his whim or mood."

For years Temperance resisted her son's pleadings to follow friends who had "gone in quest of a modicum of liberty, into the great, free North, East and West!" Worried that her son might join some of her relatives' children and leave on his own, and increasingly troubled by "petty persecutions and insults"—including white patrollers invading her home at night in search of weapons—she responded to the appeals of her Fayetteville friend John E. Patterson, already in Ohio, and made up her mind to "depart with her little ones" to "the land of opportunity." In a customary strategy of indirection, Temperance enlisted an enslaved "auntie" to approach her owner—John R. Donnell, whose wife's family had owned and emancipated John Rice Green—to ask "if he would contribute a small sum, towards the expenses of our journey; he promptly answered, 'No,' and sent this message to my mother: 'you had better remain here, amongst your friends.'" Temperance sold her little house for $225 and her friends "Ben" and "Mr. 'Jim' Green" (probably her carpenter neighbor James York Green), "came around and crated the household effects, which had not been 'auctioned' off." After seeing their possessions loaded onto the schooner *Laura Johnson*, on June 24, 1857, Temperance and her children boarded the ship to begin their journey.[120]

When the little family stopped in New York, as Temperance had arranged in advance, they found a warm welcome from old friends and fellow Episcopalians from New Bern. Richard or William Hancock showed them around the city and made sure that their possessions were properly shipped to Cleveland on the Erie Canal. On July 6 he saw the Greens off in a "day car" of the Erie Railway Company. During their twenty-four-hour journey, Temperance and her children slept in their seats and dined on provisions they had brought in hampers. At about 5:00 P.M. on July 7, 1857, the train rolled into Cleveland.

In her new home, Temperance Green again turned to her network of friends, including those from her native Fayetteville. She established herself as a seamstress and dressmaker and, seeking to place twelve-year-old John in an apprenticeship, took him to Oberlin to her friend and his namesake, bricklayer John E. Patterson, who had encouraged the family's move. Not needing an apprentice, especially a boy of small stature, Patterson suggested that Temperance take him to John H. Scott, a harnessmaker and saddler from Fayetteville and the husband of Temperance's cousin Celia. Although Green enjoyed the stimulating life of the college town, he found Scott a hard taskmaster. He ran away so often that after six weeks Temperance decided to keep him at home in Cleveland and send him to school, an opportunity that "filled [him] with joy, beyond description."[121]

Through these friends and relatives, the Greens entered an important circle of émigré North Carolinians, which was in turn part of a larger national network. At John E. Patterson's home they encountered Andrew J. Chesnutt, Temperance's distant relative from Fayetteville, who was living with the Pattersons in 1860. Two years earlier, Chesnutt and his wife, Anna

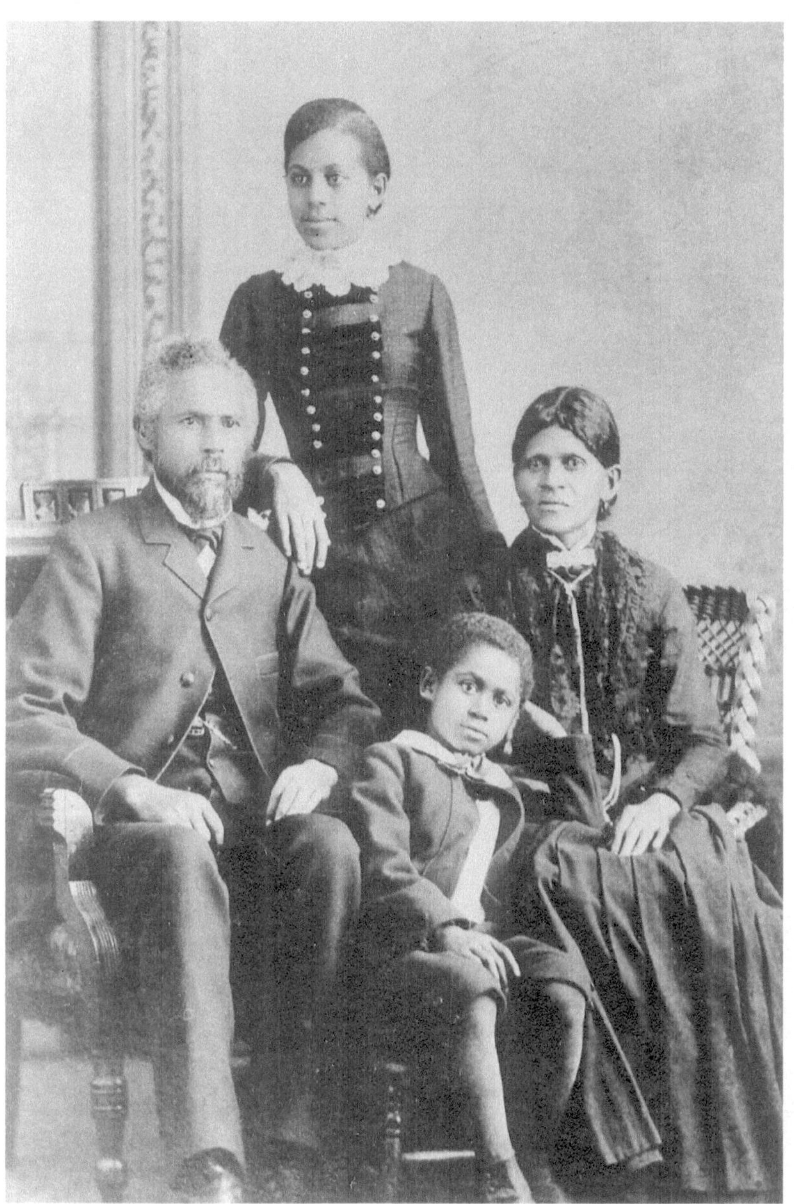

John H. Scott and family. Saddle- and harnessmaker John H. Scott was briefly the master of apprentice John Patterson Green in Oberlin, Ohio. His wife, Celia or Cecilia, was a cousin of Temperance Green. The family portrait is probably representative of photographs made of New Bern's successful black artisan families, no examples of which have been located. Courtesy of Oberlin College Archives, Oberlin, Ohio.

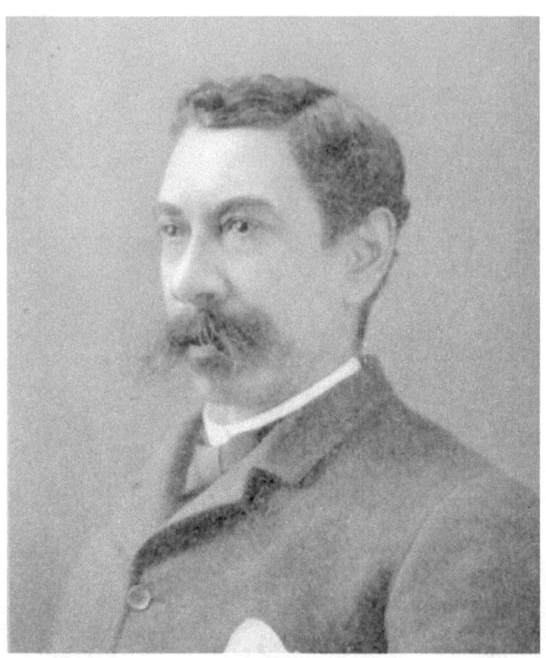

John Patterson Green. From Daniel Wallace Culp, ed., Twentieth century Negro literature, or, A cyclopedia of thought on the vital topics relating to the American Negro *(Naperville, Ill; Toronto, Can.: J. L. Nichols & Co., 1902). Courtesy of the Kellenberger Room, New Bern–Craven County Library, New Bern, North Carolina.*

Maria Sampson, had become the parents of Charles Chesnutt, who proved to be a longtime friend of John P. Green and a celebrated novelist and essayist. John E. Patterson and John H. Scott were leading abolitionists, and during his apprenticeship with Scott, John P. Green saw his master receive and assist at least one fugitive slave. In the fall of 1858, a year after Green returned to Cleveland, Scott participated in the nationally famous Oberlin-Wellington Rescue, in which black and white Oberlin men, as Green recalled, "rushed to Wellington, eight miles distant, forcibly took a fugitive slave from the custody of a United States Marshall, and set him at liberty." Scott and others were arrested, tried, and imprisoned for their actions. Temperance and her children kept abreast of the news, and young John attended a mass meeting in Cleveland where black abolitionist leader John Mercer Langston lauded the Oberlin rescuers and inspired young Green's interest in political life.[122]

A year later another of Temperance's Fayetteville acquaintances, Lewis Sheridan Leary, became an abolitionist martyr. Leary—John E. Patterson's son-in-law, a saddler from a respected Fayetteville family of color, and a former employee of John H. Scott—was killed during his role in John Brown's 1859 raid at Harper's Ferry. Visiting the Patterson home after the raid, Temperance and her children encountered the newly widowed Mary Patterson Leary and her infant daughter, Lois, then living with Mary's parents. (Mary later married abolitionist Charles H. Langston, a principal in the Oberlin-Wellington Rescue and brother of John Mercer Langston, and she became the grandmother and surrogate mother of poet Langston Hughes.)[123]

In Cleveland, Temperance Green displayed her usual industry and thrift and required the same of her children. She trained Sarah and Catharine as dressmakers and tried one more apprenticeship for John, as a tailor, which did not last long. Assisted on at least one occasion by the established citizen and fellow émigré Cicero M. Richardson, John P. Green completed his education and became a schoolteacher and a prosperous attorney. By the time of Temperance Green's death in about 1894, she had seen her son become Cleveland's first black elected official in 1873, a member of the Ohio House of Representatives in 1882–83, and the first black member of the Ohio Senate in 1892–93.[124]

STAYING HOME: NEW BERN ON THE EVE OF FREEDOM

Back in New Bern, artisans of color experienced many changes as a group and as individuals. The town's economy improved gradually in the late 1850s—with the prospect and eventually the long-awaited completion of the Atlantic and North Carolina Railroad—and the population increased as well. That growth, however, came among whites and slaves, while the number of free people of color dropped by more than 100 between 1850 and 1860 and that of free black artisans from more than sixty to about fifty. Although more black artisans worked in construction trades in 1860 than in 1850, their numbers dwindled in nearly every other craft. Many factors were involved—the arrival of white artisans, including those from the North and Europe, as the city's prospects improved; the growing mass production of many items formerly made by hand; and, not least, the departure of the leading artisans and their children—who, if they had stayed, might have taken up the reins of trade, craft training, and community leadership.[125]

It is difficult to calculate the local impact of the departure of so many of the leading black families, but it must have been profound in terms of the economic and social standing and the morale of free people of color who stayed in town. Nonetheless, artisans of color still ranked among the city's leading black property owners. Four of the five black New Bernians who owned as much as $1,000 in real estate in 1860 were artisans: dressmaker Catharine Stanly, tailoress Elizabeth Bragg, coachmaker Luke Mason, and cooper Balaam Jones. The fifth was William Pettipher, identified in 1860 as an engineer but later as a blacksmith. Artisans also numbered strongly among black New Bernians who had real estate worth between $500 and $999. Slaveholding by blacks, however, had dropped radically in New Bern, as it had statewide. Of the eight black New Bernians who owned slaves in 1850, most had died or gone north, leaving Catharine Stanly as the city's only slaveholder of color in 1860. As the owner of seven slaves, likely including some left to her by her family, she ranked at the top of the eight black slaveholders in the state.[126]

Both Catharine Stanly and Elizabeth Bragg had deep roots in the city. Each was the eldest daughter of respected free parents of color, both had family members expert in tailoring, both had remained in New Bern while kinfolk moved north, and both lived in predominantly white neighborhoods. Because they had remained single, their property belonged to them, not to their husbands. For these women, as for other women of both races, needlework offered one of the few possibilities for skilled employment. The census of 1860, the first to identify women's occupations, counted fifty-five white seamstresses and fourteen free seamstresses of color in New Bern, none of whom owned substantial property. Only a few women plied more specialized and prestigious sewing trades. There were a white milliner, a white tailoress, and a white dressmaker, the last owning $1,000 in real estate. Among free women of color, only tailoress Elizabeth Bragg (identified in the census as white) and the dressmaker Stanly sisters carried forward their family status and property ownership and practiced such prestigious specialties.[127]

Catharine Stanly and her sister Frances, aged fifty and forty, respectively, in 1860, likely attracted a prosperous white clientele, and through their own earnings and that of their slaves continued their genteel way of life until their deaths in the 1860s; their white physician referred to them as the "Misses" Stanly. Their home, in a predominantly white neighborhood, was well furnished with beds, chairs, a cupboard, card tables, a rosewood table, and a worktable for laying out patterns and cutting fabric for dresses. Their merchants' bills included purchases of fabric and trimmings. Like their parents, they could set a pretty table with a variety of cake plates, bowls, glassware, cups and saucers, two teapots and two sugar bowls, a butter dish, and four saltcellars. Their library included twelve magazines, several pamphlets, and 113 books. Frances, who survived her sister, singled out their most treasured possessions—three silver teaspoons, three silver tablespoons, a silver ladle, and a silver milk pitcher, plus "Family Portrait and Pictures" and a "Family Bible"—to be sent to family members in the North.[128]

The other leading black property owners in 1860 were artisans new to the propertied class who had begun to fill the gaps left by those who had left. The wealthiest was Luke Mason, a landless wheelwright in 1850, who by 1860 was a coachmaker with $1,200 in property, including his downtown workshop on Hancock Street, where four of his eight children were employed. Cooper Balaam Jones, an employee in merchant John D. Flanner's shop in the mid-1850s, had $1,000 worth of real estate.[129] The freeborn Edward A. Richardson, an apprentice in 1850, was in 1860 a full-fledged brickmason and a married head of household who owned real estate valued at $500. Other artisans had moved from apprentice to tradesman during the decade but without acquiring much property. Typical of many was David Wilson, who had learned the carpentry trade as an apprentice with white joiner Robert Hancock and was, at age twenty-five, a carpenter living with Jerusha Wilson, a free washerwoman aged twenty-one, probably his wife. Although David owned no real estate, he had $25 in personal property and a good reputation at his trade. His household also included his sixty-year-old mother, Rachel, and possibly his enslaved father, Peter, who lived into the 1860s.[130]

By 1860 most of the leading black artisans defined themselves differently from those of a decade earlier. Although some of the older artisans, such as James York Green and Isaac Rue, represented the manumitted generations, many of the younger ones were freeborn. In contrast to the elite families who had gone north, few of the new cohort had the deep connections with influential whites or the class identity of their predecessors. Only a few free blacks continued at the Episcopal church, such as barber Moses Kennedy, who had been freed by John Stanly and learned his trade from John C. Stanly, while John C. Stanly's daughters Catharine and Frances Stanly maintained the family's association with the First Presbyterian Church. Most of the leading artisans of color in 1860, like the majority of black churchgoers in town, belonged to the black Methodist congregation of Andrews Chapel, where they joined in fellowship with hundreds of slaves and free people of color and expressed, through hymns and psalms, their hopes for freedom and deliverance.

Black artisans' living patterns likewise showed signs of change. The northward exodus of leading families had depleted the number of free black residents in the predominantly white core areas designated as the First, Second, and Third Wards. Artisans of color, including most of those who held property—such as Luke Mason on Hancock Street and Isaac Rue and Edward A. Richardson just south of Queen—were more numerous in the racially mixed, but strongly white, Fourth and Fifth Wards just west and north of downtown.[131]

By 1860 an additional ward, the Sixth, accommodated the 1859 incorporation of the suburbs north of Queen Street, including Dryboro. A few wealthy whites lived in this ward, but by and large it had developed into a working class sector with almost equal numbers of free black and white residents. Although racial ratios varied from block to block, the Sixth Ward encompassed one of the state's principal urban concentrations of free people of color and a substantial proportion of New Bern's free black artisans. One sequence of about fifty households included some twenty-five artisans of color, including brickmasons, carpenters, coopers, painters, seamstresses, shoemakers, and wheelwrights, who lived among day laborers, draymen, fishermen, mariners, cooks, washerwomen, and housekeepers. Most were renters, but in 1860 as in 1850, the census showed several black artisan families who owned their homes there, including longtime residents tailor John Bragg and carpenter James York Green. Among the younger black craftsmen was brickmason Daniel H. Harris, a married head of household who, at age thirty-five, owned real estate valued at $800.[132]

A Family Divided and United

Representative of many artisan families in the neighborhood was the extended family of Hannah Neale, whose members adopted myriad strategies to protect and advance their status and their lives and livelihoods. Emancipated when she was about twelve years old, by 1850 Hannah was a grandmother in her mid-forties. With her first husband, Bristow or Brister Rue, Hannah had three children, George, Godfrey, and Grace. The family was torn apart when Rue was "sold away," but his wife and children kept his memory strong. Hannah subsequently married the free black boatman and Andrews Chapel leader Thomas Neale. In 1850 Godfrey, single at twenty-three and living with his mother, worked as a carpenter, and George A. Rue, aged thirty, was an educated and property-holding mechanic—a joiner by trade—and head of a household that included his wife, Ann, and their daughters Hannah, Elizabeth, and Malinda. Hannah Neale's daughter, Grace Rue Braddock, aged twenty-six and the mother of Israel and Hannah, headed her own household nearby. Hannah Neale helped Grace raise her children and supported their education: her grandson Israel Braddock Abbott, who would emerge as a political leader after the war, recalled that she had donated a dollar for his education at a local primary school.[133]

During the 1850s, all of Hannah Neale's family moved into new roles, locations, or relationships. Both sons decided to join the exodus from New Bern. Godfrey headed out for Colorado and then California. George, as we have seen, moved to New England, where he became a minister of the AME Church and was greatly admired for his eloquent preaching and his glorious singing voice. By 1860, Grace married Joseph Green, an emancipated carpenter and a leader at Andrews Chapel, and the couple and her children, Hannah and Israel, made their home with Hannah and Thomas Neale. Seventeen-year-old Israel was finishing his training with his stepfather Joseph. In the meantime, Hannah Neale had strengthened her position by becoming a property owner. In 1855, for $150, she bought from blacksmith Richard Hazel—who had moved to Cleveland—a 50 x 84 foot lot on Bragg's Alley, adjoining Dryboro, which likely included a modest house.

After living there with Hannah and her family for five years, Thomas Neale died in September 1860. Hannah commissioned a stone marker whose quality and wording affirmed his and the family's stature: "In memory of Thomas Neal, Husband of Hannah Neal, born Sept. 17, 1797, died Sept. 19, 1860, aged 63 Y's & 2 Dy's. He was a leader of the M. E. Church. He has finished his earthly labours and is now at rest with his Heavenly Father. / My husband has gone to a mansion of rest / From a region of sorrow and pain / To the glorious land by the Diety blest / Where he never can suffer again."[134]

By the eve of the Civil War, although her sons had departed for the North and West and her husband had died, Hannah Neale, along with her remaining family, was situated in her own home among friends and relatives in a neighborhood that would soon become the site of many of New Bern's leading black institutions. With the coming of war in 1861 and Union occupation in 1862, Hannah and her family—her daughter Grace and son-in-law Joseph Green, her grandson Israel Abbott, and her faraway son George A. Rue—entered new roles, for which their choices and experiences had begun to prepare them. Their lives during and after the war, as we shall see, would take dramatic new turns and would, at least for a time, bring most of the family together again.

FOUR

Worthy to Be Free, Worthy to Be Respected

Civil War, Union Occupation, and Presidential Reconstruction, 1862–1866

The fact that in spite of all law and opposition, many of us did learn to read and write, and, in spite of the evil influences and tendencies of slavery, there has always been society, some morality, and some undefiled religion among us, ought to settle the question of our capability for such things. . . . Surely the great effort of our friends at the North, and the heroic deeds of colored men on the battle field, will so far remove our difficulties, as to enable us to show to the world that we are deserving the rights and titles of citizens—a people worthy to be free—worthy to be respected.

—John Randolph, "The Capabilities of Our Race,"
Washington, North Carolina, April 1864,
Christian Recorder, May 21, 1864

In his letter to the *Christian Recorder*, John Randolph set forth his long-held hopes for freedom and citizenship at a time when such goals loomed at last as real possibilities.[1] Within days of penning his missive, the enslaved artisan and his family left their home in Washington, North Carolina, for New Bern, where he joined the growing ranks of black artisan-leadership in an almost unimaginable new world of black freedom and agency. Both towns had been occupied by Union forces for some two years when Federal ships evacuated Washington's remaining Unionists and slaves to New Bern in advance of a Confederate attack on Washington.[2] In occupied New Bern Randolph found common cause and unprecedented opportunity among black artisan leaders who were already advancing far along the path toward economic self-sufficiency and the "rights and titles of citizens." Coupling their pent-up hopes and anger with strategies born of years of experience, from early 1862 onward black artisans in New Bern cast away the bonds that had limited them and asserted themselves as men and women capable of supporting themselves and their families and as political beings focused on freedom and full citizenship.

By the time John Randolph Jr. arrived in town in the spring of 1864, New Bern was humming with activity and abuzz with political energy, and by midsummer he was taking a prominent role in the most vibrant black political arena in the state. For artisans of color, New Bern's situation during the Civil War and early Reconstruction provided a platform for action far different from most communities, North or South. From the time of Union liberation by General Burnside's troops in March 1862 onward, the nearly all-black city offered a pocket of freedom and opportunity on the edge of the Confederacy—a "Mecca of a thousand noble aspirations," as one Union soldier put it.[3]

Liberated New Bern differed from other Union-occupied sites in the South both in its urban character and in its black leadership. In 1861 Union forces captured the Sea Islands of South Carolina and Georgia, but the "contraband" colonies and camps that formed there had little in common with New Bern's urban character and experienced artisan-leadership. In contrast to those and other rural areas where northern whites strove to create a "rehearsal for Reconstruction" to demonstrate the capacities of the freedpeople, in New Bern the leadership emerged from the black community.[4]

From the first days of liberation, New Bern's artisan-leaders not only asserted their desire for freedom but outpaced Union policies in their pursuit of autonomy. Already seasoned in leadership in their churches, under occupation they could express publicly the dreams they had shared among themselves through years of oppression. In addition to empowering local people of color, the liberated city attracted other dynamic black leaders. While some had been free before the war, most were new freedmen. Together they transformed the city into one of the South's principal centers of black political leadership as they moved toward their goals of freedom and the "rights and titles of citizens." Essentially all of these leaders were artisans.

IN THE SPRING OF 1862, New Bern was a world turned upside down literally overnight. With the majority of whites, including most prominent white citizens, having "skedaddled" inland—one Union officer estimated in 1862 that only about 200 white civilians had stayed behind in a total wartime population of more than 7,000—New Bern became a city of Union soldiers and liberated black civilians. As the Yankees entered town on the heels of the departing Confederates, black New Bernians burst forth in a "grand jubilee." "Lord bless you I was afraid you would not come," exclaimed one man as he shook a Union soldier by the hand.[5]

After a brief period of uncertainty over the status of the thousands of "contrabands" coming behind Union lines, Federal military policy and the Second Confiscation Act assured their liberty in occupied New Bern. Although a few white New Bernians ventured back into town, and some northern white merchants, teachers, and missionaries followed the troops, white civilians composed a tiny minority. Former slaves occupied some vacated dwellings and shops, and Union officers established their headquarters in the mansions of the absent elite.[6] Many of the black civilians in the transformed city were there by choice and were thus self-selected for their initiative and aspirations. The majority of the city's free blacks had chosen to stay in town, and although many slaves were sent or taken inland, some were left behind, while others eluded their owners to try out life in freedom.[7] Thousands more escaped their bondage and braved distances and dangers to make their way there. From the spring of 1862 onward—for almost a year before the Emancipation Proclamation and three years before most southern blacks tasted freedom—people of color in New Bern seized the opportunity to develop their autonomy, their institutions, and their leadership in the public sphere. At war's end, these and other freedpeople

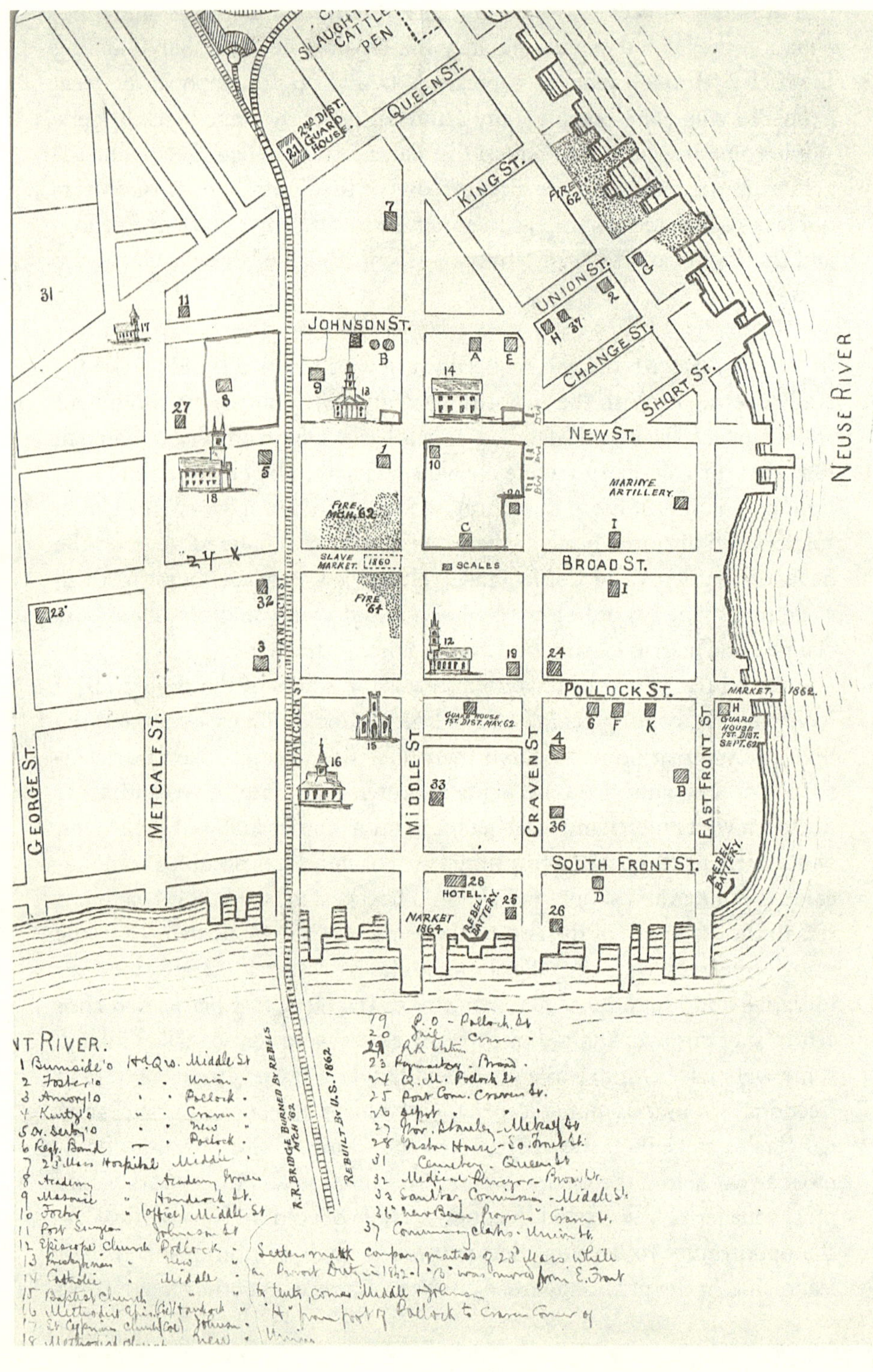
SLAUGHTER
CATTLE PEN
QUEEN ST.
2ND DIST. GUARD HOUSE
KING ST.
FIRE 62
UNION ST.
CHANGE ST.
SHORT ST.
JOHNSON ST.
NEW ST.
NEUSE RIVER
MARINE ARTILLERY
FIRE MCH. 62
SLAVE MARKET 1860
SCALES
BROAD ST.
FIRE '64
POLLOCK ST.
MARKET, 1862.
GUARD HOUSE 1ST. DIST. MAY 62.
GUARD HOUSE 1ST. DIST. SEPT. 62.
GEORGE ST.
METCALF ST.
HANCOCK ST.
MIDDLE ST.
CRAVEN ST.
EAST FRONT ST.
SOUTH FRONT ST.
REBEL BATTERY
HOTEL
MARKET 1864
NT RIVER.
R.R. BRIDGE BURNED BY REBELS MCH '62
REBUILT BY U.S. 1862
1 Burnside's Hd. Qrs. Middle St
2 Foster's . . Union .
3 Amory's . . Pollock .
4 Kurtz's . . Craven .
5 Dr. Serby's . . New .
6 Regt. Band . Pollock .
7 23d Mass Hospital Middle .
8 Academy . Academy Green
9 Masonic . Hancock St.
10 Foster . (office) Middle St
11 Post Surgeon Johnson St
12 Episcopal Church Pollock .
13 Presbyterian . New .
14 Catholic . Middle .
15 Baptist Church . .
17 St Cyprian Church (Col) Johnson .
19 P.O - Pollock St
20 Jail Craven .
23 Paymaster . Broad .
24 Q.M. Pollock St
25 Post Com. Craven St.
26 Depot . .
31 Cemetery . Queen St
32 Medical Purveyor - Broad St.
33 Sanitary Commission - Middle St.
37 Commissary clerks - Union St.

who returned or moved to New Bern built on these experiences to navigate a new world in freedom, to profit from their trades, and to claim new roles in political and community life.

THE ARTISANS WHO DOMINATED the black leadership in liberated New Bern were already accustomed to doing business with whites as well as with blacks, and a good number of them could read and write and possessed an awareness of national events. As urban artisans, most had operated with some autonomy, and as masters of their crafts, they possessed stature in the community. At Andrews Chapel, especially, slaves as well as free blacks had developed their leadership and public-speaking abilities, shared hopes for freedom, and made deep connections with their fellows. They also had long experience in attuning their behavior to the setting and situation, expressing or concealing their views according to their purpose and the race and status of their audience. These artisans, along with a few barbers who shared their experiences, formed a remarkable constellation of ambitious and talented leaders who embarked early on the path toward full citizenship.

The artisan-leadership exhibited diverse backgrounds. Most were New Bernians, some of whom had been free before the war—emancipated carpenter Joseph Green and his freeborn stepson Israel B. Abbott, and emancipated brickmason Isaac Rue and his freeborn grandson Edward Richardson—but the majority had practiced their trades in bondage until the war, including carpenter and coffinmaker Richard Tucker, blacksmith George S. Fisher, coopers Amos York and Henry H. Simmons, and brickmason Thomas Battle. Their allies included New Bern barbers John R. Good, emancipated a few years earlier, and the longtime slave Clinton D. Pierson. The local men welcomed newcomers who brought broader experiences and fresh zeal. Young plasterer George W. Price Jr. had escaped from Wil-

(Facing page): Sketch map of New Bern, 1864. Drawn by C. A. Nelson. Andrews Chapel (no. 16) is depicted near the bottom of the map, just east of the railroad tracks in the first full block of Hancock Street. Other noteworthy sites identified on the map include Burnside's headquarters (1), Academy Hospital (8), Masonic Hospital (9), Foster Hospital (10), the Episcopal church (12), the Presbyterian church (13), the Catholic church (14), the Baptist church (15), St. Cyprian's Church (17), the Methodist church (18), the Craven County Jail (20), the railroad station (21), Governor Stanly's headquarters (27), the Gaston House Hotel (28), and the cemetery (31). Courtesy of the Southern Historical Collection, University of North Carolina at Chapel Hill Library.

mington by boat in September 1862 and served briefly in the Union navy before coming to New Bern, and northern AME Zion minister James Walker Hood arrived just months before Randolph in January 1864 and assumed the pastorate of Andrews Chapel.[8]

Outstanding among the political leadership was the charismatic and elusive runaway slave brickmason Abraham Galloway. Born to an enslaved mother and a white father near Wilmington, North Carolina, Galloway had hired his own time for several years before escaping to the North. He served as a Union spy and returned to North Carolina by early 1862. Constantly in and out of New Bern, the radical advocate for freedom and equal rights galvanized the local and state movements.[9]

Watching and learning was the freeborn schoolboy Joseph C. Price, who fled Elizabeth City with his seamstress mother during the war. An apprentice to the upholsterer's trade after the war, he later embarked on a distinguished career as a minister, educator, and race leader.[10] At war's end, the artisan-leadership group expanded with the return of other New Bernians, including formerly enslaved coopers George B. Willis and Edward R. Dudley, as well as George A. Rue, the freeborn mechanic and joiner who had become a well-known AME minister in the North. As we shall see, the ensemble of leaders who gathered in the city in these heady years persisted as prominent figures for many years to come.

Artisan Trades in Wartime

For artisans of color, the liberated city provided opportunities for profitable employment in meeting the needs of soldiers and refugees, with little competition from whites. If demand dropped for fine carriages and delicate slippers, artisans still kept busy forging horseshoes, building and repairing wagons, tailoring and mending uniforms, resoling shoes and boots, and producing endless quantities of casks and barrels. Cooks and gardeners and butchers, drivers and housekeepers and barbers likewise profited from feeding and tending the soldiery. Now free to retain their earnings, skilled workers in the city took advantage of every new prospect to make money and advance their business acumen.

Artisans among the fugitives quickly went to work. Vincent Colyer, a young Quaker and artist from New York whom General Ambrose Burnside appointed as superintendent of the poor, maintained registration books in which he and his staff entered each refugee's name, age, place of origin,

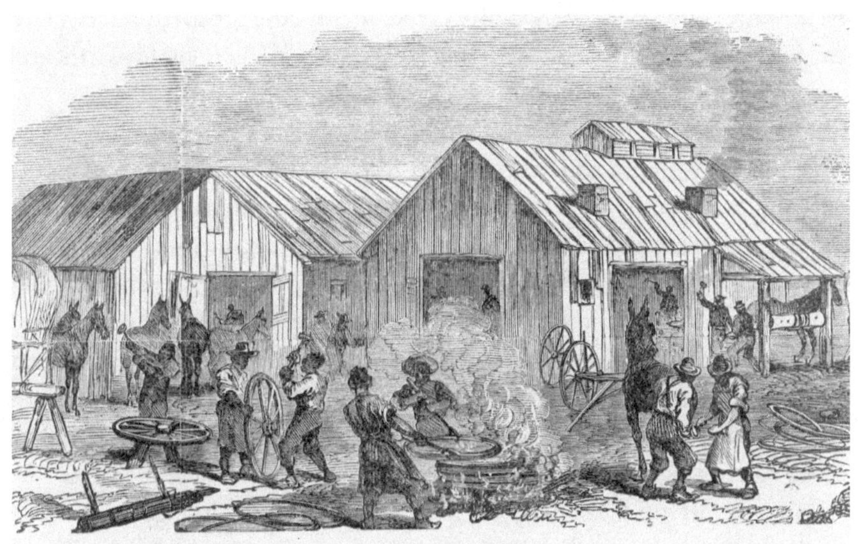

"The Freedmen's Blacksmith and Wheelwright Shop," 1862. Drawing by Vincent Colyer from Vincent Colyer, Brief Report of the Services Rendered by the Freed People to the United States Army, in North Carolina *(New York: Vincent Colyer, 1864). This is the wagon- and carriagemaking shop of Luke Mason, which included blacksmithing and wheelwrighting operations. Colyer noted that the workshop was on Hancock Street. Courtesy of the State Archives of North Carolina, Raleigh.*

family members, and previous occupation, and assigned the new arrivals to work "for which they were fitted."[11] Most of the male contrabands dug trenches, put up fortifications, and loaded and unloaded boats at the wharves, and many distinguished themselves as scouts and spies, but the new arrivals also included blacksmiths, coopers, and ship carpenters, as well as other carpenters who were assigned to making cots for the hospitals, nailing together coffins, and building and repairing docks and bridges, including the vital span across the Trent, which the Confederates had burned. Whereas Union paymasters allotted laborers about $10 a month, they paid carpenters, blacksmiths, masons, and other mechanics $1.25 to $3.00 per day.[12]

Although the throngs of refugees captured the most public attention, central to the economic and social character of liberated New Bern was the established community of black artisans already grounded in their trades, familial relationships, and congregations. Outside observers often failed to distinguish longtime New Bernians from newcomers. When Vincent Colyer claimed to depict an example of the refugees' "cheerful industry," he actually showed the workshop of Luke Mason, the prosperous free black carriage- and wagonmaker who had served a local clientele for years and was well equipped to build and repair vehicles for the Yankees.[13]

Near the end of 1864, Union administrator Horace James surveyed New Bern's black workers and received 350 responses to a handbill requesting "such colored people as were not employed by government, but were pursuing some trade, profession, or calling on their own account" to report their earnings for the year. Among the respondents, the highest-earning blacks were a few artisans and turpentine manufacturers who made upwards of $1,000 per year. Average salaries among occupational groups showed that only barbers and grocers, with more than $600 per year, exceeded artisans in their earnings: carpenters made an average of $510 per year; blacksmiths, $468; coopers, $418; and brickmasons, $402.[14]

In summing up New Bern's economic situation, including an account of the many poor people who were his principal concern, James singled out the success of its black artisans. He recalled that when most whites abandoned New Bern, they took with them "the most valuable, active, and useful of the slaves," but "the free blacks generally remained, not having the fear of 'the Yankees' before their eyes." Of these, he observed, "They are all self-supporting. Others have come in, and among them many mechanics and skilled laborers, so that New Berne has now a good supply of tradesmen, in nearly all the different branches essential to social prosperity. There are carpenters, caulkers, shipwrights, blacksmiths, masons, shoemakers, coopers, mill-wrights, engineers, carriage-makers, painters, barbers, tailors, draymen, grocers, cooks, hucksters, butchers, gardeners, fishermen, oystermen, sailors, and boatmen, with the usual supply of doctors and preachers." He concluded, "Some of these people are becoming rich; all are doing well for themselves, even in these times. They evince a capacity for business, and exhibit a degree of thrift and shrewdness, which are ample security for their future progress, if they are allowed an equal chance with their fellow-men."[15] It was, of course, that equal chance with their fellow men that would dominate freedpeople's agenda for years to come.

The African Church in Freedom

From the first days of Union liberation, New Bern's black artisan-leaders took steps to establish useful relationships with Union officers and to assume new roles in the changed city. The movement began among the black leaders of Andrews Chapel, who recognized Vincent Colyer as a potential ally who showed unusual respect for people of color. Soon after he arrived, Colyer recalled, "the Elders of the African Methodist Church" invited him to hold services to supplement the main service held by the white minister, and before long, he reported, he was "offered a salary by the freed-people, if I would take charge permanently of the congregation of St. Andrews's Colored Church."[16] The chapel elders, all artisans, included the long-free plasterer and brickmason Isaac C. Rue and others newly free: blacksmith William Ryal, carpenter-coffinmaker Richard Tucker, and carpenter Louis Williams. Other congregation leaders were Joseph Green, bricklayer Thomas C. Battle, and cooper Amos York. York, whom Colyer cited as a former slave and "a leading man among his people," soon found employment and access to military authorities as Colyer's assistant secretary.[17]

Although the churchmen did not persuade Colyer to become their pastor, they supported his interest in education for blacks, a long-standing project for their congregation, by opening their sanctuary as a schoolhouse for the hundreds of refugees. Within weeks, as Colyer recalled, Andrews Chapel, along with the old Baptist meetinghouse, hosted evening schools with over 800 pupils, young and old, of whom 600 were beginners and about 200 could already read and write.[18] In May, however, the newly arrived Union governor Edward Stanly threw the schools and the black population into disarray. When President Lincoln assigned Stanly, a Unionist native of New Bern, late of California, to serve as governor of occupied North Carolina, he instructed Stanly to follow state laws in hopes of encouraging state leaders to return to the Union.[19] In addition to his controversial decision to allow an owner to reclaim a fugitive slave, Stanly reminded Colyer that teaching slaves to read flouted state laws. Colyer closed the schools and headed north to raise opposition. Following an audience with Lincoln, Colyer returned with authority to reopen the schools; having heard the news before his arrival, local blacks greeted him with thanks and gifts. After Colyer left New Bern late that summer, Amos York wrote him a letter that captured the spirit of the times:

> Sir: —With pleasure I write these few lines to inform you that I and my family are well, and to hope that you and your family are enjoying the blessings of good health. I should have liked to have had a conversation with you before you left Newbern for good; but as I did not, I yet hope to see you again. There are great inquiries for you by

> the people of color in Newbern; they are much at a loss for they have no one now to apply to for comfort or satisfaction; no one that sympathizes with them as you did. Sir, I must say if the President of the United States was dead, the Union army could not mourn his loss more than the people of Newbern do the loss of you. The Elders of St. Andrews's Chapel, J. C. Rew, Louis Williams, William Ryol, R. M. Tucker, give their best respects to you and your family. I would like to say more, but I must close by saying if I should never meet you again in this life, I hope to meet you "In that world of spirits bright / Who take their pleasure there, / Where all are clothed in spotless white, And conquering palms they bear." I should be happy to receive a few lines from you. Your most obedient servant, Amos Yorke. August 27, 1862.[20]

Andrews Chapel's artisan-leaders persisted in seeking a minister of their choice. Through newspapers and letters, they kept abreast of developments among the national black Methodist associations—African Methodist Episcopal (AME) and African Methodist Episcopal Zion (AME Zion)—headquartered in Philadelphia and New York, respectively. They also maintained contact with friends in both associations, including the venerable Craven County native and AME Zion bishop Christopher Rush in New York and the New England AME minister and New Bern émigré George A. Rue.

National church leaders took a growing interest in bringing southern black congregations in Union-occupied areas into their folds. Both the AME and AME Zion Methodists and the predominantly white northern Methodists viewed the large congregation of Andrews Chapel as a special prize. Assigned as an AME missionary to occupied Virginia and North Carolina, in June 1862 George A. Rue headed south from New England.[21] Likely encouraged by Andrews Chapel leaders—who included his brother-in-law, carpenter Joseph Green—he hoped to bring his home church into the AME connection; tradition says that Rue had asked Green to "save" the congregation for him. During an arduous journey south, Rue ministered to fugitive slaves behind Union lines in Virginia and met with coreligionists in Washington, D.C. Because of the military situation, however, he could not obtain a pass to North Carolina; in August, sick and out of money, he turned back north. At Boston's famed Bethel AME Church on Beacon Hill, he continued his work as a passionate advocate for freedom.[22] Later that year, the northern white Methodist church assigned a white Union officer

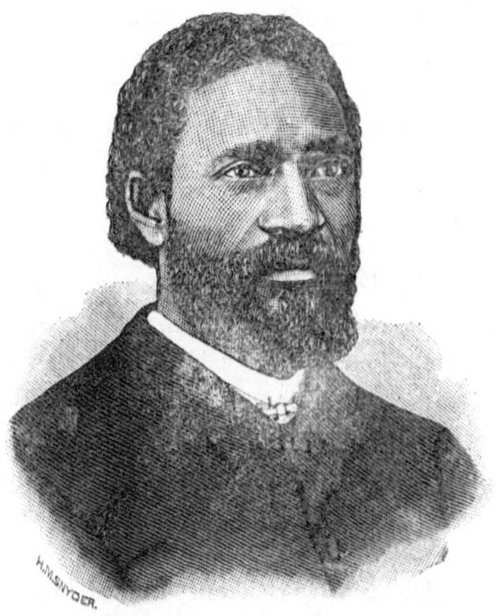

James Walker Hood. Courtesy of the State Archives of North Carolina, Raleigh.

as pastor to Andrews Chapel and other Methodist churches in occupied eastern North Carolina.[23]

Meanwhile, New Bern black Methodists in New Haven, Connecticut, who included longtime members of Andrews Chapel, appealed in 1863 to the AME Zion bishop to "send some one down to New Berne to look after our people there." After one missionary failed to arrive, the bishop selected James Walker Hood, a freeborn native of Pennsylvania who had pastored in New Haven and Bridgeport, Connecticut, and had been ordained as an elder in 1862.[24] Hood arrived in New Bern on January 20, 1864, only to find other ministers, white and black, competing to win Andrews Chapel for their denominations. Moreover, the city was reeling from a deadly smallpox epidemic; the churches were closed by military order until the epidemic subsided; and Hood soon fell ill himself.[25]

As Hood told the story, Andrews Chapel leaders, including Joseph Green, connected with him and took the situation into their own hands. Despite their old ties to AME's George A. Rue, Green and his fellow churchmen at Andrews Chapel decided to ally with Hood.[26] With the church closed and Hood lying ill, "several of the leading brethren of the church" called on Hood to report the claims made by the competing ministers. Working behind the scenes, Andrews Chapel leaders effectuated their own choice. Although public worship was forbidden during the epidemic, as Hood recalled, "it was thought that there would be no objection to a meeting of the official board, which numbered about forty members. They met in a private schoolhouse belonging to the wife of one of the members of the official board, namely, Joseph Green." At Grace Green's schoolhouse, the chapel leaders heard out Hood as well as the AME representatives and voted unanimously to unite with AME Zion. The northern white Methodist minister persisted in his claim, but Hood traveled secretly to Washington, D.C., and gained federal authorization for the congregation to choose its own pastor. He and the church board quietly arranged for him to preach on Easter (the first Sunday the churches reopened) and to reveal the federal ruling at the end of the service. With the surprise announcement acclaimed by the congregation, Andrews Chapel had a black pastor of its own choosing in a denomination with a black bishop. It became the first church in North Carolina and one of the first in the postwar South to affiliate with AME Zion.[27]

In May 1864, AME Zion Bishop J. J. Clinton—the first black bishop most New Bernians had ever seen—came from New York to hold services and ordain two congregants as deacons, blacksmith William Ryal and one Ellis Lavender. In December, Andrews Chapel hosted the state's first conference of AME Zion, which Hood cited as "the first Afro-American Conference held in that territory over which the Confederate flag had floated." The twelve delegates included Andrews Chapel's Joseph Green and Amos York, who were appointed to serve congregations at Roanoke Island and Raleigh, respectively, and joined the many black artisans who answered callings to preach the gospel.[28]

Politics and Public Life

From the first months of occupation, and well before Hood's arrival, Andrews Chapel emerged as a political as well as religious center. As black New Bernians addressed issues about which they were often a step ahead of Union policies, they held most of their meetings at Andrews Chapel. In the spring of 1862, long before the Union army accepted black soldiers, chapel leaders allowed former slave William Henry Singleton to use the meetinghouse for recruiting. Rebuffed after volunteering his service as a Union soldier, he "hired the AME Zion church [Andrews Chapel] at Newbern and commenced to recruit a regiment of colored men. I secured the thousand men and they appointed me as their colonel and I drilled them with cornstalks for guns."[29] That June, Andrews Chapel hosted one of black New Bernians' first overtly political public gatherings—an "indignation meeting held by the negroes" to object to Governor Stanly's policy on returning fugitive slaves to their owners, which was among the first southern black protests addressing that contentious issue. The policy was soon reversed, and later that summer the Second Confiscation Act gave protection to slaves taking sanctuary behind Union lines.[30]

Over the following months, freedpeople in New Bern kept abreast of fast-changing national developments. That fall, they learned of Lincoln's preliminary Emancipation Proclamation, issued on September 22, 1862, which stated that effective January 1, 1863, all persons held as slaves in states in rebellion from the Union would be free. A white Union soldier commented in November, "The Negroes are on the whole so far as I have seen more intelligent and clear headed than I fancied and are considerably interested in the President's proclamation, which many of them understand very well."[31] On January 1, 1863, many miles from home, New Bern émigré George A. Rue joined Frederick Douglass at a gathering in Boston to await a telegraph message confirming the announcement of the proclamation. Douglass recalled the moment when the news came—"It is on the wires!"—and the crowd erupted in "wild rejoicing" that "exhausted all expression." At that point, wrote Douglass, "My old friend Rue, a colored preacher, a man of wonderful vocal power, expressed the heartfelt emotion of the hour, when he led all voices in the anthem, 'Sound the loud timbrel o'er Egypt's dark sea, Jehovah hath triumphed, his people are free!'"[32]

Although in practical terms the Emancipation Proclamation confirmed the freedom already in effect in New Bern, in a broader sense it opened a new era. Its authorization of enlistment of black Union troops had an especially direct impact. In a pioneering Federal effort to recruit black soldiers from the South, during the spring of 1863 northern recruiters and black soldiers—chiefly from Massachusetts—came to New Bern to enlist volunteers for what came to be known as "the African Brigade." After a slow start, white recruiter Edward Kinsley of Massachusetts met with radical black leader Abraham Galloway, who demanded guarantees of terms for black soldiers' service before lending his support. As Kinsley recalled, Galloway and two allies, including a Mr. Randolph—possibly John Randolph Jr.—

insisted on a guarantee of fair pay and treatment for the soldiers and of benefits for their families, including care for the old and feeble, hospital jobs for the women, and teachers sent from the North to educate their children. With these assurances agreed upon, throngs of men—including many whom Singleton had recruited at Andrews Chapel—joined up as the first of some 5,000 United States Colored Troops recruited in New Bern. In the years that followed, they and thousands of other black troops proved their mettle in battle and took a decisive role in achieving the Union victory, affirming their manhood in their own eyes and the eyes of others.[33]

Few New Bern artisans chose to join these regiments. Those employed by the Union in civilian jobs earned far more at their trades than the ten dollars a month (laborers' rates) offered to the recruits, without the danger of combat. One frustrated Union officer complained that the high wages paid to black civilians made it "impossible to make much headway with recruiting." If the records of Company A of the United States Colored Troops—one of the few units for which the registrar noted the occupations of men who enlisted in New Bern—are representative, most of these recruits were farmers, sailors, and laborers; the few artisans among them were quite young, such as Samuel Mason, aged eighteen, a New Bern carpenter, and John Jones, aged nineteen, a brickmason from Halifax County. Most of the black volunteers from North Carolina were rural people and relatively poor. Some New Bern artisans enlisted in other units, including a few who served as noncommissioned officers after such positions, typically awarded to men with skilled occupations and some education, opened up for blacks. Henry Kent, a free black wheelwright in New Bern before the war, served as a sergeant in Company M, 14th U.S. Colored Heavy Artillery, at Fort Macon, North Carolina. Allen G. Oden, who enlisted in Washington, North Carolina, and served as a sergeant in Company H of the infantry, later settled in New Bern and practiced the shoemaker's trade as well as taking a leading role in civic life.[34]

Most important to New Bern's developing black artisan leadership, the recruiting campaign and the local presence of black Union soldiers strengthened the morale of the city's people of color and spurred their political participation. In New Bern during the summer of 1863 northern black recruiter Joseph E. Williams marveled at the "warmth and openness in the nature of the colored people of North Carolina" and especially at their "virtuous pride and self-respect and their natural intelligence," which captured the admiration of the northern soldiers.[35] On July 24, 1863, New Bernians

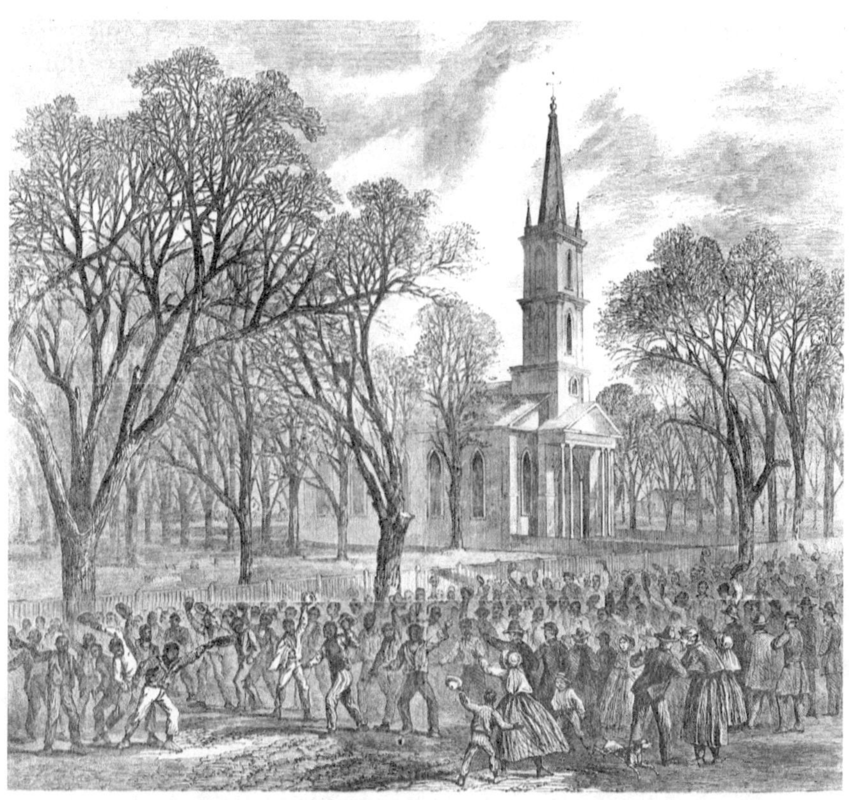

"Negro volunteers passing Episcopal Church, New Bern NC." Frank Leslie's Magazine, *February 27, 1864. The image shows Christ Episcopal Church on Pollock Street near Middle Street. The church was gutted by fire in 1871 and rebuilt on the old walls. Courtesy of the State Archives of North Carolina, Raleigh.*

witnessed a stunning event: the 1st North Carolina Colored Volunteer Infantry formed ranks and marched in parade to the city green, where freedwoman Mary Ann Starkey, a friend of Galloway and a leader in providing local aid to refugees and black soldiers, presented a regimental flag. Made in Boston with contributions from the black women of New Bern and said to have been designed by famed author Harriet Beecher Stowe, the blue silk flag featured on one side a rising sun symbolizing liberty, and on the other a Goddess of Liberty treading on a snake emblematic of "copperheads"—meaning northern supporters of the Confederacy. In a rare public speaking role for a woman, black or white, Mrs. Starkey gave a brief address on behalf of the Colored Women's Relief Association of New Bern before presenting the flag to General Edward A. Wild, who handed it to Colonel James

Beecher of the regiment, the half brother of Harriet Beecher Stowe. The ceremony—surely the first such formal and official celebration featuring black participants held in New Bern—expanded black New Bernians' vision of possibilities for their leadership in the public realm.[36] The sight of black troops became a familiar one: a year after recruiting began, the *New Bern Times* reported, "The 1st U.S. Colored Troops . . . paid our city a visit on Sunday afternoon last. They presented full ranks, and made a fine soldierly appearance. . . . The regiment contained many men of evidently an intellectual cast, and bore external evidence of having descended from the F.F.V.'s of Virginia and North Carolina."[37]

Amid these events, New Bern's black artisan-leadership and their allies expanded their ranks and their mission as they campaigned first for freedom and soon for equal rights. Sometimes working with sympathetic white Union soldiers, they organized public gatherings that featured black speakers and drew large black audiences—a radical change from the days when state and local laws forbade such gatherings. In their format and their rhetoric, these assemblies followed national models and displayed a pattern repeated in subsequent mass meetings and conventions. Reflecting the blending of the religious with the political, and dignifying each occasion with suitable ceremony, typically a chairman called the gathering to order, after which a chaplain offered a prayer and a hymn was sung, officers for the meeting were elected and committees formed to prepare resolutions. More hymns alternated with orations before the business of the meeting—the adoption of resolutions, election of delegates, or presentation of a keynote address—was concluded, often with a prayer and a final hymn. Andrews Chapel was the site of most of these gatherings.

An especially inspiring meeting came when Robert Hamilton, the black New York publisher of the AME Zion *Anglo-African* newspaper, visited New Bern in December 1863, as arranged by his friend Abraham Galloway. (Hamilton also had a local family tie: in 1859 his daughter Olivia had married Alexander H. Newton, the former brickmason's apprentice who had left New Bern for New York in 1857 and joined the Union army on December 18, 1863.)[38] Hamilton's visit reinforced the bonds between the local leadership and the larger world and energized local advocacy for equal rights.

In a report for the *Anglo-African*, William H. Johnson, a black bricklayer who served as secretary for the "Great Public Meeting in New-Bern, NC," marveled, "We have had glorious times in Newbern within the last few days." "It is but seldom that we, living far from the highway of travel, are permitted to see any of our colored friends, more especially those who are laboring for our welfare." Abraham Galloway—"our old tried and true friend"—had accompanied Hamilton to New Bern, where the well-educated barber Clinton D. Pierson was his local host. "On Sunday evening last," wrote Johnson, "Mr. Hamilton lectured in Andrews Chapel. Every seat in the house (which will seat about one thousand persons) was full."[39] At this event, Hamilton sang a version of "'the John Brown song,' entirely different from anything we had ever heard here; and the chorus was joined in with much spirit by the whole congregation." The next night, an overflow crowd gathered to cheer Hamilton's oration and to applaud Galloway's "spirited and uncompromising speech" in which he "handled secessionists and that still more defeated class, the copperheads, without gloves."[40]

After returning to New York, Hamilton wrote of the freedpeople he had met: "The material progress which they are making is really wonderful. In the town of Newbern, you will find not less than fifty shop and grocery keepers, who, although they labor under great difficulties, still are going ahead." Schools were flourishing, their population expanded by former slaves who had arrived from a radius of sixty miles and more. "If anybody supposes that the blasting and infernal system of American slavery has been able, with all its power, to begin to crush out the manhood of the colored people of the South," he said, "a visit here will entirely undeceive him." He observed, "You find here a great many naturally intelligent colored people, notwithstanding the attempts made to blot out the slightest evidence of its existence."[41]

Among the Tar Heels who had left for the North, Hamilton cited religious leaders such as AME Zion bishop Christopher Rush and William J. Alston, the Raleigh native who had apprenticed with tailor John Rice Green in New Bern and became an Episcopal minister in Philadelphia. He pointed as well to house carpenters William H. Hancock and Rigdon Green; blacksmith Richard Hazel; tailors Freeman and Albert Morris; bricklayer and plasterer Cicero M. Richardson—all New Bernians who had left in the 1850s and done well in the North. He singled out other notables still in town and prospering—his host Clinton D. Pierson, farmer Edward H. Hill, barber John R. Good, and Levin Johnson, an aged black man who "took the Congressional Globe, until they would no longer deliver it to him at the Post Office"—as men "whom oppression could not drive away (indeed some of whom could not go because they were slaves), who still hold aloft the reputation of their brethren for intelligence and industrial worth, whether absent or present."[42] Contradicting apologists for slavery who discredited black abilities, Hamilton acclaimed the New Bernians' essential qualities of artisan identity and citizenship, which they had embodied for years in quiet defiance of white stereotypes.

In 1864, spurred by changing national conditions and inspired by Hamilton's rhetoric and Galloway's dynamism, New Bern's black artisan-leaders intensified their quest for equal rights. With its minister, Hood, as an advocate for the cause, Andrews Chapel became a principal setting for political activity and played an ever more powerful role. Long before most of the nation, including President Abraham Lincoln, was prepared to address the issue of black suffrage—or even the still unresolved question of emancipation—New Bern leaders, whose self-identity was already grounded in freedom, moved boldly toward full citizenship. Along with many leaders of the day, they "drew a straight line from the Declaration of Independence to the Emancipation Proclamation," but they carried the link farther to embrace the nation's founding promises and the full legacy of equal rights.[43]

Aware of national black leaders' discussions of suffrage and cognizant of the fragility of newly won freedom, Abraham Galloway and other New Bern leaders believed that only by obtaining equal rights, especially the vote, could blacks maintain their liberty and protect themselves once the war was over. In April 1864, determined to "regain their ancient privilege, long wrested from them—the right of voting," they engaged in a remarkable assertion of their aspirations by turning directly to the highest national authority. Sharing many blacks' view of Lincoln as their special friend, the radical leader and brickmason Abraham Galloway, along with New Bern merchant and farmer E. H. Hill, barbers Clinton D. Pierson and John R. Good, minister Isaac K. Felton, and Jarvis M. Williams, a baker originally from Washington, North Carolina, slipped out of New Bern and traveled to Washington, D.C. There they "called on" President Abraham Lincoln, who welcomed them to the White House and, as they especially remembered, had them enter by the front door. At what may have been Lincoln's first such meeting with southern black leaders, they presented him with a petition on behalf of "the colored citizens of North Carolina composed alike of those born in freedom and those whose chains of bondage were severed by your gracious proclamation."[44]

Drawing upon the history of the nation and their own state, their petition invoked the principle embodied in the Declaration of Independence that "all men are created free and equal" and recalled that "the right of suffrage was exercised, without detriment, by the colored freemen of this state previous to 1835." The petition urged the president to "finish the noble work" he had begun with the Emancipation Proclamation by supporting universal manhood suffrage when the state was "reconstructed" at war's end.[45]

During their interview the New Bern men "received from Mr. Lincoln assurances of his sympathy and earnest co-operation," but no promises. Lincoln himself was far from committing to such a step at the time, though he was beginning to rethink the issue and would move in that direction in the year that followed. Whether the meeting with the black New Bernians brought him any closer to supporting black suffrage is unknown. For the North Carolinians who had met the president and for their allies, their experience was inspiring, whatever its outcome. After a public speaking tour that included a reception on May 4, 1864, at the mother Zion church in New York, the travelers returned to New Bern, where cooper Amos York presided over a mass meeting at Andrews Chapel that had gathered to hear their stories and celebrate their journey. Galloway and the other speakers transformed the gathering into a rally for equal rights.[46]

By the summer of 1864, as John Randolph Jr. witnessed after arriving from Washington, North Carolina, New Bern's dynamic black artisan-leadership had expanded its membership. At the 1864 Independence Day celebration at Andrews Chapel, presented as a fundraiser to aid wounded black soldiers, the principal speakers included not only such familiar figures as cooper Amos York and barber John R. Good, but also brickmason Edward A. Richardson, grandson of Isaac C. Rue, taking the stage for the first of many times in his civic career.[47] A month later, on August 4, Randolph mounted the podium at a meeting at Andrews Chapel to read the call in the *Anglo-African* announcing that the National Convention of Colored Citizens of the United States would be held in October in Syracuse, New York, and he was elected as secretary for the meeting. Others taking newly prominent roles at this event included freedman and blacksmith George Fisher, who chaired the meeting; freedman and cooper Henry H. Simmons, who served as cosecretary with Randolph; and the long free brickmason Daniel Harris as treasurer.[48]

The New Bernians' decision at the August gathering to send representatives to the Syracuse convention reflected their growing engagement with the national black movement for equal rights. As was probably inevitable within a growing leadership group, the choice of delegates sparked debate:

the newly arrived minister Hood favored Andrews Chapel members Ellis Lavender, Amos York, Richard Tucker, and Edward A. Richardson, while others preferred John Randolph Jr., John R. Good, and Clinton Pierson.[49] Eventually, in the midst of a yellow fever epidemic and a panic over the threat of Union conscription of New Bern freedmen, all parties united in backing a single delegate, on the grounds that the community could pay travel costs for only one representative from North Carolina—Abraham Galloway.[50]

At the Syracuse convention, which was chaired by Frederick Douglass and is considered the nation's most important meeting of black leaders during the war, Galloway was tapped to serve on key committees. Having presented President Lincoln with the petition for equal suffrage in North Carolina six months earlier, he readily joined in forming the National Equal Rights League and participated in preparing the convention's "Declaration of Wrongs and Rights," which sought freedom and equal rights for people of color as "citizens of the Republic," in terms grounded in the Declaration of Independence. After a northern speaking tour to promote the league and the declaration, Galloway returned to New Bern and promptly organized a state chapter of the Equal Rights League and five local chapters in the New Bern area.[51] These chapters—named Garnet, Galloway, Lincoln, Brown, and Clinton after important figures in the movement—included most if not all of New Bern's leading black artisans, among them the young carpenter Israel B. Abbott, who began his political career as head of the Abraham Lincoln Equal Rights League.[52]

By the end of 1864, Abraham Galloway, Israel B. Abbott, James Walker Hood, and their fellow league members had organized a grand public celebration for Emancipation Day, 1865. With the war still raging, such events occurred only in Union-liberated parts of the South. As the editor of the Unionist *North Carolina Times* of New Bern explained, for freedpeople this day had already "assumed the sanctity of the 4th of July," with Lincoln "revered in their hearts as their Washington." The event of 1865 (held on January 2 because January 1 fell on a Sunday that year) took on added excitement amid reports that promised Union victory. As Hood related, the five local Equal Rights Leagues "got up a kind of competition, each endeavoring to make the best appearance on that day" to demonstrate their strength and their hopes. Crowds began arriving in New Bern on the last days of 1864, including people from Beaufort who came by special train from Morehead City in preparation for a new day and a new year.[53]

The celebration demonstrated to all who beheld it that while the war was not yet over, a new era had indeed begun. In a spirit shared by celebrants at events taking place elsewhere in Union-occupied territory, a joyful throng cheered speeches and a flag presentation at the Union encampment at Fort Totten, then joined a parade to New Bern's Academy Green made up of ranks upon ranks of marching bands, choirs, members of the five Equal Rights leagues, the black troops of the North Carolina Heavy Artillery, and hundreds of black schoolchildren, marching school by school. Schoolteacher James O'Hara read the Emancipation Proclamation; Abraham Galloway gave another address that dealt "without kid gloves" with "Copperheads and all other kinds of reptiles"; and AME Zion bishop J. J. Clinton served as the "orator of the day." As darkness fell, the participants moved to Andrews Chapel to continue the festivities.[54]

Commending the Equal Rights Leagues for pursuing the "elevation of the race," New Bern's Unionist *North Carolina Times* editor commented, the day after the celebration, "In this transition from a state of abject degradation, to a totally new sphere, these Anglo Africans have shown a praiseworthy spirit and determination to help themselves. They have entered into the work with a vim." Some had rented land and raised crops, while others had "entered into various branches of industry." Aware that "their children were destined to move in a different path from the rugged one which they had so long traveled in," they pursued the course of education and knowledge.[55]

In the days and weeks after their Emancipation Day celebration, New Bernians anticipated the coming Union victory. New Bern and Beaufort served as bases for Federal warships on their way to bombard Fort Fisher, the massive earthworks that protected Wilmington as the South's last open port. The fort fell on January 15, 1865, and black and white Union troops soon entered Wilmington to be welcomed by thousands of rejoicing freedpeople. On February 16 and 17, New Bernians gathered at Andrews Chapel to celebrate congressional passage of the Thirteenth Amendment to the United States Constitution abolishing slavery. The event brought still more black artisans into public leadership roles. New freedman and carpenter Richard Tucker, a leader at Andrews Chapel, presided over meetings at which Galloway and Hood gave rousing speeches and Joseph Green offered the prayers, while the formerly enslaved brickmason Thomas Battle joined the committee to prepare resolutions. Commending Congress for its action, the resolutions pledged the New Bernians' undying support for Union

Emancipation Celebration in Charleston

A different emancipation celebration took place in Charleston, South Carolina, upon its liberation by Union troops. As reported in detail in the *New York Times*, on March 21, 1865, white Union officers organized newly liberated Charlestonians into a freedom parade whose themes reflected the artisanal republican traditions commonly enacted in northern cities: black artisans marched trade by trade with their tools and implements, and white-garbed black women rode in a "Car of Liberty" to celebrate their freedom in northern white terms. Black Tar Heels, however, typically planned their Emancipation Day parades to reflect themes Equal Rights League leaders invoked in their celebration in New Bern on Emancipation Day 1865, highlighting their achievements and stressing their hopes for education, military prowess, civic life, and the fight for equal rights.

New York Times, April 4, 1865; Clark, *Defining Moments*, 34–35.

victory and pointed to "streaks of light" on the horizon as portents of "the rising sun of that auspicious day in which this country shall in very truth be called the land of the free and the home of the brave."[56] These observations, like the positive words of the New Bern newspaper writer, expressed the high hopes and intentions of the growing black leadership. They would learn all too soon that as they strove to realize their hopes, they would face a new series of challenges.

Presidential Reconstruction, 1865–1866

With the war effectively over in April 1865, white and black New Bernians who had left town in 1862 began returning home to a city transformed by three years of liberation. They and those who had stayed to create new roles for themselves during the war began the struggle to remake their lives. Returning whites set about reclaiming and repairing their homes and churches. Newcomers of both races arrived in search of work and educational opportunities. Union troops still in town were soon joined by officials of the Freedmen's Bureau, which had established one of its four principal North Carolina offices in New Bern. A struggle ensued over the issue of freedmen's "place" in the new order—the tension between whites' insistence on blacks' "knowing their place" and blacks' long-deferred dream of occupying their proper place in the new American Republic.

As they asserted their new liberty and sought full citizenship, freedpeople faced bitter and sometimes violent resistance from whites alarmed by the erosion of the old racial rules and their exclusive hold on power. Even though the remaining troops and bureau officials provided some protection to blacks, whites in New Bern, as elsewhere, moved to reestablish their authority and to stifle black hopes for change. Whatever leniency whites might have shown to some blacks when the laws and customs of slavery enforced traditional hierarchies, after emancipation the old rules and paternalistic protections faded. Blacks asserting their rights often defied whites' expectations of deference. In one arena after another blacks and whites contested the outlines of a new dynamic.[57]

New Bern's black artisan-leaders were well equipped to face the new challenges. In addition to organizing the Equal Rights Leagues, even before the war ended the city's black artisans and others formed other voluntary groups that signaled their full participation in a "new epoch." To complement the white fire companies, which played an important civic leadership role as well as aiding public safety, by January 1865 black community leaders had established black volunteer fire companies, with a total membership of 150 men. Barber John R. Good and bricklayer Edward A. Richardson were officers of the Harland Company No. 1, and painter John Randolph Jr. was foreman of the Kimball Company.[58]

Renewing their pursuit of equal rights as soon as the war ended, in early May 1865—just weeks after General Robert E. Lee's surrender to Ulysses S. Grant on April 9 and Abraham Lincoln's death on April 15—black New Bernians sent a "Petition of the Colored Men of North Carolina" to the newly inaugurated President Andrew Johnson, a native of the state. The petition, datelined New Bern, May 10, was published in the *New York Herald* on May 19 and in other New York, Cincinnati, and Raleigh papers. The "undersigned, your petitioners, the colored men of the State of North Carolina," called upon the memory of their "murdered friend and father Lincoln" and cited their devotion to the Union and their military service in its cause. As free men, they sought to "show our countrymen that we can and will fit ourselves for the creditable discharge of the duties of citizenship." In short, "we want the privilege of voting." They appealed to Johnson's personal history: "As you were once a citizen of North Carolina, we need not remind you that up to the year 1835 free colored men voted in this State, and never, as we have heard, with any detriment to its interests." They urged him to "order the enrolment of all loyal men, without regard to color," in advance of elections in states returning to the Union.[59]

Although no signers' names appeared in the newspapers, similarities between this document and the petition that Abraham Galloway and his colleagues presented to President Lincoln the year before suggest the involvement of some of the same men. They were probably encouraged by—and may have encouraged—suffrage advocate and Supreme Court Justice Salmon P. Chase, who visited New Bern in early May during a tour of the South on Johnson's behalf. Immediately after meeting with citizens in New Bern and Beaufort, Chase wrote to Johnson on May 7 to encourage "the Extension of suffrage to loyal blacks." In language akin to that of the May 10 petition, he asserted his belief that the people would accept "an order for the enrollment of all loyal citizens without regard to complexion."[60]

Such an order, however, did not come about. Whatever hopes New Bern black leaders might have had in the first weeks after the end of the war, by the time their appeal was published in the *Anglo-African* on July 3, 1865, national as well as local white resistance to black suffrage had solidified. On May 29, the same day he issued an amnesty proclamation for former Confederates, President Johnson announced his reconstruction policy for North Carolina, which authorized the state to determine its own voting requirements. Thereafter, he left black suffrage issues to the states.[61]

The summer of 1865 opened a new political season, as New Bern's black artisan-leaders addressed the changing national and state realities. Although uncertainty and turmoil reigned in much of the state, Abraham Galloway and his fellow leaders in New Bern had a clear sense of their goals. Despite the fact that many whites regarded their campaign for equal rights as revolutionary and destructive, some calling Galloway "an exceedingly radical and Jacobinical spirit," for New Bern's black artisan-leaders their aim was deeply and specifically patriotic.[62] Having already made appeals to presidents Lincoln and Johnson in which they invoked the founding ideals of the American Republic and free blacks' record of voting in their state, these leaders and their allies plotted no revolution but sought peaceably to fulfill their duties, rights, and hopes as free citizens of their community and their nation.[63]

An important addition to the local black leadership was George A. Rue, the native New Bernian, joiner, and AME minister in the North, who returned home that summer. Frustrated in his effort to reach New Bern in 1862, in May 1865 he was transferred from the New England AME Conference to the new South Carolina Conference, which assigned him to New Bern. After bidding farewell to his friends in Boston, who sent him forth with a life-sized portrait of himself and a gold-lined silver cup, Rue achieved his long deferred hopes when he reached New Bern in July. He renewed relationships with his brethren and sisters at Andrews Chapel and formed a friendship with its minister, James Walker Hood. By the end of the month Rue had "already received a church and three hundred members" for AME, including a number of former Baptists.[64]

Within days of his return, Rue waded into the political fray. During his years in the North, as we have seen, he had met national abolitionist leaders, including Frederick Douglass, whose thoughts on freedom and citizenship doubtless informed his views. Like Galloway, too, Rue had become a well-known and outspoken advocate of freedpeople's rights. Whether the two had met previously or not, they surely recognized in each other kindred spirits.

Rue, along with his allies, was expert in calibrating his expression of his views to the situation at hand. Writing to the *Christian Recorder* in August on "how matters and things are going on in and around New Bern," he railed, "The returned rebels, (if devils, if you please), who are put in office as police, vent their spite upon the defenseless blacks, and often on the colored soldiers. But when they touch one of these boys, (I mean men,) it is pound for pound, drop for drop, death for death. The great question with us is: Shall traitors to our country hold the balance of power again? I give you the unequivocating answer, No! They shall die so dead, so dead, so dead: well that is enough said." Striking a calmer note, Rue added, "We are going to have a convention in Raleigh, the Lord willing, on the 29th of September, when the colored people may see eye to eye on the suffrage questions. We must be heard, and we shall be heard." He described a meeting "held in Andrews's chapel a few nights ago, to confer with each other on this vital point." Like many other black leaders, he expressed high hopes grounded in his faith in the divine plan for freedom: "Our enemies are strong, but our friends are stronger; having God on our side, we will go forward. Truth is mighty, and it will prevail!"[65]

As Rue's letter reflected, during that first postwar summer a vibrant and public freedpeople's political movement emerged in New Bern that soon extended across the state. By all accounts, Abraham Galloway was the "leading spirit." Other leaders included such longtime New Bernians as artisans Amos York and Joseph Green and barbers John R. Good and Clinton D. Pierson, and wartime arrivals John Randolph Jr., George W. Price Jr., and minister James Walker Hood.[66] All but Hood were native North Carolinians. With their leadership abilities honed by wartime experiences and having already begun the work for equal suffrage, with Galloway's encouragement they placed themselves in the vanguard of the state's black political leadership.

NEW BERNIANS AND THE NORTH CAROLINA FREEDMEN'S CONVENTION

Aware of recent freedmen's rallies in Virginia, Tennessee, and elsewhere, the New Bern leaders called a mass meeting on August 28 at Andrews Chapel to select delegates for a North Carolina Freedmen's Convention planned for the fall. Abraham Galloway brought the gathering to order, John R. Good presided, and Amos York and George W. Price Jr. served as secretaries. Explaining the purpose of the meeting, Good stated that it behooved North Carolinians to "be up with the colored people of other States, in this matter." He noted that because "the white people of this State and of the other Southern States are about to hold conventions for the purpose of reconstruction," it was "necessary that the colored people should take such steps as may influence these conventions and promote our good." After an oration by Galloway that "took the suffrage bull by the horns," the meeting agreed that the Freedmen's Convention must address suffrage along with education as essential to maintaining freedom.[67]

Overcoming concerns that Raleigh might not be a safe meeting site, those who gathered in New Bern decided that the symbolic value of meeting in the state capital outweighed the risks. The men they elected to represent New Bern as delegates—Galloway, Randolph, Good, and Rue (two artisans, a barber, and an artisan-minister)— embodied the political talent that had coalesced in the city. The meeting also appointed Galloway, Randolph, and Price to draft a circular to invite delegates from throughout the state. A soldier from Massachusetts volunteered to print 1,500 copies of the circular, and soon the three artisans' names appeared on flyers proclaiming "Freedmen of North Carolina, Arouse!" across the state. The *New Bern Daily Times*, which carried the notice "only to satisfy curiosity," warned that if the convention meant to seek "political equality," the effort would be in vain, while the *Wilmington Herald* blamed "fanatical agitators" from the North

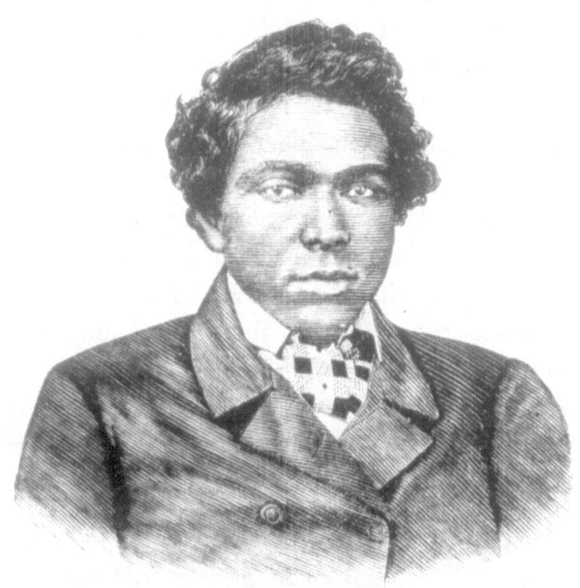

Abraham H. Galloway. From William Still, The Underground Railroad: A Record of Facts, Authentic Narratives, Letters, etc., Narrating the Hardships, Hair-Breadth Escapes, and Death Struggles of the Slaves in their Efforts for Freedom *(Philadelphia: Porter & Coates, 1872).*

for putting "wild notions" in the minds of the freedmen. George A. Rue responded in the *Herald*, "We are neither crazy, nor all so ignorant as [the editor] might think," and explained: "In our meetings we are asking for our rights, earnestly and respectfully, and shall continue asking until our demands are granted."[68]

Although the "leading spirit" was Galloway, it was also the unique and eloquent combination of Galloway, Randolph, and Rue—along with other, quieter men, such as barber John R. Good—whose work generated the August meetings and led to the convention. Others soon joined the New Bern delegation, including artisans Edward A. Richardson, Amos York, and George W. Price Jr. and minister Hood. The freedmen of the James City settlement across the Trent River from New Bern chose carpenter and minister Joseph Green to represent them, even though he resided in New Bern. In a thinly veiled threat, the *New Bern Times* warned on September 28 that James City residents should desist from sending delegates and put their physical welfare before politics: "The cool winds will whistle about [their] ears soon; and the icy breath of winter will demand more fuel and raiment.

Would it not be wisdom, then, to drop for a season the aspirations for political privileges." Green proceeded to represent James City nonetheless.[69]

In Raleigh on September 29 the New Bernians joined the gathering of 120 men of color, including many fellow artisans who journeyed from across the state to gather at the African Methodist church. Located on Edenton Street a few blocks northwest of the State Capitol, the church was also known as the Lincoln Church for a plaster bust of Abraham Lincoln attached to the wall above the pulpit along with the passage from his last inaugural address that began, "With malice toward none, with charity toward all, with firmness in the right."[70]

All observers acknowledged the pivotal role of New Bern leaders in scheduling the convention for this time and place. One "E. S.," who reported on the convention to the *Christian Recorder*, commented,

> The Eastern Counties, which have longest enjoyed freedom and the protection of the army, are evidently ahead of their less favored brethren in the central and western portion of the State, who have more recently emerged from slavery, though they are not superior to them in intelligence and in the proper appreciation of 'the situation,' and the best means to be adopted for their mutual elevation. The call for the convention originated at Newbern, and the people hereabout were scarcely consulted upon the subject. Here they deemed it impolitic and unwise to call the convention so near to, and preceding, the constitutional convention of the state, but were overruled. They are more cautious and moderate in their demands, while the delegates from below seem disposed to demand every thing in the way of civil rights.

Northern journalist John Dennett concurred: "The first steps in this matter were taken by Negroes in Newbern, and it seems to have been generally thought by the people of the central and western counties, by such of them as took any thought at all about it, that the call was issued prematurely. They would have deferred it until after the adjournment of the State Convention" so as not to "provoke resentment" from those attending that convention or to suggest "an attitude of complaint, when as yet they had suffered no injustice by state action." But the New Bernians insisted that freedpeople were "surely suffering enough" and that they should make their claims before North Carolina regained full statehood.[71]

The New Bern delegation dominated the opening events on Friday, September 29, 1865. Abraham Galloway called the meeting to order, and the officers initially selected included several New Bernians: barber John R. Good as chairman pro tem and artisans Randolph as secretary pro tem, Price as assistant secretary pro tem, and Rue as chaplain. New Bern artisans Amos York and Edward A. Richardson served on the committee on credentials. After complaints arose about giving "undue influence on the committees to Craven and other lower counties," by the end of the first day, although Hood was elected convention president, the meeting selected officers who represented other counties, with Randolph as secretary the only other New Bernian. Several delegates, among them upholsterer James H. Harris and house carpenter Stewart Ellison of Raleigh and carpenter John T. Schenck of Charlotte, like the New Bern men, took leading roles in local and state politics for years to come.[72] The format of the convention epitomized the popular combination of religious expression and a political agenda, with George A. Rue inspiring the gathering with his robust and widely admired singing of hymns and the "soul-stirring speeches for which he [was] so famous." He and other speakers at this and other freedmen's conventions across the South trumpeted a redemptive version of American history that linked the foundation of the Republic and black soldiers' role in saving the Union with equal rights for freedmen.[73]

The evolution of the North Carolina convention's position on equal rights demonstrated its leaders' sense of strategic necessities. During the first day, reiterating the goals of the mass meetings preceding the convention, Hood spoke out for equal rights under the law, including the rights to testify in court, to serve on juries, and to vote. That evening Isham Sweatt, a barber from Cumberland County; Harris, of Wake; and Galloway, of Craven likewise spoke for equal rights and a "moderate conservative course in demanding them." On the second day, the convention directed a committee consisting of James Harris of Raleigh as chair plus Isham Sweatt and New Bernians Good, Randolph, and Rue to prepare an address to the state Constitutional Convention to express "the wishes of this convention on the subject of equal rights." The evening speakers were J. P. Sampson, a member of a wealthy free black Wilmington family, late of Ohio, who was most outspoken in demanding equal rights, and Rue, who "while he earnestly demanded justice for the colored man . . . advised moderation."[74]

On the third day, matters took a different turn. On Monday morning, October 2, after much discussion, the convention voted to table the resolution "defending negro suffrage and equal rights before the law." The record is silent about what took place in the interim, which included a day's break on Sunday with an extended opportunity for private conversations. Significantly, by Sunday, the white delegates for the Constitutional Convention had arrived in Raleigh, and their presence may have encouraged the leading freedmen to reassess the situation. One observer recorded that day, "Out of the whole number elected from the 85 counties, only two are said to have obtained their seats with the knowledge of their constituents that they would favor the admission of negro testimony in courts of justice. No candidate dared to come before the people as the advocate of equal rights, or the right of suffrage for the negro." Some northern journalists credited the shift in perspective to a change in leadership, but in fact most of the same leaders persisted, including Galloway and Harris—one a radical, the latter more cautious—and Rue and Randolph, who were "radical in desire, but conservative in action." The shift in strategy probably reflected the leaders' reading of the political situation and their well-honed ability to tailor their communications with whites to suit the circumstances and thereby to navigate territory dominated by whites. However forcefully they might advocate equal rights in their own meetings and writings, they judged that any effective appeal to the Constitutional Convention required a different approach.

That afternoon, the committee appointed to draft the address—Harris, Good, Randolph, Rue, and Sweatt; two artisans, two barbers, and an artisan-minister—brought forward a document that made no mention of equal suffrage or other legal rights: "Everything that [they] thought could justly offend any class of their fellow-citizens at the South or North was carefully rejected," commented a northern journalist, and the address "breathe[d] nothing but moderation and conciliation." Even the white newspapers in Raleigh and New Bern commended the document for its restraint.[75]

The convention's resolutions, like much rhetoric of the day, universalized the traditional virtues of artisan identity as the grounding for black citizenship and equal rights: "[We] will prove by our habits of industry and respectability, that we are worthy of citizenship among the people of North Carolina." In contrast to the earlier speeches and the hopes of many of its members, the address "most respectfully and humbly" focused on freedpeople's need for protection and fair treatment and their aims for education and self-improvement. Of their rights, the document said only, "We most earnestly desire to have the disabilities under which we formerly labored removed, and to have all the oppressive laws which make unjust discrimination on account of race or color wiped from the statutes of the State. We invoke your protection for the sanctity of our family relations. Is this asking too much?" Having heard repeated white claims to the state and nation as a "white man's country" as well as schemes to colonize freedpeople in the west or other distant locales, the writers concluded: "Though associated with many memories of suffering as well as of enjoyment, we have always loved our homes, and dreaded . . . a forcible separation from them. Now that freedom and a new career are before us, we love this land and people more than ever before. Here we have toiled and suffered; our parents, wives, and children are buried here; and in this land we will remain unless forcibly driven away." The convention selected committee members Rue and Harris along with Abraham Galloway to present the document to the white convention.[76]

On the fourth and last day of their meeting, the Freedmen's Convention turned to the goals their address had skirted. On October 3, 1865, the gathering "resolv[ed] itself into a State Equal Rights League" and adopted a constitution. Stating that they were "emulating the efforts of the friends of Equal Rights in New Berne," and feeling "the stern necessity of encouraging a well ordered and dignified life," the state league set out to "secure, by political and moral means . . . the repeal of all laws and parts of laws, State and National, that make distinctions on account of color." As the convention drew to its close, by request George A. Rue sang the joyful hymn "Sound the Loud Timbrel," which for him surely recalled the thrilling night in Boston when he celebrated the Emancipation Proclamation with Frederick Douglass. In the African Church in Raleigh, the freedpeople joined in the chorus, "Sound the loud timbrel o'er Egypt's dark sea! Jehovah has triumphed: his people are free!"

A few days after the Freedmen's Convention, the state Constitutional Convention, called to meet the requirements of Presidential Reconstruction to void secession and prohibit slavery, took up the freedmen's address. Governor William Holden presented the document, and the clerk read it aloud. "Two or three members of the colored convention"—perhaps Galloway, Rue, and Harris, who had delivered it—"were in the gallery watching the fates of their address, and many significant glances were sent in that direction from the body of the house, one delegate calling the attention of another to the presence of the Negroes." After receiving the freedmen's

Carolinians in Cleveland

One last item appeared in the published proceedings of the Freedmen's Convention: a letter of September 20, 1865, from "The North Carolinians in the City of Cleaveland, Ohio, to the North Carolinians in Convention Assembled in Raleigh." Thirty-two men of color, identified by their occupations and hometowns in North Carolina, conveyed their greetings: "Brethren: We, the undersigned, former residents of the State of North Carolina, now residents of the city of Cleveland, Ohio, take this method of assuring you [of] our deep interest in your Convention about to assemble, and the great issues of enfranchisement and elevation in which you are engaged." The expatriates, twenty of whom were artisans, wrote, "May you finally triumph in establishing in your State the great idea that all 'governments derived their just powers from the consent of the governed.'" The signers included ten former New Bernians: R. G. Hoyle, Blacksmith; F. W. Morris, Mer[chant] Tailor; R. M. Green, Carpenter; B. S. Green, Pr. F. A. S., Book agent; S. H. Weaver, Tr., Plasterer; Jno P. Green, Sec., Clerk; W. H. Morris, Tinsmith; J. R. Warren, Carpenter; J. W. Stanly, Carpenter; C. M. Richardson, Plasterer (Goldsboro).

F. W. (Freeman) Morris, freed by his white father as a youth, had become a successful merchant tailor. Carpenter R. M. Green was Rigdon Green, emancipated by his brother, James York Green; and B. S. Green was Rigdon's son Benjamin. Carpenter J. W. Stanly was the grandson of John C. Stanly and son of John Stewart Stanly. John P. Green, son of the emancipated tailor John R. Green and grandson of white legislator John Stanly, had gone to Cleveland as a boy with his mother. Plasterer C. M. Richardson was the Cicero M. Richardson who had left New Bern as a boy to apprentice with Jacob Harris in Fayetteville. Among the other signers were Richardson's brothers-in-law Cicero Richardson Harris, identified as a bootmaker from Fayetteville, who later became a bishop in the AME Zion denomination, and his brother Robert Harris, a teacher from Fayetteville, who returned home to help found the school that became Fayetteville State University. Although far from home, the expatriates maintained contact with one another in their adopted city, and they shared a deep connection with their home state and old friends that lasted through the war and reached across the miles.

Convention of the Freedmen of North Carolina, Official Proceedings, 22–23.

address “respectfully,” the convention referred it to a committee for consideration. The committee recommended taking no action on the freedmen’s address, but its report left no doubt of its members’ views. Repudiating “any theoretical scheme of social and political equality” and insisting on whites’ rightful position as dispensers of all privileges, the report employed typical language of barely veiled threats to assert that the “improvement and welfare” of freedpeople depended on their traditional ties with whites rather than any “assertion of impracticable claims for social and political rights.” The committee warned against “the premature introduction of any schemes that may disturb the operations of these kindly feelings, or inflame the inherent social prejudice that exists against the colored race” and recommended deferring all matters concerning the freedmen to the new state legislature that had been elected along with governor Jonathan Worth, who replaced provisional governor William W. Holden. The legislature that convened in November postponed consideration of all such issues to the following year.[77] The Freedmen’s Convention leaders, for their part, published the proceedings of their convention, thus making a public and lasting record of both their conciliatory address to the white convention and the broader statements of their hopes and goals they had expressed during their meeting.[78]

COMMUNITY BUILDING

Back in New Bern, the convention delegates returned to their trades and civic endeavors as they and their fellow leaders worked to build up their community institutions and to regroup politically. In contrast to the dire poverty besetting many freedpeople in the state during the closing months of 1865, the economic situation for artisans and other New Bernians looked bright. Traveling across the South that winter, black Union chaplain John H. Scott of Oberlin (to whom John P. Green had been apprenticed briefly) found that in New Bern “the colored people [were] doing very well indeed. I found some ten or fifteen occupying stores, and buying and selling just as their old masters used to do. . . . I have been told that some of them have cleared over $400, and these same people were but a few years ago slaves. These are the people that our enemies say cannot take care of themselves!”[79] New Bern artisans and other black leaders promptly formed working relationships with the agents of the Freedmen’s Bureau, established in the city at war’s end, which was active on many fronts despite white opposition. In November 1865, bureau administrator Oliver Howard and his wife reported that they were teaching some 200 students at Andrews Chapel and another bureau school—probably at Rue's Chapel—which were the only "free colored schools" in town.[80]

Building on earlier accomplishments, New Bern leaders strengthened their existing church congregations and formed new ones. Black Baptists organized St. John's Missionary Baptist Church and First Baptist Church in the 1860s. From at least 1864 black Episcopalians, including brickmason Israel Harris and his family, had been worshipping at St. Cyprian's Church in the former Baptist meetinghouse; in 1866 all the black members of Christ Church transferred to St. Cyprian's, which appears to have been the first separate black Episcopal congregation in the state. Andrews Chapel AME Zion continued as the largest congregation in town, and a second AME Zion church, Clinton Chapel, founded late in 1864 and dedicated by the bishop for whom it was named, was likewise thriving. In December 1865 the second state conference of Zion met in Beaufort, where Andrews Chapel artisans Amos York and Joseph Green were ordained as elders who could serve as pastors. "From this Conference," recalled Hood, "men were sent all over N.C., from the seashore to the mountain top," to establish and serve new congregations.[81]

George A. Rue's young AME church (later known as Rue's Chapel) was also flourishing with the help of Rue's friend, the freedman, cooper, and churchman George B. Willis. According to the church history, Willis "arrived home from Dixie" about the same time Rue returned from the North in the summer of 1865, suggesting that he was one of the New Bern slaves whose owners took or sent them behind Confederate lines in advance of Union occupation. Early on, Willis demonstrated the strategic thinking that informed his effectiveness as a community leader. For a time Rue's new congregation worshipped in temporary quarters, but Willis soon devised a means to get a church built with the help of the Freedmen's Bureau. According to church history, he bought a lot and negotiated an agreement with the bureau, "whose business it was to build schoolhouses," to construct a building there. As part of the bargain, he "contracted with [bureau head] General Howard to use the church so many years as a school house, then afterwards to turn the property over to the [church] trustees, which was done." Willis purchased the lot in mid-1866 and a few years later deeded the property to the congregation, thus enabling the group to possess its own church and the autonomy that went with it. The congregation also erected a Sunday school building, a project that called upon Rue's skills as a mechanic and joiner: "The members of the church being unable to pay a Carpenter, Elder George A. Rue and J. P. Jones undertook the job."[82]

The two African Methodist ministers and their flocks enjoyed a harmonious relationship, which in turn strengthened the local black community. Despite tensions between the two groups nationally, Rue and Hood both hoped for union between them and cultivated "pulpit union" in New Bern. When black Union chaplain (later AME bishop) Henry M. Turner, likewise an advocate for national union, visited New Bern in 1865, he went to Hood's home, and Hood "searched up Rev. Brother Rue, and both together gave me a cordial welcome to their city."[83]

New Bern's artisan-leaders, along with ministers Rue and Hood, also played a central role in an important and controversial achievement late in 1865—the formation of the first black Masonic lodge in the state. This advance toward community building and uplift, initiated by some of the city's best educated and most respected men of color, evoked a response from whites that showed all too vividly the resistance blacks faced in assuming new roles as free men. On November 27, the *New Bern Daily Times* carried a story, headlined "Negro Masonry," from a recent issue of the *Anglo-African*: "Past Most-Worshipful Paul Drayton, of the National Grand Lodge, is about to resume his labors in the South, under the authority of the Most-Worshipful Grand Lodge of the State of New York. He will leave this city [New York] in a few days to dedicate and constitute 'Union Lodge' in the city of Charleston, S.C., and a King Solomon Lodge in the town of New Bern, N.C., and is also vested with full power to organize Lodges throughout the southern portion of this country."

The newspaper's white editor explained, "There is in this city, an organization called King Solomon's Lodge No. 1 of A. F. M., composed entirely and exclusively of negroes. It was established here some weeks ago."[84] Ignoring—or perhaps unaware of—local memory of the black house carpenter William H. Hancock's antebellum position as tyler in St. John's Lodge, the writer fulminated against the "gross insult" of conferring "the rites and benefits of this ancient and honorable order" upon "creatures who have just emerged from a state of bondage." He demanded that North Carolina's Grand Lodge take a stand against formation of the black lodge. As a result, leaders of the state lodge registered a complaint with the white Grand Lodge of New York, and a heated exchange ensued before the white Carolinians realized that, contrary to the report, the New York Grand Lodge had played no role in establishing the New Bern lodge. In fact, Paul Drayton was grand master

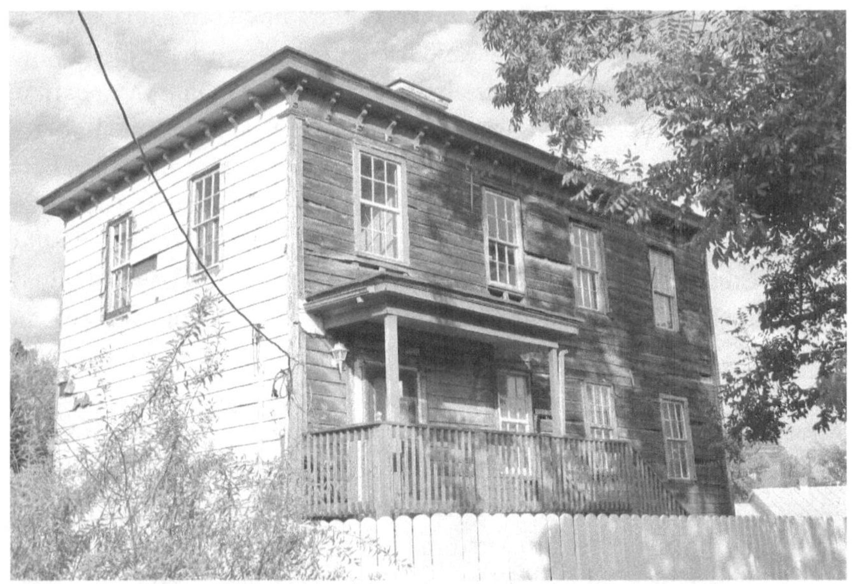

King Solomon Lodge. Photograph 2012 by Penne S. Sandbeck, New Bern, North Carolina.

of the National Compact Grand Lodge, a black organization, and James W. Hood, a devoted Mason instrumental in forming King Solomon Lodge, was associated with the black Prince Hall Lodge of New York.[85]

Despite the swirling controversy, New Bern's black Masons proceeded undeterred. Contrary to the newspaper's characterization of them as unworthy "creatures," founding members of the lodge included such accomplished and educated men as George A. Rue, John Randolph Jr., and James Hood—all recently returned from the Freedmen's Convention in Raleigh—as well as coopers Edward R. Dudley, George B. Willis, and Henry H. Simmons.[86] These artisan-leaders, like Hood, had been or would soon become prominent in public life. In the Masonic incident, as at the Freedmen's Convention, they learned all too soon that whatever benefits the war and emancipation had brought or promised for black citizens, a rising tide of white opposition countered their efforts to claim full participation in community life. They saw all the more clearly the importance of establishing Masonic lodges and other voluntary associations to complement their church homes as they addressed the new challenges of life as free people.

In 1866, as Presidential Reconstruction continued, conditions for freedmen worsened in North Carolina as throughout the South. Like other southern legislative bodies, the North Carolina legislature enacted "Negro codes" limiting freedmen essentially to the status of antebellum free blacks and affirming that only white men could vote or hold public office. As national tensions mounted over the status of freedmen, in June 1866 Congress passed the Fourteenth Amendment to the Constitution, which included clauses disqualifying certain Confederate leaders from voting and providing equal protection for all citizens without distinctions for race or color. Congress also required that each state formerly in rebellion ratify the amendment in order to be readmitted to the union. North Carolina legislators had no intention of doing so.[87]

Attuned to the developments on the state and national fronts, New Bern's black artisan-leaders intensified their campaign for their rights. When President Johnson's administration tried to discredit New Bern's Freedmen's Bureau, local leaders rose to the bureau's defense. At a public meeting in May 1866 they insisted that the bureau was essential to the protection of freedmen until such time as their rights—including the vote—were guaranteed by law. The following August, after the bureau reassigned the local bureau superintendent Col. W. W. Wiegel to Maryland, these same leaders called a mass meeting at Andrews Chapel in support of his faithful service. Joining such stalwarts as Amos York, James W. Hood, and George W. Price Jr. on the podium were two freedmen newly prominent in civic affairs: cooper Edward R. Dudley, who had returned home after spending the war with his owners at Salisbury, and shoemaker Edward Havens, formerly of Washington, North Carolina. The gathering reaffirmed the importance of the Freedmen's Bureau to freedpeople's safety and welfare until such time as they possessed the equal rights essential to their own protection.[88]

A month later, New Bernians convened again at Andrews Chapel, this time to select delegates for the second Freedmen's Convention in Raleigh, to be held in October. Those present at the gathering selected three veterans of the 1865 convention—minister and mechanic George A. Rue, barber John R. Good, and painter John Randolph Jr.—plus barber Clinton D. Pierson and carpenter-undertaker Richard Tucker. The artisan-dominated New Bern delegation again took a prominent role. At the convention, additional organizations were established, and in fact sometimes the convention itself was referred to as the "State Equal Rights League Convention of Freedmen." When the group selected officers for the State League, they included New Bernians Randolph (who for unknown reasons had not attended the convention) as corresponding secretary and John R. Good as a vice-president.[89] At the same event, the North Carolina Educational As-

Address of the Freedmen's Convention to the White and Colored Citizens of North Carolina, 1866.

FELLOW-CITIZENS:—We, the colored People of North-Carolina, in Convention assembled at Raleigh, on the 2nd, 3d, 4th and 5th days of Oct. 1866, viewing the complex condition of affairs and of public sentiment in our State, deem it our duty to present to you our grievances, our sufferings and the outrages heaped upon us, because of our helpless and disqualified position for self-defence, resulting, as we think we can prove, from no greater cause than our long and unjust political disfranchisement.

We ask you, in the spirit of meekness, is taxation without representation just? History and conscience answer no! We do not come to you in a spirit of reproach or denunciation, neither do we feel in pleading for equal rights without regard to complexional differences, that we are in the least degree selfish. Nor do we in any respect seek to lower the standard of refinement, intelligence or honor among the great and loyal people of the commonwealth of North-Carolina, by urging these questions upon your consideration at this time. We would view if possible the brightest side of the picture, which we have to present, and give to our beloved State all the honor and credit deserved for the rapid strides which this great Nation has been taking in the direction of universal emancipation and equality before the law.

You will acquiesce when we say that we can boast a little of our loyalty to the general government, in the bloody struggle through which we have just passed. Our fathers fought shoulder to shoulder with the white man in the Revolutionary war, and in the war of 1812. They did

sociation held its organizational meeting, selected George A. Rue as vice-president, and appointed carpenter Richard Tucker and brickmason Edward A. Richardson to represent Craven County on the association's board of managers.[90]

The 1866 Freedmen's Convention, unlike its predecessor, confronted political issues head-on. Although Abraham Galloway did not attend—nor did any other delegates from Wilmington—the gathering included several their duty and did it well. In the one just ended, our fathers, brothers and sons bared their breasts to the fiery storm to save the Union.

FELLOW-CITIZENS: You have taught us one good thing, which we cannot forget. It is this: "That all men are born free and equal, and that they are endowed by their Creator with inalienable rights. That among these are life, liberty and the pursuit of happiness. That to secure these rights, governments are instituted among men, deriving their just powers from the consent of the governed," &c.

FELLOW-CITIZENS: Can we look to you for protection or not, to shield us from the murderous hand? Oh, humanity, where is thy blush? Our defenceless wives and children, fathers, sons and brothers are beaten with clubs, robbed, shot and killed, in various localities, and the authorities regard it not. We beg you as white men in authority to shield our defenceless heads, and guard our little homes. We appeal to your religion and humanity. We claim by merit the right of suffrage, and ask it at your hands. We believe the day has come, when black men have rights which white men are bound to respect. We intend to live and die on the soil which gave us birth. Oh, North-Carolina, the land of our birth, with all thy faults we love thee still. Will you, oh! will you treat us as human beings, with all our rights? It is all we ask.

Your humble servants, in behalf of the State's Equal Rights League, George A. Rue, Chairman, and J. T. Schenck, H. Locket, and J. A. Sykes.

Minutes of the Freedmen's Convention . . . 1866.

men whose perspectives had changed over the intervening year. They had experienced whites' abuses of blacks, the imposition of the "black code," and the legislature's rejection of black suffrage. Despite the usual warnings from whites that blacks should avoid politics, convention president James H. Harris of Raleigh, a moderate the year before, joined Rue and others in calling unequivocally for equal rights, including suffrage.[91]

Cognizant of congressional Republicans' growing frustration with both

President Andrew Johnson and the resistant southern states, the 1866 Freedmen's Convention addressed itself not only to the legislature but also to the people of the state and to Congress. Lauding the Thirty-Ninth Congress's passage of the Freedmen's Bureau bill, the Civil Rights bill, and the Fourteenth Amendment, the convention expressed the hope that "a like spirit of justice and humanity may guide the acts of their 40th session, until legislation shall protect equally the rights of all American people, without regard to race or color, for which we shall ever pray."

George A. Rue chaired the committee appointed to prepare the "Address of the Freedmen's Convention to the White and Colored Citizens of North Carolina." His fellow committee members were carpenters John T. Schenck of Charlotte and Hardy Lockhart (Locket) of Raleigh, and T. A. Sykes (occupation unknown) of Elizabeth City, all of whom participated in postwar political life in their communities. Probably reflecting Rue's influence in its sonorous language, the 1866 address called for "the right of suffrage, in common with other citizens of the United States, in consideration of our loyalty, citizenship and merit." In their full-throated expression of their values and goals for their rightful place in the American republic, Rue and his colleagues invoked the heritage of American history and rights as their own. In a classic expression of the emerging tradition of such freedom documents, they captured the spirit as well as many of the phrases of the Declaration of Independence as they recited their complaints, declared their loyalty to their native state, and cited the record of black soldiers' service in the American Revolution and the Civil War as part of their claim to the full rights of American citizenship. As the convention concluded, once more George A. Rue was asked to lead the group in the hymn he had sung on so many occasions and whose chorus resonated anew: "Jehovah has triumphed, his people are free!"

To no one's surprise, the Conservative state legislature ignored the Freedmen's Convention address as well as refusing to ratify the Fourteenth Amendment. Yet, as Rue and his fellow leaders realized, the changing political situation in Washington offered new hope for freedpeople's campaign for equal rights.[92] Confronted with the southern states' imposition of black codes and former Confederates' return to power, after the new Congress was elected late in 1866, Radical Republicans embarked on a course that challenged the president's policies and would open the door for black political participation in North Carolina and elsewhere. During the last weeks of 1866 and the first months of 1867, New Bernians, along with other black and white southerners, waited and watched to see what course the Fortieth Congress would take when its session began in early March, and what the coming year would bring.

The year thus closed with the prospect of a new day on the political horizon. Before that day dawned, however, George A. Rue died at age forty-six on December 22, 1866. Suffering from the effects of yellow fever, after completing his work for the Freedmen's Convention he returned to his New Bern flock, while keeping abreast of news from Washington. His friend and fellow minister James W. Hood preached his funeral at the church Rue had founded the year before, and in accord with his dying wishes he was buried with Masonic honors, with his brethren from King Solomon Lodge in attendance.[93]

Within a year, Rue's allies and other black men would exercise the right to vote, and before many more months passed, his friends who had led the cause in New Bern would win public office. Some of the boldest wartime leaders moved on to advance black rights elsewhere. Hood moved to Fayetteville, where he assumed the pastorate of the AME Zion church as the next step in his long career as churchman and bishop. Brickmason Abraham Galloway and plasterer George W. Price Jr. had joined Wilmington freedpeople's struggles, and Galloway emerged as a radical leader in state politics. In New Bern, despite the loss of these key figures, seasoned artisan-leaders carried forward the empowering experiences of war and the hard lessons of early Reconstruction as they took their places as citizens of the state and nation.

FIVE

We Can and Will Do More

Artisans and Citizens, 1867–1900

We stand here as men and women, at liberty to go where we please—free to stay with our loved ones, free to work for our children and provide homes which are ours, free to worship God when, where and how we please, free to educate ourselves and our children and elevate our condition thereby higher and higher. . . . And now that we are free, we will show *to the world what we can make ourselves. The day has gone by when it was said of us we had no brain to learn. Ye who a short time ago were in the darkness and ignorance of slavery press on for knowledge—for knowledge is power. . . . Our white friends have been astonished at our progress in these few short years of our freedom, but we can and will do more. . . . Be not more anxious for houses and lands than for learning, but strive to improve in all respects. . . . By the sweat of our brow we earn our bread and lay up little by little . . . to buy homes—*our *homes, my brethren, gained by* our *earnings, applied to our use and not to our masters. . . .*

"Liberty *has triumphed and we will* ever *follow her car. Our love for our native land, these United States of America, shall never be excelled by any other class of people. This whole land is our home as much as of the white race, and we will live and act and* vote *for her prosperity."*

—Virgil A. Crawford, January 1, 1873,
New Bern Daily Times, January 3, 1873

On the tenth anniversary of the Emancipation Proclamation, New Bern cooper, freedman, and city councilman Virgil A. Crawford, like Emancipation Day orators across the South, recalled past years in bondage, affirmed recent progress, and looked forward with hope and determination.[1] His speech reiterated core values of American artisan identity—industry, thrift, and respectability—which had gained broad currency as qualities essential to black Americans' efforts to "elevate" their race. Like many national figures who tied freedmen's rights as citizens to the legacy of the American Revolution, Crawford used the classic republican trope of the "Car of Liberty" to assert their stake in the nation.[2] Highlighting local freedpeople's achievements, the black Elm City Band and Reliance Fire Company led a "cavalcade" of black citizens brought up by horse-drawn carriages conveying officials who, like Crawford, had come out of slavery to become master artisans, property owners, and civic leaders.

New Bern's artisans of color predominated in local economic, political, and social life from emancipation onward, and they did so to an extent unusual in North Carolina cities. Like white artisan republicans of the Northeast, they saw political rights as the key to all else they hoped to achieve. Using their artisan status to advance the interests of their race rather than the particular concerns of their occupational or class group, they, like Crawford, invoked the ideals of the early nation to claim their proper place in what they hoped and believed was a reborn American republic.

THE POSTWAR DECADES brought thrilling opportunities as well as severe trials for black North Carolinians. Poverty plagued many freedpeople, but others employed their skills, connections, and ambitions to make a decent living, establish their own households, and improve their children's opportunities for education and advancement. Some engaged in political life, generally as Republicans. They built up their churches and civic associations, and they worked to find long-lost family members, form stable marriages, and strengthen networks of family, friends, and neighbors. All too ironically, within a short time after they attained the freedom to operate their own businesses and profit from their skills, black artisans found themselves contending with the broad national shift away from handicrafts toward mass production that eroded the economic position of nearly all artisans in the country. Nonetheless, especially in towns, a black middle class emerged, composed mainly of successful artisans and entrepreneurs

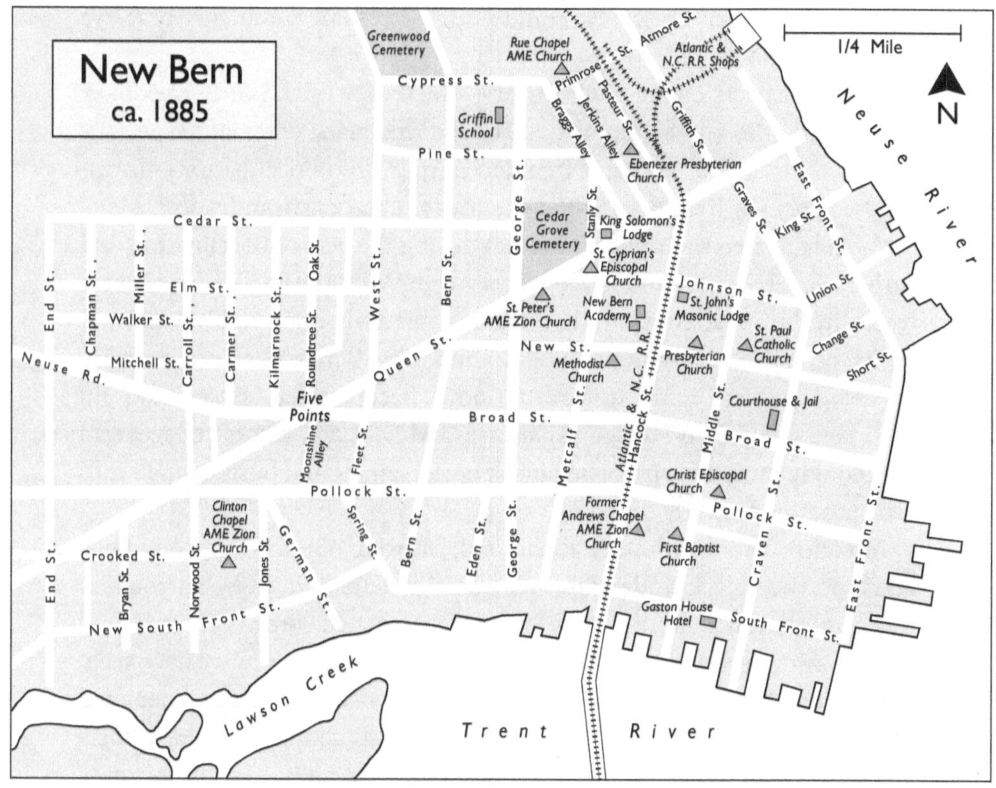

New Bern, ca. 1885. Map by Michael T. Southern

and the growing number of black citizens who entered professions hitherto closed to them.[3]

On Emancipation Day, 1873, black artisans in New Bern occupied an unusually favorable setting. Much would change by the end of the century, but in the early 1870s industrialized mass production had just begun to reorder local craft trades, and artisans like Crawford still profited from their traditional skills and maintained their economic and civic stature. As Crawford tacitly acknowledged, the Democrats' "redemption" of North Carolina from 1870 onward had assailed freedmen's political rights across the state, but New Bern's assertive artisan-leadership and strong black majority sustained the vibrant political life they had inaugurated in the mid-1860s. In 1873 Crawford had reason to believe that, by exerting their right to vote and working to learn and prosper, he and his fellow black citizens could continue to shape their future. He could assert with some confidence that "we can and will do more."

Certain aspects of the city's history—the legacy of the early free black community, the antebellum exodus of the free black elite, and especially the town's role as a mecca of freedom during Union occupation—distinguished postwar New Bern's opportunities for black artisan-leaders. Many of them had tried their political wings during the years of occupation and early Reconstruction, and in New Bern, as in Wilmington and a few other towns in the state, political life remained relatively open to black participants through Reconstruction and beyond. New Bern's black artisan-leaders also faced less competition from other occupational classes than did their counterparts in Raleigh, Charlotte, and Durham, where colleges and burgeoning industries propelled black professionals and businessmen into civic prominence early on.

In contrast to Charleston, Richmond, or even Wilmington, New Bern had a postwar black leadership that was not characterized by antebellum free status, nor was there in New Bern an entrenched elite of color to stand in the way of new leaders.[4] The years of Union occupation, as we have seen, had brought talented and ambitious newcomers of color to a town depleted of its antebellum free black elite. The new arrivals, along with newly liberated New Bernians, had honed their economic and political skills for three years before war's end. Few of the postwar artisan-leaders had the long-standing ties or kinship with the white aristocracy that characterized the earlier black elite in New Bern or many of their contemporary black leaders elsewhere.

Yet New Bern also differed from small but booming towns like Charlotte and Durham where nearly all of the black leaders were newcomers. Like their contemporaries in Wilmington and Fayetteville, New Bernians drew upon shared local stories that reached deep into the past. Memories of wartime accomplishments bolstered their sense of purpose and reinforced the relationships established during those extraordinary years. Looking further back, some New Bernians drew upon a history that stretched from the early national period's legacy of freedom and achievements, which they preserved in memory during and after the oppression of the late antebellum era. In the mid-1860s, the city's black leaders pressing for universal manhood suffrage had invoked more than once the model of free blacks' voting before 1835. White memoirists of the later nineteenth century recalled that era of black suffrage in favorable terms and cited notable free blacks such as the wealthy barber John C. Stanly and artisans Donum Montford and John Rice Green. Local newspapers continued to carry news of black New Bernians long resident in other cities, including carpenter Rigdon Green, who died in Cleveland in 1887 after an absence of some thirty years.[5]

New Bernians also carried forward personal knowledge of the past. Freedman and brickmason Thomas Battle liked to recall the days when he had worshipped with blacks and whites at the old Methodist meeting-house.[6] Virgil A. Crawford surely heard from his father and grandmother stories of how John C. Stanly, along with manumitted carpenters Bacchus Simmons and James York Green, had enabled his father to gain his liberty as a boy in 1815 and how Simmons had trained him in his trade. Isaac Rue likely repeated his own tales of slavery and liberation as he encouraged his grandson Edward A. Richardson to advance in his trade and civic roles. In immaterial as well as material ways this heritage undergirded postwar New Bernians' sense of themselves and their possibilities as they defined their new lives and identities.

"By the Sweat of Our Brow We Earn Our Bread": Artisans at Work in Freedom

Black New Bernians, young and old, epitomized the "hundreds of fine artisans" described by émigré brickmason Alexander H. Newton who "came [out] of slavery . . . able to begin at once the laying of the foundation of the history of a free people. They took up their several trades, and for both races, turned their hands to every advantage."[7] Freedmen's Bureau official Horace James had commented in 1864 that the local black artisans who plied their trades as free men during occupation demonstrated a "capacity for business" and a "degree of thrift and shrewdness" that would yield "ample security for their future progress, if they are allowed an equal chance with their fellow-men."[8] It was that equal chance that postwar artisans strove to attain and protect.[9]

In 1870, the first census taken after emancipation depicted a majority-black city of about 6,000 people bustling with scores of artisans, of whom more than two-thirds were people of color.[10] Nearly all of these black artisans were new freedpeople, newcomers, or young people who had recently come of age; only about a dozen had appeared as free artisans in New Bern in the census of 1860.[11] A large portion of the city's postwar black artisans, like most of the leaders in the group, were New Bernians who had been enslaved until the war.[12] Once established in their trades, these artisans showed notable persistence: about 40 of 190 black male artisans counted in 1870 were still in New Bern in 1880 despite a substantial drop in the overall number of artisans, and all of the leading black craftsmen enumerated in the 1870 census stayed in town for the rest of their lives.[13]

These freed craftsmen published newspaper advertisements in the 1870s that signaled their attainments and their hopes. Blacksmith Samuel Jackson was "prepared to do first-class Horse Shoeing at a very moderate price" at his shop below South Front Street. At his "Tailoring Establishment" on South Front Street, Mustipher Holly was "ready to cut and make Gentlemen's Clothing in the latest and most artistic manner" and to make old clothes "as good as new." Edward Havens invited customers to his shoemaking shop on Middle Street near Front, where he accomplished "all kinds of work in a first-class Boot and Shoemaker's line"—doing repairs "neatly and expeditiously" and making "fine or common boots and shoes . . . in the most workmanlike manner and warranted to give satisfaction."[14]

Even as liberated black artisans enjoyed new opportunities, however, state policies narrowed the paths by which black youths could gain skills for artisan careers. The end of slavery terminated whites' interests in training slaves as artisans to advance their owners' profits. The apprenticeship system for free black and white children, like most county government mechanisms, collapsed during the war, and when Craven County apprenticeship assignments resumed, the purpose had changed. No longer did the local court bind out children of either race to learn skilled trades. Focused on the control and care of impoverished and illegitimate children, court officials bound them as farmers or servants or with no occupation designated; artisans who took craft apprentices did so on their own.[15] Moreover, as national leader W. E. B. Du Bois pointed out, postwar southern white artisans, like those in the North for years, now preferred to convey skills to white youths rather than training unwanted competitors.[16]

Black artisans in New Bern took on the responsibility for conveying craft skills to black children. Of thirteen local black apprentices counted in the 1870 census and nine in 1880, only one lived in the household of a white artisan—Henry Lovick, an apprentice with Scots-born carpenter James Boyle. Some apprentices of color, such as upholsterer's apprentice Joseph C. Price, aged fifteen in 1870, and carpenter's apprentice George Eubanks, nineteen in 1880, resided with their mothers or other kinfolk and did not identify their masters, who might have been either black or white. Many black artisans, as we shall see, learned their skills from parents or grandparents. Nearly all the black apprentices who lived with nonfamily masters—such as Cicero Jones, an apprentice of cooper Virgil A. Crawford in 1870, and Joseph Taylor, an apprentice of brickmason Thomas Battle in 1880—learned their trades from master artisans of their own race.[17]

The racial makeup of local craftspeople continued along familiar lines. Black artisans, including many who had plied their trades in slavery, worked at nearly every craft, with the exceptions of gunsmithing, silversmithing, and a few other specialties dominated by whites. A few blacks and whites worked as bonnetmakers, caulkers, coppersmiths, harnessmakers, jewelers, milliners, painters, pumpmakers, shipbuilders, upholsterers, wagonmakers, and wheelwrights. Most artisans of color in 1870, however, practiced the trades of blacksmithing, bricklaying, carpentry, coopering, shoemaking, and tailoring.

As the impact of mass production spread in the 1870s and 1880s, craftsmen's prospects varied from trade to trade and place to place. Especially hard hit in New Bern was coopering, for decades an important and traditionally black craft. In 1870 the town had as many as thirty coopers, all black and most of them new freedmen, including many local leaders such as George B. Willis, Henry H. Simmons, Amos York, Edward R. Dudley, and Virgil A. Crawford. But that once-vital trade declined abruptly in response to mass production, including the establishment of a local barrel factory. By 1880 there were only ten coopers in town. Willis kept making barrels, but Simmons was working as a drayman, York identified himself as a preacher and worked at a sawmill, and Dudley and Crawford had government desk jobs. By contrast, despite the influx of cast-metal products, the city's black men maintained their strength in the blacksmith's trade. Some worked for the railroad, while others kept busy shoeing mules and horses and making and repairing vehicles and farm equipment. Freedmen operated all of the blacksmith businesses listed in the 1880 city directory: Allen Jackson, the firm of Samuel Jackson and his brother Eli, the firm of Elisha Nelson and William and Titus Rial, and George S. Fisher, who had several employees, including his sons, in his workshop.[18]

Familiar racial patterns likewise persisted in crafts customarily practiced by both races. Black cabinetmaker Miles Sheppard appeared in the city business directory, along with two white men in that trade. Even with the competition from ready-made footwear and clothing sold by local merchants, black and white shoemakers and needleworkers not only continued to make repairs and alterations but fashioned custom-made goods well into the twentieth century. Edward Havens and his sons had one of the principal shoemaking firms, while John Hawley, Mustipher Holly, and Richard Sawyer stood out among the tailors of color.[19] Richard Sawyer, a schoolboy of fourteen in 1870, was in 1880 a "seamster" living with his mother, washerwoman Lucretia Neal. He soon translated his skills into an "Up to Date Tailoring Establishment" and guaranteed "All work is of the very latest design. Suits and overcoats made to your measure of the Best Foreign and Domestic Goods."[20]

As was true before the war, gender conventions generally limited black as well as white women's artisan roles to needle crafts.[21] Many women, such as Richard Sawyer's mother, Lucretia, supported themselves and their families as washerwomen, domestic servants, and unskilled laborers. Needlework provided one of the best-paid female occupations, which was practiced by genteel women as well as those of lower social status. Seamstresses constituted the vast majority of women artisans of both races, and in 1870 the town's forty black seamstresses appeared in numbers roughly equal to their white sisters. Likewise repeating earlier trends, only a few women of either race practiced the specialized and more prestigious crafts of tailoress or dressmaker. Among the few women practicing crafts other than needlework were Dollie York and Phillis Crawford, widowed sisters of color, who made and "battened" chairs in their old age. Black or white, few women artisans owned real property, and none of the craftswomen of color possessed substantial wealth. Elizabeth Bragg, a white tailoress according to the census of 1860 and the daughter of antebellum tailor John Bragg, was listed as a "mulatto" seamstress in 1880. The single head of a household that included her siblings and her children, she was exceptional among women artisans in 1870 in owning $400 worth of real estate, which reflected her antebellum family legacy of property as well as skill.[22]

For women, unlike men, marital status affected how they or the census taker identified their occupations. Most women who were noted as having a craft occupation were single or widowed like Elizabeth Bragg and Dollie York and Phillis Crawford, while most married women, even if they practiced skilled crafts, were listed as keeping house. Tailoress Grace Harris Walker, a daughter of brickmason Israel Harris Sr., exemplified the many women whose changing family situations led to craft employment and identity. In 1870 Grace was "keeping house" for her husband, Edward Walker, and their two daughters. By 1880, however, Edward was in New

York, and Grace and her daughters had moved in with her parents. For her, returning with her children to her parents' home provided vital security and care beyond what she might have had as a single mother. To augment the household income, she found employment as a tailoress in the downtown merchant tailor shop of Bavarian tailor Adam Zang, where she worked with him, another white tailor, and a white tailoress. She was the only black woman and one of the few women of either race noted in the 1880 city directory with a skilled craft (the directory did not identify seamstresses).

Widowhood brought similar changes. Harriet Lane, a daughter of blacksmith George Fisher, was in 1880 a widow, aged thirty-three, living with her parents and employed as a dressmaker. Amanda Hawley, the wife of tailor John Hawley, appeared in the census of 1880 as "keeping house," but after John died, she was listed in 1900 as a tailoress and widowed head of a household that included her daughter Hettie Latham, a tailor, and three young grandchildren. In 1900, perhaps reflecting changing ideas of gender and employment, a greater proportion of married women were listed with skilled craft occupations than previously: of nine dressmakers of color, five were single or widowed, while four were married and living with their husbands.[23]

Whereas essentially all of New Bern's female artisans engaged in needle crafts, among the city's male artisans, a majority of whom were black, construction work was the principal employment. Construction artisans in nearly every community and of both races encountered especially complex and profound changes as mass production transformed the industry nationally and eliminated many aspects of traditional building practice.[24] On the one hand, demand for workers rose as the city grew and citizens replaced old buildings with new ones. Mass production spurred construction by making building materials cheaper, but the site-specific nature of construction still required artisans to erect the buildings.

Carpenters, the most numerous craftsmen in New Bern, built and finished hundreds of new structures from the vast supplies of lumber, flooring, weatherboards, doors, posts and pillars, shutters, banisters, mantels, and decorations pouring out of local or distant factories. Of the three carpentry firms in the business directory of 1880, two were white and one was black—McGee, Nelson, and Company—while the majority of the individuals listed as carpenters were black.[25]

Black men maintained their dominance in the brickmason's trade, which

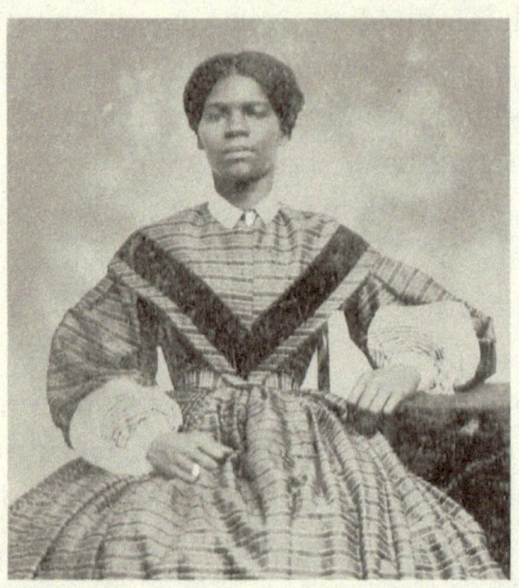

Sylvia Conner, June 5, 1863. Courtesy of Tryon Palace Historic Sites and Gardens, New Bern, North Carolina.

Sylvia Conner, Seamstress

A New Bern seamstress who gained an unusual place in the documentary record was Sylvia Conner (Connor). In 1870, as a freedwoman, aged thirty-five, she was working as a domestic servant in the household of wealthy white physician Isaac Hughes. That the census gave no indication of her sewing skills is a reminder that the number of women identified in records as seamstresses fell short of their actual numbers. In fact, Conner was a "superb seamstress" who, a few years earlier, had captured the attention of Henry A. Clapp, a young soldier from Massachusetts, when he was stationed in New Bern during the war. Taking his meals at a boardinghouse run by Sylvia's sister Mary Jane, Private Clapp admired both women and had a photographer capture their likenesses. Sylvia, he wrote, possessed "unusual refinement" and was "a woman of very good sense and well developed reflective faculties." In gratitude for the sisters' kindness in cooking and sewing for him, Henry asked his mother to send a box of clothing for them. Upon opening it, he reported, Sylvia "remarked that mother 'seemed to have guessed her taste exactly.'"

U.S. census, 1870; Penne S. Sandbeck, "Yankee Gentlemen: Daniel R. Larned, Henry A. Clapp, and New Bern's Federal Occupation," *The Palace: The Magazine of Tryon Palace* (Spring 2012), 14.

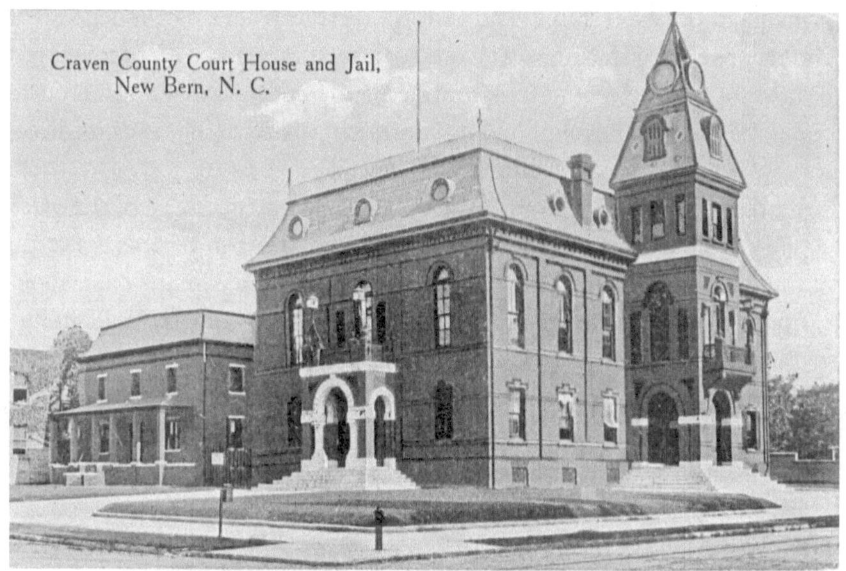

Craven County Courthouse and Jail, New Bern. One of New Bern's major construction projects in the post-Reconstruction era, it was designed by architect Samuel Sloan of Philadelphia, and the builder was John B. Lane. With construction records absent, the bricklayers and carpenters have not been identified, but most of them would have been local and regional black craftsmen. Postcard view, courtesy of the North Carolina Collection, University of North Carolina at Chapel Hill Library.

faced strong demand as the city erected brick stores and warehouses as well as elaborate masonry buildings like the Craven County Courthouse of the 1880s and the United States Post Office of the 1890s. Some specialists may have come from the North, but most of the local masons had learned their skills in slavery. All six brickmasons in the 1880 business directory were freedmen: Thomas Battle, William Fenderson, Israel Harris Sr., James and Charles Sparrow, and Stepney White. One of the few white brickmasons, William H. Jones, whom we met at the antebellum Moses Griffin School project, was known for his black "corps of bricklayers."[26]

Yet numbers did not tell the full story. While demand for construction artisans remained high, changes in production and accompanying shifts in the organization of the building industry redefined their roles and status. As carpenters and brickmasons became assemblers of manufactured items, increasingly it was no longer the master artisan but the architect and the contractor who determined the character of buildings and claimed the principal profits and status. The nationwide shift from small, independent craft shops to large businesses favored contractors, who might or might not be artisans themselves but took contracts and hired artisans and laborers to complete them.[27] The four building contractors listed in the 1880 city directory were white men who employed many black workers.

Of these, contractor Edward Pavie was named by nearly all of the black construction artisans who identified their employers in records.[28] Typical of these workmen were four who cited him in their Freedman's Bank applications—all former slaves from the immediate area. Carpenter William Rue was a New Bernian, mason John Smith was from Hyde County, and carpenters Simon Croom and James Weston were brothers from Jones County. Smith, Croom, and Weston may have come to New Bern during the war, as did Pavie, who arrived from New York in 1862 with the Union quartermaster's department. He advertised in 1872 "all kinds of carpenter work done at the lowest Cash Price. Contracts made and guaranteed." By 1870 Pavie's shop was the largest building operation in town, with twenty workmen erecting twenty-five buildings in that year alone. For twenty years they constructed stores and residences in New Bern, including rental houses in a small suburb known as "Pavie Town," which Pavie developed northwest of Dryboro for black residents, including his employees and their families.[29]

A few black building artisans ventured into more profitable sectors of the construction industry. They had seen Hardy B. Lane's carpenter son John thrive as a contractor after the war and George Bishop expand his steam-powered production of building materials. Black carpenters Daniel G. Moseley and Sylvester Mackey teamed up as contractors in the early 1890s but returned to their roles as carpenters by 1900. The *New Bern Daily Journal* of March 10, 1893, reported that carpenter and Union veteran Dennis Wadsworth had invested in manufacturing: he was erecting a building at the corner of Queen and Pollock Streets near the railroad tracks to carry on the wheelwright's business, make "truck boxes" (for shipping local produce), and "put in planing machines and machines for ornamental round and scroll work" After equipping his new facility with steam-powered machinery, Wadsworth had only a few years to test the enterprise before his death in 1897.[30]

IN NEW BERN, as most southern cities, black as well as white artisans operated their businesses downtown. The center city—which covered several blocks from the Trent River and South Front Street on the south, northward to Pollock and Broad Streets; and from East Front Street along the Neuse westward to Hancock Street and the railroad—continued as a zone of mixed uses, classes, and races through the century. While a growing number of black artisans located their shops in the increasingly black suburban sectors, not until well into the twentieth century did Jim Crow practices push out nearly all the downtown black businesses. Throughout the nineteenth century, white and black New Bernians still crossed paths and conducted their business in a racially mixed downtown.[31]

Leading black and white artisans in quiet, "clean" trades, such as shoemaking and tailoring, located their shops in the prime blocks of Middle, Craven, and South Front Streets, convenient to white as well as black customers. Their neighbors included the principal banks and hotels; the offices and shops of white attorneys and physicians, milliners, and jewelers; boardinghouses, restaurants, stores, and livery stables kept by both blacks and whites; and the shops of leading barbers, nearly all of whom were black—such as cooper Amos York's son-in-law, Hugh Banks, in 1893 a "tonsorial artist" at 93 Middle Street with "everything first class."[32] Several such businesses operated in the prime blocks of South Front Street in or near the Gaston House Hotel. Edward Havens had his shoemaking shop at "3 e Gaston House" in 1880, and tailor John Hawley was next door. Richard Sawyer worked in 1880 with white tailors Hurtt and Gaskill on Middle Street, near black tailoress Grace Walker, who was employed in the shop of white merchant tailor Adam Zang. By 1893 Sawyer was operating his own shop on South Front Street at Craven Street near tailor Mustipher Holly. Shoemaker Allen G. Oden had his shop on Craven just north of South Front, and by 1893 Havens moved his shoemaking shop from South Front to a prime block of Middle Street.[33]

Artisans typically located operations that generated heat, noise, and the threat of fire on the edges of downtown. In 1880 Samuel Jackson maintained his forge in the Trent River wharf area behind the Gaston House, and Nelson and Rial's blacksmith shop was on Craven Street below South Front. A few blocks north, carpenter and coffinmaker Richard Tucker had his shop on Pollock between George and Metcalf Streets, and Luke Mason manufactured wagons on Pollock near Hancock and the railroad tracks. At the northern edge of downtown, Eli Jackson's blacksmith shop stood at the corner of Hancock and Broad Streets, while George S. Fisher's smithy and residence were on Broad near George Street.[34] In 1900, Samuel Jackson was still hammering away at his old stand south of South Front, but most of the

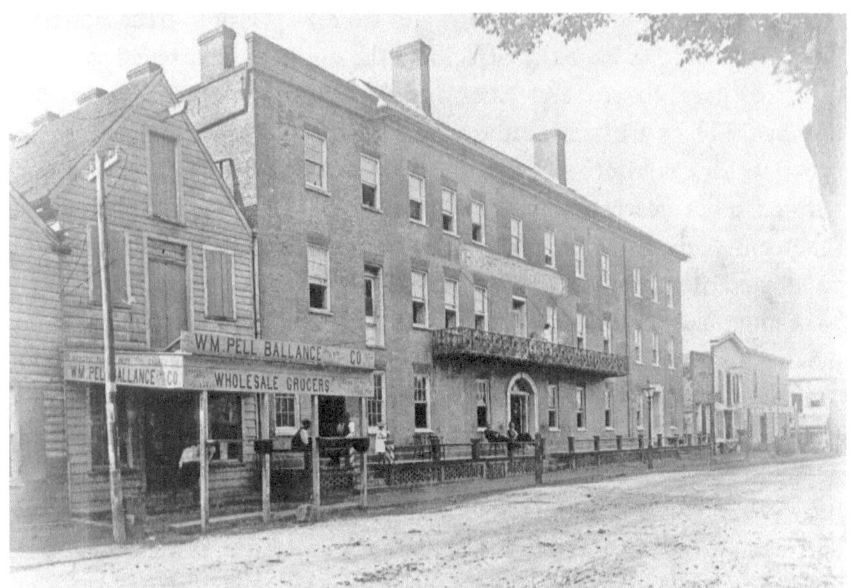

Gaston House Hotel, South Front Street. Many local black and white artisans had their shops in or near this hotel. Courtesy, Kellenberger Room, New Bern–Craven County Public Library, New Bern, North Carolina.

blacksmiths had their forges near the commercial area called Five Points at the intersection of West Broad and Queen Streets.

The blacksmiths at Five Points belonged to a growing number of black artisans and entrepreneurs who located their businesses in or near the suburban black neighborhoods. As early as the 1870s Five Points was a lively business sector centered on the "New Market House." Its location at the hinge between the racially mixed neighborhoods west and north of downtown made it convenient to customers as well as to farmers hauling goods to market. By 1880 blacksmith Allen Jackson lived and worked on Queen Street at Moonshine Alley; shoemaker Quash Slade had his shop on Queen and his home "near New Market"; and carpenter William O. Randolph was also on Queen near the market. At the same time, the eastern blocks of Queen Street near Dryboro and adjoining streets flourished as a racially mixed corridor of businesses and institutions, including the Elm City Hotel, King Solomon Lodge, St. Cyprian's Episcopal Church, and St. Peter's AME Zion Church.[35]

Throughout town, black artisans in every trade encompassed a spectrum of status and wealth. Many worked as employees or on their own on a small scale, while a few became property owners, employers, and civic leaders. As had been true before the war, wealth and status did not concentrate in specific crafts: a few artisans excelled in each trade. Whatever the initial advantages of previous free status and property ownership might have been, most of the city's successful black artisans of the postwar years had practiced their trades in bondage. More important to their success than their antebellum condition was their shared experience of a head start during Union occupation, along with their previous mastery of skills and their sense of purpose even in slavery, which they had honed during and immediately after the war.[36]

Although black artisans accumulated only modest wealth, they fared dramatically better than the general population, black or white. Since most New Bern blacks had come out of slavery without property and faced the dual challenges of race and a sluggish town economy, the local picture of black realty holding in 1870 was dismal.[37] The census of 1870, the last to show property values, indicated that only about 60 of nearly 4,000 black New Bernians owned real estate. A remarkable proportion of these black property owners—about half—were male artisans. In stark contrast to the proportion in the general population and among female artisans, about 15 percent of some 190 black craftsmen owned real estate.[38] Most had property valued at $100 to $500, and a few between $500 and $1,000. Only the top dozen property owners of color held real estate valued at $1,000 or more. Among these were artisans and freedmen Richard Tucker, George S. Fisher, Thomas Battle, and Isaac C. Rue, who owned their homes and shops and sometimes also rental property.[39] Some supplemented their craft earnings with income from other enterprises, including Tucker, who went into the coffinmaking and undertaking business and operated a store, and who, in 1869, with fellow artisans George B. Willis and Moses Bryan and their friends, barber Clinton D. Pierson, and minister Brevett W. Morris, helped found a local land and building association.[40]

Black craftsmen, like many others, struggled during the economic fluctuations of the 1870s and 1880s, especially those who lost their savings in the collapse of the Freedman's Bank in 1874. For the most part, however, the artisans who established themselves in their trades and as property owners by 1870 managed relatively well. In the late 1880s and early 1890s, artisans Virgil A. Crawford, Allen G. Oden, Edward Havens, Joseph Green, and John Randolph Jr. had real estate valued at between $100 and $600 and tools worth from $25 to $100. The handful of black New Bernians with property worth upwards of $1,000 included artisans Edward A. Richardson and Edward R. Dudley, who had rural as well as town property, while blacksmith George S. Fisher, the wealthiest black artisan in town, owned town lots and tools and equipment valued at $2,650 in 1887.[41]

Records of the national credit rating firm R. G. Dun and Company illustrate how the successful freedman Fisher fared during the 1870s. The firm, which assembled and published descriptions of selected businesspeople to assess their suitability for credit, ranked him highest among the eight black business owners they rated in town. Its reports illuminate his changing financial standing as well as the personal characteristics valued by the firm's evidently white informants.[42]

As was true before the war, the wealth of New Bern's leading black artisans fell short of that of their colleagues in richer North Carolina cities. In Wilmington in 1870, the wealthiest men of color were freedman and house carpenter Henry A. Taylor, with $5,000 in real estate, and freeborn carpenter Alfred Howe, with $3,000. Raleigh upholsterer and political leader James H. Harris had $5,000 in property, and Fayetteville's respected saddler Matthew Leary, a wealthy free man before the war, had property worth $6,000.[43] Prominent white artisans in New Bern also possessed property of higher value than did the leading black craftsmen, with some holding property worth $5,000 to $10,000 in 1870. Brickmason Thomas Battle watched his younger friend, the black real estate developer and money lender Isaac Hughes Smith, assemble a fortune of many thousands of dollars by the end of the century, but neither Battle nor any of his fellow black artisans accrued much beyond their own homes and shops, and only a few left estates worth as much as $1,000.[44]

At the same time, successful artisans of color acquired personal property to provide their families with comfortable homes and represent their respectable status. Like his antebellum predecessors, shoemaker Edward Havens furnished his family home with plenty of kitchen and dining furniture, bedsteads and featherbeds and bedspreads, rocking chairs and easy chairs, as well as such niceties as a settee, mantel ornaments, six wall pictures, and lace curtains. His library comprised one book on the Masonic order and one *Masonic Ritual*, two hymnals and a Bible, *Aesop's Fables*, a *Treatise on Plants* and a book on *Forests and Animals*, plus "1 Book: Under Ground R. R.," "Stanleys Travels in Africa," and "History American Negro." He presented himself in a manner suited to a man of standing, owning at least four suits, five coats (including one of alpaca), two derby hats and one straw

Freedman and Blacksmith George S. Fisher

Geo. S. Fisher (Negro) New Bern Blacksmith

Jan 10, 1870	Is a negro a very upright & industrious man. Has no property qualification but should not hesitate to trust him moderately.
May 1870	No change
Dec 1870	Same
June 1871	No change
Dec 1871	Worth $2,000 and industrious Negro of good character and habits
June 1872	Worth $2,000 Colored man, industrious & entitled to credit He is an exception of the Negro.
Dec 1872	Worth some $1,000. A Negro industrious & entitled to credit.
June 1873	No change
Dec 1873	No change
June 3, 1874	Worth $2,000 in real estate good character & habits and entitled to credit.
Dec 1874	No change
June 1875	Worth $1,000 to $3,000
Dec 1875	Hardworking & attentive, has some property
June 1876	Worth $2,500. Industrious & economical man
Dec 1876	Worthy man worth $2,000 to 2,500 in real estate Well worthy of credit.
May 1877	Worth $3,000 to 4,000 hardworking man worthy of reasonable credit
Dec 1877	Worth $5,000 to 6,000 a very honest man of excellent character and habits
June 1878	Lists in 1877 real estate in value at $1,875 & [personal property] valued at $200. Very worthy man of good character and habits (previous estimate too high)
Jan 1879	Lists for tax real estate $1,875 personal property $100 very industrious thrifty man *lost $2,000 by Freemen's & Savings Bank*
Sept 1879	Listed for taxation real estate $1,630 & personal $130 & personal property valued at $130. Of excellent character & standing sober & industrious. Think a desirable customer to a reasonable amount.

R. G. Dun & Co. Collection, North Carolina, Vol. 7, p. 126, Baker Library Historical Collections, Harvard Business School, Boston, Mass.

hat, two watches valued at ten dollars and five dollars apiece, and a pair of gold-rimmed eyeglasses. His craft equipment—eighty pairs of wooden lasts; a wide variety of hammers, nippers, knives, rasps, awls, and needles; a good supply of leather, thread, and buttons; several benches and desks; and a Singer sewing machine—had served him well and, coupled with his real estate, enabled his shoemaker sons to continue the family business long after his death.[45]

IN 1900 BLACK WRITER Charles Chesnutt used the changing nature of employment in Fayetteville, North Carolina, as an example to highlight the problems facing black workers everywhere. In the years just after the war, he recalled, "nearly all the mechanics were men of color," including a wealthy saddlemaker, the leading undertaker (a former cabinetmaker), and tailors, shoemakers, wheelwrights, and blacksmiths, as well as carpenters, bricklayers, and plasterers. By 1900, he found, while "colored men [were] still the barbers, blacksmiths, masons and carpenters," few practiced other crafts. He cited the "growth of manufactures and the increased ease and cheapness of transportation" as a principal cause:

> The shoes which were formerly made by hand are now manufactured in Massachusetts and sold, with a portrait of the maker stamped upon the sole, for less money than the most poorly paid mechanic could afford to make them for by hand. The buggies and wagons [formerly made in Fayetteville] are now made in Cincinnati and other Northern cities, and delivered in North Carolina for a price prohibitive of manufacture by hand. Furniture is made at Grand Rapids, coffins in one place, and clothing in still another. The blacksmith buys his horseshoes ready made, in assorted sizes, and has merely to trim the hoof and fasten them on with machine-made nails. The shoemaker has degenerated into the cobbler; the tinner merely keeps a shop for the sale of tinware.

Chesnutt believed that "in large part through the operation of social forces beyond any control on their part," the current generation of blacks had "lost their hereditary employments," which had been inadequately replaced by jobs in factories, mines, and mills. Some "younger colored people who might have learned trades" had become teachers or preachers, while too many others had drifted into "servile occupations"—"a poor substitute for the independent position of the skilled mechanic."[46]

In some respects New Bern's employment situation at century's end conformed to the picture Chesnutt painted.[47] As we shall see, some young people, including children of leading artisans, used their educations to become teachers and white-collar workers. Factories and other businesses gave jobs to whites that were not open to blacks, and a disproportionate number of blacks labored at unskilled and service work. As the importance of craft production declined, so did the proportion, if not the number, of artisans in the total population.

Yet conditions in New Bern were not as bleak as the picture Chesnutt portrayed. The city's resilient cohort of black artisans presented a different story as they persisted and even thrived at their trades and passed along their skills to the younger generation well into the twentieth century. The census of 1900, which recorded growth in the general population, also showed that the number of black craftsmen had increased substantially since 1880—from about 140 to about 185, constituting about 68 percent of the city's 270 male artisans. A few crafts had only white practitioners—a marble cutter, a bridge builder, a carriagemaker, a boilermaker, and two harnessmakers. Only black men now worked in diminished numbers as coopers, cobblers, and ship caulkers. But most artisan trades still employed both black and white practitioners, including painters, ship carpenters, shoemakers, tailors, tinners, tinsmiths, and wheelwrights. Fairly equal numbers of black and white women identified themselves as seamstresses, dressmakers, and tailoresses. In keeping with Chesnutt's observations, black men maintained their predominance among blacksmiths and in the building trades: 23 of 25 New Bern brickmasons and 95 out of about 120 carpenters were black men.

In contrast to Chesnutt's depiction, New Bern's artisans of color spanned the generations. Some of the emancipated generation of artisan-leaders died in the 1880s and 1890s, but others lived and maintained their economic and social positions through the end of the century. Old-timers also included more typical workers of modest means, such as carpenter David Wilson, who had learned his trade from white carpenter Robert Hancock before the war. Although he never became wealthy, he persisted as a carpenter both for the railroad and on his own, operated a grocery, and married, had children, and supported his mother, Rachel, in his home until her death at more than 100 years of age. Cited in 1895 as "one of the best colored carpenters of the city," at age sixty-six in 1900, Wilson was still working at his trade.[48]

Although some of the younger generation took the paths Chesnutt described—entering professions or taking servile work—the fact that the town had a healthy number of younger artisans, including some who followed in their parents' footsteps, was especially important for the persistence of the artisan trades in New Bern. James and John T. Havens operated their late father Edward's shoemaking firm under his name, and after James moved to Raleigh, John kept the business going in New Bern. Tailor Richard Sawyer not only continued at his trade well into the twentieth century but trained at least three of his sons: Annias at age fifteen was listed as an apprentice tailor in his father's household in the 1900 census; his younger brother Freeman moved to New York and earned a reputation for his elegant style; and brother Leonard worked in the metropolis with Freeman before returning home to continue the family tradition.[49] In 1900 twenty-year-old carpenter Walter Leith was in practice with his forty-year-old father, Lewis, who had come to town about 1880. Henry Clay Sparrow, a brickmason aged twenty-six in 1900, trained with his father, Charles, before embarking on a career noted for his distinctive brickwork.[50]

One local artisan of color attained a professional status unusual for blacks of his or later times. George C. Eubanks, listed as a "mulatto" carpenter's apprentice in the 1880 census, had gone to school at an unidentified institution but had returned home by 1900 to set up practice as an architect. Identified as a white man aged thirty-four in 1900, Eubanks was one of two New Bernians listed as architects at that time. The other was Herbert Woodley Simpson, the white son of a local building contractor and undertaker, who, at age twenty-nine, had a busy regional practice. In 1904 Simpson and Eubanks had their offices at 68 and 65 Broad Street, respectively, and both continued their practices well into the new century.[51]

During the years between the Civil War and the turn of the century, New Bern's artisans of color did much to differentiate their community from Chesnutt's bleak portrait. One factor was the sheer number of black craftspeople who had created a legacy of achievement and could pass along their expertise to the next generation. The leading artisans also exerted themselves to give young people opportunities for advancement, both by taking them as apprentices and, as we shall see, by stressing education as well as craft training. Moreover, they modeled for the younger generation the example of black artisans who could earn a decent living, establish families and homes, and become respected citizens and leaders. With their economic and community position grounded in the fruits of their thrift and industry, these artisan-citizens worked endlessly for the causes they saw as essential to freedom and progress for their people.

"We Will Live and Act and *Vote* for Her Prosperity": Black Artisans in Political Life

From the mid-1860s throughout the rest of the century, nearly all of New Bern's black political leaders were artisans. Black craftsmen in other cities, to be sure, also exerted leadership in political life—members of the Howe and Price families in Wilmington, Stewart Ellison and James H. Harris in Raleigh, and John T. Schenck in Charlotte—but in New Bern black artisans' political predominance was unusually strong and long lasting. These leaders included not only some of the town's most prosperous black artisans, like George Fisher and Richard Tucker, but also men such as house carpenter Israel B. Abbott, cooper Henry H. Simmons, and painter John Randolph Jr., who held only modest property.

By the beginning of Congressional Reconstruction in 1867, New Bern had lost bright stars Abraham Galloway and George A. Rue from its leadership constellation. Nonetheless, a core group of artisan-leaders carried forward the goals and ideals of those formative years into a new era of suffrage and officeholding. Several had entered political life by the end of 1865, and their brief but intense experiences with the radical figureheads of the mid-1860s had imbued them with a sense of personal as well as group identity and agency. As they showed in organizing the 1865 Freedmen's Convention, their experiences had put them on a different footing from many of their contemporaries who had spent the war years under white and Confederate rule. They joined in every opportunity to exert their rights as citizens and promote the rights and prospects of others. Far from forming a closed cadre, the wartime artisan-leaders had developed a porous and dynamic ethos that welcomed newcomers while holding fast to their values and sense of purpose.[52]

During the first months of Congressional Reconstruction, black New Bernians' hopes soared. It appeared that universal manhood suffrage was close at hand and that New Bernians would take the first steps. The *Christian Recorder* predicted on March 23, 1867, "The municipal election of Newbern NC is to be held early next month and the colored citizens of that place are determined to cast their votes in accordance with the provisions of the Reconstruction law," and quoted the *Raleigh Standard*: "The colored people of Newbern will be the first of their race in the State to vote under the Sherman act [Congressional Reconstruction]. We have no doubt they will highly appreciate the privilege and that they will so exercise it as to promote the good and glory of their country." Black artisans led in organizing the local Republican Party and hosting such events as a May visit by suffrage advocate and United States Senator Henry Wilson of Massachusetts to promote equal rights.[53]

Their hopes collided with Conservatives' intransigency. Shortly before the municipal election, scheduled for the first Monday in May, New Bernians learned that the Union military administrator, General Daniel Sickles, had suspended the election. The general took this action as a result of a meeting with North Carolina's civilian governor, Jonathan Worth. Sickles appointed white men to the local offices and delayed elections until after the Constitutional Convention required by Congress, which was scheduled for 1868.[54]

With their hopes for the May election dashed, New Bern's artisan-leaders acted as they had done many times before by turning their efforts to the day ahead. In keeping with the concurrent formation of equal rights and education state associations at the Freedmen's Convention of 1866, they placed education along with suffrage high among their priorities. On June 18, 1867, artisans Edward A. Richardson and Richard Tucker, selected as Craven County's members of the state educational association in 1866, convened a public meeting at Andrews Chapel to form a free school. With Tucker as chair, the group highlighted the interdependence of suffrage and education: "The colored people of the Southern States are about to enjoy the great right of suffrage, which is the basis of all political and social freedom and improvement . . . therefore . . . we, citizens of New Bern, accept with this privilege, the principles and responsibilities which are necessarily related to it." With "a system of universal education being necessary to the permanence of our republican institutions," they continued, "each State should make provision for the establishment and support of public schools for the education of all its youth . . . without discrimination on account of color or religious belief." They formed a local education board that comprised a "who's who" of black artisan-leaders: Virgil A. Crawford, George S. Fisher, Daniel H. Harris, William H. Johnson, John Randolph Jr., Henry H. Simmons, Richard Tucker, George B. Willis, and Amos York, with Edward A. Richardson as president.[55] These men, along with fellow artisans Israel B.

Abbott and Thomas Battle, barbers Clinton D. Pierson and John R. Good, and ministers Alexander Bass and Brevett W. Morris, reappeared regularly as members of a leadership group that contended with the host of rapidly changing conditions.

During the racial and political tensions of that first summer of Congressional Reconstruction, a series of murders and robberies struck eastern North Carolina. New Bern black leaders immediately called a "Mass Meeting of Colored Citizens" at the courthouse, on July 3, to condemn the outrages and refute racial accusations. Randolph called the meeting to order, Tucker served as chair, and Fisher, York, Richardson, and Good formed a committee to prepare "resolutions expressive of the feeling of the meeting," which appeared immediately in the local newspaper: "We the colored people of this community do, from our hearts, deprecate this awful state of things; and while we know that because colored persons are among those robbers and murders is no reason why all of us should be implicated (nor do we suppose we are). Yet we feel it to be our imperative duty as good citizens to express to our fellow citizens and to the world, our abhorance and condemnation of these most damnable acts." Declaring themselves "on the side of law and order," they pledged "ourselves and our services, whenever and wherever needed," to "bring these murderers to suffer the penalty of their crime."[56] By holding their meeting at the courthouse and stressing their status as "good citizens," they claimed their new roles and responsibilities. On the very next day, many of the same leaders took the public stage on a happier occasion, Independence Day. Crowds of celebrants paraded through town, attended races at the local track, made excursions to the beach, watched a fireworks display, and gathered at the Academy Green to hear John Randolph Jr. read the Declaration of Independence.[57]

In November 1867, thousands of black New Bern men went to the polls at last—to vote for delegates for the congressionally mandated Constitutional Convention of 1868. Black artisans figured among those whom Union officials recommended as local registrars: painter John Randolph Jr. ("very intelligent"), carpenter Richard Tucker, shoemaker Moses D. Hill; and barber Clinton D. Pierson.[58] By the appointed day, 3,108 black men and 1,509 whites had registered to vote in Craven County. They elected two white Republicans and one black: Clinton D. Pierson, who had traveled with Abraham Galloway to present the North Carolinians' suffrage petition to Abraham Lincoln back in 1864. When the state Constitutional Convention met in

Raleigh early in 1868, Pierson and his fellow delegates, including Galloway and others familiar from the freedmen's conventions, enacted numerous reforms, including the congressionally mandated manhood suffrage.[59]

In the elections that were held soon after the convention, New Bern and Craven County's enfranchised black majority and their experienced artisan-leaders made their city and county a center of Republican strength. Artisans were among the first local party officials, including Randolph and Tucker, who moved readily into the self-governance they had sought for so long. Missing from the roster was Clinton Pierson, who was suffering from the rheumatism that would lead to his death at age fifty-eight in 1870.[60] The first black legislator from Craven, elected in 1868 along with two white Republicans, was clergyman Brevett W. Morris. As one of at least twenty black men in the Republican-majority legislature, he participated in passing reforms that included public education for both races. Among the lasting achievements of this legislature was a law vital to the interests of artisans—a mechanics' lien law. Familiar in the North (thanks to the efforts of white mechanics), but previously unobtainable in North Carolina and much of the South, mechanics' lien laws assigned mechanics and other workers financial rights in the property owned by employers who failed to pay them for their work. Unanimously supported by black legislators, the law offered new safeguards to black as well as white artisans in a world commanded by the propertied class.[61]

At home, too, New Bern's veteran artisan-leaders dominated among the new officeholders. Four of the five black men chosen in 1868 as Craven County justices of the peace were artisans—Richard Tucker, Moses D. Hill, Mingo Croom, and Edward A. Richardson—with farmer Willis Pettipher the fifth. Following the reforms of 1868, town councilmen were elected by popular vote, with three at-large members and one each from the seven city wards. In the first election, in 1869, the at-large winners were white railroad businessman Edward R. Stanly, with 458 votes, and black coopers George B. Willis and Amos York, with 436 and 428 votes, respectively. Four wards elected white aldermen and three wards elected blacks—blacksmith George S. Fisher, barber John R. Good, and cooper Virgil A. Crawford.[62]

Meanwhile, state Conservatives (renamed Democrats in the 1870s) turned their energies to recapturing political power in the election of 1870, using cries of "Negro domination" in order to "redeem" the state for whites. New Bern black artisans moved unexpectedly into the heart of the conflict. With Klan atrocities mounting in much of the state, in early summer 1870

Republican governor William Holden called up state troops to quell the violence and protect the state armory in Raleigh. He commissioned Colonel George Kirk to organize a regiment from the white Unionist areas of western North Carolina and eastern Tennessee, and he asked William J. Clarke, a Confederate veteran and new Republican in New Bern, to raise a regiment from Republican counties in the east. Clarke turned to Craven County black men, who quickly filled Company H of the First Regiment, with New Bern artisans as the commissioned officers: cooper George B. Willis as captain and carpenters Israel B. Abbott and James D. Dudley (brother of cooper Edward R. Dudley) the lieutenants.[63]

Experienced in political life if not military service, Captain Willis and his fellow officers settled into their new roles, saw to the issuance of Union uniforms and weapons for a hundred men, and traveled to Raleigh on July 19 to set up camp near downtown. Along with enduring Conservatives' derision, Willis gained recognition for his capable handling of the troops during their months of guard duty. In the statewide election, held on August 4, Conservatives capitalized on the "Kirk-Holden War," as they called it, to capture a legislative majority, which they soon used to impeach and remove Governor Holden.[64] Craven County and New Bern, however, were not so easily "redeemed." George B. Willis, Edward R. Dudley, and Richard Tucker won seats in the county's all-black, all-artisan delegation in the House of Representatives, and Willis and the men of Company H returned home in September with new sheen to their reputations.

Long after the Conservatives' statewide victory of 1870, these men and other black New Bernians kept winning legislative seats in numbers that were second only to those of New Hanover County (Wilmington).[65] As the number of blacks and Republicans in the General Assembly shrank, they saw their power diminish but continued to run for and win seats nonetheless. In 1872, Israel B. Abbott outpolled Willis and joined Dudley and Tucker in the second all-black Craven delegation. Richard Tucker became the first black state senator from Craven in 1874, and cooper Henry H. Simmons was elected to the House of Representatives in 1876. Black farmer Willis Pettipher followed in 1878, and the recently arrived New Bern teacher and attorney George H. White, as we shall see, was elected to the House in 1880 and to the state senate in 1884.[66]

On the local scene, the racial balance among New Bern's aldermen continued for a time, with Willis and York retaining at-large seats in 1870 and Fisher, Crawford, and John R. Good reelected from the Fifth, Sixth, and

Craven County Black Men in the North Carolina Legislature, 1868–1898

House of Representatives

1868	Brevett W. Morris (minister)
1870	Edward R. Dudley (cooper), Richard Tucker (carpenter and undertaker), George B. Willis (cooper)
1872	Edward R. Dudley, Richard Tucker, Israel B. Abbott (carpenter)
1874	John R. Good (barber), Edward H. Hill (farmer, merchant)
1876	Henry H. Simmons (cooper)
1878	Willis D. Pettipher (farmer, deputy sheriff)
1880	George H. White (teacher and attorney)
1882	William H. Johnson (brickmason?)
1884–88	John E. Hussey (boardinghouse keeper and grocer)
1898	Isaac Hughes Smith (real estate owner and financier)

State Senate

1874	Richard Tucker (carpenter and undertaker)
1884	George H. White (teacher and attorney)

Seventh Wards.[67] Even as Conservatives took steps to shift the council balance toward their party, black as well as white Republicans still won seats, with Virgil A. Crawford a regular winner and Good elected in 1872 and York in 1874. In 1875 the legislature added four council seats to New Bern's majority-Democratic districts. Then, despite opposition from black legislators, including New Bernian Henry H. Simmons's eloquent defense of electoral principles, the Democratic legislature of 1876–77 reduced the number of wards in the city from seven to five, with one immense Fifth Ward encompassing nearly half of the city's area and much of the black population —and represented by only one alderman. Black artisans persevered on the council, with the support of the city's majority-black electorate and the Fifth Ward: Virgil A. Crawford was joined on the board by shoemaker Quash W. Slade in 1879 and 1880, carpenter E. E. Tucker in 1881, and Henry H. Simmons in 1888 and 1890.[68] By that time Crawford and Simmons were among the few black city councilmen in North Carolina.[69]

Ironically, black artisans' political opportunities took on new dimensions when Democrats gerrymandered the "Black Second" Congressional District in 1872 to isolate black-majority counties, including Craven. The resulting district became fertile political ground for black and white Republicans, who rewarded their supporters with remunerative federal appointments. Those in New Bern included Edward R. Dudley as deputy collector of revenue, Virgil A. Crawford as a collector at the U.S. Custom Office, John Randolph Jr. as a mail agent at the U.S. Post Office, and Edward A. Richardson, cited in the *New Bernian* of January 17, 1880, as "a faithful and obliging Clerk in our Post Office," who also had a brief appointment as postmaster.[70]

In 1886, after years of growing intraparty struggles in the district, carpenter and former legislator Israel B. Abbott repeated an earlier bid for the Republican congressional nomination by challenging the incumbent, the mixed-race attorney James O'Hara of Goldsboro. After a tumultuous convention, both men ran as Republicans. Seeing unexpected opportunity in the Republican stronghold, the heartened Democrats put up white New Bern attorney Furnifold Simmons. With the black and Republican vote divided, Simmons triumphed and began a political career that lasted well into the twentieth century.[71] Abbott died a few months later at age forty-four. The *New Bern Weekly Journal* of May 26, 1887, summarized his career and offered rare, if qualified, praise for a black political figure: "His education was very limited; he was not a forcible speaker, but possessed great shrewdness as a politician, rare executive ability for one of his station, and as presiding officer of a body of colored representatives disposed to be unruly, he was unexcelled."

New Bern's artisan-citizens, who dominated local black political leadership from the 1860s into the 1890s, combined their wartime experiences with the status and income associated with their trades to develop their political skills, connections, and positions. At the same time, their public service strengthened their social and economic stature. The correlation of craft occupations with political prominence persisted in New Bern longer than in most communities, even as the new generation of educated and professional blacks whom the artisans had helped nurture joined in leadership roles. Contrary to Democrats' claims that North Carolina was dominated by "Negro rule," never did black North Carolinians constitute a majority in the legislature or on a city council. Despite New Bern's majority-black electorate, only in 1868 and 1870 did blacks compose as much as half of the town council. However few their numbers, black officeholders were a source of pride to their fellow black citizens, and in New Bern they maintained their presence throughout the century.

"Press On for Knowledge—for Knowledge is Power": Striving for Education

As we have seen, New Bern's black artisan-leaders and their allies placed tremendous emphasis on education. Even conservative whites recognized that blacks would "deny themselves of any comfort to send their children to school." From emancipation onward, the issue of public schools for blacks was a highly contested part of the state's political agenda. As all parties recognized, the issue concerned not simply the quality of school facilities but the much larger political and moral question of the place of blacks in the social, economic, and political structure. Many whites claimed that blacks with too much education would not "know their place" and would demand the "social equality" and "Negro rule" that threatened the structure of southern society. For blacks, education was central to self-improvement and self-determination as they strove for their proper place as American citizens.[72]

For years New Bern had a few private schools for black students, some of them established before the war. White New Bernians (unlike some whites elsewhere) generally tolerated, and some supported, schools for blacks, and a few expressed admiration for the city's "intelligent" black citizens. The schools taught by black soldiers during the war were followed by the establishment of Freedmen's Bureau schools that operated for a few years, including one affiliated with St. Cyprian's Church; and George A. Rue's daughter Malinda Rue taught at a school sponsored by the cashier of the local Freedman's Bank. Grace Green, the local free black teacher in whose schoolhouse, as we have seen, the board of Andrews Chapel met to choose their minister in 1864, continued to instruct students for several more years. In 1870 brickmasons Edward A. Richardson and Daniel H. Harris and barber John R. Good opened an account with the Freedman's Bank as trustees of a St. Phillips School. Local parents and students embraced the opportunities: one report counted 1,489 black students and 715 whites enrolled during 1868.[73]

The brilliant young Joseph C. Price demonstrated early on the new possibilities that schooling opened to blacks. The son of an enslaved ship carpenter and a free black seamstress, he had come with his mother from

Elizabeth City to New Bern as a child during the war, and at age fifteen he was an apprentice in the upholsterer's trade as well as attending school. Price was fortunate that his mother took him to New Bern, for there he found the opportunity for schooling and matured among black leaders who modeled forward thinking and assertive action as well as encouraging his advancement. Grace Green was his beloved teacher, and he is said to have attended schools affiliated with Andrews Chapel and St. Cyprian's Church. His keen mind and winning personality impressed attentive black New Bernians, including his Sunday school teacher at Andrews Chapel—brickmason Thomas Battle—and the minister James Walker Hood, both of whom encouraged him to pursue higher education. After attending Shaw University in Raleigh in 1873 and then Lincoln University in Pennsylvania, young Price embarked on a career that gained him national and international acclaim as a minister, educator, civil rights leader, and race spokesman. Like his mentors in New Bern, he saw education as central to black advancement, and he spoke forcefully for the cause. The pride of his old friends in New Bern, the upholsterer's apprentice of 1870 was by 1882 president of AME Zion's nationally renowned Zion Wesley College, later Livingstone College, in Salisbury, North Carolina.[74]

In time, however, black children's access to education dwindled as the Freedmen's Bureau was terminated and northern support for New Bern's private black schools dropped off. The city's black artisan-leaders saw the establishment of public schools for blacks as one of the great needs of the postwar period, and to that they bent their best efforts. In 1867, as we have seen, artisan-leaders called a meeting on the interlocking topics of black suffrage and education and formed a local school board to promote public education "without discrimination on account of color or religious belief" as central to their pursuit of full citizenship.[75]

Prospects looked bright after the election of 1868. The new Republican legislature authorized public schools for both races—a first for North Carolina—and from 1868 to 1870 James Walker Hood, former minister of Andrews Chapel, served as assistant superintendent of schools for both the state and the Freedmen's Bureau and made progress toward establishing public schools for both races. But after Conservatives won control of the legislature in 1870, they ousted Hood and discouraged state support of public schools.[76]

Seeing the lay of the land, in 1870 artisans Israel B. Abbott, Edward A. Richardson, William W. Lawrence, and Edward Havens led in forming the

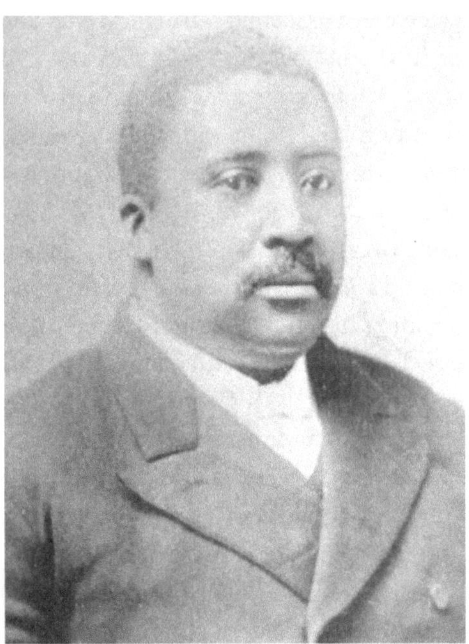

Joseph C. Price. Courtesy of the State Archives of North Carolina, Raleigh.

Young Men's Intelligent and Enterprising Association (YMIEA), with the goal of founding a local school. A larger group of artisans and their allies incorporated the New Bern Educational Association in 1872 to complement the YMIEA.[77] They recognized that the local schools for blacks fell woefully short of facilities in such towns as Charlotte, Wilmington, and Raleigh. Gradually their efforts bore fruit. In 1873 the YMIEA published a letter in the *New Bern Times* pressing local white leaders to devote more resources to public schools for black students, and in that year the trustees of the white New Bern Academy responded by lending their support to a school for black students. In 1875 the state finally mandated public schools for both blacks and whites, spurring New Bern to provide at least minimal public school facilities for black students. This action represented a step in the right direction but did not begin to meet the needs and hopes of the black population.[78]

These artisan-leaders also joined in statewide educational efforts. In mid-October 1877 the State Colored Education Convention in Raleigh brought together 140 men from across the state. Craven County citizens chose as delegates the politically experienced artisans Israel B. Abbott, John Randolph Jr., and Henry H. Simmons. In all-too-familiar language, the white editor of the *New Bernian* cautioned local blacks to concentrate on hard work and self-improvement, to avoid "bad advisors," and "give less thought to politics." He insisted that Democrats, not Republicans, had blacks' interests at heart and "were responsible for whatever educational advantages they possessed." The three New Bern delegates proceeded to Raleigh, where they joined colleagues from more than forty counties, including several familiar to them from the freedmen's conventions and legislative sessions.[79] The Education Convention's polite resolutions restated the need for "the colored people" to "assume the task of molding their own destiny as citizens of the American Republic" and reiterated that "education, morality, and industry must constitute the basis of their elevation and prosperity as a people." They made no specific demands but expressed appreciation for the legislature's and governor's support, presumably referring to the recent law mandating public schools for both races. Along with providing an occasion for educational activists to join together in defining their mutual goals, the convention set the stage for the formation of a more effective black organization, the North Carolina State Teachers Association, a few years later.[80]

New Bernians' local efforts in the wake of the 1875 law made some headway. By 1880 black students in New Bern could attend one of three "colored" public schools: School No. 1 had George H. White as principal, with Miss Kate Pettipher, a daughter of blacksmith William N. Pettipher, as assistant; No. 2 had Alexander Bass, the black Episcopal churchman, as principal and Miss Maggie Godley as assistant; and No. 3 had a Miss Tucker, likely Richard Tucker's daughter Emeline, as teacher. Blacksmith George S. Fisher served as one of the three members of the racially mixed New Bern Public School Committee.[81]

An important result of the New Bern artisans' education campaign was the arrival of the young black teacher George H. White. A native of Bladen County, North Carolina, and bearer of a new normal-school certificate from Howard University, he came to town in 1877 at age twenty-four to become the teacher and principal at the new black school. The appointment proved fortunate both for New Bern and for White. Like his near contemporary Joseph C. Price, White found opportunities in New Bern that gave him a foundation for his ascendancy as a national leader. The young teacher studied law with white Republican attorney William J. Clarke, one of the few white attorneys in the state willing to take on a black protégé. Socially, White associated mainly with the education-minded black artisan circle whose members were instrumental in founding the school and bringing him to town, and it was in association with these artisan-citizens that White matured as a political leader. He joined the First Presbyterian Church and formed connections with black Presbyterians such as John Randolph Jr., whose daughter Fannie he married on February 27, 1879, the month after he passed the state bar exam. With his background in law and his experience and connections in New Bern, he was elected to his first legislative term in 1880, and he soon became one of the state's principal black leaders, as well as a spokesman for his race and, eventually, the only black man in the United States Congress.[82]

Thanks to White's work in the legislature, New Bern became home to one of the first state-supported normal schools established to train black teachers in North Carolina. The first was present-day Fayetteville State University, which had originated in 1867 with support from the Freedmen's Bureau and was authorized as a state normal school in 1877.[83] In 1881 the state authorized four more black normal schools; one account states that White crafted the bill and persuaded white legislators to support the black schools along with white ones. New Bern and Franklinton were selected for the first school sites, followed by Plymouth and Salisbury. The State Normal Institute, as the New Bern school was known, opened in July, with White as its principal and only teacher. By 1883 it had three more teachers.[84]

In 1883 the state legislature authorized the creation of separate public graded schools for black and white children, subject to local voters' approval of the system and the additional taxes involved. Craven County's black majority, as well as its white voters, supported the measure, which both groups believed would benefit their children. When two racially segregated boards of trustees were selected, ten out of the sixteen members of the black board were artisans.[85] Most had worked for the cause of black education for years—Israel B. Abbott, Virgil A. Crawford, Edward R. Dudley, George S. Fisher, Edward A. Richardson, Henry H. Simmons, and George Willis—while shoemakers Allen G. Oden and Cicero Robbins and carpenter John Jones were newer to educational offices, if not to civic leadership. Their fellow board members were George H. White, ministers Alexander Bass and Brevett W. Morris, grocers Robert G. Moseley and Joseph Mumford, and farmer and butcher Alexander Sanders.[86] These men could take satisfaction in the attainment of state-supported public schools for blacks, including a graded school, which, while still inadequate to the size of the population, greatly strengthened local educational opportunities. The State

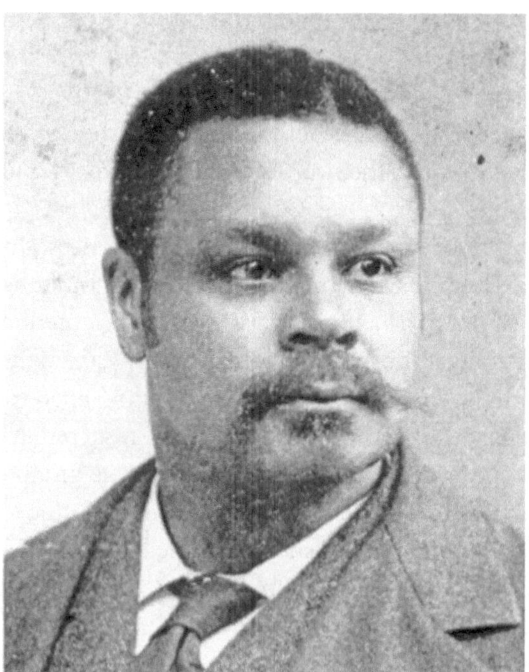

George H. White. Courtesy of the State Archives of North Carolina, Raleigh.

Normal Institute especially added luster to the town's identity and attracted students from far and wide, as well as giving local students advantages for which their parents' generation of artisans had worked so long.

"Strive to Improve in All Respects": Community and Uplift Associations

In addition to working for education, most of New Bern's leading black artisans, including all who were active in political life, participated as founders and leaders in religious, civic, and fraternal groups that supported racial uplift and blacks' development as citizens. In this area, as in economic life, they had gained a head start during Union occupation, having chosen their black minister at Andrews Chapel, formed St. Cyprian's Episcopal Church, and organized two volunteer fire companies during the war. Within months of the war's end they had founded Rue's Chapel AME congregation and King Solomon Lodge. From these early beginnings, they rapidly expanded their organizations and institutions, with politically active artisans figuring prominently among the founders and early officers. Some, such as carpenter Joseph Green and cooper Amos York, who were initially active in political life turned their focus to their ministries. Others, including brickmasons Israel Harris Sr. and Israel Harris Jr. and shoemakers Edward and John T. Havens, devoted themselves to their churches and fraternal and civic organizations.

At St. Cyprian's Episcopal Church, both of the Harrises, along with barber Moses Kennedy, served in various offices from the founding years onward and represented the parish at the racially mixed but predominantly white state diocesan conventions.[87] Presbyterians John Randolph Jr. and his extended family and George H. White led in founding Ebenezer Presbyterian Church in 1878 for the black members of First Presbyterian Church. Aided by the white church members and others, the little group constructed in 1880–81 a frame church in picturesque Carpenter Gothic style located on Pasteur Street near the railroad shops and the homes of several members. The "architect" and builder was John's carpenter brother, William O. Randolph, recently returned south from New Haven.[88]

As in previous years, the majority of black artisans, including those most active in politics, affiliated with AME and AME Zion. These associations—which included Rue's Chapel AME and Clinton Chapel AME Zion established in the 1860s, as well as Andrews Chapel AME Zion—maintained friendly relations, and in 1871 artisans from both groups were among the founders of the African Methodist Episcopal Singing School of New Bern.[89] In 1873, when the Rue's Chapel congregation laid the cornerstone for a new church, clergy present at the event included not only its pastor but also AME Zion minister Amos York and Episcopal deacon Alexander Bass.[90]

Also known as Bethel Methodist, Rue's Chapel continued to grow, with George B. Willis as a prominent leader and his son George H. Willis as the first organist. In about 1878 the congregation welcomed a native son as its pastor: Alexander H. Newton, the former brickmason's apprentice who had left for the North shortly before the war. Glad to return after an absence of twenty years, he was "received very cordially" by the church members, including several old friends. He marveled at the "great changes" in the town: "There were no slave gangs, no whipping post, no slave pen, no auction block." Instead, "a Mr. George H. White was superintendent of the public schools, (Colored); Edward Richardson was a clerk in the post office; John Willis was a deputy sheriff [actually, deputy clerk of court]; and Edward Hill, presiding elder at the AME Zion Church was a wealthy planter." New-

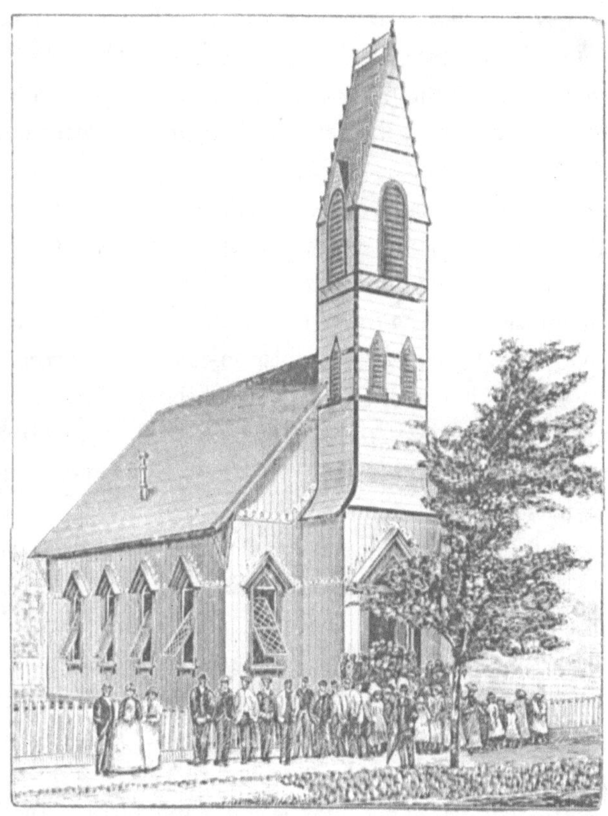

Ebenezer Presbyterian Church, New Bern. From L. C. Vass, History of the Presbyterian Church in New Bern, N.C.: With a Resume of Early Ecclesiastical Affairs in Eastern North Carolina, and a Sketch of the Early Days of New Bern, N.C. *(Richmond: Whittett and Shepperson, 1886). Courtesy of Tryon Palace Historic Sites and Gardens, New Bern, North Carolina.*

ton affirmed, "These and other men and women had made good their opportunities. They had not only welcomed the change from slavery but they had taken their places as freedmen among the citizens of this country and had demonstrated that they had in them that out of which the best citizens are made."[91]

Andrews Chapel maintained its role as a center of political as well as religious life. For several years after emancipation, the congregation—still the town's largest of either race—worshipped in the old meetinghouse on Hancock Street, and as in the past its leadership included many of the town's activist artisans, such as Richard Tucker, Thomas Battle, Virgil A. Crawford, and Edward R. Dudley. In the early 1870s, when the white Methodists decided to reclaim the old meetinghouse, the chapel congregation needed a new home on property that was indisputably theirs.[92] Crawford and Dudley, as trustees, handled the purchase of a lot on the south side of Queen Street in 1874. The congregation devoted their time and earnings to building an imposing frame edifice in Gothic Revival style, which was dedicated on August 22, 1886, and named St. Peter's AME Zion Church.[93]

In 1888 the congregation hosted the national conference of AME Zion at their new church, bringing hundreds of the faithful to New Bern and stirring many memories. Back in town for the occasion were former Andrews Chapel pastor James W. Hood, now a bishop, and Joseph Price, now president of AME Zion's Livingstone College in Salisbury.[94] Price surely greeted with pleasure bricklayer and churchman Thomas Battle, who, like Hood, had recognized Price's abilities twenty years before and encouraged him on his path to education.

A highlight of the conference was the election and consecration of two bishops, Charles Pettey and Cicero Richardson Harris. As some longtime New Bernians recognized, Harris was named for his brother-in-law, brickmason Cicero M. Richardson, who had left town for Fayetteville a half century before to learn his craft from the future bishop's father, Jacob Harris, and had become a successful citizen of Cleveland, Ohio. Cicero Richardson Harris and his brother Robert returned to Fayetteville after the war and founded the school that became the state's first black normal school in 1877, and he served as principal of present Livingstone College in its early years before Price became president. For freedpeople like Thomas Battle and Edward R. Dudley, the sight of the two black men being made bishop in a black church in New Bern represented a stunning advance from the world into which they had been born. For younger observers, the event affirmed rising hopes, and for Dudley's college-educated daughter, Sarah, it changed her life. She renewed her acquaintance with the widowed Charles Pettey, and a year later the two married. They became one of the most prominent black couples in town, and Sarah embarked on her role as an AME Zion spokeswoman for racial uplift and advancement.[95]

TOGETHER WITH THEIR CHURCH LIFE, New Bern's leading black artisans placed a high value on the civic and fraternal institutions they founded and supported. Politically active or not, they valued opportunities for leadership, fellowship, and community service in organizations that underscored their identities as citizens. When tailor Mustipher P. Holly died in 1905,

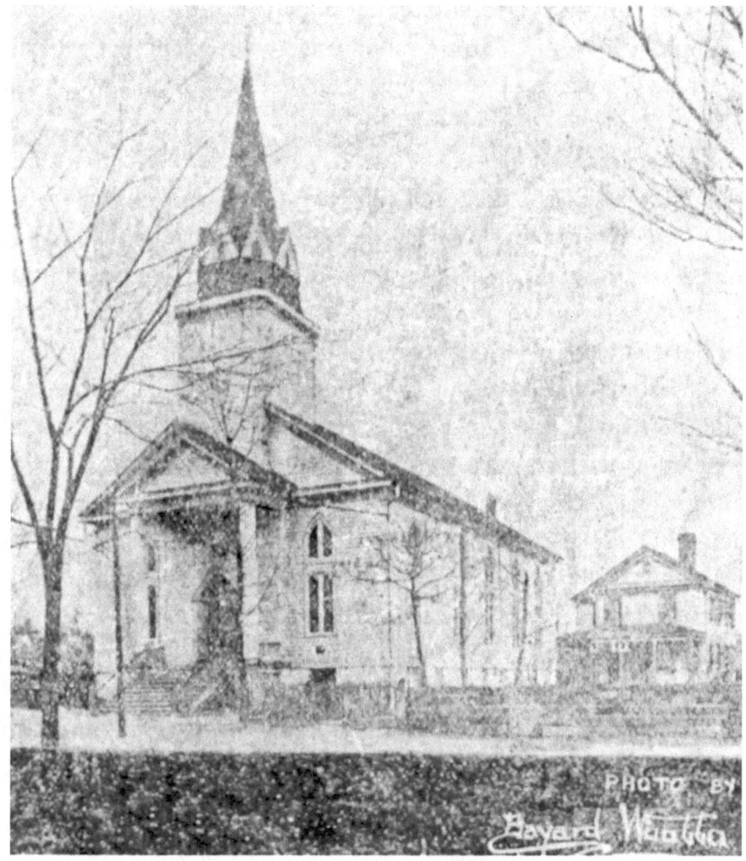

St. Peter's AME Zion Church. This shows the frame church before it was remodeled and brick veneered in the early twentieth century. Photograph by Bayard Wootten. Courtesy of the State Archives of North Carolina, Raleigh.

his possessions included his tailoring equipment, his Odd Fellows uniform, and his Masonic apron.[96] In 1871 cooper Edward R. Dudley, a passionate temperance man, founded a local unit of the Independent Order of Good Templars of New Bern as the first black chapter of that international temperance organization. The New Bern Templars included several leading black artisans who were drawn to its ideals. Like other Templars, the chapter frequently organized public events and parades to attract converts. In June 1873 it hosted a state convention of "Colored Good Templars" who marched through the town "in full regalia" for a "Grand Temperance Mass Meeting" of white and black participants at Andrews Chapel.[97]

Many other artisan-leaders likewise participated in numerous groups.

Virgil A. Crawford was a cofounder and member of the Rough and Ready Fire Company, the United Brotherhood Society of New Bern, the local educational board, and the Good Templars. Edward Havens, likewise a Mason, was a founder of the Young Men's Intelligent and Enterprising Association and the Mechanics' and Laborers' Mutual Aid Society of North Carolina. This last group, incorporated by a long list of founders chiefly from New Bern, was not a labor group but a society whose purpose was to provide death benefits to its members—usually $15 to $20, but ranging up toward $100, amounting to several days' pay for most artisans—to provide for a decent burial and help pay debts or medical expenses.[98]

Black Masonry was especially important in New Bern, as in many communities across the state and nation, and the order included most of the town's leading black artisans. For both blacks and whites, Masonry played a vital role in asserting their manhood, supporting their leadership in economic and civic life, and promoting virtuous living.[99] Along with founders George B. Willis and Henry H. Simmons, longtime members of King Solomon Lodge included Israel Harris Sr. and Edward and John Havens. Allen G. Oden and Edward R. Dudley served as worshipful masters, as did teacher and attorney George H. White, who, like tailor Mustipher Holly, became master of the state grand lodge. In 1870 King Solomon Lodge, probably drawing on the skills of its artisan members, began construction of a large frame lodge on Queen Street, near Cedar Grove Cemetery. In February 1871 they celebrated its completion with a grand ball, described in the local newspaper as "largely attended and a very enjoyable affair."[100] By 1880 there were two more black lodges—Morning Star and Zaradatha—whose officers included shoemaker Cicero Robbins and blacksmith Samuel Jackson, as well as Israel Harris Jr. and John Willis, who followed in their fathers' traditions.[101] Masons customarily took prominent roles in rituals that marked important beginnings and endings, from cornerstone-laying ceremonies to funerals. Burial services with Masonic honors constituted an important duty and benefit for members, and newspaper notices frequently announced members' deaths and invited Masonic brethren to attend their funerals as a group.[102]

Black men also gave public expression to their citizenship in military and quasi-military organizations that paralleled white groups of the day. The black New Bern Guards and New Bern Rifle Cadets, founded in 1875, marched and drilled regularly for several years; the Cadets' officers in 1880 included shoemaker Cicero Robbins as captain and cooper William

W. Lawrence as first lieutenant.[103] Black military groups not only survived but flourished under Democratic state governance. The adjutant general to Governor Zebulon Vance, whose 1876 victory had clinched the Democrats' "redemption" of the state, asserted that black militias had proved satisfactory in the past and predicted that in the event of racial conflict they would support the "conservative forces of society."[104] In 1877 the New Bern Guards and the Rifle Cadets, along with their fellow companies from Wilmington, Charlotte, Fayetteville, and Raleigh, made up two all-black battalions of the newly reorganized North Carolina State Guard. The New Bern and Raleigh companies formed the Fourth Battalion, with New Bern shoemaker and Union veteran Allen G. Oden as major, and the companies continued their public roles with governmental approval and support well into the 1880s.[105]

In 1887 New Bern black veterans, including Major Oden, established a local chapter of the Grand Army of the Republic (GAR), one of several black and white GAR posts in eastern North Carolina. Named for Colonel James Beecher, who led the African Brigade in 1863, the post had thirty-three members by 1890.[106] The sight of uniformed black veterans on the Fourth of July and especially Memorial Day vividly recalled to black New Bernians' minds the importance of black troops in achieving the Union victory. In 1897 Edward R. Dudley and other members of New Bern's three Masonic lodges conducted the cornerstone laying for a headquarters building for the Beecher post.[107] Well into the twentieth century, every year on May 30 GAR members and their friends and families processed from the post lodge to the National Cemetery to honor the Union dead. Old soldiers, like Oden, donned their Union uniforms for the occasion, and some hefted their old rifles. For some local whites, such scenes evoked events they would have preferred to forget, as well as providing a discomfiting image of potential black strength. For black participants and viewers, the GAR activities reinforced memories of their shared history and affirmed their stature as citizens and patriots.[108]

A Cooper and Civic Man

The public career of cooper George B. Willis incorporated the multiple civic roles of a busy artisan-citizen and the host of organizations that black citizens created in freedom. As we have seen, the formerly enslaved Willis had returned home "from Dixie" in the summer of 1865 and immediately joined George A. Rue in founding the AME church that became Rue's Chapel, and he served the church as a lay leader for the rest of his long life. That same year he was one of the founders of King Solomon Lodge, where he was an officer and faithful member; another local lodge was later named for him. In public life, he was a founding member of the local educational board in 1867; he was elected as one of New Bern's first black aldermen in 1869; and he led the black state militia company to Raleigh in July 1870, and in August won election to the state legislature.

In the flurry of organizational energy in New Bern during the 1870s and 1880s, Willis was frequently at the forefront. In 1870 he joined with painter John Randolph Jr. and cooper William W. Lawrence to form the Reliance Engine Company as a successor to the black fire companies formed during the war. Another company, the Rough and Ready, whose founders also included several artisans, was organized in 1874.[109] In 1871 Willis joined the Good Templars, and in 1873 he was one of the many founders of the Mechanics and Workers Mutual Aid Society of North Carolina. Following years of work for black public education, Willis was appointed to the 1883 board of trustees for the new black graded school. At his death in 1900 his estate received $99 from a "Beneficial Association" to which he belonged. Of this, $30 went to the undertaker, and the rest paid off his debts.[110]

For Willis and his fellow artisan-leaders, as for the northern white mechanics of the new republic, these organizations provided mutual support and the opportunity to develop leadership skills. For southern black artisans, in particular, such groups played vital roles in a world in which the dominant white minority sought to restrict their place and identity. In their creation of organizations that at once paralleled white organizations and provided an alternate universe of action unaffected by white definitions of their character and status, they, like millions of Americans, poured tremendous energy into the effort. They succeeded in forming institutions that, along with their churches, provided guidance and fellowship, strengthened their political and economic positions, and bolstered their local and supralocal connections.

Some associations enabled their members to demonstrate their civic presence in especially striking ways by holding large public meetings, conducting important rituals, and participating in public celebrations and parades. These elaborate parades and processions, whether formal and solemn or exuberant and jovial, underscored their group identity and allowed the participants to present a public face that differed from their everyday appearance and behavior. Crowds of both races lined the streets to watch or join the parades. Whether as Masons or Good Templars, New Bern Rifle Cadets or GAR veterans, through such elaborate and sometimes coded performances black New Bernians demonstrated their status as free people and citizens in age-old ways, presenting a public counterimage to the white stereotypes of black docility and expressing for themselves and all observers their leadership, solidarity, and pride.[111] As the winds began to blow stronger against black political participation late in the century, these organizations became ever more important to their members as the pillars on which their community life rested and the grounding for citizen leadership.

At Their Own Fireside: Families and Neighborhoods

Whatever their public roles might have been, for most of New Bern's artisans of color and their fellow freedpeople, the goal toward which they devoted their dearest hopes and strongest efforts was to establish, protect, nurture, and provide for their families—and thus to rejoice in the freedom "to stay with our loved ones," the freedom "to work for our children and provide homes which are ours," which Virgil A. Crawford had cited in his Emancipation Day speech. The wages they commanded as artisans, their activities in political life, and their participation in supportive church and civic groups—all helped freedpeople reach toward the attainment of their often long-deferred hopes for family unity, stability, and autonomy.

Long after the war ended, freedpeople held memories of the painful separations of families during slavery—memories that surely intensified their desire for stable families in freedom. Despite distance, the passage of time, and the paucity of records, many freedpeople recalled the names and stories of their parents and siblings, including those long dead or sold away. Formerly enslaved carpenter William Rue, who worked for contractor Edward Pavie, remembered that his father was a slave named Brister Rue—"never saw him"—but William's freeborn half sister, Grace Green, knew that their father had been "sold away" and was dead. Carpenter Joseph Green, Grace's husband, who was born a slave in Craven County and had lived in New Bern from age thirteen, remembered his long-dispersed family: his father, Richmond Green, had been dead for over twenty years, and his mother, Phoebe Green, was living in the North. His brother Thomas Green lived in Jones County, and brother John was in Mobile, Alabama. One sister, Mary Davis, was in New Bern, but his other sisters, Delsy, Harriet, Caroline, Chelsea, and Maria, had been "sold away." Simon Croom, the freedman and carpenter also employed by contractor Edward Pavie, knew the whereabouts of four of his brothers, including fellow carpenter James Weston in New Bern, but he also recalled his sisters Rachel, Betsy, and Jeannette, and his brothers Evans, Bright, Wright, Jack, and Emanuel—"all sold."[112]

Some fortunate slaves maintained intact families despite the threats bondage presented. Shoemaker Edward Havens and his family took pleasure in telling the story of how, as a young slave near Washington, North Carolina, he fell in love with Maria Cherry, a slave on a nearby farm. Learning that his beloved was in jeopardy of being sold after her owner's death, Edward appealed to his owner to buy her and allow them to live as man and wife. Because of the owner's esteem for Edward, the story continued, he paid the unusually large sum of $1,500 for Maria, and the two began wedded life and had the first of their children in slavery. By 1866 they were in New Bern, where they affirmed that they had been married for six years, and in 1870 their household included their children, Lilla, aged nine, Edward, seven, and James, one year old.[113]

Freed couples like the Havenses embraced their right to have legal marriages at last. In 1866, when state law authorized the registration and legal recognition of marital relationships among former slaves, artisans numbered among the local couples who thronged to register their marriages. Carpenter Joseph Green and Grace Brown had been married for eleven years; painter John Randolph Jr. and Della Redmond for fifteen years; and cooper Amos York and Desdemona McIlvane for nineteen. Widower Isaac Rue had wed his younger wife, Rachel, less than a year before. By 1870, William Rue and the brothers Simon Croom and James Weston, who had seen their families ripped apart in slavery, were married heads of households, and the two brothers and their families lived next door to one another.[114]

Carpenter and undertaker Richard Tucker and his wife Emeline, members of Andrews Chapel, had long yearned to legalize their union. Having lived as man and wife for thirty years in slavery, these parents of fifteen children were, according Freedmen's Bureau official Horace James, "not satisfied with their slave marriage, and invited me to marry them according to the laws of liberty and the word of God." With "legal marriage between slaves . . . impossible," the couple worried that they were "living in adultery and their children in illegitimacy." In December 1865, Richard and Emeline Tucker "stood together, at their own fireside, before the hymeneal altar," with “a few colored friends and several officers of the Freedmen’s Bureau, and lady teachers from the North” as guests. “They took each the other by the hand, as their lawful and wedded mate; and tears of grateful joy streamed down their serious faces, while the sanctions of our holy religion were thrown around their union of thirty years’ duration.” After the vows, “all sat down to a bountiful supper, and the past was recounted, the present enjoyed, and the future predicted.” Following the wedding feast, the couple and their friends and family joined in singing hymns, including a favorite in New Bern, “Sound the Loud Timbrel,” with its jubilant chorus, “Sound the loud timbrel o’er Egypt’s dark sea! Jehovah has triumphed, his people are free!”[115]

Family structures and household arrangements for black artisans encompassed a wide spectrum. Single, divorced, and widowed women artisans, chiefly needleworkers, might live alone, head households, or reside with kin or other people. Most single male artisans were just beginning their careers, such as carpenter William Physioc, aged twenty-four, who lodged with brickmason Israel Harris Jr. in 1880. It was not unusual for single craftspeople to stay with a parent or parents into adulthood and sometimes throughout the parents’ lives. George Eubanks, listed in the 1880 census as a “mulatto” apprentice carpenter aged nineteen, was living with his mother, the wealthy freedwoman Lucinda Stanly. After a sojourn in the North, he returned home by 1900 and stayed with her throughout her life. Many single artisans lived in boardinghouses or other settings. In what must have been an especially lively spot, Henry Harper, a forty-three-year-old wheelwright, roomed in a household headed by Kiziah Hayes, a white woman of fifty-two, along with two single black musicians, Richard Herring and Augustus Gill, aged fifty-five and thirty-five. Wagonmaker Luke Mason, a single wheelwright of sixty-eight in 1880, typified the former family men who spent their later years alone.[116]

Essentially all of the leading black artisans in postwar New Bern, however, subscribed to the ideal Virgil A. Crawford had invoked—of working to create families, support children, and “provide homes which are ours.” The single factor that most defined postwar New Bern’s artisan-leaders—more than their previous status of freedom or bondage, place of origin, or shared wartime experience—was a stable married life and membership in a strong and supportive family. Churches and fraternal groups, popular literature, and the rhetoric of national leaders all emphasized wholesome family and home life as essential to racial uplift. Like their antebellum free black predecessors, the leading artisans married and created systems of support across generations to adapt to the exigencies of fortune, separation, aging, and the frequency of early deaths.

Virgil A. Crawford himself had entered married life on September 4, 1865, when he wed Harriet Hargate, just five months after the war. In 1870 he headed a household that included Harriet, who was "keeping house," and an apprentice cooper, Cicero Jones. Ten years later the Crawfords' home included their daughter Sarah and a young cousin of Harriet's, both in school. Their situation was typical in that successful male artisans, whether black or white, usually headed households in which the wife was keeping house for her own family—a valued contrast from black women's role in slavery, when many had been forced to devote their time and energy to other women's children and households. Like the Crawfords, many artisan families included children above the age of four or five who attended school, while older children were employed in a parent's trade or other work or stayed in school into their teens or twenties.

Some artisan couples lived in the households of others—often kinfolk or artisan families—before setting up housekeeping. In 1870 blacksmith Titus Rial (Real) and his wife, Julia Anne, lodged with shoemaker Edward Havens and his wife, Maria, and their three children. By 1880 the Rials had their own household, which encompassed three generations, including a daughter, aged ten, and Julia's mother, washerwoman Dinah Garner.

Multigenerational households, which provided essential support for young and old alike, were numerous among leading artisan families. Edward and Caroline Dudley had in their home in 1880 their seven children plus Edward's mother, freedwoman Sarah Pasteur, for whom their eldest daughter, Sarah, was named. Blacksmith and freedman George S. Fisher and Mary Jane Jones, who married in October 1865, had five children at home in 1870, including John H. and Charles, apprentices in their father's trade. By 1880 their blacksmith son John H. had married and brought his wife and their child into the household, and their widowed daughter Harriet Lane was home and working as a dressmaker. Cooper Amos York and his wife Desdemona, who married in 1847 and registered their union in 1866, experienced a similar situation. In 1870 they had three children at home: Emily, at twenty-one, worked as a seamstress, and Hannah, aged twenty-three, and John T., fifteen, were both attending school. In 1880 the Yorks' household also included Amos's nephew William, a schoolboy of ten, while the grown children, Emily, John, and Hannah, were still at home.

John and Hannah were both schoolteachers, and Hannah had married and brought into the household her husband, barber Hugh Banks, and their infant son, Amos.[117]

To preserve family stability despite frequent early deaths, widowed artisans, like many other widowers and widows, remarried frequently. Painter John Randolph Jr. and his brother, carpenter William O. Randolph, were both widowed in midlife and promptly remarried. John wed a much younger woman, Kate Green, who helped raise his children from his marriage to his first wife, Della. William married Celia, the widow of his brother Lewis, and together the new couple raised the children of their previous marriages. John Randolph's daughter Fannie married schoolteacher George H. White, and the couple had a daughter, named Della after Fannie's mother. These happy events were followed by Fannie's death only a few months after her daughter's birth; White remarried and was widowed and remarried again. Some widowers married younger women and had second and third clusters of children, men such as brickmason and minister Thomas Battle, who reportedly married three times and fathered twenty-six children before and after emancipation. At age forty-five in 1870, the prosperous freedman was newly married to nineteen-year-old Annie Vashti Delmar, and their household included Thomas Battle Jr., fifteen, an apprentice in his father's trade. By 1880 Thomas and Annie had the first three of at least nine children of their own.

Artisans like Thomas Battle followed long-standing custom in passing their trade skills along to their children, thereby augmenting their workforce for a time and improving their children's prospects. Shoemaker Edward Havens, as we have seen, trained three sons, Edward Havens Jr., James, and John T., in his trade. Brickmason and Episcopal lay leader Israel Harris Sr. handed down his skills as well as his name: Israel Harris Jr. and his brother David pursued their father's trade, and in 1900 Israel Harris Jr. and his wife, Emma's, six children included seventeen-year-old Israel Harris III, representing the third generation of brickmasons in the family.[118]

Brickmasons and plasterers Edward A. Richardson and his brother Isaac, whose father was a caulker, probably learned their skills from their maternal grandfather, Isaac Rue. In 1870 Edward and his family lived only a few doors away from Rue, who at age eighty was still at his trade and one of the wealthiest black men in town. In reporting the "Death of an Old Colored Man," the *New Bernian* of January 17, 1880, recalled, "Uncle Isaac, as we learn, was born in slavery and was once the property of a colored man named Montford, but some twenty years before the late war, by thrift and industry he purchased his freedom and afterwards acquired a considerable amount of property in real estate, which is left to his grandson, E. A. Richardson." Rue noted in his will that he left the property to Edward "in consideration of his kindness to me in my old age."[119] In 1880 Isaac Richardson was a married brickmason whose son Charles was an apprentice brickmason, at age fifteen, and by 1900 brickmason Charles headed his own household and lived next door to his parents.

These artisans could also see the direction of the future and heeded Virgil A. Crawford's Emancipation Day message to "educate ourselves and our children and elevate our condition thereby higher and higher." Essentially all of New Bern's leading black artisans sent their children to at least a few years of elementary school before allowing them to begin training at a skilled trade or working at an occupation. Some stayed in school into their teens and twenties, and a few became schoolteachers themselves. By 1880, the black public schools of the 1870s, together with the new graded school and normal school, had opened doors for the rising generation to pursue white-collar professional and clerical careers essentially closed to people of color two decades before.

The *New Bern Commercial News* of October 25, 1881, carried the following announcement: "A musical and literary entertainment will be given at Stanly Hall on Tuesday, October 25, 1881, for the benefit of Ebenezer Presbyterian Church, colored." The notice was signed by Miss N. J. Scott, chairman, and George H. White, secretary, she a teacher and he the principal at the local black school. The "Order of Exercises" included choruses, solos, and duets, along with dialogues, jokes, and declamations. Featured singers and speakers included Sarah Dudley, Hattie Randolph, Oleona Pegram, Florence Randolph, John H. Fisher, and John York. A "bountiful supply of refreshments" was to be served after the performances. A review in the next day's white newspaper observed that the event was "an entire success. . . . All performed their parts admirably. The music, instrumental and vocal, was fine, and the literary efforts evinced careful training and native talent." The writer commented, "We think the colored people of New Berne are as intellectual as any in the State, and in all affairs of this sort give evidence of the influence upon the colored race of the literary culture and manners which have distinguished New Berne for so long in the history of the State."[120]

Presented as an entertainment to benefit the new church, the program also displayed to the public the fruits of local black education. Most of the performers were youths from eleven or twelve years old into their early twenties. Nearly all were the children of leading black artisans: Edward R. Dudley's daughter Sarah; Amos York's son John; George S. Fisher's son John; John Randolph Jr.'s daughter Hattie and his niece, Oleona Pegram; and William O. Randolph's daughter Florence—all of whom were attending or had attended school past the elementary grades. Most would soon translate their educational achievements into new occupational paths in New Bern or far from home.

Sarah Dudley completed the local graded school and went on Scotia Seminary in Concord, North Carolina, before returning home as a schoolteacher and marrying Bishop Charles Pettey.[121] Amos York's son John T. was teaching school. John H. Fisher began by pursuing his father George's trade as a blacksmith but gained enough schooling to become a clerk in a local bank. Oleana Pegram, a schoolgirl in her uncle John Randolph's household in 1880, continued her education at Scotia College and Fisk University and in 1889 married fellow teacher Simon Green Atkins. The couple moved to Winston-Salem to found the Slater Institute (later Winston-Salem State University), where he was the first president and she a revered teacher of English.[122] Randolph's daughter Harriet also gained an education and in 1887 married George H. Willis, the schoolteacher son of George B. Willis. This couple also moved to Winston-Salem, where George began a school and was known as "Professor" Willis. The elder Willis son, John, was practicing his father's coopering trade in 1870, but he too attended school and was employed as a clerk by 1880. Unlike his brother, he stayed in New Bern with his father and by 1880 at age thirty was the deputy clerk of the superior court.

An Artisan Family Network of Neighbors

The multigenerational artisan family of Hannah Neale, whom we met as a free family before the war, demonstrated the varied strategies, including transfers of property and household proximity, that families employed to weather changing times. Although Hannah owned only a modest property—her home in Bragg's Alley, which she had bought before the war—she took steps to protect it for her heirs. In 1864, in the midst of the war, she put her "X" on a deed transferring her property to her schoolteacher daughter, Grace Green. To ensure the efficacy of the deed despite the wartime suspension of registrations, Hannah enlisted prominent friends as witnesses—her fellow Andrews Chapel members, elders Isaac Rue, Moses Hill, and Richard Tucker, and minister James Walker Hood. Once county government was restored, she registered the deed on September 10, 1866, as one of the first recorded in New Bern after the war. On the same day, Grace deeded the property to her own daughter, seamstress Hannah Cora Brown, subject to a life estate for Grace and her husband, carpenter Joseph Green. Joseph, Grace, and Hannah Cora continued to reside there throughout their lives, and after their deaths the property went to Hannah Cora's daughters, Melissa and Alice Harris.[123]

Family support extended beyond the transfer of property. In the summer of 1865, Hannah's son George A. Rue, the distinguished AME minister and sometime mechanic, had returned home with his wife, Ann, and their daughters, Malinda (Milly) and Hannah. Late in 1866, George A. Rue's death in midlife left Ann as a single head of household with two schoolteacher daughters plus little Nealy and George, both born in New Bern. Living near Hannah Neale and Grace Green, Ann and her family could rely on family companionship and support. Also nearby was George Rue's nephew, house carpenter and political figure Israel B. Abbott. By 1870 Abbott's family included his wife, Susan, and their four young children, James, Ann, Cora, and baby Gracy. Hannah Neale, now sixty-five, lived near the Abbotts in her own household with her great-granddaughter Hannah C. Abbott, aged two, for whom she was caring while Israel and Susan managed their houseful of children and the new baby. Hannah Neale died in 1880, aged about seventy-five, having seen most of her children and grandchildren survive and flourish. In 1887, her grandson Israel Abbott died in the prime of life, not long after his loss in the tumultuous election of 1886, leaving his widow to raise their children in their home on George Street in the midst of his relatives and fellow artisan families.[124] Susan Abbott lived out her life as a widow, but in 1883 the long-widowed Ann Rue remarried, to cooper George B. Willis—the friend and fellow churchman of her late husband, George A. Rue—who had lost his longtime wife, Sarah, a few years before.[125]

"Homes Which Are Ours"

Like their antebellum predecessors, leading postwar artisans invested their earnings in providing homes for their families' security and comfort. As in the past, some artisans—including those of relatively modest means—graced their residences with genteel furnishings indicative of their standing and tastes. Mass production of furniture and household goods reduced prices and enabled a growing proportion of citizens to afford such niceties. Israel B. Abbott left his widow and seven children a small estate in 1887, which included a modicum of furniture and the family's parlor organ. For middling as well as elite families of this period, foot-pedaled parlor organs added a genteel touch as well as enabling family and friends to enjoy music at home in a new medium. Carpenter William O. Randolph and his wife, Celia, who rented their home, furnished it nicely with beds, bureaus, and chairs in their two upstairs bedrooms, and welcomed guests to a parlor fitted with a sofa, sofa chairs, pictures, a marble-top table, and their most expensive household item, an organ valued at twelve dollars.[126] William's brother John Randolph Jr. lived in similar fashion until his death in 1890. With his children grown and gone, he and Kate had in their home one bedstead and a featherbed, a "lounge," two rocking chairs, three stoves, a washstand, and a looking glass, plus numerous chairs to accommodate visiting family and friends. For John and Kate Randolph, too, a prized possession was their parlor organ, valued at fifteen dollars, around which their family could gather to sing their favorite hymns.[127]

Black artisans followed various paths in deciding where to locate their homes, depending on their economic and social status, the availability and cost of housing for rent or sale, and proximity to family, workplace, church, and fellow people of color. Throughout the nineteenth century black artisans continued in the residential patterns begun in the early nineteenth century, with some living in predominantly white areas, many in areas with fairly even numbers of both races, and an increasing number in the growing and strongly black suburban neighborhoods. As the city mushroomed during and immediately after the Civil War, freedpeople settled in nearly every part of town, but especially in the racially mixed and affordable suburban neighborhoods. As in other North Carolina cities, from Wilmington to Charlotte, while residential racial segregation accelerated faster than did the segregation of businesses, at no time in the nineteenth century were living patterns in New Bern fully segregated by race. Throughout the predominantly black and predominantly white sectors, the pattern was complicated by an often subtle patchwork of blocks that were racially mixed as well as individual blocks or clusters dominated by a single race, and certain blocks or areas distinguished by class as well as race. Reinforcing earlier trends, these patterns continued to shape the urban landscape well into the twentieth century after many prosperous whites left central New Bern for segregated streetcar suburbs.[128]

Following antebellum precedent, a few successful black artisans owned homes in the predominantly white part of town, including in 1880 George B. Willis and his family on East Front Street, just south of Queen; Richard Tucker on Metcalf Street, between Broad and Pollock; and George S. Fisher on Broad Street. George Street persisted as a racially mixed corridor that included black homeowners, with seamstress Elizabeth Bragg and her family on South Front, near George; shoemaker Edward Havens on Pollock Street, between George and Bern Streets; black carpenter Charles Disbru at Donum Montford's old corner at Broad and George; and tailor Mustipher Holly farther north on George Street, between New and Queen. The racially mixed blocks on the south side of Queen, east of George and near St. Peter's and St. Cyprian's Churches, maintained their identity and prestige into the twentieth century. A map of about 1881 showed a "School, Colored" at the corner of Johnson and Middle Streets. Established residents here included Edward A. Richardson at the corner of Queen and Johnson Streets, where he, like his grandfather Isaac Rue, lived on property the family had owned since before the war. Virgil A. Crawford and his family lived on Queen, near Metcalf, as did John Randolph Jr. and his family.[129]

From 1870 onward, however, an increasing majority of New Bern's black artisans, like most of their fellow citizens of color, lived in the racially mixed but increasingly black suburban sectors north and west of the central city. Residents ranged across the spectrum in their occupations and their accommodations, from day laborers and laundresses renting rooms or lodging to prosperous artisans who owned their own homes. There were numerous cottages and duplexes but also many two-story houses, some with the complex footprints and porches typical of the fashionable Queen Anne style. In the neighborhood west of downtown and north of New South Front Street, the racial mix continued to show a fairly even balance. Residents in 1880 included shoemaker Allen G. Oden on New South Front Street near Spring Street; and, on German (Liberty) Street, carpenter-grocer David Wilson, blacksmith William Pettiford, and clergyman Alexander Bass. Key institutions included Clinton Chapel AME Zion Church on Church Street and St. John's Missionary Baptist Church at the corner of South Front and Bryan Streets.[130]

North of Queen Street, where newly developed blocks reached westward

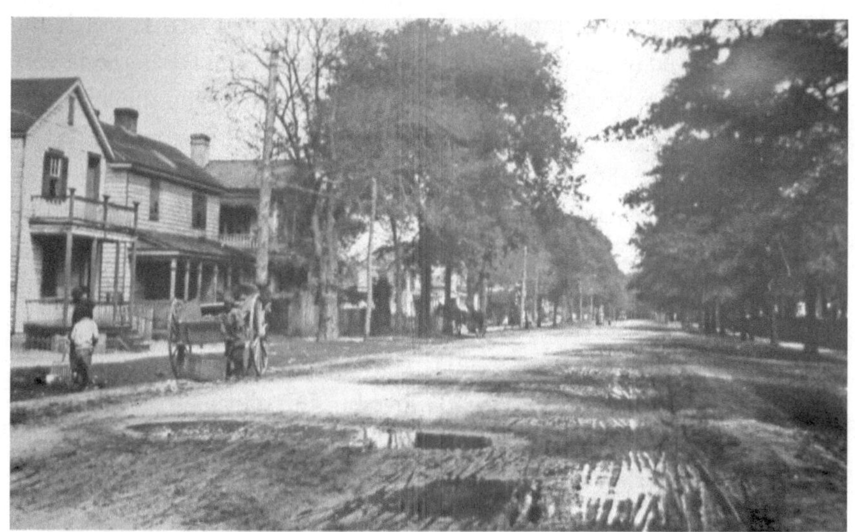

North George Street, ca. 1900, looking north from Queen Street. This is a rare photograph of the residential neighborhoods north of Queen Street before the Great Fire of 1922 leveled much of the area. Courtesy of the Kellenberger Room, New Bern–Craven County Public Library, New Bern, North Carolina.

toward Five Points and beyond, the racial mix grew increasingly black. Within the original Dryboro borders and nearby, artisan families continued the pattern of home ownership northward along George Street, including, in 1880, house carpenter and politician Israel Abbott and his family near Cedar Street, and bricklayer and Episcopal churchman Israel Harris Sr. near Pine. Amos York and his wife, Desdemona, lived on Bern Street, on property that had been hers before the war. Tailor John Hawley lived on West Street, between Queen and Cedar.

Within and east of old Dryboro, toward the railroad shops, stood such landmarks as King Solomon Masonic Lodge, facing St. Cyprian's Episcopal Church across Queen Street. Rue's Chapel AME Church was a few blocks north at Cypress Street and Bragg's Alley, up the street from the home on Bragg's Alley where Joseph and Grace Green had lived since the 1850s. In 1880, Edward R. Dudley and his family lived in a fine house at the corner of Pasteur and Primrose Streets, and bricklayer Thomas Battle and his family were almost next door, on Primrose. George H. and Fannie Randolph White lived on Pasteur, near Ebenezer Presbyterian Church, then under construction by her uncle William.[131]

By 1900 the neighborhoods north of Queen reached farther north and west, and showed both continuity and change. Amos and Desdemona York had died, but their grown children Hannah and John T. and their families made their homes there among their childhood friends. George H. White had moved in the 1880s to Johnson Street, where he lived among white neighbors. Thomas Battle and his growing family still lived in their big house on Primrose Street but had new neighbors, Sarah Dudley Pettey and her husband, Bishop Charles Pettey, who had moved into her father Edward R. Dudley's residence after he moved to his farm. Other recent arrivals included young brickmason Henry Clay Sparrow on Pasteur Street, and Edward Havens and his family, who moved from Pollock Street to a newly developed area on Willis Street, north of Primrose.[132]

In these homes and neighborhoods, whose basic character was rooted in the distant past but expanded and developed after emancipation, New Bern artisans and their friends and families built full lives around their community institutions and continued to cultivate the relationships they had established and nurtured as freedpeople. They had accomplished much that Virgil A. Crawford had envisioned in 1873. The most industrious, thrifty, and fortunate had established families and comfortable homes of their own. Black congregations had built new churches, including St. Peter's AME Zion edifice, which had been the setting for the recent national conference of Zion, and civic and fraternal groups were thriving.

When brickmason Israel Harris Sr. died at his home on north George Street in June 1897, in his eighty-first year, he and his family had lived there for some thirty years. The newspaper announced, "Members of King Solomon Lodge No. 1, F. A. M. You are hereby notified to be at your lodge this p. m. at 2:30 o'clock for the purpose of attending the funeral of Bro. Israel Harris, Sr. Visiting brethren are invited to attend." From the lodge, the Masons processed across Queen Street to St. Cyprian's Episcopal Church, where Harris had been senior warden and where his son followed him in that office. After the funeral, a throng proceeded from the church along Queen to George Street, thence northward past Harris's home and west to Greenwood Cemetery, where he was buried with Masonic honors amid the graves of his family, Masonic brethren, fellow churchmen, and neighbors.[133] Sustained by such bonds as these, black artisans drew upon their relationships as well as their craft skills to navigate the fast-changing racial and political times.

"Faithful, Industrious, Loyal People": Political Events of 1890–1900

Inventory and return of George H. White executor of Allen G. Oden Dec'd : One gun (16 shooter); 40 pairs of shoe lasts; 2 Shoemakers "Kits" and a lot of Tools and implements belonging to them; one old stove; one Grind Stone; 45 lbs. of leather worth about $10.00; one small clock; one lot of "plunder" found in shoe shop. All of the above . . . now in the hands of Dicy Oden, widow and sole devisee. May 9, 1895. . . . Cash received Burial relief, $15.00, rents received from shop, $18.50; amt received from Grand A. R., $15; Masonic Lodge, $20; Eastern Star Lodge, $15; Rent of Shop, $23.50; Sale of lot per order, $275.

—Allen G. Oden (d. 1894) estate return, filed January 17, 1896, Superior Court, Craven County Estates Papers

When attorney George H. White listed the worldly goods of shoemaker Allen G. Oden, his purpose was to fulfill his responsibility as executor of his fellow New Bernian's estate. The items he named also evoked the multifaceted identity of an accomplished artisan and citizen of the time and place. The various death benefits reflected Oden's engagement in civic groups, and most of his personal possessions betokened the craft skills that had enabled him to acquire a town lot and his workshop. The first item White noted—"One gun (16 shooter)"—was a repeating rifle of a type used effectively by Union soldiers during the war, a possession that represented Oden's service as a citizen, a sergeant in the Union Army, a major in the state guard, and commandant of the New Bern camp of the Grand Army of the Republic. It also suggested that Oden was capable of protecting himself and his wife.[134]

Another dimension of the shoemaker's identity appeared in the *New Bern Daily Journal*'s obituary for "Major A. G. Oden, a worthy colored man of this city." The newspaper presented a typical white definition of such worth—"a man of good sense, quiet and industrious" who "worked with diligence, lived according to his means, paid his way and was polite to all. He was a man who would serve as a good model to his people."[135] Such cautionary language was familiar: two years earlier the same newspaper described the prosperous blacksmith George S. Fisher as "one of the best colored men of the place," meaning that he "knew how to behave and conduct himself and did it. He was in no way obtrusive but quiet, peaceable, industrious, honest, and truthful."[136] These comments, although written from a white

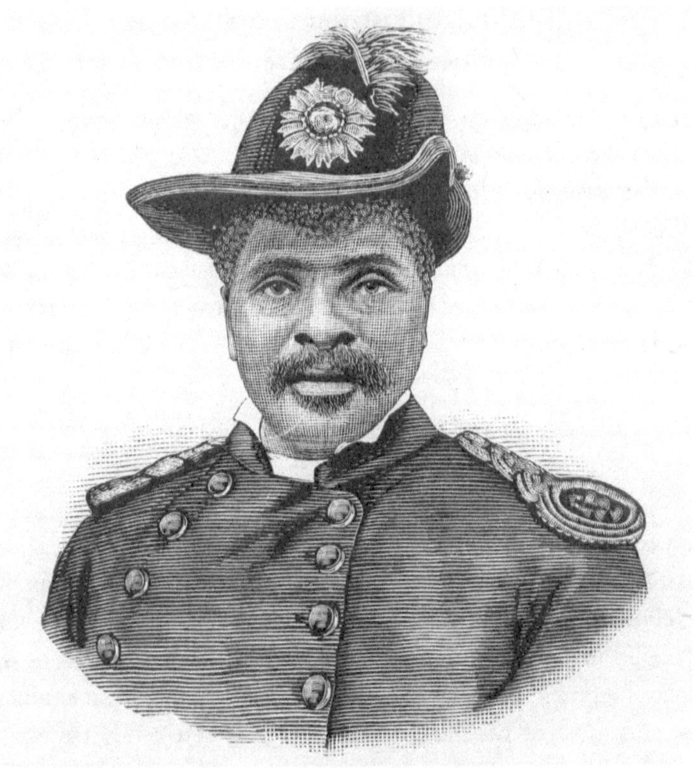

Allen G. Oden. From James Walker Hood, One Hundred Years of the African Methodist Episcopal Zion Church; or, The Centennial of African Methodism *(New York: A.M.E. Zion Book Concern, 1895). Courtesy of the North Carolina Collection, University of North Carolina at Chapel Hill Library.*

perspective, revealed the black leaders' strategies for survival and success. Like their antecedents, as well as their contemporaries, Oden and Fisher had mastered not only craft skills but the art of combining strong leadership with strategies of deference toward whites to protect themselves, their families, and their livelihoods.

One additional statement in Oden's obituary was especially relevant in the fall of 1894. The shoemaker was, according to the newspaper, "a Republican and firm in his politics, but he had no bitterness in it, and, while he was in a measure prominent in his party he never let politics interfere in his business." The phrasing implied a contrast between Oden's diplomatic approach and more "obtrusive" black Republicans such as the outspoken George H. White. During the summer and fall of 1894, as Democrats faced an unprecedented challenge from the alliance of Republicans and Populists, a "firm Republican" artisan such as Oden employed his personal as well as craft skills to ensure that his Democratic customers would not make *his* politics interfere with *their* patronage of his business.

During the 1890s black artisans found their customary societal balancing acts especially necessary amid events that alternately bolstered and threatened their political rights. The ever-broadening impact of industrialization, which contributed to the destabilization of the national and state economies, heightened political and racial tensions.[137] As we have seen, in the late 1880s and early 1890s, Democrats who claimed North Carolina as a "white man's country" had reduced black political participation even in New Bern. Still, because of the town's strong black majority and its geographical position within the "Black Second," its leading black artisans and their ally George H. White managed to win offices when few blacks in the state could still do so and to vote at a time when blacks in many southern states had been disfranchised.

Black political life began the decade at a low ebb. Although "firm" Republicans in New Bern, such as Allen G. Oden, supported black and Republican candidates in good numbers, and although black artisan-citizens Virgil A. Crawford, Henry H. Simmons, and Mustipher P. Holly (who once defeated Crawford at the polls) won seats as aldermen in the early 1890s, the success of black Republicans was exceptional.[138] After the Democratic legislature's regerrymandering in 1891 removed Craven County from the "Black Second" district to dilute the black vote, George H. White established a residence in Tarboro to qualify to run for Congress in the second district, the only one where a black candidate had a chance.

A stirring new chapter began in 1892, when North Carolina Populists (generally white, disaffected Democrats) and Republicans (dominated by white officeholders but still counting on the support of most black voters) both won substantial numbers of seats in the legislature. In 1894 the Populists and the Republicans formed a strategic alliance as "Fusionists" and won a startling legislative majority. Two years later, the Fusionists increased their majority, a white Republican captured the governor's office, and George H. White—who still maintained a home and friends in New Bern—was elected to serve as the only black member of the U.S. Congress.

On the local political scene, blacks regained much of what they had lost. After the Fusionist legislature revised the city's charter, three black men won council seats, and black New Bernians were appointed or elected to other local or state offices. While state Democrats railed against "Negro rule," Bishop Charles Pettey, the son-in-law of Edward R. Dudley, observed happily in August 1897, "We have had colored coroners and State's attorneys elected by a majority of white voters. Our representative in Congress is a colored man, George H. White, my neighbor. Throughout the State there are over 100 petty magistrates filled by colored men."[139] The number of black officeholders remained minuscule compared to the proportion of blacks in the electorate, but for people of both races the sight of blacks in such positions carried tremendous symbolic power.

Artisans were also prominent among the black New Bernians who seized a civic and military opportunity opened by the Republican governor Daniel Russell: that of forming a volunteer company to serve in the Spanish-American War. In April 1898 a "meeting of the colored citizens" organized the New Bern Riflemen. The commissioned officers were Captain James D. Dudley, the carpenter brother of cooper Edward R. Dudley, recently returned from Washington, D.C., and Lieutenants Israel Harris Jr., who followed in his father's trade as a brickmason, and John T. York, the schoolteacher who had returned to his father Amos's trade as a cooper. The company joined the Third North Carolina Regiment, authorized by Governor Russell as one of the only black-led black regiments in the war, to the fury of Democrats, who accused him of pandering to black voters.[140] In late May, the New Bern Riflemen boarded a train carrying black companies from Wilmington, Charlotte, and Raleigh to garrison duty at nearby Fort Macon. While the proximity of black soldiers at Macon and their occasional visits to New Bern galled some whites, hundreds of black citizens lined the tracks to cheer the Third Regiment on its way to Fort Macon and when the regiment departed the fort in September. Sent west to Knoxville and then to Macon, Georgia, for continued garrison duty, the New Bern Riflemen and the Raleigh, Charlotte, and Wilmington companies served until early in 1899, frustrated by assignments that kept them away from home without seeing the military action they had sought. They returned to find the state's political situation turned upside down.[141]

In the "white supremacy crusade" leading up to the election of November 1898, Tar Heel Democrats stepped up their cries of "Negro domination" and fomented fears about black men violating white women. For a time New Bern largely ignored the rhetoric. The local newspaper generally took a civil tone about black officeholders and even mocked the Raleigh *News and Observer*'s "outrage editor" for the constant headlines about black insolence and violence in Craven County. In August 1898, however, Democratic leader Charles B. Aycock made a visit to fire up white New Bernians by explaining "how vital" it was to protect their women and the "safety of the home."[142] From then on the local situation grew increasingly tense.

Because of the number of local black officials, state Democratic leaders pilloried New Bern and Craven County to arouse whites across the state. "Negroes on Top: In Craven County the White Men Are Not In It," ran a *News and Observer* headline on September 18, 1898.[143] In that newspaper's savage broadside, "Negro Rule in Craven County," the old cooper and civic leader George B. Willis could have seen caricatures of local black candidates, including his son, John B. Willis, the clerk of court who was running for register of deeds. The *New Bern Journal* got on board and warned local blacks against voting the Republican ticket by citing their "economic dependence" on whites and recalling a recent winter when "the white people of New Berne" had provided blacks with money, fuel, clothing, and food.[144]

Amid a statewide Democratic landslide on November 8, New Bern and Craven County's black voters elected businessman Isaac Hughes Smith as one of only four black men to serve in the state House of Representatives and chose John B. Willis and other black men for local offices.[145] Having fended off for the moment the triumph of the white supremacy campaign in their community, black New Bernians rejoiced to learn that their former townsman George H. White had won reelection to Congress, where he served until 1901 as the sole spokesman for their race.[146]

But soon they heard horrifying reports of the violent Democratic coup in Wilmington two days after the election. On November 10, 1898, armed white Wilmingtonians—including members of the local military company home on leave—forcibly removed the legally elected city council and killed or sent out of town many blacks and white Republicans. New Bern Democrats were dissuaded from taking similar action only by their leaders' assurances that the newly elected Democratic legislature would soon return control of local government to whites. As promised, the legislature promptly vacated New Bern's municipal offices held by blacks and other Republicans and appointed Democrats until a local election could be held. In the election held in May 1899, however, black New Bernians returned to the polls and elected four black men from the Fifth and Sixth Wards, including the cooper and Spanish-American War veteran John T. York, to serve a two-year term among the twelve aldermen.[147]

These remaining political opportunities soon vanished. Many black leaders, such as Edward R. Dudley, had hoped that the tide of white intolerance sweeping the lower South might not reach North Carolina, which had thus far avoided adopting the most oppressive measures of its sister states. They expected to fight racially charged political battles, but some had counted on thirty years of voting and their relationships with "white friends" to maintain black political participation. What they did not anticipate was the Democrats' second, scorched-earth white supremacy campaign of 1900. At stake in this election was not only the control of the legislature and the governorship, but also the elimination of blacks from politics. In 1899 the legislature crafted a constitutional amendment, adapted from Louisiana's model, to disfranchise nearly all blacks. It included a poll tax and a literacy requirement, along with a "grandfather clause" to benefit whites by allowing illiterate men to vote until 1908 if they or an ancestor had qualified to vote before January 1, 1867.[148] The *New Bern Daily Journal* of January 2, 1900, supported the amendment in language reminiscent of a preceding local newspaper's comment on black disfranchisement in 1835: although the measure might "work a hardship to the better and more respectable members of the colored race . . . that cannot be avoided at the cost of the whole white race."[149]

Well before the election, the white supremacy campaign eroded employment opportunities for black artisans. For years the Atlantic and North Carolina Railroad Company had been a major local employer of black carpenters, blacksmiths, and laborers, but in 1900 railroad president James A. Bryan, a New Bern Democrat and legislator from a white elite family, faced attacks from his own party over the company's employment of black workers. The result appeared in the *New Bern Daily Journal* of March 13, 1900, under the headline, "Negro Employees Relieved":

> It was reported yesterday that a number of the negroes in the service of the A. & N. C. railroad had been sent to the happy hunting grounds of non employment. President James A. Bryan was seen yesterday and asked about the matter. Mr. Bryan stated that he had discharged several of the negroes, adding thereby to the number that had previously been relieved to make way for white men, and that some time ago he had instructed the foreman to substitute white for colored labor whenever it was available, and that policy would continue to be pursued. . . . Mr. Bryan said [it had] been possible to make

wholesale changes without jeopardizing the interests of the road and the lives of its patrons.[150]

For black artisans and laborers employed by the railroad or elsewhere, the message could not have been clearer. However skilled they might be, and however faithfully they adhered to models of thrift and industry, under the political pressures of white supremacy, these qualities were of no consequence.

When election day rolled around, Democrats' voting frauds and threats of violence won the election for them even in New Bern. White Republican William E. Clarke, whose attorney father had mentored George H. White, called the election "a perfect farce," a "mockery from start to finish." Whites were "armed to the teeth," and when blacks came to the polls nonetheless, they were forced to hand their ballots to pollsters who "counted them as they pleased." The Democratic ticket triumphed statewide, as did the disfranchisement amendment, which took effect at the next election in 1902.[151]

Within a short time, New Bernians saw the impact of disfranchisement along with the expansion of Jim Crow laws and practices.[152] Ejected from his public position, the longtime clerk of court and register of deeds John B. Willis found work as a coachman and then as an insurance agent. When the voting registration books opened in 1902, a few members of the longtime free black families in rural Craven County came to register, but essentially none of New Bern's black political leaders did so, not even Edward R. Dudley, the son of a local white man. Apparently the only black artisan-leader who registered to vote was sixty-seven-year-old cooper, legislator, and city councilman Henry H. Simmons. Born in slavery, the aged artisan-citizen claimed early national–period white physician Edward Pasteur as his ancestor who had qualified to vote before January 1, 1867.[153]

George H. White, who had begun his political career amid New Bern's robust black artisan-citizen culture, had decided not to run again in 1900. Concluding that he could "no longer live in North Carolina and be a man," after completing his term in Congress in 1901, he followed the example of leading New Bern artisan families of the 1850s and left North Carolina, never to return. He sold his house in New Bern two years later.[154] For black New Bernians, surely White's famous 1901 valedictory rang true: "This, Mr. Chairman, is perhaps the negroes' temporary farewell to the American Congress, but let me say, Phoenix-like he will rise up some day and come again. These parting words are in behalf of an outraged, heart-broken, bruised, and bleeding, but God-fearing people, faithful, industrious, loyal people—rising people, full of potential force."[155]

Many black New Bernians joined White in the exodus. Others, however, stayed in their home communities and continued to take roles as public-spirited citizens through their churches and civic organizations. Although blacks could no longer hold public office and few could vote, black New Bernians, including numerous leading women, engaged in essentially political activity by working to advance conditions and educational opportunities for their fellow blacks. In 1902, when a black Baptist minister came to town to start an industrial institute, he made the mistake of sending out a fundraising letter to northern white Baptists that described New Bern as one of the most benighted places in the "black belt." When news of the letter reached New Bern, infuriated black citizens called a protest meeting. Denouncing the minister as an "ingrate" and deceiver, they countered his offensive description by pointing to their graded public schools, three private high schools, and the high rate of homeownership—achievements that reflected nearly forty years of work, including the efforts of artisan-leaders. "[As] for culture, refinement and moral standing," they summed up, "our citizens will compare favorably to any in the state."[156]

TWO LONGTIME CITIZENS and leading artisans in New Bern died shortly after the turn of the century: cooper Henry H. Simmons in 1904 at age seventy and shoemaker Edward Havens in 1906 at sixty-five. Their obituaries in the local white newspapers showed continuities from the themes voiced in the previous decade along with subtle but important changes. The *New Bern Weekly Journal* of July 22, 1904, lauded the "Hon Henry H. Simmons" as "one of our old and respected colored citizens he having represented this county in the Legislature and was also an ex-member of our Honorable Board of City Council."[157] Two years later, the *New Bern Daily Journal* headlined its obituary for Havens "Death of Esteemed Colored Man" and described him as "one of the best known and most highly respected colored men of the city," who "won regard from white as well as black on account of his integrity" and taught his children "the principles of success in the dignity of labor."[158]

Much of the content of these obituaries was familiar from previous years—the occupation and accomplishments of the deceased, both of the funerals held at St. Peter's AME Zion Church with Masonic honors at the burials

—but the tone differed significantly from that of the cautionary obituaries of the previous decade. In the early 1890s, black men in New Bern had possessed political power and the right of suffrage, and Republicans like Oden and Fisher presented challenges that spurred whites to publish barely veiled warnings. By 1906, the issue of black political power had been settled to Democrats' designs. With threats of "Negro rule" eliminated, white spokesmen were quick to praise "esteemed colored men" who lived up to their standards of "integrity" and "respect" and who, as the coded wording put it, taught their children the "dignity of labor" rather than aiming above their station. It was all too ironic that the newspaper called "colored citizen" Henry H. Simmons "Hon." and cited his service as a legislator and "an ex-member of our Honorable Board of City Council."[159] Just four years earlier the same newspaper had supported the amendment to ensure that no more "colored citizens" would hold local or state offices for many a year to come.

Simmons and Havens had mastered the myriad complexities required for a southern black artisan to succeed. Numbering among the "hundreds of fine artisans" recalled by Alexander H. Newton, who came out of slavery "able to begin at once the laying of the foundation of the history of a free people," they employed their craft expertise and personal strategies to earn a competency for their families and to gain respected positions in the community. Havens modeled the prosperity attainable through industry, thrift, and a carefully tailored public presentation. He established a comfortable home, trained his sons in his craft, and bequeathed them a good business at a prime address. Simmons, less wealthy, devoted his energies to political service and especially toward education for blacks. As an old man, he carried out the values of a lifetime by registering to vote in the first state election after the disfranchisement amendment took effect. From their births in slavery through their long lives as artisans and citizens, Henry H. Simmons and Edward Havens, like their fellows before and after them, used their skills, relationships, and sense of purpose to make the best of their times and their place for themselves and for those who came after them.

Conclusion

From the eve of the American Revolution to the turn of the twentieth century, skilled black workers in New Bern, North Carolina, demonstrated the multiple possibilities of crafting identities as American artisans and citizens. Like their counterparts throughout the nation, they employed techniques learned through apprenticeships or from family members to make the objects their community needed. Many simply scraped by, while some used their trade skills along with their acumen and relationships to accumulate property, establish strong families, and win business and community status. As town dwellers, they shared with other urban craftspeople the opportunities to encounter people of all classes and races, to learn new styles and new ideas, and to form new relationships. In some periods they continued traditions and personal skills learned from parents or grandparents, while at other times they met challenges that demanded new strategies to protect or advance their status.

As southern blacks, New Bern's artisans of color confronted situations different from those known to their northern and white counterparts. In an economy and a social structure based on slavery, enslaved and free black artisans contended with legal and extralegal restraints that circumscribed their work and their lives. Once freedom came, they, like white artisans, dealt with the impact of mass production on all craft trades, but they also encountered racial barriers to advancement in the industrialized economy as manufacturers, contractors, or architects. In every period, successful artisans of color mastered the complex art of calibrating competence and ambition with techniques of self-presentation and communication that best served their purposes.

For black craftspeople in New Bern and other southern cities, their circumstances might seem to offer little chance to define themselves as part of the American ideal of artisan and citizen identity. Yet through their experiences in New Bern we can see how black artisans found ways to create their own versions of American ideals that could take root in southern soil. The picture in New Bern is especially compelling because of particular factors that opened up promising opportunities: the latitude permitted slaves and free blacks by state law and local practice; the large number and proportion of black people, including accomplished free blacks; the extraordinary years of wartime freedom; and the unique political and racial conditions in the city and county after the Civil War. Black artisans found New Bern a conducive setting in which to develop valuable skills, to build up their sense of their own worth, to imagine new ways of living, and to define their goals not so much by the limits imposed by white southern society as by their own vision of their rightful place in the American Republic.

Throughout changing definitions of the meaning of race and alternating periods of opportunity and oppression, New Bern's black artisans demonstrated their resilient sense of their place as artisans and as citizens. Time and time again, they took action to improve their situations within their circumstances—or to move beyond what their circumstances seemed to allow. An enslaved brickmason dreamed of being a free master craftsman and used his skills, industry, and relationships to attain his goals; thereafter he trained and helped to free other black artisans and voted regularly for as long as the law allowed. A freeborn seamstress, wearied by hostility from whites and fearing a bleak future for her children, sold her house, packed her worldly goods, and took her children to join friends and relations in the North. An enslaved shoemaker collected some shoe leather and tools of his trade and escaped from his employer in hopes of reaching freedom by sea. An enslaved blacksmith developed his inventiveness, and when freedom came he acquired property, won public office, and campaigned for schools for black children. A freeborn carpenter augmented his wages by running a grocery and supported his widowed mother until her death at more than a hundred years of age. An enslaved house carpenter and his wife mourned their children sold away by her owner, and he worked overtime to enable his owner to buy his wife and youngest child to keep the family and their future children together. A runaway brickmason and his friends traveled to the nation's capital to appeal to the president of the United States for universal manhood suffrage. An illiterate and emancipated widow saved a dollar for her fatherless grandson to attend grammar school before starting his apprenticeship; his stepfather helped him master the carpentry trade, and he won a seat in the state legislature. An enslaved brickmason encouraged a freeborn upholsterer's apprentice to seek higher education and saw him become president of a nationally renowned college.

Such stories demonstrate these artisans' sense of agency in pursuing their goals as craftspeople, as family members, and, when possible, as citizens. More than that, they also depict the realities of artisan identity particular to the American South. They remind us that our definition of American artisan identity need not be limited by the example of one region or one race or evaluated solely by comparison with that template. Typically the American model of artisanal identity has been drawn along lines established in the early national period by northeastern urban white mechanics. Indeed, the core values and even the mottoes of those workers spread through artisan populations across the nation and into other groups as well. A few blacks in Virginia and elsewhere used radical republican rhetoric in rebelling against the slave power. Black artisans in New Bern regularly cited their industry, thrift, and respectable behavior to support their own and their family members' attempts to attain freedom as "honest and peaceable citizens."

Slaves who could not own themselves claimed some rights to the tools they used and strove to control how they spent their time away from their master's oversight. Free artisans of color guarded their rights against legal intrusions, and they and their defenders called upon the founding documents of the nation in support of their claims. With emancipation, black leaders promoting racial uplift universalized the classic artisan qualities of thrift, industry, and respectability, which had also come to define Victorian middle-class virtues, as essential for blacks who hoped to advance as American citizens. All of these ideals were interwoven with their emphasis on strong families and neighborhoods and advancement through education.

In every period, black artisans asserting their rights as citizens celebrated the ideals of American republicanism, citing the revolutionary "Car of Liberty" as a symbol of their lives as free people and invoking the language and spirit of the American Revolution, the Declaration of Independence, and the Bill of Rights in their appeals for equal rights and justice. Rejecting the claims of some that this was a "white man's country," these artisan-leaders, along with national race spokesmen, asserted with passion and determination their rights and identities as Americans.

But even as they invoked the patriotic legacy shared by their brethren in northern cities, southern black artisans showed important differences in how they employed those ideals. Northern white artisans used public and political demonstrations of their identity as republicans and citizens to assert their rightful place as an occupational and class group in the American Republic. Southern black artisans, as represented in New Bern, engaged in an opposite dynamic. Rather than promoting their own class or occupational identity, the city's black artisan-leaders used their occupational skills and status to pursue their political values: to win their freedom and enable others to do so and to work for the rights of citizenship, better education, economic opportunity, and justice for others of their race. As black southerners in a world of racial hierarchies and deference, they found that their success as artisans sometimes supported and sometimes conflicted with their sense of their rightful place as American citizens. How they confronted these issues—and myriad others that arose from the interplay of race and region, of skills and agency, and of oppression and hope—tells a vital part of the story of American artisan identity.

Appendix
Biographical Summaries

Note: The following biographical summaries encompass artisans for whom it has been possible to assemble substantial life stories beyond what is covered in the main text. I hope that further research will uncover more about the lives and careers of more of New Bern's artisans of color.

Israel Braddock Abbott

Israel Braddock Abbott (May 11, 1843–May 6, 1887) was a freeborn black house carpenter in New Bern active in political life during and after the Civil War. He was the son of Grace Rue Braddock Brown Green, a freeborn woman of color, and the nephew of her brother, the noted house joiner and minister George A. Rue.

Israel Abbott reported in 1874 that his father (see below) "died before he had completed his first year, and he was left in the care of his mother and grandmother"—Grace Green and her mother Hannah Neale. He said he had attended school until he was ten, apprenticed at the carpenter's trade for two years, and completed his training with his stepfather, Joseph Green. By 1870 Abbott owned $300 worth of real estate and $400 in personal property and headed a household that included his wife, Susan J., and their children, James E., Ann, Cora, Gracey, and Israel Abbott Jr.; by 1880 they lived on George Street between Queen and Cedar Streets.

Abbott entered political life at a young age. According to the account he gave to a biographer, early in the Civil War he was forced to work on Confederate forts, but he ran away, served briefly with a Confederate officer, escaped again in December 1861, and hid out in New Bern until the arrival of Union forces in March 1862. He "then made himself known, taking a leading part in all public meetings and enterprises among the colored people of his county, and soon became widely known and popular." Just 21 in 1864, he became a leader in the Abraham Lincoln and Frederick Douglass Equal Rights Leagues in 1864–65 and subsequently in the Republican Party.

In 1870 Abbott was chosen as lieutenant in the state militia company recruited to protect Raleigh against Klan attacks. In 1872 he was elected to the state legislature. A leader in improving local schools for blacks, he was a founder of the Young Men's Intelligent and Enterprising Association and served as a delegate to the 1877 State Colored Education Convention in Raleigh. He was active in the Good Samaritans and founded and edited that organization's newspaper, along with teacher and attorney George H. White. In 1881 Abbott and E. E. Tucker led a meeting in New Bern that organized a laborers union, which aimed to assure "reasonable compensation" for many types of workers; opposed by whites, its activities were short-lived. Abbott is best known for his ill-fated campaign for Congress in 1886. He and incumbent James O'Hara both ran on the Republican ticket, with the result that Democrat Furnifold Simmons won the election. A few months after the election, Abbott died at age 44, leaving a modest estate to his widow and children.

(The identity of Israel Braddock Abbott's father is unclear. In the census of 1850 his mother was listed as Grace Braddock, the single head of a household that included her children Israel and Hannah [Braddock]. Also in New Bern in 1850 was a free black house joiner named Israel Braddock, the married head of another local household; any relationship between him and Grace is unknown. In her Freedman's Bank application of November 13, 1869, Grace named one Israel Abbott as her first husband and George Brown as her second husband. By 1860 Grace had married Joseph Green, and her children were living with her and Joseph in her mother Hannah Neale's household, as Israel Abbott and Hannah Brown.)

Anderson, *The Black Second*; Freedman's Bank Records; "Israel B. Abbott," *Raleigh Examiner*, February 22, 1874 (Charles N. Hunter Scrapbooks,); "Israel Braddock Abbott," *North Carolina Architects and Builders: A Biographical Dictionary*, http://ncarchitects.lib.ncsu.edu/, consulted June 1, 2010; *New Bern Daily Times*, February 25, 1874; *New Bern Weekly Journal*, May 12, 1887; Watson, *A History of New Bern*.

Thomas C. Battle

Thomas C. Battle (ca. 1825–1902) was a New Bern brickmason and father of a large and notable family. According to a biography of his son William, Thomas was born a slave, married three times, and had 26 children. He prospered after emancipation, and by 1870, at age 45, he owned $1,800 in real estate and $300 in personal property. He was newly married to Annie Vashti Delmar, aged 19. Their household included Thomas's children, Thomas C. Battle Jr., a brickmason's apprentice, aged 15; and Caroline, 11. By 1880 the older children had left home, and Thomas and Annie Battle had their own children, Nancy H., aged 8; James D., 6, and Abbie, 3, plus Joseph Taylor, 17, an apprentice brickmason in their household. In this census (only), Thomas reported that his father was a native of Africa. In 1900, the Battle family was living on Primrose Street, just two doors from Sarah Dudley Pettey and her family. The Battle household included Abbie (b. 1878), Mary E. (b. 1883), Sophia (b. 1884), Lillian (b. 1890), and James L. (b. 1894). The census of 1890 has been destroyed, and the couple's other children, including William and Samuel, did not appear in the family in the censuses of 1880 or 1900.

Long affiliated with Andrews Chapel and St. Peter's AME Zion Church, Battle became a minister and was active throughout eastern North Carolina. He trained some of his sons as bricklayers but also encouraged his children to pursue education: his son William Delmar Battle learned the bricklayer's trade and was educated in the local schools, graduated from Livingstone College, studied for the ministry at Lincoln University, and became a Zion minister in the North. At Thomas Battle's death on February

1, 1902, the *New Bern Daily Journal* of February 2 recalled him as a well-known bricklayer responsible for many local buildings (not named) and as a longtime member of the Acme Lodge of the Knights of Pythias. In 1910 his widow, Annie, was working as a nurse and headed a household that included their children Abbie (Barnes), Lillian, and James. After Annie died, on August 12, 1929, the *New Bernian* of August 15 mentioned two of her and Thomas's children—John, in New Bern, and Samuel, a police sergeant in Harlem, New York. Samuel Jesse Battle's life has gained attention because of his pioneering role as a black officer in the New York police force. On August 3, 2009, the intersection of West 135th Street and Lenox Avenue in New York was dedicated as the Samuel J. Battle Plaza.

New York Daily News, August 4, 2009; "The Reminiscences of Samuel J. Battle," transcription of interview by Patrolman John Kelly, February 1960, The Oral History Collection of Columbia University, Columbia University Oral History Office, New York, 20–23, 33, partially posted at http://c250.columbia.edu/c250_celebrates/harlem_history/battle.html, consulted April 5, 2011; "William Delmar Battle," in A. B. Caldwell, ed., *History of the American Negro*, Washington, D.C., Edition (Atlanta: A. B. Caldwell Publishing Company, 1922), 261.

Elizabeth Bragg and Sarah Bragg Stanly

Elizabeth Bragg (1828–ca. 1891) and Sarah Bragg Stanly (1830–after 1880), the eldest daughters of the free "mulatto" tailor John Bragg and his emancipated wife Caroline, learned the tailoring business from their father, as did their brothers Henry and Cicero, and they continued to practice their trade throughout their lives. Elizabeth, born on November 4, 1828, and Sarah Ann, born on April 18, 1830, were both baptized at Christ Church on March 25, 1831, with their parents as sponsors. Like their mother, Caroline, they were fair skinned and were sometimes identified as white.

As noted in the entry on John Bragg, by 1850 John and Caroline and their nine children lived in a racially mixed area just north of Queen Street. Elizabeth and Sarah, aged 21 and 20, respectively, were the eldest. In 1860 Elizabeth, a single tailoress aged 31, headed one of two Bragg family households in town; hers was listed as "white" in the census and was located in another, largely white neighborhood in New Bern's Second Ward. She had $1,000 worth of real estate and $500 in personal property, and her household included Henry, a tailor; George, a butcher; and young Edwin and Frances, as well as her parents. During the late 1850s and early 1860s, when most of the family members, including the parents, John and Caroline, moved to Cleveland, Elizabeth and her brothers Henry and George stayed in New Bern; Henry evidently left or died during the 1860s.

In the late 1860s Elizabeth and Sarah and their brothers George and Edwin inherited their father's property at Queen Street and Bragg's Alley, which they sold in 1869 (CCDB 70:285–86, October 12, 1869). Elizabeth retained her home at South Front and George Streets and headed a household that included her brother George and her three children, George, Zebulon, and Caroline (aged 20, 18, and 17, respectively, in 1880). Both sons were fishermen. Caroline (Carrie) moved north in the early 1880s; she was listed in the census as a white woman and was thus known to her descendants. She married a white man, Arthur Graves, had several children, and died on June 22, 1905, in New York. (Like many other mixed-race people, Carrie could define her identity as white in the North more readily than in her native community.)

Sarah Bragg, meanwhile, had married into New Bern's leading free family of color, taking as her husband in 1852 tailor Charles S. Stanly, the youngest son of the wealthy barber John C. Stanly. Charles died in the late 1850s, leaving Sarah with four young children. In 1860 she was living in Cleveland, a 28-year-old widow and tailoress with property valued at $800; her household included her brother Cicero Bragg, 18, a tailor; and her four children, Joseph, 7; Charles, 6; Sallie, 4, and Caroline, 2, all born in North Carolina. It is not certain if Sarah moved to Cleveland before or after her husband died, but she was part of a Stanly family clan there by 1860. (Her husband's brother, schoolteacher John S. Stanly, and his family had moved there in the early 1850s; after John's death a few years later, his widow, Frances [Fanny], worked as a tailoress and headed a household that in 1860 included their three daughters; their son John, a joiner and carpenter, now headed his own household.) Sarah's parents, John and Caroline Bragg, moved to Cleveland by 1864 and lived with Sarah and her children at 162 Brownell Street until their deaths in 1866 and 1867. Sarah Bragg Stanly continued as a tailoress in Cleveland and in 1900, at age 70, was still at her craft and head of a household that included her son Joseph, a house painter. She evidently died before 1910.

CCDB; CCEP; Christ Episcopal Church, New Bern, Parish Register; Cleveland city directories via Ancestry.com. Genealogical information from Charles Steele, descendant of Caroline Bragg Graves, via email, October 2012.

John Bragg

John Bragg (ca. 1805–67), a mixed-race tailor, and his family were among New Bern's noted antebellum free black artisans. It is not known whether Bragg was born free or manumitted; he was likely connected in some way with the white John Bragg—a slaveholder who was the father of Thomas Bragg, a builder in Warren County, and thus the grandfather of Governor Thomas Bragg Jr. and General Braxton Bragg. It is possible that the tailor was the slave named John who was emancipated in 1809 by one Hannah Arthur with the support of John Bragg (*FFV*, 62). It is likely that he was the "mulatto" boy John Bragg who was apprenticed to Charles Stewart in 1814 to learn the tailor's trade and the "orphan" John Bragg, aged 14, bound to Stewart in 1818 to the same trade.

Like other local leading free families of color, John Bragg and his family affiliated with Christ Episcopal Church. In December 1827 the parish register noted the marriage of John Bragg and Caroline Ferrand (she was then about 16 years of age) at the home of John [R.] Green. Caroline was evidently the light-complexioned "female slave usually called Caroline Lane" freed in April 1827 by Stephen Ferrand with Green's support. The couple had several children who were christened at Christ Church: Elizabeth, born November 4, 1828, and Sarah Ann, born April 18, 1830, both baptized on March 25, 1831; and Stephen, George Badger, Henry, and Cicero, baptized on May 2, 1842.

By 1850 the 45-year-old tailor John Bragg owned $350 in real estate and lived with his family just north of Queen Street in Bragg's Alley. His and Caroline's children then included Elizabeth, 21; Sarah, 20; John, 18, and Stephen, 16, both carpenters; Henry, 14; George, 12; Cicero, 9; Edwin, 6; and Frances, 4. As memoirist John P. Green recalled from his boyhood, "the tailor Bragg was in the habit of carrying work to his home and performing it there, with the assistance of his good wife and other members of his family." In 1860, for reasons unknown, the census recorded some members of the family twice: one household was identified as mulatto and headed by John, who owned $250 in real estate, and another was identified as white and headed by Elizabeth, who had $1,000 worth of real estate and $500 in personal property.

Initially John and Caroline Bragg stayed in New Bern while younger members of the family joined the exodus from New Bern, including their daughter Sarah Bragg Stanly and their son Cicero. By 1864, however, John and Caroline made their home with Sarah and her children in Cleveland. Edwin also moved to the city and enlisted in the U.S. Navy. Caroline Bragg died in Cleveland in 1866 and John Bragg in 1867. In 1869 John's heirs, Elizabeth and George Bragg of Craven County and Sarah Stanly and Edwin Bragg of Cleveland, sold the property at Queen Street and Bragg's Alley, which "descended to us from our said father John Bragg" (CCDB 70:285–86, October 12, 1869).

Bassett, *Slavery in the State of North Carolina*; CCDB; Cleveland city directories via Ancestry.com.; *FFV*; Green, *Fact Stranger than Fiction*. Craven County Court Records, Court of Pleas and Quarter Sessions, 1814, 1818, and Cleveland death certificates courtesy of Charles Steele.

Virgil A. Crawford

Virgil A. Crawford (ca. 1830–97) was a black cooper active in New Bern's post–Civil War civic life. Probably enslaved until emancipation, he first appears in census records in 1870. He was apparently a grandson of Virgil Crawford (I), a free man of color whose enslaved wife, Lydia, and children, including Virgil (II), were freed in 1815 by John C. Stanly. In 1821 Virgil (II) and his sister Mary were apprenticed to freedman Bacchus Simmons—Mary, aged 7, as a spinster, and Virgil, 12, as a carpenter. This Virgil Crawford, born about 1809, was probably the father of Virgil A. Crawford, born about 1830, presumably to an enslaved mother. Virgil A. Crawford gave only his name on his Freedman's Bank application, but his brother James stated in his own application that he (James) was born in Craven County in 1844 to Gatsy Dove and Virgil Crawford (II), who was dead by 1873.

By 1870 Virgil A. Crawford, a black cooper aged 37, was established in New Bern as the owner of $150 in real estate and $150 in personal property; he was head of a household that included his wife, Harriet, 34; Cicero Jones, 18, a cooper's apprentice; and Laura Loftin, 12, a domestic servant. Virgil and Harriet Hargate (Hargett) had married on September 4, 1865. New Bern tax lists noted him with property on Queen Street in Dryboro valued at $400. In 1880 Virgil and Harriet's household included their daughter, Sarah, 11, in school, and a cousin, John Hargett. In 1880 Crawford had an appointment as the "deputy collector and messenger" at the United States Custom House and lived on Queen Street near Metcalf Street, and in 1893 he was employed by Congdon and Company's sawmill.

Crawford was New Bern's longest-serving black city councilman of the nineteenth century and one of the longest serving in the state. He began his tenure in 1870 as one of four black men elected in that year, and although the number of black councilmen dwindled as a result of new rules enacted by the Democratic legislature, he was reelected regularly from 1872 through 1894, with the exception of 1890, when he lost to tailor Mustipher Holly. In 1896 he was one of several men involved in a conflict over the legitimate council members.

He was active in Andrews Chapel and its successor, St. Peter's AME Zion Church. With James W. Hood, Joseph Green, and others he participated in the thirteenth conference of the state's AME Zion churches, held in Charlotte, and served as a delegate from North Carolina to national conferences of the denomination. He was a featured speaker at the 1873 Emancipation Day celebration, an incorporator of the Rough and Ready Fire Company No. 1, a founder of the New Bern Educational Association, and a member of the 1883 board for Craven County's graded school for black children. He died at age 67 on May 21, 1897. The *New Bern Daily Journal* of May 22 noted the death of "Councilman Crawford," an esteemed townsman, and announced his funeral, to be held on May 23 at St. Peter's AME Zion Church.

CCDB; CCEP; CCWB; Freedman's Bank Records; Greenwood Cemetery Burial Records, Kellenberger Room; M. Ruth Little, National Register Nomination, St. Peter's AME Zion Church; *New Bern Daily Times*, January 3, 1873; Watson, *A History of New Bern.*

Edward R. Dudley

Edward R. Dudley (June 10, 1840–May 18, 1913), born a slave, was a cooper by trade who taught himself to read and write and participated in political affairs for many years. He noted in his Freedman's Bank application that he was the son of Sarah Pasteur (an enslaved woman) and David Dudley (a white New Bern dentist who died several years before the Civil War). As Glenda Gilmore relates in *Gender and Jim Crow*, his maternal grandfather was Edmund Pasteur, also born a slave, who was manumitted by John C. Stanly in 1815. In 1818, Pasteur purchased from Stanly his wife, Dinah, and their daughter, Sarah, intending to free them. After Edmund's death, Sarah and her two young children, Edward and James Dudley, were sold to New Bern white businessman Richard Taylor (*Raleigh Examiner*, February 15, 1874, Charles N. Hunter Scrapbooks).

According to Dudley family tradition, when New Bern fell to Union troops in 1862, Taylor and his family moved west with their slaves to Salisbury, where Edward Dudley practiced the cooper's trade, making casks for tobacco. At the end of the war, Sarah Pasteur and her children, including Edward, returned to New Bern as free people. Edward "engaged more or less in public affairs" from 1865 onward. In 1866 Edward Dudley and Alice Shober registered their union in Craven County. About 1868, however, Edward married Caroline Elizabeth Woods and they had their first child, named Sarah for his mother, in 1869. In 1870, Dudley stated in his Freedman's Bank application that he was born in New Bern in 1840, was living on Cypress Street, and was employed by Finch and Company. Edward's brothers were James D. and Thomas. (James D., a carpenter, moved north but returned to New Bern late in the century.) The census of 1870 showed Edward, aged 30, as a mulatto cooper and head of a household that included his wife, Caroline, 31, and their one-year-old daughter Sarah, as well as Edward's mother, Sarah Pasteur, aged 50 and employed as a nurse. Edward owned real estate worth $600 and personal property valued at $300. By 1880, at age 40, he was identified as a farmer and head of a household on Primrose Street that included his mother and his wife and seven children. The oldest daughter, Sarah, gained a college education, taught school, married AME Zion Bishop Charles Pettey, and became a leader in church affairs and Progressive Era women's organizations.

Dudley took leadership roles at King Solomon Masonic Lodge and founded New Bern's Lodge of the Good Templars as the first black chapter of that international temperance organization. In 1883 he joined the first board of the county's graded public schools for black children. Originally affiliated with AME Zion, he moved to Ebenezer Presbyterian Church late in life. Dudley was among the wealthiest black people in town in the latter years of the century. In 1887 he owned 17 acres on Jack Smith Road, worth $480, and a lot on Pasteur Street, worth $150. By 1891 his land was valued at $2,025.

In 1870 Dudley was one of Craven's three black legislators, and he was reelected in 1872. He also forged relationships with white politicians. In the 1872 congressional race Dudley supported the white incumbent from the district, who defeated black candidate John Hyman of Warren County at the polls, but in the next election Dudley supported Hyman because of his stance on civil rights. Hyman won and rewarded Dudley with the position of deputy collector of revenue in New Bern. In 1882 Dudley campaigned for Orlando Hubbs, a northern-born white man who had become sheriff of Craven County, against James O'Hara in the district's Republican primary for Congress; Dudley disliked O'Hara especially because of his anti-temperance position. O'Hara won and had Dudley fired from the revenue office. In 1886, when O'Hara and New Bernian Israel B. Abbott both ran as Republicans, Dudley led a successful biracial coalition in support of white Democrat Furnifold Simmons.

Dudley retired from active public life to become a leader in the local truck-farming business. At the North Carolina Industrial, Stock and Fruit Fair, held August 26–29, 1890, in New Bern, he displayed "eggplants over 2 feet in circumference [and] pumpkins over 5 feet tall." At his death, the *New Bern Sun* of May 19, 1913, called him "one of New Bern's best negro citizens" who had been "very active in the past years for the upbuilding of his home town; was city marshal, trial justice, one of the city fathers, and for several years a member of the state legislature. He had raised a family of eight children and educated them. His oldest daughter was the wife of the late Bishop Pettey; another daughter is the wife of Archdeacon Avant. He leaves many warm friends, both white and colored." His funeral was held on May 20, 1913, at Ebenezer Presbyterian Church.

Anderson, *The Black Second*; Gilmore, *Gender and Jim Crow*; Charles N. Hunter Scrapbooks; Watson, *A History of New Bern.*

George C. Eubanks

George C. Eubanks (Eubank) (ca. 1861–after 1940?) was a New Bern carpenter who became the town's only African American architect in the early twentieth century. In 1870 the U.S. census listed him as a schoolboy, aged 8, in the household headed by his father, Allen G. Eubanks, a wealthy white auctioneer, aged 51. The household also included several other Eubanks children, all identified as white, plus Lucinda Stanly, aged 28 and identified by the census taker as a mulatto domestic servant. Lucinda was actually Allen Eubanks's former slave, his lifelong mate, and the mother of his children, including George. When Allen Eubanks died in 1877 he left his considerable fortune to Lucinda and named her as his executrix and guardian of the children. Like many mixed-race individuals, George and his mother and siblings were sometimes identified in records as white and sometimes as "mulatto." In 1880 the census listed 19-year-old George as a carpenter's apprentice living in Lucinda's household, which also included his two brothers and a sister. All were listed as mulatto.

After completing his apprenticeship, New Bern tradition recounts, George went north to study architecture and was back in New Bern by 1900, listed as an architect and carpenter and living with his mother. Both were noted as white. New Bern city directories of the 1910s and 1920s listed him as an architect—sometimes white, more often with "*," designating a person of color—with his office on Broad Street. Lucinda died in 1925 or 1926. In 1930 the census showed George as a black architect in New Bern, but he was not listed there in 1940. He may be the George Eubank listed in the census of 1940 as a white man from North Carolina living on 134th Street in New York City. Little is known of Eubanks's architectural work. The only New Bern building attributed to him is the two-story, brick Stanly Building (1912–13) at Middle and Broad Streets, which was built for his mother, who owned extensive downtown property.

CCEP; CCWB; NBCD (1880, 1893, 1904).

George S. Fisher

George S. Fisher (June 4, 1822–September 3, 1892), blacksmith and civic leader, learned and practiced his craft in slavery and within a few years of emancipation became one of the wealthiest black men in New Bern. As an enslaved youth he was apprenticed by his owner to white mechanic Zaccheus Slade, who subsequently hired Fisher to work for him. His whereabouts during the war are not documented.

After the war he moved quickly into local civic and business leadership. In 1867 he joined the local education board and was one of the New Bern black leaders who held a meeting to promote calm amid a flurry of violence in eastern North Carolina. He was one of the town's first black councilmen, elected in 1869. He served on the racially mixed school board in 1880 and as one of the trustees for the black graded school authorized in 1883. He operated the town's leading blacksmith shop, where he employed his sons and other blacksmiths. His shop and residence were located on Broad Street. In 1870, at age 49, Fisher was one of the largest black property owners in New Bern: the census for that year showed him as owner of $1,500 in real estate and $300 in personal property. By 1887 his property was valued at $2,650.

Fisher also took action to stabilize his family. On October 16, 1865, he and [Mary] Jane Jones legalized their longtime union. In 1870 their household included their children Tettitha, aged 20; John H., 16; Charles, 14; Sarah F., 13; and George Fisher Jr., 10. John and Charles were apprentices at their father's trade. By 1880 their daughter Hannah Lane had married and returned home and was employed as a dressmaker. Fisher and his family affiliated with St. Peter's AME Zion Church. His funeral was held there on September 6, 1892, and he was interred at Greenwood Cemetery.

The local newspaper carried an unusually detailed account of his life, headed "A Good Colored Man Gone." It stated that he had belonged before the war to "Mrs. Elizabeth Smith, mother of Mrs. J. J. Howard, of this city" and that as a youth he had "learned the blacksmith trade in the carriage shop of Mr. Zacheus Slade and followed it through life." Possessed of extraordinary skill, "He once took a diploma at the New Berne Fair for the best display of home-made implements of this class. Not only was he industrious but he was saving with what he made. Even while in slavery these traits asserted themselves and at night and during the half holidays given to him by Mr. Slade who hired him from his owner, he would work, make money and take care of it afterward. He had thus accumulated considerable of his own by the time the war broke out and he lost by the war over a thousand dollars of his savings in [State?] bank notes" (*New Bern Daily Journal*, September 6, 1892).

Craven County Tax Records, NCA&H; Freedman's Bank Records.

Abraham Galloway

Abraham Galloway (1837–70) was a radical advocate for freedom and equal rights, active on the national scene, who played a vital role in New Bern's and North Carolina's movement toward black rights and equality. He was born in slavery in Smithville (now Southport), North Carolina, not far from Wilmington. The son of Hester Hankins, an enslaved woman, and John Wesley Galloway, a white man, he belonged to his mother's owner, Milton Hankins. Galloway moved to Wilmington, learned the brickmason's craft, and worked at that trade for a few years, paying much of his earnings to his owner. In 1857 he escaped by ship to the North and spent some time in Kingston, Ontario, where he continued in his trade.

He soon created a remarkable life as a radical leader and important Union spy. He traveled widely before and during the Civil War and made the acquaintance of abolitionist leaders. He married Martha Ann Dixon of Beaufort, North Carolina, in 1863. His story has been told fully in David Cecelski's biography, *The Fire of Freedom: Abraham Galloway and the Slaves' Civil War*.

A brief but important part of Galloway's career involved his activities in New Bern. He was in and out of the town during the Civil War, spurring others to take action toward securing liberty and equal rights. In New Bern he took a key role in 1863 in the recruitment of local men for the United States Colored Troops. In 1864 he led the visit by black New Bernians to President Abraham Lincoln to present a petition for voting rights. He also represented the state at the Syracuse convention of black Americans and served as a vice-president and on key committees. He organized chapters of the Equal Rights League in and near New Bern and took a principal role at the 1865 Emancipation Day celebration in New Bern.

Galloway was the "moving spirit" in promoting New Bern's black political movement at war's end and in organizing the Freedmen's Convention in Raleigh in 1865. At that convention he was a key speaker and was one of three men delegated to deliver the convention's address to the white Constitutional Convention. After participating in the Freedmen's Convention, Galloway moved to Wilmington, where he worked for equal rights, taking a more radical stance than many of his contemporaries. He represented New Hanover County in the legislature and was a leader at the state Constitutional Convention of 1868. Galloway died of fever on September 1, 1870, at age 33, and his funeral drew thousands of mourners.

Cecelski, *The Fire of Freedom.*

James York Green

James York Green (ca. 1790–1860s) was born a slave and trained as a carpenter before being freed in 1812. He was identified by his full name on the petition that his owner, William B. Green, made to the court for permission to free him on September 13, 1812. The petition was also signed by William's brother Thomas A. Green; William and Thomas were apparently white carpenters. James York Green's mother, Violet, was a slave who belonged to Thomas by 1818; whether William or Thomas was his father is unknown. The petition cited him as "tolerable . . . at the Carpenters trade, a sober, honest and industrious fellow."

Immediately after his manumission, Green married Mary Neal on September 26, 1812. By 1814 he had acquired the first of several tracts of real estate. In 1815 he began taking free black apprentices to his trade, and he continued to do so for ten years. Green also moved quickly to help others obtain their freedom. On March 17, 1815, he joined the recently freed carpenter Bacchus Simmons in posting bond in support of John C. Stanly's petition to emancipate Lydia, the widow of Virgil Crawford, and her five children. On September 12, 1816, Green joined bricklayer and plasterer Donum Montford in posting bond to free Abram Moody Russell Allen. In 1818, Green was able to free his mother, Violet, and his brother Rigdon, whom he had bought from their owners for that purpose. He had purchased his mother at auction from Thomas A. Green in 1817 for $250; how he acquired his brother is not known.

Censuses from 1830 onward show Green and his family residing in Dryboro. His household in 1830 and 1840 included four slaves as well as free people of color. By 1850, at age 60, he owned real estate worth $500 and lived with his wife, Mary, 59, and James Green, aged 8, likely a grandchild. Little is known of James and Mary's children, except that James York Green Jr. married Mary Ann Ransom in Craven County in 1849 and in 1850 was listed in the census as a tailor, born about 1823, living a few doors from his parents. James Y. Green was active in First Presbyterian Church. Although many of Green's fellow artisans of color, including his brother Rigdon, went north in the 1850s, James Y. and Mary Green stayed in New Bern. In 1860 the 70-year-old carpenter owned $600 in real estate and $50 in personal property. He died in the 1860s, as indicated in a deed record of September 27, 1869 (CCDB 70:42–43).

CCDB; *FFV*; Vass, *History of the Presbyterian Church.*

John Rice Green

John Rice Green (1793–1850) was a New Bern tailor who gained his freedom as a young man in 1818 and became one of the wealthiest free black people in town. His son, John Patterson Green, stated that he was the son of Congressman John Stanly (1774–1833) and the slave Sarah Rice (d. 1821) and that he was known as John Rice during his early life, his mother later adding the last name Green. Sarah Rice and her son belonged to Mary Jones Spaight, the widow of Governor Richard Dobbs Spaight, whom Stanly killed in a duel in 1802. John was apprenticed as a slave to white tailor Reuben Bell, and he worked during his off hours and saved his money to gain his freedom. In 1818, aged about 25, he was emancipated by Richard Dobbs Spaight Jr. (CCDB 41:12). Sarah, who was emancipated in 1816 in accord with Mrs. Spaight's will of 1808, died in 1821.

Once free, Green moved quickly to attain property and status. In 1819, only a year free, he purchased a town lot (411 Johnson Street) in a fashionable section, where by 1820 he had built a handsome Federal-style residence that still stands, considerably enlarged. He also owned other real estate, including a brick building on South Front Street. Green's slaves included Peter Henrion, whom he bought in 1820 (CCDB 42:96), carpenter Peter Dewey (CCDB 45:486), Maria (CCDB 47:317), and Henry, Nicey, and Tempe (CCDB 47:376). He manumitted some of his slaves and assisted in emancipating others. Green also took free black apprentices, including William Alston and Richard Harris. He was a devoted member of Christ Episcopal Church. He married Sally McClure in 1819; she died in 1837, and later that year he married Temperance Durden, a freeborn woman from Fayetteville. John and Temperance had three children, Sarah Rice, Catharine Stanly, and John Patterson Green.

Despite his success in his trade, in the late 1840s Green encountered financial problems and was forced to sell most of his property. The family moved from their home on Johnson Street to another dwelling, which subsequently burned. Before his death in 1850, he took steps to protect a modest house in Dryboro for his wife and children, who lived there for several years (CCDB 60:288). In 1857, Temperance sold the property and moved with their children to Cleveland, where their son John Patterson Green eventually became a political leader and state legislator.

CCDB, CCEP, CCW; Christ Episcopal Church, New Bern, Parish Register; Green, *Fact Stranger than Fiction*; Sandbeck, *The Historic Architecture of New Bern.*

Joseph Green

Joseph Green (1822–89), a carpenter active in New Bern's mid-nineteenth-century political and church affairs, was born in rural Craven County, and from age 13 onward he lived in New Bern. How and when he became free is not yet known; in his Freedman's Bank application of 1869, he identified his parents as Richmond and Phoebe Green. With his first wife, Susan Green, Joseph had three children: Elisha, Henry, and Joseph Green Jr. He also had two "outsider" children, including Moses Green, who served in the 35th Regiment, Company E, of the Union army. In 1854 Joseph Green married Grace Rue Brown, a schoolteacher with two children. In 1860 they were living in the household of Grace's mother and stepfather, Hannah and Thomas Neale, along with Grace's children, Hannah Cora Brown and Israel B. Abbott, the latter of whom Joseph helped to master carpentry skills.

Although Joseph Green participated briefly in politics, serving as a delegate at the 1865 Freedmen's Convention in Raleigh, his primary focus was as a churchman. He was part of the board of Andrews Chapel that decided in 1864 to accept James W. Hood as their minister and to ally with AME Zion. He attended the first state Conference of Zion that December and was listed as a deacon. In 1865, at the second conference, held in Beaufort, he was one of six men ordained as elders (thus qualified as pastors) who were sent thenceforth to various posts in North Carolina. In 1876 he served as one of North Carolina's delegates to the national AME Zion conference in Louisville, Kentucky. In time, Green's travels were limited by Grace's declining health; she died in 1884, after suffering from paralysis for years. Joseph died on September 20, 1889, at age 67, as reported in the *New Bern Daily Journal* of September 21, 1889; five days later, the *Journal* announced, "At the regular meeting of the Ministerial Association of New Berne and vicinity, in the St. Cyprian [Episcopal] school house," the group memorialized Green as "an exemplary minister of the A. M. E. Zion church with which he was identified as one of the pioneers in this state."

Hood, *One Hundred Years*; Mobley, *James City*; Sherrill, "A Negro School-Master of the 1870's."

Rigdon M. Green

Rigdon M. Green (ca. 1797–1887), a mixed-race house carpenter who was born a slave, learned his trade and could read and write by 1818, when he was emancipated by his brother James York Green. James, emancipated six years earlier by his owner, William B. Green, had purchased his mother, Violet, and his brother Rigdon in order to emancipate them. Rigdon was probably the son of a white man, possibly William B. or his brother Thomas A. Green.

Within two years of his emancipation, Rigdon Green was living in Fayetteville, where in 1820 he took an apprentice, Robert Hazle (Hazel), to the carpenter's and joiner's trades. In 1826 he moved to Edenton, where he acquired property in land and slaves, and in 1827 took a free mixed-race apprentice, Goldsmith Lloyd, to the house carpenter's trade. In 1827 Green returned briefly to New Bern to marry Caroline Allen at Christ Episcopal Church; the couple's bondsman was tailor John R. Green. Soon after moving to Edenton, Green learned of rumors accusing him of receiving and circulating David Walker's abolitionist publication, the *Appeal*. He published a notice in the *Edenton Gazette* of October 7, 1830, to counter rumors that he had tried "to influence the colored population to seek a redress of their pretended wrongs" by lending a friend a copy of a paper, the "Rights of All," published "by a colored man" in Bellville, New Jersey. He explained that he had received the paper unsolicited and had not promoted it. Rigdon and Caroline and their children stayed in Edenton until about 1845, when they returned to New Bern, where they and two apprentices and three slaves were living in 1850.

In about 1850 Rigdon and Caroline Green sent their older children to Ohio for their educations, and by the end of the decade, they had moved to Cleveland to reunite the family. Green continued in his trade as house carpenter, and the family lived in a predominantly white neighborhood. Their household in 1860 included son Benjamin, also a carpenter, and his young family. Green was associated with Trinity, St. Peter's, and Grace Episcopal Churches in Cleveland. An account of his life from a Cleveland obituary was carried in the *New Bern Daily Journal* of March 2, 1887.

ACNC; CCAB; CCDB; Chowan County Apprentice Bonds and Deeds, Chowan County Records, NCA&H; *Edenton Gazette*, October 7, 1830; *FFV*; *New Bern Daily Journal*, March 2, 1887.

Temperance Durden Green

Temperance Durden Green (ca. 1813–ca. 1894), a freeborn seamstress and tailoress, was a native of the Scots-settled area around Fayetteville and Clinton and part of an extended family that included the Chestnut (Chesnutt) family. As related by her son John Patterson Green, she traced her free ancestry through her mother to a white woman and an enslaved man, and her father was also white. In 1837, at age 24, she married the widower John Rice Green, the prosperous, emancipated New Bern tailor twenty years her senior. They had three children, Sarah Rice Green, Catharine Stanly Green, and John Patterson Green. For several years, the family enjoyed a genteel, middle-class lifestyle in New Bern. But John R. Green encountered financial problems in the 1840s, and after his death in November 1850 Temperance and their three children moved into a modest house on lot #11 on Cedar Street in Dryboro, the purchase of which her husband had arranged to protect her from his debts (CCDB 60:288).

Temperance maintained her family through her work as a highly skilled needlewoman. In 1857 she sold her house for $225 (CCDB 64:103) and moved with her children to Cleveland, Ohio. There she bought a modest house and continued to ply her sewing skills, along with her daughters, while son John waited tables as well as attending school. She saw her son succeed as a student at Union Law College, a lawyer, and an Ohio legislator. Temperance Green died at age 81, probably in 1894.

CCDB; Green, *Fact Stranger than Fiction*.

William H. Hancock and Richard Mason Hancock

William H. Hancock (ca. 1803–after 1888) and his son Richard Mason Hancock (1832–99) were free carpenter-joiners of color who began their lives in New Bern and moved north to New Haven and Chicago, gaining respect in every community in which they lived. William H. Hancock learned his skills and came of age during New Bern's early national period of fine building and of opportunities for artisans of color. It is not known whether he was born free or freed as a child, nor have his parents been identified. He was probably connected to the prominent white Hancock family, who had lived in Craven and Carteret Counties since the early colonial period; in adulthood, his middle initial "H." distinguished him from New Bern's white William Hancock. Records show that on September 12, 1817, William Hancock, a free black boy aged 14, was apprenticed to Uriah Sandy to learn the carpenter's trade. In 1819 Sandy undertook construction of one of the city's most prestigious buildings—First Presbyterian Church—in which he was assisted by local builders John Dewey and Martin Stevenson. The building was dedicated in 1822. As Sandy's apprentice, William Hancock would have worked regularly on the project.

William became a leading member of New Bern's community of free artisans of color. He affiliated with Christ Episcopal Church, where he and his wife, Mary Ann, had their children baptized, including Richard Mason (born December 21, 1832, baptized May 15, 1833, and named for the rector, Richard Sharp Mason), Frances (born in 1835), William (baptized 1840), and Mary Emma (born and baptized in 1845). Hancock qualified to vote, along with other free men of color, until 1835. In 1839 Elizabeth Buckley bequeathed a small but well-finished house (which still stands) at 419 George Street to "Mary Handcock, a free colored woman, wife of Will. H. Handcock, a free colored man a carpenter." It is not known whether the Hancocks resided there. In 1850 the census taker recorded William, aged 45, as head of a household that included Mary and their seven children, ranging in age from Richard, a carpenter, aged 18, down to the baby, Coleston. The adults and older children were all literate. William H. Hancock had the unusual distinction of becoming a member and tyler of St. John's Masonic Lodge from as early as 1846 until as late as 1852.

Hancock and his family joined the early waves of artisans of color who emigrated to the North in the 1850s. In about 1853 or 1854 they moved to New Haven, Connecticut. In 1860 William and Mary Hancock's household there included their older children Fanny (Frances), Laura, and William, all working at craft trades; Charles, aged 7, born in North Carolina; and Cicero, aged 5, and Caroline, 3, born in Connecticut. In 1880 William and Mary Hancock were still in New Haven, and, at age 75, William was still a house carpenter. By 1886, an account written about Richard noted that "His father, William H. Hancock, is a hale old gentleman, still alive, residing at Chicago, Illinois." In 1888 both William and Richard were listed as registered voters in Chicago. William H. Hancock's death date, sometime after 1888, is not yet known.

Richard Mason Hancock (November 22, 1832–1899), eldest son of William H. Hancock, followed in his father's trade. He was educated at a local private school, probably the one operated by John S. and Fanny Stanly, before entering an apprenticeship with his father at age 13. Upon completing his training and coming of age he moved to New Haven and practiced his trade as a joiner, employed by two white firms, Atwater and Treat and Doolittle and Company. (He may have been the joiner of that name who lived in New Haven in 1849, though he was back in New Bern in 1850 before moving north for good.)

In New Haven, Richard married Mary Beman, the daughter of a prominent minister, Amos Beman of New Haven. The couple soon moved to Lockport, New York, where Richard worked as a ship carpenter building canal boats, then went to work for the Holly Manufacturing Company for four years and mastered the specialized craft of patternmaking, "a branch of the trade that requires first of all a complete mastery of carpentry, besides an acquaintance with higher mathematics, a knowledge of draughting and the constant exercise of the very best judgment" (Simmons, *Men of Mark*, 406–7). Richard and Mary had two children, George and Fanny, before Mary died in 1861; her death at age 24 on July 9 in Lockport, was reported in the *New York Tribune* of July 19, 1861.

In 1862 Richard moved to Chicago, where he became a patternmaker for the Eagle Works Manufacturing Company, described at the time as the largest machine and boiler shop and foundry in the West. After two years, he was promoted to foreman of the pattern department, in charge of fourteen white men. He subsequently became head of the pattern shop at the Liberty Iron Works. Richard was remarried in 1867, to Jane Watkins, and in 1870 their household included his two children from his first marriage. By 1880 he was widowed again; he and his son George were living in a boardinghouse.

Richard M. Hancock gained national attention when he was featured in *Men of Mark: Eminent, Progressive and Rising* (1887), a Cleveland publication that highlighted accomplished men of color throughout the nation. He remained in Chicago for the rest of his life and was a prominent citizen, a Mason, and a leading layman at St. Thomas's Episcopal Church. He appeared as a patternmaker in Chicago city directories through 1898. He is evidently the R. M. Hancock who died in Chicago on June 4, 1899.

Lisa M. Boone, "Richard Mason Hancock," in Wilson, *African American Architects*, 187–88; CCDB; Chicago and New Haven city directories via Ancestry.com; Christ Episcopal Church, New Bern, Parish Register; Green, *Fact Stranger than Fiction*; Simmons, *Men of Mark*.

Israel Harris Sr. and Israel Harris Jr.

Israel Harris Sr. (b. ca. 1816–17, d. June 28, 1897) and his son Israel Harris Jr. (b. ca. 1850–53, d. 1919) were freedmen and brickmasons who came to New Bern from Washington, North Carolina, probably during the Civil War. Although neither man accumulated wealth, both were prominent as family men, Episcopal churchmen, and Masonic leaders.

In his Freedman's Bank application of 1871, Israel Harris Jr. named Israel and Eliza as his parents and listed as his siblings David, Eliza, Rebecca, Louisa, Hannah, and Gracie. He stated that he was born in Washington, North Carolina and was brought up there and in New Bern, and that the family was living on George Street near the Griffin School. In 1870 the Harris household comprised Israel Harris Sr. and Eliza and their children Louisa, 20; Israel Harris Jr., 18; Becky, 15; Eliza, 13; and David, 12. Their grown daughters, Hannah and Grace, had married and left home, though Grace returned home by 1880 with her two daughters. By that time, Israel Harris Jr. had married Emma Bell and the couple had established their home on Jerkins Alley, a few blocks east of his parents.

Israel Harris Sr. devoted his energies to his church and his lodge. His obituary in the *New Bern Daily Journal* of June 30, 1897, described him as a "well-known" brickmason who had died in his eighty-first year. "He was for over fifty years a faithful member of St. Cyprian's Episcopal church, being one of the first Vestrymen elected, and was Senior Warden at the time of his death. He has also been Secretary of King Solomon's Lodge for thirty consecutive years, holding the position at the time of his death." His funeral was held at St. Cyprian's and he was buried at Greenwood Cemetery with Masonic honors.

Israel Harris Jr. followed in his father's footsteps. He and Emma had at least seven children, including brickmasons Israel Harris III and Charles. He served St. Cyprian's as vestryman and senior warden and a delegate to diocesan conferences, and he was worshipful master of Zaradatha Masonic Lodge. In 1898 he joined the New Berne Riflemen for service in the Spanish-American War and was selected as the company's second lieutenant. His obituary in 1919 cited him as a lay reader at St. Cyprian's, a former city councilman, a "high" Mason, and a brickmason "much respected by white citizens."

Freedman's Bank Records; *Morning New Bernian*, November 11, 1919; *New Bern Daily Journal*, June 30, 1897, and April 26, 1898.

Edward Havens and Sons

Edward Havens (ca. 1841–1906), a freedman, and his sons John T., James H., and Edward Havens Jr. established a successful shoemaking business in New Bern that continued from the 1860s into the 1940s. The family came from Washington, North Carolina, where they were likely connected with the white mercantile family of the same name. They may have moved to New Bern in 1864, along with others evacuated from Washington on the eve of a Confederate attack, or arrived after the war.

Edward and Maria Cherry were in New Bern in 1866, where they registered their marriage of six years. Their household in 1870 included their children, Lilla, 9; Edward,

7; and James, 1, plus Sophia Havens, 14, and Marcella Havens, 15, who were possibly Edward's sisters or nieces. When Edward Havens Sr. opened Freedman's Bank accounts for his three children in 1873, the family was living on Hancock Street. Edward's brother Henry, who also moved to New Bern, cited in his Freedman's Bank application of 1871 his sister Martha Havens in Brooklyn and his parents Danzy Smith and Delia Havens. By 1880, Edward and Maria Havens, identified as being aged 39 and 36, had in their household their children Lilla, 18, "at service"; Edward, 16, a shoemaker with his father; and James H., 10; Susan, 7; and John T., 5, in school.

In 1880 Havens's boot- and shoemaker's shop was on South Front Street, near the Gaston House Hotel, and his residence was on Pollock Street, between Muddy Street and George Street. Maria Havens died soon after 1880, and Edward married his second wife, Margaret, in about 1888. Within a few years, Havens moved his shop to 130½ Middle Street, and James and John joined in the business. By 1900 Edward and Margaret had moved their residence to Willis Street, north of Queen, and their household included his sister Martha, a cook, aged 60, who had come back south from Brooklyn, and 20-year-old shoemaker Nathaniel Robinson.

Although Havens was not prominent in political life, he participated in community affairs, belonging to St. Peter's AME Zion Church and King Solomon Masonic Lodge. His obituary reported that he had been a Mason for more than fifty years, "serving as past master, secretary, and deputy of the Third district." He was a founder of the Young Men's Intelligent and Enterprising Association and the Mechanics' and Laborers' Mutual Aid Society of North Carolina. At his death in 1906, he was cited as an "esteemed colored man" who had "conducted a shoe making and repairing business in this city for forty years." His estate included a fully equipped shoemaker's shop and a comfortably furnished residence.

After Edward's death, James and John continued the business under his name for a time. By 1910 James had moved to Raleigh, married, and was working as a shoemaker. Lilla married William W. Lawrence Jr. and stayed in New Bern until her death in 1918. Shoemaker John lived a long life as a prominent New Bernian, a Mason, churchman, and "society man." He rented a two-story building on Middle Street, where he had his shoe shop downstairs, while his family lived upstairs. In 1910 his household included his wife, Emma, and their four daughters, along with Emma's mother, May Dudley; by 1920 John and Emma had two more daughters. John T. Havens's death, at age 76, was reported in the *New Bern Sun-Journal* of October 6, 1951. He was survived by Emma and their six daughters—Mary Nixon and Edna Adams, of New Bern; Sarah Louise Lewis, of Los Angeles; Estelle Kenan and Thelma Burrus, of Brooklyn, New York; and Mabel Havens, of New York City. Emma later moved to New York to join family members.

Hatch, *Autobiography*; NBCD (1880, 1893, 1904); *New Bern Daily Journal*, August 5 and August 16, 1906.

Richard Hazel

Richard Hazel (ca. 1811–between 1870 and 1880), a free black blacksmith, prospered at his trade in antebellum New Bern, owning some $2,000 in real estate in 1850, before joining fellow New Bernians in leaving for Ohio. His parentage, early life, and training are not yet known, but he may have been a member of the local free black family whose surname was variously spelled Hazel, Hazle, Hassle, Hasele, and Hazzle.

The Christ Episcopal Church parish register noted Richard's marriage, on December 11, 1833, to Ann Nash (Nash Ann) Newton; they had obtained a marriage bond the day before, with leading free black carpenter William H. Hancock as their bondsman. Nash Ann (or Ann Nash) Newton came from an established family of color: her father was the master carpenter, Thomas Newton, who had gained his freedom in 1808 and freed his wife, Sarah, in 1811. Nash Ann was probably born shortly after her mother was freed.

By 1850, Richard Hazle, 39, identified in the census as black and a blacksmith, was head of a household that included his wife, Ann, 39, and daughters Ann, 16; Elizabeth, 14; Mary, 10; and son Francis, 9 months. Also in the household were Ann's mother, Sarah Newton, 80; and free youths of color who were probably apprentices. Hazel bought and sold several lots in town, including some in Dryboro, during the 1850s. Hazel earned a lasting reputation as a man of stature and thrift. Historian John Bassett's white informant, D. W. Hurt of Goldsboro, remembered him as a "blacksmith of means." John Patterson Green recalled, "One of the well to do and most highly respected of the families which affiliated with that social circle was, Mr. Richard G. Hazle, a man of pure Negro blood, and his family. Mr. Hazle was a blacksmith by trade, and also owned a small bakery, which was managed by his worthy wife and daughters. One of his daughters was a student, and graduated from Oberlin College, during the latter years of the 'fifties.'"

Richard and Ann Hazel's daughters Ann and Elizabeth both attended Oberlin College. Richard and Ann moved to Cleveland to be near them between 1855 and 1860. By 1860 Richard, aged 49, was operating a grocery in Cleveland as well as practicing his trade. His and Ann's household included Ann, 21; Elizabeth, 19; Mary, 18; Frank S., 10; and John D., 9. Their daughter Ann evidently died in 1862. In 1870—as witnessed by a notary in Cleveland (CCDB 70:592)—Richard G. and Ann N. Hazle of Cleveland sold lot #1 on Queen Street in Dryboro to the trustees of "King Solomon's Lodge #23 of Free Masons in the City of New Bern," on which the lodge erected their new building in that year. Richard Hazel died between 1870 and 1880. In 1880, his widow, Ann, was recorded in the census as living on Webster Street, with her occupation as "Living at ease." Two children remained with her, Lizy N., 30, and John, 23, both employed at a bleachery.

CCDB; Cleveland city directories via Ancestry.com.

Samuel Jackson

Samuel Jackson (ca. 1844–1904) was a long-lived New Bern blacksmith. Like essentially all the blacksmiths active in town shortly after the Civil War, he had learned and practiced his trade in slavery. Unlike some of his contemporary artisans, he did not take a prominent role in politics, but he maintained his business over the years and earned the respect of the community.

Jackson reported in his Freedman's Bank application in 1870 that he was 26 years old and resided on Muddy Street in New Bern. He worked for himself and at that time had his shop on Middle Street. (In 1871 "Jackson & Bro." blacksmiths, with a shop on Middle Street, applied for a Freedman's Bank account; this firm likely comprised Samuel and his brother Eli.) Samuel Jackson further reported that he was born in the Big Swift Creek area of Craven County and his parents were Jack Nelson, who had died of fever in 1864, and Fannie Nelson, who died in 1865. He identified two brothers still living, Edward J., aged 19, and Eli J., aged 30, and two who had died, Joe, of smallpox, and Amos, killed in the 12th Cavalry. His sisters were Tilla (Lilla?), who was dead, and Lucretia, 22; Malinda, 15; and Violet, 20. In 1870 Samuel was a widower, his wife, Rosannah Ernull, having died two years before; and he had two children, Sarah, aged 7, and Frances, aged 6.

By 1880 he had moved his shop to a location on South Front Street at the rear of the Gaston House Hotel, and the census showed him as a blacksmith, aged 50, sharing a home with his wife, Lucy, 45, who ran a boardinghouse, and daughters Fannie (Frances) and Minnie. According to the city directory, the family lived on South Front Street between Hancock and Middle Streets, not far from his blacksmith shop. His brother Eli had his shop in 1880 at the corner of Broad and Hancock Streets and lived in Bragg's Alley. Samuel maintained his operation south of the Gaston House throughout his life. At his death the *New Bern Daily Journal* of December 28, 1904, noted that the "aged and well known colored blacksmith" had done business for many years on South Front Street and was "respected by all who had dealings with him."

Freedman's Bank Records; NBCD (1880).

Park Lawrence

Park Lawrence (ca. 1770?–1871) was one of the few New Bern artisans recognized as a native of Africa. "Old colored man—Park Lawrence, died Weds. Night—Uncle Park Lawrence . . . a notable character," reported the *New Bern Daily Times* of August 18, 1871. "His history was an interesting one. He was a native of Africa, and was brought to this country in his 25th year. He consequently spoke his native African dialect fluently, and his descriptions of Africa were amusing as well as interesting. His English was never as perfect as that usually used by colored people, and quickly betrayed his African birth. When brought to this country he was sold to the Lawrence family, from whom he took his name, but subsequently belonged to the Hatch family. He learned the carpenter trade, became a good mechanic, and learned also to read. He is the uncle of Mr. W. W. Lawrence of this city. His home is at the end of Griffith St."

Park Lawrence's exact age and his connection with the Hatch family are not documented, but he did belong to the Lawrence family, and he was consistently identified as a native of Guinea. His handiwork remains unidentified, making it impossible to discern if his craftsmanship reflected influences from his native country. In 1820, in the division of the estate of William Lawrence, the widow Catharine received "Park, a carpenter," along with Retta and her infant son Harry and Old Dinah. An 1845 inventory of Catharine Lawrence's estate included "Negro Man Park Freed by the Will."

In 1860 Parker Lawrence appeared in the census as a free black carpenter, aged 90, illiterate, and born in Guinea. He headed a household that included Amy Lawrence, 80, black, born in North Carolina, and probably his wife; and Amy Wiggins, 25, black, doing housework. The census of 1870, which was frequently inaccurate on ages, listed him as only 75 years old. Blind by that time, he was identified as a carpenter from Guinea, head of a household consisting of Easter Gaskins, 45, keeping house, and Park Gaskins, 15, a carpenter's apprentice. Given the statements about his early life, the 1860 age estimate seems more likely, which suggests that he was about 101 years old at his death in 1871.

CCEP.

Lucas Mason

Lucas Mason (ca. 1812–84), generally known as Luke, was a free black wagon- and carriagemaker in New Bern before and after the Civil War. Although he was a substantial property owner, he does not appear to have been part of the civic leadership.

He may have been the free man of color by the same name listed in Jones County in the census of 1840. By 1850 he was living in New Bern, listed as a 38-year-old black wheelwright and head of a household that included his wife, Penny, 30; their children, Joseph, 9; Lewis, 8; William, 7; Samuel, 6; Elcey, 4; and Moses, 1; and an apprentice, John B. Moseley, 15. By 1860 Mason, probably a widower, was a coachmaker, who had in his home his children Lewis, 16; Samuel, 13; Moses, 11; Caroline, 9; Lucinda, 7; and Mary, 5. Although he never learned to write—consistently signing papers with an "X"—he acquired property that made him one of New Bern's wealthier men of color by 1860. The 1860 census noted him with $1,200 in real estate and $400 in personal property; tax records listed his property as lot #55 on Hancock Street and part of lot #96 on Broad Street (these two valued at $800), as well as part of lot #510 on Broad Street ($300).

During the Civil War, Union soldiers likely kept Mason's shop busy. After the war, however, he lost much of his property through mortgages and disputes; it is possible that his illiteracy put him at a disadvantage. In 1870 he was listed as a wagonmaker with real estate valued at $500 and personal property at $300. His household included his son Moses, 21, a blacksmith, and daughters Lucinda and Mary. Next door were his son Joseph, 25, a wagonmaker, and his family. In 1871 and 1872 Luke Mason still owned lot #255 (his shop) on Hancock Street. By 1880 he had returned to the wheelwright's trade and lived alone. He died in 1884 and was buried from Rue's Chapel.

CCDB; Craven County Tax Records, Kellenberger Room; NBCD (1880).

Donum Montford

Donum Montford (Mumford) (1771–1838) was one of the wealthiest and most prominent free black artisans in antebellum New Bern. Born in slavery, he was part of a generation of artisans who gained their freedom and thrived at their trades during the early national period. Little is known of Montford during his life in slavery, much or all of it spent in the ownership of the elite white Cogdell family, but well before he was emancipated in 1804, aged about 33, he had learned and practiced the plasterer's and brickmason's trades.

At his death in 1787, Richard Cogdell had left some of his slaves to his wife Lydia, for life, and thereafter to go to their youngest child, Lydia; his estate included a slave called Donum. On September 10, 1804, Lydia Cogdell and her widowed daughter Lydia Cogdell Badger sold a slave named Donum to John C. Stanly, who emancipated him the next day. Two years later, on March 3, 1806, Lydia Cogdell gave to Montford the young slave Abram Moody Russell (later Allen), whom Montford was to train in the bricklayer's and plasterer's trade and emancipate when he was 26. Montford met the conditions and freed Abram at age 21.

A few years after obtaining his own liberty, Montford married Hannah Bowers, a free woman of color, on January 18, 1809. According to New Bern memoirist John D. Whitford's account published in the *New Bern Weekly Journal*, January 17, 1905, "Hannah Mumford the wife of Donum, was much lighter in color than himself and a number of years his junior [senior] in age. She was the nurse of Wm. Gaston, when his father was butchered by the Tories on the 20th day of August, 1781." Both Donum and Hannah Montford were "colored communicants" of Christ Episcopal Church.

As a free man, Montford established himself as a substantial property owner who possessed town lots, farmland, and slaves. He owned his home, which stood at the northeast corner of Broad and George Streets. By 1820, he headed a household of 12 free people of color and 22 slaves and was thus one of the principal slaveholders among New Bern artisans. The free people in his household included himself and Hannah, plus ten younger men aged from 14 to 45, probably his apprentices and employees. There were also 14 female slaves and 8 males, the last of whom included a boy under 14, 6 men aged 14 to 45, and 1 man over 45. Ten years later, the household included 9 free young males of color, 7 male slaves (3 over 55), and 3 female slaves. As far as is known, Montford had only one child, Nelson, born about 1809 into slavery. Nelson worked with his father as a youth, and in 1828 Donum Montford manumitted him to ensure his future in freedom.

Donum Montford took numerous apprentices, all evidently children of color. His first apprentice, assigned to him by the court, was Jacob Harris, aged eight, bound to him to learn the brickmason and plasterer's trade on June 10, 1807, and many others followed. Among the slaves he trained was Ulysses, "a plasterer by trade, who served his time with Donum Mumford, in the town of New Bern afterwards worked at his business upwards of four years, in Hyde County." Montford helped others gain their freedom by helping post bond for manumissions, including that for a slave named Douglas in 1811. Only a few documented building projects record Montford's involvement. These include the John R. Donnell house (1816–18), the Craven County Jail (1821–25), and a project for Tyrrell County planter Ebenezer Pettigrew in 1819. Montford also served with prominent local men (all white) in 1832 to examine and approve structural repairs to Christ Episcopal Church.

During the late 1820s and the 1830s Montford, like other New Bernians, encountered financial problems that led him to mortgage much of his property, but he still left a good estate in land, slaves, and personal possessions. He left to Hannah many household items—including a family Bible, which has not been located. From the estate, his heir and executor, Abram Allen, bought his musket, and Hannah bought his shotgun; John Gill purchased brick molds and some old window sash; and carpenter James Y. Green bought his grindstone. Montford bequeathed to Hannah the "Negro Woman Dinah, Boy Alexander, Isaac Rue for life." His other slaves, who probably went to Abram Allen, included "old man" Bob, Dick, and Jim Carney. Donum Montford died on July 11, 1838, and was buried from Christ Church on July 12, 1838, at Cedar Grove Cemetery. He was followed by Hannah, who died on May 23, 1846.

Bishir, "Black Builders in Antebellum North Carolina"; Bishir, "Philadelphia Bricks for New Bern Jail"; Carraway, *Crown of Life*, 139; CCDB; CCEP; CCWB; John R. Donnell Letter and Account Book, SHC; Herzog, "The Early Architecture of New Bern"; Miller, "Recollections"; *Norfolk and Portsmouth (Va.) Herald*, February 2, 1818; Pettigrew Family Papers, NCA&H; Sandbeck, *The Historic Architecture of New Bern*; John D. Whitford, "Historical Reminiscences," *New Bern Weekly Journal*, January 17, 1905; Whitford, "Home Story of a Walking Stick."

Thomas Newton

Thomas Newton (d. 1826) was born a slave and mastered the carpenter's trade before he was freed as an adult in 1808. Known in slavery as Tom Newton, he took the name Thomas upon his manumission. He was manumitted by Sarah Wood(s), the widow and executrix of his former owner, Benjamin Wood(s); it is possible that he was formerly one of the many slaves owned by planter and governor Abner Nash, who had at least three slaves named Tom and owned some of Newton's family members.

In 1811 Newton freed his wife, Sarah, who had belonged to John Devereux before Newton bought her with the intent of manumission. In 1818 Newton freed his son Macklin, a shoemaker by trade, whom he had received in 1812 by the will of Margaret Nash Haslin, a daughter of former governor Abner Nash. Newton's other children included a son, Mars, born about 1793, and a daughter, Ann Nash, born about 1811, probably after her mother, Sarah, was freed. (The names Mars and Macklin also appear in the inventory of Abner Nash's slaves.) At his death in 1826, Thomas Newton left his residence, on part of lot #371 at Norwood and Narrow Streets, to Sarah; most of his tools to his son Mars; his brass candlesticks to Ann; and a few tools to his apprentice Kelso Davis.

In 1838 Thomas and Sarah Newton's daughter Ann Nash married blacksmith Richard Hazel, one of New Bern's leading free black artisans, at Christ Episcopal Church, and in 1850 the couple's household included their children plus her widowed mother Sarah Newton, aged 80. By 1860 Richard and Ann Newton Hazel had moved to Cleveland. Mars Newton continued in the carpentry trade in Washington, North Carolina, probably by 1830, when his wife Clarissa Newton was listed as a head of household among neighbors who included emancipated New Bern artisans Virgil Crawford and Abram M. Allen. In 1850 carpenter Mars Newton, 57, was head of a household in Washington that included Clarissa and five children. One of Mars Newton's apprentices was the enslaved carpenter Stewart Ellison (1832–99) who moved to Raleigh and became a postwar contractor, civic leader, and legislator. Most of Mars Newton's family moved to New York or New Haven.

CCAB; CCDB; CCEP; CCW; "Stewart Ellison," *DNCB*.

Allen G. Oden

Allen G. Oden (July 8, 1840–September 29, 1894) was a freedman, Union veteran, and shoemaker active in postwar New Bern's civic affairs, especially the AME Zion church and the Grand Army of the Republic.

The principal account of Oden's life comes from his fellow churchman James Walker Hood. Hood wrote that Oden was born in Beaufort County, North Carolina, on July 8, 1840, and that when he was eight years old, "his parents were sold from him, and he grew up without a father's or mother's care." (In 1860 more than 90 slaves were held by members of the Oden family in Beaufort County.) Oden enlisted as a soldier at Washington, North Carolina, in 1863 and, according to Hood, was "awarded a medal by General Grant for bravery in the battle of Newmarket, Va., which was lost or misplaced by the commanding officer of his company, and it never reached his hands. In July, 1866, he was honorably discharged from the army." Military records, as well as veterans' and pension records, show that Oden (Odin) enlisted on June 16, 1863, in Washington and served as a sergeant in the 36th Regiment of the U.S. Colored Troops.

After his discharge, as Hood related, Oden taught school and supplemented his pay by working "in the shingle swamps." Seeking to better his opportunities, in 1872 Oden "entered into a bargain with a Mr. Charles Jones to teach him vocal music in return for learning the shoemaking trade in his shop. Oden was not long in acquiring all that Jones knew about the business, and then a Northern man agreed to complete his education on that line in consideration of a money loan. Before the loan was paid he was enabled to make a comfortable living from his trade." He also affiliated with AME Zion and from 1872 onward was "an active worker in the Church, societies, and politics." He attended the state AME Zion conferences from 1878 onward and attended the national conference in New Bern in 1888 as a lay delegate and the 1892 conference in Pittsburgh as a "ministerial delegate."

Entering New Bern civic affairs, Oden, according to Hood, was elected county coroner three times and served on the New Bern board of aldermen from the Fifth Ward. He was a "Master of King Solomon's Lodge No. 1, A. O. of F. A. M.; President of the Relief Society D. G. M. of Masons; and W. P. of the Eastern Star. He has also served as Judge Advocate in the North Carolina Department of the Grand Army of the Republic." He also served on the board established in 1883 for the black graded school.

Likely because of his status as a Union veteran and former sergeant, Oden also served in the local black militia, and in 1877, when black militia groups formed two all-black battalions of the North Carolina State Guard, Oden was chosen as major of the Fourth Battalion, made up of the New Bern and Raleigh men. He was frequently referred to thereafter as Major Oden. In 1887 he and other New Bern black veterans established a local chapter of the Grand Army of the Republic, one of several black and white GAR posts in eastern North Carolina. Named for Colonel James Beecher, who led the African Brigade in 1863, the post had 33 members by 1890.

By 1880 Allen and his wife Dicy (Dicey) were living on New South Street near Spring Street in New Bern; he was employed as a shoemaker and she at an "eating house." His real estate in 1887 included the property on New South Front Street, worth $400, and a lot on Craven Street, worth $150, probably his workshop. He and Dicey apparently had no children. The *New Bern Daily Journal* of September 30, 1894, reported that the respected shoemaker had died on the previous day and was to be buried that afternoon from Clinton Chapel AME Zion Church. He left his widow a comfortably furnished home and death benefits from his numerous organizations.

Annual Report of the Adjutant-General of the State of North Carolina for the Year 1877 to the Commander-in-Chief (Raleigh: State Printer, 1878), 7; Craven County Tax Records, NCA&H; Hood, *One Hundred Years*; pension and military records via Ancestry.com. On the GAR in New Bern, see http://rblong.net/encgar/Beecher/index.html, consulted November 4, 2011.

John Randolph Jr.

John Randolph Jr. (1827–90) was a painter by trade who was living in New Bern by the mid-1860s. Born in slavery to a large family in Washington, North Carolina, he became an eloquent spokesman for equal rights and a leader in political life during and after the Civil War. He was the son of John Randolph Sr. (ca. 1805–after 1880) and Harriet Ore Randolph; his siblings included William O., Henry T., Louis, Edward, and Fanny Randolph. It is likely that the family evacuated Washington for New Bern in 1864 in advance of the Confederate attack on Washington.

In New Bern John Randolph Jr. became a leader in civic life, a Mason at King Solomon Lodge, a founder of the Reliance Fire Company in 1870, and a founding member of Ebenezer Presbyterian Church, organized from First Presbyterian Church; his father was one of the three original "ruling elders" of the Ebenezer congregation. He and his wife and children resided on Queen Street, and most of his extended family lived nearby in adjoining neighborhoods north of Queen. Never wealthy, he prospered sufficiently to own his family home: the city tax list of 1887 listed his property on Queen Street with a value of $400, in addition to which he had tools worth $50 and personal items worth $25. Randolph's family had stayed close in slavery and continued in freedom to emphasize stability and upward mobility for the younger generation. In 1866 John Randolph Jr. and Della Redmond affirmed that they had been man and wife for fifteen years. By 1870, Della had died and John was remarried to Kate (Catherine) Green, a native of Warren County. John, 41, and Kate, aged 20, had in their home four of John and Della's children: William, aged 15, a hotel waiter; and John, 13; Fanny, 12; and Lewis, 10, all in school. Hattie, aged 5, made her home with John's sister, Fanny Randolph Nelson.

Randolph advocated equal rights and education for blacks. His letter, "The Capabilities of Our Race" (dated April, from Washington, North Carolina, and published in the May 21, 1864, *Christian Recorder*), asserted that the "heroic deeds of colored men on the battle field" showed that blacks deserved "the rights and titles of citizens." In New Bern from the summer of 1864 onward he pursued these goals. He was prominent in the mass meetings of black citizens held in August 1865 to call for the Freedmen's Convention in Raleigh, and, along with Abraham Galloway and George C. Price Jr., signed the notices headed "*Freedmen of North Carolina, Arouse!*" that were published in newspapers across the state to attract delegates to the convention. At the convention in Raleigh, which began on September 29, 1865, Randolph served on important committees and helped craft the convention's address to the (white) Constitutional Convention. When the North Carolina Equal Rights League was organized, he served on the committee that wrote its constitution. He did not attend the second Freedmen's Convention in Raleigh in 1866, but was elected nonetheless as corresponding secretary for the league. Back in New Bern, in 1867 Randolph was among the Craven County registrars for the election of delegates to the 1868 upcoming Constitutional Convention. He, Israel B. Abbott, and Henry H. Simmons represented Craven County at the state Colored Educational Convention in Raleigh, and he worked to improve schools for black students. By 1880, Randolph had an appointment as a mail agent, a well-paid government position that resulted from his support of Republican congressional candidates.

In 1879 John and Della Randolph's eldest daughter, Fannie, married George H. White, a Howard University–educated schoolteacher and attorney. In 1880 Fannie died at age 22, leaving George with their infant daughter, Della, named for Fannie's mother. John and Della's youngest daughter Hattie married George H. Willis, and the couple moved to Winston-Salem. John and Kate Randolph's niece Oleana Pegram, who had lived with them in New Bern as a schoolgirl, trained as a teacher at Scotia College and Fisk University, married teacher Simon Green Atkins and helped found Slater Institute (later Winston-Salem State University). The *New Bern Daily Journal* of November 25, 1890, reported John Randolph's death on November 22, 1890, at age 63 years. His funeral took place at Ebenezer Presbyterian Church, and he was interred in Greenwood

Cemetery. His heirs included his widow, his children Lewis, William, and Hattie Randolph Willis, and his granddaughter Della M. White.

CCDB; CCEP; *Convention of the Freedmen of North Carolina, Official Proceedings*; *Minutes of the Freedmen's Convention . . . 1866*; New Bern Taxables, Craven County Tax Records, NCA&H; Vass, *History of the Presbyterian Church.*

Edward A. Richardson

Edward A. Richardson (ca. 1830–96) was a freeborn black plasterer and bricklayer from New Bern who became active in the city's post–Civil War political and civic life. He was part of a close-knit artisan family who acquired and retained property before and after the war.

Edward was the son of Simon Richardson and Sarah Rew (Rue) Richardson, free black people who married in Craven County in February 1830. Simon was one of many men in the long-established Richardson family who pursued the caulker's trade and other crafts over the generations. Sarah was the daughter of bricklayer and plasterer Isaac C. Rue. At the time of Sarah's birth to a free black mother, Isaac was enslaved, but he was freed by Donum Montford's will of 1838 and became one of the wealthiest men of color in New Bern. In 1850 Edward Richardson was a plasterer, aged 19, and living with his parents and his siblings who included Miles, 18, also a plasterer; Eliza, 15; Isaac, 12; and Ann, 3. The family lived within a few doors of Sarah's father, Isaac Rue, aged 63, and it is more than likely that he taught Edward and his brothers Miles and Isaac his trade. In 1851 Edward married Maria Collins, and by 1860 the couple and their two children were living next door to Isaac Rue; both men were listed as owning $500 in real estate. Tax lists showed Edward Richardson as owner of part of lot #333 on Queen Street, valued at $300, and Isaac Rue with half of lot #332, worth $200. By 1860 Edward's younger brother, Isaac, was a 22-year-old brickmason whose household included his wife, Georgianna, and their baby, Isaac, who later followed his father in the plastering trade.

The family weathered the war and held on to their property. In 1869–72, Edward held lot #333 on Queen Street; his grandfather retained lot #332 on Johnson Street and other property; and other members of the family owned small amounts of property in town. In 1870 the census taker recorded that Edward and Maria Richardson lived a few households away from Isaac Rue. Edward's parents, Simon and Sarah Richardson, were living next door to their son Isaac, a 32-year-old black bricklayer, and his family. When Isaac Rue died in 1880 the *New Bernian* of January 17, 1880, reported that the 93-year-old brickmason had left his "considerable amount" of real estate to Edward. In 1887 the local tax list recorded that Richardson, at age 55, owned 82½ acres on Trent Road, worth $495, and various town properties: he had lots on Queen Street worth $125 and $800, on Johnson Street worth $200, and on Good Street worth $350. He also had two mules valued at $125, tools valued at $100, and other personal property worth $75.

Edward A. Richardson was one of the few freeborn black New Bernians who entered local political leadership after the Civil War. His whereabouts and activities during the war are unknown, but from early 1865 onward he participated regularly in civic life. He was a founder and officer of the Harland Fire Company No. 1, formed by January 1865. He was a delegate at the Freedmen's Convention of 1865, and although he was not a delegate at the second convention in 1866, he and carpenter-undertaker Richard Tucker were chosen to represent Craven County on the board of the North Carolina Educational Association. In June 1867 he was elected chairman of the local "Educational Board" formed to establish a public school for blacks. He held the important county office of justice of the peace. He helped found and lead such uplift groups as the 1870 Young Men's Intelligent and Enterprising Association and the 1873 Mechanics and Laborers Mutual Aid Society of North Carolina. In 1883 he led the list of men who formed the board of trustees for the new graded school for black children.

By 1880, according to the *New Bernian* of January 17, 1880, Richardson had a federal patronage position and was working as "a faithful and obliging Clerk in our Post Office." In 1884, his support of congressional candidate James O'Hara garnered Richardson an appointment as postmaster at New Bern, one of the most important post offices in the Second Congressional District. His term lasted only from July 18, 1884, until June 11, 1885, when he was replaced by a Democrat. However brief, his holding of the office was an important chapter in his life. His obituary in the *New Bern Weekly Journal* of February 27, 1896, described him as "a prominent colored man" who was "well known to many of our city owing to his public position, he being postmaster under Garfield and bore a good name as far as we ever heard." His funeral took place at St. Peter's AME Zion Church.

Anderson, *The Black Second*; Craven County Tax Records, NCA&H.

George A. Rue

George A. Rue (ca. 1820–66) was a New Bern "mechanic" and joiner who moved north in the early 1850s, then returned to New Bern in 1865, where for a brief period he became an important religious and political leader.

Rue was the son of an emancipated woman, Hannah Rue Neale, and her husband, Bristow or Brister Rue, an enslaved man who was sold away. According to her grandson Israel B. Abbott, Hannah was freed when she was about 12 years old (*New Bern Daily Times*, February 25, 1874). Hannah's other children with Rue were Godfrey, a carpenter who left New Bern between 1850 and 1860 for Colorado and later California; and Grace Maria Rue Green (born ca. 1823), the mother of Israel Abbott and Hannah Cora Brown and the wife of carpenter Joseph Green. In 1850 George A. Rue, a free black mechanic, headed a household that included his wife, Ann, 26, and daughters, Hannah, 4, and Malinda, aged 1. He owned $300 in real estate. (Some accounts have indicated that George A. was from the North, but he was a native New Bernian.)

George A. Rue and his family joined the vanguard of free black New Bernians who went north. By 1852, he was in New Haven, Connecticut, where the city directory identified him as a joiner with the title, "Rev.," suggesting that he had served as a minister at Andrews Chapel. In 1855 he was ordained as a deacon associated with the New England Conference of the AME denomination. He was assigned by 1860 to a congregation in Newport, Rhode Island, and then to Boston's Bethel Church, now the Charles Street AME Church. Ordained as an itinerant elder (pastor) in 1861, in 1862 Rue tried to make his way to New Bern to bring Andrews Chapel into the AME association, but military conditions forced him to turn back. (In 1864 AME Zion missionary James Walker Hood brought the congregation into that connection.) Active as a preacher and abolitionist in the North during the war, Rue was acquainted with Frederick Douglass and other notables, and he gained a reputation not only as a preacher but as a powerful singer, best known for the liberation song, "Sound the Loud Timbrel."

At the end of the war Rue was transferred from the New England Conference to the South Carolina Conference of AME and in May 1865 was assigned to New Bern. By late summer he had begun forming the congregation that became known as Rue's Chapel AME Church, and he had entered into the local political leadership's campaign for equal rights. He reported to the *Christian Recorder* on August 18, 1865, "In Goldsborough [west of New Bern] there is some trouble among our people and their enemies, from whom I have just made my escape, but the good work is still going on. It is not prudent to go very far east of Newbern yet." He commented, "Our people in Newbern can now speak their mind more freely than they did in former days. Thank God for this great change!"

Along with the radical leader Abraham Galloway and others, Rue participated in the New Bern meetings that called for the first North Carolina Freedmen's Convention in Raleigh in the fall of 1865, and he took a prominent role at the convention, serving on key committees, including the body that prepared the address to the white Constitutional Convention. After one of his speeches, a reporter noted, "Mr. Rue's effort was well-received, as it deserved to be. His remarks were spiced with humor, and while he earnestly demanded justice for the colored man, he advised moderation and proved conclusively that nothing could be gained by violence."

At the second Freedmen's Convention, in 1866, Rue again took a leading role and helped draft the address of the convention. Not long after concluding his work at the convention, George A. Rue died on December 22, 1866, at age 46, after suffering for months from the effects of yellow fever (*Christian Recorder*, February 2, 1867).

"Brief History of the Founding of Rue Chapel A. M. E. Church"; *Convention of the Freedmen of North Carolina, Official Proceedings*; Dickerson, "George A. Rue"; Freedman's Bank Records; Green, *Methodist Meeting House*; New Haven city directories via Ancestry.com.

Isaac C. Rue

Isaac C. Rue (Rew) (ca. 1788–1880), a bricklayer and plasterer, spent at least a half century in slavery and more than thirty years as a free man. He was one of the best known and most prosperous of many black artisans who plied the "trowel trades" in New Bern during the mid-nineteenth century. In the 1830s and possibly earlier he belonged to the emancipated plasterer and bricklayer Donum Montford. Nothing is known of Rue's parents, his early years and training, or when or how he came into Montford's possession. In his will of 1838, Montford bequeathed Rue to his widow, Hannah Montford, for her lifetime and specified that he was to be freed at her death, which occurred in 1846.

Rue was free by 1850, when he was listed in the census as a plasterer with real estate valued at $500 and one male slave, aged 19. His household included his wife, Phillis, 52; daughters Angelina, 9, and Laura, 7; plus Miles Richardson, 17, a house carpenter and probably a relative by marriage. Isaac's daughter Sarah Rue (born ca. 1812) married Simon Richardson, a free black caulker, in 1830; their son Edward A. Richardson probably learned his trade from his grandfather. (It remains unknown whether Isaac Rue was related to Brister Rue, the father of George A. Rue and other freeborn children of Hannah Neale.)

Isaac Rue was widowed in the early 1860s and married Rachel Franks in 1865. He served as an elder at Andrews Chapel and its successor, St. Peter's AME Zion Church. In 1870 the census indicated that he was among the wealthiest black people in New Bern, owning $2,000 worth of real estate and $200 in personal property. The *New Bernian* of January 17, 1880, reported at his death that he was a native of the county and for nearly eighty years a resident of New Bern. He died at his home on Queen Street in his 93rd year and left his "considerable amount of property in real estate" to his grandson Edward A. Richardson.

CCDB; CCEP; CCWB; Wilson, "Negroes Who Owned Slaves."

Henry H. Simmons

Henry H. Simmons (1834–July 20, 1904) was a freedman and cooper active in wartime and postwar civic life in New Bern. A native of New Bern, he named as his parents Larry and Mary, both of whom were dead by the early 1870s. He reported in 1902 that he was a descendant of Edward Pasteur, a socially prominent white physician in the early national period.

By the mid-1860s Simmons was active in New Bern civic life. In the summer of 1864 he served as treasurer at a local public meeting concerning the Syracuse equal-rights meeting, and by January 1865 he had joined in founding the Harland Fire Company, one of the town's first two black volunteer fire companies. He was a charter member of King Solomon Masonic Lodge, established in New Bern that fall. In 1873 he was in Wilmington, North Carolina, where he signed his Freedman's Bank application with a flourish and listed his place of residence at 11th and Market Streets. He and his wife, Emily, had children Hugh W. and Susan Jane. By 1880 he was back in New Bern and employed as a drayman, and his and Emily's household included Hugh and younger children Edward, Henry, and Mary. In 1900 he was again working as a cooper and was head of a household that included his second wife, Emma, a washerwoman, and his daughter Mary.

Simmons represented Craven County in the 1876–77 legislature—the first session after the end of Reconstruction—where he and other black legislators strove with little success to protect black citizens' rights against a Democratic majority. He was a New Bern city councilman in 1888 and 1890. With other artisan-leaders, he represented the county at the State Colored Educational Convention in 1877 and served on the board of trustees for the black graded school in Craven County in 1883. In 1902 he registered to vote, one of the few leading blacks in New Bern to do so. At his death at age 70, the *New Bern Weekly Journal* of July 22, 1904, referred to him as "one of our old and respected colored citizens." His funeral was held at St. Peter's AME Zion Church and he was buried with Masonic honors.

Craven County Voting Records, 1902, NCA&H; Freedman's Bank Records; Logan, "Black and Republican"; Watson, *A History of New Bern*.

Richard Tucker

Richard Tucker (ca. 1818–81), carpenter and coffinmaker, was born and practiced his trade in slavery in New Bern. He was among the black artisans who were born too late to earn their freedom but through their skills and personal attributes were well prepared for freedom and grasped the reins of economic and political leadership when liberty came. Tucker's parentage is unknown; he had a brother named Jupiter, also a carpenter. In slavery, Richard and his wife Emeline (Emiline) had many children, some of whom were sold away by her owner, Raymond Castix. Richard earned and saved money to enable his owner, John Flanner, to purchase Emeline and their youngest child. Richard and Emeline married in December 1865, at a wedding attended by many friends and family. Among their children were Frank (who completed a Freedman's Bank application), Edward, and Amelia.

By 1862 Tucker was an elder at Andrews Chapel, and he continued his service to Andrews Chapel, later St. Peter's AME Zion Church, and in many civic associations. In 1866 he was a delegate to the second Freedmen's Convention in Raleigh, and along with Edward A. Richardson was one of Craven County's two members of the board of the North Carolina Educational Association organized at that meeting. Back home, in 1867 he and Richardson called a local meeting to promote education, and he was elected president of the resulting educational organization. He chaired numerous public meetings and was registrar for the 1867 election of delegates for the 1868 Constitutional Convention. He served as a justice of the peace and was elected to the state legislature in 1870 and 1872. He became Craven County's first black state senator in 1874.

Tucker diversified his prospects by entering the coffinmaking and undertaking business. Horace James, an official of the Freedmen's Bureau, wrote in 1866, "Richard Tucker has been known to me ever since our occupation of this State (North Carolina) as a leading and influential colored man in Newbern. He reads and writes a little, talks well, and is a person of character and standing. He is by trade a carpenter and undertaker, and is a devout class leader in the St. Andrew's Methodist Church." Tucker also ran a store and became one of the most prosperous black artisans in town. In 1870 his real estate was valued at $1,000. One of the few black artisans who maintained their homes as well as their workshops in the central city, he had his shop and residence on Pollock Street, between George and Metcalf Streets.

The 1870 U.S. census showed Tucker, who had evidently lost his wife Emeline and remarried, as head of a household that included his wife Celia, plus children Emeline, Fanny, Elizabeth, and Richard Tucker Jr. In 1880 he was living on Metcalf Street with a wife named Annie, and his daughter Emeline was still in the household. In 1878 Tucker was described by Lachlan Vass, minister at the First Presbyterian Church, as "a prominent colored man who has been a member of N. Carolina Senate from Craven Co.—about 60 or 65 years old; bright and enterprising Negro; with two daughters teaching school." Vass reported that Tucker had operated a small store in his house immediately after the war and in 1878 was cultivating some 50 or 60 acres of cotton. Tucker died in 1881.

Horace James, "A Freedman's Wedding," 1866, in *Household Reading: Selections from the Congregationalist, 1849–1866* (Boston: Galen James and Company, 1867); Elizabeth Vass Wilkerson, ed., *The Diary of Rev. L. C. Vass, D. D., Chaplain, Stonewall Brigade* (Laurens, S.C.: privately published, 2008).

George B. Willis

George B. Willis (1823–1900) was a freedman and cooper in New Bern who became active in post–Civil War political, civic, and religious life. According to the history of Rue's Chapel AME Church, he returned to New Bern "from Dixie" in the summer of 1865 and helped George A. Rue organize the congregation and obtain property for a building. He became the first superintendent of the Sunday school, the first choir leader, and its first local preacher. An early member of King Solomon Lodge, in later years he was honored by the naming of another local Masonic lodge for him.

Long active in public life, Willis was elected in 1869 as one of the city's first black aldermen. He served as captain of Company H, the black militia group that went to Raleigh in the summer of 1870 to protect the capital from the Klan, and in the election that summer won a legislative seat, as did fellow New Bernians Edward R. Dudley and Richard Tucker; the next year Israel Abbott defeated him at the polls. Willis was a founder of the local educational board formed in 1867 and served on the board of trustees appointed in 1883 for New Bern's black graded school. He helped found the Reliance Bucket and Axe Company in 1870, the Independent Order of Good Templars of New Bern in 1871, and the Mechanics and Laborers Mutual Aid Society of North Carolina in 1873.

In 1866, along with many other freedpeople in New Bern, George B. Willis and Sarah Bryan(t) affirmed that they had lived as man and wife for 20 years. In 1870 he and Sarah had six children in their home: John B., aged 20, pursuing his father's trade as a cooper, and Susan, 19, a seamstress; plus Julia, 15; George H., 14 (in school); Alex R., 10; and

Darp, 3. In 1880 their children still at home were John B., an office clerk; George H., working as a servant; and Arah, aged 9. The family lived on East Front Street near the corner of Queen Street.

Willis was widowed and remarried in 1883 to Ann Rue, the widow of AME minister George A. Rue; the January 15, 1885, *Christian Recorder* identified him as "Rev. George B. Willis, a local deacon of our Church." After being widowed again, Willis remarried in about 1892 and in 1900 at age 76, Willis was living with his wife, Jennie, aged 47. Next door on East Front Street lived his son John B. and his family. When George Willis died in June 1900, his estate received $99.00 from the "Beneficial Association," possibly the Mechanics and Laborers Mutual Aid Society of North Carolina, which he had helped establish in 1873. It covered most of his bills, including $30.00 to the undertaker.

George and Sarah Willis had educated their children and enabled them to pursue white-collar careers. Their son John died in 1926 in New Bern, a retired bookkeeper, aged 76, after a career that included service as clerk of court and register of deeds before 1900. In 1887 their son George Hamilton Willis married Hattie Randolph, a daughter of local political leader John Randolph, and they moved to Winston, later Winston-Salem, where he established a school and worked as a bookkeeper. He died in Winston-Salem in 1935.

"Brief History of the Founding of Rue Chapel A. M. E. Church"; CCDB; CCEP; McGuire, "The Making of a Black Militia"; NBCD (1880, 1893).

Amos York

Amos York (Yorke) (February 18, 1818–February 24, 1885) was a cooper, churchman, and political leader who appeared first in the record in New Bern in 1862 as an assistant secretary to Union official Vincent Colyer, who described him as a runaway slave, a "worthy Christian," and "a leading man among his people."

By 1862, and likely before, Amos York was a leader in Andrews Chapel, which in 1864 allied with AME Zion and later became St. Peter's AME Zion Church. He participated in the first state Conference of Zion in New Bern in December 1864 and was listed as a preacher. Ordained an elder in 1865, he served as secretary for subsequent conferences. Continuing to work as a cooper, he identified himself primarily as a minister and is described as having served as pastor of Clinton Chapel AME Zion Church. In 1876 and 1880 he was one of North Carolina's delegates to the national AME Zion conferences. In civic life, York took a prominent role as chair or secretary of public meetings during the war, and he was a member of the 1865 Freedmen's Convention in Raleigh; a member of the local educational board formed in 1867; and one of the first black city council members in 1869, an office to which he was reelected in 1874.

As a young man Amos York had a son, James Cornelius York, born in New Bern about 1837, whose mother, Hannah, died when the boy was about two years old. James followed his father in his trade in New Bern. In about 1847 Amos married Desdemona McIlvane, a union they registered in 1866. Their children included Emily Burnetta,

Hannah, and John Timothy; the latter two became schoolteachers, and John T. was active in civic leadership. In 1880 the Yorks' household also included schoolboy William York (noted as a son in the census, but a nephew in Amos's will), plus Hannah's husband, barber Hugh Banks, and their baby, Amos Banks.

Amos York accrued a modest amount of property. He was recorded in the 1869 list of New Bern taxables as owner of lot #47 on Bern Street, valued at $500, and he also acquired additional property. His will bequeathed to John T. a lot on Cedar Street; to James, part of a lot on the street "from the Neuse River to the railroad"; to Hannah Ann Banks, the "front half" of lot #47; to Emily Bernetta Powell (wife of Noah Powell since 1883), the other half of that lot. To William, he left a lot on Main Street in Kinston. Desdemona received the remainder of his property and served as executor. Amos and Desdemona were buried in Greenwood Cemetery, where their adjoining markers are among the oldest dated stones original to the cemetery. One reads, "Rev. Amos York, born Feb. 18, 1818, died Feb 24, 1885," the other, "Desdemona, wife of Rev. Amos York, born Dec. 25, 1817, died May 15, 1891." Not far away is a small marker inscribed, "In Memory of / Amos York / the Son of Dester Money and Amos York / Born July 28th, 1858 / Died / November 28th. 1863 / Aged / 5 years and 4 months. / 'Suffer little children to / come unto me, and forbid / them not; for of such is / the kingdom of God.'"

Later in the nineteenth century, John T. York changed his occupation from schoolteaching to coopering, which he had learned from his father. In 1900 he and his wife, Angeline, were living on Bern Street next to his sister Hannah Banks and her husband and son. He also developed as a civic leader, serving as a lieutenant in the New Berne Riflemen during the Spanish-American War and as a town alderman from 1899 to 1903.

CCDB; CCEP; CCW; Colyer, *Brief Report of the Services Rendered*; Freedman's Bank Records; New Bern Taxables, Kellenberger Room; New Bern Town Council Minutes, NCA&H.

Notes

Abbreviations

ACNC	James H. Craig, *The Arts and Crafts in North Carolina* (Winston-Salem: Museum of Early Southern Decorative Arts, 1965)
CCAB	Craven County Apprentice Bonds and Records, North Carolina State Archives, Raleigh
CCDB	Craven County Deed Books, Craven County Register of Deeds Office, New Bern; and microfilm, North Carolina State Archives, Raleigh
CCEP	Craven County Estates Papers, North Carolina State Archives, Raleigh
CCW	Craven County Wills, North Carolina State Archives, Raleigh
CCWB	Craven County Will Books, Craven County Courthouse, New Bern; and microfilm, North Carolina State Archives, Raleigh
DNCB	William S. Powell, ed., *Dictionary of North Carolina Biography*, 6 vols. (Chapel Hill: University of North Carolina Press, 1979–96)
FFV	William L. Byrd III, *In Full Force and Virtue: North Carolina Emancipation Records, 1713–1860* (Westminster, Md.: Heritage Books, 2007)
Kellenberger Room	Kellenberger Room, New Bern–Craven County Public Library, New Bern
MESDA	Museum of Early Southern Decorative Arts, Winston-Salem, N.C.
NBCD (1880)	*Chas. Emerson and Co.'s Newbern Directory, 1880–1881* (Raleigh: Edwards, Broughton, 1880; reprint, LaVergne, Tenn.: Bibliolife, 2009)
NBCD (1893)	*Business Directory of the City of New Berne, N.C.: To Which is Added Historical and Statistical Matter of Interest* (Raleigh: Edwards, Broughton, 1893)
NBCD (1904)	*New Bern, N.C. Directory, 1904–1905* (Richmond: Hill Directory Company, 1904)
NCA&H	North Carolina State Archives, Office of Archives and History, North Carolina Department of Cultural Resources, Raleigh
SHC	Southern Historical Collection, University of North Carolina Library, Chapel Hill
SLF	Freddie L. Parker, ed., *Stealing a Little Freedom: Advertisements for Slave Runaways in North Carolina, 1791–1840* (New York: Garland Publishing, 1994)

Introduction

1. Young, *The Grey Album*, 21.

2. See Bishir, "Black Builders in Antebellum North Carolina."

3. The topic of differing "social environments" for free blacks is emphasized in Bristol, *Knights of the Razor*, 72.

4. On nineteenth-century definitions of social position through work identity, see Upton, "Pattern Books and Professionalism." A substantial body of literature documents American craftsmen as members of communities and trade groups and as bellwethers of technological, economic, and social change. Especially relevant to this study are Rock, Gilje, and Asher, *American Artisans: Crafting Social Identity*, and Barnes, *Artisan Workers in the Upper South*. See also Bridenbaugh, *The Colonial Craftsman*; Garrison, *Two Carpenters*; and Lounsbury, *Essays in Early American Architecture*. On North Carolina, see Bishir, Brown, Lounsbury, and Wood, *Architects and Builders in North Carolina*; Bivins, *The Furniture of Coastal North Carolina*; and M. Ruth Little, *Sticks and Stones: Three Centuries of North Carolina Gravemarkers* (Chapel Hill: University of North Carolina Press, 1998).

5. Bishir, Brown, Lounsbury, and Wood, *Architects and Builders in North Carolina*, 111 and 187–90, on Wilmington, North Carolina; and Gillespie, *Free Labor in an Unfree World*, on Georgia.

6. John Urmston to the Society for the Propagation of the Gospel, July 2, 1711, in Saunders, ed., *The Colonial Records of North Carolina*, 1:764; Brickell, *The Natural History of North-Carolina*, 275; Fries et al., *Records of the Moravians*, 2:780. *American Farmer* (Baltimore) 9 (January 1828): 353, reproduces Charles Fisher's comments to the North Carolina House of Commons. On the term "mechanic," see Lounsbury, *An Illustrated Glossary*, 229.

7. Among many studies that consider the work of black artisans are Du Bois, *The Negro Artisan*; Thompson, *Flash of the Spirit*; Carll-White, "The Role of the Black Artisan in the Building Trades"; and Vlach, *By the Work of Their Hands*. Black artisans also appear in more general works such as Koger, *Black Slaveowners*; Wade, *Slavery in the Cities*; Berlin, *Slaves without Masters*; Martin, *Divided Mastery*; and Foner, *Reconstruction*.

Studies of specific black artisans in North Carolina include Franklin, "James Boon, Free Negro Artisan"; Bishir, "Black Builders in Antebellum North Carolina"; and Marshall and Leimenstoll, *Thomas Day*. Histories of North Carolina that mention black artisans include Bassett, *Slavery and Servitude in the Colony of North Carolina*, and *Slavery in the State of North Carolina*; Johnson, *Ante-Bellum North Carolina*; Crow, Escott, and Hatley, *A History of African Americans in North Carolina*; and, particularly important to this study, Franklin, *The Free Negro in North Carolina*.

8. Most local studies of urban black artisans in the South treat the colonial, early national, and antebellum periods. On Virginia, see Barnes, *Artisan Workers in the Upper South*; Sidbury, *Ploughshares into Swords*; Bogger, *Free Blacks in Norfolk*. On Baltimore, see Steffen, *The Mechanics of Baltimore*, especially 32–45; and Tina H. Sheller, "Freemen, Servants, and Slaves: Artisans and the Craft Structure of Revolutionary Baltimore Town," in Rock, Gilje, and Asher, *American Artisans: Crafting Social Identity*, 17–32. Cov-

ering later periods and other cities are Powers, *Black Charlestonians*, and Blassingame, *Black New Orleans*.

9. Marshall and Leimenstoll, *Thomas Day*; and John Michael Vlach, "Philip Simmons: Afro-American Blacksmith," in Vlach, *By the Work of Their Hands*, 127–60.

10. Among several works on Keckley (Keckly) is Jennifer Fleischner, *Mrs. Lincoln and Mrs. Keckly: The Remarkable Story of the Friendship Between a First Lady and a Former Slave* (New York: Broadway Books, 2003).

11. Sidbury, *Ploughshares into Swords*, and Egerton, *Gabriel's Rebellion*. On Frederick Douglass as an enslaved caulker in Baltimore before launching his career as a national racial and political leader, see Hahn, *A Nation under Our Feet*, 23, and Douglass, *The Life and Times of Frederick Douglass*, 122–35. Of the 1,509 black officeholders of the Reconstruction period featured in Foner, *Freedom's Lawmakers*, at least 362 were artisans, and several of the 243 political leaders identified as ministers combined their calling with craft occupations (Foner, xx–xxi).

12. Gilmore, *Gender and Jim Crow*; Cecelski, *The Fire of Freedom*.

13. In *Ploughshares into Swords*, 2–3, Sidbury cites the prevalence of broad statewide, regional, and national studies of slaves and other Americans of color, and stresses the need for and value of "seeking answers in a more localized place" and portraying the contours of black life in a single locale.

14. My findings draw upon and parallel those in Franklin, *The Free Negro in North Carolina* and Johnson, *Ante-Bellum North Carolina*, as well as such broader studies as Wade, *Slavery in the Cities*; Berlin, *Slaves without Masters*; Hahn, *A Nation under Our Feet*; and the works of C. Vann Woodward, especially *The Strange Career of Jim Crow*.

15. On race as a social construction—"a product of history, not of nature"—see for example Fields, "Ideology and Race in American History," 152.

16. My thinking about this perspective on New Bern's black artisans has been stimulated by essays in Rock, Gilje, and Asher, *American Artisans: Crafting Social Identity*, especially Gilje, "Introduction: Identity and Independence"; Sidbury, "Slave Artisans in Richmond"; and Gillespie, "Planters in the Making." Gilje's introduction provides a succinct description of the development of American artisan identity and opportunities for further study; quote, xv. The classic and pioneering work on this topic is Wilentz, *Chants Democratic*.

17. On parades and portraits, see Harry R. Rubenstein, "With Hammer in Hand: Working-Class Occupational Portraits," in Rock, Gilje, and Asher, *American Artisans: Crafting Social Identity*, 176–98.

18. Gilje, "Introduction: Identity and Independence," quotes, xx.

19. For displays of artisan republican identity in Savannah and Augusta, Georgia, see Gillespie, *Free Labor in an Unfree World*, 36–65; and in Petersburg, see Barnes, *Artisan Workers in the Upper South*, 105–13.

20. See white artisans' complaints about black competition in antebellum North Carolina in Bishir, Brown, Lounsbury, and Wood, *Architects and Builders in North Carolina*, 111, 190. On Georgia, see Gillespie, *Free Labor in an Unfree World*, 156–71. Barnes, *Artisan Workers in the Upper South*, 106–10, notes (110) that "when Petersburg artisans

chose to organize in the face of economic distress, they used the republican language of citizenship to lash out at free blacks only."

21. Gillespie, "Planters in the Making." See Bishir, "Jacob W. Holt," and Bishir, Brown, Lounsbury, and Wood, *Architects and Builders in North Carolina*, 157–59, on white artisans in North Carolina who owned or hired enslaved artisans.

22. Sidbury, "Slave Artisans in Richmond," uses the example of Richmond to raise such questions about artisan identity among slaves in the urban South (quotes, 4–5).

23. Thomas Newton, petition to emancipate Sarah, 1811, *FFV*, 111.

24. This discussion reflects arguments presented in Hahn, *A Nation under Our Feet*, especially "Looking Out from Slavery," 1–10.

25. *Christian Recorder*, October 28, 1865.

26. Gilmore, *Gender and Jim Crow*, 1.

Chapter 1

1. Green, *Fact Stranger than Fiction*, 36. On "communal intimacy" among blacks and whites in small antebellum towns, see Tolbert, *Constructing Townscapes*, 187–223.

2. On New Bern generally, see Watson, *A History of New Bern*, and Sandbeck, *The Historic Architecture of New Bern*.

3. Quote, Joseph Blount Cheshire, "Wilmington," in Lyman H. Powell, ed., *Historic Towns of the Southern States* (New York and London: G. P. Putnam's Sons, 1904), 219.

4. Quote, Francis Asbury, 1802, in Johnson, *Ante-Bellum North Carolina*, 120. The Governor's Residence, now often referred to as Tryon Palace, burned in 1798 and was reconstructed in the 1950s; it is now part of Tryon Palace Historic Sites and Gardens.

5. Ann Blount Pettigrew to Mary Williams Bryan, February 12, 1827 (Lemmon, *The Pettigrew Papers*, 2:80); Ann Pettigrew to Ebenezer Pettigrew, December 30, 1824 (2:51). See also Ann Blount Pettigrew to Mary Williams Bryan, April 20, 1824 (2:41).

6. Descendants of early settlers of color in the county have persisted in rural Craven County and adjoining Carteret County to the present (author, personal conversations, 2007, with Bernard George, New Bern, and David Cecelski, Durham, whose families are from these areas). Heinegg, "Free African Americans," observes that a high proportion of the earliest recorded free people of color in North Carolina were natives of Virginia, including many who had been free in Northampton County, Virginia, and settled in Craven County, including the Carter, Copes, Driggers, George, and Johnston families, while the Dove family came from Maryland. Heinegg notes that in 1790 the chief concentrations of such people in North Carolina were in Northampton, Halifax, Bertie, Craven, Granville, Robeson, and Hertford Counties. Except for Craven and Robeson, these counties lie near the Virginia border. I have not found a specific explanation for the unusual number of free people of color coming to colonial Craven County.

7. See Franklin, *The Free Negro in North Carolina*, 35–36; Watson, *A History of New Bern*, 43; Berlin, *Slaves without Masters*, 6. Quote, *Proceedings and Debates of the Convention of North Carolina*, 351. Indicating the early prevalence of interracial relationships, North Carolina laws of 1715 and 1741 imposed fines on any white man or woman "in-

termarrying with Indians, Negroes, Mustees, or Mulattoes" and punished indentured white women who had mixed-race children by extending their indentures and apprenticing the children.

8. U.S. census, 1790; Franklin, *The Free Negro in North Carolina*, 8–9, 14–19. Franklin notes (18) that in 1790 whites constituted 73.2 percent of North Carolina's population, slaves 25.5 percent, and free blacks 1.27 percent.

9. Watson, *A History of New Bern*, 307.

10. Worsley, "Catholicism in Antebellum North Carolina," 407; quote, Bishop John England to William Gaston, June 28, 1839, William Gaston Papers, SHC, transcript provided to author by Stephen C. Worsley.

11. Information on Methodism in New Bern, including Andrews Chapel, comes from Green, *Methodist Meeting House*; quote from Wait, ibid., 69. A Baptist congregation in New Bern, formed in 1809, worshipped in a frame meetinghouse on Metcalf Street near Queen Street. The congregation probably included slaves as well as whites, but little is known about its early black members, and judging from Wait's comments, it evidently attracted relatively few black worshippers. The old Baptist Church is pictured in Green, *A New Bern Album*, 177.

12. Ebenezer Pettigrew to Ann Blount Pettigrew, January 5, 1830 (Lemmon, *The Pettigrew Papers*, 2:130); John Herritage Bryan to Ebenezer Pettigrew, July 3, 1834 (Lemmon, *The Pettigrew Papers*, 2:237–38).

13. *New Bern Daily Times*, May 22, 1865.

14. See "Memorial, R. Road," Legislative Petitions, NCA&H, 1850, seeking a railroad to connect New Bern to the Central Railroad (the North Carolina Railroad) to increase profits from the city's agricultural hinterland and forest industries.

15. Although there were once many nineteenth-century gravestones for people of color in New Bern's Cedar Grove Cemetery, most have been lost. Many were destroyed in the wholesale move of Cedar Grove's black graves in 1913 and thereafter to Greenwood to make room for white burials in Cedar Grove. One stone that remained at Cedar Grove for a time was recorded in a WPA survey—that of "Daniel" [Donum] Montford, dated 1838—but it has disappeared. The stone for Sally Green (John R. Green's first wife, d. March 29, 1837) also escaped removal in 1913 and is one of the few remaining in Cedar Grove for a person of color. Author's visits to Cedar Grove and Greenwood Cemeteries with John B. Green III.

16. Green, *A New Bern Album*, 177. Black Baptists formed their own congregations in the mid- and late 1860s.

17. The name Andrews Chapel (also Andrew's, Andrew, St. Andrew's) probably honored Allen S. Andrews, the first minister assigned separately to the black congregation (Green, *Methodist Meeting House*, 64–65).

18. U.S. censuses. Some of the 1840–50 increase in the number of free people of color reflects the 1850 census taker's inclusion within New Bern of a few suburban areas formerly treated as rural, but the growth was also real, reflecting new arrivals and natural increase among those already free. Although Wilmington had fewer free blacks than

did New Bern, the Cape Fear city was known for the unusual autonomy of its slaves. See Bishir, "Black Builders."

19. U.S. censuses. In 1850 Petersburg had 2,616 free people of color, 4,729 slaves, and 6,665 whites. As noted in Lebsock, *The Free Women of Petersburg*, 11, in 1860 about half the population of the city of more than 18,000 was black, and about one third of those were free people.

20. In 1850 the census showed that of 4,581 New Bernians, almost 60 percent—2,727—were people of color, including 1,997 slaves and 800 free. In North Carolina, only Wilmington, with a total population of 7,264, had more people of color—3,683 including 3,031 slaves and 652 free blacks—who constituted about 50 percent of the population. By 1860, both cities had grown and the number and the proportion of people of color declined. New Bern's 1860 population of 5,432 included 2,872 black people (52 percent of the total)—2,383 enslaved and 689 free; Wilmington had 9,552 people, of whom 4,350 (45 percent) were black—3,777 slaves and 573 free. New Bern's free black population in 1850 was about 17 percent (almost 1 in 5) of the total population and about 29 percent of the total black population. In 1850 Petersburg had 2,616 free people of color, 4,729 slaves, and 6,665 whites. Charleston (with its majority-black population, most of whom were slaves) and New Orleans (with a majority of white people) had free black populations of under 10 percent of their total populations. Even though New Bern's free black population shrank while its total population grew by 1860, its 689 free blacks still constituted about 12 percent of the total, exceeding Wilmington in numbers and proportion and exceeding most southern cities in proportion.

21. Barrett, *The Civil War in North Carolina*, 43–44, 66–130.

22. *Anglo-African*, January 16, 1864; Greenwood, *First Fruits of Freedom*, 33.

23. Cecelski, "Abraham Galloway," especially 181. See also Watson, *A History of New Bern*, 369–427. On fugitive slaves coming into Union lines as a political action throughout the South, see Hahn, *A Nation under Our Feet*, 68–89.

24. Colyer, *Brief Report of the Services Rendered*, 51–55. See also *Christian Recorder*, June 21, 1862; Browning, "Visions of Freedom," 77–78; Browning, *Shifting Loyalties*, 76–80; and Greenwood, *First Fruits of Freedom*, 43–48, quote, 48.

25. NBCD (1880), quote, 36–37; NBCD (1893).

26. NBCD (1880).

27. According to Kenzer, *Enterprising Southerners*, 38–39, in 1870 Craven County had 8 out of 126 North Carolina black businesses assessed by the national credit rating firm of R. G. Dun & Co. Representation in the Dun listings, often cited as an indicator of enterprise, does not necessarily imply a successful business: many of those listed were described in negative terms and deemed unworthy for credit. Presumably the list does indicate entrepreneurs who were seeking credit to maintain or expand their businesses. Frenise A. Logan notes that in 1880 the successor firm of Dun and Barlow listed 80 black-owned businesses in North Carolina, with 10 of them in New Bern. Nine years later, of 175 such businesses listed in the state, 17 were in New Bern (Logan, *The Negro in North Carolina*, 112–13). Dun's lists represented but a fraction of the tradesmen of color

in New Bern. In 1933 the Dun company merged with a principal competitor to become Dun and Bradstreet.

28. On politics in this period, see Watson, *A History of New Bern*, 469–519, and Anderson, *The Black Second*.

29. For an example of a chance discovery—a drawing on a board—giving evidence of the design process and authorship in colonial Virginia, see Carl R. Lounsbury, "'An Elegant and Commodious Building': William Buckland and the Design of the Prince William County Courthouse," *Journal of the Society of Architectural Historians* 46 (September 1987): 228–40. A contrasting situation occurs in the case of Milton, North Carolina, cabinetmaker Thomas Day, for whom extensive documentation and local tradition exist, as well as a substantial body of documented and attributed furniture and interior woodwork that displays an identifiable style. See Marshall and Leimenstoll, *Thomas Day*.

Chapter 2

1. I have used a skilled worker's day's pay as the principal benchmark for comparison of monetary amounts. This has proved more accurate for New Bern than reference to current dollar amounts based on inflation over the years. Not only did relative values of specific items vary markedly from present-day values, but the inflation-based charts suggest overall cost multipliers much smaller than New Bern figures indicate. Inflation-rate sources generally indicate a multiplier of about 15 times between 1810 and 2010. However, comparison of actual costs of labor, property, and goods in ca. 1810 New Bern and those of 2010 show a multiplier of at least 100 and sometimes twice that. For example, in 1810–20 a skilled white or free black carpenter or brickmaker in New Bern made from $1 to $2 *per day* (typically upwards of 10 hours per day). Today a good carpenter or brickmason in a mid-level North Carolina city earns from $20 to $35 *per hour.* Costs of such items as real estate, tools, clothing, and food rose at various rates. A modestly priced town lot sold for $50–$80 in 1820 and a prime one for perhaps $500 to $1,000. A custom-tailored "great coat" for a rich lawyer cost $6.25 in 1834. Comparable items cost *at least* 100 times as much in 2010, and land runs higher.

2. On the significance of artisans' tools, see Sidbury, "Slave Artisans in Richmond," in Rock, Gilje, and Asher, *American Artisans*, 49, 55, and Gilje, "Introduction," in ibid. For a rare instance of such artisan displays in North Carolina, see Bishir, Brown, Lounsbury, and Wood, *Architects and Builders in North Carolina*, 187–88, on the activities of craftsmen constructing the State Capitol in Raleigh in the 1830s.

3. Minutes, Court of Pleas and Quarter Sessions, Rowan County, North Carolina, vol. 7 (1800–1807), p. 299, May 7, 1805, MESDA.

4. Donum Montford, Estates Papers, CCEP.

5. "A Citizen," *New Bern Spectator*, December 9, 1831, on New Bern's "golden age."

6. Ships and Merchants Shipping Records, 1830–1831, Craven County Records, NCA&H, cited in Cecelski, *The Waterman's Song*, 42. On the Sparrow family of shipbuilders, see Herzog, "The Early Architecture of New Bern," 347–51.

7. John R. Donnell Letter and Account Book. See Sandbeck, *The Historic Architecture of New Bern*, on the Donnell house and on Asa King, who also executed fine carpentry work at the Eli Smallwood house. Donnell was the son-in-law of the late Richard Dobbs Spaight Sr. and Mary Jones Spaight.

8. Treasurer of Public Building Accounts, Craven County Records, NCA&H; Bishir, "Philadelphia Bricks for New Bern Jail." Maintenance and repair of the eighteenth-century Craven County Courthouse likewise involved the work of various free artisans and their slaves. In 1825, Donum Montford and his crew accomplished whitewashing and repairs, for which he charged 12 shillings 6 pence per day for his own work and that of his son Nelson as well as for Annanias and Richard, while Daniel, perhaps an apprentice, earned 10 shillings a day. Montford also recorded work by women and girls—Siply, Nelly, Lydia, Rachel, Ginny, and Sally—on unspecified tasks; enslaved women commonly worked as field hands, but it is rare to find records of their work on construction projects. These women earned for Montford three shillings per day. In 1827 white house carpenter Martin Stevenson worked six days on the courthouse at the rate of 17 shillings 6 pence per day, while his "man Daniel" worked there for eleven days at 10 shillings per day and his "boy Emanuel" seven days at 6 shillings. In 1828 Stevenson did additional carpentry at the courthouse, assisted by Daniel, John, Alford, and Emanuel. Treasurer of Public Building Accounts, Craven County Records, NCA&H.

9. Bristol, *Knights of the Razor.* See also Franklin, *The Free Negro in North Carolina*, 140, and Berlin, *Slaves without Masters*, 235–36.

10. John C. Stanly account with Edward Graham, 1813, Graham Daves Collection, NCA&H. See n. 8 above for Montford's pay rates.

11. Green, *Fact Stranger than Fiction*, 43, and Schweninger, "John Carruthers Stanly." Franklin, *The Free Negro in North Carolina*, 170–79, on Chavis.

12. See Berlin, *Slaves without Masters*, 234–38, on racially identified and "stigmatized" occupations in Richmond, Charleston, and elsewhere.

13. Although there were some enslaved silversmiths in Charleston, none of New Bern's silversmiths—such as William Tisdale and Freeman Woods—is known have employed black silversmiths. Tisdale's estate included two slaves, a man and a woman, but nothing is known of their skills, and Woods's estate included no slaves. William Tisdale and Freeman Woods, Estates Papers, CCEP; Mary Reynolds Peacock, "Freeman Woods," *DNCB*. See Carll, "The Role of the Black Artisan," 173–75, on the slave silversmith Joe, trained by jeweler John Paul Grimke.

14. Sam, *Wilmington Sentinel and General Advertiser*, February 26, 1789. Although some New Bern furniture makers owned slaves, their estates inventories did not identify them by trade. Thomas Youle and Richard and Joseph Hall, Estates Papers, CCEP; transcripts in research files, MESDA. See also furniture makers William Brooks and Thomas Oliver, Wills, CCW, as owners of slaves whose skills are not cited. John S. Clements took the free black youth Bill Johnston, aged fifteen, to the chairmaker's trade on September 10, 1817 (*ACNC*, 190); and turner William Carter, a county resident, took as apprentices to his trade the free black youths Stephen Lewis in 1787, Gabe Moore in 1789, and Martin and Sharper Black in 1793 (*ACNC*, 145, 146, 150).

15. On these and other white artisans in early national–period New Bern, see Sandbeck, *The Historic Architecture of New Bern*; Herzog, "The Early Architecture of New Bern"; Bivins, *Furniture*; and *ACNC*.

16. These and other names of slave artisans appear in Farlow, "Black Craftsmen in North Carolina," Part I (February 1985), 10–13, and Part II (May 1985), 91–103. Many more enslaved artisans' names appear in runaway advertisements, wills, emancipation records, deeds, and estate inventories.

17. Hancock in Green, *Fact Stranger than Fiction*; Bragg in Miller, "Recollections," 461.

18. Whitford, "Home Story of a Walking Stick," 140–41.

19. Ibid., 100.

20. See Franklin, *The Free Negro in North Carolina*, and Bassett, *Slavery in Colonial North Carolina* and *Slavery in the State of North Carolina*, on regulations affecting people of color.

21. Walter Clark, ed., *The State Records of North Carolina* (Goldsboro: Nash Brothers for the State of North Carolina, 1905), vol. 24 (Laws 1777–88), 823. See Colonial and State Records of North Carolina, docsouth.unc.edu/csr/, consulted February 8, 2013.

22. Wade, *Slavery in the Cities*, 80–92, depicts the widespread difficulties urban whites had in regulating blacks' activities.

23. New Bern Town Council Minutes, 1797–1828, New Bern City Hall, transcript courtesy of John B. Green III.

24. Schweninger, "John Carruthers Stanly," indicates that the Revolutionary spirit of manumissions dwindled generally in the early nineteenth century. But Franklin, *The Free Negro in North Carolina*, 19–27, notes the continuation of manumissions through the period in this state.

25. Johnson, *Ante-Bellum North Carolina*, 562–63. Quote, ibid., from Stephen Grellet, a French-born Quaker convert and missionary who toured the United States and preached in New Bern in March 1825. See *Memoirs of the Life and Gospel Labours of Stephen Grellet* (1877), Google Books.

26. Degler, *The Other South*. Thanks to Jeffrey Crow and Harry Watson for sharing their perspectives on this topic.

27. Degler, in *The Other South*, 38, singles out William Gaston as a rare example of a white political leader who showed concern for the situations of both slaves and free people of color. In 1832 Gaston delivered a famous statement to students at the University of North Carolina condemning slavery, and in the landmark decision by the North Carolina Supreme Court in the case of *State v. Will* (1834) he asserted that a slave was entitled to resist a white man to save his own life. Gaston described Will as "a human being" who, though "degraded indeed by slavery," had "organs, dimensions, senses, affections, and passions like our own." As noted in the next chapter, John Stanly opposed certain restrictions imposed on free blacks in 1826, including limitations on their freedom of movement.

28. Some observers have claimed that slave artisanry was inherently inferior to that of whites (for example Bridenbaugh, *The Colonial Craftsman*, 31, 120, 138, 140). In fact, both enslaved and free craftsmen produced work of every level of quality, and in North

Carolina, at least, many of the finest buildings of the antebellum era were built entirely or in part by enslaved artisans. Bishir, "Black Builders."

29. Abraham, *North Carolina Gazette*, February 26, 1778, Windley, *Runaway Slave Advertisements*, 448–49. James York Green, *FFV*, 89.

30. Sam, *Carolina Federal Republican*, February 1, 1817, MESDA. Nelson, *Carolina Sentinel*, April 17, 1824, Herzog, "The Early Architecture of New Bern," 336. John Oliver and administrators' advertisements, *Carolina Sentinel*, June 2, 1821, and May 24, 1823.

31. For estimates of numbers of slave artisans based on the number of slaves owned by free artisans, see Berlin and Gutman, "Natives and Immigrants," 1194; and Sidbury, "Slave Artisans in Richmond, Virginia," in Rock, Gilje, and Asher, *American Artisans*, 50.

32. John F. Brevard to Alexander Brevard, December 4, 1812, Brevard Papers, quoted in Johnson, *Ante-Bellum North Carolina*, 540.

33. Mary Jones Spaight, Estates Papers and Will, CCEP and CCW.

34. Ann Blackledge, Will, CCWB B:277.

35. Green, *Fact Stranger than Fiction*, quotes, 11, 13; CCEP; CCAB.

36. Ulysses, *Norfolk and Portsmouth (Va.) Herald*, February 2, 1818, MESDA; see also *New Bern Spectator*, February 6, 1830.

37. *Stephen Forbes v. John Oliver*, Civil Actions Papers, Craven County Court Records, NCA&H.

38. *Carolina Federal Republican*, July 6, 1816 and October 19, 1816.

39. John R. Donnell Letter and Account Book.

40. *Carolina Federal Republican*, July 6, 1816 and October 19, 1816; Shadrach Fulsher, Will, CCWB A:212.

41. Cupid, *Carolina Federal Republican*, May 17, 1817, *SLF*, 528–29. The tall, "well made," and "yellow" shoemaker had taken the items from the shop of a Mr. Fluellin (probably his employer) after being "persuaded" to run away with his free black wife, Eliza Turner. He belonged to an orphan whose guardian was seeking the slave's return.

42. *Wilmington Sentinel and General Advertiser*, February 26, 1789, MESDA.

43. *Norfolk and Portsmouth Herald*, February 2, 1818, MESDA; and *Carolina Sentinel*, January 18, 1837, *SLF*, 668.

44. Green, *Fact Stranger than Fiction*, 12 (quotes); Parker, *Running for Freedom*, 40–41. See Johnson, *Ante-Bellum North Carolina*, 542–43, on the legislative debate in the 1820s over teaching slaves to read or write.

45. Green, *Fact Stranger than Fiction*, 10–13, quotes, 11, 13; CCEP; CCAB.

46. Tailor Reuben Bell died in 1811, by which time Green was about eighteen years old. The kind "Frenchman, Durand" might have been John Louis Durand (1787–1854), a native New Bernian of French descent who became a prominent white tailor and merchant, and with whom Green had subsequent business dealings. One "Lewis Durong" (phonetic spelling for Durand?) was apprenticed at age fourteen to tailor Bell in September 1800.

47. Colonial Governors' Papers, NCA&H, Box 8, transcripts in research files, MESDA. Other white artisans on the project were bricklayer Thomas Lippiner and plasterer Da-

vid Cawthon, who did not name their workers. No known records identify the artisans who built the palace in 1767–70.

48. Ibid.

49. On slave hiring, see especially Sidbury, "Slave Artisans in Richmond, Virginia"; Takagi, *"Rearing Wolves to Our Own Destruction"*; Wade, *Slavery in the Cities*, 38–54; Bishir, "Black Builders"; and Martin, *Divided Mastery*. These sources suggest that slave hiring elsewhere in the South operated in much the same way as in New Bern.

50. Johnson, *Ante-Bellum North Carolina*, 531–32, quote 532, from Frederick Nash, James Iredell, and William H. Battle, *The Revised Statutes of the State of North Carolina* (Raleigh: Turner and Hughes, 1837), vol. 1, chap. 111, sec. 21, and Session Laws, 1827, chap. 92 (quote, 726).

51. New Bern Town Council Minutes, 1797–1828, New Bern City Hall, transcript courtesy of John B. Green III.

52. See Bishir, Brown, Lounsbury, and Wood, *Architects and Builders in North Carolina*, 111, on an 1802 legislative petition from Wilmington white artisans objecting to the illegal practice of slaves being allowed to hire their own time, take contracts, and hire other slaves to complete these contracts.

53. *John Oliver v. Uriah Sandy and Stephen Forbes*, March Term, 1821, Civil Actions Papers, Craven County Court Records, NCA&H.

54. *Carolina Sentinel*, June 2, 1821 and May 24, 1823, Herzog, "The Early Architecture of New Bern," 336; John R. Donnell Letter and Account Book; CCDB 44:57.

55. John R. Donnell Letter and Account Book.

56. Ibid.; Sandbeck, *The Historic Architecture of New Bern*.

57. John R. Donnell Letter and Account Book. The terms "find" or "found" in this context referred to supplying food and drink and possibly lodging or clothing.

58. Ibid.

59. Green, *Fact Stranger than Fiction*, 50.

60. David Witherspoon, Will, CCW. David Witherspoon's son John—his only child with Mary Whiting Jones Nash Witherspoon, the widow of Gov. Abner Nash—was John Knox Witherspoon, later a noted Presbyterian minister. See John Knox Witherspoon, Abner Nash, and Frederick Nash, *DNCB*.

61. James Sanders, Will and Estates Papers, CCWB A:156, CCEP.

62. On Vail see *Carolina Federal Republican*, July 6, 1816 and October 19, 1816, in Munson, *Citizens of Craven County North Carolina*; Benners Vail, Estates Papers, CCEP. The list of slaves in Vail's estate, made December 31, 1817, included the following men identified as artisans: Bob, 31, house carpenter, valued at $800; Jim, 28, caulker and ship carpenter, $750; Ben, 38, sawyer, $500; Harry, 44, blacksmith, $250; Emanuel, 44, cooper, $350; Simon, 30, cooper, $800; Nelson, 20, shoemaker, $600. In all, Vail's estate included 23 enslaved men, 13 women, and 14 children.

63. Richard Dobbs Spaight Sr. and Mary Jones Leach Spaight, Estates Papers, CCEP. Richard and Mary Spaight's children were Richard Dobbs Spaight Jr. (later governor, unmarried, 1796–1850); Charles and William, who died young; and Margaret (1800–31),

who married John R. Donnell (1789–1864) and left him a widower with children and in possession of her slaves and other property.

64. Will and Estates Papers of Mary Sanders, CCWB A:348, CCEP, and of Thomas Hyman, CCWB 136:287, CCEP.

65. Samuel Latham, November 21, 1822, published in December 7, 1822, *Carolina Sentinel*, *SLF*, 637; *Norfolk Herald*, July 1, 1814, MESDA.

66. Kay and Cary, *Slavery in North Carolina*, 259; Parker, *Running for Freedom*, 147.

67. *North Carolina Gazette*, July 7, 1797, *SLF*, 19; *New Bern Spectator*, May 15, 1832, *SLF*, 776. By 1832 Morehead had begun the textile manufacturing enterprises that would grow into an empire at Leaksville and neighboring areas. John Motley Morehead, *DNCB*.

68. Frank Burr, *Carolina Sentinel*, April 15, 1820, *SLF*, 620; CCDB 43:173, 212, August 3 and 13, 1822. John Devereux and Thomas Pollock, *DNCB*.

69. Frank Burr, *Carolina Sentinel*, April 15, 1820, *SLF* 620; Bacchus Hill, *Carolina Sentinel*, June 15, 1822, *SLF* 635; Allen Woodard, *Carolina Sentinel*, May 18, 1822, *SLF* 633.

70. *Carolina Sentinel*, December 8, 1821, *SLF*, 632; R. Powell, Smithfield, Johnston County, November 4, 1825, *Carolina Sentinel*, December 3, 1825. *SLF*, 647.

71. Bill, a runaway cooper "well known in New Bern," *New Bern Spectator*, March 10, 1837, *SLF*, 786.

72. Glasgow O'Neill, "so well-known in Wilmington and the immediate neighborhood . . . that a description of his person is unnecessary," *Cape Fear Recorder*, October 16, 1824, *SLF*, 569.

73. *Edenton Encyclopedia Instructor*, May 31, 1800, *SLF*, 332.

74. *Carolina Sentinel*, June 3, 1820, *SLF*, 621. Jacob, *Norfolk Herald*, July 1, 1814, MESDA. Parker, *Running for Freedom*, 47–49, on warning captains of vessels.

75. Henry B. Mitchell, *Carolina Sentinel*, October 10, 1829, *SLF*, 659, and *New Bern Spectator and Literary Journal*, May 7, 1831, *SLF*, 773.

76. *FFV*, 111–112. In 1808 merchants John Devereux and William Hollister assisted the widow Sarah Woods in emancipating Thomas Newton in accord with her husband's wishes.

77. On emancipation laws, see Franklin, *The Free Negro in North Carolina*, 19–34, and Bassett, *Slavery in the State of North Carolina*, 29–38. *Laws of the State of North Carolina enacted in the year 1818* (Raleigh: Thomas Henderson, State Printer, 1819), chap. 13, pp. 21–22. See *FFV*, 311–18, for texts of North Carolina's emancipation laws. Although most accounts give the date for the shift from county to superior court as 1830, the provision seems to have been in effect from 1818. See Berlin, *Slaves without Masters*, 29, on manumission as "a slaveholder's prerogative throughout the South, except in North Carolina," which required meritorious service and court permission. See Franklin, *The Free Negro in North Carolina*, 20–23, on county courts' lack of concern regarding meritorious service.

78. Schweninger, "John Carruthers Stanly," quote, 169; Franklin, *The Free Negro in North Carolina*, 19–34; Berlin, *Slaves without Masters*, 29–35.

79. *FFV*, 88.

80. Ibid., 87.

81. Ibid., 101.

82. CCDB 41:12, May 26, 1818, ; CCDB 41:120. See Bassett, *Slavery in the State of North Carolina*, 31–32.

83. CCW; CCEP; *FFV*, 316. Larry was jointly owned by Conway and a business partner.

84. *FFV*, 37–126. In addition to manumission petitions in Craven County Records at NCA&H (published in *FFV*), deed books also contain deeds for these and other manumissions, and court records include further examples.

85. Schweninger, "John Carruthers Stanly." Stanly emancipated Brister and Boston in October 1828. For a list of slaves Stanly mortgaged in May 1828, see CCDB 45:439. Franklin, *The Free Negro in North Carolina*, 31, identifies Stanly as "the most influential free Negro in the manumission movement."

86. CCDB 36:489, September 10, 1804; CCDB 42:282, September 11, 1804; Richard Cogdell, Will and Estates Papers, CCWB A:218, CCEP.

87. *The Narrative of Lunsford Lane, Formerly of Raleigh, N.C., Embracing an Account of His Early Life, the Redemption by Purchase of Himself and Family from Slavery, and His Banishment from the Place of His Birth for the Crime of Wearing a Colored Skin. Published by Himself* (Boston: 1842), 16. Electronic edition, http://docsouth.unc.edu/neh/lanelunsford/. There had been a family dispute over Richard Cogdell's will that might have made the double transaction advisable; CCDB 33:305, April 4, 1799, Richard Cogdell [Jr.] to Thomas Badger and wife Lydia.

88. CCDB 37:10, March 3, 1806; *FFV*, 95–96.

89. Badger-Cogdell Bible, photocopy of transcription, Kellenberger Room. The transcription from the original Bible was made by John D. Whitford and is in the John D. Whitford Papers, NCA&H. The whereabouts of the original is unknown. The Bible, with entries for several families apparently inscribed by Lydia Cogdell Badger, is also variously referred to as the Badger Family Bible and the Cogdell Family Bible. Abram Allen is described in *Richmond Daily Dispatch*, November 22, 1864, http://www.perseus.tufts.edu/hopper/text?doc=Perseus%3Atext%3A2006.05.1227%3Aarticle%3D8, consulted April 26, 2010. In his will of 1838, Montford identified Allen as his nephew, but particulars of the kinship are not known.

90. Bassett, *Slavery in the State of North Carolina*, 45–46.

91. Green, *Fact Stranger than Fiction*. John P. Green noted the tensions between the Stanly and Spaight families, which grew worse after John Stanly killed Richard Dobbs Spaight Sr. in a duel. For a signed engraving of Stanly, probably identical to the one he gave to his son John R. Green, see John Stanly, Lithograph by Pendletons, Boston, from a painting by Ford, n.d. Series P2, North Carolina Collection Photographic Archives, Wilson Library, University of North Carolina at Chapel Hill. Posted at http://www.lib.unc.edu/ncc/ref/nchistory/sept2005/images.html.

92. Samuel Chapman, Will, CCW.

93. CCEP; CCW; *FFV*, 61–62; CCDB 37:916–17; CCAB.

94. *FFV*, 114, 79, 76; Green, *Fact Stranger than Fiction*, 14, 18.

95. *FFV*, 113.

96. *FFV*, 77, 78, 114, 115, 46, 48, 87, 111. When Robert Lisbon freed his daughters Myrtilla and Evelina in 1813 and 1816, respectively, he had the help of their former owner, Frederick Divoux; *FFV* 78, 115. On leading white attorneys, including George E. Badger and James W. and John H. Bryan, representing black clients, see Franklin, *The Free Negro in North Carolina*, 85–86.

97. *FFV*, 99–100. Supporting James York Green's emancipation were William B. Green's brother Thomas A. Green, J. Mastin, M. Stephens, M. E. Green, John Green, William Mitchell, and Thomas Wadsworth; *FFV*, 89. See also CCDB 41:120.

98. *FFV*, 87–88.

99. Information on Amelia Green from Patricia M. Samford, "'With Much Toil and Industry: Amelia Green and her Family's Quest for Freedom," unpublished manuscript, 2006, courtesy of Patricia M. Samford. See also Schweninger, "John Carruthers Stanly," for connections between Stanly and Amelia Green's family.

100. Donum Montford petition, 1827, John H. Bryan Papers, East Carolina University Library Special Collections, Greenville, North Carolina; *FFV*, 73–74. A Nelson Monford was listed in the U.S. census in Pitt County in 1830 as a single free black male aged 10–23. I have not found him in any other records. He was evidently born to a slave mother at about the same time Montford married the long-free Hannah Bowers.

101. *FFV*, 82, 121–22; Abner Nash, Estates Papers, CCEP. Among Nash's 110 slaves were those with names that appear later among emancipated persons: three Macklins, three Toms, Virgil, Mars, Bacc[h]us, Phoebe, and J. Newton. Frederick Nash, attorney, legislator, and chief justice of the state supreme court, moved from New Bern to Hillsborough in 1807. Frederick Nash, *DNCB*.

102. *FFV*, 87. Edward Graham (New Bern) to Frederick Nash (Hillsborough), November 23, 1809, stated that "Hancock" (probably the white William Hancock) had sold Bacchus and Sukey to William Conway and J. C. Stanly for $600, Edward Graham Papers, NCA&H. Stanly is not named in Conway's petition. I have found no deeds for the transfer of Bacchus and Sukey among any of the parties involved.

103. *Carolina Federal Republican*, February 15, 1812 (death notice of Margaret Haslin). Thomas Newton and others gave bond for Macklin's liberation in December 1818. Margaret's husband, Thomas Haslin, had bequeathed to her the slaves she had inherited from her father; Thomas Haslin, Will, CCWB B:19, July 26, 1792, proved 1797. Written at the bottom of Margaret Haslin's 1808 petition to emancipate her slave Phoebe was a note, "Mrs. Sarah Wood to emancipate mulatto man named Thomas Newton," suggesting Mrs. Haslin's interest in Newton's freedom and the possibility that he had been a Nash slave. (Sarah Woods obtained court permission to free Newton, and John Devereux and William Hollister submitted the successful petition in November 1808.) An April 1812 inventory of Mrs. Haslin's estate named slaves Grace, Macklin, John Newton, Sam, and Sanders (?), plus other slaves' names that were marked through—Rachel and her children, Kittey, Kelser, and Hannah—whom Haslin decided to give to John C. Stanly; Margaret Haslin, Will and Estates Papers, CCW, CCEP. It is possible that this Hannah of the Nash connection was the woman later known as Hannah Neale, treated in chapters 3 and 5, who was born ca. 1802–6 and identified by her grandson Israel B.

Abbott as having been freed when she was about twelve. For Stanly emancipating the slaves in 1816, see *FFV*, 79. In an undated but related petition, John C. Stanly noted that Margaret Haslin had bequeathed Rachel to him "with an injunction that he should procure the liberation" of the slaves; *FFV*, 121.

104. Virgil Crawford, Will and Estate Papers, CCW, CCEP; *FFV*, 82. The sale of Crawford's other property totaled $547.84, and his debts were $471.32. Although North Carolina law gave no legal standing to marital unions between free and enslaved people, in this and many other cases both the participants and others referred to the couples as husband and wife, and I have followed that approach.

105. CCAB; *FFV*; U.S. censuses, 1830–80. Bacchus Simmons to Lydia Crawford, CCDB 58:146 and CCDB 55:306; and Craven County Tax Book, 1849, Tryon Palace.

106. Pettigrew Family Papers, NCA&H; *ACNC*, 346, 353; Chowan County Deed Book M2: 329, Chowan County Records, NCA&H.

107. Amelia Green Estate Papers, CCEP.

108. *Kelcy Davis v. John C. Stanly*, in Schweninger, "John Carruthers Stanly," 179–81.

109. Thomas Newton, Will, CCW; Donum Montford, Estates Papers, CCEP.

110. On apprenticeship practices in early North Carolina, see Bishir, Brown, Lounsbury, and Wood, *Architects and Builders in North Carolina*, 33–38.

111. Franklin, *The Free Negro in North Carolina*, 123, 165. Franklin notes, 165, that when a bill came to the legislature in 1826–27 to repeal the requirement to teach "colored apprentices" to read and write, the measure was postponed indefinitely.

112. For apprenticeship laws and practices, see Franklin, *The Free Negro in North Carolina*, 122–30, and Zipf, *Labor of Innocents*, especially 8–17. On racial restrictions on marriages, see Franklin, *The Free Negro in North Carolina*, 35–39 and 184–85. Franklin counted 95 free children of color as apprentices in all occupations in the period 1800–1824. Thirty-two occupations were represented. Among boys, coopers were most numerous in 1800–1824, and spinsters were by far the most numerous among girls. There were probably more apprentices of color than this: as described in n. 120 below, not all free apprentices of color were identified by race in apprentice bonds.

113. Zipf, *Labor of Innocents*, 26, on the 1801 provision.

114. Franklin, *The Free Negro in North Carolina*, 125.

115. On Baltimore, see Rockman, *Scraping By*, 50. On North Carolina, see *ACNC* and Franklin, *The Free Negro in North Carolina*, 122–29.

116. CCAB. See Sandbeck, *The Historic Architecture of New Bern*, on these white builders.

117. CCAB. These apprentices were Jim and Peter Bradock and Elisha and Mackey Gregory.

118. Ibid.

119. Ibid.

120. For Craven County, counting only the apprentices explicitly identified as persons of color underestimates the total number of apprentices of color. Usually, but not always, apprentice bonds mentioned if a child was a person of color or an orphan or both; for white children, no race was indicated. Some counties printed separate forms

for free black children. Craven County's printed apprentice bonds typically used the word "orphan" but in many cases made no mention of color, simply leaving a space for the names of apprentice and master. Although sometimes the scribe added a phrase indicating that the child named was a free boy or girl of color, often no one took the trouble to identify the child's race. Thus there are many Craven County apprentice bonds where no race was noted but where other evidence identifies the child as a free person of color. One such indication is an apprentice's surname typically or exclusively associated with a local free black family, as was the case with Elijah Copes, apprenticed to carpenter James Y. Green in 1823; no race was noted in the bond, but Copes was a common surname among Craven County free blacks, and Green was a man of color. Two girls noted only as orphans—Sukey and Eliza George, aged sixteen and thirteen, respectively—were bound out in 1821 to one Robert Woods as "sempstresses"; their surname suggests that they came from the numerous Craven County free black George family. A more certain indication that the apprentice was a free person of color is the presence of a document accompanying the apprentice bond in which the master or mistress guaranteed not to take the child from the county, as required by law for free black apprentices.

121. Evidence indicates that all the children apprenticed to black New Bern artisans were people of color. It was very unusual for a white artisan to work for a black employer; an exception appears in the case of Caswell County cabinetmaker Thomas Day, who employed some white artisans. Marshall and Leimenstoll, *Thomas Day*, 29–30.

122. Parish Register, Christ Episcopal Church, New Bern, copy at Kellenberger Room; *Acts of the North Carolina General Assembly*, vol. 24 (1786–87), chap. 58, 783–84: "An Act to Emancipate Hannah, Alias Hannah Bowers, a Person of Mixed Blood, Belonging to the Estate of the Late Alexander Gaston Deceased."

123. Parish Register, Christ Episcopal Church, New Bern, copy at Kellenberger Room; *FFV*, 115, 116.

124. Green, *Fact Stranger than Fiction*; Parish Register, Christ Episcopal Church, New Bern, copy at Kellenberger Room.

125. On racial residential patterns in other North Carolina cities, including the much later trend toward separation elsewhere, see Hanchett, *Sorting Out the New South City.*

126. On only a few pages of the 1820 census of New Bern are races of the persons named differentiated by the presence or absence of titles. Information on living patterns in the following paragraphs is derived from U.S. censuses for Craven County unless otherwise noted.

127. Miller, "Recollections," 461. On black sectors in late antebellum Richmond, see Takagi, *"Rearing Wolves to Our Own Destruction,"* 96–98; and in Petersburg, Barnes, *Artisan Workers in the Upper South*, 132–33.

128. Craven County Tax Records, 1815, NCA&H, posted at Kellenberger Room web site;; U.S. census, 1820, New Bern and Craven County. Bacchus Simmons, emancipated in 1811 (CCDB 38:93–94), bought lot #357 from John C. Stanly for eighty dollars in the same year (CCDB 39:519–21).

129. See CCDB 37:114 for the plat of Dryboro (lots 1–76) by Sarah Dry Smith and her

husband Benjamin Smith, a governor. She had inherited the property from her father, William Dry. Census records suggest that free people of color lived in this area "on the south side of the Neuse" before they acquired lots there. For deeds involving property in this area, see, for example, CCDB 40:199 (1816); CCDB 62:171 (1833); CCDB 62:226 (1838). The emancipated carpenter James York Green lived in Dryboro and owned property there and elsewhere: in 1814 he bought two lots in Dryboro (CCDB 39:288, 295); in 1816 he bought lot #352 across Queen Street at Craven Street (CCDB 39:664); and he continued to acquire property in Dryboro and elsewhere (CCDB 39:671, 769). A deed of 1827 (CCDB 45:168) refers to a lot sold by John C. Stanly to Elizabeth Hatch, where her slave Isa resided. General information on Dryboro comes from Hanchett and Little, *The History and Architecture of Long Wharf and Greater Duffyfield*, 55–56. Dryboro and nearby streets were not incorporated into New Bern until 1859, but from 1840 onward the census counted some residents of the area as part of New Bern. See Watson, *A History of New Bern*, 295, on annexation of Dryboro and creation of the Sixth Ward to accommodate it.

130. Craven County Tax List, 1815, NCA&H, posted at Kellenberger Room web site; CCDB, various deeds.

131. CCDB 47:317; CCDB 42:96; CCDB 45:486; and CCDB 47:376.

132. Despite extensive literature on the topic of slaveholding among free people of color, there is little consensus about black slaveholders' motives. See Franklin, *The Free Negro in North Carolina*, 162; Schweninger, "John Carruthers Stanly"; Larry Koger, *Black Slaveowners*; and Berlin, *Slaves without Masters*, 270–77. Carter G. Woodson's early study, *Free Negro Owners of Slaves in the United States in 1830* (Washington: Association for the Study of Negro Life and History, 1924; reprint, Westport Conn.: Negro Universities Press, 1968), has been the subject of much discussion, which is summarized in Koger, *Black Slaveowners*, 80–101, and David L. Lightner and Alexander M. Ragan, "Were African American Slaveholders Benevolent or Exploitative? A Quantitative Approach," *Journal of Southern History* 71, no. 3 (August 2005): 535–55. The analysis of black slaveholders' motives that most closely parallels the situation in New Bern appears in Koger, *Black Slaveowners*, describing free blacks who owned slaves for both benevolent and economic reasons.

133. Miller, "Recollections," 461. Donum Montford, Will, CCWB C:423. See "Donum Montford," Appendix, for the 1820 and 1830 U.S. census records of the members of his household. In 1828, Montford mortgaged several tracts of land plus his slaves Toney, 58; Jim Carney, 28; Annis, 34, and her children Lewis, Fanny, William, and Sally; and Isaac, aged about 30. CCDB 45:361. In 1831, he mortgaged "old woman Dinah" and her sons John and Alexander. CCDB 48:154. Montford named six slaves in his will of 1838: Dinah, Boy Alexander, "old man" Bob, Dick, Jim Carney, and Isaac (Rue). CCWB C:43.

134. Green, *Fact Stranger than Fiction*.

135. Ibid. John P. Green stated that Sarah Rice chose not to give her son his father's last name (Stanly) because of bad blood between the Spaight and Stanly families, and that she named him John Rice and added Green later, for a white New Bernian she had nursed.

136. Rigdon Green obituary, *New Bern Daily Journal*, March 2, 1887.

137. CCDB; Carraway, *Crown of Life*, 139; "Account settled with John R. Green," May 1834, John R. Donnell Letter and Account Book.

138. Schweninger, "John Carruthers Stanly," 174–75, 186; plan of "Original Purchasers of Pews," 174. All the priced pews were on the main floor, and except for Stanly the other original pew owners were whites of some stature. Most blacks occupied the galleries. Stanly owned pews 34 and 35 in a rear corner, each of which cost $150. These were two pews behind that of white heiress Mary McKinley, whose pew 31 likewise cost $150. More expensive pews ranged from $200 to $350.

139. Green, *Fact Stranger than Fiction*, 13; Carraway, *Crown of Life*, 121–25. Carraway notes, 173–74, that Mason conducted Sunday evening services "for the benefit of the coloured people" in 1826; in 1833 Bishop Levi Ives mentioned a black Episcopal congregation in New Bern; and another such group was formed in the 1840s. She describes St. Cyprian's organization "soon after" the Civil War as "the first permanent one of the kind here" (174).

140. Parish Register, Christ Episcopal Church, New Bern, copy at Kellenberger Room; Green, *Fact Stranger than Fiction*, 13.

141. Green, *Fact Stranger than Fiction*, 10. These four houses are the principal known residences of antebellum free people of color in New Bern. All stand in the central section of town. See in Sandbeck, *The Historic Architecture of New Bern*, the following: Amelia Green (Green-Hollister) House, ca. 1790–1810, moved back from Broad Street on George Street, p. 417; John C. Stanly (Stanly-Allen) House (ca. 1804), 405 Johnson Street, pp. 277–78; John C. Stanly (Stanly-Bishop) House (ca. 1800–1810, purchased by Stanly ca. 1815), 501 New Street, pp. 250–51; and John R. Green House (ca. 1820), 411 Johnson Street, pp. 279–80 (John R. Green sold this house and moved to a smaller house that subsequently burned). All have been substantially altered since their original construction. Another example of houses associated with free blacks is the Euphemia Tinker House (ca. 1800–1810), 419 George Street (p. 419), which Sandbeck describes as having been bequeathed in 1839 to Mary Hancock, the wife of free black carpenter William H. Hancock, and after 1846 owned by white men who used it for rental purposes; the one-and-one-half story frame dwelling typifies many small-scale side-passage plan houses in early national period New Bern. In addition, Sandbeck notes that the much-altered "Federal-Period Cottage" (ca. 1790–1820) at 211 Broad Street (p. 225) was owned by local free black men Robert Lisbon, John C. Stanly, and John Rice Green.

142. Sandbeck, *The Historic Architecture of New Bern*, 440–43, 448–49; Green, *Fact Stranger than Fiction*, 15.

143. Miller, "Recollections," 461; "Bits of the History of New Berne," *New Bern Daily Journal*, October 8, 1882.

144. Miller, "Recollections," 460. See Watson, *A History of New Bern*, 308–9, and Franklin, *The Free Negro in North Carolina*, 108–9. CCDB; CCW; New Bern Taxables Lists, Craven County Tax Lists, 1816–19, NCA&H (microfilm). Craven County Tax Lists, 1815, in Treasurer's and Comptroller's Papers, County Settlements with the State, Tax Lists, NCA&H (microfilm), located and transcribed by Victor Jones and posted at http://

newbern.cpclib.org/research/tax/1815tax.htm. February 10, 2013. A few men of color, including John C. Stanly and Donum Montford, possessed the fifty acres required to vote for the state senate. Deeds show that several other men of color acquired property between 1819 and 1835, but no tax lists are known to survive from those years.

145. *New Bern Federal Republican*, August 13, 1814; Watson, *A History of New Bern*, 308–9. Stanly defeated "Col. Pasteur"—Edward Pasteur, who had been Richard Dobbs Spaight's second in the infamous 1802 duel in which Stanly killed Spaight. The two taxpayers cited were probably John C. Stanly and Donum Montford, the largest property owners of color noted in the 1816–19 New Bern Taxables Lists, Craven County Tax Records, NCA&H.

146. Stanly, *A Military Governor*, on voting, 16; quote, 23.

Chapter 3

1. This summary of the situation of urban blacks in the antebellum South is adapted from Goldfield, *Region, Race, and Cities*, 105.

2. For an account of a free black carpenter's requests to white men to write passes and serve as local protectors, see Franklin, "James Boon, Free Negro Artisan."

3. Louis D. Henry (*DNCB*) was a native of New Jersey whose mother came from New Bern; after graduating from Princeton he studied law in New Bern with his uncle, Edward Graham. He fled to New York in 1813 after killing his college friend, Thomas Stanly (youngest son of John Wright Stanly and part of a duel-prone family) in a duel, but later settled in Fayetteville.

4. James W. Bryan's petition to free Webber described her as a "favorite slave of his father" who had belonged "from the time of her birth" to the Bryans and rendered meritorious service in attending the elder Bryan's long illnesses; *FFV*, 122–23.

5. *FFV*, 122–23; CCDB 43:228; CCDB 45:168, 170, 171, 172; Catherine Webber, Will, CCWB C:426. See Schweninger, "John Carruthers Stanly," 176–77, on Stanly's friendship with Bryan.

6. In 1830 the U.S. census listed Jacob Harris in Fayetteville as the head of a free black household. He died by 1850, and his widow, Charlotte, headed a household of seven children, including brickmasons William and Joseph, 23 and 19. A near neighbor was carpenter Moses Harris, 45, possibly a kinsman; his household included Anna M. Sampson, 18, who later married Andrew J. Chesnutt and became the mother of writer Charles Chesnutt.

7. U.S. census; Cumberland County Marriage Bonds, Cumberland County Records, NCA&H.

8. U.S. census, 1850, 1860; Catherine Webber, Will, CCWB C:426.

9. U.S. censuses; Lynda Vestal Herzog and Catherine W. Bishir, "Bennett G. Flanner," http://ncarchitects.lib.ncsu.edu. Herzog, "The Early Architecture of New Bern," 334–35 (Stevenson). John M. Roberts (New Bern) to Duncan Cameron, February 20, 1833, Cameron Papers, SHC, concerning Asa King.

10. Hardy B. Lane to David Paton, July 14, 1839, Capitol Building Papers, Treasurer's and Comptroller's Papers, NCA&H.

11. Familiar local artisans, black and white, continued to get such jobs as repairs and additions to public buildings. Craven County Treasurer of Public Building Accounts, NCA&H.

12. The Newbern Mechanics Association was formed in 1841 and incorporated in 1844 (Watson, *A History of New Bern*, 337). I have found no references to its activities.

13. Whitford, "Home Story of a Walking Stick," 329.

14. Bishir, Brown, Lounsbury, and Wood, *Architects and Builders in North Carolina*, 217–18; U.S. census, 1850, 1860; Herzog, "The Early Architecture of New Bern," 291, 337.

15. On the "dividing point" see Bassett, *Slavery in the State of North Carolina*, 7. Bassett (9) credits the "victory" of the pro-slavery faction in the state primarily to the Nat Turner Rebellion and abolitionist agitation in the North along with the rise of cotton production. Johnson, *Ante-Bellum North Carolina*, 611.

16. Franklin, *The Free Negro in North Carolina*, 123–25, and Zipf, *Labor of Innocents*, 27–29.

17. Johnson, *Ante-Bellum North Carolina*, 584–85, on the 1826 law and controversy.

18. Franklin, *The Free Negro in North Carolina*, 67–74, on the "Free Negro Code." See *FFV*, 311–18 for copies of emancipation laws.

19. Charles Edward Morris, "Panic and Reprisal: Reaction in North Carolina to the Nat Turner Insurrection, 1831." *North Carolina Historical Review*, 62, no. 1 (1985): 29–52.

20. Ibid., quote, 47.

21. Watson, *A History of New Bern*, 308–9; *New Bern Spectator*, December 2, 1831; *New Bern Sentinel*, December 7, 14, 1831. Besides the Bryans, the other members of the committee were James C. Stevenson, Thomas Watson, and Benjamin F. Blackledge. The background of the election that spurred the petition is complex. The special election of November 28, 1831, was held after the legislature was elected because Charles Spaight, younger brother of Richard Dobbs Spaight Jr., died before he could take office. The seat had been held earlier by John Stanly. After Stanly's stroke forced him to vacate the seat in 1827, his friend William Gaston filled the seat and was reelected to it for a full term in 1829–31. After Charles Spaight's sudden death, Democrat Charles Shepard and John Stanly's son Edward, a Federalist, announced as candidates. Edward Stanly said he would withdraw if William Gaston—his father John's dear friend—could be persuaded to run, which occurred shortly before the election (*New Bern Spectator*, November 25, 1831). Charles Shepard's sister Mary was the wife of John H. Bryan.

22. *New Bern Spectator*, December 9, 1831; *New Bern Sentinel*, December 14, 1831; Franklin, *The Free Negro in North Carolina*, 107–8. See petition in Legislative Petitions, NCA&H, December 15, 1831.

23. *Proceedings and Debates of the Convention of North Carolina*, and Franklin, *The Free Negro in North Carolina*, 107–16. *Fayetteville Carolina Observer*, June 16, 1835, cited in Franklin, *The Free Negro in North Carolina*, 115.

24. Charles B. Shepard to John H. Bryan, July 9, 1838, John Herritage Bryan Collection, NCA&H, quoted in Johnson, *Ante-Bellum North Carolina*, 564.

25. James Y. Green and Richard G. Hazel to Gen. Alexander F. Gaston, February

29, 1844, William Gaston Papers, SHC. My attention was called to this document by Degler, *The Other South*, 39, citing Edward F. McSweeney, "Judge William Gaston of North Carolina," in Thomas F. Meehan et al., eds., *Historical Records and Studies* (New York: United States Catholic Historical Society, 1926), Vol. 17, 181, 184. See also Gertrude S. Carraway, *Years of Light: History of St. John's Lodge, No. 3, A. F. & A. M. New Bern, North Carolina, 1772–1944* (New Bern: Owen G. Dunn Company, 1944), 52. McSweeney and Carraway probably drew upon Henry G. Connor's published 1914 speech, "William Gaston." In it, Connor quoted the free blacks' statement at length and commented, "I have thought that none of the eulogies speak more eloquently, or set forth more strongly, the virtues of William Gaston, the man, than those adopted by the 'free people of color' of the town of his nativity, and his home." Henry G. Connor, "William Gaston," in *Addresses at the Unveiling and Presentation of the Bust of William Gaston by the North Carolina Bar Association . . . November 24, 1914* (Raleigh: Edwards and Broughton Printing Co., 1915), 46. Only the original letter in the William Gaston Papers gives a fuller text and names the free black leaders involved.

26. Quote, Stanly, *Military Governor*, 23. Green, *Methodist Meeting House*, 64–65.

27. Stanly, *Military Governor*, 34. The free black schoolteacher that Stanly cited was probably Grace Green, whose husband, carpenter Joseph Green, had been enslaved but was free by 1860.

28. Catherine Webber (CCWB C:426) left lot #5 and another lot in Dryboro and the residue of her estate to Cicero Richardson, whom she identified as the son of her daughter Sally Webber. See Cicero Richardson of New Bern to Alex Mitchell, deed, February 11, 1840, on the sale of property in Dryboro, parts of lots 8 and 49, for $23 (CCDB 54:239); the property was identified as having been sold to Catherine by John C. Stanly.

29. Hollister Account Book, microfilm, NCA&H; U.S. census, 1850. Julie Hipps, "Black Builders in New Bern, 1790–1840: The Carpenters and Masons," unpublished research paper, 2002, Tryon Palace Research Department, identifies carpenter Lane as the principal builder. See also Sandbeck, *The Historical Architecture of New Bern*, 236.

30. Cicero Richardson was identified as a resident of Wilmington when, on November 15, 1842, he sold parts of Dryboro lots 51 and 52 to Joshua Scott of New Bern for $45 (CCDB 56:352).

31. For white blacksmith Silas Burns of Massachusetts in Raleigh, see Bishir, Brown, Lounsbury, and Wood, *Architects and Builders in North Carolina*, 467, n. 158.

32. CCAB; Herzog, "The Early Architecture of New Bern," 338. William Hilton also took John Harris, a free black youth, as a mason's apprentice in 1845.

33. Moses Griffin, Estates Papers, CCEP.

34. U.S. censuses, 1850, 1860; New Bern Tax Records, 1815, 1860. See Herzog, "The Early Architecture of New Bern," and Sandbeck, *The Historic Architecture of New Bern*, on these and other artisans.

35. Franklin, *The Free Negro in North Carolina*, 67–74, on the "Free Negro Code." *FFV*, 311–18.

36. 1830–31 law, as clarified in 1836–37, in *FFV*, 315–18. John Good was emancipated

by the General Assembly of 1854–55, as requested by his owner, manufacturer George Bishop.

37. Hardy B. Lane Sr., Estates Papers, CCEP, and U.S. censuses. Lane's slave carpenter Donum is probably the Donum Wadsworth who plied his trade in New Bern as a free man from the mid-1860s until his death in 1880.

38. Catherine W. Bishir, *The House Marina Built: Cherry Hill* (Warrenton: Cherry Hill Foundation, 2004), 5, 23.

39. Mary McKinley, Estates Papers, CCEP.

40. Receipt of C. Dewey, May 15, 1835, Cameron Family Papers, SHC.

41. John M. Roberts (New Bern) to Duncan Cameron, February 20, 1833; and Paul Cameron to Duncan Cameron, November 1834, Cameron Family Papers, SHC.

42. Paul Cameron to Duncan Cameron, November 1834, Cameron Family Papers, SHC. On these white builders, see Bishir, Brown, Lounsbury, and Wood, *Architects and Builders in North Carolina*, and http://ncarchitects.lib.ncsu.edu.

43. Scipio, quote, Bassett, *Slavery in the State of North Carolina*, 45. Scipio Hughes purchases, John Oliver, Estates Papers, CCEP. Some slaveholders allowed slaves to live as "virtually free," such as Henry Taylor, an enslaved carpenter from Cumberland County, whose white father and owner allowed him to move to Wilmington and establish a business from which he emerged as one of the richest black men in postwar Wilmington. See "Henry Taylor," at http://ncarchitects.lib.ncsu.edu and Weiss, *Robert R. Taylor.*

44. George Fisher obituary, *New Bern Daily Journal*, September 6, 1892; U.S. censuses, 1850, 1860, 1870.

45. Moses Griffin, Estates Papers, CCEP.

46. Horace James, "A Freedman's Wedding," 1866, in *Household Reading: Selections from the Congregationalist, 1849–1866* (Boston: Galen James and Company, 1867); White, *"Somebody Knows My Name."*

47. Parker, *Running for Freedom*, 51–52.

48. *New Bern Spectator*, December 30, 1836, *SLF* 784.

49. *New Bern Weekly Journal*, October 25, 1854. This newspaper was formerly *The Advance.*

50. Cecelski, *The Fire of Freedom*, 17.

51. The census of 1850 showed that New Bern's free black artisans included at least 6 blacksmiths, 7 bricklayers or brickmasons, 9 carpenters, 3 caulkers, 6 coopers, 5 joiners, 5 mechanics (including a bricklayer and a joiner), 1 painter, 3 plasterers, 6 shoemakers, 10 tailors, and 1 wheelwright. There were no white blacksmiths, bricklayers, plasterers, or caulkers listed in the census, but all the other trades were represented, plus specialists like 2 watchmakers, 2 silversmiths, and 1 gunmaker. Carpenters were most numerous among white artisans (15) as well as free black ones. The census of 1860 showed similar patterns but a greater number of specialties among whites and an increase in construction workers of both races. That census was the first to show occupations for females, by far the most numerous being seamstresses (about 55 white and 14 free black). The free black artisans enumerated in the census of 1860 included at least 2 blacksmiths, 10 brickmasons, 15 carpenters, 1 coachmaker, 4 coopers, 2 dressmakers, 1 engineer, 1

plasterer, 14 seamstresses, 6 shoemakers, 3 tailors, 1 tailoress, 2 wheelwrights, and 1 tinsmith.

52. Petitions, 1829, Craven County, from Digital Library on American Slavery, http://library.uncg.edu/slavery/index.aspx, consulted March 21, 2010. CCWB D:153. William Morris, Estates Papers, CCEP. In 1830 William Morris headed a household in which all the other members, including the "mulatto" children, were listed as slaves; by 1840 the "mulatto" children in the household were listed as free (U.S. censuses, 1830, 1840). In 1838 Morris amended his will to place in trust a tract of land "to permit my woman Patty to use and enjoy said piece of ground" for her lifetime, after which it was to go to Harriet, Albert, and Freeman. Morris named as new executors Hardy Whitford and John L. Durand. At Morris's death in 1848, neither Patty nor the three children were listed among his many slaves—all of whom were sold. His executor noted on a list of household items and ten shares of bank stock, "This property was devised to Pattey." On Freeman and Albert Morris as well-regarded tailors, see Bassett, *Slavery in the State of North Carolina*, 45.

53. William and Catharine Lawrence, Estates Papers, CCEP; *New Bern Daily Times*, August 18, 1871. Park Lawrence does not appear in the 1850 census but does appear in 1860 and 1870.

54. Donum Montford, Will, CCWB C:423. See also will of Mary McKinley (CCWB D:13), who died in 1840. She expressed her desire to free her slaves and stated, "If the laws of the State forbid that, and no relaxation of the strict rule can be pursued in this behalf then my Executors are directed to carry the said slaves out of the State and then to those parts where they can be manumitted and there cause them to be emancipated and set free from slavery." Her slaves were freed (Mary McKinley, Estates Papers, CCEP).

55. CCDB 42:282; CCW; CCEP; U.S. censuses, 1850–80; Parish Register, Christ Episcopal Church, New Bern, copy at Kellenberger Room (burials, 1846).

56. CCAB. David Wilson, Freedman's Bank application, via http://www.ancestry.com. The *New Bern Daily Journal*, September 23, 1895, "Death of a Colored Centenarian," stated that Rachel Wilson was born about 1792.

57. Franklin, *The Free Negro in North Carolina*, 123, 165. Franklin notes, 165, that when a bill came to the legislature in 1826–27 to repeal the requirement to teach "colored apprentices" to read and write, the measure was postponed indefinitely.

58. Whether a similar pattern developed in other communities is not known; since apprentice bonds do not state the race of the master, it is impossible to discern such a trend without separate knowledge of the masters' racial identity.

59. CCAB, 1820s–1850s.

60. CCAB, 1820s–1850s. Franklin, *The Free Negro in North Carolina*, 125, shows that in Craven County free black apprentices were bound to a greater variety of skilled trades in the period 1800–1824 than in the period 1825–60. In the latter period the number of black children bound as farmers (i.e. farm laborers) rose from two to twenty-four, and for the first time such children were bound to the service occupations of body servant, house servant, and waiter, categories not represented in the earlier period. Franklin's

numbers are probably low because, as has been noted, some apprentices of color were not so identified in the apprentice bonds.

61. On northern cities' objections to black apprentices in white shops, see Barnes, *Artisan Workers in Petersburg*, 141–42.

62. CCAB; Hardy B. Lane, Estates Papers, CCEP.

63. U.S. census, 1850. In 1850 Castix, the owner of twenty-one slaves, had $3,000 invested in a shoemaking enterprise in which he employed four male and forty female workers who produced 300 pairs of shoes a year with a value of $2,400.

64. CCAB. On the Flanner house, see Sandbeck, *The Historic Architecture of New Bern*, 273–74: a chalked inscription on a joist reads, "October 17, 1855," and the names "Marshall" and "Willis" are also visible.

65. Simmons, *Men of Mark*; "Israel B. Abbott," Charles N. Hunter Scrapbooks; Green, *Fact Stranger than Fiction*, 30; U.S. censuses.

66. Green, *Fact Stranger than Fiction*, 15–17.

67. Newton, *Out of the Briars*, 19–25; quote, 19; U.S. census, 1850.

68. Newton, *Out of the Briars*, 22.

69. Ibid., 24, 25.

70. Ibid., 25, 26, 110; quote, 123. Alexander H. Newton's likeness is featured on a monument to his regiment, dedicated in 2008 in New Haven.

71. James West Bryan to John H. Bryan, June 7, 1854, John Herritage Bryan Collection, vol. 6.5, NCA&H.

72. U.S. census, 1850. Lydia Crawford's date of birth is not certain. She appeared as a head of household in the censuses of 1830 and 1840, in the age grouping of 36 to 54 years old. The censuses of 1850, 1860, and 1870 indicated various birth years for her of 1800, 1805, and 1794, respectively. By 1815, when her husband Virgil died, the couple had five children. Even if Lydia was born in 1794, to have had five children by age twenty-one would have made her a very young mother—not impossible in a time when women as young as fourteen or fifteen had children.

73. U.S. census, 1850.

74. "New Bern within the Memory of the Oldest Inhabitant, 1830–1860," undated manuscript by Lavinia Cole Roberts (Mrs. F. C. Roberts), in Elizabeth Moore, "Records of Craven County, North Carolina," vol. 1, 1960, Elizabeth Moore Collection.

75. Although antebellum censuses of New Bern listed only the names of residents and not street addresses, it is possible to discern living patterns through known property owners. There is no city directory for the period.

76. U.S. census, 1850. In Wilmington, North Carolina, the 1850 census taker counted all the white people first and then started a new page for free people of color. The census taker of 1860 proceeded in a geographical order that shows that free people of color lived in various parts of Wilmington.

77. In Petersburg most free blacks had their homes and businesses across the Appomattox River from downtown, and in Richmond free and enslaved blacks lived mainly in the area near the waterfront, factories, and railroad facilities. On Petersburg, see

Barnes, *Artisan Workers*, 132; and on Richmond, see Takagi, *Rearing Wolves*, 96–98, and Tyler-McGraw, *At the Falls*, 113.

78. U.S. census, 1850, and Craven County Deeds, various dates, CCDB. Richard G. Hazel's "Bake House" occupied the southwest corner of lot #251 at the intersection of Broad and Middle Streets; he sold the buildings to John Jones for $500 in 1853 (CCDB 61:159–60).

79. U.S. census, 1850.

80. Green, *Fact Stranger than Fiction*, 43–44.

81. Ibid. See Gatewood, *Aristocrats of Color*, and Schweninger, *Black Property Owners*.

82. U.S. censuses, 1850, 1860.

83. Donum Montford, Will, CCWB C:423; U.S. censuses.

84. Green, *Fact Stranger than Fiction*, 22.

85. Freeman Woods, Donum Montford, Estates Papers, CCEP.

86. U.S. census, 1850. Franklin, *The Free Negro in North Carolina*, 169, indicates that in 1850 Craven County had forty-six free black children enrolled in school, a number exceeded only by Robeson and Wake Counties. The 1860 census did not note any free black children in New Bern as attending school.

87. Green, *Fact Stranger than Fiction*, 42.

88. There were some exceptions for free children who went away to school, such as the children of the Caswell County cabinetmaker Thomas Day, who attended Wesleyan Academy in Wilberforce, Massachusetts, and returned home without encountering problems, likely because of Day's stature in the community. Marshall and Leimenstoll, *Thomas Day*, 48–50.

89. Green, *Fact Stranger than Fiction*, 43, 44; Ellen NicKensie Lawson and Marlene D. Merrill, eds., *The Three Sarahs: Documents of Antebellum Black College Women* (New York and Toronto: Edwin Mellen Press, 1984), 47–54, photograph of Ann Stanly, 46; Rigdon Green obituary, *New Bern Daily Journal*, March 2, 1887.

90. Vass, *History of the Presbyterian Church*, 146–47. Members whom Vass listed as hosting prayer groups included "Thos. Sparrow, Jno. Jones, E. Hawes, O. Dewey, Robt. Hay, J. Y. Green, C. Slover, M. Stevenson, Wm. Taylor, and Capt. R. Fisher." Although it seems unlikely that as a free black James York Green would have been included in these prayer groups, he appears to be the only James Y. Green in town.

91. Green, *Fact Stranger than Fiction*, 43–44; James West Bryan to John H. Bryan, June 7, 1854, John Herritage Bryan Collection, vol. 6.5, NCA&H.

92. A tyler or tiler is a Masonic officer who serves as a guard at the door. Voorhis, *Negro Masonry in the United States*, 76; "D." in *New Bern Daily Journal*, August 27, October 8, 1882 ("D" has been identified as John D. Whitford). Green, *Fact Stranger than Fiction*, 56–57. In *Negro Masonry in the United States*, 76, Voorhis quotes "'A Centennial History of Morning Star Lodge, 1793–1893, of Worcester, Massachusetts' by Edward S. Nason, 1894," 220, on the black tyler in New Bern. Voorhis also notes, "The Proceedings of the Grand Lodge of NC show Brother William H. Hancock (sometimes spelled Handcock), to whom this item refers, as Tyler of the lodge for 1849, 50, 51, and 52, and as a member

for several years afterward. . . . Brother Hancock petitioned St. John's Lodge on April 8, 1846. He was initiated April 13, passed May 7 and raised on June 1, 1846."

93. See Johnson, *Ante-Bellum North Carolina*, 572–81, on the reaction against abolitionism and its impact on free blacks.

94. Franklin, *The Free Negro in North Carolina*, 136–40, quote 136; James H. Boykin, *The Negro in North Carolina prior to 1861* (New York: Pageant Press, 1958), 26; Bishir, "Black Builders," 89–91. On similar events in Georgia, see Gillespie, *Free Labor in an Unfree World*, 157–59.

95. A printed petition headed "Memorial from Sundry Citizens of ~~Craven~~ Beaufort County," dated June 19, 1850, was received in December 1850 (Legislative Petitions, 1850–1851, General Assembly Records, NCA&H). I have not found a version from Craven signers.

96. *New Bern Weekly Journal* (formerly the *Advance*), October 25, 1854.

97. *New Bern Weekly Journal*, November 29, 1854.

98. During the late 1850s, white mechanics organized to object to tax laws and practices that favored the slaveholding class (through their enslaved workers) at the expense of white craftsmen. In Wilmington, when white mechanics destroyed a building under construction by slave contractors, the local elite condemned the white men's action. See also state authorities' condemning other white mechanics' protests and petitions as arraying "labor" against "property," and as a "monstrous-agrarian-leveling" threat on a par with abolitionism. Bishir, Brown, Lounsbury, and Wood, *Architects and Builders in North Carolina*, 187–90.

99. "The Election," *New Bernian*, July 9, 1852. On November 2, 1852, in the *New Bernian*, "Veritas" reaffirmed the need for the election officials to do their duty; Watson, *A History of New Bern*, 311. Craven County Election Returns, 1835, 1847–1853, 1854–1856, Craven County Records, NCA&H.

100. *New Bern Weekly Journal*, October 25, 1854.

101. *Anglo-African*, January 16, 1864.

102. Colyer, *Brief Report of the Services Rendered*; Alfred S. Roe, *The Twenty-Fourth Regiment, Massachusetts Volunteers, 1861–1866* (Worcester, Mass.: Twenty-Fourth Veteran Association, 1907), 136.

103. Franklin, *The Free Negro in North Carolina*, quote, 156. Franklin points out (160, 237) that the number of North Carolina slaveholders of color dropped from 191 in 1830, with a total of 620 slaves, to 8 in 1860 who owned 25 slaves among them.

104. Franklin, *The Free Negro in North Carolina*, 208, and Johnson, *Ante-Bellum North Carolina*, 571, on the Williams family. For North Carolina contributors (including Andrews Chapel) to the American Colonization Society, see Franklin, 238–46. For North Carolina subscribers (all in New Bern) to the *African Repository*, see, for example, *African Repository* 35 (1859), published by the American Colonization Society (via http://books.google.com).

105. Green, *Fact Stranger than Fiction*, 20.

106. Green, *Fact Stranger than Fiction*, 44–45. See Berlin, *The Making of African Amer-*

ica, on the principal "passages" of millions of African Americans, which involved much larger numbers of people.

107. Richard Brodhead, ed., *The Journals of Charles W. Chesnutt* (Durham: Duke University Press, 1993), 134, entry for March 30, 1880.

108. Dickerson, "George A. Rue." New Haven City Directory, 1852, via http://www.ancestry.com. Home of Yale University and many abolitionists, in 1850 New Haven had the highest percentage of black residents of any northern city, and it attracted many more black southerners during the ensuing decade.

109. William Henry Ferris, *The African Abroad: Or, His Evolution in Western Civilization, Tracing His Development Under Caucasian Milieu*, Volume 2 (New Haven: Tuttle, Morehouse & Taylor Press, 1913), Google eBook, 699–700; quote, 700. Those cited included carpenters William Hancock, Charles L. McLynn, Anthony Skinner, John Groves, and Willis Bonner, and blacksmiths John Lane and John Godett. U.S. censuses, 1850, 1860; New Haven City Directory, 1856, via http://www.ancestry.com.

110. In 1852 in New York Richard M. Hancock witnessed a power of attorney deed to his father William (who was still in New Bern) from New York residents Cornelius and Catharine S. Sawyer and Mary Richardson, formerly of New Bern, authorizing William to sell their lot #22 in Dryboro in New Bern (CCDB 61:17). (Cornelius Sawyer was a free black blacksmith.) On Hancock's employers and subsequent career, see "Richard M. Hancock," in Simmons, *Men of Mark*. On Mary Beman, daughter of minister Amos Beman, see *New York Tribune*, July 19, 1861.

111. Davis, *Black Americans in Cleveland*, 17–18, 29, 36 (quote), 63–74. See also Allan Peskin, ed., *North into Freedom: The Autobiography of John Malvin, Free Negro, 1795–1880* (Cleveland: Press of Western Reserve University, 1966), 8–19, on the unusual character of Cleveland's citizens of color in the 1850s.

112. U.S. censuses, 1850, 1860. The number of North Carolinians of color in Ohio rose from about 1,360 in 1850 to more than 2,200 by 1860. These figures do not include the many light-skinned persons of mixed race who were identified as white in the censuses. Cicero Richardson's move to Cleveland is indicated by the ages and birthplaces of his children.

113. Davis, *Black Americans in Cleveland*, 56–57, quoting *The Liberator*, November 20, 1857, 56. Green, *Fact Stranger than Fiction*, 59, described Morris as "one of the most intelligent, conservative and genteel colored men then residing in Cleveland or elsewhere, in the United States."

114. Davis, *Black Americans in Cleveland*, 67, citing the *Cleveland Leader*, July 15, 1859, and *Morris v. Sanborn et al.*, ibid., 163, citing the *Cleveland Gazette*, January 3 and July 11, 1903. Morris ran his well-regarded business in Cleveland until his death in 1902 at the age of eighty-two. See *Post*, February 18, 1903 (clipping, Charles N. Hunter Scrapbooks,). On Ohio laws affecting voting rights of mixed-race men who were more than half white, see Peskin, *North into Freedom*, 82.

115. U.S. censuses, 1850, 1860. Richard Hazel died between 1870 and 1880.

116. Rigdon Green obituary, *New Bern Daily Journal*, March 2, 1887. Except for Ben-

jamin, I have not located Rigdon Green's children in either Ohio or North Carolina censuses. On Bishop Ravenscroft, identified by a contemporary as an evangelical and a "High-Churchman," see "John Stark Ravenscroft," *DNCB*. In 1860 Rigdon and Caroline Green and their son Benjamin and his wife and children were living in Cleveland in a white neighborhood; the census taker listed them without indicating their race, implying that they were white.

117. Caroline and John Bragg died in Cleveland in 1866 and 1867, respectively (Cleveland City Directories via http://www.ancestry.com and copies of death certificates for Caroline and John Bragg, courtesy of Charles Steele, October 2012).

118. To protect his family's security, in anticipation of his death in 1850, John R. Green, with the help of his black friends Shade and Ann Green and white merchant Jeremiah N. Allen, arranged to have a modest house in Dryboro sold to Allen and placed in trust for Temperance until after his death. Green, *Fact Stranger than Fiction*, stated that John R. Green transferred the property to Shade Green. Deeds indicate that Ann Green (Shade's wife) sold the property for $150 to trustee Jeremiah N. Allen in 1850 in a deed registered in 1851 (CCDB 60:228). The deed, registered after John R. Green's death, explained that Allen as trustee was to hold the property for Temperance so long as she was a married woman, and therefore a *feme covert*, and to deliver it to her after her husband's death. Jeremiah Allen is probably J. N. Allen, a white merchant from Rhode Island listed in New Bern in the census of 1860. He and Temperance Green sold the property in 1857 to Zaccheus Brown (CCDB 64:103, registered 1857). The property was later incorporated into Cedar Grove Cemetery. A descendant of Shade Green identifies Ann Green as his wife; his death date is unknown (Rosemary Clifford McDaniel, email to John B. Green III, New Bern, copy forwarded by Green to author, May 3, 2012). John P. Green was only about five years old when his father died and would have known of these events mainly from his mother.

119. Green, *Fact Stranger than Fiction*, 22.

120. Ibid., 22, 47–50, second quote, 49. John Patterson was bondsman for Temperance and John R. Green's marriage in Cumberland County in 1837.

121. Ibid., 53–72; last quote, 72.

122. U.S. census, Cleveland and Oberlin, 1860; William Cheek and Aimee Lee Cheek, *John Mercer Langston and the Fight for Black Freedom, 1829–1865* (Urbana and Chicago: University of Illinois Press, 1996), 339. A. J. (Andrew Jackson) Chesnutt, a freeborn native of Fayetteville, married Anna Maria Sampson, also of North Carolina; their children included Charles Chesnutt, born in Cleveland in 1858. Anna Maria and Charles Chesnutt do not appear in the 1860 census. The family moved to Fayetteville after the war. Reaves, *Strength through Struggle*, 382.

123. Joshua Howard, "Tar Heels at Harpers Ferry, October 16–18, 1859," http://www.nccivilwar150.com/history/john-brown-nc.htm, consulted August 15, 2010; U.S. census, 1860. Lewis Leary was a son of Matthew N. Leary, a prominent free black saddler and citizen of Fayetteville and longtime associate of John Patterson. Matthew Leary Jr. followed in his father's trade in Fayetteville and held local offices during Reconstruction. His younger brother, John Sinclair Leary, graduated from Howard University in

1871 and had a distinguished law career in North Carolina, serving as the founding dean of Shaw University's Law School. Foner, *Freedom's Lawmakers*, 129–30.

124. Green, *Fact Stranger than Fiction*; U.S. censuses.

125. Unless otherwise noted, all information in this section comes from the U.S. census of 1860 for New Bern and Craven County and from Craven County Tax Records, Kellenberger Room, 1860, 1861.

126. Franklin, *The Free Negro in North Carolina*, 236.

127. Elizabeth Bragg was one of many free people of color whose light complexion evoked ambiguous racial definitions. The census of 1860 listed her as a white woman and head of a household that included her parents and some of her siblings, also identified as white. When a local official listed Henry and George Bragg among New Bern taxables (for property Elizabeth owned) in 1860, he drew the diagonal marks enumerating Henry and George right on the line between the columns for black and white polls. Craven County Tax Records, 1860, Kellenberger Room.

128. Catharine and Frances (Francis) Stanly, Estates Papers, CCEP. The sisters' estates were not settled and recorded until after the war. According to John D. Whitford's article in the *New Bern Weekly Journal*, December 27, 1904, the sisters spent their mature years in a small house on New Street (no longer standing), to which their father John C. Stanly had moved late in life after residing in two larger houses elsewhere in town.

129. U.S. census; Craven County Tax Records, Kellenberger Room, 1860, 1861; Green, *Fact Stranger than Fiction*, 29–30.

130. Freedman's Bank Record, David Wilson, New Bern, via http://www.ancestry.com.

131. U.S. census, 1860.

132. Ibid.

133. U.S. censuses, 1850, 1860.

134. CCDB 63:103. Craven County Tax Records, Kellenberger Room, 1860, note Neale's ownership of a 50 x 84 foot lot on Green's Alley, improved. Evidently Green's Alley was also or soon known as Bragg's Alley. Thomas Neal(e) gravestone, Greenwood Cemetery.

Chapter 4

1. Randolph's letter, dated April 1864, was published in the *Christian Recorder* of May 21, 1864. Because it was signed simply John Randolph, it is not certain whether the writer was the painter and political leader John Randolph Jr. or his father John Sr., a hotel waiter, but it was probably the politically active younger man. Thanks to David Cecelski for this reference and others and for sharing his copies of period newspapers, especially the *Anglo-African*. For an in-depth study of this period in New Bern, see Cecelski, *The Fire of Freedom*. John Randolph Jr.'s brother Henry noted in his Freedman's Bank application (1870) that he had been born in and grew up in Washington; he was residing in New Bern at age twenty-eight in 1870 along with other members of his extended family.

2. On the evacuation of Washington, see the May 1 report in the *Christian Recorder*, May 14, 1864. Given the April letter sent from Washington and John Randolph Jr.'s

emergence in New Bern political leadership early that summer, it seems likely that the family came with the others rescued from Washington in May 1864. A visitor late in 1864 commented on the "almost entire absence of negroes" in Washington, with the exception of five or six free blacks still there. Notable among these was the aged brickmason and Episcopalian Abram M. Allen, freed by Donum Montford almost fifty years before, who remained "true to the South" and refused to leave. *Richmond Daily Dispatch*, November 22, 1864, http://www.perseus.tufts.edu/hopper/text?doc=Perseus%3Atext%3A2006.05.1227%3Aarticle%3D8, consulted December 8, 2008. See also Abram M. Allen, Washington, North Carolina, to Eliza Ellison, Wilson, North Carolina, October 30, 1864, Henry Alderson Ellison Papers, SHC.

3. James Emmerton, 1862, quoted in Browning, *Shifting Loyalties*, 85. On occupied New Bern, see Browning, *Shifting Loyalties*; Greenwood, *First Fruits of Freedom*; and Cecelski, *The Fire of Freedom*.

4. Rose, *Rehearsal for Reconstruction*. Although there were ventures in black autonomy in other Union-occupied areas, the Port Royal experience is the best known because of Rose's classic work. See also Hahn, *A Nation under Our Feet*, 72–82, for fugitive slaves' political activities in other Union-held locations in the South, including contraband camps and colonies.

5. "Skedaddled" in *Anglo-African*, January 16, 1864. For estimate of remaining whites, Browning, *Shifting Loyalties*, 58. An estimated seven trains with 120 cars carried away "most of the town's white (and some of its black) population" (Browning, 57). See also Watson, *A History of New Bern*, 399. Last quote, Greenwood, *First Fruits of Freedom*, 33.

6. See Brasher, *The Peninsula Campaign*, and Gregory P. Downs, *Declarations of Dependence: The Long Reconstruction of Popular Politics in the South, 1861–1908* (Chapel Hill, University of North Carolina Press, 2011), 47–51, on black refugees coming behind Union lines at Fortress Monroe, Virginia, in 1861, which formed the background to the events in New Bern and elsewhere.

7. One exception was the emancipated barber and Episcopalian Moses Kennedy (Canada, Canaday), who joined the white elite—"our people"—to go inland. Whitford, "Home Story of a Walking Stick," 144.

8. On George W. Price Jr., see Reaves, *Strength through Struggle*, 449–51; Bishir, *Bellamy Mansion*, 26–30, 46, 55; and Gould, *Diary of a Contraband*, 28–29, 113, 271–72. Price ran away and boarded a Union ship on September 22, 1862, along with enslaved plasterer William Gould and others, but on November 10, Gould recorded (*Diary of a Contraband*, 113) that "George P—-e" and two other men deserted while ashore at Beaufort. Gould and Price kept in touch afterwards (see list of correspondents, 1864, in Gould, *Diary of a Contraband*, 307). Price subsequently became a political leader in Wilmington. On Hood, see Martin, *For God and Race*.

9. Cecelski, *The Fire of Freedom*.

10. Joseph C. Price, *DNCB*.

11. I have been unable to find this registration book, though it may exist somewhere in federal records. Brasher, *The Peninsula Campaign*, depicts a situation in Virginia where the Union was slow to employ fugitive slaves to help build fortifications. In New

Bern in March 1862, the Union soldiers put the fugitives to work right away on fortifications and other projects.

12. Colyer, *Brief Report of the Services Rendered*, 34–35, 9. On wages, see Reid, "Raising the African Brigade," 289.

13. Colyer, *Brief Report of the Services Rendered*, 9. Colyer (1825–88) was a Quaker, an accomplished artist, and a humanitarian who worked often with the poor. Later he gained fame for his paintings of the American West.

14. James, *Annual Report*, 10–12. He heard from 350 people, nearly all men, whose combined incomes totaled $151,562. Of these, 110 reported annual incomes between $500 and $1,000; 18 earned upwards of $1,000 a year, 4 above $2,000, and 2 above $3,000. The *Anglo-African* also published James's report on January 28, 1865. On James, see Mobley, *James City*, 26–42. From 1863 to 1865, he held positions as Union chaplain, superintendent of the poor, superintendent of Negro affairs for North Carolina, and assistant commissioner for the Freedmen's Bureau in North Carolina. He was instrumental in establishing the freedpeople's village, later called James City after him, across the Trent from New Bern.

15. James, *Annual Report*, 10–12.

16. Colyer, *Brief Report of the Services Rendered*, 36, 35. According to Green, *Methodist Meeting House*, 70, "The last minister sent to Andrews Chapel by the Methodist Episcopal Church, South was Nathan A. Hooker. He was first assigned to the church in 1860 and reappointed in December 1861. How much of this second appointment he served is unknown."

17. Colyer, *Brief Report of the Services Rendered*, 59. Colyer and York evidently used the term "elders" more loosely at this point than was typical of the AME and AME Zion denominations. In those bodies, an ordained elder serves as a pastor qualified to administer the sacraments and must previously have served as a deacon; an ordained deacon, a step below an elder in authority, assists the elder in Holy Communion and with other ministerial duties. Both are called Reverend. A licensed preacher is one who is recognized as having discerned a call to preach and demonstrated his qualifications. More loosely, anyone who preaches is often called a preacher. Reginald F. Hildebrand to author, email, October 26, 2012. After Andrews Chapel affiliated with Zion in 1864, these categories were put into effect, as shown in Hood's accounts of that year.

18. As noted by Greenwood in *First Fruits of Freedom*, 39–41, Colyer worked in cooperation with Horace James, then chaplain of the 25th Massachusetts Volunteer Infantry; the teachers included several soldiers. See Greenwood's analysis of the Colyer-Stanly contretemps, 41–47.

19. Old-time New Bernians remembered Edward Stanly as the son of Congressman John Stanly, and some recognized him as the half brother of the emancipated tailor John R. Green.

20. Colyer, *Brief Report of the Services Rendered*, 59–60.

21. Dickerson, "George A. Rue," 46–47, notes that Rue, a licensed preacher for some years, was ordained as an itinerant deacon in 1855 and as an itinerant elder in 1861.

22. Rue's reports on his journey were published in various issues of the *Christian*

Recorder in 1862. Dickerson, "George A. Rue," 49, notes that Rue was reassigned from the congregation in Newport to Bethel Church in Boston. Located at that time on Anderson Street on Beacon Hill, the venerable black congregation was an important center of abolitionism and a haven for runaway slaves before and during the Civil War. During Rue's tenure it hosted the New England Annual Conference of AME in 1864. After the war the congregation acquired a new church on Charles Street and took its present name, Charles Street AME Church. See http://charlesstreetame.org/about.php, consulted October 21, 2012.

23. Edward S. Redkey, "Henry McNeal Turner, Black Chaplain in the Union Army," in John David Smith, ed., *Black Soldiers in Blue*, 349. Because the secretary of war had authorized northern denominations to take over churches in the occupied South, northern Methodists, including white Union chaplains, claimed black as well as white Methodist congregations in the occupied zones.

24. Martin, *For God and Race*, 34–43, 47–58; and Hood, *One Hundred Years* (quote, 85).

25. Hood, *One Hundred Years*, 85–86 and 289.

26. According to the church history of Rue's Chapel, Rue had written to his "brother-in-law Rev. James [Joseph] Green to save St. Andrew's Chapel for him, as he had found a church which had colored bishops, but before Rev. Rue could come home, Bishop Hood (then Rev. Hood) had run the blockade with General Ben. Butler and immediately took charge of St. Andrew's Chapel, telling people that he represented a church having Negro Bishops." "Brief History of the Founding of Rue Chapel A. M. E. Church."

27. Hood, *One Hundred Years*, 289–95. Shortly after the Andrews Chapel leaders voted to ally with AME Zion, Hood also brought into Zion the black Methodists of Purvis Chapel in nearby Beaufort; local circumstances permitted the entire Beaufort congregation to vote on the matter before Andrews Chapel did so.

28. Hood, *One Hundred Years*. Ellis Lavender (trade unknown) was identified by Hood as a refugee from Washington, North Carolina. In 1863 he was serving as a minister in Washington: the *Anglo-African* of January 16, 1863, reported several marriages at which he had officiated there. He later affiliated with another denomination. Martin, *For God and Race*, 60, 85; and Hood, *Sketch of the Early History*. "War was still raging," recalled Hood of the convention, but "nevertheless Bishop Clinton with his missionaries, gathered around a stove on a cold winter day and laid the foundation for that structure which towers up so grandly to-day." The twelve men included Bishop Joseph J. Clinton; elders John Williams, Ellis Lavender, J. W. Hood, and E. H. Hill; deacons W. J. Moore, H. W. Jones, David Gray, Joseph Green, Sampson Copper, and Abel Ferribee; and preacher Amos York.

29. Singleton, *Recollections of My Slavery Days*, 8. He was referring to Andrews Chapel, AME Zion from 1864.

30. Stanly, *A Military Governor*, 21–22, describes this meeting in detail. See also Greenwood, *First Fruits of Freedom*, 44–45.

31. Oliver W. Peabody to Mary Peabody, November 20, 1862, Oliver W. Peabody Papers, Massachusetts Historical Society, Boston, Massachusetts, quoted in Browning, "Visions of Freedom and Civilization," 78. On contraband policies and the Emancipa-

tion Proclamation, see Hahn, *A Nation under Our Feet*, 70–74, and Reid, *Freedom for Themselves*, 2–6.

32. Douglass, *The Life and Times of Frederick Douglass*, 255–56.

33. Reid, "Raising the African Brigade," 266–72; quote, 266; Cecelski, "A Radical and Jacobinical Spirit," 179–81, 187–91; Edward Kinsley, "Raising the First North Carolina Colored Regiment," 7–10, Edward W. Kinsley Papers, Special Collections and University Archives, W. E. B. Du Bois Library, University of Massachusetts Amherst. Kinsley's account of his secret meeting with Galloway refers to a "Mr. Randolph," who along with an "Uncle Isaac" joined in the negotiations. Kinsley gave no first name for Randolph, whom he identified as a minister of the Methodist church. Cecelski, *The Fire of Freedom*, 73–74, 79, identifies Mr. Randolph as John Randolph Jr., thus indicating that John Randolph Jr. was in New Bern with Galloway in 1863. If so, he seems to have left, probably returning to Washington; not until mid-1864 did he begin to appear in accounts of meetings in New Bern.

34. Reid, "Raising the African Brigade," 285–89, quote 289; and *Freedom for Themselves*, 29–40. In Company B, the registrar identified all the recruits as laborers, and when Company C's men signed up in June in Washington, North Carolina, the registrar left the "occupation" line blank. On the fact that most black troops recruited in North Carolina were rural, poor, and illiterate, see Richard Reid, "USCT Veterans in Post–Civil War North Carolina," in Smith, *Black Soldiers in Blue*, 395. On Kent, see Reid, *Freedom for Themselves*, 222, from "Sergeant Henry Kent," Civil War Pension Files, RG 15, National Archives, Washington, D.C., via http://www.ancestry.com; he left a widow, Mary E. Kent, in New Bern. On Oden, see 1890 Veterans Schedule, New Bern, North Carolina, via http://www.ancestry.com; and Hood, *One Hundred Years*, 621.

35. Joseph E. Williams, report of July 18, 1863, in *Christian Recorder*, July 25, 1863.

36. *Christian Recorder*, August 15, 1863; Cecelski, "A Radical and Jacobinical Spirit," 180, 188.

37. *New Bern Times*, April 20, 1864. "F.F.V." refers to the "First Families of Virginia," a common term for that state's aristocracy.

38. Newton, *Out of the Briars*, 31, on his enlistment in New Haven in the 29th Regiment, Connecticut Colored Volunteer Infantry.

39. Report from New Bern, December 23, 1863, in *Anglo-African*, January 9, 1864. See also *Anglo-African*, January 16, 1864. William H. Johnson, more than likely the same man, was identified as a bricklayer in New Bern after the war.

40. Report from New Bern, December 31, 1863, in *Anglo-African*, January 16, 1864.

41. Ibid.

42. Ibid.

43. "Straight line," Clark, *Defining Moments*, 33.

44. Quotes, *Anglo-African*, May 14, 1864, which published the petition. Cecelski, *The Fire of Freedom*, 115–27, provides a full account of the meeting with Lincoln and the subsequent speaking tour and identifies the backgrounds of the delegates (115). He states (115) that this appears to have been Lincoln's first meeting with black leaders from the South.

45. Cecelski, *The Fire of Freedom*, 117.

46. Ibid. The *New Bern Times*, May 21, 1864, carried an account of the New Bernians' journey copied from the *Anglo-African*. The New York reception of May 4, held at the mother Zion church, was described in the *Anglo-African* of May 14, 1864, and the issue of July 2 carried a report dated June 15, 1864, about the subsequent meeting in New Bern. By early 1864 Lincoln had begun to rethink his ideas on black suffrage and even suggested to the governor of Louisiana the notion of allowing "some of the colored people" to vote. Franklin, *Reconstruction after the Civil War*, 21–22. On Lincoln's evolving ideas on black suffrage in 1865 see Eric Foner, *The Fiery Trial: Abraham Lincoln and American Slavery* (New York: W. W. Norton and Company), 317–19.

47. *Anglo-African*, July 30, 1864.

48. Letter of August 4, 1864, in *Anglo-African*, August 20, 1864.

49. Both sides sent missives to the *Anglo-African* on the subject. Letter of August 31, 1864, in *Anglo-African*, September 17, 1864; letter of September 24, 1864, in *Anglo-African*, October 8, 1864.

50. *Anglo-African*, September 17 and October 8, 1864. See also Cecelski, *The Fire of Freedom*, 134–37.

51. See Cecelski, "A Radical and Jacobinical Spirit," 190–91, and *The Fire of Freedom*, 138–57, on Galloway at the Syracuse convention.

52. *Anglo-African*, January 28, 1865; "Israel B. Abbott," newspaper clipping, Charles N. Hunter Scrapbooks.

53. *Anglo-African*, January 28, 1865; *North Carolina Times*, December 15, 1864.

54. J. W. H. (Hood), *Anglo-African*, January 28, 1865. On other Emancipation Day parades in this period, see Mitch Kachun, *Festivals of Freedom: Memory and Meaning in African American Emancipation Celebrations* (Amherst: University of Massachusetts Press, 2003), 97–119, and Clark, *Defining Moments*, 17–55.

55. *North Carolina Times*, January 7, 1865.

56. *Anglo-African*, March 11, 1865. Meanwhile, as William Lloyd Garrison reported in *The Liberator*, a mass meeting of blacks and whites in Boston celebrated the passage of the Thirteenth Amendment on February 4, 1865, and the evening was concluded with the singing of "Sound the Loud Timbrel," led by a "Mr. Rue" (George A. Rue) whom he identified as the pastor of the black Methodist church in Boston. James M. McPherson, *The Negro's Civil War: How American Blacks Felt and Acted during the Civil War for the Union* (revised edition, New York: Vintage Books, 2003), 52.

57. See Hodes, *White Women, Black Men*, especially 147–48, on growing white animosity toward postwar black male autonomy and political power.

58. *North Carolina Times*, January 28, January 31, 1865; *Anglo-African*, March 11, 1865.

59. *New York Herald*, May 19, 1865; Bergeron, *The Papers of Andrew Johnson*, 57–58. The petition also appeared in the *New York Times*, the *New York Evening Post*, the *Cincinnati Enquirer*, and a Raleigh newspaper (Justin Eastwood, University of Tennessee Library, email to author, October 10, 2011). No manuscript version has been located in the Johnson Papers at the University of Tennessee Library, nor is there any known list of the

signers. Thanks to Earl Bell and Jeffrey Crow for calling my attention to the petition in the published Johnson papers.

60. On Chase's visit to New Bern in May and his description of conversations with black and white leaders there and elsewhere, see Salmon P. Chase to Andrew Johnson, May 7, 1865, from Beaufort, North Carolina, in Brooks D. Simpson, LeRoy P. Graf, and John Muldowny, eds., *Advice after Appomattox: Letters to Andrew Johnson, 1865–1866* (Knoxville: University of Tennessee Press, 1987), 19–20, and 23–29. Chase's involvement in the New Bern petition has not been documented but it seems likely, given his visit to New Bern at the time, the similarity of the language about the "enrollment" of citizens, and how quickly and widely the petition was published.

61. Ibid., 26, on the *New York Herald* viewpoint; 32, on that newspaper condemning Chase as a "negro-worshipper"; and 40, on Johnson's May 29 policy on suffrage. See also Franklin, *Reconstruction after the Civil War*, 42.

62. Cecelski, "A Radical and Jacobinical Spirit," 191.

63. See Hahn, *A Nation under Our Feet*, 104–10, on similar, earlier efforts in Tennessee and Louisiana.

64. This account draws mainly on Green, *Methodist Meeting House*, and Rue's 1865 reports to the *Christian Recorder*. Rue thanked his friends in Boston for their gifts in a letter to the *Christian Recorder* published on July 1, 1865.

65. George A. Rue, letter, August 28, 1865, *Christian Recorder*, September 9, 1865.

66. Hahn, *A Nation under Our Feet*, 120–27, on other freedmen's conventions in the South during the summer and autumn of 1865. Hahn's analysis of the leadership of these groups—whom he calls "America's true Jacobins" (120)—in various southern states points out parallels with the leadership in North Carolina, though it appears that natives of the state were unusually predominant in the Raleigh convention.

67. Rue, letter, August 28, 1865, *Christian Recorder*, September 9, 1865. *New Bern Daily Times*, August 30, 1865 (a Wednesday), describes the meeting held on the previous Monday night. The meeting of August 22 was reported in the *New Bern Daily Times*, August 23, 1865, as cited in Alexander, *North Carolina Faces the Freedmen*, 184.

68. *New Bern Daily Times*, August 28 and 31, 1865, and *Wilmington Herald*, September 27 and 29, 1865, quoted in Alexander, *North Carolina Faces the Freedmen*, 20. See also Greenwood, *First Fruits of Freedom*, 81–83, and Cecelski, *The Fire of Freedom*, 180–82, on the August meetings. George A. Rue, August 28, 1865, *Christian Recorder*, September 9, 1865.

69. Alexander, *North Carolina Faces the Freedmen*, 64–66, and *New Bern Daily Times*, September 28, 1865. Quote from Mobley, *James City*, 52. For analysis of the 1865 Freedmen's Convention, see Alexander, *North Carolina Faces the Freedmen*, 17–31, and Cecelski, *The Fire of Freedom*, 185–88. For firsthand reports, see Dennett, *The South as It Is*, 147–65; Andrews, *The South since the War*, 56–65; "Colored Convention in North Carolina," September 29–October 1, 1865, *Christian Recorder*, October 28, 1865; and *Convention of the Freedmen of North Carolina, Official Proceedings*.

70. The "African" Methodist congregation in Raleigh subsequently became St. Paul's

AME Church. Quote from Dennett, *The South as It Is*, 149–50. "Colored Convention in North Carolina," September 29–October 1, 1865, *Christian Recorder*, October 28, 1865.

71. "Colored Convention in North Carolina," September 29–October 1, 1865, *Christian Recorder*, October 28, 1865; Dennett, *The South as It Is*, 148–49.

72. Alexander, *North Carolina Faces the Freedmen*, 26; "Colored Convention in North Carolina," September 29–October 1, 1865, *Christian Recorder*, October 28, 1865. Other officers besides Hood and Randolph included assistant secretary, W. Cawthorn of Warren County; treasurer, J. R. Caswell of Wake; and chaplain, Alexander Bass of Raleigh (an Episcopalian who soon moved to New Bern). See Harris and Ellison in *DNCB*, and Schenck in Greenwood, *Bittersweet Legacy*, especially 47–48.

73. See Hahn, *A Nation under Our Feet*, 122, for parallels.

74. *Convention of the Freedmen of North Carolina, Official Proceedings*; Dennett, *The South as It Is*, 148–49. Quote, Andrews, *The South since the War*, 60.

75. *Convention of the Freedmen of North Carolina, Official Proceedings*; "Colored Convention in North Carolina," September 29–October 1, 1865, *Christian Recorder*, October 28, 1865. The record is ambiguous on why the convention changed its approach on equal rights in preparing the address to the Constitutional Convention. Given the timing, it may have reflected the convention leaders' assessment of the views of the white convention delegates who arrived on Sunday. Hamilton, *Reconstruction in North Carolina*, 150, credits to Galloway and Harris the omission of the suffrage issue from the freedmen's address. Alexander, *North Carolina Faces the Freedmen*, 28, notes that "the Harris committee was dominated by the supposedly more radical faction." Last quote, Dennett, *The South as It Is*, 153.

76. See Cecelski, *Fire of Freedom*, 187, on the inclusion of Galloway in this group.

77. Alexander, *North Carolina Faces the Freedmen*, 35; Dennett, *The South as It Is*, 161–62, first quote 161; Andrews, *The South since the War*, 75–79, quote, 78.

78. *Convention of the Freedmen of North Carolina, Official Proceedings*, 22–23. The list of 32 North Carolinians in Cleveland included 20 artisans, 3 barbers, 2 students, a teacher, a soldier, a railroad agent, a book agent, and a clerk. Besides New Bern their home towns included Raleigh, Chapel Hill, Fayetteville, Goldsboro, Kinston, and Wilmington.

79. *Christian Recorder*, December 9, 1865.

80. Oliver Howard, November 12, 1865, and Mrs. C. G. Howard, November 1865, in *The Freedmen's Record* 1, no. 12 (December 1865), http://mac110.assumption.edu/aas/Reports/fr12-1865.html, consulted May 9, 2010.

81. *Anglo-African*, March 11, 1865, on Clinton Chapel. Hood, *Sketch of the Early History*, 85.

82. Willis's role is described in "Brief History of the Founding of Rue Chapel A. M. E. Church." Robert Primrose to George B. Willis, deed for lot #8 (formerly William Hollister's) for $125, July 10, 1866 (CCDB 70:366); and Primrose to Willis, deed for lot #23 (formerly William Hollister's) for $100, June 10, 1866 (CCDB 70:365). George B. Willis to Lewis Williams and others, trustees of AME church in New Bern, for $1, lot #8, northeast corner of Cypress Street and Bragg's Alley, (CCDB 73:313). On Rue's handiwork in building the Sunday school building, see *Christian Recorder*, October 19, 1891.

83. *Christian Recorder*, July 29 and December 30, 1865; on "pulpit union," see *Christian Recorder*, January 20, 1866. Edwin S. Redkey, "Henry McNeal Turner," in Smith, *Black Soldiers in Blue*, 337–60.

84. *New Bern Daily Times*, November 27, 1865.

85. Ibid. Paul Drayton died in Charleston on December 17, 1865. On black Masonic lodges in North Carolina, see Kenzer, *Enterprising Southerners*, 66–75. He notes, 148, that while some accounts give 1866 as the founding date for King Solomon Lodge, an unpublished history of black masonry in North Carolina, "Steps of Prince Hall," by Major S. Hight, dates it in 1865. On the controversy between the North Carolina and New York Grand Lodges, see Voorhis, *Negro Masonry in the United States*, 50–51, 119–21. On Hood, see Martin, *For God and Race*, 38. Hood was also instrumental in founding lodges in Wilmington, Raleigh, and Fayetteville, which with New Bern organized a state Grand Lodge in 1870; Hood served as grand master for fourteen years.

86. Simmons was identified at the time of his death as "one of the charter members of the King Solomon Lodge No 1 A. F. & A. M. of this city." *New Bern Weekly Journal*, July 22, 1904.

87. On local and state developments in this period, see Watson, *A History of New Bern*; Alexander, *North Carolina Faces the Freedmen*; Hamilton, *Reconstruction in North Carolina*; Escott, *Many Excellent People*, 113–95; and for the national context, Foner, *Reconstruction*; and Hahn, *A Nation under Our Feet*.

88. Alexander, *North Carolina Faces the Freedmen*, 80–81; S. W. Laidler to Thaddeus Stevens, May 7, 1866, "Letters to Stevens," quoted in ibid., 80; *New Bern Weekly Times*, August 21, 1866.

89. Alexander, *North Carolina Faces the Freedmen*, 81–95; quote, 82, *New Bern Daily Times*, September 14, 1866. On Randolph, see his letter in *Minutes of the Freedmen's Convention . . . 1866*, 20, and Watson, *A History of New Bern*, 430.

90. Other officers of the formally organized North Carolina Equal Rights League included Wake County's James H. Harris as president, J. R. Caswell and Stewart Ellison as vice-presidents, and W. H. Anderson as recording secretary. James Bowman of Cumberland County became treasurer. Other officers of the Educational Association included president James O'Hara of Wayne County, who had been in New Bern earlier; vice-presidents John T. Schenck of Mecklenburg and H. Locket of Wake; secretary William Cawthorn of Warren; and treasurer Moses Patterson of Wake; *Minutes of the Freedmen's Convention . . . 1866*, 28–29. Except for O'Hara, most of these men, like the New Bernians, were artisans.

91. The following account is from *Minutes of the Freedmen's Convention . . . 1866*.

92. See Hamilton, *Reconstruction in North Carolina*, 187–88, on a bill introduced in Congress on December 13, 1866 (the same day the North Carolina legislature rejected the Fourteenth Amendment) by Thaddeus Stevens, at the behest of North Carolina white Republicans, to establish Reconstruction in North Carolina, including limited black suffrage—universal male suffrage, qualified by property ownership or the ability to read and write, but not by race. The bill was not acted upon.

93. *Christian Recorder*, February 2, 1867; "Brief History of Rue's Chapel."

Chapter 5

1. *New Bern Daily Times*, January 3, 1873, cited in Brundage, *The Southern Past*, 95. On Crawford's family background, see Chapter 2.

2. Brundage, *The Southern Past*, 55–104, on the idea that black public celebrations on Emancipation Day, Memorial Day, and the Fourth of July countered stories told by whites through monuments, pageants, books, and film. Brundage points out (94–99) parallels between Crawford's speech and others of similar times and purposes.

3. Greenwood, *Bittersweet Legacy*, describes this process in Charlotte. See also Gavins, "The Meaning of Freedom," and Kenzer, *Enterprising Southerners*, including an analysis of the occupations and backgrounds of blacks active in postwar political life (86–106).

4. Greenwood, *Bittersweet Legacy*, 43, cites the lack of a preexisting black elite in Charlotte. The New Bern leaders contrast with those depicted by Kenzer, *Enterprising Southerners*, especially 43, who finds that most successful postwar North Carolina entrepreneurs of color were free before the war.

5. Whitford, "Home Story of Walking Stick," and Miller, "Recollections." *New Bern Daily Journal*, March 2, 1887.

6. Thomas Battle obituary, *New Bern Daily Journal*, February 2, 1902.

7. Newton, *Out of the Briars*, 23.

8. James, *Annual Report*, 10–12.

9. Generally craft unions in North Carolina, for either or both races, were few and short-lived throughout the nineteenth century, a situation that continued in the twentieth century. No craft union for blacks is known to have developed in New Bern. Israel B. Abbott organized a short-lived workers' union in 1881, which encompassed primarily laborers and did not last long. Watson, *A History of New Bern*, 520.

10. Of about 330 artisans (not including apprentices) in the city of not quite 6,000 souls in 1870, about 230—or about 70 percent—were black. Among about 85 females listed as artisans (chiefly seamstresses), slightly over half were women of color. By contrast, about 190, or 76 percent, of New Bern's approximately 250 male artisans were black.

11. Free artisans of color shown in both the 1860 and 1870 censuses include the following: Israel B. Abbott, Elizabeth Bragg, James Dove, Joseph Green, Park Lawrence, Isaac Rue, David Wilson, Moses Hill, William H. Johnson, Luke Mason, David Richardson, Edward A. Richardson, and William Pettiford. (There was more than one New Bern man named William [H.] Johnson in the period. William Pettiford was variously identified over time as a laborer, an engineer, and a blacksmith.)

12. Of the 61 New Bern black artisans who filled out applications for Freedman's Bank accounts from 1869 through 1873, 27 were natives of Craven County, all but two from New Bern; 4 came from neighboring states; and the rest were natives of other North Carolina counties, including some who had grown up in New Bern. These figures may or may not be representative of the larger black artisan population. The bank applications do not specify whether the applicant had been enslaved, but in several cases personal evidence indicates the applicant's former situation as a slave.

13. There was a substantial drop in the number of black artisans between 1870 and

1880; in the latter year the census recorded about 140 black male artisans and about 35 black female artisans. All population figures given here are approximate because of the errors possible at several stages, including the census taker's initial record and my own identification and counting. As noted elsewhere, the 1870 census is especially prone to errors and omissions, particularly for black people. Some artisans known to be in town at a certain time do not appear in the census, such as brickmason and plasterer Edward A. Richardson, absent from the 1880 census but present in the 1880 city directory. Persistence among women is hard to estimate because of surname changes at marriage. Of the leading artisans of the 1870s and 1880s, those free before the war included Isaac C. Rue and his grandson Edward A. Richardson, house carpenter Israel B. Abbott, and wagonmaker Luke Mason and his sons. Most of the leading artisans after the war, however, were freedmen who had come to the fore during wartime occupation and immediately afterward. They included New Bernian carpenter Richard Tucker, blacksmith George S. Fisher, brickmason Thomas Battle, and coopers Amos York, Edward R. Dudley, Virgil A. Crawford, Henry H. Simmons, and George B. Willis. Others, including painter John Randolph Jr., shoemaker Edward Havens, and bricklayers Isaac Harris Sr. and Isaac Harris Jr., arrived from Washington, North Carolina. Those who moved to New Bern in the 1870s included shoemaker and Union veteran Allen G. Oden and carpenter William O. Randolph, painter John's brother. Younger men, such as tailor Mustipher Holly and shoemaker John T. Havens, entered their trades in the 1870s and 1880s, followed by others in the 1890s, including some third-generation artisans in their families.

14. *New Bern Daily Nut Shell*, December 1, 1879 (Jackson and Holly), and February 23, 1876 (Havens).

15. CCAB. Zipf notes in *Labor of Innocents*, chaps. 2 and 3, that in the North Carolina counties in her study, unlike Craven County, the number of black apprenticeships rose after the war, including some arranged by the Freedmen's Bureau. Like Craven County, records in those counties indicate emphasis on social control, not transfer of craft skills.

16. Du Bois, *The Negro Artisan*, 23.

17. U.S. censuses, 1870, 1880.

18. Some, if not all, of the Jackson men were related: "Jackson & Bro.," blacksmiths, with a shop on Middle Street, applied for a Freedman's Bank account in 1871. George S. Fisher obituary, *New Bern Daily Journal*, September 6, 1892. The one white blacksmith in New Bern in 1870—Patrick Trenwith, a native of Ireland—was, like several local white artisans, an immigrant who had learned his skills in a different environment; NBCD (1880); U.S. censuses, 1870, 1880. It should be noted that the NBCD (1880) listed only one business (that of Allen Jackson) among the blacksmith businesses as "c," for colored, but the individual listings in the directory showed that all of the men listed as blacksmiths were black. Racial identities are usually more reliably designated in the individual listings in the directory than in the business section.

19. NBCD (1880), U.S. censuses, 1870, 1880. The names Holly and Holley, rare in Craven County, were common in northeastern North Carolina counties, such as Bertie

and Chowan, suggesting that some of the New Bern group came from that area. Tailor Mustipher (Mustapher) P. Holly was listed as M. P. Harley in the 1880 census and M. P. Holley in the 1893 city directory.

20. NBCD (1904). Nine of the thirteen boot- and shoemakers' businesses cited in the 1880 directory and two of the five tailoring businesses were operated by men of color. No shoemaking firms appeared in the 1893 directory, but there were two white- and two black-run tailoring shops.

21. U.S. censuses, 1870, 1880.

22. U.S. censuses, 1860, 1870, 1880.

23. U.S. censuses, 1880, 1900.

24. On changes in the production of building materials and their effect on artisans, see Lounsbury, "The Wild Melody of Steam," 193–239. Unlike for the antebellum era, for the postwar period no known records identify the artisans who worked on specific New Bern projects.

25. NBCD (1880). Although the business listing denoted the carpentry firm of McGee and Nelson as white, its principals were black: Benjamin McGee, Samuel Nelson, Isaac Brown, and Benjamin Beasley.

26. William Jones in Herzog, "The Early Architecture of New Bern," 340; *New Bern Times*, December 14, 1871.

27. Lounsbury, "The Wild Melody of Steam," 259–72.

28. Carpenters identified as Pavie employees in NBCD (1880) were William Barrum, Archie Blunt, Charles Disbrew, Abram Dudley, William James, Abe Jones, Henry J. Long, James West, and Charles Whitfield. The censuses of 1870 and 1880 list others.

29. Freedman's Bank Records; *New Bern Daily Times*, June 15, 1871, August 29, 1871, and June 10, 1872; *New Bern Daily Journal*, August 12, 1891, and July 15, 1882. On Pavie, see Herzog, "The Early Architecture of New Bern," 325–28. Herzog notes as Pavie projects in 1869 the J. E. Nash store, the Sebastian Bangert market house, and a house for George Claypool at his marble works; and in 1871 a commercial building for merchants Baer and Eppler, a saloon and dwelling on Middle Street for F. Ulrich, and a mansard-roofed "cottage" for William Dunn. A remodeling of the George Allen store on Pollock Street was underway when Pavie died in 1891. On Pavie Town (Pavietown) see Hanchett and Little, *The History and Architecture of Long Wharf and Greater Duffyfield*, 60. See also "Edward Pavie," http://ncarchitectsandbuilders.ncsu.edu, consulted July 30, 2010.

30. *New Bern Daily Journal*, March 10, 1893; Civil War Pension Record, Dennis Wadsworth, 1867, via http://www.ancestry.com. On Wadsworth's 1893 shop, see Sanborn Insurance Map, 1893, and Dennis Wadsworth, Estates Papers, 1897, CCEP, including a full inventory of his steam-powered equipment and his traditional carpentry tools.

31. For similar patterns in Charlotte, see Hanchett, *Sorting Out the New South City*, 37–45.

32. NBCD (1893). On black barbers, see Bristol, *Knights of the Razor*, 120–48. Barbers typically had separate shops for black and white customers; whether tailors and shoemakers followed similar policies in this period is not clear.

33. These locations are found in the city directories of 1880 and 1893. Urban renewal

projects of the mid- to late twentieth century destroyed all of the buildings on the south side of South Front Street and nearby Trent River wharf area, with the exception of the Federal-period Harvey mansion on South Front. For photographs of some of these, see Green, *New Bern Album*.

34. NBCD (1880).

35. In contrast to NBCD (1880), the NBCD (1893) generally omitted coverage of the Five Points area. The NBCD (1904) reinstated some coverage of the area.

36. Some freedpeople likely benefited from their antebellum relationships with prominent whites, such as blacksmith George S. Fisher, who had earned the esteem of his antebellum employer, businessman Zaccheus Slade, and may have profited from that connection.

37. Available figures on local property ownership in this period are unreliable. Property values given in the 1870 census—the last to list property values—vary widely from the more reliable Craven County tax lists for 1869–71, Kellenberger Room. The 1870 census, which was based on the census taker's conversations with household members, showed more people as real estate owners, and often gave a different (usually higher) property value, than did tax lists. Only tax lists specified what town lots or other property the person owned.

38. U.S. census, 1870.

39. Ibid.

40. Several citizens, including black and white Republicans, incorporated in 1869 the Newbern Co-operative Land and Building Association, which proposed to sell shares of $200 each, to a total capital stock of $500,000. *Public Laws of the State of North Carolina, Passed by the General Assembly at its Session 1868–1869* (Raleigh: M. S. Littlefield, State Printer and Binder, 1869), 252.

41. Craven County Tax List, 1887, microfilm, NCA&H, transcribed by Ansley Wegner. Of the few tax lists surviving for New Bern in the late nineteenth century, the 1887 list is the most complete and legible. It shows the following ages and property values for known artisans of color: Virgil Crawford, 54, Queen Street, $600; Allen G. Oden, 46, New South Front Street, $400, and Craven Street, $150; Edward Havens, 47, Jenkins (Jerkins) Alley (for wife), $150; Joseph Green, 65, Bragg's Alley, $100; John Randolph, 56, Queen Street, $400; Edward Richardson, 55, 82½ acres on the Trent Road, $495, Queen Street, $125 and $800, Johnson Street, $200, Good Street, $350; George S. Fisher, 63, Broad, Pollock, and Short Streets and Scotts Alley, $2,650; Edward R. Dudley, town and rural property, $730 in 1887 (by 1891 his landholdings were worth $2,025). It also listed attorney George H. White, 34, Pasteur Street, $250, Primrose and Cedar, $100.

42. R. G. Dun & Co. Collection, North Carolina, vol. 7, p. 29, Baker Library Historical Collections, Harvard Business School, Boston, Mass.

43. Kenzer, *Enterprising Southerners*, 88–94, and U.S. census, 1870.

44. New Bern's sluggish economy limited the wealth of even its most successful men of color. With the exception of real estate dealer and money lender Isaac Hughes Smith (who with at least $100,000 worth of property emerged as one of the richest black men in North Carolina in the 1890s), no postwar-period black New Bernians

remotely rivaled the wealth of the black economic elite elsewhere in the state or nation. On a regional scale, as Schweninger has shown, the definition of "prosperous" southern blacks after the war entailed property worth at least $20,000. In addition to I. H. Smith, the few very prosperous blacks in North Carolina included industrialist Warren C. Coleman in Concord, brickmaker Richard Fitzgerald in Durham, and former brickmason and barber John Merrick, who emerged in Durham at the end of the 1890s as a banking and insurance leader. All three had links with the Duke family of Durham. Schweninger, *Black Property Owners*; Kenzer, *Enterprising Southerners*, 86–106; and "Isaac Hughes Smith," *DNCB*.

45. Edward Havens Estates Papers, CCEP.

46. Charles Chesnutt, "The Free Colored People of North Carolina," *Southern Workman* 31 (March 1902): 136–41, http://faculty.berea.edu/browners/chesnutt/Works/Essays/free.html, consulted December 9, 2010. Chestnutt was born in Ohio to parents from Fayetteville, North Carolina, and moved with them back to Fayetteville after the war.

47. NBCD (1893) had business listings for 22 white craftsmen and only 9 black ones—blacksmiths Samuel Jackson, Joseph McDaniel, and W. R. Edwards; shoemakers Edward Havens, Allen G. Oden, and J. C. Waters; tailor M. P. Holly, and contractors D. G. Moseley and S. Mackey. These numbers reflected the racial orientation of the directory more than the actual number of artisans.

48. *New Bern Daily Journal*, September 23, 1895.

49. U.S. censuses, 1870–1900. Author's telephone interview, December 2, 2011, with Carol Sawyer Hicks, New Bern; notes in possession of author. Tailor Mustipher Holly at age forty employed his son Bradley as his apprentice in 1900.

50. Author's telephone interview, November 30, 2011, with Carolyn Bland, New Bern; notes in possession of author. Local tradition cited by Mrs. Bland credits Henry Clay Sparrow with planning and rebuilding St. Peter's AME Zion Church after the fire of 1922. U.S. census, 1900.

51. U.S. censuses, 1880, 1900, and NBCD (1904).

52. On leadership groups among postwar black citizens elsewhere, see Gatewood, *Aristocrats of Color*; Schweninger, *Black Property Owners*; and especially Greenwood, *Bittersweet Legacy*. Reaves, *Strength through Struggle*, shows that many members of Wilmington's postwar black leadership, including Henry Taylor, the Howes, the Prices, the Valentines, and the Sampsons, came from free or "virtually free" families prominent in the city before the war.

53. *Christian Recorder*, March 23, 1867; *New Bern Republican*, May 2, 1867.

54. *New Bern Republican*, May 4, 1867, published the order cancelling the New Bern municipal election. Sickles's announcement came after his meeting at his headquarters in Charleston with North Carolina's Conservative civilian governor Jonathan Worth, at which Sickles conceded that "no municipal elections should be held until after the meeting of the [Constitutional] convention." On Worth's role, see Edward McPherson, *A Political Manual for 1868, Including a Classified Summary of the Important Executive, Legislative, Politico-Military, and General Facts of the Period from April 1, 1867, to July 15,*

1868 (Washington, D.C.: Philips and Solomons, 1868), 317, and Hamilton, *Reconstruction in North Carolina*, 222–23, citing Correspondence Relative to Reconstruction, and Sickles to U. S. Grant, April 18, 1867.

55. *New Bern Republican*, July 30, 1867, in Watson, *A History of New Bern*, 451.

56. *New Bern Republican*, July 6, 1867. The July 3 meeting chaired by Tucker included as speakers and leaders Randolph, York, Richardson, and Fisher, plus Thomas Battle, John R. Good, and clergymen Alexander Bass and Brevett Morris.

57. *New Bern Republican*, July 6, 1867; Watson, *A History of New Bern*, 449.

58. On New Bern men as registrars, see Watson, *A History of New Bern*, 432; and "Register of Registrars," vols. 1 and 2 (1867), Records of the Assistant Commissioner for the State of North Carolina, Bureau of Refugees, Freedmen and Abandoned Lands, 1865–1870, RG 105, National Archives, Washington, D. C., transcription courtesy of David Cecelski.

59. Hamilton, *Reconstruction in North Carolina*, 253–93; see 254 for a list of black delegates to the Constitutional Convention. Hamilton cites James H. Harris, James Walker Hood, and Abraham Galloway as leaders at that meeting.

60. Watson, *A History of New Bern*, 436; *New Bern Daily Republican*, December 30, 1868. Pierson died of "acute rheumatism" at age fifty-eight in January 1870 (U.S. census, Manuscript Mortality Schedule, 1870, via http://www.ancestry.com).

61. Balanoff, "Negro Legislators in the North Carolina General Assembly"; Crow, Escott, and Hatley, *A History of African Americans in North Carolina*, 85. Other black legislators, including formerly enslaved carpenters John R. Page of Chowan and Stewart Ellison of Wake, also introduced bills to help mechanics and other workers in this session, but these failed.

62. Watson, *A History of New Bern*, 439–40.

63. McGuire, "The Making of a Black Militia Company." Thanks to the author for sharing a prepublication version of his article, which is the first study to focus attention on Clarke's regiment and the black troops of Company H. McGuire states that James D. Dudley subsequently moved to Washington, D.C., where he held a government position, but later returned to New Bern and served as an officer during the Spanish-American War.

64. Ibid.

65. Watson, *A History of New Bern*, 469–74; Anderson, *The Black Second*, 5. According to Powell, *North Carolina through Four Centuries* (Chapel Hill: University of North Carolina Press, 1989), 431, Craven County had 14 black legislators during the period 1868–99, New Hanover had 15, and Edgecombe had 11. No other county had as many as 10.

66. Logan, "Black and Republican," 311–46. The legislature of 1876–77 revised the charters in Wilmington, Raleigh, Tarboro, Elizabeth City, Fayetteville, and Kinston to assure white majorities on town councils and boards of aldermen. This session did pass a few laws of benefit to blacks, including authorization of the first state-supported black normal school, now Fayetteville State University. See Logan, *The Negro in North Carolina*, especially 56–63, on the election law of 1877 and further restrictions in 1889.

67. U.S. census, 1870. The results reflected the racial ratios in the seven wards.

"Population of Civil Divisions Less Than Counties," *Ninth Census of the United States, 1870* (Washington, D.C.: Government Printing Office, 1872), 222. In 1870 there were 146 blacks and 530 whites in the First Ward; 257 blacks and 367 whites in the Second; 293 blacks and 345 whites in the Third; 226 blacks and 231 whites in the Fourth; 1,027 blacks and 402 whites in the Fifth; 1,396 blacks and 78 whites in the Sixth, and 484 blacks and 67 whites in the Seventh.

68. Watson, *A History of New Bern*, 438, 471, 476.

69. A few black New Bernians were appointed to county offices by Democratic legislatures. See Edmonds, *The Negro in Fusion Politics*, 50–51, on the 1877 legislature's (controversial) appointment of black justices of the peace in eastern counties; and NBCD (1880).

70. Anderson, *The Black Second*, 5, 115.

71. Ibid., 132–40; Gilmore, *Gender and Jim Crow*, 7–10; Watson, *A History of New Bern*, 479–81. Simmons won with 15,158 votes to O'Hara's 13,060 and Abbott's 5,020. In 1888 Simmons lost his congressional seat to black Republican Henry Cheatham of Vance County. In 1898 he became chairman of the state Democratic Party and was a principal architect of the white supremacy crusades of 1898 and 1900. He was elected to the United States Senate in 1900 and served there until 1930. Watson, *A History of New Bern*, 481; Simmons, *DNCB*.

72. On the political dimensions of black education, see Escott, *Many Excellent People*, 136–37, 166, 180. First quote, David Schenck Diary, July 4, 1873, SHC, at 180.

73. Watson, *A History of New Bern*, 451, 454.

74. U.S. censuses, 1870, 1880. See Price in *DNCB* and Crow, Escott, and Hatley, *A History of African Americans in North Carolina*, 102–3. For Price's speech of 1890 on education and the "Negro problem," see http://www.blackpast.org/?q=1890-joseph-c-price-education-and-problem, consulted July 23, 2012.

75. *New Bern Republican*, July 30, 1867.

76. Martin, *For God and Race*, 75–76, on Hood as superintendent. On Democrats' opposition to state support for public schools after 1870, see Escott, *Many Excellent People*, 180.

77. *Public Laws of the State of North-Carolina, Passed by the General Assembly, 1872–1873*, 91. Most of the New Bern Educational Association's twenty incorporators were artisans active in public life—Israel B. Abbott, Edward A. Richardson, Richard Tucker, Thomas Battle, Virgil A. Crawford, Moses T. Bryan, George Fisher, William Lawrence, Miles Sheppard, E. E. Tucker, John Randolph Jr., Edward R. Dudley, and George B. Willis—together with their allies Alexander Bass and John R. Good. They, along with barber John M. Banton, clerk John Dixon, grocer George Physic, and shoemaker George W. Stanly, demonstrated the breadth and depth of black New Bernians' concern for education of the younger generation.

78. Watson, *A History of New Bern*, 568.

79. Mobley, *James City*, 69, quoting the *New Bernian*, September 8, 22, and October 6, 1877; Watson, *A History of New Bern*, 568–69.

80. *Educational Weekly*, December 13, 1877, http://ir.uiowa.edu/cgi/viewcontent

.cgi?article=1047&context=edweek, consulted July 9, 2012. Escott notes in *Many Excellent People*, 180, that many of these same leaders took part in the North Carolina State Teachers Association in the 1880s.

81. NBCD (1880).

82. Justeson, *George Henry White*, 33–56.

83. The first principal at the Fayetteville school was Robert Harris, the son of Fayetteville brickmason Jacob Harris. His brother, Cicero Richardson Harris, later a bishop, also taught there, as did writer Charles Chesnutt.

84. Watson, *A History of New Bern*, 569, 573. Justeson, *George Henry White*, 77–81, on White's role in the legislature and as principal. In 1887 the black normal school moved to Goldsboro, though for several years it held summer teachers' institutes in New Bern.

85. The graded school law of 1883 provided that the black graded schools could be supported by taxes on blacks, the white ones by taxes on whites, an arrangement that proved controversial and worked to the detriment of black schools. On Craven County's vote, see Watson, *A History of New Bern*, 570–73, quote 572. See also Gavins, "The Meaning of Freedom," 189, on the graded school law.

86. The school that came to be known as the West Street Graded School began in a frame structure, which burned and was replaced in the early twentieth century by a brick building. Initially housing the primary grades, it later included a high school and served as a center of community life.

87. "History of St. Cyprian's Episcopal Church," typescript, ca. 2007 (photocopy in St. Cyprian's Episcopal Church survey file, Survey and Planning Branch, State Historic Preservation Office, Office of Archives and History, North Carolina Department of Cultural Resources, Raleigh). St. Cyprian's founding date is usually given as 1866, but on an 1864 map of the city (see Chapter 4) a drawing of "St. Cyprian's (col.)" appears at the junction of Metcalf, Johnson, and Queen Streets where the present church stands. In 1871, when the officers of the church applied for a Freedman's Bank account, barber Moses Kennedy was head of the vestry and Israel Harris was treasurer. See Harris obituary, *New Bern Daily Journal*, June 30, 1897. In 1880 or 1881 St. Cyprian's received its first black priest, Peter William Cassey, son of prominent Philadelphia abolitionist Joseph Cassey; a barber like his father, he had gone to San Francisco and worked at his trade before entering the priesthood in San Jose. He stayed in New Bern until 1894. http://www.blackpast.org/?q=aaw/cassey-peter-william-1831, consulted July 21, 2012; and Carraway, *Crown of Life*, 215.

88. Vass, *History of the Presbyterian Church*. According to Vass, the original members of the black congregation were John Randolph Sr., John Randolph Jr., Julius Willis, Caroline Barham, Livinia Willard, George H. White, Caesar Lewis, William O. Randolph, Jane Coats, L. Palmer, and William W. Lawrence. The first "ruling elders" were John Randolph Sr., Willis, and White.

89. On the African Methodist Singing School, see *Private Laws of the State of North-Carolina, Passed by the General Assembly* (Raleigh: Holden & Wilson, 1871). Founders included Virgil A. Crawford, Cicero Robbins, Amos York, and Edward R. Dudley.

90. *New Berne Weekly Times*, August 21, 1873.

91. Newton, *Out of the Briars*, 110–12. Newton evidently began his ministry at Rue's Chapel in 1878 and left two years later for an assignment in Morristown, New Jersey.

92. *New Bern Daily Journal*, May 22 and May 23, 1888, and Martin, *For God and Race*, 188. The *Star of Zion* publication was founded in New Bern by AME Zion members and eventually moved to Charlotte. Sanborn Insurance Maps (North Carolina Collection, University of North Carolina at Chapel Hill, and NCA&H, at http://www.lib.unc.edu/dc/ncmaps/) indicate that the old Andrews Chapel meetinghouse on Hancock Street was razed between 1893 and 1898.

93. M. Ruth Little, "St. Peter's A. M. E. Zion Church," National Register of Historic Places nomination, 1997. By the early twentieth century the frame church was brick veneered or rebuilt in brick; it burned in 1922.

94. Martin, *For God and Race*, 116–17.

95. Gilmore, *Gender and Jim Crow*, 12–13.

96. M. P. Holly, Estates Papers, CCEP.

97. New Bern Templars included Dudley's fellow coopers Virgil A. Crawford and George B. Willis; carpenters Moses Bryan and Lewis Williams; bricklayers Daniel H. Harris and Israel Harris Sr., and tailor Mustipher Holly. *New Bern Daily Times*, June 12, 1873; Charles N. Hunter Scrapbooks.

98. *Public Laws and Resolutions, Together with the Private Laws, of the State of North Carolina, Passed by the General Assembly at Its Session 1872–1873* (Raleigh: Stone & Uzzell, 1873). The men listed first among the many incorporators of the mutual aid society included carpenters Israel B. Abbott and Moses T. Bryan; brickmasons Edward A. Richardson, Daniel H. Harris, Thomas C. Battle, and Israel Harris; shoemakers Cicero Robbins and Edward Havens; painter John Randolph Jr.; carpenter and undertaker Richard Tucker; blacksmith George S. Fisher; cabinetmaker and turner Miles Shepard; and coopers William W. Lawrence, George B. Willis, Edward R. Dudley, Henry H. Simmons, Virgil A. Crawford, and Amos York.

99. On black Masonry in nineteenth-century North Carolina, see Kenzer, *Enterprising Southerners*, 69–75.

100. On March 1, 1870, the trustees of King Solomon Lodge—coopers William W. Lawrence, Edward R. Dudley, and Henry H. Simmons—purchased Dryboro lot #1 on Queen Street from Richard and Ann Hazel of Cleveland, who had moved there from New Bern in the 1850s (CCDB 70:592, witnessed by a notary in Cleveland, Ohio). Richard Hazel, the free black blacksmith, acquired lot #1 in 1855 from James York Green (CCDB 64:303), who purchased it from Sarah Bland in 1838 (CCDB 63:403). Quote, *New Bern Daily Times*, February 23, 1871.

101. By 1880, the city also had a chapter of the Masonic affiliate group, the Eastern Star, which included both men and women. It included shoemakers Cicero Robbins and Allen G. Oden, and its officers were Oden's wife Dicey; Lucy Tucker, the wife of carpenter E. E. Tucker; and Celia Randolph, the wife of carpenter William O. Randolph. NBCD (1880).

102. NBCD (1880).

103. NBCD (1880). On black military organizations in Wilmington, see Reaves, *Strength through Struggle*, 333–42.

104. *Annual Report of the Adjutant-General of the State of North Carolina for the Year 1877 to the Commander-in-Chief* (Raleigh: State Printer, 1878), 7.

105. Ibid. According to Reaves, *Strength through Struggle*, 342, in 1899 the legislature forbade black men from service in the state guard. *New Bern Daily Journal*, October 21, 1894, on Allen G. Oden.

106. Reid, *Freedom for Themselves*, 307, states that the Beecher GAR post in New Bern was formed by 1871. The Library of Congress web site indicates that the T. A. Lyons Camp 57 of the Department of Virginia and North Carolina was the white camp in New Bern and Beecher 22 was the black camp. See http://www.loc.gov/rr/main/gar/appendix/virginia.html, consulted April 14, 2010. The Beecher post's history gives a founding date of 1887 and states that it continued to operate until about 1914; http://rblong.net/encgar/Beecher/index.html, consulted November 4, 2011. Thanks to Josh Howard and Chris Meekins for research assistance on this topic.

107. *New Bern Daily Journal*, November 27, 1897.

108. On black Union veterans at Memorial Day events, see Brundage, *The Southern Past*, 69–70. The national date for Decoration Day, later called Memorial Day, was May 30 for many years. Southern states designated various "Confederate Memorial Days"—May 10 in North Carolina.

109. Watson, *A History of New Bern*, 562, and http://www.archive.org/stream/lawsresolutions0187374nor/lawsresolutions0187374nor_djvu.txt, consulted November 6, 2011. Artisans Virgil A. Crawford, Samuel Jackson, James D. Dudley, and brickmason Israel Harris Jr. were among the founders of the Rough and Ready Company. Both groups are listed in NBCD (1880). On the convention of black fire companies from across the state in Raleigh, see Reaves, *Strength through Struggle*, 198.

110. George B. Willis, Estates Papers, CCEP.

111. It is not clear how long the Equal Rights Leagues were active in New Bern.

112. Freedman's Bank Records, via http://www.ancestry.com.

113. Hatch, *Autobiography*; White, *"Somebody Knows My Name"*; U.S. census, 1870.

114. U.S. census, 1870.

115. Horace James, "A Freedman's Wedding," 1866, in *Household Reading: Selections from the Congregationalist, 1849–1866* (Boston: Galen James and Co., 1867).

116. U.S. censuses, 1870, 1880; unless otherwise noted information in the following paragraphs comes from those records.

117. On Edward R. Dudley and his daughter Sarah Dudley Pettey, see Gilmore, *Gender and Jim Crow*, 1–29.

118. Emma Harris reported in the 1900 census that she and Israel had been married for 23 years and that she had 7 children living out of 18.

119. Isaac C. Rue, Will, CCWB E:244. In 1860 Edward owned part of lot #333 on Queen Street, valued at $300, while Isaac owned half of lot #332 on Johnson Street, worth $200. The Craven County Tax Book of 1874 (Tryon Palace) listed Rue as owning

part of lot #332, valued at $250, and lot #32 on Queen Street in Dryboro, valued at $50. His will identified the Johnson Street property as his home and that on Queen as "adjoining the lot whereon Daniel Harris now lives." Edward A. Richardson appears in the NBCD (1880) but not in the U.S. census of 1880.

120. Watson, *A History of New Bern*, 575–76. *New Bern Commercial News*, October 25 and 26, 1881. N. [Nancy] J. Scott was a teacher at the normal school and later George White's second wife. Justeson, *George Henry White*, 53–56.

121. U.S. censuses, 1870, 1880; Gilmore, *Gender and Jim Crow*.

122. Oleana Pegram Atkins's death certificate stated that she was born in Charlotte to one Fanny Howz but did not identify her father, thus leaving unclear her relationship to Kate or John Randolph. A building at Winston-Salem State University is named in her honor.

123. Hannah Neale to Gracy Green, August 4, 1864, registered September 10, 1866 (CCDB 67:364), and Joseph Green and Gracy Green to Hannah C. Brown, September 9, 1866, registered September 10, 1866 (CCDB 67:366). Tucker, Rue, and Hood witnessed the second deed, which also gave Grace and Joseph life estates in the property. The property eventually descended to Grace's granddaughters Alice and Melissa Harris, presumably Hannah Cora's children.

124. CCDB, CCW, CCEP.

125. *Christian Recorder*, January 15, 1885.

126. Israel B. Abbott and William O. Randolph, Estates Papers, CCEP.

127. John Randolph Jr., Estates Papers, CCEP.

128. See *Gray's New Map of New Bern, Craven County, North Carolina* (ca. 1880), NCA&H, for a vivid illustration of racial distribution.

129. Locations from NBCD (1880) and Sandbeck, *The Historic Architecture of New Bern*.

130. Despite the loss of most of the nineteenth-century buildings in these areas to fire and urban renewal, a few houses of the postwar years still stand. See Hanchett and Little, *The History and Architecture of Long Wharf and Greater Duffyfield*, and Sandbeck, *The Historic Architecture of New Bern*. Further research may identify the owners or occupants of the few nineteenth-century buildings that survive. The process is complicated by the fact that many of the surviving houses have been moved or greatly altered or both.

131. The 1880 census listed George and Fannie White on Pasteur Street. NBCD (1880) listed White's residence at the corner of Primrose and Jenkins Alley. The 1887 Craven County Tax List (NCA&H) noted him with property on both Pasteur and Primrose streets.

132. U.S. census, 1900. See also NBCD (1893) and NBCD (1904).

133. *New Bern Daily Journal*, June 30, 1897.

134. Allen G. Oden, Estates Papers, CCEP. The sixteen-shooter used during the Civil War was followed by an improved repeating rifle, the famed Winchester rifle.

135. *New Bern Daily Journal*, September 30, 1894.

136. Ibid., September 6, 1892.

137. On politics in this period, see Crow, Escott, and Hatley, *A History of African Americans in North Carolina*, 95–118.

138. Virgil A. Crawford served for 17 years as councilman until he was defeated in May 1890 by Mustipher P. Holly. Crawford was reelected in 1891, 1892, 1893, and 1894. In 1896 a contretemps developed among competing groups of aldermen, whose members included Virgil A. Crawford and Cicero Robbins, but it is not clear which candidates finally won seats. John B. Green III to author, emails, October 2012.

139. Charles C. Pettey, *Raleigh Gazette*, August 28, 1897, quoted in Gilmore, *Gender and Jim Crow*, 78.

140. See Gilmore, *Gender and Jim Crow*, 78–82, on black New Bernians and other North Carolinians in the Spanish-American War.

141. *New Bern Daily Journal*, May 29–31, 1898; Watson, *A History of New Bern*, 489.

142. Gilmore, *Gender and Jim Crow*, 88, 94.

143. Raleigh *News and Observer*, September 18, 1898, quoted in Hanchett and Little, *The History and Architecture of Long Wharf and Greater Duffyfield*, 13.

144. Broadside entitled "Negro Rule in Craven County" [1898], North Carolina Collection, University of North Carolina at Chapel Hill; Watson, *A History of New Bern*, 488–99; quote, 488.

145. On Smith, see Edmonds, *The Negro in Fusion Politics*, 106–8.

146. Watson, *A History of New Bern*, 492; "George Henry White," *DNCB*.

147. Watson, *A History of New Bern*, 493–95. Elected from the Fifth Ward in 1899 were Thomas McCarthy and J. J. Moseley, and from the Sixth, J. T. York and W. H. Johnson. Elected from the Fifth Ward in May 1901 were McCarthy and N. J. Cobb, and from the Sixth, again J. T. York and W. H. Johnson. (Except for York's, I have not been able to identify these men's occupations with certainty in the 1900 census.) Their terms ended in May 1903. New Bern Town Council Minutes, 1890–1908, NCA&H (microfilm). Vol. 8: 99–238.

148. See Gilmore, *Gender and Jim Crow*, 119–26, for a concise explanation of the disfranchisement amendment, which took effect in 1902. If all the blacks who had white ancestors or free black ancestors who voted before 1867 had used this provision, black registration in 1902–8 would have been much higher than it was.

149. *New Bern Daily Journal*, January 2, 1900, cited in Watson, *A History of New Bern*, 495.

150. *New Bern Daily Journal*, March 13, 1900, cited in Watson, *A History of New Bern*, 496. James Augustus Bryan (see *DNCB*), a son of attorney James West Bryan and a nephew of John Herritage Bryan, served in the Confederate army and after the war owned large amounts of property. He was president of the Atlantic and North Carolina Railroad Company and the National Bank of New Bern. See Mobley, *James City*, on Bryan's relationship with James City, which was located on land he acquired through his wife, Mary Spaight Shepard, a descendant of Governor Richard Dobbs Spaight Sr.

151. Watson, *A History of New Bern*, 498. William E. Clarke was the son of attorney William J. Clarke, who died in 1886 (*DNCB*). He attributed the Democratic victory and

ratification of the disfranchisement amendment directly to his townsman Furnifold Simmons and called upon "a just God in heaven who will exact a strict account of him."

152. The Raleigh *News and Observer* estimated on November 4, 1902, from reports from Democrats, that after the amendment took effect in 1902, only 4.6 percent of black men in North Carolina registered to vote. Gilmore, *Gender and Jim Crow*, 125.

153. Craven County Election Records, NCA&H. The Craven County registration lists did not identify voters by race; they did include several members of the Godett(e) and George families, names associated with longtime free people of color in rural Craven County.

154. George H. White, *Defense of the Negro Race: Charges Answered* (Washington, D.C.: [Government Printing Office], 1901), quoted in Gilmore, *Gender and Jim Crow*, 117. See Sandbeck, *The Historic Architecture of New Bern*, 286, on White's sale of his house on Johnson Street in 1903, by which time White was residing in Washington, D.C. White was the last black congressman until 1928, the last from the South until 1972, and the last from North Carolina until 1992 (Crow, Escott, and Hatley, *A History of African Americans in North Carolina*, 211).

155. Justeson, *George Henry White*, 311.

156. Gilmore, *Gender and Jim Crow*, 142–43.

157. *New Bern Weekly Journal*, July 22, 1904.

158. *New Bern Daily Journal*, August 5 and 16, 1906.

159. *New Bern Weekly Journal*, July 22, 1904.

Bibliography

Web Sites

http://docsouth.unc.edu/ (*Documenting the American South*. Includes published and unpublished documents posted by the University of North Carolina at Chapel Hill)

http://ncarchitects.lib.ncsu.edu/ (*North Carolina Architects and Builders: A Biographical Dictionary*. Includes biographical information, searchable by location and name, for several black artisans in New Bern. An original digital publication of North Carolina State University Libraries, Raleigh)

http://newbern.cpclib.org/research/resources.html (Includes primary materials from multiple sources, including NCA&H, transcribed and posted by the New Bern–Craven County Public Library, New Bern)

http://www.hpo.ncdcr.gov/NR-PDFs.html. (Includes National Register of Historic Places nominations for North Carolina. Original nomination forms are at the National Park Service, Washington, D.C., and copies and supplementary materials are at the State Historic Preservation Office, Office of Archives and History, Department of Cultural Resources, Raleigh.)

Original Government Documents Accessible on the Web via Ancestry.com (http://www.ancestry.com)

Freedman's Bank Records

Military and Pension Records

North Carolina Death Records

North Carolina Marriage Records

United States Censuses, Manuscript Population Schedules, and Slave Schedules, 1790–1910

Manuscripts and Archival Material

Amherst, Massachusetts

Special Collections and University Archives, W. E. B. Du Bois Library, University of Massachusetts Amherst

Edward W. Kinsley Papers

Chapel Hill, North Carolina

Southern Historical Collection, University of North Carolina Library

Cameron Family Papers

John R. Donnell Letter and Account Book, Bryan Family Papers

Henry Alderson Ellison Papers
William Gaston Papers
Durham, North Carolina
David M. Rubenstein Rare Book and Manuscript Library, Duke University
Charles N. Hunter Scrapbooks, Charles N. Hunter Papers.
Greenville, North Carolina
East Carolina University Library Special Collections
John H. Bryan Papers
Elizabeth Moore Collection
New Bern, North Carolina
Craven County Courthouse
Craven County Will Books
Craven County Register of Deeds Office
Craven County Deed Books
Kellenberger Room, New Bern–Craven County Public Library
Christ Episcopal Church, New Bern, Parish Register (photocopy of original at Christ Church, New Bern)
Greenwood Cemetery Burial Records, microfilm
Greenwood Cemetery Gravestone Records, microfilm
New Bern Tax Lists, 1860–72, broken series
New Bern City Hall
New Bern Town Council Minutes, 1797–1828
Tryon Palace Historic Sites and Gardens, Carraway Library
Craven County Tax Books, 1849, 1874, 1899
Raleigh, North Carolina
North Carolina State Archives
Badger-Cogdell Family Bible, transcript, John D. Whitford Collection (whereabouts of original unknown)
John Herritage Bryan Collection
Chowan County Records
Colonial Governors' Papers, Box 8
Craven County Records: Apprentice Bonds and Records, Civil Actions Papers, Court Records, Deeds, Election Returns, Estates Papers, Miscellaneous Records, Ships and Merchants Shipping Records (1830–31), Slaves and Free Negroes File, Tax List (1887), Treasurer of Public Building Accounts, Voting Records, Wills
Graham Daves Collection
Edward Graham Collection
Hollister Account Book, microfilm
Legislative Petitions, General Assembly Records
New Bern Town Council Minutes, broken series
Pettigrew Family Papers
Slave Collection

Treasurer's and Comptroller's Papers
Craven County Tax Lists, 1815, County Settlements with the State, Tax Lists, NCA&H (microfilm), at http://newbern.cpclib.org/research/tax/1815tax.htm. February 10, 2013
John D. Whitford Papers
Winston-Salem, North Carolina
Museum of Early Southern Decorative Arts
Research Files

Frequently Cited Newspapers and Periodicals

Anglo-African
Christian Recorder
Star of Zion
New Bern, North Carolina: various newspapers, on microfilm, Kellenberger Room, New Bern–Craven County Library, New Bern, and North Carolina State Archives, Raleigh. (The city name was variously spelled in the titles of these newspapers, as elsewhere, New Berne, Newbern, Newberne, and New Bern.)

Published Primary Sources:
Travelers' Accounts, Memoirs, Directories, Records of Conventions

Andrews, Sidney. *The South since the War: As Shown by Fourteen Weeks of Travel and Observation in Georgia and the Carolinas*. Boston: Ticknor and Fields, 1866.
Bergeron, Paul H., ed. *The Papers of Andrew Johnson*. Vol. 8, *May–August, 1865*. Knoxville: University of Tennessee Press, 1989.
Business Directory of the City of New Berne, N.C.: To Which is Added Historical and Statistical Matter of Interest. Raleigh: Edwards and Broughton, 1893.
Chas. Emerson and Co.'s Newbern Directory, 1880–1881. Raleigh: Edwards, Broughton, 1880. Reprint, Charleston, S.C.: BiblioLife, 2009.
Colyer, Vincent. *Brief Report of the Services Rendered by the Freed People to the United States Army, in North Carolina*. New York: Vincent Colyer, 1864. Eastern North Carolina Digital Library, http://digital.lib.ecu.edu/historyfiction/fullview.aspx?id=cob. January 20, 2010.
Convention of the Freedmen of North Carolina. Official Proceedings. [Raleigh]: n. p., 1865.
Dennett, John Richard. *The South as It Is: 1865–1866*. Edited and with an introduction by Henry M. Christman. New York: Viking, 1965.
Douglass, Frederick. *The Life and Times of Frederick Douglass, Written by Himself: His early life as a slave, his escape from bondage, and his complete history*. 1892. Reprint, New York: Dover Publications, 2003.
Fries, Adelaide L., Douglas LeTell Rights, Minnie J. Smith, and Kenneth G. Hamilton, eds. *Records of the Moravians in North Carolina*. 11 vols. Raleigh: North Carolina Historical Commission, 1922-69.
Green, John P. *Fact Stranger than Fiction: Seventy-Five Years of a Busy Life, with*

Reminiscences of Many Great and Good Men and Women. Cleveland: Riehl Printing, 1920. Documenting the American South. University Library, University of North Carolina at Chapel Hill, http://docsouth.unc.edu/southlit/greenfact/green.html. March 23, 2010; June 20, 2012.

Hatch, Isaiah Prophet. *An Autobiography of I. P. Hatch of New Bern, N.C.; and an Early History of Craven, Jones, Pamlico, Carteret and Lenoir Counties*. New Bern, n.d., ca. 1923.

Hood, James Walker. *One Hundred Years of the African Methodist Episcopal Zion Church; or, The Centennial of African Methodism*. New York: A.M.E. Zion Book Concern, 1895. Documenting the American South. University Library, University of North Carolina at Chapel Hill, http://docsouth.unc.edu/church/hood100/menu.html. April 10, 2010.

———. *Sketch of the Early History of the African Methodist Episcopal Zion Church*. Charlotte, N.C.: A.M.E. Zion Publishing House, 1914. Documenting the American South. University Library, University of North Carolina at Chapel Hill, http://docsouth.unc.edu/church/hood/. January 31, 2013.

James, Horace. *Annual Report of the Superintendent of Negro Affairs in North Carolina, 1864*. Boston: W. F. Brown, 1865.

Lemmon, Sarah McCulloh, ed. *The Pettigrew Papers*. 2 vols. Raleigh: North Carolina Department of Cultural Resources, Division of Archives and History, 1971, 1988.

Miller, Stephen F. "Recollections of Newbern fifty years ago." In *Our Living and Our Dead*, vol. 1, no. 4. Raleigh: N.C. Branch [of] the Southern Historical Society, 1874, http://digital.lib.ecu.edu/historyfiction/fullview.aspx?id=mir. January 17, 2012.

Minutes of the Freedmen's Convention, Held in the City of Raleigh, on the 2nd, 3rd, 4th, and 5th of October, 1866. Raleigh: Standard Book and Job Office, 1866.

New Bern, N.C. Directory, 1904–1905. Richmond: Hill Directory Company, 1904, via Ancestry.com.

Newton, A. H. *Out of the Briars: An Autobiography and Sketch of the Twenty-ninth Regiment Connecticut Volunteers*. N.p.: privately published, 1910. Reprint, Miami, Fla.: Mnemosyne Reprinting, 1969.

Proceedings and Debates of the Convention of North Carolina, Called to Amend the Constitution of the State, Which Assembled at Raleigh, June 4, 1835. Raleigh: Joseph Gales and Son, 1836.

Reid, Whitelaw. *After the War: A Tour of the Southern States, 1865–1866*. New York: Howard and Hulbert, 1880.

Singleton, William Henry. *Recollections of My Slavery Days*. Peekskill, N.Y.: Highland Democrat, 1922. Documenting the American South. University Library, University of North Carolina at Chapel Hill, http://docsouth.unc.edu/neh/singleton/. January 31, 2012.

Stanly, Edward. *A Military Governor Among Abolitionists: A Letter from Edward Stanly to Charles Sumner*. New York: privately published, 1865, http://www.archive.org/details/militarygovernoroostan. November 2, 2011.

Whitford, John D. "Bits of History" and "Historical Reminiscences," *New Bern Daily Journal* (1880s) and *New Bern Weekly Journal* (1900–1905), posted at http://newbern.cpclib.org/research/whitford/index.htm. April 12, 2013.

Wilkerson, Elizabeth Vass, ed. *Diary of Rev. L. C. Vass, Chaplain, Stonewall Brigade.* Laurens, S.C.: privately published, 2008.

Published and Unpublished Secondary Sources

Alexander, Roberta Sue. *North Carolina Faces the Freedmen: Race Relations during Presidential Reconstruction, 1865–1867.* Durham: Duke University Press, 1985.

Anderson, Eric. *Race and Politics in North Carolina, 1872–1901: The Black Second.* Baton Rouge: Louisiana State University Press, 1981.

Balanoff, Elizabeth. "Negro Legislators in the North Carolina General Assembly, July, 1868–February, 1872." *North Carolina Historical Review* 49, no. 1 (January 1972): 22–55.

Barnes, L. Diane. *Artisan Workers in the Upper South: Petersburg, Virginia, 1820–1865.* Baton Rouge: Louisiana State University Press, 2008.

Barrett, John G. *The Civil War in North Carolina.* Chapel Hill: University of North Carolina Press, 1963.

Bassett, John Spencer. *Slavery and Servitude in the Colony of North Carolina.* Baltimore: Johns Hopkins University Press, 1896. Reprint, [Whitefish, Mont.]: Kessinger Publishing, n.d.

———. *Slavery in the State of North Carolina.* Baltimore: Johns Hopkins University Press, 1899. Reprint, New York: AMS Press, 1972.

Berlin, Ira. *The Making of African America: The Four Great Migrations.* New York: Viking, 2010.

———. *Slaves without Masters: The Free Negro in the Antebellum South.* New York: Pantheon Books, 1975. 2nd edition, New York: New Press, 2007.

Berlin, Ira, and Herbert G. Gutman. "Natives and Immigrants, Free Men and Slaves: Urban Workingmen in the Antebellum American South." *American Historical Review* 88 (December 1983): 1175–1200.

Bishir, Catherine W. "Black Builders in Antebellum North Carolina." *North Carolina Historical Review* 61, no. 4 (October 1984): 422–61. Reprinted in Catherine W. Bishir, *Southern Built: American Architecture, Regional Practice.* Charlottesville: University of Virginia Press, 2006.

———. "Jacob W. Holt, an American Builder." *Winterthur Portfolio* 16, no. 1 (Spring 1981): 1–32. Reprinted in Catherine W. Bishir, *Southern Built: American Architecture, Regional Practice.* Charlottesville: University of Virginia Press, 2006.

———. *North Carolina Architecture.* Chapel Hill: University of North Carolina Press, 1990.

———. "Philadelphia Bricks for New Bern Jail." *APT Bulletin* (Association for Preservation Technology) 10, no. 4 (Spring, 1977): 62–66. Reprinted in Catherine W. Bishir, *Southern Built: American Architecture, Regional Practice.* Charlottesville: University of Virginia Press, 2006.

Bishir, Catherine W., Charlotte V. Brown, Carl R. Lounsbury, and Ernest H. Wood III. *Architects and Builders in North Carolina: A History of the Practice of Building.* Chapel Hill: University of North Carolina Press, 1990.

Bivins, John, Jr. *The Furniture of Coastal North Carolina.* Winston-Salem and Chapel Hill: Published by the Museum of Early Southern Decorative Arts and distributed by the University of North Carolina Press, 1988.

Blassingame, John W. *Black New Orleans, 1860–1880.* Chicago: University of Chicago Press, 1973; Phoenix edition, 1976.

Bogger, Tommy L. *Free Blacks in Norfolk, Virginia, 1799–1860: The Darker Side of Freedom.* Charlottesville: University Press of Virginia, 1997.

Brasher, Glenn David. *The Peninsula Campaign and the Necessity of Emancipation: African Americans and the Fight for Freedom.* Chapel Hill: University of North Carolina Press, 2012.

Brewer, James Howard. "Legislation Designed to Control Slavery in Wilmington and Fayetteville." *North Carolina Historical Review* 30, no. 2 (April 1953): 155–66.

Brickell, John. *The Natural History of North-Carolina.* Dublin: James Carson, 1737. Reprint, Murfreesboro, N.C.: Johnson Publishing Company, 1968.

Bridenbaugh, Carl. *The Colonial Craftsman.* Chicago: University of Chicago Press, 1961.

"Brief History of the Founding of Rue Chapel A. M. E. Church, 1865, by George A. Rue," undated typescript by "Church Secretary, Rue Chapel A. M. E. Church, New Bern, N.C."

Bristol, Douglas Walter, Jr. *Knights of the Razor: Black Barbers in Slavery and Freedom.* Baltimore: Johns Hopkins University Press, 2009.

Brodhead, Richard, ed. *The Journals of Charles W. Chesnutt.* Durham: Duke University Press, 1993.

Browning, Judkin. *Shifting Loyalties: The Union Occupation of Eastern North Carolina.* Chapel Hill: University of North Carolina Press, 2011.

———. "Visions of Freedom and Civilization Opening before Them: African Americans Search for Autonomy during Military Occupation in North Carolina." In *Struggles over Change: North Carolinians in the Era of the Civil War and Reconstruction,* edited by Paul D. Escott, 69–100. Chapel Hill: University of North Carolina Press, 2008.

Brundage, W. Fitzhugh. *The Southern Past: A Clash of Race and Memory.* Cambridge: Belknap Press of Harvard University Press, 2005.

Byrd, William L., III. *Against the Peace and Dignity of the State: North Carolina Laws Regarding Slaves, Free Persons of Color, and Indians.* Westminster, Md.: Heritage Books, 2007.

———. *In Full Force and Virtue: North Carolina Emancipation Records, 1713–1860.* Westminster, Md.: Heritage Books, 2007.

Carll-White, Mary Allison. "The Role of the Black Artisan in the Building Trades and the Decorative Arts in South Carolina's Charleston District, 1760–1800." Ph.D. diss., University of Tennessee, 1982.

Carraway, Gertrude S. *Crown of Life: History of Christ Church, New Bern, N.C., 1715–1940*. New Bern: Owen G. Dunn, Publisher, 1940.

Carter, Wilmoth. *The Urban Negro in the South*. New York: Vantage Press, 1962.

Cecelski, David S. *The Fire of Freedom: Abraham Galloway and the Slaves' Civil War.* Chapel Hill: University of North Carolina Press, 2012.

———. "A Radical and Jacobinical Spirit: Abraham Galloway and the Struggle for Freedom in the Maritime South." In David S. Cecelski, *The Waterman's Song: Slavery and Freedom in Maritime North Carolina*. Chapel Hill: University of North Carolina Press, 2001.

Clark, Kathleen Ann. *Defining Moments: African American Commemoration and Political Culture in the South, 1863*. Chapel Hill: University of North Carolina Press, 2005.

Craig, James H. *The Arts and Crafts in North Carolina*. Winston-Salem: Museum of Early Southern Decorative Arts, 1965.

Crow, Jeffrey J. *The Black Experience in Revolutionary North Carolina*. Raleigh: North Carolina Department of Cultural Recources, Division of Archives and History, 1977.

Crow, Jeffrey J., Paul D. Escott, and Flora J. Hatley. *A History of African Americans in North Carolina*. Raleigh: North Carolina Department of Cultural Resources, Division of Archives and History, 2002.

Curry, Leonard P. *The Free Black in Urban America 1800–1850: The Shadow of the Dream*. Chicago: University of Chicago Press, 1981.

Davis, Russell H. *Black Americans in Ohio's City of Cleveland: George Peake, the First Black Settler, to Carl Stokes, the First Black Mayor.* Washington, D.C.: Associated Publishers for the Association for the Study of Negro Life and History in cooperation with the Western Reserve Historical Society, 1972; reprint, 1985.

Degler, Carl N. *The Other South: Southern Dissenters in the Nineteenth Century*, 1974. Reprint, Gainesville: University Press of Florida, 2000.

Dennett, John Richard. *The South as It Is: 1865–1866*. New York: Viking Press, 1965.

Dickerson, Dennis C. "George A. Rue: Missionary Minister in New England & North Carolina." *The A. M. E. Church Review* 117, no. 381 (January–March 2001): 46–54.

Dill, Alonzo Thomas, Jr. "Public Buildings in Craven County." *North Carolina Historical Review* 20, no. 4 (October 1943): 301–26.

Du Bois, William E. Burghardt. *The Negro Artisan*. Atlanta: Atlanta University Press, 1902. Reprint, Charleston, S.C.: BiblioLife, n.d.

Edmonds, Helen. *The Negro in Fusion Politics in North Carolina, 1894–1901*. Chapel Hill: University of North Carolina Press, 1951.

Egerton, Douglas R. *Gabriel's Rebellion: The Virginia Slave Conspiracies of 1800 and 1802*. Chapel Hill: University of North Carolina Press, 1993.

Escott, Paul D. *Many Excellent People: Power and Privilege in North Carolina, 1850–1900*. Chapel Hill: University of North Carolina Press, 1985.

———, ed. *North Carolinians in the Era of the Civil War and Reconstruction*. Chapel Hill: University of North Carolina Press, 2008.

Evans, W. McKee. *Ballots and Fence Rails: Reconstruction on the Lower Cape Fear.* 2nd edition. New York: Norton Library, 1974.

Farlow, Gale. "Black Craftsmen in North Carolina." *North Carolina Genealogical Society Journal* 11, no. 1 (February 1985): 2–13, and no. 2 (May 1985): 91–103.

Fields, Barbara J. "Ideology and Race in American History." In *Region, Race, and Reconstruction: Essays in Honor of C. Vann Woodward*, edited by J. Morgan Kousser and James M. McPherson, 143–77. New York: Oxford University Press, 1982.

Foner, Eric. *Freedom's Lawmakers: A Directory of Black Officeholders during Reconstruction*. Revised edition. Baton Rouge: Louisiana State University Press, 1996.

———. *Reconstruction: America's Unfinished Revolution, 1863–1877.* New York: Harper and Row, 1988. Paperback edition, Perennial Classics, 2002.

Franklin, John Hope. *The Free Negro in North Carolina, 1790–1860*. Chapel Hill: University of North Carolina Press, 1943.

———. "James Boon, Free Negro Artisan." *Journal of Negro History* 30 (April 1945): 150–80. Reprinted in John Hope Franklin, *Race and History: Selected Essays, 1938–1988*, 206–26. Baton Rouge: Louisiana State University Press, 1989.

———. *Reconstruction after the Civil War.* Chicago: University of Chicago Press, 1961, reprint, 1994.

Garrison, J. Ritchie. *Two Carpenters: Architecture and Building in Early New England, 1799–1859*. Knoxville: University of Tennessee Press, 2006.

Gatewood, Willard B. *Aristocrats of Color: The Black Elite, 1880–1920*. Bloomington: Indiana University Press, 1991. Reprint, Fayetteville: University of Arkansas Press, 2000.

Gavins, Raymond. "The Meaning of Freedom: Black North Carolina in the Nadir." In *Race, Class, and Politics in Southern History: Essays in Honor of Robert F. Durden*, edited by Jeffrey J. Crow, Paul D. Escott, and Charles L. Flynn Jr., 175–215. Baton Rouge: Louisiana State University Press, 1989.

Gilje, Paul A. "Introduction: Identity and Independence. The American Artisan, 1750–1850." In *American Artisans: Crafting Social Identity, 1750–1850*, edited by Howard B. Rock, Paul A. Gilje, and Robert Asher, xi–xx. Baltimore: Johns Hopkins University Press, 1995.

Gillespie, Michele. *Free Labor in an Unfree World: White Artisans in Slaveholding Georgia, 1789–1860*. Athens: University of Georgia Press, 2000, 2004.

———. "Planters in the Making: Artisanal Opportunity in Georgia, 1790–1830." In *American Artisans: Crafting Social Identity, 1750–1850*, edited by Howard B. Rock, Paul A. Gilje, and Robert Asher, 33–47. Baltimore: Johns Hopkins University Press, 1995.

Gilmore, Glenda Elizabeth. *Gender and Jim Crow: Women and the Politics of White Supremacy in North Carolina, 1896–1920*. Chapel Hill: University of North Carolina Press, 1996.

Goldfield, David. *Region, Race, and Cities: Interpreting the Urban South*. Baton Rouge: Louisiana State University Press, 1997.

Gould, William B., IV. *Diary of a Contraband: The Civil War Passage of a Black Sailor.* Stanford: Stanford University Press, 2002.

Green, John Burgwyn, III. *Methodist Meeting House: The Early History of Centenary United Methodist Church, New Bern, North Carolina.* New Bern: privately published, 2002.

———. *A New Bern Album: Old Photographs of New Bern, North Carolina, and the Surrounding Countryside.* New Bern: The Tryon Palace Commission, 1985.

Greenwood, Janette Thomas. *Bittersweet Legacy: The Black and White "Better Classes" in Charlotte, 1850–1910.* Chapel Hill: University of North Carolina Press, 1994.

———. *First Fruits of Freedom: The Migration of Former Slaves and Their Search for Equality in Worcester, Massachusetts, 1862–1900.* Chapel Hill: University of North Carolina Press, 2009.

Hahn, Steven. *A Nation under Our Feet: Black Political Struggles in the Rural South from Slavery to the Great Migration.* Cambridge: Belknap Press of Harvard University Press, 2003.

Haley, John H. *Charles N. Hunter and Race Relations in North Carolina.* Chapel Hill: University of North Carolina Press, 1987.

Hamilton, J. G. de Roulhac. *Reconstruction in North Carolina.* Columbia University Studies in History, Economics and Public Law, vol. 58, no. 141. New York: Columbia University, 1914. Reprint, Gloucester, Mass.: Peter Smith, 1964.

Hanchett, Thomas W. *Sorting Out the New South City: Race, Class, and Urban Development in Charlotte, 1875–1975.* Chapel Hill: University of North Carolina Press, 1998.

Hanchett, Thomas W., and M. Ruth Little. *The History and Architecture of Long Wharf and Greater Duffyfield: African American Neighborhoods in New Bern, North Carolina. A Report Prepared for the City of New Bern Historic Preservation Commission.* New Bern: City of New Bern Historic Preservation Commission, 1994.

Heinegg, Paul. "Free African Americans of Virginia, North Carolina, South Carolina, Maryland and Delaware," http://freeafricanamericans.com/. March 21, 2010.

Herzog, Lynda Vestal. "The Early Architecture of New Bern, North Carolina, 1750–1850." Ph.D. diss., University of California, Los Angeles, 1977.

Hildebrand, Reginald F. *The Times Were Strange and Stirring: Methodist Preachers and the Crisis of Emancipation.* Durham: Duke University Press, 1995.

Hipps, Julie. "Black Builders in New Bern, 1790–1840: The Carpenters and the Masons." Unpublished research paper, 2002. Copy courtesy of Tryon Palace Research Department.

Hirsch, Susan E. *Roots of the American Working Class: The Industrialization of Crafts in Newark, 1800–1860.* Philadelphia: University of Pennsylvania Press, 1978.

Hodes, Martha. *White Women, Black Men: Illicit Sex in the Nineteenth-Century South.* New Haven: Yale University Press, 1997.

Johnson, Guion Griffis. *Ante-Bellum North Carolina: A Social History.* Chapel Hill: University of North Carolina Press, 1937.

Justeson, Benjamin R. *George Henry White: An Even Chance in the Race of Life*. Baton Rouge: Louisiana State University Press, 2012.

Kay, Marvin L. Michael, and Lorin Lee Cary. *Slavery in North Carolina, 1748–1775*. Chapel Hill: University of North Carolina Press, 1995.

Kenzer, Robert C. *Enterprising Southerners: Black Economic Success in North Carolina, 1865–1915*. Charlottesville: University Press of Virginia, 1997.

Kimball, Gregg D. *American City, Southern Place: A Cultural History of Antebellum Richmond*. Athens: University of Georgia Press, 2000.

Koger, Larry. *Black Slaveowners: Free Black Slave Masters in South Carolina, 1790–1860*. Jefferson, N.C.: McFarland, 1985. Reprint, Columbia: University of South Carolina Press, 1995.

Lebsock, Suzanne. *The Free Women of Petersburg: Status and Culture in a Southern Town, 1784–1860*. New York: W. W. Norton and Company, 1984.

Logan, Frenise A. "Black and Republican: Vicissitudes of a Minority Twice Over in the North Carolina House of Representatives, 1876–1877," *North Carolina Historical Review* 61, no. 3 (July 1984): 311–46.

———. *The Negro in North Carolina, 1876–1894*. Chapel Hill: University of North Carolina Press, 1964.

Lounsbury, Carl R. *Essays in Early American Architectural History: A View from the Chesapeake*. Charlottesville: University of Virginia Press, 2011.

———. *An Illustrated Glossary of Early Southern Architecture and Landscape*. New York: Oxford University Press, 1994.

———. "The Wild Melody of Steam." In Catherine W. Bishir, Charlotte V. Brown, Carl R. Lounsbury, and Ernest H. Wood III. *Architects and Builders in North Carolina: A History of the Practice of Building*, 193–239. Chapel Hill: University of North Carolina Press, 1990.

Marshall, Patricia Phillips, and Jo Ramsay Leimenstoll. *Thomas Day: Master Craftsman and Free Man of Color*. Chapel Hill: University of North Carolina Press, 2010.

Martin, Jonathan D. *Divided Mastery: Slave Hiring in the American South*. Cambridge, Massachusetts: Harvard University Press, 2004.

Martin, Sandy Dwayne. *For God and Race: The Religious and Political Leadership of AMEZ Bishop James Walker Hood*. Columbia: University of South Carolina Press, 1999.

McGuire, Samuel B. "The Making of a Black Militia Company: New Bern Troops in the Kirk-Holden War, 1870." *North Carolina Historical Review*, forthcoming.

Mobley, Joe A. *James City: A Black Community in North Carolina, 1863–1900*. Raleigh: North Carolina Department of Cultural Resources, Division of Archives and History, 1981.

Munson, Barry. *1814–1818*. Vol. 1 of *Citizens of Craven County North Carolina and Vicinity*. Privately published, 2006.

Parker, Freddie L. *Running for Freedom: Slave Runaways in North Carolina, 1775–1840*. New York: Garland Publishing, 1993.

——. *Stealing a Little Freedom: Advertisements for Slave Runaways in North Carolina, 1791–1840*. New York: Garland Publishing, 1994.
Powell, William S., ed. *Dictionary of North Carolina Biography.* 6 vols. Chapel Hill: University of North Carolina Press, 1979–96.
Powers, Bernard E., Jr. *Black Charlestonians: A Social History, 1822–1885*. Fayetteville: University of Arkansas Press, 1994.
Reaves, William M. *"Strength through Struggle": The Chronological and Historical Record of the African-American Community in Wilmington, North Carolina, 1865–1950*. Edited by Beverly Tetterton. Wilmington: New Hanover County Public Library, 1998.
Reid, Richard M. *Freedom for Themselves: North Carolina's Black Soldiers in the Civil War Era*. Chapel Hill: University of North Carolina Press, 2008.
——. "Raising the African Brigade: Early Black Recruitment in Civil War North Carolina." *North Carolina Historical Review* 70, no. 3 (July 1993): 266–301.
"The Reminiscences of Samuel J. Battle." Transcript of interview by Patrolman John Kelly. February 1960. The Oral History Collection of Columbia University, Columbia University Oral History Office, New York. Partially posted at http://c250.columbia.edu/c250_celebrates/harlem_history/battle.html. April 5, 2011.
Rock, Howard B., Paul A. Gilje, and Robert Asher, eds. *American Artisans: Crafting Social Identity, 1750–1850*. Baltimore: Johns Hopkins University Press, 1995.
Rockman, Seth. *Scraping By: Wage Labor, Slavery, and Survival in Early Baltimore.* Baltimore: Johns Hopkins University Press, 2009.
Rose, Willie Lee. *Rehearsal for Reconstruction: The Port Royal Experiment*. New York: Bobbs-Merrill, 1964. Reprint, New York: Oxford University Press, 1976.
Sandbeck, Peter B. *The Historic Architecture of New Bern and Craven County, North Carolina*. New Bern: Tryon Palace Commission, 1988.
Saunders, William L., ed. *The Colonial Records of North Carolina*. 10 vols. Raleigh: P. M. Hale, Printer to the State, 1886–90.
Schweninger, Loren. *Black Property Owners in the South, 1790–1915*. Urbana: University of Illinois Press, 1990; Illini Books edition, 1997.
——. "John Carruthers Stanly and the Anomaly of Black Slaveholding." *North Carolina Historical Review* 47, no. 2 (April 1990): 159–92.
Sherrill, Josephine Price. "A Negro School-Master of the 1870's." *Journal of Negro History* 30, no. 2 (Spring 1961): 163–72.
Sidbury, James. *Ploughshares into Swords: Race, Rebellion, and Identity in Gabriel's Virginia, 1730–1810*. Cambridge and New York: Cambridge University Press, 1997.
——. "Slave Artisans in Richmond, Virginia, 1780–1810." In *American Artisans: Crafting Social Identity, 1750–1850*, edited by Howard B. Rock, Paul A. Gilje, and Robert Asher, 48–62. Baltimore: Johns Hopkins University Press, 1995.
Simmons, William J. *Men of Mark: Eminent, Progressive and Rising.* Cleveland: George M. Rewell, 1887. Documenting the American South. University Library, University of North Carolina at Chapel Hill, http://docsouth.unc.edu/neh/simmons/simmons.html. April 10, 2012.

Smith, John David, ed. *Black Soldiers in Blue: African American Troops in the Civil War Era*. Chapel Hill: University of North Carolina Press, 2002.
Stavisky, Leonard. "The Origins of Negro Craftsmanship in Colonial America." *Journal of Negro History* 32 (July 1947): 417–29. Reprinted in James E. Newton and Ronald L. Lewis, eds. *The Other Slaves: Mechanics, Artisans, and Craftsmen*, 183–91. Boston: G. K. Hall, 1978.
Steffen, Charles G. *The Mechanics of Baltimore: Workers and Politics in the Age of Revolution, 1763–1812*. Urbana: University of Illinois Press, 1984.
Takagi, Midori. *"Rearing Wolves to Our Own Destruction": Slavery in Richmond, Virginia, 1782–1865*. Charlottesville: University Press of Virginia, 1999.
Thompson, Robert Farris. *Flash of the Spirit: African and Afro-American Art and Philosophy*. New York: Vintage Books, 1983.
Tolbert, Lisa C. *Constructing Townscapes: Space and Society in Antebellum Tennessee*. Chapel Hill: University of North Carolina Press, 1999.
Tyler-McGraw, Mary. *At the Falls: Richmond, Virginia, and Its People*. Chapel Hill: University of North Carolina Press, 1994.
Upton, Dell. "Pattern Books and Professionalism: Aspects of the Transformation of Domestic Architecture in America, 1800–1860." *Winterthur Portfolio* 19, nos. 2/3 (Summer/Autumn 1984): 107–50.
Vass, L. C. *History of the Presbyterian Church in New Bern, N.C.: With a Resume of Early Ecclesiastical Affairs in Eastern North Carolina, and a Sketch of the Early Days of New Bern, N.C.* Richmond: Whittett and Shepperson, 1886.
Vlach, John Michael. *By the Work of Their Hands: Studies in Afro-American Folklife*. Charlottesville: University Press of Virginia, 1991.
Voorhis, Harold Van Buren. *Negro Masonry in the United States*. New York: Henry Emmerson, [1940]. Reprint, [Whitefish, Mont.]: Kessinger Publishing, 1996.
Wade, Richard. *Slavery in the Cities: The South, 1820–1860*. New York: Oxford University Press, 1964.
Watson, Alan D. *A History of New Bern and Craven County*. New Bern: Tryon Palace Commission, 1987.
Weiss, Ellen. *Robert R. Taylor and Tuskegee: An African American Architect Designs for Booker T. Washington*. Montgomery: New South Books, 2012.
White, Burnetta McGhee. *"Somebody Knows My Name": Marriages of Freed People in North Carolina, County by County*. Athens, Ga.: Privately published, 1995.
Whitford, John D., "The Home Story of a Walking Stick: Early History of the Biblical Recorder and Baptist Church at New Bern, N.C., told in every day talk." New Bern: typescript, 1899. Copy in John D. Whitford Papers, NCA&H.
Wilentz, Sean. *Chants Democratic: New York City and the Rise of the American Working Class, 1788–1850*. 25th anniversary edition. New York: Oxford University Press, 2004.
Wilson, Calvin Dill. "Negroes Who Owned Slaves." *Popular Science Monthly* 81 (November 1912): 483–94.

Wilson, Dreck Spurlock, ed. *African American Architects: A Biographical Dictionary, 1865–1945*. New York: Routledge, 2004.

Windley, Lathan A. *Virginia and North Carolina*. Vol. 1 of *Runaway Slave Advertisements: A Documentary History from the 1730s to 1790*. Westport, Conn.: Greenwood, 1983.

Wood, Peter H. *Black Majority: Negroes in Colonial South Carolina from 1670 through the Stono Rebellion*. New York: W. W. Norton, 1974; paperback edition, 1996.

Woodward, C. Vann. *The Strange Career of Jim Crow*. New York: Oxford University Press, 2002. First published 1955.

Worsley, Stephen C. "Catholicism in Antebellum North Carolina." *North Carolina Historical Review* 55, no. 4 (October 1983): 399–430.

Young, Kevin. *The Grey Album: On the Blackness of Blackness*. Minneapolis: Grey Wolf, 2012.

Acknowledgments

It is a pleasure to recall the many people who have made this book possible. Its history began during research in the 1970s for *Architects and Builders: A History of the Practice of Building* (1990) by Catherine W. Bishir, Charlotte V. Brown, Carl R. Lounsbury, and Ernest Wood III, with research assistance from J. Marshall Bullock and William Bushong. We sought to learn more about the often unsung people who created our state's architecture. Combing records for evidence of architects and building craftsmen uncovered an unexpected wealth of information about black artisans from the colonial period onward. Thanks especially to Marshall Bullock for locating many obscure references. Some of these findings appeared in my article, "Black Builders in Antebellum North Carolina," in 1984, and a smaller portion made its way into *Architects and Builders*. New Bern stood out as the home of several such craftsmen, including the free black plasterer and brickmason Donum Montford.

Twenty years later, I returned to the topic. I wanted to learn more about black artisans of various trades in a single community through time and thus to dig a deeper, narrower hole into the past and concentrate on a smaller cast of characters. New Bern, known for its craft traditions and its strong black history, seemed to be a promising choice. As described below, the support of Kay Williams, director of Tryon Palace Historic Sites and Gardens, and Jeffrey Crow, deputy secretary of Archives and History, Department of Cultural Resources, confirmed the selection. As it has turned out, New Bern's well-documented history and accessible resources provided far more information than I anticipated, and I have learned a far richer story than I ever imagined could be found.

I am happily indebted to the previous research of the many people who have studied New Bern's history, including its African American heritage. Every student of New Bern history owes a debt to two early memoirists: Stephen Miller, who described the town of the 1820s in his "Recollections of Newbern fifty years ago," and John D. Whitford, who recorded his memories of his long life in New Bern as well as interviewing many elderly black and white New Bernians, and published these stories in "Home Story of a Walking Stick" and in the series "Bits of History" and "Historical Reminiscences" that appeared in local newspapers from the early 1880s to 1905.

More recent studies of New Bern include Thomas W. Hanchett and M. Ruth Little, *The History and Architecture of Long Wharf and Greater Duffyfield: African American Neighborhoods in New Bern, North Carolina*; Lynda Vestal Herzog, "The Early Architecture of New Bern, North Carolina, 1750–1850"; Alan D. Watson, *The History of New Bern and Craven County*; Peter B. Sandbeck, *The Historic Architecture of New Bern and Craven County*; and David S. Cecelski, *The Fire of Freedom*.

I am grateful for the patient researchers who have faithfully transcribed and published original documents relevant to New Bern. The Museum of Early Southern Decorative

Arts (MESDA) in Winston-Salem has assembled material on decorative arts and artisans including those in New Bern, much of which appears in James Craig's *Arts and Crafts in North Carolina*. Vital to this project have been Freddie Parker's *Stealing a Little Freedom: Advertisements for Slave Runaways in North Carolina, 1791–1840* and William L. Byrd III's *In Full Force and Virtue: North Carolina Emancipation Records, 1713–1860*. Genealogists and others have transcribed, published, and indexed thousands of local records, especially for the colonial and antebellum periods, and genealogist Eula Pearl Beauchamp accomplished this for the manuscript population schedules of the 1870, 1880, and 1900 United States censuses for Craven County. The web site Ancestry.com, like other similar sources, also makes accessible vast amounts of information transcribed by hundreds of hands and formatted in ways that give access to data and original documents otherwise difficult or impossible to locate; this site has been invaluable to this study, especially in the search for people who left New Bern and would have been impossible to track to their new homes without such research tools. Likewise essential has been the stunning access to information provided by Google and other search engines that have turned up information all across the web and the nation.

Thanks to the institutions that have collected, preserved, and made available New Bern records. These include the Office of Archives and Records in the North Carolina Department of Cultural Resources in Raleigh, the North Carolina Collection and Southern Historical Collection at the University of North Carolina Library in Chapel Hill, and especially relevant for this study, the Kellenberger Room at the New Bern–Craven County Library in New Bern, which collects regional historical materials and makes key records accessible through its web site.

I am also grateful for the generous and knowledgeable help of many friends and colleagues. One of the great pleasures of studying the history of North Carolina is the network of people who willingly share their expertise and lend support to fellow students of that history.

For essential assistance in research I am thankful to John B. Green III and Victor Jones, the librarians at the Kellenberger Room, who have been helpful far beyond the call of duty in finding references in newspapers and elsewhere and in sending me clues they encountered in their own work. John's frequent contributions and patient responses to my queries have been central to this project.

At Archives and History, North Carolina Department of Cultural Resources, thanks go to historians Michael Hill, Josh Howard, and Ansley Wegner of the Research Branch, and to the archivists at the Search Room of the North Carolina State Archives, including Doug Brown, Kim Anderson, Chris Meekins, and the late George Stevenson. At the University of North Carolina in Chapel Hill, thanks to Robert Anthony, Stephen Fletcher, Keith Longetti, Jason Tomberlin, Matt Turi, Tim West, and other staff of the North Carolina Collection and the Southern Historical Collection at the University of North Carolina Library for their assistance in obtaining images. I am grateful to Sally Gant at MESDA and to Justin Eastwood at the University of Tennessee Library for their help in tracking down information at their institutions. In New Bern, I thank Deborah Morefield and Nancy Mansfield for help in obtaining quality photographs of key buildings and

Dean Knight for helping track down records. Thanks to David Cecelski, Robert Kenzer, and Charles Steele for sharing their research materials.

Generous friends have also done me the great favor of reading all or portions of this manuscript and providing encouragement and suggestions that have improved the work, including Betsy Cromley, Jeffrey Crow, Clifton Ellis, Thomas Hanchett, Reginald Hildebrand, Michael Hill, Kim Hoagland, Kate Hutchins, Ruth Little, Carl Lounsbury, Virginia Price, William S. Price, Penne Sandbeck, Peter Sandbeck, Michael Southern, Dell Upton, Camille Wells, Peter Wood, and two anonymous readers for the University of North Carolina Press. I owe special thanks to Penne Sandbeck for her unstinting help in taking photographs and tracking down information and historic photographs and to my friend and colleague Michael Southern for creating the maps that embody his unique sense of history and place.

It is a pleasure and a privilege to work with the University of North Carolina Press. I am grateful for the encouragement, patience, and skills of editor David Perry, a friend through thick and thin for more than twenty-five years, who devoted essential efforts to bringing this book into reality. For this book I also offer my thanks to managing editor Ron Maner, editorial assistant Caitlin Bell-Butterfield, copyeditor Shirley Werner, and designer Heidi Perov, as well as to director of marketing Dino Battista, copywriter Beth Lassiter, director of publicity Regina Mahalek, and director of development Joanna Ruth Marsland. Special thanks go to two New Bern friends of history, Nelson McDaniel and Robert Mattocks, for their roles in enabling *Crafting Lives* to be priced for a wide readership, and to them as well as other donors, listed in the front matter, for their generous contributions.

Two people simply made this project possible from the first glimmer through the completion of the manuscript. When I was trying to develop an idea into a project, Jeffrey Crow of Archives and History not only offered moral support but suggested that the project might fit within the educational goals of New Bern's Tryon Palace Historic Sites and Gardens. Kay Williams, longtime director of Tryon Palace, immediately saw the potential of the project in furthering the institution's mission of broadening knowledge of the importance of people of color in the history of the palace, New Bern, and North Carolina. Working with Jeff and with Freddie Parker, chair of the African American History Advisory Committee of Tryon Palace, Kay lost no time in setting up the project in the autumn of 2006.

Through Kay's efforts, my research was supported by the Wachovia Foundation's funding of Tryon Palace's "One History/Many Stories" project for African American history educational programming and exhibits. The assistance of the Wachovia Foundation, now the Wells Fargo Foundation, is acknowledged with thanks, together with the Tryon Palace Council of Friends and the African American History Advisory Committee of Tryon Palace. I appreciate the wisdom and good company of committee members Sydney Barnwell, Sharon Bryant, Jeffrey Crow, David Dennard, Bernard George, John Haley, Michele Lanier, and Freddie Parker.

Kay showed her usual positive and resourceful creativity and offered guidance, trust, and help from her enthusiasm for the original concept through the subsequent years of research, writing, and revisions. She was always eager to hear news of fresh discoveries, sympathetic at setbacks, and ready to enjoy a good laugh. She and I shared the camaraderie of having been English majors in the 1960s and part of a generation eager to expand the understanding of American history beyond the versions we had grown up with. Although she did not live to see the book published, Kay was delighted to know that the manuscript was accepted by the University of North Carolina Press in September 2012. This book is dedicated to her memory and her legacy of devoted and effective service to the cause of history. Without Kay this book would never have come about.

Finally, I thank John Bishir, who has supported this idea from the beginning, and who has been sounding board, cheerleader, reader of more drafts than imaginable, and my dear companion on visits to New Bern as through life.

Catherine W. Bishir
Raleigh
February 2013

Index

Abbott, Israel Braddock (carpenter), 155, 217, 241, 330 (n. 11), 331 (n. 13); biographical summary, 259–60; in civic organizations, 221–22, 224, 283, 336 (nn. 71, 77), 338 (n. 98); early life, 149–50, 155, 260, 270; family of, 240, 243, 259–60, 285; organizes union, 330 (n. 9); owns real estate, 243; political roles of, 12, 170, 213, 217–19, 260, 265, 283, 289

Abbott, Susan, 240

Abolitionism and abolitionists, 125, 137, 138, 139, 144–45, 267, 271, 286; southern whites' reaction to, 102, 103, 106, 133–35, 136

Abraham (apprentice house carpenter), 52

Abraham (carpenter, shoemaker), 51

Abraham (carpenter), 46

Abram (apprentice cooper), 52

Abram (brother of runaway blacksmith), 64

Abram (cooper), 41

"Address of the Freedmen's Convention to the White and Colored Citizens of North Carolina" (1866), 188–89, 190

African Brigade. *See* U.S. Colored Troops

African Methodist Episcopal (AME) Church, 31, 160, 226. *See also* Rue, George A.; Rue's Chapel AME Church

African Methodist Episcopal Singing School, 226

African Methodist Episcopal Zion (AME Zion) Church, 3, 160, 162, 226; national conference in New Bern, 228. *See also* Andrews Chapel; Clinton Chapel; St. Peter's AME Zion Church

Allen, Abram Moody Russell(brickmason, plasterer): early life and manumission of, 46–47, 54, 72, 73, 74, 88, 89, 279; executor and heir of Donum Montford, 80, 121, 280; takes apprentices, 84; in Washington, N.C., 100, 281, 322 (n. 2)

Allen, Eliza, 126

Allen, Jeremiah N., 320 (n. 118)

Allen, Mary, 126

Alston, William J. (apprentice tailor, minister), 123, 131, 167, 269

America (cooper), 41

American Revolution: black soldiers' service in, 47–48, 188, 190; New Bern leaders in, 23, 70, 71, 76; principles and rhetoric of, invoked by black artisan-leaders, 14, 168, 174, 194; spirit of, related to manumissions, 49, 68, 76, 95, 105

Anderson, W. H., 329 (n. 90)

Andrews, Allen S., 297 (n. 17)

Andrews Chapel (Andrew Chapel; Andrew's Chapel; St. Andrew's Chapel), 27–28, 107, 148, 154 (ill.), 221, 227–28, 229; affiliates with AME Zion, 161–62; leaders at, 110, 149, 159, 160, 240, 260, 264, 270, 286, 287, 288, 290; as political meeting site, 162–63, 166–69, 171, 175, 176, 187, 214, 227, 229; as schoolhouse, 159, 184, 221. *See also* Hood, James Walker; Methodist Meeting House; St. Peter's AME Zion Church

Antislavery sentiment, 25, 49, 133

Apprenticeships, 6, 10, 45, 47, 52–53, 60, 79, 80–83, 98–100, 121–25; apprentice bonds, 81, 121–22, 307 (nn. 112, 120), 315 (n. 60); assigned by courts, 83–84, 121–22; black masters of apprentices, 17, 47, 80, 83–84, 122–23, 198, 199, 122, 212; for free black children, 44–45, 81, 103, 121–23; laws concerning, 81; practices after Civil War, 198–99; for slaves, 52–53, 117; teaching apprentices to read and write, 81, 122; tools given to, 38, 80; white masters of black apprentices, 54, 81–83, 122–23, 198. *See also individual artisans*

Architects, 203, 212. *See also* Eubanks, George C.; Hawks, John; Nichols, William; Paton, David

Architecture, New Bern, 9; antebellum, 112,

114; colonial period, 23; early national period, 24, 42, 58; post–Civil War, 32, 201, 203 ; regional influence of, 44
Artisanal republicanism, 14
Artisan-citizenship, 68–69, 78, 80, 83, 93–96, 135, 219. *See also* Artisan-leaders, black; Voting rights, for North Carolina blacks
Artisan identity: American, 9, 12, 14, 38; among black New Bernians, 15–18, 46, 67
Artisan-leaders, black, 17, 67, 96, 196, 211; church affiliations of, 89–91, 131, 147, 225–28; defend Freedmen's Bureau, 187; form civic and fraternal organizations, 106–7, 173, 185–86, 228–32; form stable families, 235–37; in military roles, 216–17; and North Carolina Freedmen's conventions, 176–83; in occupied New Bern (1862–1865), 55, 152, 155–56, 158, 160, 166, 168; organize tribute to William Gaston, 106–7; political activities of in postwar era, 174–75, 194–96, 215–19, 245, 331 (n. 13); pursue equal rights, 166, 168–70, 173–75, 187; promote education for black students, 110–11, 130–31, 214, 220–24, 238–39. *See also* North Carolina Freedmen's Conventions
Artisans: importance to pre-industrial economy, 10, 40–44; pay rates for, 44–45, 55, 114, 115, 128; tools of (*see* Tools); women as (*see* Women artisans)
—black (postwar): continuity among, 197–98, 211–12; decline in apprenticeships, 197–98; form and support families, 235–41; gender definitions of, 200–201; number of, 197, 211; location of workshops, 204–6; ownership of real estate, 207–8, 240–44; racial makeup of crafts, 199; residential patterns among, 240–44; status of, 210–12; trades practiced, 198–204. *See also* Artisan-leaders, black; Contractors; Mass production, impact on artisans
—enslaved, 6, 7, 11, 40, 50–66; as church leaders, 110; in colonial period, 10; complaints of whites about, 134; craft skill levels of, 10, 51; economic importance of, 10; financial values of, 51–52, 303 (n. 62); gender roles of, 11; hiring practices, 56–61, 115, 116, 115–18; literacy among, 54–55; numbers of (unknown), 45, 115; owned by nonartisans, 46; as runaways, 62–66, 118; tools supplied to, 53, 58–59, 61; trades practiced by, 45, 51; working alongside whites, 41, 42, 43, 55, 82. *See also* Apprenticeships; Manumissions; Marriages; Slaves
—free black (antebellum), 39–40; church affiliations of, 89–91, 131, 146–47; in "colored society," 87–93, 129; complaints by whites about, 133–34; continuity among, 112–14; departures of, 136–44; number of, 119, 145; as real estate owners, 86–87, 148, 149; residential patterns among, 86–87; status of, 9–11, 87–93, 126, 129–30; trades practiced by, 45–46, 101. *See also* Apprenticeships; Families, black artisan; Manumissions; Marriages; Slaveholders; *and specific artisans*
—white: antebellum continuity among, 111–12; elite attitudes toward, 101; complaints from, 1850s, 133; enter manufacturing, 101–2; hire and own slaves, 58–60, 69; leave New Bern, 100; list of, in antebellum New Bern, 101; list of, in early national period, 45–46; number of, 119; status of, 9–10, 14–15; take black and white apprentices, 54, 81–82, 121–23; trades practiced by, 45–46, 112–14, 146, 199–203, 205, 211; wealth of, 208. *See also* Bell, Reuben; Bishop, George; Buxton, Jarvis; Charlotte, William; Dewey, John; Durand, John Louis; Flanner, Bennett; Hall, Joseph; Hall, Richard; Hancock, Robert; Hay, Robert; Jones, William H.; King, Asa; Lane, Hardy B., Jr.; Lane, Hardy B., Sr.; Lane, John; Mitchell, Joshua; Moore, Wallace; Oliver, John; Rains, Gabriel; Sandy, Uriah; Stevenson, Martin; Tisdale, Nathan; Tisdale, William; West, John; Willis, Alonzo; Woods, Freeman; Zang, Adam
Artisan trades, racial composition of: during early national period, 45–46; in 1850, 314 (n. 51); post–Civil War, 197, 199, 200, 201, 211, 330 (n. 10), 331 (n. 18), 332 (n. 20)
Asbury, Francis, 25

Atkins, Oleona Pegram, 238, 239
Atkins, Simon Green, 239
Atlantic and North Carolina Railroad, 27, 145, 250
Aycock, Charles B., 249

Badger, George E., 72, 73, 89
Badger, Lydia Cogdell, 71, 72, 73, 83, 89
Baltimore, Md., compared with New Bern, 7, 11, 28, 50
Banks, Hannah York, 237
Banks, Hugh (barber), 205, 237, 291
Banton, John M. (barber), 336 (n. 77)
Baptists, 25, 27, 31, 184, 297 (n. 11)
Barbers, 9, 44–45, 71, 205, 210; earnings of, 45, 158; as political and community leaders, 155, 176, 215. *See also* Banks, Hugh; Good, John R.; Kennedy, Moses; Pierson, Clinton D.; Stanly, John Carruthers
Barrum, William (carpenter), 332 (n. 28)
Bass, Alexander, 215, 223, 224, 242, 336 (n. 77)
Bassett, John, 73
Battle, Annie Vashti Delmar, 237, 260
Battle, Samuel Jesse, 261
Battle, Thomas C. (brickmason, minister), 197, 199, 203, 208, 215, 227, 228, 243, 244, 331 (n. 13); biographical summary, 260–61; church affiliation, 110, 159, 221, 227, 228; in civic organizations, 336 (n. 77), 338 (n. 98); family of, 237, 243–44, 260–61; minister, 237; owns real estate, 207; political roles of, 155, 171, 215
Battle, Thomas C., Jr. (apprentice brickmason), 237, 260
Battle, William Delmar (brickmason, minister), 260
Battle, Samuel J., 261
Beasley, Benjamin (carpenter), 332 (n. 25)
Beecher, James, 231
Bell, Reuben (tailor), 41, 45, 52, 54, 269
Ben (blacksmith), 60, 61
Ben (carpenter), 58–59, 82
Ben (sawyer), 303 (n. 62)
Berry, John (brickmason), 116
Bibles, family, 73, 131, 147, 208
Bill (carpenter), 115
Bill (cooper), 41
Biracial work forces: common practice, 10, 21, 41, 42, 54–55, 82, 112; examples of, 42–43, 54–55, 112, 201; white objections to, 133, 134, 316 (n. 61)
Bishop, George (cabinetmaker, carpenter, manufacturer), 101, 204
Black, Martin (apprentice turner), 300 (n. 14)
Black, Sharper (apprentice turner), 300 (n. 14)
"Black Code," 102
Blackledge, Ann, 52
Blackledge, Benjamin F., 312 (n. 21)
Blackledge, William, 52
Blacksmiths, 41, 44, 63, 112–13, 157, 199, 205–6, 210–11, 250; as apprentices, 81; average earnings of, in 1864, 158; location of shops, 205–6; racial distribution among, 45, 112–13, 199, 211; tools of, 61. *See also* Fisher, George S.; Hazel, Richard G.; Hughes, Scipio; Jackson, Allen; Jackson, Eli; Jackson, Samuel; Pettipher, William; Rial, Titus; Rial, William; Trenwith, Patrick; Willoby
Blunt, Archie (carpenter), 332 (n. 28)
Bob (carpenter), 303 (n. 62)
Bonner, Willis (carpenter), 319 (n. 109)
Boston (barber), 71
Boston (carpenter), 42
Bowers, Hannah. *See* Montford, Hannah Bowers
Bowman, James, 329 (n. 90)
Bowman, Thomas (blacksmith), 46
Boyle, James (carpenter), 198
Braddock, Grace. *See* Green, Grace
Braddock, Israel (house joiner), 260
Bradock, Peter (apprentice carpenter), 307 (n. 117)
Bragg, Braxton, 262
Bragg, Caroline (Carrie), 261–62
Bragg, Caroline Ferrand, 85, 91, 140, 261
Bragg, Cicero (tailor), 123, 140, 261, 262, 263
Bragg, Elizabeth (tailoress), 123, 140, 146, 200, 242, 262–63, 330 (n. 11); biographical summary, 261–62; family of, 200, 261–62; owns real estate, 127, 146, 200, 242; racial identification of, 146, 200, 321 (n. 127)
Bragg, George, 140, 321 (n. 127)
Bragg, Henry (tailor), 123, 140, 261, 263, 321 (n. 127)
Bragg, John (father of carpenter Thomas Bragg), 262

Bragg, John (tailor), 41, 80, 85, 101, 130, 148, 261; biographical summary, 262–63; family of, 85, 91 111, 123, 262–63; good reputation of, 46; moves to Cleveland, Ohio, 140; owns real estate, 86, 129, 130, 148
Bragg, John, Jr. (carpenter), 263
Bragg, Sarah (tailoress). *See* Stanly, Sarah Bragg
Bragg, Stephen (carpenter), 123, 263
Bragg, Thomas, Jr., 262
Bragg, Thomas, Sr. (carpenter), 118, 262
Brickell, John, 10
Brickmasons, 45–46, 98, 114; earnings of, 114, 158; racial distribution among, 45, 113–14, 201–3, 211; role as master builders, 43–44. *See also* Allen, Abram Moody Russell; Battle, Thomas C.; Battle, Thomas C., Jr.; Berry, John; Flanner, Bennett; Galloway, Abraham; Harris, Daniel H.; Harris, Israel, Jr.; Harris, Israel, Sr.; Harris, Jacob; Jones, William H.; Mitchell, Joshua; Montford, Donum; Moore, Wallace; Newton, Alexander Herritage; Richardson, Cicero M.; Richardson, Edward A.; Rue, Isaac C.; Sparrow, Charles; Sparrow, Henry Clay; Sparrow, James
Brister (barber), 71
Brown, Hannah Cora (seamstress), 240
Brown, Isaac (carpenter), 332 (n. 25)
Brown, William Wells, 139
Bryan, Abram, 90
Bryan, Henry E., 124
Bryan, James A., 250, 341 (n. 150)
Bryan, James West, 97, 99, 104, 105, 126, 132
Bryan, John Herritage, 76, 97, 99, 104
Bryan, Mary Spaight Shepard, 312 (n. 21), 341 (n. 150)
Bryan, Moses T. (carpenter), 207, 336 (n. 77), 338 (nn. 97, 98)
Bryan v. Wadsworth, 90
Burgwin, George H., 76
Burns, Silas (blacksmith), 313 (n. 31)
Burnside (Paul Cameron House), 116
Burnside, Ambrose, 28, 29, 156
Burr, Frank (brickmason), 64, 88
Buxton, Jarvis (carpenter, cabinetmaker), 55, 56
Cabinetmakers, 45. *See also* Bishop, George; Buxton, Jarvis; Rains, Gabriel; Sam; Shepard, Miles; West, John
Cameron, Duncan, 116
Cameron, Paul, 116
Carpenters, 43, 51, 54–55, 112, 157, 179, 190, 201, 203, 204, 211; average earnings of, in 1864, 158; racial distribution among, 45, 100–101, 112, 201, 210, 211. *See also* Abbott, Israel Braddock; Ben; Bishop, George; Boston (carpenter); Buxton, Jarvis; Dewey, Jack; Dewey, John; Dudley, James D.; Ellison, Stewart; Green, James York; Green, Joseph; Green, Rigdon M.; Hancock, Robert; Hancock, William H.; Lane, Hardy B., Jr.; Lane, Hardy B., Sr.; Lane, John (carpenter); Lisbon, Robert; Newton, Thomas; Oliver, John; Randolph, William O.; Rue, George A.; Sandy, Uriah; Simmons, Bacchus; Stevenson, Martin; Tucker, Richard; Wilson, David
Carriage makers, 112
Carter, William (turner), 300 (n. 14)
Carter family, 82
Cassey, Peter William (barber, minister), 337 (n. 87)
Castix, Raymond (shoemaker), 117, 122
Caswell, J. R., 329 (n. 90)
Caulkers, 61, 81, 158, 199, 211, 284. *See also* Richardson, Simon
Cawthon, David (plasterer), 303 (n. 47)
Cawthorn, William, 329 (n. 90)
Cedar Grove Cemetery, 27, 91, 280, 297 (n. 15)
Cemeteries. *See* Cedar Grove Cemetery; Greenwood Cemetery
Chairmakers. *See* Crawford, Phillis; Hay, Robert; York, Dollie
Chapman, Isabel, 75
Chapman, Nathan (carpenter), 74
Chapman, Samuel, family of, 74
Charles, 43
Charleston, S.C.: compared with New Bern, 7, 8, 11, 22, 28, 50, 196; emancipation parade in, 172
Charlotte, N.C., compared with New Bern, 26, 30, 31, 196, 241
Charlotte, William (painter), 45

Chase, Salmon P., 174
Chavis, John, 44
Cheatham, Henry, 336 (n. 71)
Chesnutt, Andrew Jackson, 142
Chesnutt, Anna Maria Sampson, 142, 311 (n. 6)
Chesnutt, Charles, 137, 144, 210
Christ Episcopal Church, 25, 89, 90, 91, 131, 165 (ill.), 184
Civil War, effects in New Bern, 33, 117, 152–72; black artisan leaders during, 152–56, 159, 170; black political life during, 163, 166–72; church activities during, 159–62; contrabands during, 29, 30, 153, 157; craft employment during, 156–58; epidemics during, 161–62, 170; recruitment of black Union troops during, 162–66; and strategic position of New Bern, 28; Union capture and occupation of New Bern, 8, 12, 28–30, 152–72
Clapp, Henry A., 202
Clarke, William E., 251
Clarke, William J., 217, 223
Clements, John S., 300 (n. 14)
Cleveland, Ohio, as destination for black emigres from New Bern, 100, 131, 137–45, 149, 182, 197, 228, 261–63, 269, 271, 276, 281, 320
Clinton, J. J., 162, 171
Clinton Chapel AME Zion Church, 184, 226, 242
Cobb, N. J., 341 (n. 147)
Cogdell, Lydia Duncan, 71, 72, 73, 89
Cogdell, Richard, 71
Coleman, Warren C., 334 (n. 44)
"Colored society," 87–88, 129
Colored Women's Relief Organization of New Bern, 165
Colyer, Vincent, 156, 159, 323 (n. 13)
Company H, First Regiment North Carolina State Troops, 217, 289
Conner, Mary Jane, 202
Conner (Connor), Sylvia (seamstress), 202, 202 (ill.)
Conservative Party, 214, 216, 217
Construction trades: antebellum, 21, 42, 44, 79, 98, 112, 145; postwar changes in, 201, 203, 204
Contrabands during Civil War, 29–30, 152, 157
Contractors, 42, 203–4
Conway, Robert W. (carpenter), 74, 90
Conway, William (blacksmith), 41, 62, 69–70, 77
Coopers, 41, 61, 63, 81, 112, 148, 157; average earnings of, in 1864, 158; essential to antebellum economy, 44; numbers of, decline after 1870, 199, 211; among postwar artisan-leaders, 155–56. *See also* Crawford, Virgil A.; Dudley, Edward R.; Jones, Balaam; Simmons, Henry H.; Spelman, Asa; Willis, George B.; York, Amos; York, John T.
Craft artifacts, scarcity of New Bern–made examples, 33–34
Craft training. *See* Apprenticeships
Craven County Courthouse (eighteenth century), 300 (n. 8)
Craven County Courthouse and Jail (1880s), 203, 203 (ill.)
Craven County Jail (1820s), 42, 44 (ill.)
Crawford, Harriet Hargate, 236
Crawford, Lydia, 78, 126, 268
Crawford, Mary (apprentice spinster), 263
Crawford, Phillis (chairmaker), 200
Crawford, Virgil, I (farmer and carpenter), 76, 77–78, 126
Crawford, Virgil, II (apprentice carpenter, mechanic), 78, 281
Crawford, Virgil A. (cooper), 12, 78, 197, 199, 224, 242, 331 (n. 13), 336 (n. 77); biographical summary, 263–64; church affiliation of, 227–28, 337 (n. 89); in civic organizations, 214, 230, 338 (nn. 97, 98), 339 (n. 109); Emancipation Day speech of, 193; family of, 236, 244, 263–64; owns real estate, 207, 333 (n. 41); political roles of, 193–94, 216, 218, 219, 224, 247
Croom, Mingo (painter), 216
Croom, Simon (carpenter), 204; family of, 234
Cupid (shoemaker), 53

Daniel (brickmason), 42
Davis, Kelso (Kelcy; carpenter), 80, 280
Day, Thomas (cabinetmaker), 11, 120, 308 (n. 121), 317 (n. 88)
Declaration of Independence: language and principles of, cited by black leaders, 67,

168, 170, 190, 257; read at Independence Day celebration in 1867, 215
Denby, Joshua (brickmason), 114
Dennett, John, 178
Devereux, Frances Pollock, 64
Devereux, John, 64, 66, 67
Dewey, Charles, 116
Dewey, Jack (Dewey's Jack; carpenter), 116–17
Dewey, John (carpenter), 45, 82, 272
Dewey, Peter (carpenter), 88
Dick (blacksmith), 64
Dick (carpenter), 118
Disbru (Disbrew), Charles (carpenter), 242, 332 (n. 28)
Disfranchisement amendments: in 1835, 105–6; in 1900, 250, 251
Dixon, James (apprentice carpenter), 123
Dixon, John, 336 (n. 77)
Donnell, John R., 89, 142, 300 (n. 7), 304 (n. 63); hires out enslaved artisans, 53, 58–60; residence of, 42, 43 (ill.), 280
Donum (carpenter), 115
Douglas, 74
Douglass, Frederick, 11, 163, 170, 175, 286
Dove, Bill (apprentice carpenter), 83
Dove, James (artisan), 330 (n. 11)
Dove, Lewis (apprentice plasterer, mason), 84
Dove family, 81
Dressmakers, 11, 13, 17, 70, 146, 200, 201, 211, 236, 267, 271; racial distribution of, 211, 314 (n. 51). *See also* Green, Temperance Durden; Lane, Harriet; Stanly, Catharine Green; Stanly, Frances
Drummond, William (builder), 116–17
Dry, William, 309 (n. 129)
Dryboro (suburb of New Bern), 86–87, 123, 128, 129, 141, 148, 149, 206, 308–9 (n. 129); artisans residing in, 243, 263, 268, 269, 271, 276, 313 (nn. 28, 30), 338 (n. 100)
Du Bois, W. E. B., 198
Dudley, Abram (carpenter), 332 (n. 28)
Dudley, Caroline, 236
Dudley, Edward R. (cooper), 12, 156, 199, 251, 289, 331 (n. 13), 336 (n. 77); biographical summary, 264–65; church affiliation, 227–28; 265; in civic organizations, 186, 229, 230, 231, 338 (nn. 98, 100); family of, 228, 236, 239, 264–65; owns real estate, 208, 333 (n. 41); political roles of, 187, 217, 218, 219, 224; residence of, 243, 244
Dudley, James D. (carpenter), 217, 248, 265, 339 (n. 109)
Dudley, Sarah. *See* Pettey, Sarah Dudley
Durand, John Louis (tailor), 45, 55

Ebenezer Presbyterian Church, 226, 227 (ill.), 337 (n. 88)
Edenton, N.C., 28, 48, 57, 65, 79, 123, 270–71
Edmond, 43
Education: for antebellum free blacks, 45, 110–11, 131, 137–39, 149, 317 (n. 86); for apprentices, 81, 121–22; artisan-leaders organize to improve, 17, 214, 220–25, 230, 232; blacks strive for, 17–18, 171, 180, 194, 220–25, 252, 267; central to black freedom and advancement, 176, 211, 220, 239; and education board in 1866, 214; New Bern Educational Association, 222–23; North Carolina Educational Association, 187–88, 214; North Carolina State Teachers Association, 223; public education, 214, 216, 223–24; of slaves, 54, 103, 110–11, 135; State Colored Education Convention, 222–23. *See also* Schools for black students
Edwards, W. R. (blacksmith), 334 (n. 47)
Elijah (carpenter), 42
Ellison, Stewart (carpenter), 179, 213, 281, 329 (n. 90), 335 (n. 61)
Elm City Band, 194
Elm City Hotel, 206
Emancipation Day: in 1865, 170–71, 172; in 1873, 193–95
Emancipation Proclamation, 163, 168–69; reading of, 171
Emancipations. *See* Emancipation by will; Manumissions
Emancipation by will, 69, 72, 75, 76, 77, 115–16, 120, 136
Emanuel (cooper), 303 (n. 62)
Emigration of free black artisans from New Bern, 100, 136–44
Episcopal churches. *See* Christ Episcopal Church; St. Cyprian's Episcopal Church
Equal rights: appeal to Abraham Lincoln for, 168; appeal to Andrew Johnson for,

173–74; and founding documents of nation, 95, 168, 170, 179; of freedmen, in 1814, 95; sought by artisan-leaders, 156, 166, 168–69, 174, 197, 214, 257; strategies concerning, at North Carolina Freedmen's Conventions, 179–90
Equal Rights Leagues: national, 170; New Bern area chapters, 17, 170, 171, 173; North Carolina State Equal Rights League organized, 181, 187; statement by, 188–89
Eubanks, George C. (apprentice carpenter, architect), 198, 212, 235; biographical summary, 266; family of, 235, 266

Families, black artisan: as antebellum free black elite, 87, 89–93, 129–32, 146, 200; craft training by members of, 41, 123, 145, 150, 210, 212, 237; departure of, 136–40, 147, 149; among early free black families in Craven County, 24, 46, 82, 251; establishing and protecting, 7, 84–85, 150, 164, 181, 208, 236, 237, 244; extended, 126, 127, 147, 148, 239–40; importance to status and success, 126, 235–36; manumission of members of, 67, 70, 73, 74, 75–76; networks of, 76–78, 98, 100, 239–40; runaways aided by, 64; separated in slavery, 15, 20, 61, 74, 117–18, 148, 233–34; in slavery, 117, 123, 126, 234; sought by freedpeople, 233–34; supported through artisan skills, 14, 67, 126; uniting, 13, 118, 194, 234; and women's household roles in freedom, 235. *See also* Education; Marriages; *individual artisans*
Fayetteville, N.C., 27, 98–100, 105, 137, 191, 208, 210; black militia from, 231; compared with New Bern, 8, 26, 28, 31, 48, 57, 86, 112, 113, 196, 208; decline in artisan trades in, 210; former residents of, in Cleveland and Oberlin, Ohio, 100, 137, 139, 141, 142–45, 182, 183, 228, 271; free black community in, 100; leading blacks artisans of, 208, 210; New Bern artisans in, 79, 98, 99, 100, 139, 270
Fayetteville State University, 224, 228
Federalist Party, 94
"Federal-Period Cottage," 310 (n. 141)
Felton, Isaac K., 164
Female artisans. *See* Women artisans
Fenderson, William (brickmason), 203
Ferguson, Boston (tailor), 74
Fire companies, 173, 230
First Baptist Church, 184
First North Carolina Colored Volunteer Infantry, 165
First Presbyterian Church, 58, 82, 272; congregation of, 89, 147
Fisher, Charles (apprentice blacksmith), 236, 267
Fisher, George S. (blacksmith), 155, 199, 331 (n. 13); biographical summary, 266–67; in civic organizations, 214, 223, 224, 336 (n. 77), 338 (n. 98); early life of, 117; family and household of, 201, 236, 238–39, 266–67; location of workshop and residence, 205, 242; obituary of, 245; owns real estate, 207–9; political roles of, 169, 213, 215, 216–17, 223, 253; report on, by R. G. Dun, 209
Fisher, John H. (apprentice blacksmith), 236, 238, 239, 267
Fisher, Mary Jane Jones, 236
Fitzgerald, Richard (brickmaker), 334 (n. 44)
Five Points (commercial area), 206, 243
Flanner, Bennett (brickmason), 45, 89, 100
Flanner, John D., 114, 118, 123, 147
Forbes, Stephen, 42, 53, 58
Fourteenth Amendment, 187, 190
Free blacks (antebellum): as apprentices, 122; assist in freeing slaves, 72, 74, 75, 76; disfranchisement of, 105–6; emancipate slaves by will, 89, 120; forbidden to buy, apprentice, or hire slaves, 136; forbidden to enter or reenter state, 103, 131; freedom to travel, 79, 98, 103; leave New Bern, 136–45; lose rights, 135–36; manumit slaves, 71, 72, 75, 76; number of, in New Bern, 119; own real estate, 129; own slaves, 130; petitions and protests against, 133–34; remain in New Bern after Union capture, 153, 158; voting rights of, 16, 87, 104–6, 173; wealth of, 130. *See also* Artisans—free black; Residential patterns in New Bern, racial
Freedman's Bank, 204, 207, 210, 220, 260, 263, 264, 270, 274, 275, 277, 287, 288
Freedmen's Bureau, 172, 183, 184, 187, 190, 197, 235; operates schools, 220, 221, 224

Freedmen's Conventions. *See* North Carolina Freedmen's Conventions
Freedom, imagining, 6
Fulsher, Shadrach (carpenter), 53
Fulsher, Thomas, 53
Fusionists, 33, 247

Gabriel (blacksmith), 11, 57
Galloway, Abraham (brickmason), 177 (ill.); biographical summary, 267–68; at constitutional convention of 1868, 216; early life of, 118, 156; negotiates recruitment of black Union troops, 163; and North Carolina Freedmen's Convention of 1865, 174–81; political roles of, 165–68, 188, 191, 213, 216, 268, 286, 335 (n. 59); presents petition to Abraham Lincoln, 168; proponent of equal rights, 168–71, 174–79; returns to Wilmington, 191; at Syracuse National Convention of Colored Citizens, 170
Garner, Dinah, 236
Gaskins, Park (apprentice carpenter), 278
Gaston, Alexander (father of William), 85
Gaston, Alexander (son of William), 107
Gaston, Margaret, 85
Gaston, William, 24, 65, 85, 95, 103, 104, 133, 144; assists in manumissions, 75; defends franchise for free blacks, 105; defends human rights of blacks, 49, 301 (n. 27); impact of death on blacks, 107, 133; political roles of, 94, 104; supported by black voters, 94, 104; supreme court justice, 90; tribute from free blacks at death, 106–7, 108–9
Gaston House Hotel, 205, 206 (ill.)
George, 53
George, Eliza and Sukey (apprentice seamstresses), 342 (n. 153)
George family, 24, 342 (n. 153)
Gildersleeve, John, 51
Gill, Augustus, 235
Godett, John (blacksmith), 319 (n. 109)
Godett(e) family, 24, 81, 342 (n. 153)
Godley, Maggie, 223
Good, John R. (barber), 164, 167, 170, 215, 220; in civic organizations, 173, 336 (n. 77); emancipated, 155, 313 (n. 36); in North Carolina Equal Rights League, 187; and North Carolina Freedmen's Conventions, 177, 179–80, 187; political roles of, 168, 169, 170, 176, 216, 217, 218
Gooding, Jacob, 124
Good Samaritans, 259
Good Templars, 31, 229
Gould, William B. (plasterer), 322 (n. 8)
Graham, Edward E., 45, 88, 94, 99; assists in manumissions, 49–50, 67, 74–75, 77; reads law with John Jay, 50; supported by black voters, 50, 94
Grand Army of the Republic (GAR): James Beecher Post, 231; T. A. Lyons Camp, 339 (n. 106)
Gravestones, 91–93, 94 (ill.), 149, 297 (n. 15)
Great Fire of 1922, 34, 35, 338 (n. 93)
Green, Amelia (spinner), 12, 79, 80, 85; manumits family members, 75, 76, 79; residence of, 91, 310 (n. 141)
Green, Ann, 130, 320 (n. 118)
Green, Benjamin S. (carpenter), 131, 182, 271
Green, Caroline Allen, 91, 131, 140, 234
Green, Catharine (Catherine) Stanly (dressmaker), 70, 141, 145, 269, 271
Green, Grace (Rue/Braddock/Brown), 148, 149, 150, 221, 233, 234, 243, 260, 313 (n. 27); owns real estate, 239, 240; schoolteacher, 162, 220, 221
Green, Harriet, 76, 234
Green, James York (carpenter), 46, 140, 142, 280; acquires and frees mother and brother, 69, 75; assists in freeing slaves, 72, 74, 78, 197; biographical summary, 268–69; church affiliation of, 132; early life of, 51, 65; employs apprentices, 83, 84, 122, 308 (n. 120); family of, 69, 84, 268–69; leader in tribute to William Gaston, 106–9; manumission of, 68; owns real estate, 86–87, 95, 129–30, 148, 309 (n. 129); owns slaves, 88. *See also* Green, Rigdon
Green, James York, Jr. (tailor), 269
Green, John Patterson, 73, 119, 129–32, 141, 142, 144 (ill.), 145, 182
Green, John Rice (tailor), 6, 11, 46, 67, 111, 136, 141, 197; assists in manumissions, 74, 78, 85; biographical summary, 269; church

affiliation of, 89–91, 132; deportment of, 6, 93; early life in slavery, 51, 52, 54, 60, 65; employs apprentices, 123, 167; family of, 85, 111, 137, 269; financial reverses of, 101, 127, 130, 141; manumission of, 69; owns real estate, 87, 141, 310 (n. 144), 320 (n. 118); owns slaves, 88, 130; residence of, 85, 91, 92 (ill.), 310 (n. 141); son of John Stanly, 73, 89, 95; speaker at tribute to William Gaston, 106. *See also* Green, John Patterson; Green, Temperance Durden; Rice, Sarah
Green, Joseph (carpenter, minister), 243, 259, 330 (n. 11); biographical summary, 270; church affiliation of, 110, 159, 160, 162; in civic organizations, 336 (n. 77); family of, 149, 233–34, 240, 270; minister, 162, 171, 184, 226; and North Carolina Freedmen's Convention, 177, 270; owns real estate, 207, 333 (n. 41); trains stepson, 149, 260. *See also* Green, Grace; Rue, George A.
Green, Mary Davis, 233
Green, Mary Neal, 84
Green, Nancy, 75, 76
Green, Phoebe, 233
Green, Princess, 75
Green, Richmond, 233
Green, Rigdon M. (carpenter), 46, 65, 89, 167, 182, 268; apprentices of, 123; biographical summary, 270–71; church affiliation of, 91, 140; death of, 197; family of, 91, 129, 131, 270–71; hires slaves, 115–16; manumission of, 69, 75, 268; moves to Cleveland, Ohio, 140; moves to Fayetteville and Edenton, 79; owns slaves, 130. *See also* Green, James York
Green, Sally (Sarah) McClure, 85, 91; gravestone of, 297 (n. 15)
Green, Sarah Rice (dressmaker), 141, 145, 271
Green, Shadrach (Shade; plasterer), 60, 130, 320 (n. 118)
Green, Temperance Durden (dressmaker, tailoress, seamstress), 11, 13, 129, 141–42, 269; biographical summary, 271; family of, 141, 271; moves to Cleveland, Ohio, 17, 141–42, 144, 145; skills of, 141. *See also* Green, John Rice
Green, Thomas A., 233, 268
Green, Violet, 69, 75
Green, William B., 74
Greenwood Cemetery, 27, 244, 267, 274, 283, 291, 297 (n. 15)
Gregory, Elisha (apprentice carpenter), 307 (n. 117)
Gregory, Mackey (apprentice carpenter), 307 (n. 117)
Grellet, Stephen, 301 (n. 25)
Groves, John (carpenter), 319 (n. 109)
Guillet, Michael (trunkmaker?), 83
Gunsmiths, 45, 112, 199

Hall, Joseph (cabinetmaker), 45
Hall, Richard (cabinetmaker), 45
Hamilton, Robert, 125, 135, 167
Hancock, Coleston, 126, 272
Hancock, John, 119
Hancock, Mary (Mary Ann), 126, 132, 310 (n. 141)
Hancock, Mary Beman, 138
Hancock, Richard Mason (joiner, ship carpenter, patternmaker), 123, 126, 131, 132, 138, 142, 272; biographical summary, 273
Hancock, Robert (carpenter), 101, 112, 121, 123, 147
Hancock, William H. (carpenter), 46, 101, 112, 129, 142, 167, 276, 310 (n. 141); apprentice, 82; biographical summary, 272; church affiliation of, 132; employs apprentices, 123; family of, 101, 111, 123, 126, 129, 137, 272; moves to Chicago, 272; moves to New Haven, Conn., 138; owns real estate, 87; owns slaves, 130; tyler in white Masonic lodge, 132, 135, 185. *See also* Hancock, Richard Mason
Handicrafts, 40–41, 101, 194, 195
Harland Fire Company No. 1, 173
Harper, Henry (wheelwright), 235
Harris, Alice, 240
Harris, Charles (brickmason), 272
Harris, Charlotte, family of, 311 (n. 6)
Harris, Cicero Richardson (bootmaker, teacher, minister), 100, 139, 337 (n. 83); becomes bishop, 182, 228
Harris, Daniel H. (brickmason), 101, 148, 169, 214, 220, 338 (nn. 97, 98)

Harris, David (brickmason), 237
Harris, Emma, 237
Harris, Israel, Jr. (brickmason), 230, 235, 237, 248, 339 (n. 109); biographical summary, 274
Harris, Israel, Sr. (brickmason), 184, 203, 226, 237, 244; biographical summary, 273–74; church affiliation of, 226; family of, 200, 237, 273–74; in civic organizations, 230, 244, 338 (nn. 97, 98); residence of, 243
Harris, Israel, III (brickmason), 237, 274
Harris, Jacob (brickmason), 83, 84, 98, 99, 228, 279
Harris, James H. (upholsterer), 179, 180, 181, 189, 208, 213, 329 (n. 90), 335 (n. 59)
Harris, John (apprentice brickmason), 313 (n. 32)
Harris, Joseph (brickmason), 311 (n. 6)
Harris, Melissa, 240
Harris, Moses (carpenter), 311 (n. 6)
Harris, Richard (apprentice tailor), 269
Harris, Robert (mechanic, teacher), 100, 182, 228, 337 (n. 83)
Harris, Thomas (apprentice cooper), 83
Harris, William (brickmason), 311 (n. 6)
Harry (blacksmith), 61
Harry (blacksmith), 303 (n. 62)
Harry (cooper), 90
Haslin, Margaret Nash, 77
Haslin, Thomas, 306 (n. 103)
Hatch, Ann B., 52
Hatch, Charles, 61
Hatch, Durant, 64, 65
Hatch, Elizabeth, 86, 309 (n. 129)
Hatch, Richard B., 52
Havens, Edward (shoemaker), 198, 200, 205, 208, 226, 242, 244, 253, 331 (n. 13), 334 (n. 47); biographical summary, 274–75; in civic organizations, 221, 226, 230, 338 (n. 98); family of, 234, 236, 237, 244, 274–75; locations of workshops, 205; obituary of, 252; owns real estate, 207, 242, 333 (n. 41); political roles of, 187; trains sons, 212, 237
Havens, Edward, Jr. (shoemaker), 237, 274, 275
Havens, James H. (shoemaker), 212, 237; biographical summary, 274–75
Havens, John T. (shoemaker), 226, 230, 237, 274, 275, 331 (n. 13); biographical summary, 275
Havens, Maria Cherry, 234, 236
Hawks, John (architect), 23, 45
Hawley, Amanda (tailoress), 201
Hawley, John (tailor), 200, 201, 205, 243
Hay, Robert (chair and cabinetmaker), 45
Hayes, Kiziah, 235
Hazel, Ann (daughter of Richard G. and Ann N. Hazel), 131
Hazel, Ann Nash Newton, 126, 131, 140, 338 (n. 100)
Hazel, Elizabeth, 131
Hazel (Hasle), Garrison (apprentice brickmason), 83
Hazel (Hasele), Henry (apprentice carpenter), 83
Hazel (Hasle), Patience (apprentice spinster), 83
Hazel, Richard G. (blacksmith), 101, 106, 107, 112, 126, 127, 129, 131, 140, 167, 281; biographical summary, 276; family of, 111, 137, 276; owns real estate, 130, 338 (n. 100)
Hazel (Hasele, Hazle), Robert (apprentice carpenter, joiner), 79, 83, 270
Henrion, Peter, 88
Henry, 88
Henry (ship carpenter), 42
Henry, Elizabeth, 90
Henry, Louis D., 99
Herring, Richard, 235
Hill, Edward H., 167, 168, 218, 226
Hill, Moses D. (shoemaker), 122, 215, 216, 330 (n. 11)
Hilton, William (brickmason), 313 (n. 32)
Hiring of slaves. *See* Artisans—enslaved: hiring practices; Self-hiring of slaves
Holden, William, 181, 217
Hollister, William, 112, 304 (n. 76); house of, 113 (ill.)
Holly, Bradley (apprentice tailor), 334 (n. 49)
Holly (Holley), Mustipher (Mustapher) P. (tailor), 198, 200, 228, 230, 331 (n. 13), 332 (n. 19); in civic organizations, 230, 338 (n. 97); location of workshop, 205; owns real estate, 242; political roles of, 247, 264
Hood, James Walker, 156, 161 (ill.), 187, 191, 228, 281; Masonic leader, 186; minister

at Andrews Chapel, 161–62, 170–71, 184, 185, 221, 228, 240; and North Carolina Freedmen's Convention, 175–77, 179; state school official, 221
Households, black artisan: household and personal possessions in, 130–31, 147, 208, 240–41; multigenerational, 126, 148, 236; nonrelated members of, 85, 126, 199, 235, 236. *See also* Families, black artisan; Residential patterns in New Bern, racial
Howard, Oliver, 183
Howe, Alfred (carpenter), 208
Howe, William Tryon, 75
Howe family, 213, 334 (n. 52)
Hoyle, R. G. (blacksmith), 182
Hubbs, Orlando, 265
Hughes, Isaac, 117, 202
Hughes, Langston, 145
Hughes, Scipio (blacksmith), 117
Hurtt and Gaskill (tailors), 305
Hussey, John E., 218
Hyman, John, 265
Hyman, Thomas (blacksmith), 61–62

Indentures. *See* Apprenticeships
Independent Order of Good Templars, 31, 229
Internal improvements, 26, 100
Isa, 86, 309 (n. 129)
Isaac (shoemaker), 65

Jack (apprentice carpenter), 52
Jack (carpenter), 60
Jackson, Allen (blacksmith), 199, 306, 331 (n. 18)
Jackson, Eli (blacksmith), 199, 205, 277
Jackson, Samuel (blacksmith), 198, 199, 205, 230, 334 (n. 47), 339 (n. 109); biographical summary, 276–77
Jacob (brickmason), 43
Jacob (carpenter), 62
James (blacksmith), 63
James, Horace, 158, 197, 323 (n. 14)
James, William (carpenter), 332 (n. 28)
James City, N.C., 30
Jay, John, 50
Jim (carpenter), 55, 56
Jim (caulker, ship carpenter), 303 (n. 62)
Jim (shoemaker), 61
Jim Crow laws and practices, 205, 251
Joe (brickmason), 114
Joe (tanner), 46
Johnson, Abbey (apprentice spinster), 83
Johnson, Andrew, 173, 174, 190
Johnson, Jacob, 121
Johnson, Levin, 167
Johnson, Polly (apprentice spinster), 83
Johnson, Rebecca, 121
Johnson, Richard (apprentice plasterer), 83
Johnson, William H. (brickmason), 126, 166, 214, 218, 330 (n. 11), 341 (n. 147)
Johnston, Bill (apprentice chairmaker), 300 (n. 14)
Jones, Abe (carpenter), 332 (n. 28)
Jones, Balaam (cooper), 119, 146, 147
Jones, Cicero (apprentice cooper), 199, 236, 263
Jones, Hugh, 71
Jones, John (brickmason), 164
Jones, John (carpenter), 224
Jones, William H. (brickmason), 114, 203

Keckly, Elizabeth (dressmaker), 11
Kennedy, Moses (barber), 147, 226, 322 (n. 7)
Kent, Henry (wheelwright), 136
Kimball Fire Company, 173
King, Asa (carpenter), 42, 45, 100, 116
King Solomon Lodge: artisan members of, 186, 230, 232, 265, 274, 275, 282, 287, 289; burial ceremonies held by, 191, 230, 244; founding of, 185–86, 329 (n. 85); lodge hall, 186 (ill.), 206, 230, 243, 276
Kinsley, Edward, 163
Kirk, George, 217
"Kirk-Holden War," 217
Knights of Pythias, Acme Lodge, 261

Lane, Caroline, 130
Lane, Frederick (carpenter), 101, 122
Lane, Hannah (dressmaker), 267
Lane, Hardy B., Jr. (carpenter), 101, 122
Lane, Hardy B., Sr. (carpenter), 45, 54, 89, 101, 112, 114, 120, 122
Lane, Harriet (dressmaker), 201, 236
Lane, John (blacksmith), 319 (n. 109)
Lane, John (carpenter), 101, 122, 127, 204
Lane, Lunsford, 71
Langston, Charles H., 145

Langston, John Mercer, 144, 145
Larry (blacksmith), 69–70
Latham, Hettie (tailor), 201
Lavender, Ellis, 162, 170, 324 (n. 28)
Lawrence, Catharine, 120
Lawrence, Park (carpenter), 120, 330 (n. 11); biographical summary, 277–78
Lawrence, William W. (cooper), 82–83, 231, 336 (n. 77), 338 (nn. 98, 100); founds fire company, 232
Lawson (plasterer), 43
Lawson Creek, 23, 35, 86
Leary, John Sinclair, 320 (n. 123)
Leary, Lewis Sheridan (saddler), 145
Leary, Mary Patterson, 145
Leary, Matthew, Jr. (saddler), 320 (n. 123)
Leary, Matthew N. (saddler), 208, 320 (n. 123)
Leith, Lewis (carpenter), 212
Leith, Walter (carpenter), 212
Lewis, Elizabeth (apprentice seamstress), 121
Lewis, Sally, 121
Lewis, Stephen (apprentice turner), 300 (n. 14)
Liberia, 133, 136
Lincoln, Abraham, 29–30, 168–69, 170, 173, 178
Lincoln, Mary Todd, 11
Lippiner, Thomas (brickmason), 55
Lisbon, Myrtilla, 75
Lisbon, Robert (carpenter), 74, 75, 84, 87, 95, 310 (n. 141)
Lisbon, Venus, 75
Little family, 122
Livingstone College, 221, 228, 260
Lloyd, Goldsmith (apprentice carpenter), 79, 270
Lockhart (Locket), Hardy, 190
Long, Henry J. (carpenter), 332 (n. 28)
Long, Tom (apprentice carpenter), 82
Lovick, Henry (apprentice carpenter), 198

Mackey, Sylvester (carpenter, contractor), 204, 334 (n. 47)
Mallett (carpenter), 55
Manumissions, 16, 46, 67–78; by emancipated blacks, 68, 70–72, 74–76; by family members, 73–74, 76–78; financial barriers to, 103, 115; frequency of, in New Bern, 49, 68, 70; laws concerning, 67–68, 90, 114–15; by leading whites, 49, 52, 76–77; legal barriers to, 114–15, 120; petitions for, 66–67, 68–69; process of, 69; white attorneys assisting in, 49–50, 67, 74–75, 76
Maria, 88
Marriages: importance of, for antebellum free blacks, 84, 85, 126–27; importance of, for freedpeople, 234–36; recorded in Christ Church Parish Register, 25, 85; remarriages frequent, 237; and spouses separated in slavery, 148; between whites and blacks, 81, 126
—slave: between slaves, 84, 117, 234; between slaves and free people, 20, 81, 85, 121, 126, 236; no legal standing for, 234; registered and legalized, 66, 234–35
Mary (apprentice seamstress), 83
Mason, Cicero (apprentice carpenter), 123
Mason, Joseph (wagonmaker), 278
Mason, Lucas (Luke; wheelwright, coachmaker, wagonmaker), 146, 147, 148, 158, 235, 330 (n. 11), 331 (n. 13); biographical summary, 278; shop of, 157 (ill.), 205
Mason, Moses (blacksmith), 278
Mason, Richard Sharp, 25
Mason, Samuel (carpenter), 164
Masonic lodge(s), 31, 185–86; antebellum white, black tyler in, 132–33; cornerstone laying by, 230; George B. Willis Lodge, 232; Morning Star Lodge, 230; Prince Hall Lodge (New York), 186; Zaradatha Lodge, 230, 274. *See also* King Solomon Lodge; St. John's Masonic Lodge
"Mass Meeting of Colored Citizens" (July 1867), 215
Mass production, impact on artisans, 101–2, 145, 194–95, 199, 201, 210
McCabe, Rachel, 65
McCarthy, Thomas, 341 (n. 147)
McClure, Jacob, 90
McDaniel, Joseph (blacksmith), 334 (n. 47)
McGee, Benjamin (carpenter), 203 (n. 25)
McGee, Nelson, and Company (carpenters), 201
McKinley, Mary, 115, 310 (n. 138), 315 (n. 54)
McLin (McLynn), Charles L. (carpenter), 123, 319 (n. 109)
McLin, Thomas, 42

Mechanics, competition among, 133, 318 (n. 98)
Mechanics' and Laborers' Mutual Aid Society of North Carolina, 230, 232
Mechanics' lien law, 216
Merrick, John (brickmason, barber), 334 (n. 44)
Methodist churches, 27, 89, 111
Methodist Meeting House, 25, 107
Miller, Stephen, 86, 88, 93, 94
Milliners, 199, 205
Mingo (carpenter), 115
Mitchel, Alexander, 52
Mitchell, Henry, 66
Mitchell, Joshua (brickmason), 42, 43, 45, 89
Mitchell, William (apprentice carpenter), 123
Montford (Mumford), Donum (plasterer, brickmason), 40–42, 46, 50, 67, 79, 91, 99–100, 127, 131, 196, 268, 287, 311 (nn. 144, 145); advertisement placed by, 37–39; assists in freeing slaves, 49, 68, 72, 74, 76, 268; biographical summary, 279–80; church affiliation of, 131; death of, 111; deportment of, 93; employs apprentices, 53, 54, 72, 80, 83–84, 122; family of, 84, 279–80; financial reverses, 101, 130; frees slaves, 114, 121; gravestone of, 297 (n. 15); manumission of, 49, 71–72; as new freedman, 78–79; owns real estate, 87, 95, 127, 310 (n. 144); owns slaves, 12, 54, 88–89, 90, 130, 287, 309 (n. 133); petition to manumit son, 76; relationships with whites, 89, 90, 95; residence of, 85, 130–31, 242; in slavery, 40, 51, 71; wages made, 45, 300 (n. 8); work at Craven County Jail, 42–43; work at John R. Donnell house, 42. *See also* Allen, Abram Moody Russell; Montford, Hannah Bowers; Montford, Nelson; Rue, Isaac C.; Stanly, John Carruthers
Montford, Hannah Bowers, 38, 83, 84–85, 91, 95, 112, 121, 130–32, 279, 287
Montford, Nelson (brickmason, plasterer), 76, 89, 279
Moore, Elijah (apprentice carpenter), 82
Moore, Gabe (apprentice turner), 300 (n. 14)
Moore, Wallace (brickmason), 42, 45
Morehead, John Motley, 64
Morris, Albert (tailor), 120, 167
Morris, Brevett W., 207, 215, 216, 218, 224
Morris, Freeman W. (tailor), 120, 126, 137, 139–40, 167, 182
Morris, Hannah, 126
Morris, Harriet, 120
Morris, Maria, 139
Morris, Patty, 120
Morris, W. H. (tinsmith), 182
Morris, William S., 120
Moseley, Daniel G. (carpenter, contractor), 204, 334 (n. 47)
Moseley, J. J., 341 (n. 147)
Moseley, John B. (apprentice wheelwright), 278
Moseley, Robert G., 224
Moses Griffin School, 5 (ill.), 114
Mumford, Joseph, 224

Nash, Abner: family of, frees slaves, 76–78; slaves of, 64, 65, 280, 306 (n. 101)
Nash, Frederick, 76–77
National Convention of Colored Citizens of the United States, 169–70
National Equal Rights League, 170
Nat Turner Rebellion, 98, 103, 105
Neal, Lucretia, 200
Neale, Hannah, 148, 239, 240, 306 (n. 103)
Neale, Thomas, 149
"Negro codes," 186–87
"Negro rule," 248, 249, 253
Nelson (shoemaker), 303 (n. 62)
Nelson, Elisha (blacksmith), 199
Nelson, John, 51
Nelson, Samuel (carpenter), 332 (n. 25)
Nelson and Rial (blacksmiths), 205
New Bern (Newbern, Newberne, New Berne), N.C.: as colonial capital, 23; compared with other cities, 7, 8, 11, 22, 26, 28, 30, 31, 50, 86, 113, 196, 208, 212, 217, 241; economy of, 23, 26–27, 30–31, 100, 145; geographic position of, 22–23; historical overview of, 20–35; interracial interactions and proximity in, 20–22, 25, 40, 42, 46–48, 50, 85–86, 89, 131–32, 148, 204–6, 241–45; political wards in, 148, 216, 336 (n. 67); population of, 22, 23, 24–25, 27, 28, 30, 31, 145, 153; racial and social climate in, 8, 39, 46, 49–50, 106, 134–36, 153, 172–73, 247–51; racial composition

of, 24, 28, 32, 86, 127, 145, 148, 153, 241–43, 335 (n. 67); religious denominations in, 25, 31; town plan of, 22, 23, 32. *See also* Architecture, New Bern; Civil War, effects in New Bern
New Bern Academy, 222
Newbern Co-operative Land and Building Association, 333 (n. 40)
New Bern Educational Association, 222, 336 (n. 77)
New Bern Guards, 230, 231
Newbern Mechanics Association, 101
New Bern Rifle Cadets, 230, 231
New Bern Riflemen, in Third North Carolina Regiment, 248
New Haven, Conn., as destination for black émigrés from New Bern, 137, 138
Newton, Alexander Herritage (apprentice brickmason, plasterer, minister), 123, 124, 125, 131, 166, 197, 226–27, 253
Newton, Macklin (shoemaker), 77, 280
Newton, Mars (carpenter), 80, 280–81
Newton, Mary, 123, 125, 126, 129
Newton, Olivia Hamilton, 125, 167
Newton, Sarah, 66–67, 127
Newton, Thaddeus, 123, 129
Newton, Thomas (Tom; carpenter), 16, 46, 65, 74, 77, 78, 79, 80, 84, 95, 127, 276; biographical summary, 280–81; family of, 67, 77, 80, 280–81; owns real estate, 86, 87, 145; petition to free wife, 66–67
Nicey, 88
Nichols, William (carpenter, architect), 46
North Carolina Constitutional Conventions: of 1835, 105; of 1865, 180, 183; of 1868, 215, 216
North Carolina Educational Association, 187
North Carolina Equal Rights League, 181, 329 (n. 90)
North Carolina Freedmen's Conventions: of 1865, 176–80; of 1866, 187–90
North Carolina State Guard, 231, 282
North Carolina State Teachers Association, 223

Oberlin, Ohio, as destination for black émigrés from New Bern, 139–40
Oberlin School and College (Oberlin, Ohio), 131
Oberlin-Wellington Rescue, 144
Oden, Allen G. (shoemaker), 164, 205, 245, 331 (n. 13), 334 (n. 47); biographical summary, 281–82; in civic organizations, 230, 231; major in State Guard, 231, 246 (ill.); obituary of, 245; owns real estate, 207, 242, 333 (n. 41); political roles of, 224, 246–47, 282
Oden, Dicey (Dicy), 245, 282, 338 (n. 101)
Officeholders, black New Bernians as: aldermen (town councilmen), 32, 194, 216, 217, 218, 232, 247, 249, 251, 252, 341 (n. 147); clerk of court, 249; federal appointments, 219; justices of the peace, 336 (n. 69); register of deeds, 249; state legislators, 32, 215, 216, 217, 218, 224, 232, 249, 251, 252, 335 (n. 65); trustees of Craven County school board, 224–25, 232
O'Hara, James, 171, 219, 260, 265, 329 (n. 90)
Oliver, John (carpenter), 43, 45, 51, 53, 58, 59, 82, 117
Oliver, Joseph, 58
Oliver, Samuel, 58

Page, John R. (carpenter), 335 (n. 61)
Painters, 158, 199. *See also* Charlotte, William; Randolph, John, Jr.; Wade, Benjamin; Whitfield, Thomas
Pasteur, Edward, 251, 311 (n. 145)
Pasteur, Sarah, 236
Paton, David, 101
Patterson, John E. (brickmason), 141, 142, 144
Patterson, Moses, 329 (n. 90)
Pavie, Edward (contractor), 204, 233, 234, 332 (nn. 28, 29)
Paxton, William (carpenter), 52
Pay rates for artisans, 44–45, 157, 158, 164
Peggy (apprentice trunkmaker), 83
Pegram, Oleona (Oleona Pegram Atkins), 238, 239
Pepsi-Cola, 31
Petersburg, Va., 11, 28, 86
Pettey, Charles, 228, 244, 248
Pettey, Sarah Dudley, 228, 238, 239, 244, 265
Pettipher (Pettiford), William (engineer, blacksmith), 146, 223, 242, 330 (n. 11)

Pettigrew, Ebenezer, 79
Pettipher, Kate, 223
Pettipher, Willis D., 216, 217, 218
Phoebe, 77
Physic, George, 336 (n. 77)
Physioc, William (carpenter), 235
Pierson (Pearson), Clinton D. (barber), 135, 155, 167, 207; political roles of, 168, 170, 176, 187, 215–16
Plasterers: among apprentices, 81; racial distribution among, 114, 210, 314–15 (n. 51). *See also* Allen, Abram Moody Russell; Green, Shadrach; Montford, Donum; Newton, Alexander Herritage; Price, George W., Jr.; Richardson, Cicero M.; Richardson, Edward A.; Rue, Isaac C.; Ulysses
Pollock, Mr., 64
Pompey (Pomp; carpenter), 55, 56
Populist Party, 33, 247
Presbyterian congregations, 25, 31, 107, 131
Price, George W., Jr. (plasterer), 155, 176, 177, 179, 187, 191, 322 (n. 8); family of, 213, 334 (n. 52)
Price, Joseph C. (apprentice upholsterer, minister, educator), 156, 198, 220–21, 222 (ill.), 228

Race, definitions and meaning of, 13, 106
Rachel, and family, 77
Racial deference, strategies of, 5, 6, 16, 47–48, 87, 93, 159, 173, 245–47, 253
Rains, Gabriel (cabinetmaker), 45, 85
Raleigh, N.C.: African Methodist Church (St. Paul's AME Church) in, 178; artisans in, 113, 116, 208, 212, 213; black military companies from, 231, 248; black population of, 31, 208; Company H state troops in, 217; compared with New Bern, 26, 28, 31, 86, 113, 196, 208, 217, 221, 222; as state capital, 23. *See also* North Carolina Freedmen's Conventions; State Colored Education Convention
Ralph, Mark (carpenter), 62
Randolph, Celia, 237, 241, 338 (n. 101)
Randolph, Della Redmond, 234, 237
Randolph, Florence, 238, 239
Randolph, Hattie, 238, 239
Randolph, Henry T., 282
Randolph, John, Jr. (painter): biographical summary, 282–84; church affiliation, 226; in civic organizations, 173, 186, 214, 232, 336 (n. 77), 338 (n. 98); family of, 224, 234, 236, 237, 239, 282–84, 321 (n. 1); letter from, 151, 321 (n. 1); moves from Washington, N.C., to New Bern, 152, 164; and North Carolina Freedmen's Conventions, 176, 177; owns real estate, 207, 213, 333 (n. 41); political roles of, 152, 162, 164, 169, 170, 179, 180, 187, 215, 216, 219; residence of, 241, 242
Randolph, John, Sr., 282, 337 (n. 88)
Randolph, Kate Green, 237, 241
Randolph, Lewis, 237
Randolph, William O. (carpenter), 206, 226, 237, 241, 282, 331 (n. 13)
Reconstruction, 12, 32, 152, 196; Congressional, 213–17; Presidential, 172–91
Reliance Fire Company (Reliance Axe and Bucket Company), 194, 232, 289
Religious revivals, 25
Republican Party, 32, 33, 190, 214, 216, 247
Residential patterns in New Bern, racial, 21, 85–86, 127–29, 241–44; compared with other cities, 7, 8, 28, 31, 86, 241
Revere, Paul, 14
Rial, Julia Anne, 236
Rial (Real), Titus (blacksmith), 199, 236
Rial, William (blacksmith), 199
Rice, Sarah, 52, 73, 269; gravestone of, 93, 94 (ill.). *See also* Green, John Rice
Richardson, Charles (apprentice brickmason), 238
Richardson, Cicero M. (brickmason, plasterer), 98, 99, 100, 111, 139, 145, 167, 182, 228
Richardson, David (artisan), 330 (n. 11)
Richardson, Edward A. (brickmason, plasterer): apprentice, 147; biographical summary, 284–85; in civic organizations, 173, 188, 214, 220, 221–22, 336 (n. 77), 338 (n. 98); family of, 123, 147, 237, 284–85; and North Carolina Freedmen's Convention, 177, 179; owns real estate, 147, 148, 208, 238, 333 (n. 41); political roles of, 169,

170, 215, 216, 219, 224, 226; residence of, 148, 242. *See also* Rue, Isaac C.
Richardson, Isaac (brickmason, plasterer), 123, 237, 284
Richardson, Isaac, Jr. (plasterer), 284
Richardson, Miles (carpenter), 287
Richardson, Miles (plasterer), 284
Richardson, Robert, 139
Richardson, Sarah Ann Harris, 100, 139
Richardson, Sarah Rue, 127
Richardson, Simon (caulker), 127, 287
Richmond, Va., 15, 57, 127; compared with New Bern, 7, 8, 11, 22, 28, 50, 86, 196
"Rip Van Winkle State," 26, 100
Robbins, Cicero (shoemaker), 224, 230, 338 (nn. 98, 101), 341 (n. 138)
Robinson, Nathaniel (shoemaker), 275
Roman Catholic congregations, 25, 31
Romey, 43
Rough and Ready Fire Company, 230, 232
Rue, Ann, 149, 240
Rue, Bristow (Brister), 148, 233
Rue, Elizabeth, 149
Rue, George A. (mechanic, joiner): AME minister and missionary, 125, 160, 184, 185–87; biographical summary, 285–86; in Boston, 160, 163, 175, 323 (n. 22); death of, 191, 240; family of, 111, 148, 220, 259, 285–86; founds Rue's Chapel AME Church, 125, 231; and Frederick Douglass, 138, 163; moves to New England, 137–38; and North Carolina Freedmen's Conventions, 174–83 passim, 187–89; owns real estate, 130; political roles of, 156, 174, 187; singer, 163, 181, 190. *See also* Rue's Chapel AME Church
Rue, Godfrey (carpenter), 148, 149, 285
Rue, Grace. *See* Green, Grace
Rue, Hannah, 149
Rue, Isaac C. (brickmason, plasterer): biographical summary, 286–87; church affiliation of, 110, 159, 240; family of, 111, 112, 123, 234, 237, 238, 284, 287; freed by will, 89, 114, 121; obituary, 237–38; owns real estate, 130, 238, 207, 238; owns slave, 130; persistence in New Bern, 101, 136, 147, 155, 197, 237–38, 330 (n. 11), 331 (n. 13); probably trains grandsons, 123, 238; residence of, 127, 148; in slavery, 89, 112, 284, 309 (n. 133); work at William Hollister House, 112; work at Moses Griffin School, 114
Rue, Malinda, 149, 220
Rue, Rachel, 234
Rue, William (carpenter), 204, 233, 234
Rue's Chapel AME Church, 184, 226, 243
Runaway slaves, 62–66, 118
Rush, Christopher, 160, 167
Russell, Abram Moody. *See* Allen, Abram Moody Russell
Russell, Daniel, 248
Ryal (Ryol), William (blacksmith), 159, 160, 162

St. Cyprian's Episcopal Church, 184, 206, 220, 226, 243
St. John's Masonic Lodge: gathering of free blacks at, 106–7; William H. Hancock as tyler in, 132, 185
St. John's Missionary Baptist Church, 184, 242
St. Peter's AME Zion Church, 206, 228, 229 (ill.)
Sam (apprentice blacksmith), 38
Sam (cabinetmaker, carpenter), 45, 54
Sam (carpenter, seaman), 46, 51
Sampson, J. P., 179
Sampson family, 334 (n. 52)
Sanders, James (blacksmith), 60
Sanders, Mary, 61
Sandy, Uriah (carpenter), 45, 58, 59, 82, 272
Sawyer, Annias (apprentice tailor), 212
Sawyer, Catharine S., 319 (n. 110)
Sawyer, Cornelius (blacksmith), 138, 319 (n. 109)
Sawyer, Freeman (tailor), 212
Sawyer, Leonard (tailor), 212
Sawyer, Richard (tailor), 200, 205, 212
Schaw, Robert, 75
Schenk, John T. (carpenter), 179, 190, 213, 329 (n. 90)
Schools for black students: antebellum, 110–11, 131, 135, 149; during Civil War, 159, 167, 171; graded, 223, 224, 232, 252, 336 (n. 85); normal, 224, 228; postwar, 184, 214, 220–23, 236–39; St. Phillips School,

220; West Street School, 336 (n. 85). *See also* Education; Livingstone College; Oberlin School and College
Scott, Celia (Cecelia), 142, 143 (ill.)
Scott, John H. (harnessmaker, saddler), 142, 144, 145; family of, 143 (ill.); Union chaplain, 183
Scott, Joshua, 313 (n. 30)
Seamstresses, 11, 13, 17, 146, 200, 330 (n. 10); as apprentices, 81, 83, 121. *See also* Bragg, Elizabeth; Conner, Sylvia; Green, Temperance Durden
Second Confiscation Act (1862), 30, 153, 163
Second Congressional District ("Black Second"), 8, 32, 219, 247
Self-hiring of slaves, 56–57, 115, 117, 134
Shepard, Charles B., 104, 106
Shepard (Sheppard), Miles (cabinetmaker, turner), 199, 336 (n. 77), 338 (n. 98)
Shepard, William, 62
Ship carpenters, 42, 123, 157, 211
Shoemakers, 53, 63, 158, 198, 199, 205, 211; apprentices, 81, 199–200; craft equipment of, 210, 245; decline among, 210. *See also* Castix, Raymond; Havens, Edward; Havens, John T.; Hill, Moses D.; Oden, Allen G.; Robbins, Cicero; Slade, Quash W.
Sickles, Daniel, 214
Silversmiths, 41, 45, 112, 199. *See also* Tisdale, William; Woods, Freeman
Simmons, Bacchus (carpenter), 78–79, 80, 84, 86, 87, 95, 263, 268; assists in freeing slaves, 77, 78, 197; manumission of, 68–69
Simmons, Furnifold, 219, 260, 265, 342 (n. 151)
Simmons, Henry H. (cooper), 199; artisan-leader, 155, 331 (n. 13); biographical summary, 287–88; in civic associations, 186, 214, 230, 338 (nn. 98, 100); obituary of, 252–53; owns real estate, 213; political roles of, 169, 217, 218, 223, 224, 247, 252, 283; registers to vote in 1902, 251; at State Colored Education Convention, 223
Simmons, Phillip (blacksmith), 11
Simmons, Sukey, 68–69, 77, 84
Simon (carpenter), 53, 59
Simon (cooper), 303 (n. 62)
Simpson, Herbert Woodley (architect), 212
Singleton, William Henry, 162–63
Skin color, 73, 129, 321 (n. 127)
Skinner, Anthony (carpenter), 319 (n. 109)
Skinner, Charles (apprentice carpenter), 123
Slade, Quash W. (shoemaker), 206, 218
Slade, Zaccheus (mechanic), 117, 266
Slater Institute (later Winston-Salem State University), 239
Slaves: enslaved children of white fathers, 70, 73, 74, 89; families protected, 118, 234; families separated, 20, 61–62, 118, 233–34; hiring practices, 56–61, 115–18; insurrections, white fear of, 98, 102, 103, 104, 133, 134; literacy among, 10, 54, 67, 135; marriages not legal, 81, 85; marriages registered, 234; owned by parents, 73–74, 75, 76; regulations concerning, 19–20; relationships with whites, 20–21; runaways, 61–66, 118, 156; surnames of, 64–65; teaching of to read and write forbidden, 103
—population of: in New Bern in 1800 and 1820, 25; in New Bern in 1850, 28; in Craven County in 1790, 24
See also Artisans—enslaved; Contrabands during Civil War; Emancipation by will; Manumissions; Marriages
Slaveholders: blacks as, 12, 38, 43, 45, 70, 77, 79, 88–89, 130, 146, 309 (n. 132); opposed to slavery, 49; primarily nonartisans, 51
Sloan, Samuel (architect), 203
Smith, Benjamin, 309 (n. 129)
Smith, Elizabeth, 117
Smith, Isaac Hughes, 208, 218, 249
Smith, John (mason), 204
Smith, John F., 74
Smith, Sarah Dry, 308 (n. 129)
Spaight, Charles G., 60, 312 (n. 21)
Spaight, Mary Jones, 52, 61, 93, 269
Spaight, Richard Dobbs, Jr., 52, 69, 88, 89, 94, 95, 269, 303 (n. 63)
Spaight, Richard Dobbs, Sr., 61, 269, 303 (n. 63), 305 (n. 91)
Spanish-American War, 248
Sparrow, Charles (brickmason), 203, 212

Sparrow, Henry Clay (brickmason), 212, 244, 334 (n. 50)
Sparrow, James (brickmason), 203
Sparrow, Thomas (ship builder), 42, 45
Spelman, Asa (cooper), 47–48, 49
Spelman family, 24
Spooner (carpenter), 55
Stanly, Ann Cogdell, 72
Stanly, Benjamin (barber), 45
Stanly, Catharine Green (dressmaker), 45, 70, 127, 130, 140, 146–47
Stanly, Charles S. (tailor), 45, 140, 262
Stanly, Edward, 30, 95, 111, 159, 312 (n. 21)
Stanly, Edward R., 216
Stanly, Eunice, 70
Stanly, Fanny (Frances; tailoress, schoolteacher), 111, 127, 131, 140, 262
Stanly, Frances (dressmaker), 45, 127, 130, 140, 146–47
Stanly, George W. (shoemaker), 336 (n. 77)
Stanly, James G., 64
Stanly, John, 30, 70, 104, 106, 111; assists in manumissions, 49–50, 72, 75, 147; congressman, 73; defends rights of free blacks, 49, 103, 133; father of John Rice Green, 73, 89, 95, 269; legislator, 103, 312 (n. 21); supported by black voters, 94, 95
Stanly, John (joiner, carpenter), 45, 127, 182, 262
Stanly, John Carruthers (barber), 45, 70, 71, 93, 130, 147, 197; apprentices of, 83; church affiliation of, 89–90; early life and emancipation, 70; family of, 70, 72, 74, 84, 87, 130, 137, 140, 147, 262; frees and assists in freeing slaves, 70, 71, 72, 75, 77, 78, 90, 99, 197, 263, 264, 268; loses wealth, 111, 130; owns real estate, 70, 86, 87, 130, 308 (n. 128), 309 (n. 129), 311 (nn. 144, 145), 313 (n. 27); residences of, 70, 85, 91, 310 (n. 141), 321 (n. 128); slaves owned by, 70, 80, 305; son of John Wright Stanly, 70; taxpayer eligible to vote, 95
Stanly, John Stewart: emancipated, 70; family of, 127, 131; moves to Cleveland, Ohio, 140; operates school for free blacks, 44, 111, 131; owns real estate, 87; owns slaves, 130; son of John C. Stanly, 45, 70; taxpayer eligible to vote, 95
Stanly, John Wright, 70, 73
Stanly, Kitty Green, 70, 75, 89
Stanly, Lucinda, 235, 266
Stanly, Osborne (joiner), 45
Stanly, Sarah Bragg (tailoress), 123, 131, 140; biographical summary, 262–63
Stanly, Thomas, 311 (n. 3)
Stanly Building, 266
Starkey, Mary Ann, 165
Star of Zion, 338 (n. 92)
State Colored Education Convention, 222, 259
State Normal Institute, 224, 225
State v. Will (1834), 301 (n. 27)
Stevenson, James C., 312 (n. 21)
Stevenson, Martin (carpenter), 45, 59, 100, 272, 300 (n. 8)
Stewart, Alexander, 70
Stewart, Charles (tailor), 262
Stewart, Lydia Rellier, 70, 89
Suffrage. *See* Disfranchisement amendments; Voting rights for North Carolina blacks
Sweatt, Isham (barber), 179, 180
Sykes, T. A., 190

Tailoresses, 11, 13, 141, 200, 201, 205, 211, 242. *See also* Bragg, Elizabeth; Green, Temperance Durden; Stanly, Sarah Bragg
Tailors, 6, 80, 88, 112, 123, 139, 140, 158, 201, 210, 212, 314 (n. 51); apprenticeships of, 52, 54, 81, 123; own real estate, 86, 91, 129–30, 148; racial distribution of, 112, 199, 211, 332 (n. 20), 334 (n. 47); shop locations, 198, 205. *See also* Bell, Reuben; Bragg, John; Durand, John Louis; Green, John Rice; Hawley, John; Holly, Mustipher; Morris, Albert; Morris, Freeman; Sawyer, Richard; Zang, Adam
Taylor, Henry A. (carpenter), 208, 314 (n. 43), 334 (n. 52)
Taylor, Joseph (apprentice brickmason), 199
Tempe, 88
Thornton, James (apprentice carpenter), 82
Tinker, Euphemia, 310 (n. 141)
Tinners and tinsmiths, 211
Tisdale, Nathan (silversmith), 45

Tisdale, William (silversmith), 41, 127
Tom (blacksmith), 61
Tom (brother of runaway blacksmith), 64
Tom (ship carpenter), 42
Tony (plasterer), 43
Tools (craft), 61, 124–25, 172, 210; for enslaved artisans, 53, 58–59, 61; ownership of, 15, 53, 59, 80, 207, 257; significance of, 14, 38, 79–80
Travel restrictions on slaves and free blacks, 78–79, 98, 103
Trenwith, Patrick (blacksmith), 331 (n. 18)
Tryon, William, 23
Tryon Palace, 23, 55
Tucker, E. E. (carpenter), 218, 259, 336 (n. 77)
Tucker, Emeline (daughter of Richard and Emeline Tucker), 223
Tucker, Emeline (wife of Richard Tucker), 117, 118, 234
Tucker, Jupiter (carpenter), 288
Tucker, Richard (carpenter, undertaker): biographical summary, 288–89; church affiliation of, 110, 159, 160, 227, 240; in civic organizations, 188, 214, 336 (n. 77), 338 (n. 98); family of, 117–18, 223, 234–35, 288–89; location of workshop, 204; as new freedman, 155; and North Carolina Freedmen's Convention, 187; owns real estate, 207, 242; political roles of, 170, 171, 187, 215, 216, 217, 218; in slavery, 110, 114, 117–18, 123
Turner, Henry M., 185

Ulysses (plasterer), 53, 54, 279
United Brotherhood Society, 230
U.S. Colored Troops, 163, 164, 166, 281
U.S. Post Office (New Bern), 203
Upholsterers. *See* Harris, James H.; Price, Joseph C.
Urmston, John, 10

Vail, Benners, 53, 61
Vail, Elizabeth, 61
Vesey, Denmark (carpenter), 11
Voting rights for North Carolina blacks, 93–95, 104–6, 173

Wade, Benjamin (Ben; painter), 42, 46, 112
Wadsworth, Dennis (carpenter), 204
Wadsworth, Donum (carpenter), 314 (n. 37)
Wadsworth, William, 90
Wagonmakers, 112. *See also* Mason, Lucas
Wait, Samuel, 25
Walker, David, *Walker's Appeal, in Four Articles* (1829), 103, 271
Walker, Grace Harris (tailoress), 200–201, 205
Warren, J. R. (carpenter), 182
Waters, J. C. (shoemaker), 334 (n. 47)
Watson, Thomas, 312 (n. 21)
Weaver, S. H. (plasterer), 182
Webber, Catherine (Caty), 99
West, John (carpenter, cabinetmaker), 55
Weston, James (carpenter), 204, 234
Wheelwrights, 148, 199, 210, 211. *See also* Kent, Henry; Mason, Lucas; Wadsworth, Dennis
White, Fannie Randolph, 224, 237, 243
White, George H., 225 (ill.), 246, 259, 333 (n. 41); attorney, 224–25, 245; church affiliation of, 226; congressman, 247, 249, 251–52; educator, 217, 223, 224, 226, 238; family of, 237, 283; legislator, 217, 218, 224; Masonic leader, 230; residences of, 243, 244, 247
White, Nancy J. Scott, 238, 340 (n. 120)
White, Stepney (brickmason), 203
"White supremacy crusade," 33, 248, 250, 251
Whitfield, Charles (carpenter), 332 (n. 28)
Whitfield, Thomas (Tom; painter), 65, 66
Whitford, Hardy (shoemaker), 121
Whitford, John D., 47, 132
Will (carpenter), 55, 56
Williams, Daniel (tanner), 136
Williams, Jarvis M., 168
Williams, Louis (carpenter), 159, 160, 338 (n. 97)
Willis, Alonzo (apprentice carpenter, manufacturer), 101, 122
Willis, Ann, 240
Willis, George B. (cooper), 156, 199, 207, 239, 240, 242, 249; biographical summary, 289–90; captain of state militia Company H, 217; church affiliation of, 184, 186, 226; in civic organizations, 186,

214, 230, 231, 232, 336 (n. 77), 338 (nn. 97, 98); family of, 289–90; political roles of, 216, 217, 218, 224, 232
Willis, George H., 226, 239
Willis, Harriet Randolph, 239
Willis, John B. (cooper), 226, 230, 239, 249, 251, 289, 290
Willis, Susan (seamstress), 289
Willoby (Willoughby; blacksmith), 41, 60, 61, 69–70
Wilmington, N.C., 27, 28, 30, 31, 48, 57, 64, 75, 100, 112, 171, 249; black artisan families in, 213; black militia companies from, 231, 248; black property owners in, 130, 208; coup of 1898, 33, 249; compared with New Bern, 8, 26, 28, 30, 31, 50, 86, 113, 196, 208, 217, 241; Abraham Galloway in, 118, 156, 191; and North Carolina Freedmen's Conventions, 176–77, 179, 188
Wilson, David (carpenter), 121, 147, 211, 242, 330 (n. 11)
Wilson, Henry, 214
Wilson, Jerusha, 147
Wilson, John (apprentice carpenter), 123
Wilson, John (apprentice shoemaker), 121
Wilson, Marshall (apprentice carpenter), 123
Wilson, Peter, 121, 147
Wilson, Rachel, 121, 147, 211
Windsor (carpenter), 53
Winston-Salem State University, 239
Witherspoon, David, 60
Witherspoon, John Knox, 60, 303 (n. 60)
Witherspoon, Mary Whiting Jones Nash, 303 (n. 60)
Women artisans, 11, 200–203, 211; blacks and whites share gendered craft roles, 11, 200; households of, 235; marital status and artisan identity, 200; needle crafts predominant among, 146; number of 146, 314 (n. 51), 200, 211; own real estate, 146, 200; racial distribution among, 146, 200, 211; as slaveholders, 146. *See also* Dressmakers; Milliners; Seamstresses; Tailoresses
Woodard, Allen (carpenter), 64
Woods, Benjamin, 65, 67
Woods, Freeman (silversmith), 41, 45, 130
Woods, Sarah, 304 (n. 76), 306 (n. 103)
Worth, Jonathan, 183, 214

York (carpenter), 42
York (Yorke), Amos (cooper), 179, 199, 244; biographical summary, 290–91; church affiliation of, 110, 159, 337 (n. 89); in civic organizations, 214, 338 (n. 98); family of, 234, 236, 239, 244, 290–91; grave marker of, 291; letter from, 159–60; minister, 162, 184, 226; as new freedman, 159, 330 (n. 13); and North Carolina Freedmen's Convention, 177, 179; political roles of, 169, 170, 176, 187, 216, 290; residence of, 243, 244; in slavery, 110, 155, 159
York, Desdemona McIlvane, 234, 236, 243, 244, 291
York, Dollie (chairmaker), 200
York, Emily (seamstress), 236
York, Hannah, 244
York, James Cornelius (cooper), 290
York, John T. (cooper), 238, 239, 244, 249, 341 (n. 147)
Youle, Thomas (cabinetmaker), 45
Young Men's Intelligent and Enterprising Association, 222, 230

Zang, Adam (tailor), 201, 205

www.ingramcontent.com/pod-product-compliance
Lightning Source LLC
LaVergne TN
LVHW050954080826
845145LV00006B/1496
* 9 7 8 1 4 6 9 6 2 6 5 7 4 *